Lecture Notes in Artificial Intelligence 12325

Subseries of Lecture Notes in Computer Science

Series Editors

Randy Goebel
  University of Alberta, Edmonton, Canada
Yuzuru Tanaka
  Hokkaido University, Sapporo, Japan
Wolfgang Wahlster
  DFKI and Saarland University, Saarbrücken, Germany

Founding Editor

Jörg Siekmann
  DFKI and Saarland University, Saarbrücken, Germany

More information about this series at http://www.springer.com/series/1244

Ute Schmid · Franziska Klügl ·
Diedrich Wolter (Eds.)

KI 2020: Advances in Artificial Intelligence

43rd German Conference on AI
Bamberg, Germany, September 21–25, 2020
Proceedings

 Springer

Editors
Ute Schmid ⓘ
Universität Bamberg
Bamberg, Germany

Franziska Klügl ⓘ
Örebro University
Örebro, Sweden

Diedrich Wolter ⓘ
Universität Bamberg
Bamberg, Germany

ISSN 0302-9743   ISSN 1611-3349   (electronic)
Lecture Notes in Artificial Intelligence
ISBN 978-3-030-58284-5   ISBN 978-3-030-58285-2   (eBook)
https://doi.org/10.1007/978-3-030-58285-2

LNCS Sublibrary: SL7 – Artificial Intelligence

This Springer imprint is published by the registered company Springer Nature Switzerland AG
The registered company address is: Gewerbestrasse 11, 6330 Cham, Switzerland

Preface

This proceedings volume contains the papers presented at the 43rd German Conference on Artificial Intelligence (KI 2020), held during September 21–25, 2020, hosted by University of Bamberg, Germany. Due to COVID-19, KI 2020 was the first virtual edition of this conference series.

The German conference on Artificial Intelligence (abbreviated KI for "Künstliche Intelligenz") has developed from a series of unofficial meetings and workshops, starting 45 years ago with the first GI-SIG AI meeting on October 7, 1975. GI-SIG AI is the Fachbereich Künstliche Intelligenz (FBKI) der Gesellschaft für Informatik (GI). As a well-established annual conference series it is dedicated to research on theory and applications across all methods and topic areas of AI research. While KI is primarily attended by researchers from Germany and neighboring countries, it warmly welcomes international participation.

KI 2020 had a special focus on human-centered AI with a particular focus on AI in education and explainable machine learning. These topics were addressed in a panel discussion as well as in a workshop. The conference invited original research papers and shorter technical communications as well as descriptions of system demonstrations on all topics of AI. Further, the submission of extended abstracts summarizing papers that had recently been presented at major AI conferences was encouraged.

KI 2020 received more than 70 submissions from 13 countries which were reviewed by three Program Committee members each. The Program Committee, comprising 53 experts from 8 countries, decided to accept 16 submissions as full papers, 12 as technical contributions, and 4 as pre-published abstracts.

The program included six invited talks:

- Anthony G. Cohn, University of Leeds, UK: "Learning about Language and Action for Robots"
- Hector Geffner, Institució Catalana de Recerca i Estudis Avançats and Universitat Pompeu Fabra, Spain: "From Model-free to Model-based AI: Representation Learning for Planning"
- Jana Koehler, DFKI, Germany: "10^{120} and Beyond: Scalable AI Search Algorithms as a Foundation for Powerful Industrial Optimization"
- Nada Lavra, Jožef Stefan Institute, Slovenia: "Semantic Relational Learning"
- Sebastian Riedel, Facebook AI Research and University College London, UK: "Open and Closed Book Machine Reading"
- Ulli Waltinger, Siemens Corporate Technology, Germany: "The Beauty of Imperfection: From Gut Feeling to Transfer Learning to Self-Supervision"

The main conference was supplemented with five workshops and seven tutorials. In addition to the annual doctoral consortium, a student day was introduced encouraging students – from high-school as well as from bachelor and master programs – to present their AI projects. Although COVID-19 complicated KI 2020 in several regards, it was a pleasure to organize this traditional annual event. We are grateful to our co-organizers, Matthias Thimm (workshops and tutorials chair), Tanya Braun (doctoral consortium chair), Jens Garbas (demo and exhibition chair), as well as to Johannes Rabold and the Fachschaft WIAI for organizing the student day, and to Klaus Stein for technical support. Student volunteers and support from local administrators (especially Romy Hartmann) was essential for the smooth (virtual) running of the conference. They supported us not only with generating a virtual city tour, but with many organizational details. We also want to thank the University of Bamberg for their generous support.

We thank the Program Committee members and all additional reviewers for their effort and time they invested in the reviewing process. Our appreciation also goes to the developers of EasyChair; their conference management system provides great functionalities that helped to organize the reviewing process and generate this volume. Last but not least, we would like to thank Christine Harms and the GI Geschäftsstelle for the registration support and Springer for publishing the proceedings and sponsoring the Best Paper Award.

We hope the conference was enjoyed by all who participated.

July 2020

Ute Schmid
Franziska Klügl
Diedrich Wolter

Organization

Program Committee

Klaus-Dieter Althoff	German Research Center for Artificial Intelligence (DFKI), Universität Hildesheim, Germany
Martin Atzmüller	Tilburg University, The Netherlands
Franz Baader	TU Dresden, Germany
Christoph Beierle	FernUniversität in Hagen, Germany
Christoph Benzmüller	Freie Universität Berlin, Germany
Ralph Bergmann	University of Trier, German Research Center for Artificial Intelligence (DFKI), Germany
Tarek R. Besold	Alpha Health, Telefonica Innovation Alpha, Spain
Tanya Braun	University of Lübeck, Germany
Ulf Brefeld	Leuphana University of Lüneburg, Germany
Gerhard Brewka	Leipzig University, Germany
Manfred Eppe	University of Hamburg, Germany
Christian Freksa	University of Bremen, Germany
Ulrich Furbach	University of Koblenz-Landau, Germany
Johannes Fürnkranz	Johannes Kepler University Linz, Austria
Barbara Hammer	Bielefeld University, Germany
Malte Helmert	University of Basel, Switzerland
Joachim Hertzberg	Osnabrück University, German Research Center for Artificial Intelligence (DFKI), Germany
Andreas Hotho	Julius Maximilians University of Würzburg, Germany
Steffen Hölldobler	TU Dresden, Germany
Eyke Hüllermeier	Paderborn University, Germany
Gabriele Kern-Isberner	TU Dortmund University, Germany
Matthias Klusch	German Research Center for Artificial Intelligence (DFKI), Germany
Franziska Klügl	Örebro University, Sweden
Stefan Kopp	Bielefeld University, Germany
Ralf Krestel	Hasso Plattner Institute, University of Potsdam, Germany
Bernd Ludwig	Universität Regensburg, Germany
Thomas Lukasiewicz	University of Oxford, UK
Till Mossakowski	Otto von Guericke University Magdeburg, Germany
Ralf Möller	University of Lübeck, Germany
Jörg P. Müller	Clausthal University of Technology, Germany
Bernhard Nebel	University of Freiburg, Germany
Heiko Paulheim	University of Mannheim, Germany
Ute Schmid	University of Bamberg, Germany

Lars Schmidt-Thieme	University of Hildesheim, Germany
Claudia Schon	University of Koblenz-Landau, Germany
Lutz Schröder	Friedrich-Alexander-Universität Erlangen-Nürnberg, Germany
Daniel Sonntag	German Research Center for Artificial Intelligence (DFKI), Germany
Myra Spiliopoulou	Otto von Guericke University Magdeburg, Germany
Steffen Staab	University of Stuttgart, Germany, and University of Southampton, UK
Frieder Stolzenburg	Harz University of Applied Sciences, Germany
Heiner Stuckenschmidt	University of Mannheim, Germany
Michael Thielscher	The University of New South Wales, Australia
Matthias Thimm	University of Koblenz-Landau, Germany
Paul Thorn	Heinrich Heine University Düsseldorf, Germany
Ingo J. Timm	University of Trier, Germany
Sabine Timpf	University of Augsburg, Germany
Anni-Yasmin Turhan	TU Dresden, Germany
Toby Walsh	The University of New South Wales, Australia
Diedrich Wolter	University of Bamberg, Germany
Stefan Woltran	Vienna University of Technology, Austria
Stefan Wrobel	Fraunhofer IAIS, University of Bonn, Germany
Özgür Lütfü Özçep	University of Lübeck, Germany

Additional Reviewers

Alrabbaa, Christian	Klügl, Peter
Borgwardt, Stefan	Lee, Jae Hee
Boukhers, Zeyd	Leemhuis, Mena
Brinkmeyer, Lukas	Lienen, Julian
Bruckert, Sebastian	Lima, Oscar
Cramer, Marcos	Lüth, Christoph
Demirović, Emir	Malburg, Lukas
Eisenstadt, Viktor	Maly, Jan
Eriksson, Salomé	Matthiesen, Jennifer
Ferber, Patrick	Menges, Raphael
Glauer, Martin	Mohammed, Hussein
Gromowski, Mark	Nau, Dana
Haldimann, Jonas Philipp	Neubauer, Kai
Hartwig, Mattis	Omeliyanenko, Janna
Hoffmann, Maximilian	Pfannschmidt, Karlson
Höllmann, Mark	Potyka, Nico

Rabold, Johannes
Reuss, Pascal
Rieger, Ines
Rudolph, Yannick
Sauerwald, Kai
Schiff, Simon
Schlör, Daniel

Schoenborn, Jakob Michael
Schwartz, Tobias
Seitz, Sarem
Siebert, Sophie
Stock, Sebastian
Zehe, Albin
Zeyen, Christian

Contents

Abstracts of Pre-published Papers

Technical Contributions

Full Contributions

Two Algorithms for Additive and Fair Division of Mixed Manna

Martin Aleksandrov$^{(\boxtimes)}$ and Toby Walsh

Technical University Berlin, Berlin, Germany
{martin.aleksandrov,toby.walsh}@tu-berlin.de

Abstract. We consider a fair division model in which agents have positive, zero and negative utilities for items. For this model, we analyse one existing fairness property (EFX) and three new and related properties (EFX$_0$, EFX^3 and EF1^3) in combination with Pareto-optimality. With general utilities, we give a modified version of an existing algorithm for computing an EF1^3 allocation. With $-\alpha/0/\alpha$ utilities, this algorithm returns an EFX^3 and PO allocation. With absolute identical utilities, we give a new algorithm for an EFX and PO allocation. With $-\alpha/0/\beta$ utilities, this algorithm also returns such an allocation. We report some new impossibility results as well.

Keywords: Additive fair division · Envy-freeness · Pareto-optimality

1 Introduction

Fair division of indivisible items lies on the intersection of fields such as social choice, computer science and algorithmic economics [15]. Though a large body of work is devoted to the case when the items are goods (e.g. [11,19,22,26]), there is a rapidly growing interest in the case of mixed manna (e.g. [5,13,25]). In a mixed manna, each item can be classified as *mixed* (i.e. some agents strictly like it and other agents strictly dislike it), *good* (i.e. all agents weakly like it and some agents strictly like it), *bad* (i.e. all agents weakly dislike it and some agents strictly dislike it) or *dummy* (i.e. all agents are indifferent to it).

An active line of fair division research currently focuses on approximations of envy-freeness (i.e. no agent envies another one) [18]. For example, Aziz et al. [4] proposed two such approximations for mixed manna: EF1 and EFX. EF1 requires that an agent's envy for another agent's bundle is eliminated by removing one particular item from these agents' bundles. EFX strengthens EF1 to any non-zero valued item in these bundles, increasing the agent's utility or decreasing the other agent's utility. However, they study only EF1 and identify improving our understanding of EFX as an important open problem for mixed manna:

> *"Our work paves the way for detailed examination of allocation of goods/chores, and opens up an interesting line of research, with many problems left open to explore. In particular, there are further fairness concepts that could be studied from both existence and complexity issues, most notably envy-freeness up to the least valued item (EFX)* [14].*"*

© Springer Nature Switzerland AG 2020
U. Schmid et al. (Eds.): KI 2020, LNAI 12325, pp. 3–17, 2020.
https://doi.org/10.1007/978-3-030-58285-2_1

We make in this paper a step forward in this direction. In particular, we study not only EFX but also *new* properties, all stronger than EF1. For example, one such property is *envy-freeness by parts up to some item*: $EF1^3$. This ensures EF1 independently for the set of all items, the set of goods and the set of bads (i.e. the different parts). Another such property is *envy-freeness by parts up to any item*: EFX^3. This requires EFX for each of the different parts of the set of items. Yet a third such property is EFX_0. This one extends the existing envy-freeness up to any (possibly zero valued) good from [24] to any (possibly zero valued) bad by relaxing the non-zero marginal requirements in the definition of EFX. We will shortly observe the following relations between these properties.

$$EFX_0 \Rightarrow EFX \quad EFX^3 \Rightarrow EFX \quad EF1^3 \Rightarrow EF1 \quad EFX^3 \Rightarrow EF1^3$$

We analyse these properties in isolation and also in combination with an efficiency criterion such as Pareto-optimality (PO). PO ensures that we cannot make an agent happier without making another one unhappier. More precisely, we ask in our work whether combinations of these properties can be guaranteed, and also how to do this when it is possible. Our analysis covers three common domains for *additive* (i.e. an agent's utility for a set of items is the sum of their utilities for the items in the set) utility functions: *general* (i.e. each utility is real-valued), *absolute identical* (i.e. for each item, the agents' utilities have identical magnitudes but may have different signs) as well as *ternary* (i.e. each utility is $-\alpha$, 0 or β for some $\alpha, \beta \in \mathbb{R}_{>0}$).

Each of these domains can be observed in practice. For instance, if a machine can perform a certain task faster than some pre-specified amount of time, then its utility for the task is positive and, otherwise, it is negative. Thus, multiple machines can have mixed utilities for tasks. Further, consider a market where items have prices and agents sell or buy items. In this context, the agents' utilities for an item have identical magnitudes but different signs. Finally, a special case of ternary utilities is when each agent have utility -1, 0, or 1 for every item. This is practical because we need simply to elicit whether agents like, dislike or are indifferent to each item. A real-world setting with such utilities is the food bank problem studied in [1].

We give some related work, formal preliminaries and motivation in Sects. 2, 3 and 4, respectively. In Sect. 5, we give a polynomial-time algorithm (i.e. Algorithm 1) for computing an $EF1^3$ allocation with general utilities. We also prove that an EFX^3 allocation, or an EFX_0 allocation might not exist even with ternary identical utilities. In Sect. 6, we give a polynomial-time algorithm (i.e. Algorithm 2) for computing an EFX and PO allocation with absolute identical utilities, and show that Algorithm 1 returns an $EF1^3$ and PO allocation. In Sect. 7, we show that Algorithm 1 returns an $EF1^3$ and PO allocation with ternary utilities, whereas Algorithm 2 returns an EFX and PO allocation. Finally, we give a summary in Sect. 8.

2 Related Work

For indivisible goods, EF1 was defined by Budish [12]. Caragiannis et al. [14] proposed EFX. It remains an open question whether EFX allocations exist in problems with general utilities. Recently, Amanatidis et al. [2] proved that EFX allocations exist in *2-value* (i.e. each utility takes one of two values) problems. In contrast, we show that EFX and PO allocations exist in problems with ternary (i.e. $-\alpha/0/\beta$) utilities, which are special cases of 3-value problems. Barman, Murthy and Vaish [7] presented a pseudo-polynomial time algorithm for EF1 and PO allocations. Barman et al. [8] gave an algorithm for EFX and PO allocations in problems with identical utilities. Plaut and Roughgarden [24] proved that the *leximin* solution from [17] is also EFX and PO in this domain. Although this solution maximizes the minimum agent's utility (i.e. the egalitarian welfare), it is intractable to find in general [16]. In our work, we give a polynomial-time algorithm for EFX and PO allocations in problems with absolute identical utilities, and show that this welfare and EFX^3 are incompatible.

For mixed manna, Aziz et al. [4] proposed EF1 and EFX. They gave the double round-robin algorithm that returns EF1 allocations. Unfortunately, these are not guaranteed to satisfy PO. They also gave a polynomial-time algorithm that returns allocations which are EF1 and PO in the case of 2 agents. Aziz and Rey [6] gave a "ternary flow" algorithm for leximin, EFX and PO allocations with $-\alpha/0/\alpha$ utilities. With $-\alpha/0/\beta$ utilities, we discuss that these might sadly violate EFX^3 even when $\alpha = 1, \beta = 1$, or EFX when $\alpha = 2, \beta = 1$. By comparison, we give a modified version of the double round-robin algorithm that returns EF1^3 allocations in problems with general utilities, EF1^3 and PO allocations in problems with absolute identical utilities and EFX^3 and PO allocations in problems with $-\alpha/0/\alpha$ utilities. Other works of divisible manna are [9,10], and approximations of envy-freeness for indivisible goods are [3,14,21]. In contrast, we study some new approximations and the case of indivisible manna.

3 Formal Preliminaries

We consider a set $[n] = \{1, \ldots, n\}$ of $n \in \mathbb{N}_{\geq 2}$ agents and a set $[m] = \{1, \ldots, m\}$ of $m \in \mathbb{N}_{\geq 1}$ indivisible items. We assume that each agent $a \in [n]$ have some *utility* function $u_a : 2^{[m]} \to \mathbb{R}$. Thus, they assign some utility $u_a(M)$ to each bundle $M \subseteq [m]$. We write $u_a(o)$ for $u_a(\{o\})$. We say that u_a is *additive* if, for each $M \subseteq [m]$, $u_a(M) = \sum_{o \in M} u_a(o)$. We also write $u(M)$ if, for each other agent $b \in [n]$, $u_a(M) = u_b(M)$.

With additive utility functions, the set of items $[m]$ can be partitioned into *mixed items*, *goods*, *bads* and *dummies*. Respectively, we write $[m]^{\pm} = \{o \in [m] | \exists a \in [n] : u_a(o) > 0, \exists b \in [n] : u_b(o) < 0\}$, $[m]^{+} = \{o \in [m] | \forall a \in [n] : u_a(o) \geq 0, \exists b \in [n] : u_b(o) > 0\}$, $[m]^{-} = \{o \in [m] | \forall a \in [n] : u_a(o) \leq 0, \exists b \in [n] : u_b(o) < 0\}$ and $[m]^{0} = \{o \in [m] | \forall a \in [n] : u_a(o) = 0\}$ for the sets of these items. We refer to an item o from $[m]^{+}$ as a *pure good* if $\forall a \in [n] : u_a(o) > 0$. Also, we refer to an item o from $[m]^{-}$ as a *pure bad* if $\forall a \in [n] : u_a(o) < 0$.

We say that agents have *general* additive utilities if, for each $a \in [n]$ and each $o \in [m]$, $u_a(o)$ could be any number from $\mathbb{R}$. Further, we say that they have *absolute identical* additive utilities if, for each $o \in [m]$, $|u_a(o)| = |u_b(o)|$ where $a, b \in [n]$, or *identical* additive utilities if, for each $o \in [m]$, $u_a(o) = u_b(o)$ where $a, b \in [n]$. Finally, we say that agents have *ternary* additive utilities if, for each $a \in [n]$ and each $o \in [m]$, $u_a(o) \in \{-\alpha, 0, \beta\}$ for some $\alpha, \beta \in \mathbb{R}_{>0}$.

An *(complete) allocation* $A = (A_1, \ldots, A_n)$ is such that (1) A_a is the set of items allocated to agent $a \in [n]$, (2) $\bigcup_{a \in [n]} A_a = [m]$ and (3) $A_a \cap A_b = \emptyset$ for each $a, b \in [n]$ with $a \neq b$. We consider several properties for allocations.

Envy-Freeness Up to One Item. Envy-freeness up to one item requires that an agent's envy for another's bundle is eliminated by removing an item from the bundles of these agents. Two notions for our model that are based on this idea are EF1 and EFX [4].

Definition 1 (EF1). *An allocation A is* envy-free up to some item *if, for each $a, b \in [n]$, $u_a(A_a) \geq u_a(A_b)$ or $\exists o \in A_a \cup A_b$ such that $u_a(A_a \setminus \{o\}) \geq u_a(A_b \setminus \{o\})$.*

Definition 2 (EFX). *An allocation A is* envy-free up to any non-zero valued item *if, for each $a, b \in [n]$, (1) $\forall o \in A_a$ such that $u_a(A_a) < u_a(A_a \setminus \{o\})$: $u_a(A_a \setminus \{o\}) \geq u_a(A_b)$ and (2) $\forall o \in A_b$ such that $u_a(A_b) > u_a(A_b \setminus \{o\})$: $u_a(A_a) \geq u_a(A_b \setminus \{o\})$.*

Plaut and Roughgarden [24] considered a variant of EFX for goods where, for any given pair of agents, the removed item may be valued with zero utility by the envious agent. Kyropoulou et al. [20] referred to this one as EFX_0. We adapt this property to our model.

Definition 3 (EFX_0). *An allocation A is* envy-free up to any item *if, for each $a, b \in [n]$, (1) $\forall o \in A_a$ such that $u_a(A_a) \leq u_a(A_a \setminus \{o\})$: $u_a(A_a \setminus \{o\}) \geq u_a(A_b)$ and (2) $\forall o \in A_b$ such that $u_a(A_b) \geq u_a(A_b \setminus \{o\})$: $u_a(A_a) \geq u_a(A_b \setminus \{o\})$.*

An allocation that is EFX_0 further satisfies EFX. Also, EFX is stronger than EF1. It is well-known that the opposite relations might not hold.

Envy-Freeness by Parts. Let $A = (A_1, \ldots, A_n)$ be a given allocation. We let $A_a^+ = \{o \in A_a | u_a(o) > 0\}$ and $A_a^- = \{o \in A_a | u_a(o) < 0\}$ for each $a \in [n]$. Envy-freeness by parts up to one item ensures that EF1 (or EFX) is satisfied in each of the allocations A, $A^+ = (A_1^+, \ldots, A_n^+)$ and $A^- = (A_1^-, \ldots, A_n^-)$.

Definition 4 ($EF1^3$). *An allocation A is* envy-free by parts up to some item *(EF1-EF1-EF1 or $EF1^3$) if the following conditions hold: (1) A is EF1, (2) A^+ is EF1 and (3) A^- is EF1.*

Definition 5 (EFX^3). *An allocation A is* envy-free by parts up to any item *(EFX-EFX-EFX or EFX^3) if the following conditions hold: (1) A is EFX, (2) A^+ is EFX and (3) A^- is EFX.*

With just goods (bads), EF1[3] (EFX[3]) is EF1 (EFX). With mixed manna, an allocation that is EF1[3] also satisfies EF1, one that is EFX[3] satisfies EFX, and one that is EFX[3] satisfies EF1[3]. The reverse implications might not be true.

Pareto-Optimality. We also study each of these fairness properties in combination with an efficiency criterion such as Pareto-optimality (PO), proposed a long time ago by Vilfredo Pareto [23].

Definition 6 (PO). *An allocation A is* Pareto-optimal *if there is no allocation B that* Pareto-improves *A, i.e.* $\forall a \in [n]$: $u_a(B_a) \geq u_a(A_a)$ *and* $\exists b \in [n]$: $u_b(B_b) > u_b(A_b)$.

4   Further Motivation

We next further motivate the new properties EF1[3] and EFX[3] by means of a simple example. Consider a birthday party where Bob invites his new friends Alice and Mary. Bob has 3 pieces of his favourite *strawberry cake* (value is 1) and 2 pieces of the less favorable to him *chocolate cake* (value is 0). Bob also hopes that some of his guests would be willing to help him *washing up the dishes* and *throwing away the garbage* after the party. Alice and Mary arrive and it turns out that both like only chocolate cake (value is 1), and dislike any of the household chores (value is −1) as does Bob. How shall we allocate the 5 goods (i.e. all pieces of cake) and the 2 chores?

For EF1 (EFX) and PO, we shall give the strawberry cake to Bob and one piece of the chocolate cake to each of Alice and Mary. As a result, Bob gets utility 3 whereas Alice and Mary get each utility 1. If we want to maximize the egalitarian welfare, we should assign both chores to Bob. Doing so preserves EF1 (EFX) and PO for all items. However, it violates EF1[3] (EFX[3]). Indeed, Bob might be unhappy simply because they have to do both chores instead of sharing them with Alice and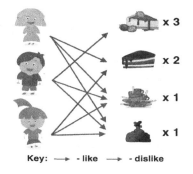

Mary. This means that an EF1 (EFX) allocation might not satisfy EF1[3] (EFX[3]). In contrast, achieving EF1[3] (EFX[3]) avoids assigning both chores to Bob. For example, asking Bob to wash up the dishes and Alice to throw away the garbage, or vice versa is EF1[3] (EFX[3]). Other such options share the chores between Bob and Mary, and Alice and Mary. However, none of these maximizes the egalitarian welfare. This means that EF1[1] (EFX[3]) might be incompatible with this objective.

5   General Additive Utilities

We begin with general utilities. An EF1 allocation in this domain can be computed in $O(\max\{m^2, mn\})$ time. For this purpose, we can use the existing *double round-robin* algorithm from [4]. However, this algorithm may fail to guarantee PO because an agent might pick a bad for which some other agent have zero utility.

Example 1. *Consider* 2 *agents and* 2 *items, say* a *and* b. *Define the utilities as follows:* $u_1(a) = -1$, $u_1(b) = -1$ *and* $u_2(a) = -1$, $u_2(b) = 0$. *In this problem, the double round-robin algorithm is simply a round-robin rule with some strict priority ordering of the agents. Wlog, let agent 1 pick before agent 2. Wlog, let agent 1 pick* b. *Now, agent 2 can only pick* a. *The returned allocation gives utility* -1 *to agent 1 and utility* -1 *to agent 2. By swapping these items, agent 1 receive utility* -1 *and agent 2 receive utility* 0. *Clearly, this is a Pareto-improvement.* □

In response, we modify slightly the double round-robin algorithm by adding an extra preliminary phase where each dummy item/non-pure bad is allocated to an agent who has zero utility for it: Algorithm 1. As we show, this modified version gives us an $EF1^3$ allocation that is PO not only with $-1/0/1$ utilities but also with any ternary utilities, as well as with absolute identical utilities.

Theorem 1. *With general utilities, Algorithm 1 returns an* $EF1^3$ *allocation in* $O(\max\{m^2, mn\})$ *time.*

Algorithm 1. An $EF1^3$ allocation (see the Appendix for a complete version).

1: **procedure** MODIFIED DOUBLE ROUND-ROBIN($[n], [m], (u_1, \ldots, u_n)$)
2:      $M^0 \leftarrow \{o \in [m] | \forall b \in [n] : u_b(t) \leq 0, \exists c \in [n] : u_c(t) = 0\}$
3:      $\forall a \in [n] : A_a \leftarrow \emptyset$
4:      **for** $t \in M^0$ **do**   ▷ allocate all dummies/non-pure bads
5:          pick $a \in \{b \in [n] | u_b(t) = 0\}$
6:          $A_a \leftarrow A_a \cup \{t\}$
7:      $B \leftarrow$ DOUBLE ROUND-ROBIN($[n], [m] \setminus M^0, (u_1, \ldots, u_n)$)
8:      **return** $(A_1 \cup B_1, \ldots, A_n \cup B_n)$

Proof. The double round-robin algorithm returns an EF1 allocation, and so B is EF1. Consider B^+ and B^-. Let there be $qn - p$ pure bads for some $q, p \in \mathbb{N}$ with $p < n$. The algorithm creates p "fake" dummy items for which each agent has utility 0, and adds them to the set of pure bads. Hence, the number of items in this set becomes qn. Thus, the agents come in a round-robin fashion according to some ordering of the agents, say $(1, \ldots, n-1, n)$, and pick their most preferred item in this set (i.e. all pure bads and "fake" dummies) until all of them are allocated. This is EF1 for the pure bads. Hence, B^- is EF1.

Further, the agents come in a round-robin fashion by following the reversed ordering, i.e. $(n, n-1, \ldots, 1)$, and pick their most preferred good until all mixed items and goods are allocated. If an agent has no available item which gives them strictly positive utility, they pretend to pick a new "fake" dummy item for which they have utility 0. This is EF1 for the mixed items and goods. Hence, B^+ is also EF1 which implies that B is EF1[3]. Finally, extending B to all items, by allocating each dummy item/non-pure bad to someone who holds zero utility, preserves EF1[3]. This means that the returned allocation is EF1[3]. □

We move to stronger properties. For example, EFX[3] allocations in our setting might not exist. The rationale behind this is that an agent may get their least valued bad in an attempt of achieving EFX for the bads. As a result, removing this bad from their bundle might not be sufficient to eliminate their envy of some other agent who receive positive utility for a good and a bad.

Proposition 1. *There are problems with 2 agents and ternary identical utilities for 1 pure goods and 2 pure bads, in which no allocation is EFX[3].*

Proof. Suppose that there are 2 agents and 3 items. We define the utilities as follows: $u(a) = -1$, $u(b) = -1$, $u(c) = 2$. We note that one EFX allocation gives items a, b and c to agent 1 and no items to agent 2. However, there is no allocation that satisfies EFX[3].

We observe that there are two EFX allocations of the pure bads, i.e. $A = (\{a\}, \{b\})$ and $B = (\{b\}, \{a\})$. Further, we observe that there are two EFX allocations of the pure good, i.e. $C = (\{c\}, \emptyset)$ and $D = (\emptyset, \{c\})$. By the symmetry of the utilities, we consider only A, C and D.

If we unite ("agent-wise") A and C, then $u(A_2 \cup C_2 \setminus \{b\}) = 0 < 1 = u(A_1 \cup C_1)$. Therefore, the union of A and C is not EFX and, therefore, EFX[3]. If we unite A and D, then $u(A_1 \cup D_1 \setminus \{a\}) = 0 < 1 = u(A_2 \cup D_2)$. Again, the union of A and D violates EFX[3]. Similarly, for B, C and D. □

By comparison, EFX allocations exist in 2-value problems with goods [2]. It follows immediately that EFX[3] allocations exist in such problems. From this perspective, we feel that our impossibility result compares favorably to this possibility result because such allocations may not exist in 2-value problems with goods and bads.

Even more, this result also implies that no EFX allocation satisfies EF1[3] and no EF1[3] allocation satisfies EFX in some problems with identical and ternary utilities. As a consequence, any allocation that could be returned by Algorithm 1 might violate EFX. These implications are also true for the stronger version EFX$_0$ in problems where such allocations exist.

However, EFX$_0$ allocations might also not always exist. The reason for this might be the presence of dummies. One may argue that such items could be removed. However, some web-applications on Spliddit for example ask agents to announce items (e.g. inherited items) and utilities but the system has no access to the actual items and, therefore, cannot remove the dummies [14].

Proposition 2. *There are problems with 2 agents and ternary identical utilities for 1 pure good and 1 dummy, in which no allocation is EFX_0.*

Proof. Suppose that there are 2 agents and 2 items, say a and b. We define the utilities as follows: $u(a) = 1$ and $u(b) = 0$. We argue that there is no EFX_0 allocation in this problem. To see this, we make two observations. Firstly, with the given set of items, it is impossible that both agents obtain the same utility, as the individual utilities are integers and their sum is odd. Secondly, EFX_0 for the agents in this problem where a dummy item is present requires that both agents have the same utility. This follows by the definition of EFX_0.   □

In contrast, a natural restriction of EFX_0 to goods is achievable in problems with 2 agents and general utilities [24], or *any* number of agents and 0/1 utilities [2]. By Propositions 1 and 2, it follows that neither EFX^3 nor EFX_0 can be achieved in combination with PO, or even a weaker efficiency notion such as *completeness* (i.e. all items are allocated), in general.

6   Absolute Identical Additive Utilities

We continue with absolute identical utilities. Requiring such utilities is not as strong as requiring just identical utilities. To see this, consider agents 1, 2 and items a, b. Define the utilities as $u_1(a) = 3$, $u_1(b) = 2$ and $u_2(a) = 3$, $u_2(b) = -2$. The absolute values of these utilities are identical but their cardinal values are not, e.g. $|u_1(b)| = |u_2(b)| = 2$ but $u_1(b) = 2, u_2(b) = -2$.

By Proposition 1, $EF1^3$ and EFX are incompatible in this domain. Nevertheless, we can combine each of them with PO. For example, Algorithm 1 returns an allocation that satisfies PO besides $EF1^3$. The key reason for this result is that in such problems there are no items that are bads (goods) for some agents and dummy for other agents.

Theorem 2. *With absolute identical utilities, Algorithm 1 returns an $EF1^3$ and PO allocation.*

Proof. $EF1^3$ follows by Theorem 1. We note that each allocation that gives at least one mixed item to an agent who values it strictly negatively can be Pareto-improved by moving this item to an agent who values it strictly positively. Therefore, such an allocation is not Pareto-optimal. We also note that each other allocation, including the returned one, maximizes the sum of agents' utilities because it achieves the maximum utility for each individual item. Such an allocation is always Pareto-optimal.   □

At the same time, we can compute an EFX and PO allocation in polynomial time. For this task, we propose a *new* algorithm: Algorithm 2. We let $M(o) = \max_{a \in [n]} u_a(o)$ denote the maximum utility that an agent derives from item o. Further, let us arrange the items in non-increasing absolute maximum utility order by using the following tie-breaking rule.

Ordering σ_m: Wlog, $|M(1)| \geq \ldots \geq |M(m)|$. Initialize σ_m to $(1, \ldots, m)$. While there are two items s and t from $[m]$ such that $|M(s)| = |M(t)|$, $M(s) > 0$, $M(t) < 0$ and t is right before s in σ_m, do move s right before t in σ_m. Thus, within items with the same absolute maximum utilities, σ_m gives higher priority to the mixed items/goods than to the pure bads.

Algorithm 2 allocates the items one-by-one in such an ordering σ_m. If the current item t is mixed or pure good, then Algorithm 2 gives it to an agent who has currently the minimum utility among the agents who like the item. If item t is pure bad, then Algorithm 2 gives it to an agent who has currently the maximum utility. Otherwise, it gives item t to an agent with zero utility.

Theorem 3. *With absolute identical utilities, Algorithm 2 returns an EFX and PO allocation in $O(\max\{m \log m, mn\})$ time.*

Algorithm 2. An EFX and PO allocation.

1: **procedure** MINIMAX$([n], [m], (u_1, \ldots, u_n))$
2:    $\forall a \in [n] : A_a \leftarrow \emptyset$
3:    $\sigma_m \leftarrow (1, \ldots, m)$, where $|M(1)| \geq \ldots \geq |M(m)|$ and, within items with tied absolute maximum utilities, mixed items/goods come before pure bads
4:    **for** $t \in \sigma_m$ **do**
5:       **if** t is mixed item or good **then**
6:          $N \leftarrow \{b \in [n] | u_b(t) > 0\}$
7:          MinUtil$(A) \leftarrow \{b \in N | u_b(A_b) = \min_{c \in N} u_c(A_c)\}$
8:          pick $a \in$ MinUtil(A)
9:       **else if** t is pure bad **then**
10:          MaxUtil$(A) \leftarrow \{b \in [n] | u_b(A_b) = \max_{c \in [n]} u_c(A_c)\}$
11:          pick $a \in$ MaxUtil(A)
12:       **else** $\triangleright$ t is dummy item or non-pure bad
13:          pick $a \in \{b \in [n] | u_b(t) = 0\}$
14:       $A_a \leftarrow A_a \cup \{t\}$
15:    **return** $(A_1, \ldots, A_n)$

Proof. For $t \in [m]$, we let A^t denote the partially constructed allocation of items 1 to t. Pareto-optimality of A^t follows by the same arguments as in Theorem 2, but now applied to the sub-problem of the first t items. We next prove that A^t is EFX by induction on t. This will imply the result for EFX and PO of A^m (i.e. the returned allocation).

In the base case, let t be 1. The allocation of item 1 is trivially EFX. In the hypothesis, let $t > 1$ and assume that the allocation A^{t-1} is EFX. In the step case, let us consider round t. Wlog, let the algorithm give item t to agent 1. That is, $A_1^t = A_1^{t-1} \cup \{t\}$ and $A_a^t = A_a^{t-1}$ for each $a \in [n] \setminus \{1\}$. It follows immediately by the hypothesis that each pair of different agents from $[n] \setminus \{1\}$ is EFX of each other in A^t. We note that t gives positive, negative or zero utility to agent 1. For this reason, we consider three cases for agent $a \in [n] \setminus \{1\}$ and agent 1.

Case 1: Let $u_1(t) > 0$. In this case, t is mixed item or pure good (good) and $u_1(A_1^t) > u_1(A_1^{t-1})$ holds. Hence, agent 1 remain EFX of agent a by the hypothesis. For this reason, we next show that agent a is EFX of agent 1. We consider two sub-cases depending on whether agent a belong to $N = \{b \in [n] | u_b(t) > 0\}$ or not. We note that $1 \in N$ holds because of $u_1(t) > 0$.

Sub-case 1 for $a \to 1$: Let $a \notin N$. Hence, $u_a(t) \leq 0$. As a result, $u_a(A_1^{t-1}) \geq u_a(A_1^t)$ holds. Thus, as A^{t-1} is EFX, we derive that $u_a(A_a^t) = u_a(A_a^{t-1}) \geq u_a(A_1^{t-1} \setminus \{o\}) \geq u_a(A_1^t \setminus \{o\})$ holds for each $o \in A_1^{t-1}$ with $u_a(o) > 0$. We also derive $u_a(A_a^t \setminus \{o\}) = u_a(A_a^{t-1} \setminus \{o\}) \geq u_a(A_1^{t-1}) \geq u_a(A_1^t)$ for each $o \in A_a^t$ with $u_a(o) < 0$. Hence, agent a is EFX of agent 1.

Sub-case 2 for $a \to 1$: Let $a \in N$. Hence, $u_a(t) > 0$. Moreover, $u_a(A_a^{t-1}) \geq u_1(A_1^{t-1})$ by the selection rule of the algorithm. For each item $o \in A_1^{t-1}$, we have $u_1(o) = u_a(o)$ if o is pure good, pure bad or dummy item, and $u_1(o) \geq u_a(o)$ if o is mixed item. Therefore, $u_1(A_1^{t-1}) \geq u_a(A_1^{t-1})$ or agent a is envy-free of agent 1 in A^{t-1}.

We derive $u_a(A_a^t) = u_a(A_a^{t-1}) \geq u_a(A_1^{t-1}) = u_a(A_1^t \setminus \{t\})$ because $A_a^t = A_a^{t-1}$ and $A_1^t = A_1^{t-1} \cup \{t\}$. Furthermore, $u_a(A_1^t \setminus \{t\}) \geq u_a(A_1^t \setminus \{o\})$ for each $o \in A_1^{t-1}$ with $u_a(o) > 0$ because $u_a(o) \geq u_a(t)$ holds due to the ordering of items used by the algorithm.

We now show EFX of the bads. We have $u_a(A_a^t \setminus \{o\}) = u_a(A_a^{t-1} \setminus \{o\}) \geq u_a(A_1^{t-1}) + u_a(t) = u_a(A_1^t)$ for each $o \in A_a^{t-1}$ with $u_a(o) < 0$ because $|u_a(o)| \geq u_a(t)$ holds due to the ordering of items used by the algorithm. Hence, agent a is EFX of agent 1.

Case 2: Let $u_1(t) < 0$. In this case, t is pure bad and $u_a(A_1^t) < u_a(A_1^{t-1})$ holds. That is, agent 1's utility decreases. By the hypothesis, it follows that agent a remain EFX of agent 1 in A^t. For this reason, we only show that agent 1 remain EFX of agent a.

$1 \to a$: We have $u_1(A_1^{t-1}) \geq u_a(A_a^{t-1})$ by the selection rule of the algorithm. For each item $o \in A_a^{t-1}$, we have $u_a(o) = u_1(o)$ if o is pure good, pure bad or dummy item, and $u_a(o) \geq u_1(o)$ if o is mixed item. We conclude $u_a(A_a^{t-1}) \geq u_1(A_a^{t-1})$ and, therefore, $u_1(A_1^{t-1}) \geq u_1(A_a^{t-1})$. Hence, agent 1 is envy-free of agent a in A^{t-1}.

Additionally, it follows that $u_1(A_1^t \setminus \{t\}) \geq u_1(A_a^t)$ holds because $A_1^t \setminus \{t\} = A_1^{t-1}$ and $A_a^t = A_a^{t-1}$. Due to the order of the items, we have $|u_1(b)| \geq |u_1(t)|$ for each $b \in A_1^t$ with $u_1(b) < 0$. Hence, $u_1(A_1^t \setminus \{b\}) \geq u_1(A_1^t \setminus \{t\}) \geq u_1(A_a^t)$ for each $b \in A_1^t$ with $u_1(b) < 0$.

At the same time, $u_1(A_1^{t-1}) \geq u_1(A_a^{t-1} \setminus \{g\})$ for each $g \in A_a^{t-1}$ with $u_1(g) > 0$. Again, due to the order of the items, $u_1(g) \geq |u_1(t)|$. Therefore, $u_1(A_a^t \setminus \{g\}) \leq u_1(A_a^t) - |u_1(t)| = u_1(A_a^{t-1}) - |u_1(t)| \leq u_1(A_1^{t-1}) - |u_1(t)| = u_1(A_1^t)$. Consequently, $u_1(A_1^t) \geq u_1(A_a^t \setminus \{g\})$ for each $g \in A_a^t$ with $u_1(g) > 0$.

Case 3: Let $u_1(t) = 0$. In this case, t is dummy item or non-pure bad. Hence, $u_a(A_1^{t-1}) \geq u_a(A_1^t)$ and $u_1(A_1^t) = u_1(A_1^{t-1})$ hold. That is, agent 1's utility does not change. By the hypothesis, this means that they remain EFX of each agent a and also each agent a remains EFX of them in A^t.

Finally, computing maximum values takes $O(mn)$ time and sorting items takes $O(m \log m)$ time. The loop of the algorithm takes $O(mn)$ time. □

For problems with identical utilities, Aziz and Ray [6] proposed the "egal-sequential" algorithm for computing EFX and PO allocations. By Theorem 3, Algorithm 2 also does that. However, we feel that such problems are very restrictive as they do not have mixed items unlike many practical problems.

Corollary 1. *With identical utilities, Algorithm 2 returns an EFX and PO allocation.*

Algorithm 2 allocates each mixed item/good to an agent who likes it, and each dummy item/non-pure bad to an agent who is indifferent to it. As a consequence, the result in Theorem 3 extends to problems where, for each mixed item/good, the likes are identical and, for each pure bad, the dislikes are identical.

Corollary 2. *With identical likes (i.e. strictly positive utilities) for each mixed item, identical likes for each good and identical dislikes (i.e. strictly negative utilities) for each pure bad, Algorithm 2 returns an EFX and PO allocation.*

7 Ternary Additive Utilities

We end with ternary utilities. That is, each agent's utility for each item is from $\{-\alpha, 0, \beta\}$ where $\alpha, \beta \in \mathbb{R}_{>0}$. We consider two cases for such utilities.

7.1 Case for Any α, β

By Proposition 1, it follows that an EFX[3] allocation might not exist in some problems even when $\alpha = 1$ and $\beta = 2$. However, we can compute an EF1[3] (notably, also EF1-EFX-EFX) and PO allocation with Algorithm 1.

Theorem 4. *With ternary utilities from $\{-\alpha, 0, \beta\}$ where $\alpha, \beta \in \mathbb{R}_{>0}$, Algorithm 1 returns an EF1[3] and PO allocation.*

Proof. The returned allocation is EF1[3] by Theorem 1. This one achieves the maximum utility for each individual item. Hence, the sum of agents' utilities in it is maximized and equal to β multiplied by the number of goods plus β multiplied by the number of mixed items minus α multiplied by the number of pure bads. In fact, this holds for each allocation that gives each mixed item/good to an agent who has utility β, and each dummy/non-pure bad to an agent who has utility 0. Each other allocation is not PO and does not Pareto-dominate the returned allocation. Hence, the returned one is PO. □

One the other hand, we already mentioned after Proposition 1 that each allocation returned by Algorithm 1 in such problems may violate EFX. However, Algorithm 2 returns an EFX and PO allocation in this case.

Theorem 5. *With ternary utilities from* $\{-\alpha, 0, \beta\}$ *where* $\alpha, \beta \in \mathbb{R}_{>0}$, *Algorithm 2 returns an EFX and PO allocation.*

Proof. This is where the ordering used by the algorithm plays a crucial role. If $\beta \geq \alpha$, we note that all mixed items and goods are allocated before all pure bads and all of these are allocated before the remaining items (i.e. dummy items and non-pure bads). If $\beta < \alpha$, we note that all pure bads are allocated before all mixed items and goods and all of these are allocated before the remaining items. Further, we observe that agents have identical likes for each mixed item or each good (i.e. β), and identical dislikes for each pure bad (i.e. $-\alpha$). Therefore, the result follows by Corollary 2. □

By comparison, the "ternary flow" algorithm of Aziz and Rey [6] may fail to return an EFX allocation even with $-2/1$ utilities. To see this, simply negate the utilities in the problem from Proposition 1. This algorithm allocates firstly one good to each agent and secondly the bad to one of the agents. This outcome violates EFX.

7.2   Case for $\alpha = \beta$

In this case, we can compute an EFX³ and PO allocation with Algorithm 1. Although we consider this a minor result, we find it important because it is the only one in our analysis when EFX³ and PO allocations exist.

Theorem 6. *With ternary utilities from* $\{-\alpha, 0, \alpha\}$ *where* $\alpha \in \mathbb{R}_{>0}$, *Algorithm 1 returns an EFX³ and PO allocation.*

Proof. The returned allocation is EF1¹ and PO by Theorem 4. With general (and, therefore, ternary) utilities, an allocation that is EFX³ also satisfies EF1³ because EFX is a stronger property than EF1, but the opposite implication might not be true. In fact, with utilities from $\{-\alpha, 0, \alpha\}$, the opposite implication also holds. Indeed, if an allocation is EF1 for a given pair of agents, then removing some good from the envied agent's bundle or removing some bad from the envy agent's bundle eliminates the envy of the envy agent. But, the envious agent likes each such good with α and each such bad with $-\alpha$. Hence, such an allocation is EFX. This implies that an EF1³ allocation is also EFX³ in this domain. □

By Theorem 5, Algorithm 2 returns an EFX and PO allocation in this case. However, this one might falsify EFX^3 even when $\alpha = 1$ (see motivating example). The same holds for the "ternary flow" algorithm of Aziz and Rey [6] because it maximizes the egalitarian welfare when $\alpha = 1$ (see motivating example).

8   Conclusions

We considered additive and fair division of mixed manna. For this model, we analysed axiomatic properties of allocations such as EFX_0, EFX^3, EFX, $EF1^3$, EF1 and PO in three utility domains. With general utilities, we showed that an $EF1^3$ allocation exists and gave Algorithm 1 for computing such an allocation (Theorem 1). With absolute identical or $-\alpha/0/\beta$ utilities, this algorithm returns an $EF1^3$ and PO allocation (Theorems 2 and 4). With $-\alpha/0/\alpha$ utilities, it returns an EFX^3 and PO allocation (Theorem 6).

With absolute identical utilities, we gave Algorithm 2 for computing an EFX and PO allocation (Theorem 3). With ternary utilities, this algorithm also returns such an allocation (Theorem 5). We further proved two impossibilities results (Propositions 1 and 2). In particular, with ternary identical utilities, an EFX_0 allocation, or an EFX^3 allocation might not exist. We leave for future work two very interesting open questions with general utilities. Table 1 contains our results.

Table 1. Key: ✓-possible, ×-not possible, P-polynomial time, $\alpha, \beta \in \mathbb{R}_{>0} : \alpha \neq \beta$.

Property	General utilities	Ident. & abs. utilities	$-\alpha/0/\beta$ utilities	$-\alpha/0/\alpha$ utilities
$EF1^3$	✓, P (Theorem 1)			
$EF1^3$ & PO	open	✓, P (Theorem 2)	✓, P (Theorem 4)	
EFX & PO	open	✓, P (Theorem 3)	✓, P (Theorem 5)	
EFX^3		× (Proposition 1)		
EFX^3 & PO				✓, P (Theorem 6)
EFX_0		× (Proposition 2)		

A   A Complete Version of Algorithm 1

For reasons of space, we presented a short version of Algorithm 1 in the main text. We present in here a complete version of it.

Algorithm 1. An EF1^3 allocation.

1: **procedure** MODIFIED DOUBLE ROUND-ROBIN($[n], [m], (u_1, \ldots, u_n)$)
2:      $M^0 \leftarrow \{o \in [m] | \forall b \in [n] : u_b(t) \leq 0, \exists c \in [n] : u_c(t) = 0\}$
3:      Allocate each item from M^0 to an agent who has utility 0 for it. We let A denote this allocation.
4:      $M^- \leftarrow \{o \in [m] \setminus M^0 | \forall a \in [n] : u_a(o) < 0\}$
5:      Suppose $|M^-| = qn - p$ for some $q, p \in \mathbb{N}$ with $p < n$. Create p "fake" dummy items for which each agent has utility 0, and add them to M^-. Hence, $|M^-| = qn$.
6:      Let the agents come in some round-robin sequence, say $(1, \ldots, n-1, n)$, and pick their most preferred item in M^- until all items in it are allocated.
7:      $M^+ \leftarrow \{o \in [m] \setminus M^0 | \exists a \in [n] : u_a(o) > 0\}$
8:      Let the agents come in the round-robin sequence $(n, n-1, \ldots, 1)$ and pick their most preferred item in M^+ until all items in it are allocated. If an agent has no available item which gives them strictly positive utility, they pretend to pick a "fake" dummy item for which they have utility 0.
9:      Remove the "fake" dummy items from the current allocation and return the resulting allocation. We let B denote this allocation.
10:      **return** $(A_1 \cup B_1, \ldots, A_n \cup B_n)$

References

1. Aleksandrov, M., Aziz, H., Gaspers, S., Walsh, T.: Online fair division: analysing a food bank problem. In: Proceedings of the Twenty-Fourth IJCAI 2015, Buenos Aires, Argentina, July 25–31, 2015, pp. 2540–2546 (2015)
2. Amanatidis, G., Birmpas, G., Filos-Ratsikas, A., Hollender, A., Voudouris, A.A.: Maximum Nash welfare and other stories about EFX. CoRR abs/2001.09838 (2020)
3. Amanatidis, G., Birmpas, G., Markakis, V.: Comparing approximate relaxations of envy-freeness. In: Proceedings of the Twenty-Seventh International Joint Conference on Artificial Intelligence, IJCAI 2018, Stockholm, Sweden, July 13–19, 2018, pp. 42–48 (2018)
4. Aziz, H., Caragiannis, I., Igarashi, A., Walsh, T.: Fair allocation of indivisible goods and chores. In: Proceedings of the Twenty-Eighth International Joint Conference on Artificial Intelligence, IJCAI-19, pp. 53–59. International Joint Conferences on Artificial Intelligence Organization, July 7 2019
5. Aziz, H., Moulin, H., Sandomirskiy, F.: A polynomial-time algorithm for computing a Pareto optimal and almost proportional allocation. CoRR abs/1909.00740 (2019)
6. Aziz, H., Rey, S.: Almost group envy-free allocation of indivisible goods and chores. In: Bessiere, C. (ed.) Proceedings of the Twenty-Ninth International Joint Conference on Artificial Intelligence, IJCAI-20, pp. 39–45. International Joint Conferences on Artificial Intelligence Organization, July 2020. main track
7. Barman, S., Krishnamurthy, S.K., Vaish, R.: Finding fair and efficient allocations. In: Proceedings of the 2018 ACM Conference on EC 2018, pp. 557–574. ACM, New York (2018)
8. Barman, S., Krishnamurthy, S.K., Vaish, R.: Greedy algorithms for maximizing Nash social welfare. In: Proceedings of the 17th International Conference on Autonomous Agents and MultiAgent Systems, AAMAS 2018, Stockholm, Sweden, July 10–15, 2018, pp. 7–13 (2018)

9. Bogomolnaia, A., Moulin, H., Sandomirskiy, F., Yanovskaia, E.: Dividing BADS under additive utilities. Soc. Choice Welfare **52**(3), 395–417 (2018)
10. Bogomolnaia, A., Moulin, H., Sandomirskiy, F., Yanovskaya, E.: Competitive division of a mixed manna. Econometrica **85**(6), 1847–1871 (2017)
11. Brams, S.J., Taylor, A.D.: Fair Division - From Cake-Cutting to Dispute Resolution. Cambridge University Press, Cambridge (1996)
12. Budish, E.: The combinatorial assignment problem: approximate competitive equilibrium from equal incomes. J. Polit. Econ. **119**(6), 1061–1103 (2011)
13. Caragiannis, I., Kaklamanis, C., Kanellopoulos, P., Kyropoulou, M.: The efficiency of fair division. Theory Comput. Syst. **50**(4), 589–610 (2012)
14. Caragiannis, I., Kurokawa, D., Moulin, H., Procaccia, A.D., Shah, N., Wang, J.: The unreasonable fairness of maximum Nash welfare. In: Proceedings of ACM Conference on EC 2016, Maastricht, The Netherlands, July 24–28, 2016, pp. 305–322 (2016)
15. Chevaleyre, Y., Dunne, P., Endriss, U., Lang, J., Lemaitre, M., Maudet, N., Padget, J., Phelps, S., Rodrguez-Aguilar, J., Sousa, P.: Issues in multiagent resource allocation. Informatica **30**, 3–31 (2006)
16. Dobzinski, S., Vondrák, J.: Communication complexity of combinatorial auctions with submodular valuations. In: Proceedings of the Twenty-fourth Annual ACM-SIAM Symposium on Discrete Algorithms. SODA 2013, Society for Industrial and Applied Mathematics, Philadelphia, PA, USA, pp. 1205–1215 (2013)
17. Dubins, L.E., Spanier, E.H.: How to cut a cake fairly. Am. Math. Monthly **68**(11), 1–17 (1961)
18. Foley, D.K.: Resource allocation and the public sector. Yale Econ. Essays **7**(1), 45–98 (1967)
19. Hugo, S.: The problem of fair division. Econometrica **16**, 101–104 (1948)
20. Kyropoulou, M., Suksompong, W., Voudouris, A.: Almost envy-freeness in group resource allocation. In: Proceedings of the Twenty-Eighth International Joint Conference on Artificial Intelligence, IJCAI 2019, pp. 400–406. International Joint Conferences on Artificial Intelligence Organization, August 2019
21. Lipton, R.J., Markakis, E., Mossel, E., Saberi, A.: On approximately fair allocations of indivisible goods. In: Proceedings of the 5th ACM Conference on EC, New York, NY, USA, May 17–20, 2004, pp. 125–131 (2004)
22. Moulin, H.: Fair Division and Collective Welfare. MIT Press, Cambridge (2003)
23. Pareto, V.: Cours d'Économie politique. Professeur á l'Université de Lausanne. vol. I. pp. 430 1896. vol. II. pp. 426. F. Rouge, Lausanne (1897)
24. Plaut, B., Roughgarden, T.: Almost envy-freeness with general valuations. In: Proceedings of the 29th Annual ACM-SIAM Symposium on Discrete Algorithms, SODA 2018, New Orleans, LA, USA, January 7–10, 2018, pp. 2584–2603 (2018)
25. Sandomirskiy, F., Segal-Halevi, E.: Fair division with minimal sharing. CoRR abs/1908.01669 (2019)
26. Young, H.P.: Equity - In Theory and Practice. Princeton University Press, Princeton (1995)

Dynamic Play via Suit Factorization Search in Skat

Stefan Edelkamp[✉]

University of Koblenz-Landau, Post Box 201 602, 56016 Koblenz, Germany
stefan.edelkamp@gmail.com

Abstract. In this paper we look at multi-player trick-taking card games that rely on obeying suits, which include Bridge, Hearts, Tarot, Skat, and many more. We propose mini-game solving in the *suit factors* of the game, and exemplify its application as a single-dummy or double-dummy analysis tool that restricts game play to either trump or non-trump suit cards. Such factored solvers are applicable to improve card selections of the declarer and the opponents, mainly in the middle game, and can be adjusted for optimizing the number of points or tricks to be made. While on the first glance projecting the game to one suit is an over-simplification, the partitioning approach into suit factors is a flexible and strong weapon, as it solves apparent problems arising in the phase transition of accessing static table information to dynamic play. Experimental results show that by using mini-game play, the strength of trick-taking Skat AIs can be improved.

1 Introduction

Computer game-playing AIs have shown outstanding performances in perfect-information board games like Go, Chess, and Shogi [26,27], and in multi-player, non-trick-taking card games like Poker [2]. As state-of-the-art programs are still playing considerable worse than human experts, there is a growing research interest in studying incomplete information multi-player trick-taking games, like Bridge [4], or Skat [5,20,21].

Many existing card-playing AIs perform some sort of machine learning on a large selection of expert games [7,10,19,28], often mixed with information-set sampling and open-card game play [4]. Especially in the opening stage of the trick-taking game such as the bidding stage or the first card to issue, static recommendation tables suggest cards by selecting and analyzing the feature vectors of human records [5].

In this paper, we consider Skat [24,25], a popular three-player international card game (see Fig. 1). For the single declarer, determined in a bidding stage, and the two opponents, we derived an approximation of winning probabilities from millions of expert games [5]. This goes down to associating statistical information to *card groups*, i.e., the patterns of cards within a certain *suit*. Depending on the game being played, card groups contain eight cards (Null), seven non-trump

© Springer Nature Switzerland AG 2020
U. Schmid et al. (Eds.): KI 2020, LNAI 12325, pp. 18–32, 2020.
https://doi.org/10.1007/978-3-030-58285-2_2

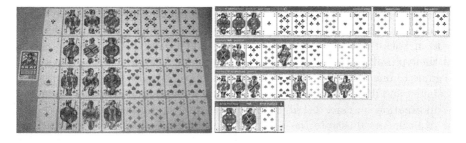

Fig. 1. Skat competition game cards, international deck, partitioned into suits (left, image credits: thanks to Sönke Kraft/Arnulf zu Linden); review of Skat game played on our Server with Skat taken and put, as well as first trick being played (right). The declarer plays Grand.

cards (Suit and Grand), and four trump cards (Grand), or eleven trump cards (Suit). Once cards in the suits have been played, this static group information, however, is no longer accurate.

By the vast amount of possible hands in a deal, and an even larger number of different trick-taking play in card games, there is a limit of what an expert game information can actually provide. While one can infer and store reliable statistical recommendations for the first cards to play, for later tricks in the middle game, this information is blurred, as with the cards that have already been played, the lookup tables associated to card groups loose precision. For example, it makes a great difference, whether or not the highest card of the game is still in play. The aim of the paper, therefore, is to obtain dynamic information in the suit *factors* of the game, where a factor is a projection of the card game to one of its suit. The contributions of the paper are as follows.

1. Devising a single- and double-dummy mini-game open card game solver that efficiently determines the outcome of a game between the declarer and the opponent(s); restricted to either one trump or non-trump suit, suggesting the card with the best possible payoff in optimal open card play. Card recommendations of different factors are compared for the overall suggestion.
2. Introduce several applications of mini-game solving for improving dynamic play and to determine the best possible card in a suit for the declarer and/or the opponent(s). We will address non-trump play in Grand and trump play in Suit games.
3. As the single-dummy solver becomes available in circumstances. Where suits are not obeyed, the knowledge of the distribution of cards at least in the suits is maintained and updated accordingly. Effectively the two player with the remaining suit cards play a two-player game.
4. For the double-dummy algorithm, we save high non-trump cards from being played too eagerly to save tricks and points for the declarer.
5. Experimental findings based on playing series of thousands of high-quality games show the impact of the mini-game searches in improving the playing strength of an existing Skat AI.

The paper is structured as follows. After kicking off with a motivation of two scenarios for Suit factorization, we briefly look into recent algorithmic developments in trick-taking card games, including PIMC and $\alpha\mu$ [4]; their strength and their pitfalls. Then, we turn to factorizing the search space by projecting the game to one of its suits (trump or non-trump). We provide the essentials of the single- and double-dummy implementation we used, and give insights in how the information on card distributions in each suit is updated within the game. The experiments illustrate the potential of the factorization method, which we wrap-up with concluding comments.

2 Two Scenarios

2.1 Trump Card Selection in Suit

Once the distribution of cards in one suit has been clarified, e.g., by one player not obeying a suit, the game projected to that suit, essentially, is a two-person game. To monitor and improve trump play of the opponents, the knowledge of the players is maintained and updated in *knowledge vectors/sets* $\overline{K_{ij}}$, containing the cards that due to the cards being played, Player i knows that Player (or Skat) j must not have [6]. The opponent player, who ran out of cards in that suit acts as a *dummy* (known terminology in Bridge), putting high cards in her partner's trick and low cards in the declarer's ones. In such *trump factor* of the game, we assume the declarer to be strong, and, once a trick gets lost, to receive back the right of issuing the next card. Similarly, if the declarer is about to issue a card, she can start the double-dummy analysis.

2.2 Standing Card Selection in Grand

For the declarer to select a non-trump card in Grand, we integrate statistical information tables for choosing the card to build what we call a *standing group*. After a few cards have been played, however, the accuracy of the information gained from a millions of games drops significantly, resulting in a rising need of a dynamic analysis.

Surely, towards the end of the game, we can apply additional plausibility tests. If the declarer already has 50 points, we should prefer playing an Ace to seal the deal, even if the analysis tells us to build groups by using a low-value card. Similarly, if the opponents already have 47 points, we avoid finessing the 10 with issuing a Queen.

Suppose as an example, we are playing Grand and are analyzing ♠. The declarer is about to open a trick and to have hand cards ♠A, ♠Q, ♠9 with ♠8 being already played. We have that ♠10, ♠K, ♠7 are the possible opponent cards. According to the hyper-geometric distribution there is a 78.9% chance of the opponent cards to be partitioned into 2:1 cards, and with probability of 21.1% for a partitioning into 3:0 cards. For the factor analysis of standing cards in Table 1 we assume that if one opponents run out of cards they lift the other with 10 points, while no foreign points are given to the declarer. As a result issuing ♠A is worse by about 5 points on average than playing ♠9.

3   Limits of Perfect Information Monte-Carlo Sampling

The main challenge is that based on the impartial knowledge about the cards, there is uncertainty in the players' belief of the real card distribution. Moreover, card playing conventions enable to transfer card information transfer among the players. There have been notable recent suggestions on how to organize the search in trick-taking games, so that the search maintains information (alias belief) sets instead of singleton cards.

Counter-factual regret minimization (CFR) [31] has been established as a very powerful tool for the selection of moves in incomplete information games, but the search trees generated for its application in trick-based card play are widely considered to be currently too deep for a timely analysis [7].

Table 1. Skat factor analysis for all possible opponent card distributions; numbers: points lost to the opponents by the declarer, percentage of games being affected according to the hyper-geometric distribution, influence equals points time percentage (left), expected average, maximum and minimum points made by the opponents, rounded to full integers (right).

Opp.'s card	Card played	Points	Prob [%]	Influence
♠10, ♠K, ♠7	♠A	34	21.1%	7.17
♠10, ♠K, ♠7	♠Q	37	21.1%	7.81
♠10, ♠K, ♠7	♠9	34	21,1%	7.17
♠10, ♠K	♠A	20	26.3%	5.26
♠10, ♠K	♠D	13	26.3%	3.42
♠10, ♠K	♠9	10	26.3%	2.63
♠10, ♠7	♠A	20	26.3%	5.26
♠10, ♠7	♠Q	13	26.3%	3.42
♠10, ♠7	♠9	10	26.3%	2.63
♠K, ♠7	♠A	14	26,3%	3.68
♠K, ♠7	♠Q	17	26.3%	4.47
♠K, ♠7	♠9	14	26.3%	3.68

	♠ A	♠Q	♠9
aver. Points	21	19	16
max. Points	34	37	34
min. Points	14	13	10

Perfect information Monte-Carlo sampling (PIMC) as introduced by Levy [15] is currently still one the best algorithmic options for dealing with imperfect information in trick-taking card games. It has already been used in Ginsberg's popular Bridge-playing program GIB [8], and taken on to other trick-taking games like Skat [7,11,13], or Spades/Hearts [29]. An attempt for the analysis of PIMC is made by Long [16]. The algorithmic take in PIMC is, at each decision point to select a card, to evaluate a larger sample of the belief space and call a double-dummy solver for each of the worlds, followed by selecting the card with maximum score. Furtak [7] has proposed *recursive Monte-Carlo search* to improve PIMC. Several limitations have been identified for Bridge play as matters of *strategy fusion* and *non-locality* by [4], leading to the $\alpha\mu$ search algorithm(s) that lifts some of them. The main observation is that even if the full belief space would be sampled and analyzed, the individual searches in PIMC may lead to contradicting card proposals. The main contribution of $\alpha\mu$ is to devise Pareto optimality into the search process and increase the look-ahead (parameter M) in PIMC for a better exploration/exploitation trade-off. The increase in running time is reduced by further pruning rules. In its nestedness the recursive strategy shares similarities with *nested Monte-Carlo search* [3,30] or *nested rollout policy adaptation* [23].

4 Factorized Search

Factorizing the search is a concept well-known from combinatorial game theory [1] and has been applied to endgame play in Computer Go [18]. The main approach, readily applicable to simple games such as Nim and put forward to a divide-and-conquer search strategy is to decompose the larger game into several smaller ones, whose combination exactly solve the original game [17]. With this paper we aim much lower, and look at mini-searches in the factors for each of the suits (either trump or non-trump) to approximately solve the overall game through addressing some of the problems in dynamically optimizing play; e.g., providing card suggestions for the case, when information about card become clarified, possibly due to non-obeying suits.

Our so-called mini-game solver is widely usable to bridge the opening of the trick-taking stage, where we can apply reliable statistical information for proper card recommendations, to the endgame, where we can analyze the entire belief-space. We give some examples in the game of Skat, but the approach is applies many other trick-taking card games as well. In particular, mini-game search can be used, e.g,

- for book-keeping trumps in opponent play, where we have to select a trump card and evaluate the strength of the play against the declarer. Suppose ♣ is trump, that the declarer issues ♡J, and is known to have ♣J,♣Q,♣9,♣8 as remaining cards in her hand, with one opponent bailing out on trump. The other opponent has ◇J,♣A,♣10, so that in trump 28 points are available. If we further set that the declarer gets back the right to open a trick, mini-game search determines that, assuming optimal play, 17 points are at reach for the declarer, suggesting to play card ♣10 first, on ♣J playing ◇J second, holding back the ♣A for the 11 points difference.
- For book-keeping non-trumps for the opponents. If we were to know that the declarer has ◇A,◇K,◇9, and ◇7 in one suit and the others three of the total seven cards are located at one opponent, then she knows that she has to overtake an issued no-value card played by the declarer with the Q to save the ◇10. Similarly, for ◇10, ◇K, ◇9 in the declarer's hand the opponents will be able to secure the Ten, if the Ace is held with two other cards.
- for the analysis of standing cards as an estimate on the number of tricks in a suit that will go home eventually. The first card to issue can be extracted from expert rules, but in the middle game, this lacks dynamic information about trick-taking. The number of tricks (if any) to be secured by the opponents can be counted and indicate, which card the declarer has to show. Based on this information in the endgame it is even possible to detect so-called non-trump or trump *forks*.

Given a formal definition of a game that describes of the hands and moves, it is straight-forward to derive one for a mini-game by simply projecting all its card sets in the hand and moves to the currently analyzed suit ϕ. One could use *extensive form game* $G = (N, A, H, Z, \rho, \sigma, u, I)$ with factor $G \downarrow \phi = (N, A \downarrow \phi, H \downarrow \phi, Z \downarrow \phi, \rho \downarrow \phi, \sigma \downarrow \phi, u \downarrow \phi, I \downarrow \phi)$, where N is the set of players and H is the set of non-terminal states in the game. is defined as the history of all actions taken Z is the set of terminal histories. $H \cap Z = \emptyset$ and $H \cup Z = S$ is the set of all states in the game. Z corresponds to the set of leaf nodes in a game tree. Utility function $u_i : Z \rightarrow \mathbb{R}$ gives a real-valued payoff to player i given that the game ends at state $z \in Z$. $\rho : H \rightarrow N$ is a function that defines which player is to move in state $h \in H$. $A(h)$ is the set of moves available in state h. $\sigma : H \times A \rightarrow S$ is the state transition function that maps a non-terminal state and action to a new state. For all $h_1, h_2 \in H$ and $a_1, a_2 \in A$ if $\sigma(h_1, a_1) = \sigma(h_2, a_2)$ then $h_1 = h_2$ and $a_1 = a_2$. Information sets I are partitions of non-terminal states that players cannot tell apart. When $|I| = 1$ for all I we are in a perfect information game. As we generate all possible open card distributions, in mini-game search, we look at a series of perfect information games only.

While in principle possible wrt. the requested brevity and contribution of the paper, we avoid mapping the rules of Skat into extensive form games in full detail. As the number of projected hand cards may vary among the players, additional rules for filling up the hands of the opponents, and of obeying have to be found if a player runs out of cards. It is also often requested to modify the rules of issuing a trick, as in some cases we may want the alter the right to issue the trick. Other than this the playing rules are the same as in the original game, making it a game tree abstraction.

5   The Power of Suit Partitioning

Following early work of Lasker [14], it has mathematically been motivated and, later on, empirically been shown that for variants of the Null-Games (Null, Null-Hand, Null-Ouvert, Null-Ouvert-Hand, the misére game variants in Skat), approximating the winning probabilities $P_w(h)$ of a hand h multiplying the projected ones $P_w(h \downarrow s)$ in each suit, $s \in \{\clubsuit, \spadesuit, \heartsuit, \diamondsuit\}$ is astonishingly accurate [5], so that

$$P_w(h) \approx \prod_{s \in \{\clubsuit, \spadesuit, \heartsuit, \diamondsuit\}} P_w(h \downarrow s).$$

If the hand h is represented as a set of cards and s is represented by the set of all cards in a suit, then $P_w(h \downarrow s) = P_w(h \cap s)$.

We use bit-vectors for card sets. Patterns in each suit are indexed. For a suit of eight cards in the Null game we have the *card group* $CG_8(h, s) = h \downarrow s \in \{0, \ldots, 255\}$. For non-trump we have groups $CG_7(h, s)$ and for trump play either $CG_{11}(h, s)$ (Suit), or CG_4 (Grand). In GG_k there are at most 2^k hands. Given that there are three different players and cards that already been played, pre-computing all possible card combination for a fast lookup in a hash table is cumbersome and leads to large tables. In the static variant, where the groups have not been touched during trick play, we generate tables of size 2^k with the probabilities for winning have to be pre-computed using the large amount of stem games. The concept of such table is present for many different aspects of the Skat game like color change, first cards to issue, cutting cards, etc.

Unfortunately, the statistical information does not easily cover on-going games, as the CGs are affected by the removal of cards being played. As an example of the concept of dynamic suit partitioning is the computation of safe cards, since a hand of the declarer in a Null game is safe (100% certain), if it is safe in each of the suits [12].

For trump games (Grand/Suits) the concept of accumulating static information in each suit (either trump or non-trump cards only) is also reflected in some of the features of a hand, to determine the winning probability. One such feature is the number of trump aces and non-trump aces and tens, or free suits, which are empty groups. A critical one is estimating the number of *standing cards* in each suit, a player expects to win. The approximation of standing cards are added for the entire hand,

$$standing(h) = \sum_{s \in \{\clubsuit, \heartsuit, \spadesuit, \diamondsuit\}} standing(h \downarrow s),$$

where $standing(h \downarrow s) = standing(h \cap s)$. For estimating $standing(h \downarrow s)$ statistical information is collected.

While this works well for bidding, for Skat putting and for the early stages of trick play, the dynamic evolution of CGs, e.g., for standing cards, this proves to be a real challenge. Note that the algorithm for detecting safe suits and hands that takes into account the cards being played is not easily to be extended, as in trump games the right to issue cards often changes, and we necessarily need to count tricks and points.

Therefore, a dynamic concept of standing cards is needed, which we call *mini-games*, i.e., the reduction of the overall game to one suit or the set of trump cards, aggregating the values for the entire game, possible averaging with respect to the amount of uncertainty in the cards. In mini-games, only cards in one suit, are issued. To overcome the problem we use an open card mini-game solver, the *mini-glassbox*.

6   Mini-Glassbox Search

Open alias dummy card solving is a search using a glassbox by having with perfect information that is not necessarily present but may be sampled. There are single-dummy and double-dummy variants of the mini-glassbox search algorithm (MGB-SDS and MGB-DDS for short). These algorithms compute the best playing card wrt. the optimization objective and the trick's starting condition, while assuming optimal play of the opponents. The search spaces in the mini-games are so small that for the sake of performance, we omit transposition table pruning [22], as the total exploration efforts in these state spaces are negligible and the gain in the number of explored nodes are dominated by re-initializing the hash table after each invocation of the solver.

Our exploration algoithm for such open card solvers, is decomposed into decision procedure on a given threshold for the point and embedded in a binary search for computing the optimum (a paradigm also known as *moving test driver*, cf. e.g., [12]).

6.1   Single-Dummy Mini-Glassbox Solver

The simplest case is given if one of the three players is known not to have a card of a certain (non-trump or trump) suit s, e.g. by not obeying s. Then, the mini-game reduces to only two parties that remain to hold cards of s in their hands. Except of the cards put in the Skat, full knowledge of all cards in s is known. There are also other measures monitoring the play to deduce if one player cannot have any card of a certain kind, as one may generally assume that the lowest-value card is given to the trick owned by the opposing party, and the highest-value card to the trick owned by the own party.

In practice the single-dummy variant of the mini-game solver applies to trump play in suit games in order to decide on the trump card for an opponent to obey, or to a player to decide whether or not to start issuing trump cards from top to bottom. At this stage of the game it has been clarified that the other player has no trump card left.

The algorithm counts the number of points the declarer can cash in, and assumes optimal play of both parties. Notice a few subtle insights. While the result of the trick is correctly distributed to the players, the next turn will always be at the declarer's site, which compensates for the fact that s/he tries to win

```
MiniSingle::AND(playable)
  if (!playable)
    return opoints + sum(h[1]) < maximum - limit;
  while (playable)
    index = select(playable); bitindex = (1<<index);
    h[0] &= ~bitindex; played |= bitindex;
    t[0] = index; rval = -1;
    if (|played| mod 2 == 0)
      turn = winner(1,0);
      score = VALUE(t[0]) + VALUE(t[1]);
      if (turn) opoints += score; else dpoints += score;
      t1 = t[1]; t[0] = t[1] = -1;
      rval = (opoints >= maximum-limit) ? 0
        : (dpoints > limit) ? 1 : AND(h[0]);
      t[1] = t1;
      if (turn) opoints -=score; else dpoints -= score;
    else
      rval = OR(h[1]);
    t[0] = -1;
    played &= ~bitindex; h[0] |= bitindex;
    playable &= ~bitindex;
    if (rval == 1) return 1;
  return 0;
```

Fig. 2. Single-dummy mini-glassbox solver for declarer node, counting points.

and is assumed to get back to play with the stronger by-hand. The reasoning is that the declarer will get his/her right to issue the card. The single-dummy algorithm is given in Fig. 2, so that there are two players, of which we selected the declarer node. The algorithm is tuned for speed. It uses bitvectors for the hands, played, and playable cards. Function select extracts one bit in the set (via constant-time processor instructions), winner determines the leader in a trick. Hand cards are $h[j]$, table cards are $t[j]$, with j being Player $j \in \{0, 1, 2\}$, If the declarer (Player 0) runs short of playable trumps, all remaining cards are counted for the opponents (opoints). Otherwise, a card is selected, and the search continues.

There are some further issues to be solved, as some cards may be already present on the table. They also influence the maximum of points that can be obtained. As we count points, we take into account the value of the partner card in the first trick.

6.2 Double-Dummy Mini-Glassbox Solver

The double-dummy version of the mini-glassbox solver is shown in Fig. 3, also for the declarer's turn. Besides being defined for three players, it aligns with the notation of variables in the single-dummy version of Fig. 2.

The double-dummy mini-glassbox solver shares similarities with the double-dummy solver for the overall game. But the search space is much smaller, as the game is restricted to only one suit. Again, we skip transposition table pruning to avoid cleaning the hash table. For the standing card *value* we use the solver

```
MiniDouble::AND(playable)
  if (!playable) return dpoints > limit;
  while (playable) {
    index = select(playable); bitindex = (1<<index);
    h[0] &= ~bitindex; played |= bitindex;
    t[0] = index; rval = -1;
    if (|played| mod 3 == 0)
      turn = winner(1,2,0);
      score = 1;
      if (turn) opoints += score; else dpoints += score;
      t1 = t[1], t2 = t[2];
      t[0] = t[1] = t[2] = -1;
      rval =
        (opoints >= maximum-limit)? 0:
        (dpoints > limit)? 1:
        (turn==1 && h[0] && h[1] & suit)? OR1(h[1]):
        (turn==2 && h[0] && h[2] & suit)? OR2(h[2]):
        AND(h[0]);
      t[1] = t1; t[2] = t2;
      if (turn) opoints -=score; else dpoints -= score;
    else
      rval = OR1(playable_cards(h[1]));
    t[0] = -1;
    played &= ~bitindex; h[0] |= bitindex;
    playable &= ~bitindex;
    if (rval == 1) return 1;
  return 0;
```

Fig. 3. Double-dummy mini-glassbox solver for declarer node, counting tricks.

for counting the number of tricks, while for computing the optimal card we also count points as illustrated in the motivating example. As we see there are now three players AND, OR1, and OR2.

In this case we want the number of tricks as a measure about to generate standing non-trump cards for the declarer. Again the decision variant for a given threshold is shown. An example for the algorithm for building standing cards is as follows. Assume the declarer has A, K, 8, 7 in some arbitrary suit, and plays the 8.

Case 1. Both opponents obey the suit, then only one card is in the opponents hands, and the ace is the highest card, so that the declarer gets all tricks if she plays from above, as she has three standing cards.

Case 2. One opponent does not have a remaining card in the requested suit. If the 10 drops immediately, the AS wins all further tricks, given that she issues from highest- to lowest-value card. If one opponent overtakes the trick with the Queen, the declarer has to take the Ace to loose the 7. For this case she only has 2 standing cards.

For the glassbox solver after a trick has been collected and counted for the correct party, we impose that the declarer gets the right to issue the next card, only if there is no other card of the suit that can be played.

Padding with irrelevant cards aligns the number of cards to the one of the declarer if needed. When we were to count points, opponent cards become padded with high cards, with their value is not being counted in a declarer's trick.

```
MiniDouble::solve(h0,h1,h2,play,P0,P1,P2,start)
  left = -1, right = maximum;
  while (true)
    if (left == right-1)
      return right;
    limit = (left+right)/2;
    x = MGBS(h0,h1,h2,play,P0,P1,P2,start);
    if (!x) right = limit; else left = limit;

MiniDouble::find(h0,h1,h2,first) {
  pad1 = count(h0) - count(h1) + (first != -1);
  pad2 = count(h0) - count(h2) + (first != -1);
  h1 = pad(h1,pad1);
  h2 = pad(h2,pad2);
  maximum = count(h0) + (first != -1);
  if (first == -1)
    return solve(h0,h1,h2,0,-1,-1,-1,0);
  else
    return solve(h0,h1,h2,(1<<first), first,-1,-1,1);
  return v;

MiniDouble::distribute(decl,opps,o0,o1,first)
  if (opps == 0)
   return find(decl,h0,h1,first);
  index = select(opps); bit = (1<<index);
  aver1 = distribute(decl,opps & ~bit,o0 | bit, o1,first);
  aver2 = distribute(decl,opps & ~bit,o0, o1 | bit,first);
  return aver1 + aver2;
```

Fig. 4. Calling the Mini double-dummy glassbox solver for all distributions of opponent cards.

Of course this again is only an approximation. Setting the turn for the next trick neglects the play in the other suits and trump cards. Always assigning it to the declarer neglects finessing the cards, which is an important factor in almost all trick-taking games.

The binary search optimization algorithm for the exact value assuming optimal play is called for each possible card distribution of the opponents. As this distribution might be uneven, to allow playing on, we pad cards of different suits to the opponents.

It is well-known that the number of cards in a suit follow a hyper-geometric distribution [9]. In Fig. 4 we illustrate how to generate all possible remaining opponent hands, given the hand for the declarer. The algorithm is recursive and puts all possible cards still to distribute in either the one or the other hand until no opponent card remains. The result of evaluating all calls with the mini-glassbox solver is added, and later on averaged for the number of possible distributions.

7   Experiments

In the experiments we look at 10,000 Suit games in of all types $t \in \{\diamondsuit, \heartsuit, \spadesuit, \clubsuit\}$ and an equal number of Grand games. In a three-player pure AI game we replay the deal of human expert games, using the human Skat, and the human game chosen. We also ran the AIs on 3,600 random deals on our Skat server.

While the mini-glassbox (MGB) solving approach is more general and can be modified to different objectives, we decided to evaluate a) single-dummy mini-glassbox search for better trump play in Suit games, optimizing the number of points; and b) double-dummy search for better non-trump play in Grand games, optimizing the number of points and tricks. Our computer has an Intel(R) Core(TM) i7-8565 CPU @ 1.8 GHz and 16 GB RAM given to an Oracle Linux VM. The programming language was C++ (gcc, version 7.4.0 Ubuntu-8.04.1).

Single-Dummy Mini-Game Search for Playing and Obeying Trump in Suit Games. We extracted 10,000 Skat expert Suit games and added the MGB solver to the opponents. Once the monitor of the knowledge base has derived that there are only two hands remaining that have trump cards, it calls the MGB to help selecting a trump card according to the suggested outcome of the solver.

The obtained empirical results are presented in Table 2. We separate between the play with and without the support of the MGB solver, and further partition with respect to a) the Human game play outcome and b) the outcome of an open card (retrospective) solver for the entire game. The advances in this case are visible but moderate. We see that with the support of the MGB solver the opponents are able to win 32 more games against the same AI for the declarer.

Table 2. Suit games without and with opponent support of a Mini-Glassbox analysis.

	Human wins	Glassbox wins	Computer wins	Count	Percentage	CPU time
Without MGB	0	0	0	763	7.6%	
	0	0	1	756	7.6%	
	0	1	0	58	0.6%	
	0	1	1	271	2.7%	
	1	0	0	462	4.6%	
	1	0	1	1,250	12.5%	
	1	1	0	244	2.4%	
	1	1	1	6,196	62.0%	
Total (Wins)	8,152	6,769	8,473	10,000	100%	633 s
With MGB	0	0	0	776	7.8%	
	0	0	1	743	7.4%	
	0	1	0	57	0.6%	
	0	1	1	272	2.7%	
	1	0	0	467	4.7%	
	1	0	1	1,245	12.5%	
	1	1	0	259	2.6%	
	1	1	1	6,181	61.8%	
Total (Wins)	8,152	6,769	8,441	10,000	100%	647 s

Double-Dummy Mini-Game Search for Standing Cards in Grand Games. In the second set of experiments, we took 10,000 Skat expert Grand games and added the MGB solver to find the declarer's best card to issue; via generating standing cards in each of the non-trump suits. As described above, we generated all possible distributions of the non-trump suit and compared the standing card value gain between the different playing options.

The results are presented in Table 3. The opponents are able to win 160 more games. This advance of declarer play is a significant improvement, as the number of games won was already close to the the the maximum of 10,000 games: almost 30% of the previously lost games, are now won by the new AI for the declarer.

In both cases, the performance offset is acceptable, as the average time of an entire game is below 0.1 s and includes all file handling, pre-computation efforts and the open-card analysis of the entire game. We also see, that the AI declarer wins significant more games than the human one. This might indeed be a sign of superior computer play, but also an indication that the AI opponents are not yet strong enough.

Overall. We also played 3,600 games of various kinds on our skat server with three fully independent Skat AI clients. We included suit factorization and endgame support [6] for both the declarer and the opponents after trick 5 with a belief-space size of at most 100 (see Fig. 4). Including bidding the entire simulation took 19.82 m in total. Of the 3,600 games, 154 games were folded (4.27%). We applied a rating of the games that is also used in competitions. For this, the average playing strength for a series of 36 games was $(88, 157 + 89, 522 + 94, 797) \cdot (3, 600/3, 446)/(3 \cdot 100) \approx 950$.

Table 3. Grand games without and with declarer support of a Mini-Glassbox analysis.

	Human wins	Glassbox wins	Computer wins	Count	Percentage	CPU time
Without MGB	0	0	0	135	1.4%	
	0	0	1	274	0.2%	
	0	1	0	15	0.2%	
	0	1	1	140	1.4%	
	1	0	0	178	1.8%	
	1	0	1	658	6.6%	
	1	1	0	229	2.3%	
	1	1	1	8,371	83.7%	
Total (Wins)	9,436	8,755	9,443	10,000	100%	794 s
With MGB	0	0	0	121	1.2%	
	0	0	1	288	2.8%	
	0	1	0	8	0.1%	
	0	1	1	147	1.5%	
	1	0	0	134	1.3%	
	1	0	1	702	7.0%	
	1	1	0	134	1.3%	
	1	1	1	8,466	84.6%	
Total (Wins)	9,436	8,755	9,603	10,000	100%	902 s

Table 4. Results on 3,600 games for random deals played on the Skat server, with AI bidding, skat putting, and trick-taking play. For each player the first row shows points, games won, games lost, and estimated card strength.

result	35057	935	173	8.67	36052	964	185	8.74	40027	999	190	8.81
+ (won Games - lost Games) x 50	38100	762			38950	779			40450	809		
+ turned games x 40	15000	375			14520	363			14320	358		
total	88157				89522				94797			

8   Conclusion

Factorized card-game solving is an almost universally applicable technique to optimize trick-taking play in cases, where the remaining hands among the players are either known exactly or the information set can be enumerated completely. The approach is based on projecting a game to its suits and combining the result of the according game factors. It is applied for the declarer or the opponents to optimize the number of tricks or points, assuming the game is not already won in the current trick. The players optimize dynamic card play, since after one trump trick static information on average distribution and probabilities is no longer available. As one means, the declarer can use it for a dynamic computation of non-trump standing cards. Similarly, all players can optimize trump play. We can also use it for approximating the number of declarer points for announcing *Schneider* and *Schwarz*.

The approach of mini-game open card solving is a tool to improve card selection in Skat. Although much information about all the other cards in the game is neglected, and given that we combine the exploration results directly to an evaluation of the overall search space, compared to combinatorial game theory, the factorized approach of optimally solving partial problems helps in many cases for choosing the best card.

Acknowledgments. Thanks to Rainer Gößl for his invaluable help as a skat expert.

References

1. Berlekamp, E.R., Conway, J.H., Guy, R.K.: Winning Ways for Your Mathematical Plays, Vol. 1–4. A K Peters (2001)
2. Bowling, M., Burch, N., Johanson, M., Tammelin, O.: Heads-up limit hold'em poker is solved. Commun. ACM **60**(11), 81–88 (2017)
3. Cazenave, T.: Nested Monte-Carlo search. In: International Joint Conference on Artificial Intelligence (IJCAI), pp. 456–461 (2009)
4. Cazenave, T., Ventos, V.: The $\alpha\mu$ search algorithm for the game of Bridge. CoRR, abs/1911.07960 (2019)
5. Edelkamp, S.: Challenging human supremacy in Skat. In: Symposium on Combinatorial Search (SOCS), pp. 52–60 (2019)
6. Edelkamp, S.: Representing and reducing uncertainty for enumerating the belief space to improve endgame play in Skat. In: European Conference on Artificial Intelligence (ECAI) (2020)
7. Furtak, T.M.: Symmetries and search in trick-taking card games. Ph.D. thesis, University of Alberta (2013)
8. Ginsberg, M.: Step toward an expert-level Bridge-playing program. In: International Joint Conference on Artificial Intelligence (IJCAI), pp. 584–589 (1999)
9. Gößl, R.: Der Skatfuchs - Gewinnen im Skatspiel mit Mathematische Methoden. Selfpublisher. Dämmig, Chemnitz, Available from the Author or via DSKV Altenburg (2019)
10. Keller, T., Kupferschmid, S.: Automatic bidding for the game of Skat. In: German Conference on Artificial Intelligence (KI), pp. 95–102 (2008)
11. Knorr, F.: Ein selbstkalibrierender Spieler für Skat. Master's thesis, Universität Passau (2018)
12. Kupferschmid, S.: Entwicklung eines Double-Dummy Skat Solvers mit einer Anwendung für verdeckte Skatspiele. Master's thesis, Albert-Ludwigs-Universität Freiburg (2003)
13. Kupferschmid, S., Helmert, M.: A Skat player based on Monte-Carlo simulation. In: Computers and Games, pp. 135–147 (2006)
14. Lasker, E.: Das verständige Kartenspiel. August Scherl Verlag, Berlin (1929)
15. Levy, D.N.L.: The million pound bridge program. In: Heuristic Programming in Artificial Intelligence (1989)
16. Long, J.R.: Search, inference and opponent modelling in an expert-caliber Skat player. Ph.D. thesis, University of Alberta (2011)
17. Müller, M.: Computer go as a sum of local games an application of combinatorial game theory. Ph.D. thesis, ETH Zürich (1995)
18. Müller, M.: Decomposition search: a combinatorial games approach to game tree search, with applications to solving Go endgames. In International Joint Conference on Artificial Intelligence (IJCAI), pp. 578–583 (1999)

19. Rebstock, D.: Improving AI in Skat through Human Imitation and Policy Based Inference. Master's thesis (2019)
20. Rebstock, D., Solinas, C., Buro, M.: Learning policies from human data for Skat. CoRR, abs/1905.10907 (2019)
21. Rebstock, D., Solinas, C., Buro, M., Sturtevant, N.R.: Policy based inference in trick-taking card games. CoRR, abs/1905.10911 (2019)
22. Reinefeld, A., Marsland, T.A.: Enhanced iterative-deepening search. IEEE Trans. Pattern Anal. Mach. Intell. **16**(7), 701–710 (1994)
23. Rosin, C.D.: Nested rollout policy adaptation for Monte Carlo tree search. In: International Joint Conference on Artificial Intelligence (IJCAI), pp. 649–654 (2011)
24. Schettler, F., Kirschbach, G.: Das große Skatvergnügen. Urania Verlag, Leipzig, Jena, Berlin (1988)
25. Schubert, H.: Das Skatspiel im Lichte der Wahrscheinlichkeitsrechnung. J. F. Richter, Hamburg (1887)
26. Silver, D.A.H., et al.: Mastering the game of Go with deep neural networks and tree search. Nature, **529**, 484 (2016)
27. Silver, D., et al.: Mastering Chess and Shogi by self-play with a general reinforcement learning algorithm. Technical Report 1712.018, arxiv (2017)
28. Solinas, C.: Improving Determinized Search with Supervised Learning in Trick-Taking Card Games. Master's thesis (2019)
29. Sturtevant, N.R., White, A.M.: Feature construction for reinforcement learning in hearts. In: Computers and Games, pp. 122–134 (2006)
30. Winands, M.H., Björnsson, Y., Saito, J.-T.: Monte-carlo tree search solver. Comput. Games **5131**, 25–36 (2008)
31. Zinkevich, M., Johanson, M., Bowling, M., Piccione, C.: Regret minimization in games with incomplete information. In: Advances in Neural Information Processing Systems, pp. 1729–1736 (2008)

Dynamic Channel and Layer Gating in Convolutional Neural Networks

Ali Ehteshami Bejnordi$^{(\boxtimes)}$ and Ralf Krestel

University of Passau, Passau, Germany
ehteshami.bahador@gmail.com, ralf.krestel@uni-passau.de

Abstract. Convolutional neural networks (CNN) are getting more and more complex, needing enormous computing resources and energy. In this paper, we propose methods for conditional computation in the context of image classification that allows a CNN to dynamically use its channels and layers conditioned on the input. To this end, we combine lightweight gating modules that can make binary decisions without causing much computational overhead. We argue, that combining the recently proposed channel gating mechanism with layer gating can significantly reduce the computational cost of large CNNs. Using discrete optimization algorithms, the gating modules are made aware of the context in which they are used and decide whether a particular channel and/or a particular layer will be executed. This results in neural networks that adapt their own topology conditioned on the input image. Experiments using the CIFAR10 and MNIST datasets show how competitive results in image classification with respect to accuracy can be achieved while saving up to 50% computational resources.

Keywords: Conditional computation · Channel and layer gating · CNN · ResNet · Image classification

1 Introduction

Conditional computation is a new emerging field in deep learning [3,4]. Conditional computation aims to dynamically allocate resources in a neural network conditionally on the data. Conditional computation can be implemented in different ways such as dynamic execution of different sub-networks inside the main network or different layers or filters. Such models could allow running of different computation graphs conditioned on the input. For example, images that are easier may need less layers/filters or even shallower sub-branches in the network for making a prediction, while more complex examples may warrant the use of more computational resources in the network.

The most obvious benefits of conditional computation is saving resources at inference time. This is because the network is able to dynamically use parts of its units conditioned on the input. While the original base network can have a very large number of parameters and Multiply-accumulate operations (MAC), due to

© Springer Nature Switzerland AG 2020
U. Schmid et al. (Eds.): KI 2020, LNAI 12325, pp. 33–45, 2020.
https://doi.org/10.1007/978-3-030-58285-2_3

the dynamic structure of the network during inference, the resulting model may use a much lower average number of parameters and MACs.

The other advantage of conditional computation can be related to the formation of mixture of experts [11] inside the network. By gating individual components inside a network, we can make the parts that are active more specialized for the specific input, while other elements (filters/layers or sub-networks) may be specialized to perform well on other types of inputs. The idea of mixture of expert neural networks has been previously explored. Early works trained independent expert models to do different tasks and then joined the models and used a gating unit that could select the right model for the given input. Conditional computation, offers a generalized way of forming mixture of experts inside a neural network in which there is potentially a single expert model per example.

Dynamic capacity networks (DCN) [1] picked-up this idea by using a high capacity and a low capacity sub-network. The low capacity sub-network analyzes the full image, while the high capacity sub-network only focuses on task-relevant regions identified by the low capacity part.

In this paper, we propose to combine channel and layer gating using lightweight gating modules that can make binary decisions (1 for execution and 0 otherwise), saving computational costs, while maintaining high performance.

2   Related Work

There are several works in recent literature on conditional computation that successfully use gating to learn conditional layers/features in their networks. In this section we review and discuss several approaches for implementing conditional computation for computer vision applications.

2.1   Conditional Computation in Neural Networks

Stochastic Times Smooth Neurons. Bengio et al. [4] introduced stochastic times smooth neurons as gating units for conditional computation that can turn off large chunks of the computation performed within a deep neural network. The proposed gating units can produce actual zero for certain irrelevant inputs and hence lead to a sparsity that greatly reduces the computational cost of large deep networks. Even though stochastic gates perform non-smooth functions such as thresholds, the authors show that it is possible to obtain approximate gradients by introducing perturbations in the system and observing the effects.

The proposed stochastic neurons were used in the context of conditional computation to dynamically select parts of some computational graph for execution, given the current input. This work was among the first to show that a dynamic computational saving could be obtained without any significant loss in performance.

2.2 Layer Gating

Independence of Layers in Residual Neural Networks. Many of the modern CNNs are based on the recently proposed residual neural networks. In traditional architectures such as AlexNet [14] or VggNet [16], inputs are processed via low-level features in the first few layers up to task specific high-level features in the very deep layers. However, the identity skip-connection in residual networks allows the data to flow from any layers to any subsequent layer [19]. In a study by Veit et al. [19], it was shown that removing single layers from residual networks at test time does not cause a significant drop in performance. This is in sharp contrast to traditional architectures such as AlexNet and VGG which have a dramatic performance drop after a layer removal. This shows that layers in ResNets [8] exhibit a significant degree of independence and that residual networks can be viewed as a collection of many paths, instead of a single very deep network. Motivated by these results, several methods were proposed for skipping execution of layers inside a network conditioned on the input such as convolutional neural networks with adaptive inference graph (ConvNet-AIG) [18] and SkipNet [20].

Convolutional Networks with an Adaptive Inference Graphs. Veit et al. [18] proposed a CNN architecture called convolutional neural networks with adaptive inference graph (ConvNet-AIG) that dynamically decides whether the current layer should be activated or not based on the input it receives. This allows constructing adaptive inference graphs conditionally on the input. This is achieved by training a set of gating units. Specifically, ConvNet-AIG [18] works with residual networks (ResNets) architecture [8] that are gated at each layer. The gating function is actually a basic neural network that can get the same featuremap that goes to a ResNet block as the input. The gating network makes a binary decision whether a layer should be enabled or turned off for the given input.

In ConvNet-AIG [18], the gating unit computes the global average pooling of the input and shrinks the entire featuremap into a vector size of $1 \times 1 \times C$, where C is the number of input channels. This vector is then passed to two fully connected layers that generate an output. This output has two nodes for two decisions: on meaning executing the layer, and off meaning skipping the layer. Technically, selecting the maximum between these two decisions for learning the gating function is a bad idea. If the network only considers this maximum decision, it might end up learning trivial solutions (For example, the gate may learn to remain always on or always off regardless of the input). Besides that taking the hard argmax function of the output is not differentiable. To circumvent this problem, the authors used the Gumbel-max trick [7]. Gumbel sampling is a strategy that allows us to sample from a discrete distribution.

The major limitation of this method is that it is not able to save computation on a more fine-grained level. In ConvNet-AIG [18], gates are only defined for each individual ResNet block (skip a whole block). It makes sense to enable more fine-grained gating such as gating of filters of the convolutional layers.

Skipping Layers Using Long Short-Term Memory Gates. SkipNet [20] is another method that can dynamically skip a layer in a ResNet architecture in a similar fashion. The authors use Long Short-term Memory (LSTM) [9] modules as the gating units for their network. For skipping redundant layers, the gating blocks of SkipNet [20] use a binary decision similar to ConvNet-AIG [18]. To overcome the problem of non-differentiable discrete decision Wang et al. [20] proposed a hybrid algorithm that is a combination of supervised learning and reinforcement learning.

The gating module of SkipNet [20] is composed of a global average pooling layer and one 1×1 convolutional layer and also one LSTM layer. This recurrent gating design allows it to take benefits of LSTM architecture and reduces the cost of a CNN network inference time while at the same time achieving better results. SkipNet [20] bypasses fewer layers for difficult samples like dark or noisy images and skips more layers for easy images. However, in comparison to ConvNet-AIG [18] it achieves lower performance. One major problem with SkipNet [20] is that its accuracy drops rapidly as it saves more compute.

2.3   Gating Individual Filters/Channels

GaterNet [5] is a gating architecture that learns a complete convolutional network jointly and in parallel with the original network, and tries to gate individual filters in the base model. This method, however, comes at a high extra computation cost which may not be necessary. The authors proposed a gater network that extracts the features of the input and then based on these features gates the filters of main network. Chen et al. employed Improved SemHash trick [12] to make discrete gate functions differentiable during the backward pass. Unfortunately, the authors do not report any information about the MAC count or trade-off points between the accuracy and MAC-saving for different sparsity levels. This makes comparison of their approach with other methods challenging.

Dynamic channel pruning [6] is another recently proposed method that selects individual features to be turned on/off based on the input. This is done by choosing the top-k ranked features that should be executed for the specific input. Gao et al. [6] proposed using Feature Boosting and Suppression (FBS) method. This method uses auxiliary blocks that determine the importance of the output of a convolutional layer based on the input it receives. The authors showed that the Feature Boosting and Suppression method can improve the execution time 5 times faster than VGG-16 and 2 times faster than ResNet-18 while at the same time the reduction in accuracy is less than 0.6%.

Bejnordi proposed a model [2] which performs a more fine-grained level skipping by learning to execute filters inside a residual block conditioned on the input. The authors also proposed the batch-shaping loss to encourage the network to learn more conditional features. More recently, a new residual block was proposed where a gating module learns which spatial positions to evaluate exploiting the fact that not all regions in the image are equally important for the given task. The major benefit of our method is the ability of saving more computation cost rather than other methods. This architecture allows the model to gate a channel in a convolutional layer or a whole layer of residual block based on the input it receives.

3 Dynamic Layer and Channel Gating

In this work, we design a neural network architecture that enables fine-grained filter gating as well as layer-gating of whole residual blocks of convolutional neural networks. Unlike GaterNet [5] that gates individual channels using a learned auxiliary network, we use very light-weight gating modules similar to the ones used in ConvNet-AIG [18] for gating the filters and layers in each layer. Our proposed solution is called dynamic layer and channel gating (DLCG).

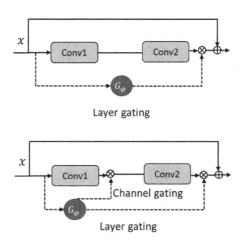

Fig. 1. Overview of different mechanism for gating a residual network. The top shows the layer gating approach proposed by Veit et al. [18]. The ResNet block in the bottom shows our proposed joint channel and layer gating (DLCG). In DLCG, we use a single gating module G_ϕ to jointly gate filters and layers

3.1 Proposed Gating Architecture

Figure 1 shows an overview of different gating strategies we consider in our work: Layer gating as proposed by Veit et al. [18], and our proposed joint channel and layer gating (DLCG). As shown in the lower part of the figure, we learn a single gating module to jointly gate layers and filters in the residual block.

3.2 The Structure of Our Gating Module

The aim of the gating module G_ϕ is to estimate the relevance of a layer or filter given the input features. The gating module should have a light design (low MAC consumption) to not undermine the value of conditional computation, while at the same time operate in an input dependent fashion and make smart decisions for activating channels or layers in the block. Beside that, the gates should make binary decisions. A gate with a soft output will not be useful. While a hard zero means we can skip the computation of a unit, a soft value such as 0.3 means we should still give some attention to the current unit and hence no computational saving will be obtained.

Our gating modules have a light and efficient structure inspired by the gating modules of ConvNet-AIG [18]. An overview of our gating module is presented in Fig. 2. Our gating module takes the incoming featuremap to the residual block as input and applies a global average pooling to reduce the input dimension to $1 \times 1 \times N$, where N is the number of channels in the input featuremap. This step significantly reduces the computation costs of the gating network and is similarly used in Squeeze and Excitation networks [10]. This representation is obtained through:

$$z_c = \frac{1}{H \times W} \sum_{i=1}^{H} \sum_{j=1}^{W} x_{i,j,c} \tag{1}$$

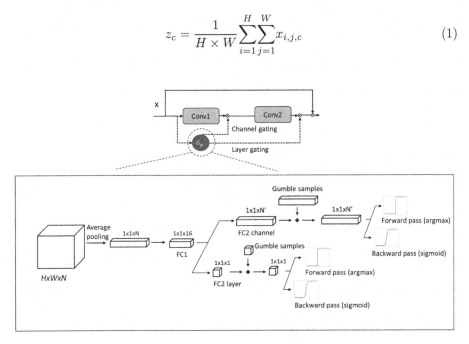

Fig. 2. Illustration of the gating module structure for our joint channel and layer gating network

This representation is then fed to a small MLP with a first fully connected layer with 16 neurons. This fully connected layer is a shared layer for both channel and layer gating. The output of this layer is passed to a ReLU non-linearity. After that, there are two separate heads, one for channel gating and one for layer gating (see Fig. 2). The fully connected layer on the channel gating head generates the output probabilities for gating individual filters $\hat{\alpha}_i$, where $i \in \{1, 2, \cdots, N'\}$, and N' denotes the number of channels in the first convolutional layer of the ResNet block. Note that each element in the output of this gating network is an independent binary gate $\hat{\alpha}_i$ responsible to choose to either execute or skip the computation of the filter i in the first convolutional layer of the ResNet block.

For layer gating, we use a fully connected layer that linearly projects the feature to a single output $\hat{\beta}$ (single gate) whose output determines if the current residual block should be executed or not. All the gates are trained using the Gumbel max trick [7] with sigmoid relaxation.

Note that during inference, we first look at the output of the layer gating and if it chooses to skip the layer, we do not perform any channel gating and the whole ResNet block is skipped. And in case the gate decides to execute the block, we proceed with the channel gating unit.

3.3   Sparsity Objective

Consider a gated classification model which only uses the task loss (e.g. categorical cross-entropy) to optimize the network. The gradients coming from the task loss could be back-propagated through the gating units. The most trivial solution for the gating units would be to make sure all the gates are always on. In this case, we end up with a network that is equivalent to a model trained without any gating units. Ideally, however, we would like the units and layers in the network to be input dependent. That means we want the gates to be on when the specific layer/filter is relevant for the current input and to be off if otherwise. To encourage this behaviour we use a sparsity objective which penalizes the gates for being always on.

Target Loss. In ConvNet-AIG [18], the sparsity is achieved by defining a loss function that encourages each layer to be executed at a certain target rate. The target rate can take a value between 0 and 1 representing the overall execution percentage of a layer. The execution rate is penalized in a mini-batch of data. The loss term is expressed as:

$$L_{target} = \sum_{l=1}^{N} (\bar{z}_l - t)^2 \tag{2}$$

in which t is the target rate and is a parameter selected by the user during training and $\bar{z}_l$ represents the fraction of images that are executed for a certain layer l and N is the total number of ResNet blocks. The total loss for optimizing the layer gated network is then obtained by summing up the normal loss function L_C (categorical cross-entropy) and the target rate loss L_{target}:

$$L_{AIG} = L_C + L_{target} \tag{3}$$

In practice, the best results in ConvNet-AIG [18] were achieved by manual setting of target rates per layer and following a lot of heuristics and hyperparameter tuning. For example, the target rate of the initial layers and layers at the end of the network were set to 1 while the intermediate layers were given lower target rates as they seemed to be more prunable.

Target-Free Sparsity Loss. Unlike ConvNet-AIG [18], we propose to remove the target rate. This would allow different layers/channels to take varying dynamic execution rates. This way, the network may automatically learn to use more units for a specific layer and less for another, without us having to determine a target rate in advance. Besides that, we give weight to the sparsity loss by the coefficients λ and γ which control the pressure on the sparsity loss for layer gating and channel gating, respectively. The resulting loss equation for layer gating is, therefore:

$$L_{l-sparsity} = \sum_{l=1}^{N} \bar{z}_l^2 \tag{4}$$

And for the case of channel gating we have:

$$L_{ch-sparsity} = \sum_{f=1}^{K} \bar{z}_{ch}^2 \tag{5}$$

where z_{ch} denotes the fraction of images which activate a specific gate that gates whole layers, and K is the total number of filters that are gated in the network. Therefore, the final objective for joint channel and layer gating of our DLCG network is:

$$L_{DLCG} = L_C + \lambda L_{l-sparsity} + \gamma L_{ch-sparsity} \tag{6}$$

We optimize this loss with mini-batch stochastic gradient descent. To generate different sparsity levels for our gating network we set different values for our λ and γ coefficients.

4   Experiments

Evaluation Metrics. Top-1 and top-5 accuracies [14] are the measures that are used to evaluate the performance of algorithms for image classification tasks such as the ImageNet [14] or CIFAR [13] classification. Top-1 accuracy describes that the classifier gives the highest probability to the target label. Top-1 accuracy is also known as the normal accuracy and is widely used in benchmarks to rank different algorithms. Top-5 accuracy is mostly common when the number of classes are very large such as for ImageNet classification (1000 classes). Since we apply our model to MNIST and CIFAR10 classification tasks, we only report the top-1 accuracy.

Also for evaluating the computation cost of the model we report multiply-accumulate operations count (MAC). This measure gives us a good criterion of how fast our model is in practice. The computation time of a layer in a CNN architecture mostly depends on the MAC operations performed on that layer during the convolutional operation. The MAC count for a standard convolutional layer is $(H \times W \times C) \times (K \times K \times C')$. Where $(H \times W \times C)$ represents the dimension of the input featuremap and $(K \times K \times C')$ represents the spatial size of filters times the number of filters in the convolutional layer. By gating a specific filter we affect the number of filters C' that are applied to the input. Note that gating filters not only reduces the MAC count of the current layer, but also affects the MAC count of the following layer because the input dimension to the next layer is automatically reduced.

To get better insight into the effectiveness of the gating architectures, we also plot the MAC versus Accuracy curve to see how saving computation affects the accuracy of the gated models.

Table 1. Results of the experiment on the CIFAR10 dataset for our joint channel and layer gating architecture (DLCG) with different sparsity loss coefficients

Gate loss factor		Average activation rate		Accuracy	GMAC
Layer	Channel	Layer	Channel		
0.09	0.15	0.399	0.215	88.96	0.0076
0.07	0.12	0.464	0.262	89.67	0.0089
0.09	0.10	0.405	0.272	89.87	0.0091
0.05	0.10	0.564	0.305	90.59	0.0115
0.05	0.07	0.677	0.388	91.55	0.0145
0.02	0.03	0.727	0.548	91.99	0.0206
0.00	0.03	0.992	0.591	92.49	0.0232
0.00	0.05	0.999	0.791	92.74	0.0320
0.00	0.00	0.999	0.880	92.86	0.0353

4.1 Experiments on CIFAR10

For evaluation of our approach, we use the CIFAR10 dataset [13]. CIFAR10 is a popular dataset for the task of image classification consisting of 10 categories It contains of 50000 images for training and 10000 images for testing of size 32×32 pixels.

Training Configuration for CIFAR10 Classification. We used ResNet20 [8] as the base network for our CIFAR10 experiments. We trained our joint layer and channel gated models using stochastic gradient descent with Nesterov momentum [17]. The network was trained for a total of 400 epochs with a batch size of 256. At the start of training, the learning rate was set to 0.1. We followed a step policy for learning rate drop and divided the initial learning rate by a factor of 10 at epochs 200, 300 and 375. The weight decay for the parameters of the network was set to $5e^{-4}$. We did not apply weight decay to any of the parameters of the gating modules (weights or biases).

We used random cropping and random horizontal flipping as data augmentation to improve the generalization of our model. To generate trade-off points for our MAC-accuracy curve, we experimented with different values of λ and γ for the sparsity objectives.

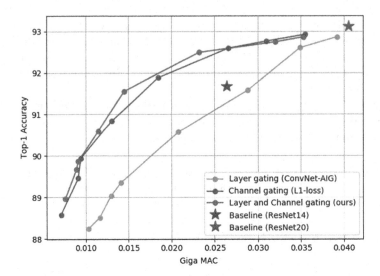

Fig. 3. The top-1 accuracy vs MAC count curve for the three gating architectures trained on CIFAR10 dataset

Results on CIFAR10: We present the result of our DLCG model in Table 1 with different accuracy vs mac trade-offs. This model is performing consistently better than ConvNet-AIG [18] as shown in Fig. 3. We additionally compare the results to the case in which we only use channel gating. The accuracy of our DLCG model is slightly higher than a sole channel gated model as well. We argue that the major performance gain comes from the channel gating modules and that is clear from the significant performance gap between channel gating alone and ConvNet-AIG [18].

In Fig. 3, we show the trade-off between MAC count and accuracy for the three different gating schemes: ConvNet-AIG [18] and channel gating as well as joint channel and layer gating. Note that in all MAC count calculations, we also include the overhead of the gating modules (less than 0.03%).

From the results, it is obvious that our proposed gating models outperform ConvNet-AIG [18] by a large margin. In this plot we also present the performance of two baseline models: ResNet20 and ResNet14 without any gating. As can be seen, ResNet14 without gating outperforms a gated ConvNet-AIG [18] model at a similar MAC count. This result is surprising, because in such a case one would prefer to use a ResNet14 model rather than a ConvNet-AIG [18] model with a ResNet20 backbone. This result questions the entire value of conditional computation. Our ResNet20 based gated models, in contrast, outperform ResNet14 non-gated baseline by a large margin at a similar MAC count. This is highly desirable, as it means we can take a large capacity neural network (such as ResNet20) and sparsify it to the size of a smaller network (such as ResNet14), while getting a much higher accuracy than the smaller non-gated model.

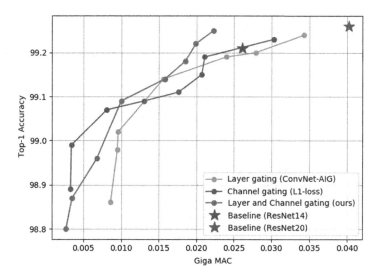

Fig. 4. The top-1 accuracy vs MAC count curve for the three gating architectures trained on MNIST dataset

4.2 Experiments on MNIST

To verify our results from the CIFAR10 dataset, we additionally evaluated our approach on the smaller MNIST dataset [15]. MNIST is a database of handwritten digits from 0 to 9. Each image is available in the form of a grayscale image with a size of 28×28 pixels. This dataset contains 60000 images for training and 10000 images for testing.

Figure 4 shows the top-1 accuracy versus MAC count curve for the three gating scenarios: layer gating, channel gating, and joint channel and layer gating (DLCG). As can be seen, our DLCG model outperforms the channel gating model and also the ConvNet-AIG [18] model (layer gating) in high accuracy ranges. DLCG outperforms ConvNet-AIG [18] at all trade-off points and shows that the addition of a more fine-grained gating mechanism could be beneficial for conditional computation neural networks.

5   Conclusions and Future Work

In this paper, we studied conditional computation models for vision applications. An important limitation in conventional neural network architectures is their fixed static graph. The deep learning models we train for various tasks are largely task- and context-agnostic. This implies that regardless of the input, all elements of the network are executed. This shortcoming may render such models inefficient in many real-world applications such as running models on mobile devices. Therefore, we focused on the design of a convolutional neural network that can dynamically utilize its units conditioned on the input image. In particular, we presented a joint layer and channel gating architecture, that can decide to activate or deactivate channels in a convolutional layer or a whole residual block based on their relevance to the specific input.

Our empirical evaluations show that channel gating alone can outperform layer gating methods such as ConvNet-AIG [18] by a large margin on the MNIST and CIFAR10 datasets. This increase in performance could be attributed to the fine-grained nature of our architecture design. Rather than saying a whole residual block with all its computation units are irrelevant for the input, we decide the computation saving at the fine-grained channel level. Our joint layer and channel gating show some improvement over channel gating alone, but not significantly as most of the computational saving comes from the channel gating operations. Overall, our proposed gating architecture provides improved efficiency and classification accuracy.

We speculate that the reason why channel gating alone may perform as good as joint channel and layer gating could be as follows. The gating module generally produces very sparse channel gating solutions in each ResNet block which would lead to significant saving in computation. However, the small number of filters which are remaining active are necessary to achieve a high performance. Therefore, the model generally prefers to choose some filters from each layer (albeit small in number) rather that skipping the entire block.

A highly desirable aspect of our proposed gating approach is that we can take a large capacity neural network such as ResNet20 and sparsify it to the size of a smaller network such as ResNet14, while achieving a much higher accuracy than this small non-gated model (ResNet14).

There are many future research directions. One would be to use the batch-shaping loss proposed in [2] for our model. We think our joint channel and layer gating architecture could potentially benefit from this loss. It would additionally be useful to evaluate the performance of our method on the larger scale ImageNet dataset.

Another direction would be to integrate early exiting methods to our model to not only save computation by gating individual filters and layers but also exit the whole model at an early stage in case the model is already certain about the decision regarding an easy example. This way, the model can choose to skip huge amount of computation for easier examples.

References

1. Almahairi, A., Ballas, N., Cooijmans, T., Zheng, Y., Larochelle, H., Courville, A.: Dynamic capacity networks. In: International Conference on Machine Learning, pp. 2549–2558 (2016)
2. Bejnordi, B.E., Blankevoort, T., Welling, M.: Batch-shaping for learning conditional channel gated networks. In: International Conference on Learning Representations (2020). https://openreview.net/forum?id=Bke89JBtvB
3. Bengio, E., Bacon, P.L., Pineau, J., Precup, D.: Conditional computation in neural networks for faster models. arXiv preprint arXiv:1511.06297 (2015)
4. Bengio, Y., Léonard, N., Courville, A.: Estimating or propagating gradients through stochastic neurons for conditional computation. arXiv preprint arXiv:1308.3432 (2013)

5. Chen, Z., Li, Y., Bengio, S., Si, S.: You look twice: Gaternet for dynamic filter selection in CNNs. In: The IEEE Conference on Computer Vision and Pattern Recognition (CVPR), June 2019
6. Gao, X., Zhao, Y., Dudziak, L., Mullins, R., Xu, C.-Z: Dynamic channel pruning: Feature boosting and suppression. In: International Conference on Learning Representations (2019). https://openreview.net/forum?id=BJxh2j0qYm
7. Gumbel, E.J.: Statistical theory of extreme values and some practical applications. NBS Appl. Math. Ser. **33** (1954)
8. He, K., Zhang, X., Ren, S., Sun, J.: Deep residual learning for image recognition. In: Proceedings of the IEEE Conference on Computer Vision and Pattern Recognition, pp. 770–778 (2016)
9. Hochreiter, S., Schmidhuber, J.: Long short-term memory. Neural Comput. **9**(8), 1735–1780 (1997)
10. Hu, J., Shen, L., Sun, G.: Squeeze-and-excitation networks. In: Proceedings of the IEEE Conference on Computer Vision and Pattern Recognition, pp. 7132–7141 (2018)
11. Jacobs, R.A., Jordan, M.I., Nowlan, S.J., Hinton, G.E., et al.: Adaptive mixtures of local experts. Neural Comput. **3**(1), 79–87 (1991)
12. Kaiser, Ł., Bengio, S.: Discrete autoencoders for sequence models. arXiv preprint arXiv:1801.09797 (2018)
13. Krizhevsky, A.: Learning multiple layers of features from tiny images. Technical report. Citeseer (2009)
14. Krizhevsky, A., Sutskever, I., Hinton, G.E.: Imagenet classification with deep convolutional neural networks. In: Advances in Neural Information Processing Systems, pp. 1097–1105 (2012)
15. LeCun, Y., Bottou, L., Bengio, Y., Haffner, P., et al.: Gradient-based learning applied to document recognition. Proc. IEEE **86**(11), 2278–2324 (1998)
16. Simonyan, K., Zisserman, A.: Very deep convolutional networks for large-scale image recognition. arXiv preprint arXiv:1409.1556 (2014)
17. Sutskever, I., Martens, J., Dahl, G., Hinton, G.: On the importance of initialization and momentum in deep learning. In: International Conference on Machine Learning, pp. 1139–1147 (2013)
18. Veit, A., Belongie, S.: Convolutional networks with adaptive inference graphs. In: Proceedings of the European Conference on Computer Vision (ECCV), pp. 3–18 (2018)
19. Veit, A., Wilber, M., Belongie, S.: Residual networks behave like ensembles of relatively shallow networks. Conference on Neural Information Processing Systems (NIPS) (2016)
20. Wang, X., Yu, F., Dou, Z.-Y., Darrell, T., Gonzalez, J.E.: SkipNet: Learning dynamic routing in convolutional networks. In: Ferrari, V., Hebert, M., Sminchisescu, C., Weiss, Y. (eds.) ECCV 2018. LNCS, vol. 11217, pp. 420–436. Springer, Cham (2018). https://doi.org/10.1007/978-3-030-01261-8_25

Contour-Based Segmentation
of Historical Printings

Norbert Fischer, Alexander Gehrke, Alexander Hartelt, Markus Krug,
and Frank Puppe[✉]

Chair of Artificial Intelligence, University of Wuerzburg, Würzburg, Germany
{norbert.fischer,alexander.gehrke,alexander.hartelt,markus.krug,
frank.puppe}@informatik.uni-wuerzburg.de

Abstract. The automatic transcription of historical printings with OCR has made great progress in recent years. However, the correct segmentation of demanding page layouts is still challenging, in particular, the separation of text and non-text (e.g. pictures, but also decorated initials). Fully convolutional neural nets (FCNs) with an encoder-decoder structure are currently the method of choice, if suitable training material is available. Since the variation of non-text elements is huge, the good results of FCNs, if training and test material are similar, do not easily transfer to different layouts. We propose an approach based on dividing a page into many contours (i.e. connected components) and classifying each contour with a standard Convolutional neural net (CNN) as being text or non-text. The main idea is that the CNN learns to recognize text contours, i.e. letters, and classifies everything else as non-text, thus generalizing better on the many forms of non-text. Evaluations of the contour-based segmentation in comparison to classical FCNs with varying amount of training material and with similar and dissimilar test data show its effectiveness.

Keywords: Page segmentation · Connected components · State of the art.

1 Introduction

Digitization of historical documents allows for an easy access of invaluable works of our past. This would allow access without strict conditions and the requirement to physically visit a library or museum for research. Digitization of a large quantity of historical printings can also severely influence the quality and the speed of new findings in terms of research questions, when not only a limited amount of resources, but a vast amount of resources is available in computer readable formats. The digitization of entire library stocks requires the support of intelligent and high quality automation in order to finish the tasks in a reasonable amount of time.

The digitization process of historical books usually consists of a multitude of different steps, each coming with their own challenges for automatic systems.

© Springer Nature Switzerland AG 2020
U. Schmid et al. (Eds.): KI 2020, LNAI 12325, pp. 46–58, 2020.
https://doi.org/10.1007/978-3-030-58285-2_4

While the scanning process still requires manual intervention, the detection of the layout and the recognition of the textual characters can be greatly supported with modern day automation.

A typical OCR-Workflow (Reul et al., 2019) with a scan as input and plain text as output consists of the following four steps: pre-processing, segmentation, text recognition (core OCR) and post-processing. Pre-processing converts the image in a standard binary (or sometimes grayscale) format and deals with artefacts of the scan-process, e.g. dewarping to rectify a distorted scan, denoising or despeckling to clean up the scan and cropping the printing area to remove unwanted scan periphery. Segmentation separates text regions from non-text regions (e.g. images) and often provides finer grained classes for text regions like running text, marginalia, headings etc. broken down in text lines with a reading order. The core OCR step gets a text line as input and a transcription as output. Due to many factors the OCR for historical printings is not perfect. Consequently, a post-correction step using e.g. statistical information and linguistic background knowledge is often added for correction of transcription errors.

At the time of writing no pipeline exists that is able to fully automatically produce a quality which suffices and does not need manual post-correction of any sort. One of the key-findings of the project OCR-D[1] was, that an automatic segmentation based on a pre-processed scan is still the worst component in the OCR-workflow. Recent advances in layout recognition mainly focused on pixel-based methods, centred around fully convolutional neural networks that are arranged in an encoder-decoder architecture.

In this work we present an alternative way to achieve state of the art results of historical layout analysis using connected components (from now on referred to as contours) as input to our neural network. The idea is that the contours of individual characters are very similar throughout pages of documents of the same origin, while the contours that appear in images show more variety and can not be compressed as efficiently by an encoder-decoder architecture. A classifier can be tuned on the features of the contours that appear many times on the pages and the resulting features can be used to decide whether the contour is part of a text region or an image region. Our intuition behind this approach is that while a sliding window (as is the case in a regular CNN) may be able to extract features from every part of the image, it is unlikely to focus on contours, thus missing the notion of "letters" and therefore has to approximate it or use other features of text.

This work is structured as follows: In Sect. 2 we present previous work and their results on the task of historical page segmentation, followed by the presentation of the data sets we utilized in this work in Sect. 3. Our main contribution, the neural network based on contours is presented in Sect. 4 and the experiments we conducted are explained in Sect. 5. The discussion of our results in comparison to a pixel classifier is given in Sect. 6 and the paper is concluded in Sect. 7.

---

[1] https://ocr-d.de/.

2   Related Work

Fig. 1. In the left image each of the areas enclosed by red borders is a superpixel generated by the SLIC algorithm (compactness = 1, segments count = 3000). In the right image every contour (i.e. region with connected pixels) is treated as a separate region. Some contours are highlighted with a different color for illustration (Color figure online).

This section gives an overview over the existing supervised techniques for the layout analysis. In general, the approaches can be classified into three distinct groups:

- superpixel-approach grouping similar pixels to so-called superpixels
- pixel-classifier trained with different classes like text and image
- base-line detection of virtual lines beneath letters in a text row

The *superpixel approach* is pursued in the works of Chen et al. (2016a) and (2016b). The first step in this approach is to separate the page into super pixels using the *Simple Linear Iterative Clustering* (SLIC)-algorithm (Noh and Woodward, 1976). SLIC groups pixels with similar visual properties into a single so-called super pixel. Each super pixel is subsequently classified with a convolutional neural network into different regions. The authors report pixel accuracies of up to 96% on historical documents. This approach shares similarities with the method presented in this paper. The first similarity being that the classification is done on a local snippet of the image without any further information about the context, but their approach relies heavily on the quality of the resulting super pixels, since errors that occur during preprocessing usually can not be recovered. Figure 1 shows the difference of the input segmented using SLIC and the input segmented into contours. We reimplemented the approach of the authors as best as possible but could not achieve results anywhere near state-of-the-art. Our work is therefore based on connected components and is inspired by the success of Bukhari et al. (2010) who used a Multi-layer-Perceptron and reached evaluation accuracies of over 95%.

A *pixel-classifier* predicts a single mask for an entire page in a single prediction pass with the neural network. This approach was first applied for page segmentation by Long et al. (2015) and further extended by Wick and Puppe (2018) for historical documents. The idea is that making use of a fully convolutional encoder-decoder structure also allows the algorithm to focus on a further neighborhood of a single pixel (as opposed to the approach using superpixels).

An application of the *base-line* approach for historical documents was presented in the work of Grüning et al. (2019). Their network structure, called the ARU network, can be seen as a combination of two individual networks that are trained in an end-to-end setting. The first network is a variation of the classical U-net (Ronneberger et al., 2015) with the convolutional layers being replaced by residual blocks to obtain more stability during training. The second part of the network called A-net produces an attention feature map which is later combined with the results of the first subnetwork. The result of that network undergoes some post processing steps, yet again involving super pixels before the final prediction occurs. Because only baselines are extracted, the output must be adapted in further steps to the segmentation output of the other algorithms.

3   Data

During this work, we used two different data sets for our experiments. The first one is used as a test set exclusively for evaluation and originates from the project OCR-D and is a collection of many different printings between the 16th and 19th century. The individual 170 pages in that data set have been selected to represent a large variety of different layouts. Instead of using the original data set, we removed the periphery of the pages (that is, we removed any borders and clipped the page content to its actual content) imitating the effect of the preprocessing step in the OCR-Workflow (see above)[2].

The second data set referred to as *Layout ground truth* (LGT) is used for training and is a compilation of several different early prints from the 14th up to the 16th century. In total, LGT comprises 4933 pages with 1515 pages containing at least one image.

Finding a suitable data set is not easy. We experimented for about a year with data sets derived from the DTA (Deutsches Text Archiv). In their data sets, the regions are labeled using bounding boxes which we found to be insufficient in many cases and yielding too bad results when we used it to train our algorithms.

---

[2] https://gitlab2.informatik.uni-wuerzburg.de/ocr4all-page-segmentation/evaluation-datasets.

4   Contour-Based Page Segmentation

This section describes our approach to segment between textual regions and image regions based on individual contours. The first step is to determine all connected components using the Block-Based Connected Components algorithm Chang et al. (2015) provided by OpenCV. For each connected component, an axis-aligned bounding box is extracted and reshaped, so that a single network can be used to deal with inputs of different sizes. This reshaping distinguishes two cases: The first case arises when the resulting bounding box is smaller than the required input of the network. We applied a downscaling approach using a linear intrapolation while retaining the aspect ratio of the original bounding box. Any resulting border areas are treated as background pixels. The second case deals with connected components that are smaller than the required network input. These components are enlarged using linear extrapolation and subsequently binarized by applying a thresholding function. The resulting pixel values are normalized to reside in the interval $[0, 1]$.

4.1   CNN-Architecture

The resulting image snippet is then fed into a CNN (depicted in Fig. 2). The network consists of three convolution-pooling blocks applied in a linear fashion and a feature reduction using two fully-connected layers and a subsequent softmax classification. During training, the parameters are tuned using the cross-entropy loss function.

Since not every part of the image is part of a connected component, we complement the CNN-architecture with a customized post-processing routine, which is described in the next section.

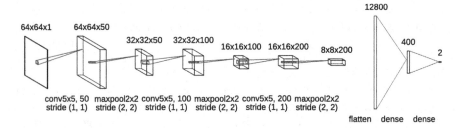

Fig. 2. The neural network architecture for the contour based approach to distinguish between text regions and non-text (e.g. image) regions. The architecture is a classical convolution and pooling network, which subsequently is reduced to just two values for the prediction of the final class.

4.2   Post-processing

We developed a sophisticated model to post-process the results of our contour based network in order to overcome its main weakness classifying each contour independently without using information from neighboring contours. For example, pixels of a letter might be faded thus splitting a letter in parts, so that the remaining contours don't resemble a letter anymore. In addition, historical printings contain a lot of noise, which might resemble e.g. a dot in the text. These problems are enlarged by the fact that all contours are scaled up or down to the same size as input to the CNN.

The main idea of the post-processing is therefore to improve the initial predictions using context information by a rule-based algorithm. For very small contours, this is simply an adaption to their neighbor contours. "Normal" contours are grouped to regions with different techniques (see below) and all contours within a region take over the majority class of the contours of that region (with the nice side effect, that letters within an image might change their class from letter to image). A special case are decorated initials, which are widespread in historical printings. They resemble a letter, but should be treated as an image. They are recognized by their bigger size relative to a text line. The post-processing produces a final mask that is returned as the page segmentation. In the following, the eight steps of the post-processing are described in more detail, an exemplary output is shown in Fig. 3:

1. Adaptation of small contours: This first post-processing step reclassifies small contours. A small contour is a contour with a diagonal that is shorter than 5 times the median height of all text boxes (denoted as $\bar{h}$, as determined by the classifier). The bounding box is extended by $\bar{h}$ in all directions and the neighboring boxes are taken into account. If 85% of all foreground pixels in the extended box show a different class, then the class is changed.

2. Recognition of text lines We utilize a recursive version of k-means. We start with all text blocks and cluster them into two clusters. If the y-coordinates of the resulting cluster centers differ by at least $0.6 \cdot \bar{h}$, then k-means is applied recursively on both clusters, else the clusters are assumed to only contain text blocks of the same line.

3. Column detection After text lines have been found, they are split into columns. For this, the text block in the previously detected lines are sorted using their x-coordinates and a split is introduced if the distance between two sorted neighboring text blocks is larger than $2 \cdot \bar{h}$.

4. Separation of decorated initials Since in our data, decorated initials are labelled as images, this step has the goal to split initials from the remaining text blocks. A text block is identified as a decorated initial if the height of the first text box is larger than 1.8 times the maximum height of all other boxes of the same line.

5. Reconstruction of text areas For each text line, we create a bounding box that contains all text blocks of that line. The algorithm to detect text areas starts with a line and creates a list of candidate lines that might be merged with the current line. A candidate line may not differ by more than $1.5 \cdot \bar{h}$ at the left and right x-coordinates. The final grouping is decided by the differences in y-direction of the line centres. Neighboring candidate lines are merged until a candidate is found with a distance of more than $2.5 \cdot \bar{h}$ to the nearest candidate (using the centres of the lines respectively). Each resulting cluster can then be treated as a text area with all ungrouped lines being their own area.

6. Classification of the resulting text blocks This step creates a polygon around each previously detected text area. If at least 50% of the foreground of that polygon consists of text blocks, then all containing elements are treated as text, otherwise they are treated as an image region. This step gets rid of some elements that are misclassified, e.g. a small region that was previously labelled as an image that is actually found inside a text area.

7. Classification of the image regions This step has the purpose to predict rectangular shapes for every image region. In this algorithm, we apply an iterative optimization routine based on simulated annealing. At first, initial predictions of rectangles are produced using selective search (Uijlings et al., 2013). The second step filters these rectangles so that only rectangles remain which contain at least one image pixel and show no overlap to text regions of more than 5% and are not completely contained by a larger rectangle. The remaining rectangles are then independently readjusted to their individual local neighborhood by either randomly shrinking or extending them in a random direction. Each rectangle after that morphological transformation is scored using a fitness function:

$$\Delta F = (\Delta p_i - 10 \cdot \Delta p_t - 0.05 \cdot \Delta p_b) \cdot 500$$

with Δp_i being the difference in image pixels, Δp_b the difference in background pixels and Δp_t the difference in textual pixels when compared to the initial rectangle.

If the fitness function is either positive or the evaluation of the inequality $\exp \frac{\Delta F}{T} > \rho$ holds (with ρ being a random number in $[0, 1[$ and T starting at 10.000 the candidate rectangle is replaced by the candidate rectangle in the next iteration.

8. Final classification This final step takes the resulting mask and readjusts the class labels by majority voting of the classified foreground pixels of each contour. On a tie, we label the contour as an image.

5   Experiments

In this work, the primary goal is to show that using the contours of a page and the application of a CNN results in state of the art segmentation results, when only classifying in two categories of regions (text and non-text regions). For this, we conducted two different experiments.

Fig. 3. The left image shows the prediction of the contour classifier. The image in the middle depicts the text and image regions detected by the post-processing algorithm. The rightmost image shows the corrected prediction when using the results of the post-processing. Contours / regions belonging to the text class are colored in green while non-text elements are illustrated in blue (Color figure online).

5.1 In-Domain Experiment

In the in-domain experiment we train our contour based classifier, as well as our baseline (see Sect. 5.3) on the LGT data in a fivefold setting. For this experiment, foreground pixels labelled as background in the ground truth are counted as non-text pixels.

5.2 Cross-Domain Experiment

In the cross-domain experiment the pixel classifier and the contour based approach are compared on the OCR-D test set with its 170 scans, which is completely different from the LGT training set. This setting is more realistic for the ultimate goal of a fully automatic OCR-Pipeline. We vary the amount of training data using the full LGT data set and a balanced subset using only those pages containing at least one image.

Foreground pixels, which are not labelled as text or non-text in the ground-truth pose an issue for the evaluation. Such pixels could either be remnants of the page's periphery, degradation or dirt on the original document or noise induced by the binarization method. Therefore we conduct the evaluation using two different methods: in the first method (with background) we count foreground-pixels not labelled as text or non-text as non-text pixels, therefore including all elements on the page. For the second method (without background) we ignore all foreground-pixels, which aren't labelled as text or non-text in the ground truth, as well as all "random" pixels belonging to a contour with 8 pixels or less.

As the main metrics for the evaluation we used the foreground pixel accuracy (FgPA) (Wick and Puppe, 2018) and the F1 scores on the text and non-text class, respectively. Additionally, we report the precision and recall scores for each class.

Only pixels in the foreground are considered for the calculation of all the metrics. For all of these measures, we count each foreground-pixel individually as either correctly or incorrectly classified based on the prediction and the label of the pixel in the ground truth.

5.3 Experimental Settings

The exact parameters for replication of our experiments are given in this section. Our code for both, the pixel classifier[3] and the contour based approach[4] are made available.

Hyperparameter Pixel classifier: The pixel classifier uses a total of 7 convolutional layers in the encoder, each layer uses a kernel size of $[5, 5]$ and a stride of $[2, 2]$. The amount of the encoder filters grows: 20, 30, 40, 40, 60, 60. After every second convolutional layer, we apply a single max-pooling layer. The decoder is composed of five deconvolutional layer with 80, 60, 40, 30 and 20 filters respectively. Each deconvolutional layer gets access to a former convolutional layer of the encoder using skip connections. All activation functions used are rectifier linear units. The pixel classifier is trained using Adam with a batchsize of 1 and a learning rate of 10^{-4} and a cross-entropy loss. Training is carried out for 100 epochs and stopped if no improvements on validation data could be achieved for 30 epochs. The pixel classifier uses a post-processing step by a majority vote on the pixels of each contour labeling all pixels of the contour either as text or non-text.

Contour Classifier: The contour based classifier had three convolutional layers with 50, 100 and 200 filters respectively, each having the size of $[5, 5]$. We trained using a batchsize of 64 using Adam and a learning rate of 10^{-4}.

6   Discussion

Table 1. Results of the in-domain experiment of the contour and pixel classifier with training on the full LGT data set and evaluation of one split in a five fold scenario. We report the averaged results of pixel-wise Precision, Recall and F1 in percent.

Approach	$FgPA$	P_{text}	R_{text}	$F1_{text}$	P_{img}	R_{img}	$F1_{img}$
Pixel-classifier	99.5	99.5	99.9	99.7	99.3	97.9	98.6
Contour-Classifier (with post-proc.)	98.8	99.3	98.7	99.3	94.2	99.1	96.6

---

[3] https://gitlab2.informatik.uni-wuerzburg.de/ls6/ocr4all-pixel-classifier.

[4] https://gitlab2.informatik.uni-wuerzburg.de/s331055/contour-classifier-clean.

Table 2. Results of cross-domain experiment of the contour- and pixel-classifier with training on the full or reduced (balanced) LGT dataset and evaluation on the OCR-D dataset with or without small background contours removed. All results are the average of a ten fold. We report the results of pixel-wise Precision, Recall and F1 in percent as well as the standard deviation for the ten models.

	Contour-based segmentation								Pixel-classifier			
Training dataset (LGT):	Full				Balanced				Full		Balanced	
Post-processing	Yes		No		Yes		No		No		No	
Eval with or without background	W/o	With	W/o	With	W/o	With	W/o	With	W/o	With	W/o	With
FgPA	**98.9**	97.6	97.0	96.8	*98.9*	97.6	97.1	97.0	**99.1**	98.6	*98.3*	97.7
Standard Deviation	0.06	0.20	0.29	0.30	0.09	0.11	0.30	0.30	0.14	0.15	0.27	0.27
Text F1	**99.4**	98.7	98.4	98.2	*99.4*	98.7	98.5	98.3	**99.5**	99.3	*99.1*	98.8
Standard Deviation	0.03	0.11	0.16	0.17	0.05	0.06	0.17	0.17	0.07	0.08	0.15	0.15
Text Precision	**99.7**	99.5	99.4	99.2	*99.7*	99.5	99.3	99.2	**99.6**	99.4	*99.8*	99.6
Standard Deviation	0.06	0.05	0.09	0.14	0.08	0.05	0.16	0.16	0.06	0.07	0.04	0.07
Text Recall	**99.1**	97.9	97.3	97.2	*99.2*	97.9	97.6	97.5	**99.4**	99.1	*98.4*	97.9
Standard Deviation	0.09	0.22	0.37	0.38	0.15	0.14	0.45	0.46	0.11	0.15	0.32	0.36
Non-Text F1	**92.6**	86.7	80.6	82.3	*92.6*	86.6	81.4	83.1	**93.4**	91.7	*88.9*	87.4
Standard Deviation	0.36	0.98	1.38	1.30	0.54	0.54	1.39	1.22	0.94	0.88	1.59	1.27
Non-Text Precision	**89.4**	80.2	71.8	74.8	*89.7*	79.9	73.6	76.6	**92.0**	90.3	*81.5*	80.5
Standard Deviation	0.92	1.67	2.55	2.36	1.69	1.05	3.37	3.10	1.38	1.51	2.91	2.61
Non-Text Recall	**96.0**	94.4	92.0	91.7	*95.6*	94.6	91.2	91.1	**94.9**	93.3	*97.7*	95.5
Standard Deviation	0.75	0.57	1.20	1.53	1.07	0.59	2.21	1.88	0.82	0.75	0.57	0.74

Table 3. Evaluation of the fraction of the exact errors that occurred on both approaches in relation to the total errors of the approach. The results are reported in percent. Both approaches only have about 1/3 of their errors in common.

Training LGT-Data	Balanced		Full	
Eval with or w/o background	With	W/o	With	W/o
Contour classifier	28.4%	30.4%	24.9%	32.3%
Pixel classifier	30.1%	19.0%	42.8%	37.6%

The results of the in-domain experiment with a fivefold cross-validation within the LGT full data are listed in Table 1. It shows very good results for the Pixel-Classifier with an overall foreground pixel accuracy (FgPA) of 99.5%, with an F1-Score for text-pixels of 99.7% and for non-text pixels of 98.6%. The contour classifier shows also good results for FgPA and F1-score for text around 99%, but the F1-score for non-text contours drops to 96.6%. However, this scenario

Fig. 4. Comparison of demanding images from the OCR-D evaluation dataset classified with both approaches illustrating their different kinds of errors. The upper row shows the predictions of the contour-classifier with post-processing, whereas the lower row shows the predictions of the pixel-classifier. Contours colored in green or blue have been classified as text or as non-text respectively. Typical errors of the contour-classifier are decorated letters in headlines, because they are much less frequent than normal letters and have a much higher variation, so there were too few examples available for them in the training material. The pixel-classifier does not show such clear error patterns (Color figure online).

may be seen as an upper bound, what results can be achieved, since usually the algorithms classify pages different from the training set which is evaluated by the cross-domain experiment.

The results of the cross-domain experiment with the OCR-D data set are shown in Table 2. It contains two training sets, the full LGT data set with 4933 pages and a reduced, "balanced" version, where only the 1515 pages with at least one image are used. The contour classifier has nearly the same evaluation results on both data sets, because it uses an internal parameter balancing the number of text and non-text contours in a relation of 5 : 1, so that it does not use the additional text pages in the full LGT data set. Post-processing improves the result of the contour classifier. The pixel classifier does not profit from this post-processing, therefore we omitted the results (however it post-processes its raw classification results by a majority vote over pixels within a contour, see above). Removing background pixel as well as small contours with less than 8 pixel, improves the results of both classifiers. The main results are printed in bold in table 2: The contour classifier is slightly better when trained on the smaller balanced LGT data set and the pixel classifier achieves better scores when trained on the full LGT data set with a small lead of less than 1% in FgPA, Text F1 and Non-Text F1, respectively, which is however not significant taking the standard deviations into account, in particular the relatively high standard deviations for Non-Text F1, precision and recall. We conducted a further experiment to investigate, whether both approaches misclassify the same contours. The results are shown in table 3 and example pages are shown in Fig. 4. It turns out that both approaches misclassify different pixels: when training with the full LGT data set and evaluating without background pixels (with post-processing) only about 32%–37% of all misclassified pixel were the same in both approaches. In the setting using the balanced LGT data set for training, this proportion drops to only 19% to 30% of identical pixel errors in relation to all pixel errors. Including the background pixels, the percentages of identical pixel errors are slightly higher, but similar. We conclude, that both approaches achieve similar results for segmenting text and non-text in historical printings, but produce different errors. This heterogeneity can be utilized by a combination of both approaches.

7   Outlook

In this work, we showed that an approach that uses connected components as its input yields comparable results to a state of the art pixel classifier on a completely different data set it was trained on. We expect to improve upon our results with the contour based approach if we experiment with Conditional Random Fields (Lafferty et al., 2001) and modern Graph Neural Networks (Scarselli et al., 2008) to integrate the context of neighboring contours and page layout information directly. Improvements should not be restricted to the contour based approach. We showed that a pixel classifier is less robust to a change of the domain. For this purpose future experiments with modern attention mechanism could further improve upon the pixel classifier. Combining both approaches by e.g. confidence voting or using the approach of base line detection for text lines as additional information source is a further promising approach, since about 2/3 of their pixel errors are different.

References

Bukhari, S.S., Al Azawi, M.I.A., Shafait, F., Breuel, T.M.: Document image segmentation using discriminative learning over connected components. In Proceedings of the 9th IAPR International Workshop on Document Analysis Systems, pp. 183–190 (2010)

Chang, W.-Y., Chiu, C.-C., Yang, J.-H.: Block-based connected-component labeling algorithm using binary decision trees. Sensors **15**(9), 23763–23787 (2015)

Chen, K., Liu, C.-L., Seuret, M., Liwicki, M., Hennebert, J., Ingold, R.: Page segmentation for historical document images based on superpixel classification with unsupervised feature learning. In: 2016 12th IAPR Workshop on Document Analysis Systems (DAS), pp. 299–304. IEEE (2016a)

Chen, K., Seuret, M., Liwicki, M., Hennebert, J., Liu, C.-L., Ingold, R.: Page segmentation for historical handwritten document images using conditional random fields. In: 2016 15th International Conference on Frontiers in Handwriting Recognition (ICFHR), pp. 90–95. IEEE (2016b)

Grüning, T., Leifert, G., Strauß, T., Michael, J., Labahn, R.: A two-stage method for text line detection in historical documents. Int. J. Doc. Anal. Recogni. (IJDAR) **22**(3), 285–302 (2019)

Lafferty, J.D., McCallum, A., and Pereira, F.C.N.: Conditional random fields: Probabilistic models for segmenting and labeling sequence data. In: Proceedings of the Eighteenth International Conference on Machine Learning, ICML 2001, pp. 282–289, San Francisco, CA, USA. Morgan Kaufmann Publishers Inc. (2001)

Long, J., Shelhamer, E., Darrell, T.: Fully convolutional networks for semantic segmentation. In: Proceedings of the IEEE Conference on Computer Vision and Pattern Recognition, pp. 3431–3440 (2015)

Noh, W.F., Woodward, P.: SLIC (Simple Line Interface Calculation). In: Proceedings of the Fifth International Conference on Numerical Methods in Fluid Dynamics, June 28–July 2, Twente University, Enschede, Lecture Notes in Physics, vol. 59. Springer, Berlin, Heidelberg (1976). https://doi.org/10.1007/3-540-08004-X_336

Reul, C., Christ, D., Hartelt, A., Balbach, N., Wehner, M., Springmann, U., Wick, C., Grundig, C., Büttner, A., Puppe, F.: OCR4all - An open-source tool providing a(semi-)automatic OCR workflow for historical printings. Appl. Sci. **9**(22), 4853 (2019)

Ronneberger, O., Fischer, P., Brox, T.: U-Net: Convolutional networks for biomedical image segmentation. In: Navab, N., Hornegger, J., Wells, W.M., Frangi, A.F. (eds.) MICCAI 2015. LNCS, vol. 9351, pp. 234–241. Springer, Cham (2015). https://doi.org/10.1007/978-3-319-24574-4_28

Scarselli, F., Gori, M., Tsoi, A.C., Hagenbuchner, M., Monfardini, G.: The graph neural network model. IEEE Trans. Neural Netw. **20**(1), 61–80 (2008)

Uijlings, J.R., Van De Sande, K.E., Gevers, T., Smeulders, A.W.: Selective search for object recognition. Int. J. Comput. Vis. **104**(2), 154–171 (2013)

Wick, C., Puppe, F.: Fully convolutional neural networks for page segmentation of historical document images. In: 2018 13th IAPR International Workshop on Document Analysis Systems (DAS), pp. 287–292. IEEE (2018)

Hybrid Ranking and Regression for Algorithm Selection

Jonas Hanselle[(✉)] [iD], Alexander Tornede [iD], Marcel Wever [iD],
and Eyke Hüllermeier [iD]

Heinz Nixdorf Institute and Department of Computer Science,
Paderborn University, Paderborn, Germany
{jonas.hanselle,alexander.tornede,marcel.wever,eyke}@upb.de

Abstract. Algorithm selection (AS) is defined as the task of automatically selecting the most suitable algorithm from a set of candidate algorithms for a specific instance of an algorithmic problem class. While suitability may refer to different criteria, runtime is of specific practical relevance. Leveraging empirical runtime information as training data, the AS problem is commonly tackled by fitting a regression function, which can then be used to estimate the candidate algorithms' runtimes for new problem instances. In this paper, we develop a new approach to algorithm selection that combines regression with ranking, also known as learning to rank, a problem that has recently been studied in the realm of preference learning. Since only the ranking of the algorithms is eventually needed for the purpose of selection, the precise numerical estimation of runtimes appears to be a dispensable and unnecessarily difficult problem. However, discarding the numerical runtime information completely seems to be a bad idea, as we hide potentially useful information about the algorithms' performance margins from the learner. Extensive experimental studies confirm the potential of our hybrid approach, showing that it often performs better than pure regression and pure ranking methods.

Keywords: Algorithm selection · Hybrid loss optimization · Combined ranking and regression

1 Introduction

Algorithm selection (AS) refers to the task of automatically selecting an algorithm from a set of candidate algorithms, which appears to be most suitable for a given instance of a problem class. A typical application of AS is the selection of solvers for computationally hard problems on a per-instance basis. Prominent examples of such problems include the Boolean satisfiability problem (SAT) [24] and the travelling salesman problem (TSP) [15]. Depending on the specific problem class, different criteria can be considered for assessing candidate algorithms. Especially important in this regard is an algorithm's efficiency measured in terms of its runtime.

© Springer Nature Switzerland AG 2020
U. Schmid et al. (Eds.): KI 2020, LNAI 12325, pp. 59–72, 2020.
https://doi.org/10.1007/978-3-030-58285-2_5

On the basis of empirical runtime information, i.e., observations of runtimes on training instances, the AS problem is typically tackled by fitting regression functions, one per algorithm, to predict the runtime on new query instances [5,24]. Collecting the predictions for all algorithms, the presumably fastest one is then selected. Regression-based approaches proved to perform well in practice, often improving over the algorithm that performs best on average, also known as the single best solver (SBS), by orders of magnitude [24].

In spite of this practical success, one may wonder whether AS should indeed be tackled as a regression problem. First, since selection is eventually based on the *comparison* of the predicted runtimes, regression appears to be an unnecessarily difficult problem. Indeed, prediction errors could be tolerated as long as they do not change the *ranking* of the algorithms, or even less, the presumably best algorithm. From this point of view, one may also question symmetric loss functions like the squared error loss, as commonly used in regression. For example, if algorithms A and B have runtimes of, respectively, 10 and 13 min, the estimates 12 and 11 min are clearly better than 5 and 9 min in terms of the squared error. However, whereas the former switch the order of the two algorithms, the latter will still promote the faster algorithm, namely A.

These considerations may suggest to tackle AS as a ranking instead of a regression problem, and indeed, ranking methods from the field of preference learning have been used for constructing algorithm selectors [6,8,18,21,22]. Such models are learned from data comprised of problem instances together with respective rankings of the candidate algorithms. Data of that kind can often be collected more easily than precise numerical runtimes, which is another advantage of ranking methods. For example, if algorithm A finished before a given timeout is reached, while algorithm B did not, the preference $A \succ B$ can still be derived as training information, even if the concrete runtime of B is not known.

However, the ranking-based approach could be criticized as well, namely for ignoring potentially useful training information about the actual runtimes, if available, and the performance margins between algorithms. For example, a runtime of 2 min for algorithm A and 2.1 min for B leads to the same ranking $A \succ B$ as a runtime of 2 min for A and 200 min for B.

In this paper, we propose a hybrid approach to algorithm selection that combines both approaches, ranking and regression, hoping to benefit from the best of the two worlds: simplifying the learning task and solving the right problem while providing sufficiently detailed information such that concrete runtime information and margins between candidate algorithms are taken into account. To this end, we make use of hybrid loss functions [20]. Following a more formal description of the AS setting in the next section, our approach will be detailed in Sects. 3 and 4.

Our experimental evaluation in Sect. 5 confirms the potential of the proposed hybrid approach, which proves beneficial for several of the investigated scenarios. More specifically, optimizing our hybrid regression and ranking loss improves over optimizing the pure regression respectively ranking loss in terms of various metrics, eventually yielding a better performing algorithm selector.

2   Algorithm Selection

In the (per-instance) algorithm selection problem, first introduced by Rice [17], one is concerned with automatically selecting the most suitable algorithm from a set of candidate algorithms $\mathcal{A} = \{A_1, \ldots, A_K\}$ for a specific instance $I \in \mathcal{I}$ of an algorithmic problem class such as the Boolean satisfiability problem (SAT). Formally, the goal is to find a mapping $s \colon \mathcal{I} \to \mathcal{A}$, also referred to as *algorithm selector*, from a problem instance space $\mathcal{I}$ to the set of candidate algorithms $\mathcal{A}$, which optimizes a costly-to-evaluate performance measure $m \colon \mathcal{I} \times \mathcal{A} \to \mathbb{R}$ of interest. The arguably most relevant example of such a measure, which is also considered in this paper, is runtime. The optimal algorithm selector (the oracle) is defined as

$$s^*(I) := \arg\min_{A \in \mathcal{A}} \mathbb{E}\left[m(I, A)\right], \tag{1}$$

for $I \in \mathcal{I}$, where the expectation accounts for the potential randomness of the algorithm (and any other random effects causing the performance of A on I to be non-deterministic).

2.1   Existing Approaches

To evaluate the performance measure m, an algorithm normally needs to be run on a given problem instance. This makes an exhaustive search over the algorithm space $\mathcal{A}$ computationally intractable or at least extremely costly. To circumvent this problem, a surrogate model $\widehat{m} \colon \mathcal{I} \times \mathcal{A} \to \mathbb{R}$ can be used to estimate the performance. Such models, which should be cheap to evaluate, are trained on data collected from previous algorithm runs. A feature extraction function $f \colon \mathcal{I} \to \mathbb{R}^d$ is used to compute d-dimensional feature representations of problem instances, which then allow for modeling the algorithm performance as functions of instance features. To keep the notation simple, we will not distinguish between I and $f(I)$ in the remainder of this paper; instead, we denote both a problem instance and its feature representation by I. Using such a model, the canonical algorithm selector will suggest the algorithm A with the lowest predicted runtime on the instance I:

$$\hat{s}(I) := \arg\min_{A \in \mathcal{A}} \widehat{m}(I, A) \tag{2}$$

A natural choice for $\widehat{m}$ is an algorithm-specific regression model $\widehat{m}_k \colon \mathcal{I} \to \mathbb{R}$, directly estimating the runtime achieved by an algorithm $A_k \in \mathcal{A}$ on a problem instance of interest $I \in \mathcal{I}$ [7].

   Early work on such surrogates can be found in [12], where the authors tackle the winner determination problem for the CPLEX solver. They demonstrate that, under certain conditions, the hardness of an instance represented by features, i.e., the expected performance of an algorithm on that instance, can be learned using machine learning approaches. Both linear and nonlinear models (multivariate adaptive regression splines [5]) were successfully applied for modeling the hardness of an instance (with respect to the root mean squared error).

In one of the earlier versions of the well-known algorithm selection approach Satzilla [24], the authors leverage such empirical hardness models on a per-algorithm basis. To this end, they learn one linear model per algorithm using ridge regression, which estimates its performance for unseen instances based on associated features.

Similarly, restart strategies are selected based on conditional runtime prediction models in [6]. These models are inferred through ridge linear regression conditioned on the satisfiability of an instance. Instead of directly selecting an algorithm based on the predicted runtime, the authors of [4] use regression techniques in a more indirect way: The runtimes predicted by random forests are used to map instances into another feature space, in which k-nearest neighbor methods are then applied to make the final selection.

As already explained in the introduction, an accurate prediction of runtimes is a sufficient but not necessary condition for selecting the best performing algorithm. Actually, such a selection rather corresponds to a *classification* instead of a regression problem, with the algorithms playing the role of the classes. Training a classifier, however, has a number of disadvantages. For example, by looking at the best algorithm only, large parts of the training data would be ignored. Likewise, recommendations are not very informative in this setting, as they do not differentiate between the (presumably) non-optimal algorithms. Alternatively, the AS problem could also be tackled as a *ranking* task, which can be seen as a compromise between classification and regression.

Ranking methods have been developed in the field of preference learning. Specifically relevant in the context of AS is so-called *label ranking* (LR) [23]. Here, instances are associated with rankings over a set of choice alternatives, in our case algorithms. Thus, training data is of the form

$$(I, A_1 \succ \cdots \succ A_z) \in \mathbb{R}^d \times \mathcal{R}(\mathcal{A}), \tag{3}$$

where $\mathcal{R}(\mathcal{A})$ is the set of all total orders on $\mathcal{A}$, and $A_i \succ A_j$ suggests that algorithm A_i performs better than algorithm A_j. What is then sought is a model $h : \mathbb{R}^d \to \mathcal{R}(\mathcal{A})$, which, given an instance $I \in \mathcal{I}$ (resp. its feature representation $f(I)$), predicts a ranking over the set of candidate algorithms $\mathcal{A}$. A recommendation can then be derived from that ranking, for example in the form of the top-1 or more generally top-k candidates. An example of label ranking applied to AS can be found in [6], where the authors infer rankings of collaborative filtering algorithms for instances of recommendation problems. Similarly, the authors of [8] use neural network based LR techniques to select meta-heuristics for travelling salesman problem instances.

In [22], *dyadic* approaches to ranking and regression are presented, which do not only leverage instance but also algorithm features, allowing one to select from an extremely large set of algorithms. A ranking method based on the Plackett-Luce model is shown to perform very well in a setting with many algorithms and very few training data, called *extreme algorithm selection*. Similarly, [14] leverage a ranking approach motivated from a Bayesian perspective, where the joint utility score of a pair of algorithms for an instance is defined in terms of the difference of the individual utility scores.

For a comprehensive and up-to-date survey of methods for algorithm selection, we refer to [10].

3   Hybrid Ranking and Regression Losses

There are several motivations for casting AS as a (label) ranking instead of a regression problem. As already explained, ranking not only appears to be the simpler task, but actually also the "right" problem. Indeed, the goal of AS is better reflected by a (non-symmetric) ranking than by a (symmetric) regression loss. Besides, precise numerical performance degrees are not always observable, for example when an algorithm is timed out, leading to missing or censored data in the case of regression, while preferences can still be derived. On the other hand, if precise performances are available, then considering only the qualitative part of the training information, namely the order relations, comes with a certain loss of information. For example, information about the algorithms' actual performance degrees, and the differences between them, may provide useful information about the reliability of a (pairwise) comparison.

These considerations suggest that both aspects should be taken into account when training an algorithm selector: predicted runtimes should first of all match the order of algorithms, and if possible, even be close to the actually observed runtimes. This could be accomplished by training the predictor with a hybrid loss function that combines both aspects into a single criterion.

Therefore, we propose the use of hybrid ranking and regression approaches for the AS problem. To this end, we model the performance of each algorithm in the candidate set $A_k \in \mathcal{A}$ in terms of a scoring function $v_k \colon \mathcal{I} \to \mathbb{R}$. As will be seen, the scoring function is in direct correspondence to the performance measure m_k, though not necessarily the same. The overall scoring model v is then given by $v(I, A_k) := v_k(I)$. Similar to the original combined regression and ranking approach presented by Sculley [20], our hybrid loss functions are based on a convex combination of a ranking term L_{RANK} that imposes ordering constraints between the individual predictions $v_k(I)$, $k \in [K] := \{1, \dots, K\}$, and a regression term L_{REG} that relates v_k to the actual runtime $m(I, A_k)$ achieved by algorithm A_k on the respective instance I.

3.1   Training Data

As training data, we assume (possibly incomplete or partial) information about the performance of algorithms on a set of training instances $I_1, \dots, I_N \in \mathcal{I}$:

$$\mathcal{D} := \Big\{ \big(I_n, m'_1(I_n), \dots, m'_K(I_n) \big) \Big\}_{n=1}^{N}, \tag{4}$$

where $m'_k(I_n)$ is information about the performance (runtime) of algorithm A_k on the instance I_n. Usually, $m'_k(I_n)$ is the runtime itself, however, the performance is also allowed to be unknown ($m'_k(I_n) = \perp$), for example because the algorithm has not been executed. Moreover, $m'_k(I_n)$ might be censored information about the true performance. A practically motivated example of such information is a timeout $(m'_k(I_n) = TO)$: algorithm A_k has been run on I_n, but not till the end, because it did not terminate within a given time frame.

From the information about each of the N instances I_n, we construct a set of training examples R_n for a regression learner and a set of training examples P_n for a preference learner. For regression, if $m'_k(I_n) \neq \perp$, we include an example $(I_n, y_{k,n})$ which is normalized by the timeout T_{max}, namely $y_{k,n} = 1$ if $m'_k(I_n) = TO$ and $y_{k,n} = m'_k(I_n)/T_{max}$. In the case where $m'_k(I_n) = \perp$, no information about A_k is included in R_n.

The set P_n consists of pairwise preferences of the form $A_i \succ A_j$, suggesting that algorithm A_i performed better on I_n than algorithm A_j. We include such a preference, which we formally represent as (I_n, i, j), whenever one of the following conditions holds:

- $m'_i(I_n) \notin \{\perp, TO\}$, $m'_j(I_n) \notin \{\perp, TO\}$, $m'_i(I_n) < m'_j(I_n)$,
- $m'_i(I_n) \notin \{\perp, TO\}$, $m'_j(I_n) = TO$.

3.2   Loss Functions

As already said, the overall loss of a model v on a dataset $\mathcal{D}$ is a convex combination of a ranking and a regression loss:

$$L(\mathcal{D}, v) := \lambda L_{\text{RANK}}(\mathcal{D}, v) + (1 - \lambda) L_{\text{REG}}(\mathcal{D}, v) , \tag{5}$$

where the hyperparameter $\lambda \in [0, 1]$ can be tuned to balance the two objectives. Setting $\lambda = 0$ corresponds to a pure regression model, whereas $\lambda = 1$ results in a pure ranking model.

In general, any ranking loss L_{RANK} and any regression loss L_{REG} can be used to instantiate our generic framework. Here, we model the latter in terms of the mean squared error (MSE)

$$L_{\text{REG}}(R_n, v) := \frac{1}{|R_n|} \sum_{(I_n, y_{k,n}) \in R_n} \left(v_k(I_n) - y_{k,n} \right)^2 . \tag{6}$$

The overall loss $L_{\text{REG}}(\mathcal{D}, v)$ is then obtained by averaging (6) over all N training instances.

For ranking, we consider the squared hinge ranking loss given by

$$L_{\text{RANK}}(P_n, v) := \binom{|P_n|}{2}^{-1} \sum_{(I_n, i, j)} \ell\left(\epsilon - v_i(I_n) + v_j(I_n) \right) , \tag{7}$$

where $\epsilon \in \mathbb{R}^+$ is a margin and $\ell(x) = (\max\{0, x\})^2$. This loss function is a smooth convex approximation of the simple 0/1 loss and enforces a margin effect in the sense that, to have a loss of 0, the two predictions must be correctly ordered and have a distance of at least ϵ. Again, the loss on the entire data, $L_{\text{RANK}}(\mathcal{D}, v)$ is obtained by averaging over all N training instances. For computational reasons, since $L_{\mathrm{RANK}}(P_n, v)$ contains a quadratic number of preferences, one may consider approximating this loss by sampling a subset of these preferences.

As an alternative to the squared hinge ranking loss (7), we also consider the following loss:

$$L_{\mathrm{RANK}}(P_n, v) := \binom{|P_n|}{2}^{-1} \sum_{(I_n, i, j)} \ell\big(v_i(I_n), v_j(I_n)\big), \tag{8}$$

with

$$\ell(x, y) = \log\big(\exp(-x) + \exp(-y)\big) + x. \tag{9}$$

This loss corresponds to the negative log-likelihood of observing a pairwise preference under the Plackett-Luce (PL) model for ranking data [13,16], which is commonly used in preference learning and label ranking [3].

4   Models and Optimization

For modeling the scoring functions $v_k \colon \mathcal{I} \to \mathbb{R}$, we consider three types of models, namely linear models, quadratic models, and feed-forward neural networks. Linear models define the score of an algorithm $A_k \in \mathcal{A}$ for a specific problem instance $I \in \mathcal{I}$ in terms of a linear combination of the instance features:

$$v_k(I) = \boldsymbol{w}_k^T I, \tag{10}$$

where $\boldsymbol{w}_k \in \mathbb{R}^d$ are the model parameters. To model quadratic relationships, a polynomial feature transformation $\phi \colon \mathbb{R}^d \to \mathbb{R}^{d(d+1)/2}$ is applied that maps the instance features to all monomials of degree 2. Consequently, the quadratic models are described by weight vectors $\boldsymbol{w}_k \in \mathbb{R}^{d(d+1)/2}$. We summarize all model parameters in a single parameter set $\boldsymbol{W} = \{\boldsymbol{w}_k \,|\, A_k \in \mathcal{A}\}$. Since all loss terms are convex, their convex combination (5) remains convex, and their minimization can be accomplished using gradient-based optimization methods. We apply the L-BFGS-B algorithm [2,25] for this task. To avoid overfitting, we employ weight decay by adding a regularization term $R(\boldsymbol{W}) = \gamma \sum_{k=1}^{K} \sum_{j=1}^{d} [\boldsymbol{w}_k]_j^2$, which can be adjusted by setting $\gamma \in \mathbb{R}$ to an appropriate value.

The neural network is given by a simple feed-forward architecture as illustrated in Fig. 1.

We adapt the training procedure from [19] for our setting of hybrid ranking and regression. For adjusting the model's weights $\boldsymbol{W}$, backpropagation is applied. The *Adam* optimizer [11] was selected as a gradient-based optimization method for minimizing the loss function. Regularization is implemented in terms of *early stopping*. Before the training procedure starts, a fraction of the original training dataset is selected as a validation set and removed from the training data. During the training, the model's loss on this validation set is computed periodically. A rising validation loss is an indicator of overfitting, thus the training procedure is stopped if an increase in the validation loss is observed for several consecutive checks. Afterwards, the model parameters are fixed to the set of weights that achieved the best validation loss during training.

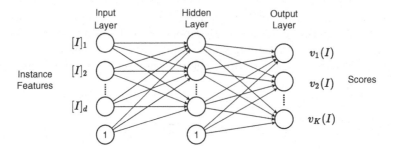

Fig. 1. Architecture of the neural network. Problem instance feature descriptions are fed into the input layer. The nodes of the fully connected hidden layer use a sigmoidal activation function in order to learn non-linear relationships. The nodes in the output layer use the identity as an activation function. Here, $[I]_j$ denotes the j-th entry of the instance feature vector.

5   Evaluation

In order to evaluate the performance of the proposed hybrid ranking and regression approach to the algorithm selection problem, we make use of the *ASlib* benchmark [1]. This benchmark contains several AS *scenarios*, which are collections of performance data of algorithms achieved on several problem instances. As we consider runtime as a selection criterion in the scope of this paper, we evaluated our approach using scenarios from the algorithmic problem domains of Boolean satisfiability (SAT), mixed integer programming (MIP), constraint satisfaction (CSP), and container pre-marshalling (CPMP).

5.1   Performance Metrics

For assessing the performance achieved by the proposed approaches, we consider both ranking measures as well as specific algorithm selection measures. Ranking measures quantify how well the ranking over algorithms according to their predicted performance corresponds to the ranking implied by their true performance. We represent a ranking of the algorithms $\{A_1, \ldots, A_K\}$ in terms of a mapping $\pi \colon [K] \to [K]$, such that $\pi(k)$ is the position of the algorithm A_k in the ranking — allowing for ties,[1] we may have $\pi(i) = \pi(j)$ for $i \neq j$. One prominent measure is the rank correlation coefficient Kendall's tau [9]. Given a ground truth ranking π and a predicted ranking $\hat{\pi}$, Kendall's τ is defined as

$$\tau(\pi, \hat{\pi}) = \frac{C - D}{\sqrt{(C + D + T_\pi) \cdot (C + D + T_{\hat{\pi}})}}, \tag{11}$$

where C is the number of correctly ordered pairs $((\pi(i) - \pi(j))(\hat{\pi}(i) - \hat{\pi}(j)) > 0)$, D is the number of incorrectly ordered pairs $((\pi(i) - \pi(j))(\hat{\pi}(i) - \hat{\pi}(j)) < 0)$,

---

[1] Ties are mainly caused by timeouts in the "ground truth" data but rarely occur in the predicted performances.

and T_π and $T_{\hat\pi}$ are the number of ties in ranking π and $\hat\pi$, respectively. Kendall's τ takes values in $[-1, 1]$, where $\tau(\pi, \hat\pi) = 1$ means that the rankings $\hat\pi$ and π are in perfect agreement and $\tau(\pi, \hat\pi) = -1$ the exact opposite (one of them is the reversal of the other one).

A widespread performance measure in the field of AS with respect to runtime is the penalized average runtime with a penalty factor of 10 (PAR10). Typically, the algorithms for the problem domains considered in this paper are not run for an indefinite amount of time until they eventually terminate, but are rather aborted after a predefined timeout is exceeded. The PAR10 score simply averages the runtime achieved by the selected algorithms for all problem instances of a scenario and accounts for timed out runs with 10 times the timeout as their runtime. We ignore feature costs, i.e., the runtime of the feature extraction function f, when computing PAR10 scores, as not all of the considered scenarios provide this information.

5.2   Evaluation Setup

The experimental results were obtained by conducting a 10-fold cross validation. In each fold, a fraction of 90% of a scenario's problem instances and the corresponding algorithm performances was used for training the algorithm selector, and the remaining 10% were used as a test set. For each scenario, we used the full set of features provided by ASLib [1]. Missing feature values were imputed with the feature's mean. Afterwards, feature values were standardized before training the models. Algorithm runtimes are given in terms of the PAR10 format, i.e., timed out runs are accounted for with 10-times the timeout. As the set of pairwise preferences P_n grows quadratically in the number of candidate algorithms, we approximate it by a sample $\hat{P}_n$ containing at most 5 pairwise algorithm comparisons for each instance. Should this number of comparisons not be available, we sample the maximum number of possible comparisons.

To evaluate the influence of the hyperparameter λ on the predictive performance, we conducted the experiments for $\lambda \in \{0.0, 0.1, \ldots, 1.0\}$. For training the linear and quadratic models, we set the regularization parameter $\gamma = 10^{-3}$ and ran the L-BFGS-B [2,25] algorithm for at most 100 iterations in order to minimize the loss functions. For the neural network-based approaches, we used the *Adam* [11] optimizer with a learning rate of $\eta = 10^{-3}$ for minimizing the loss functions and a batch size of 128. The architecture consists of a single hidden layer with 32 nodes, each using the sigmoid activation function $t \mapsto \frac{1}{1+e^{-t}}$. For early stopping, a fraction of 0.3 of the original training data is used as a validation set. We compute the loss on this validation set every 8 epochs and stop the training procedure if it increases for 8 consecutive checks. After the training, the model weights are set to the values for which the best validation loss was observed. If early stopping does not apply, the training procedure is stopped after a maximum number of 1,000 epochs. We evaluated the performance metrics for six independent runs on different random seeds and aggregated them by averaging the results.

The implementation of the proposed approaches including a documentation is provided on GitHub.[2]

5.3 Results

In the following, we discuss the results obtained by the experimental evaluation for all considered approaches, i.e., the two ranking loss functions in combination with the mean squared error as regression loss: the linear models (PL-LM, Hinge-LM), the quadratic models (PL-QM, Hinge-QM), and the neural networks (PL-NN, Hinge-NN). Figure 2 shows the average Kendall's τ rank correlation achieved by each of the proposed approaches for several values of λ. Recall that lower values of λ correspond to emphasizing the regression objective while higher values correspond to emphasizing the ranking objective. At first glance, we observe a tendency that larger values for λ lead to better rankings. Notably, however, in various cases the peak performance is not achieved for $\lambda = 1$, but rather for a proper compromise between ranking and regression. Consider for example the MIP-2016, SAT11-RAND or SAT11-HAND scenario, for which several of the proposed approaches achieve their peak performance for intermediate λ values.

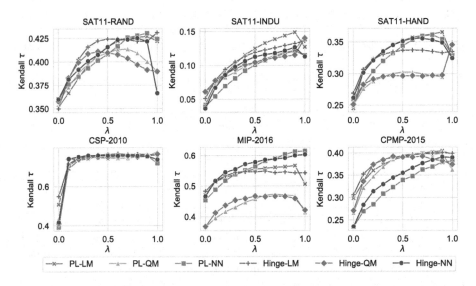

Fig. 2. Average Kendall's τ rank correlation coefficient achieved by the proposed approaches for different values of λ on a variety of AS scenarios. In multiple cases, an intermediate setting of $\lambda \in (0, 1)$ achieves a better rank correlation than pure regression ($\lambda = 0$) or pure ranking ($\lambda = 1$).

Figure 3 shows the PAR10 scores achieved by the proposed approaches. Again, we observe that neither pure regression nor pure ranking achieve the

---

[2] https://github.com/JonasHanselle/CoRRAS.

best performance consistently. Instead, a combination of the two appears to be favorable for most of the AS scenarios. Especially in the CSP-2010 and the MIP-2016 scenarios, the best performances, i.e. lowest PAR10 scores, are achieved for most of the proposed models when considering a hybrid ranking and regression loss.

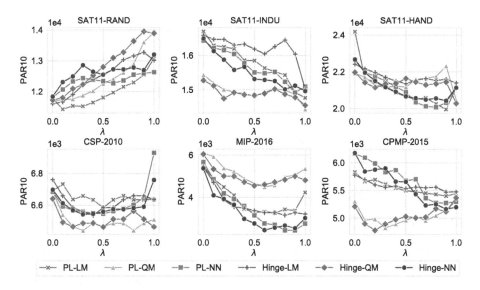

Fig. 3. Penalized average runtime achieved by selecting the top ranked algorithm predicted by the proposed models for each problem instance of the considered AS scenario.

Table 1 shows the number of scenarios for which a pure regression approach ($\lambda = 0$), a pure ranking approach ($\lambda = 1$), or a hybrid ranking and regression approach ($\lambda \in \{0.1, \ldots, 0.9\}$) achieves the best performances according to Kendall's τ and the PAR10 score. Regarding the rank correlation, unsurprisingly none of the proposed models achieved the best performance with the pure regression setting. The hybrid ranking and regression results are either on par with pure label ranking results or ahead of them. With respect to the PAR10 scores, hybrid regression and ranking performs the best for all model-loss combinations. Overall, for the majority of model-scenario combinations, a hybrid regression and ranking approach performs the best. While setting the hyperparameter λ to an intermediate value yields promising results, we could not reliably identify an optimal default value for this parameter. Instead, as can be seen in the plots in Figs. 2 and 3, the value for which the best performance is achieved depends both on the model and the scenario at hand.

Table 1. Number of scenarios for which each configuration achieved the best (average) performance according to Kendall's τ coefficient resp. PAR10 score. Recall that $\lambda = 0$ means pure regression, $\lambda \in (0, 1)$ a hybrid approach, and $\lambda = 1$ pure ranking.

Model	τ			PAR10		
	$\lambda = 0$	$\lambda \in (0, 1)$	$\lambda = 1$	$\lambda = 0$	$\lambda \in (0, 1)$	$\lambda = 1$
PL-LM	0	6	0	0	5	1
PL-QM	0	3	3	1	3	2
PL-NN	0	4	2	1	5	0
Hinge-LM	0	4	2	1	4	1
Hinge-QM	0	3	3	1	3	2
Hinge-NN	0	5	1	1	4	1

6   Conclusion

In this paper, we advocated the use of hybrid ranking and regression for the algorithm selection problem, mainly with the objective to tackle the "right" problem—which is selection, or, more generally, ranking—while not losing potentially useful numerical information about observed performances (runtimes). The proposed framework is built upon optimizing combined loss functions that take both regression and ranking criteria into account. We investigated three classes of models for estimating algorithm performances, namely linear models, quadratic models, and non-linear models in the form of neural networks. The results obtained by our experimental evaluation confirm that considering both ranking and regression objectives often leads to better algorithm choices than solely relying on one of the two objectives.

The proposed approaches rely on minimizing a convex combination of a ranking and a regression loss function. We investigated the squared hinge ranking loss and a ranking loss based on the Plackett-Luce model in combination with the mean squared error as a regression loss. In future work, we plan to further elaborate on suitable hybrid losses and to investigate the performance of other combinations. Of particular interest are regression methods for censored data, as these allow for modeling timeouts in a theoretically sound way. Another important question concerns the influence of the hyperparameter λ, which balances the regression and the ranking objectives. As we did not observe a suitable default value, it would be interesting to identify properties of algorithm selection scenarios that seem to influence the optimal choice of this parameter, i.e., which allow for deciding which of the two objectives, regression or ranking, should be emphasized more.

Acknowledgements. This work was supported by the German Federal Ministry of Economic Affairs and Energy (BMWi) within the "Innovationswettbewerb Künstliche Intelligenz" and the German Research Foundation (DFG) within the Collaborative Research Center "On-The-Fly Computing" (SFB 901/3 project no. 160364472).

The authors also gratefully acknowledge support of this project through computing time provided by the Paderborn Center for Parallel Computing (PC^2).

References

1. Bischl, B., et al.: Aslib: A benchmark library for algorithm selection. Artif. Intell. **237**, 41–58 (2016)
2. Byrd, R.H., Lu, P., Nocedal, J., Zhu, C.: A limited memory algorithm for bound constrained optimization. SIAM J. Sci. Comput. **16**(5), 1190–1208 (1995)
3. Cheng, W., Dembczynski, K., Hüllermeier, E.: Label ranking methods based on the Plackett-Luce model. In: Proceedings of the 27th International Conference on Machine Learning (ICML-10), June 21–24, 2010, Haifa, Israel, pp. 215–222. Omnipress (2010)
4. Collautti, M., Malitsky, Y., Mehta, D., O'Sullivan, B.: SNNAP: Solver-based nearest neighbor for algorithm portfolios. In: Blockeel, H., Kersting, K., Nijssen, S., Železný, F. (eds.) ECML PKDD 2013. LNCS (LNAI), vol. 8190, pp. 435–450. Springer, Heidelberg (2013). https://doi.org/10.1007/978-3-642-40994-3_28
5. Friedman, J.H.: Multivariate adaptive regression splines. Ann. Stat., 1–67 (1991)
6. Haim, S., Walsh, T.: Restart strategy selection using machine learning techniques. In: Kullmann, O. (ed.) SAT 2009. LNCS, vol. 5584, pp. 312–325. Springer, Heidelberg (2009). https://doi.org/10.1007/978-3-642-02777-2_30
7. Hutter, F., Xu, L., Hoos, H.H., Leyton-Brown, K.: Algorithm runtime prediction: Methods & evaluation. Artif. Intell. **206**, 79–111 (2014)
8. Kanda, J., Soares, C., Hruschka, E., de Carvalho, A.: A meta-learning approach to select meta-heuristics for the traveling salesman problem using MLP-based label ranking. In: Huang, T., Zeng, Z., Li, C., Leung, C.S. (eds.) ICONIP 2012. LNCS, vol. 7665, pp. 488–495. Springer, Heidelberg (2012). https://doi.org/10.1007/978-3-642-34487-9_59
9. Kendall, M.G.: The treatment of ties in ranking problems. Biometrika **33**(3), 239–251 (1945)
10. Kerschke, P., Hoos, H.H., Neumann, F., Trautmann, H.: Automated algorithm selection: Survey and perspectives. Evol. Comput. **27**(1), 3–45 (2019)
11. Kingma, D.P., Ba, J.: Adam: A method for stochastic optimization. In: 3rd International Conference on Learning Representations, ICLR 2015, San Diego, CA, USA, May 7–9, Conference Track Proceedings (2015)
12. Leyton-Brown, K., Nudelman, E., Shoham, Y.: Learning the empirical hardness of optimization problems: The case of combinatorial auctions. In: Van Hentenryck, P. (ed.) CP 2002. LNCS, vol. 2470, pp. 556–572. Springer, Heidelberg (2002). https://doi.org/10.1007/3-540-46135-3_37
13. Luce, R.D.: Individual choice behavior. John Wiley, Oxford, England (1959)
14. Oentaryo, R.J., Handoko, S.D., Lau, H.C.: Algorithm selection via ranking. In: Proceedings of the Twenty-Ninth AAAI Conference on Artificial Intelligence, January 25–30, 2015, Austin, Texas, USA, pp. 1826–1832 (2015)
15. Pihera, J., Musliu, N.: Application of machine learning to algorithm selection for TSP. In: 26th IEEE International Conference on Tools with Artificial Intelligence, ICTAI 2014, Limassol, Cyprus, November 10–12, pp. 47–54. IEEE Computer Society (2014)
16. Plackett, R.L.: The analysis of permutations. J. Roy. Stat. Soc. Ser. C (Appl. Stat.) **24**(2), 193–202 (1975)

17. Rice, J.R.: The algorithm selection problem. Adv. Comput. **15**, 65–118 (1976)
18. de Sá, C.R., Soares, C., Knobbe, A.J., Cortez, P.: Label ranking forests. Exp. Syst. **34**(1) (2017)
19. Schäfer, D., Hüllermeier, E.: Dyad ranking using Plackett-Luce models based on joint feature representations. Mach. Learn. **107**(5), 903–941 (2018). https://doi. org/10.1007/s10994-017-5694-9
20. Sculley, D.: Combined regression and ranking. In: Proceedings of the 16th ACM SIGKDD International Conference on Knowledge Discovery and Data Mining, Washington, DC, USA, July 25–28, pp. 979–988 (2010)
21. Tornede, A., Wever, M., Hüllermeier, E.: Algorithm selection as recommendation: From collaborative filtering to dyad ranking. In: CI Workshop, Dortmund (2019)
22. Tornede, A., Wever, M., Hüllermeier, E.: Extreme algorithm selection with dyadic feature representation. CoRR abs/2001.10741 (2020)
23. Vembu, S., Gärtner, T.: Label ranking algorithms: A survey. In: In: Fürnkranz J., Hüllermeier E. (eds.) Preference Learning, pp. 45–64. Springer, Heidelberg (2010). https://doi.org/10.1007/978-3-642-14125-6_3
24. Xu, L., Hutter, F., Hoos, H.H., Leyton-Brown, K.: Satzilla: Portfolio-based algo-rithm selection for SAT. J. Artif. Intell. Res. **32**, 565–606 (2008)
25. Zhu, C., Byrd, R.H., Lu, P., Nocedal, J.: Algorithm 778: L-BFGS-B: Fortran sub-routines for large-scale bound-constrained optimization. ACM Trans. Math. Softw. **23**(4), 550–560 (1997)

Conditional Reasoning and Relevance

Steffen Hölldobler[1,2]([✉])

[1] Technische Universität Dresden, Dresden, Germany
`sh@iccl.tu-dresden.de`
[2] North Caucasus Federal University, Stavropol, Russian Federation

Abstract. The *Weak Completion Semantics* is a computational and nonmonotonic cognitive theory based on the three-valued logic of Łukasiewicz. It has been applied to adequately model – among others – the suppression task, the selection task, syllogistic reasoning, and conditional reasoning. In this paper we investigate the case where the antecedent of a conditional is true, but its consequent is unknown. We propose to apply abduction in order to find an explanation for the consequent. This allows to derive new conditionals which are necessarily true. But it also leads to two problems, viz. that consequents should not abduce themselves and that the antecendent of a conditional should be relevant to its consequent. We propose solutions for both problems.

Keywords: Human reasoning · Conditional reasoning · Logic · Nonmonotonicity · Relevance · Weak Completion Semantics

1 Introduction

Classical binary logic is often considered as a normative theory in the psychology of reasoning. Oaksford and Chater [28] have identified five fundamental problems for this – as they call it – *old* paradigm, viz. that it is knowledge poor, that background knowledge must be consistent, that there can be no learning, that it is monotonic, and that it concentrates on individual reasoning. Indeed, many data from experiments show that participants do not seem to apply classical binary logic in their reasoning, cf. [3,21].

Somewhat surprisingly, after their initial analysis, Oaksford and Chater jump to the probabilistic paradigm. However, there appears to be an alternative to both, the old, classical binary logic paradigm as well as to the probabilistic paradigm, which may be called the *new, multi-valued, and nonmonotonic logic paradigm*. This paradigm has been extensively studied within the fields of artificial intelligence and logic programming since the 1970s and it has the additional advantage of being computational. Recently, it has also been applied to human reasoning by Stenning and van Lambalgen [33,34]. They have proposed a two-stage process: in the first stage, reasoning is towards a logic program; in a second stage, reasoning is with respect to the program.

Based on the ideas underlying the approach of Stenning and van Lambalgen the *Weak Completion Semantics* has been developed [16]. It is mathematically

© Springer Nature Switzerland AG 2020
U. Schmid et al. (Eds.): KI 2020, LNAI 12325, pp. 73–87, 2020.
https://doi.org/10.1007/978-3-030-58285-2_6

sound [17], computational, and has been applied to different human reasoning tasks including the suppression [7] and the selection task [8]. In syllogistic reasoning [29], the *Weak Completion Semantics* has outperformed all other cognitive theories discussed in [21] including PSYCOP [32] as well as the mental [18] and the verbal models theory [31].

. The *Weak Completion Semantics* has also been applied to conditional reasoning [5,6]. In particular, a method called *minimal revision followed by abduction* (MRFA) was proposed to evaluate conditionals. In this paper we will consider the case, where the antecedent of a conditional is evaluated to true whereas its consequent is evaluated to unknown. We will pursue the idea to consider such a consequent as an observation and to apply abduction in an attempt to explain it. This leads to two problems. Firstly, a consequent should not abduce itself. Secondly, the antecedent should be relevant to the consequent. But how should relevance be defined?

The main contribution of this paper is the development of a model-theoretic notion of relevance and its incorporation into the MRFA procedure such that the two abovementioned problems are solved.

The paper is organized as follows. In Sect. 2 the *Weak Completion Semantics* and the MRFA procedure are illustrated. In Sect. 3 we will present our idea and the problems which may occur. Three different notions of relevance will be developed in Sects. 4, 5, and 6. It will turn out that the first two are inadequate. We will build the third notion of strong relevance into the MRFA procedure and apply it to several examples in Sect. 7. In the final Sect. 8 we put our contribution in perspective. We assume readers to be familiar with logic (e.g. [15]), logic programming (e.g. [23]), and abductive logic programming [20].[1]

2   The Weak Completion Semantics

In a nutshell, the *Weak Completion Semantics* consists of five steps: (1) Reasoning towards a program. (2) Weakly completing the program. (3) Computing its least model under Łukasiewicz logic. (4) Reasoning with respect to the least model. (5) If necessary, applying abduction.

To illustrate the *Weak Completion Semantics* as well as its evaluation of conditionals we consider the *suppression task* [3]. It is a set of twelve experiments where subjects were given a fact and one or two conditionals as background knowledge and were asked to draw conclusions. The experiments showed that in certain contexts subjects reject previously drawn conclusions. This holds for valid as well as for invalid conclusions with respect to two-valued classical logic. In this paper, rather than adding a fact like *she has an essay to write* to the background knowledge and asking whether subjects are willing to conclude that *she will study late in the library* we will evaluate the conditional *if she has an essay to write, then she will study late in the library*.

---

[1] Usually, abductive frameworks come with integrity constraints. In this paper we assume that the set of integrity constraints is empty, but the presented approach can be straightforwardly extended by non-empty sets of integrity constraints.

Suppose that the conditional *if she has an essay to write, then she will study late in the library* is given as background knowledge. Stenning and van Lambalgen have proposed that reasoning towards a program should lead to

$$\mathcal{P}_1 = \{\ell \leftarrow e \wedge \neg ab_e, \ ab_e \leftarrow \bot\},$$

where ℓ and e denote that she will study late in the library and that she has an essay to write, respectively, ab_e is an abnormality predicate which is assumed to be false, and $\bot$ is a truth constant denoting falsehood. They consider a conditional not as a truth functional connective but as a license for inferences, and the abnormality predicate is used to represent this principle. Weakly completing program $\mathcal{P}_1$ we obtain[2]

$$wc\,\mathcal{P}_1 = \{\ell \leftrightarrow e \wedge \neg ab_e, \ ab_e \leftrightarrow \bot\}.$$

As shown in [17], each weakly completed program has a unique least model[3] under the three-valued logic of Łukasiewicz [24]. This model can be computed as the least fixed point of a semantic operator introduced by Stenning and van Lambalgen. Reasoning is then performed with respect to this least model. In the example, the least model $\mathcal{M}_{\mathcal{P}_1}$ of $wc\,\mathcal{P}_1$ maps the atom ab_e to false and the atoms e and ℓ to unknown.

Suppose that given $\mathcal{P}_1$ as background knowledge we would like to evaluate the conditional *if she has an essay to write, then she will study late in the library (if e then ℓ)* with respect to the weak completion of $\mathcal{P}_1$. Its antecedent e is unknown under $\mathcal{M}_{\mathcal{P}_1}$. In this case, MRFA[4] considers e as an observation that should be explained. It can be explained by abducing the (minimal) explanation $e \leftarrow \top$, where $\top$ is a truth constant denoting truth. Adding this fact to $\mathcal{P}_1$ we obtain[5]

$$\mathcal{P}_2 = \{\ell \leftarrow e \wedge \neg ab_e, \ ab_e \leftarrow \bot, \ e \leftarrow \top\}.$$

Its weak completion is

$$wc\,\mathcal{P}_2 = \{\ell \leftrightarrow e \wedge \neg ab_e, \ ab_e \leftrightarrow \bot, \ e \leftrightarrow \top\},$$

whose least model $\mathcal{M}_{\mathcal{P}_2}$ maps the atoms e and ℓ to true and the atom ab_e to false. Consequently, the conditional *if e then ℓ* is mapped to true, which corresponds to the results of the first experiment reported in [3].

In this example, we could have simply added the fact $e \leftarrow \top$ to the program $\mathcal{P}_1$ to obtain the same result. But in other experiments the addition of a definition for the antecedent of a conditional is not sufficient and abduction is needed.

---

[2] Weak completion differs from Clark's completion [4] in that undefined atoms – like e in this example – are not mapped to false but to unknown.

[3] Let $I^\top$ and $I^\bot$ be the sets of ground atoms mapped to true and false, respectively, by an interpretation I. For interpretations I_1 and I_2 we define $I_1 \subseteq I_2$ if and only if $I_1^\top \subseteq I_2^\top$ and $I_1^\bot \subseteq I_2^\bot$. This allows to partially order the set of interpretations.

[4] See the Appendix for a complete specification of MRFA.

[5] This is the program proposed in [34] to model the first experiment reported in [3].

E.g., suppose we want to evaluate the conditional *if she will study late in the library, then she has an essay to write (if ℓ then e)* given the background knowledge $\mathcal{P}_1$. $\mathcal{P}_1$ contains already a definition for ℓ and it does not seem to be particularly meaningful to add $\ell \leftarrow \top$ to it. However, applying abduction we find that adding $e \leftarrow \top$ to $\mathcal{P}_1$ explains ℓ. Hence, the conditional *if ℓ then e* is evaluated to true, which corresponds again to the experimental results reported in [3].

Now suppose that the conditional *if the library stays open, then she will study late in the library* is added to the background knowledge $\mathcal{P}_1$. Following [34] and reasoning towards a program we obtain

$$\mathcal{P}_3 = \{\ell \leftarrow e \wedge \neg ab_e,\ \ell \leftarrow o \wedge \neg ab_o,\ ab_e \leftarrow \neg o,\ ab_o \leftarrow \neg e\},$$

where o denotes that the library will stay open and ab_o is another abnormality predicate. The library not being open is an abnormality with respect to ab_e. Likewise, not having a reason to go to the library is an abnormality with respect to ab_o and having an essay to write is the only reason in this scenario so far. Weakly completing the program $\mathcal{P}_3$ we obtain

$$wc\,\mathcal{P}_3 = \{\ell \leftrightarrow (e \wedge \neg ab_e) \vee (o \wedge \neg ab_o),\ ab_e \leftrightarrow \neg o,\ ab_o \leftrightarrow \neg e\},$$

whose least model $\mathcal{M}_{\mathcal{P}_3}$ maps the atoms ℓ, e, o, ab_e, and ab_o to unknown. Suppose that considering this extended background knowledge we would like to evaluate the conditional *if e then ℓ* again. Its antecedent e is unknown given the background knowledge, but as before it can be explained by the explanation $e \leftarrow \top$. Adding this explanation to the program $\mathcal{P}_3$ we obtain

$$\mathcal{P}_4 = \{\ell \leftarrow e \wedge \neg ab_e,\ \ell \leftarrow o \wedge \neg ab_o,\ ab_e \leftarrow \neg o,\ ab_o \leftarrow \neg e,\ e \leftarrow \top\}.$$

Its weak completion is

$$wc\,\mathcal{P}_4 = \{\ell \leftrightarrow (e \wedge \neg ab_e) \vee (o \wedge \neg ab_o),\ ab_e \leftrightarrow \neg o,\ ab_o \leftrightarrow \neg e,\ e \leftrightarrow \top\},$$

whose least model $\mathcal{M}_{\mathcal{P}_4}$ maps the atom e to true, the atom ab_o to false, and the atoms ℓ, o, and ab_e to unknown. Hence, the conditional *if e then ℓ* is now unknown contrary to being evaluated to true earlier. This shows that the *Weak Completion Semantics* is nonmonotonic and can model suppression.

As a forth example consider the *shooting of Kennedy scenario* discussed in [1]: *If Oswald shot, then the president was killed. If somebody else shot, then the president was killed. Oswald shot.* Reasoning towards a program we obtain

$$\mathcal{P}_5 = \{k \leftarrow os \wedge \neg ab_{os},\ k \leftarrow ses \wedge \neg ab_{ses},\ ab_{os} \leftarrow \bot,\ ab_{ses} \leftarrow \bot,\ os \leftarrow \top\},$$

where k, os, ses denote that Kennedy was killed, Oswald shot, and somebody else shot, respectively, and ab_{os} as well as ab_{ses} are abnormality predicates which are assumed to be false. Its weak completion is

$$wc\,\mathcal{P}_5 = \{k \leftrightarrow (os \wedge \neg ab_{os}) \vee (ses \wedge \neg ab_{ses}),\ ab_{os} \leftrightarrow \bot,\ ab_{ses} \leftrightarrow \bot,\ os \leftrightarrow \top\},$$

whose least model $\mathcal{M}_{\mathcal{P}_5}$ maps the atoms os and k to true, ab_{os} and ab_{ses} to false, and ses to unknown.

Suppose that given this background knowledge we want to evaluate the counterfactual *if Oswald did not shoot Kennedy in Dallas, then Kennedy was not killed in Dallas (if $\neg os$ then $\neg k$)*. Its antecedent $\neg os$ is false in $\mathcal{M}_{\mathcal{P}_5}$. In order to satisfy the antecedent, we have to revise $\mathcal{P}_5$. Within MRFA this can be (minimally) done by replacing $os \leftarrow \top$ by the assumption $os \leftarrow \perp^6$ to obtain

$$\mathcal{P}_6 = \{k \leftarrow os \wedge \neg ab_{os},\ k \leftarrow ses \wedge \neg ab_{ses},\ ab_{os} \leftarrow \perp,\ ab_{ses} \leftarrow \perp,\ os \leftarrow \perp\}.$$

Its weak completion is

$$wc\,\mathcal{P}_6 = \{k \leftrightarrow (os \wedge \neg ab_{os}) \vee (ses \wedge \neg ab_{ses}),\ ab_{os} \leftrightarrow \perp,\ ab_{ses} \leftrightarrow \perp,\ os \leftrightarrow \perp\},$$

whose least model $\mathcal{M}_{\mathcal{P}_6}$ maps the atoms os, ab_{os} and ab_{ses} to false, and k and ses to unknown. Consequently, the conditional *if $\neg os$ then $\neg k$* is unknown.

3   An Idea and Two Problems

Herein, we consider conditionals of the form *if $\mathcal{A}$ then $\mathcal{C}$*, where antecedent $\mathcal{A}$ and consequent $\mathcal{C}$ are consistent sets of literals[7] and $\mathcal{A}$ is true but $\mathcal{C}$ is unknown given the background knowledge. As an example – adapted from [27] – consider a scenario where a person has observed that a liquid spilled on blue litmus paper has colored the paper red, but otherwise has forgotton basic chemistry. Then, from the observer's perspective, the antecedent of the conditional *if a liquid turns blue litmus paper red, then it is acidic* is true, but the consequent is unknown.

We conjecture that often humans are unsatisfied if they cannot assign true or false to the consequent of a conditional and continue to reason about it. The idea pursued in this paper is to consider an unknown consequent as an observation that should be explained. We apply abduction [20] in order to find an explanation for such a consequent. In that case, if the explanation is added to the antecedent, a *new* conditional arises which is necessarily true.

For example, in the *suppression task* the conditional *if e then ℓ*[8] is evaluated to unknown given the background knowledge $\mathcal{P}_4$. But its consequent ℓ can be explained by $o \leftarrow \top$. Consequently, the *new* conditional *if she has an essay to write and the library stays open, then she will study late in the library* can be derived and is known to be true. In the *shooting of Kennedy scenario* the conditional *if $\neg os$ then $\neg k$* is evaluated to unknown given the background knowledge $\mathcal{P}_6$. But its consequent $\neg k$ can be explained by $ses \leftarrow \perp$. Consequently, the *new*

---

[6] Phan Minh Dung has suggested to call expressions of the form $A \leftarrow \perp$ *assumptions* as they can be overwritten by any other definition for A. E.g., $wc\{A \leftarrow \perp\} = \{A \leftrightarrow \perp\}$, whereas $wc\{A \leftarrow \perp,\ A \leftarrow \top\} = \{A \leftrightarrow \top \vee \perp\}$. $\neg A$ holds in the former, but A holds in the latter example showing that negation is by default and is defeasible.

[7] A set of literals is consistent iff it does not contain an atom and its negation.

[8] In case of singleton sets we often drop the curly brackets and write e instead of $\{e\}$.

conditional *if Oswald did not shoot Kennedy in Dallas and nobody else did, then Kennedy was not killed in Dallas* can be derived and is known to be true.

However, the idea leads to two problems. Firstly, it should be impossible that the consequent of a conditional can abduce itself. For example, the conditional *if ¬os then ¬ses* is unknown given the background knowledge $\mathcal{P}_6$. But its consequent *¬ses* can be explained by *ses ← ⊥* and, hence, the conditional *if Oswald did not shoot Kennedy in Dallas and no one else shot, then no one else would have* is known to be true, but appears to be meaningless. As has been pointed out by Johnson-Laird and Byrne [19], a conclusion is worth drawing if it preserves semantic information, be parsimonious, and states something new. In the case of abduction, the given background knowledge is preserved and a (minimal) explanation is added to the antecedent of the given conditional such that its consequent becomes true. But the explanation should be something new which does not involve the consequent.

Secondly, a conditional like *if she is studying late in the library, then lightning will occur* may be evaluated to true given the background knowledge $\mathcal{P}_2 \cup \{lightning \leftarrow \top\}$. But such an evaluation does not seem to be very helpful as there is no connection between her studying late in the library and the occurrence of lightning. Rather, we need to check whether the antecedent of a true conditional is related or *relevant* to its consequence. This is a long-standing issue which has already been discussed in e.g. [13,14,25] and is central to relevance theory (see e.g. [10] or [26]). In logic programming, relevance has received some attention in the attempt to query logic programs by conditionals (see e.g. [2]), but this does not seem to be a recent issue anymore. In all approaches that we have examined, relevance is treated proof theoretically and is quite involved. To the best of our knowledge, there does not exist a common understanding on how relevance shall be defined in the context of human reasoning.

4   Relevance Through Dependencies

In logic programming, the *depends* relation is often used in the analysis of programs, where an atom A *depends* on an atom B if and only if A and B are in the transitive closure of the following relation: Given a program $\mathcal{P}$, atom A *directly depends on* atom B if and only if $\mathcal{P}$ contains a rule of the form $A \leftarrow Body$ and either B or $\neg B$ occurs in *Body*. As an example, consider the program

$$\mathcal{P}_7 = \{t \leftarrow ps \wedge \neg ab_t, \ ab_t \leftarrow \bot, \ p \leftarrow ps \wedge \neg ab_p, \ ab_p \leftarrow \bot\}$$

encoding that usually *pipe smokers (ps) have tobacco (t)* and *pipe smokers have a pipe (p)*. ab_t and ab_p are abnormality predicates which are assumed to be false. In this program, the atom t depends on ps and ab_t, whereas p depends on ps and ab_p, but neither does p depend on t nor does t depend on p.

We may define *relevance through dependencies* as follows: atom B is *relevant* to atom A if and only if A depends on B. In the program $\mathcal{P}_7$, neither p is relevant to t nor t is relevant to p. Assume that we would like to evaluate the conditional *if somebody has a pipe then he/she has tobacco (if p then t)* given the background knowledge $\mathcal{P}_7$. The least model $\mathcal{M}_{\mathcal{P}_7}$ of the weak completion of $\mathcal{P}_7$ maps the atoms ps, p, and t to unknown and ab_t and ab_p to false. Applying MRFA we can explain *having a pipe* by the (minimal) explanation that the person is a *pipesmoker*. Adding the explanation $ps \leftarrow \top$ to the program $\mathcal{P}_7$ we obtain

$$\mathcal{P}_8 = \{t \leftarrow ps \wedge \neg ab_t, \ ab_t \leftarrow \bot, \ p \leftarrow ps \wedge \neg ab_p, \ ab_p \leftarrow \bot, \ ps \leftarrow \top\}.$$

Now, p, t as well as *if p then t* are mapped to true by the least model $\mathcal{M}_{\mathcal{P}_8}$ of

$$wc\,\mathcal{P}_8 = \{t \leftrightarrow ps \wedge \neg ab_t, \ ab_t \leftrightarrow \bot, \ p \leftrightarrow ps \wedge \neg ab_p, \ ab_p \leftrightarrow \bot, \ ps \leftrightarrow \top\}.$$

Thus, p influences t with respect to the background knowledge $\mathcal{P}_8$. But, p is still irrelevant to t. Hence, this definition of relevance does not meet our intention and we look at developing notions of relevance which may.

5   Weak Relevance

In order to define a better notion of relevance we will make use the following function: *deps* assigns to a given program $\mathcal{P}$ and a given consistent set $\mathcal{S}$ of literals the set of facts, i.e. rules of the form $B \leftarrow \top$, and assumptions, i.e. rules of the form $B \leftarrow \bot$, occurring in $\mathcal{P}$, on which the literals occurring in $\mathcal{S}$ depend:

$$deps(\mathcal{P}, \mathcal{S}) = \{B \leftarrow Body \in \mathcal{P} \mid Body \in \{\top, \bot\} \text{ and there exists } A \in \mathcal{S} \text{ or}$$
$$\neg A \in \mathcal{S} \text{ such that } A \text{ depends on } B\}.$$

Returning to the previous example, we find

$$deps(\mathcal{P}_8, \{t\}) = \{ps \leftarrow \top, ab_t \leftarrow \bot\}$$

and

$$deps(\mathcal{P}_8, \{p\}) = \{ps \leftarrow \top, ab_p \leftarrow \bot\}.$$

With the help of the function *deps* we can now define the following – let's call it – *weak* notion of relevance given a conditional *if A then C*: antecedent A and consequence C are *weakly relevant to one another with respect to a program $\mathcal{P}$* if and only if

$$(A \cup deps(\mathcal{P}, A)^{\downarrow}) \cap (C \cup deps(\mathcal{P}, C)^{\downarrow}) \neq \emptyset,$$

where

$$\mathcal{Q}^{\downarrow} = \{A \mid A \leftarrow \top \in \mathcal{Q}\} \cup \{\neg A \mid A \leftarrow \bot \in \mathcal{Q}\}$$

and $\mathcal{Q}$ is a program containing only facts and assumptions. In words, A and C are weakly relevant to one another if and only if there is at least one common literal occurring in A and the set of literals on which A depends as well as in C and the set of literals on which C depends. This appears to be a generalization of the *variable sharing principle* applied in relevance theory (see e.g. [26]) in that a shared variable (or literal) must not just occur in A and C, but may also occur in the set of literals on which A and C depend.

Applied to the program $\mathcal{P}_8$ and the conditional *if p then t* we find

$$(\{p\} \cup \{ps, \neg ab_p\}) \cap (\{t\} \cup \{ps, \neg ab_t\}) = \{ps\} \neq \emptyset.$$

The atoms p and t are weakly relevant to one another with respect to $\mathcal{P}_8$.

As another example consider the conditional *if Joe is winning in the million Euro lottery then he is rich* and the program

$$\mathcal{P}_9 = \{rich\,X \leftarrow win\,X \wedge \neg\,ab\,X,\ ab\,X \leftarrow \bot,\ win\,joe \leftarrow \top,\ rich\,joe \leftarrow \top\}$$

encoding the background knowledge that usually *if somebody is winning in the million Euro lottery (win) then this person is rich (rich), Joe is winning, Joe is rich*, and ab is an abnormality predicate which is assumed to be false for all X. The fact $rich\,joe \leftarrow \top$ may be due to Joe inheriting a fortune when his aunt died some years ago and, thus, is completely independent of playing in the million Euro lottery. Considering the ground instance $g\,\mathcal{P}_9$ of $\mathcal{P}_9$ by replacing the variable X with the constant *joe* we find

$$deps(g\,\mathcal{P}_9, \{win\,joe\}) = \emptyset$$

and

$$deps(g\,\mathcal{P}_9, \{rich\,joe\}) = \{win\,joe \leftarrow \top,\ ab\,joe \leftarrow \bot\}.$$

Hence,

$$(\{win\,joe\} \cup \emptyset) \cap (\{rich\,joe\} \cup \{win\,joe, \neg\,ab\,joe\}) = \{win\,joe\} \neq \emptyset$$

and we conclude that *win joe* is weakly relevant to *rich joe* with respect to $g\,\mathcal{P}_9$. But, this does not seem to correctly represent the background knowledge encoded in program $g\,\mathcal{P}_9$, because the truth of *win joe* has no influence on the truth of *rich joe*. The atom *rich joe* will always be true in the least model $\mathcal{M}_{g\,\mathcal{P}_9}$ of

$$wc\,g\,\mathcal{P}_9 = \{rich\,joe \leftrightarrow (win\,joe \wedge \neg\,ab\,joe) \vee \top,\ win\,joe \leftrightarrow \top,\ ab\,joe \leftrightarrow \bot\}$$

because $(win\,joe \wedge \neg\,ab\,joe) \vee \top$ is semantically equivalent to $\top$.

6   Strong Relevance

In this section we will develop a better notion of relevance which is called *strong relevance*. In order to do so, we need the following function: *def* assigns to a program $\mathcal{P}$ and a set $\mathcal{S}$ of literals the set of program clauses defining $\mathcal{S}$, i.e.,

$$def(\mathcal{P}, \mathcal{S}) = \{A \leftarrow Body \in \mathcal{P} \mid A \in \mathcal{S} \text{ or } \neg A \in \mathcal{S}\}.$$

Let $\mathcal{P}$ be a program encoding the background knowledge and $\mathcal{M}_\mathcal{P}$ be the least model of the weak completion of $\mathcal{P}$. Furthermore, let $\mathcal{A}$ as well as $\mathcal{C}$ be consistent sets of literals and consider the conditional *if $\mathcal{A}$ then $\mathcal{C}$*. Its antecedent $\mathcal{A}$ is *strongly relevant to* its consequent $\mathcal{C}$ *with respect to* $\mathcal{P}$ if and only if $\mathcal{A}$ and $\mathcal{C}$ are true under $\mathcal{M}_\mathcal{P}$, but $\mathcal{C}$ is not true under $\mathcal{M}_{\mathcal{P}'}$, where $\mathcal{M}_{\mathcal{P}'}$ is the least model of the weak completion of $\mathcal{P}' = \mathcal{P} \setminus (def(\mathcal{P}, \mathcal{A}) \cup deps(\mathcal{P}, \mathcal{A}))$. The idea behind strong relevance is to check whether the consequent $\mathcal{C}$ looses support as soon as the support of the antecedent $\mathcal{A}$ is withdrawn. One should observe that in contrast to weak relevance, strong relevance is not symmetrical.

In order to check whether the atom $win\,joe$ is strongly relevant to the atom $rich\,joe$ with respect to the program $g\,\mathcal{P}_9$, we firstly need to check that both atoms are true in $\mathcal{M}_{g\,\mathcal{P}_9}$, which is indeed the case. Thereafter, with

$$def(g\,\mathcal{P}_9, \{win\,joe\}) = \{win\,joe \leftarrow \top\}$$

and

$$deps(g\,\mathcal{P}_9, \{win\,joe\}) = \emptyset$$

we find

$$g\,\mathcal{P}_9' = g\,\mathcal{P}_9 \setminus \{win\,joe \leftarrow \top\} =$$
$$= \{rich\,joe \leftarrow win\,joe \wedge \neg\,ab\,joe,\ ab\,joe \leftarrow \bot,\ rich\,joe \leftarrow \top\}.$$

The least model $\mathcal{M}_{g\,\mathcal{P}_9'}$ of the weak completion of $g\,\mathcal{P}_9'$ maps the atom $rich\,joe$ to true and the atom $win\,joe$ to unknown. Thus, $rich\,joe$ does not loose support as soon as the support for $win\,joe$ is withdrawn. In other words, even if Joe is not winning, he will still be rich. $win\,joe$ is not strongly relevant to the atom $rich\,joe$ with respect to the program $g\,\mathcal{P}_9$.

Returning to the conditonal $if\ p\ then\ t$ and the program $\mathcal{P}_8$, we find that the atoms p and t are true under $\mathcal{M}_{\mathcal{P}_8}$. Let

$$\mathcal{P}_8' = \mathcal{P}_8 \setminus \{p \leftarrow ps \wedge \neg ab_p,\ ab_p \leftarrow \bot,\ ps \leftarrow \top\} = \{t \leftarrow ps \wedge \neg ab_t,\ ab_t \leftarrow \bot\}.$$

Hence, because the least model $\mathcal{M}_{\mathcal{P}_8'}$ of the weak completion of $\mathcal{P}_8'$ maps the atom t to unknown, the antecedent p is strongly relevant to the consequent t with respect to the program $\mathcal{P}_8$.

Consider the conditional $if\ e\ then\ \ell$ and the program $\mathcal{P}_4$. Because $\mathcal{M}_{\mathcal{P}_4}$ maps the antecedent e to true and the consequent ℓ to unknown, e is not strongly relevant to ℓ with respect to $\mathcal{P}_4$. Now consider the program

$$\mathcal{P}_{10} = \mathcal{P}_4 \cup \{o \leftarrow \top\}.$$

Its weak completion is

$$wc\,\mathcal{P}_{10} = \{\ell \leftrightarrow (e \wedge \neg ab_e) \vee (o \wedge \neg ab_o),\ ab_e \leftrightarrow \neg o,\ ab_o \leftrightarrow \neg e,\ e \leftarrow \top,\ o \leftrightarrow \top\}.$$

We find that $\mathcal{M}_{\mathcal{P}_{10}}$ maps the atoms e, o, and ℓ to true, whereas it maps the atoms ab_e and ab_o to false. Furthermore, with

$$def(\mathcal{P}_{10}, \{e\}) = \{e \leftarrow \top\}$$

and

$$deps(\mathcal{P}_{10}, \{e\}) = \emptyset$$

we obtain

$$\mathcal{P}'_{10} = \mathcal{P}_{10} \setminus \{e \leftarrow \top\}$$
$$= \{\ell \leftarrow e \wedge \neg ab_e, \; \ell \leftarrow o \wedge \neg ab_o, \; ab_e \leftarrow \neg o, \; ab_o \leftarrow \neg e, \; o \leftarrow \top\}.$$

The least model $\mathcal{M}_{\mathcal{P}'_{10}}$ of the weak completion of program $\mathcal{P}'_{10}$ maps the atom o to true, the atom ab_e to false, and the atoms ℓ, e, and ab_o to unknown. Hence, the antecedent *she has an essay to write* is strongly relevant to the consequent *she will study late in the library* with respect to the program $\mathcal{P}_{10}$.

As a last example consider the conditional *if she has an essay to write and the library is open then she will study late in the library* and the program $\mathcal{P}_{10}$. In order to check whether the antecedent $\{e, o\}$ is strongly relevant to the consequent ℓ with respect to the program $\mathcal{P}_{10}$ we recall that $\mathcal{M}_{\mathcal{P}_{10}}$ maps the atoms e, o, and ℓ to true. With

$$def(\mathcal{P}_{10}, \{e, o\}) = \{e \leftarrow \top, o \leftarrow \top\}$$

and

$$deps(\mathcal{P}_{10}, \{e, o\}) = \emptyset$$

we now obtain

$$\mathcal{P}''_{10} = \mathcal{P}_{10} \setminus \{e \leftarrow \top, \; o \leftarrow \top\}$$
$$= \{\ell \leftarrow e \wedge \neg ab_e, \; \ell \leftarrow o \wedge \neg ab_o, \; ab_e \leftarrow \neg o, \; ab_o \leftarrow \neg e\}.$$

The least model $\mathcal{M}_{\mathcal{P}''_{10}}$ of the weak completion of $\mathcal{P}''_{10}$ maps all atoms to unknown. Hence, the antecedent $\{e, o\}$ is strongly relevant to the consequent ℓ with respect to the program $\mathcal{P}_{10}$.

7   Extending MRFA by Strong Relevance

We will modify the case where the antecedent of a conditional is mapped to true of the procedure *minimal revision followed by abduction* (MRFA) in three ways: Firstly, by checking whether for true conditionals the antecedent is strongly relevant to the consequent, secondly, by allowing abduction in case the antecedent is true and the consequence is unknown, and thirdly, by disallowing that a consequent abduces itself. Let *if $\mathcal{A}$ then $\mathcal{C}$* be a conditional, $\mathcal{P}$ a program, $\mathcal{A}_{\mathcal{P}}$ be the set of abducibles for the program $\mathcal{P}$, $\mathcal{M}_{\mathcal{P}}$ be the least model of the weak completion of the program $\mathcal{P}$, and $\mathcal{C}^{\uparrow} = \{A \leftarrow \top \mid A \in \mathcal{C}\} \cup \{A \leftarrow \bot \mid \neg A \in \mathcal{C}\}$. We are interested in the three cases where $\mathcal{M}_{\mathcal{P}}$ maps $\mathcal{A}$ to true:

If $\mathcal{M}_{\mathcal{P}}$ maps $\mathcal{A}$ and $\mathcal{C}$ to true
   then if $\mathcal{A}$ is strongly relevant to $\mathcal{C}$ with respect to $\mathcal{P}$
      then the value of the conditional *if $\mathcal{A}$ then $\mathcal{C}$* is true
      else the conditional is meaningless.

If $\mathcal{M}_{\mathcal{P}}$ maps $\mathcal{A}$ to true and $\mathcal{C}$ to false
   then the value of the conditional *if $\mathcal{A}$ then $\mathcal{C}$* is false.

If $\mathcal{M}_{\mathcal{P}}$ maps $\mathcal{A}$ to true and $\mathcal{C}$ to unknown
   then the value of the conditional *if $\mathcal{A}$ then $\mathcal{C}$* is unknown and
      if $\mathcal{X} \subseteq \mathcal{A}_{\mathcal{P}} \setminus \mathcal{C}^{\top}$ explains $\mathcal{C}$
      and $\mathcal{A} \cup \mathcal{X}^{\downarrow}$ is strongly relevant to $\mathcal{C}$ with respect to $\mathcal{P} \cup \mathcal{X}$
      then the value of the conditional *if $\mathcal{A} \cup \mathcal{X}^{\downarrow}$ then $\mathcal{C}$* is true.

As before, we expect explanations to be minimal. For the cases where $\mathcal{M}_{\mathcal{P}}$ maps $\mathcal{A}$ to false or unknown, the reader is refered to the Appendix and the literature [5,6] as they do not play a role in the idea and the problems discussed in this paper. However, the case where $\mathcal{M}_{\mathcal{P}}$ maps $\mathcal{A}$ to false was presented in the *shooting of Kennedy scenario* in Sect. 2. It was just meant to show that counterfactuals can be treated by *minimal revision followed by abduction* as well. In the paper, we have also discussed various examples, where the antecedent $\mathcal{A}$ was unknown but could be explained by abduction. The name MRFA, however, was given due to the case where $\mathcal{M}_{\mathcal{P}}$ maps $\mathcal{A}$ to unknown and abduction alone cannot explain $\mathcal{A}$. In particular, in [6] it was shown that there are examples within the *firing squad scenario* introduced in [30] which cannot be solved by abduction alone. In this case, a minimal revision step is added before abduction is applied. The complete extended MRFA procedure is listed in the Appendix.

The first two steps of the extended MRFA procedure should be obvious, but the third step needs clarification. Given a program $\mathcal{P}$, the set of abducibles $\mathcal{A}_{\mathcal{P}}$ usually consists of all facts and assumptions for atoms which occur only in the bodies of rules in $\mathcal{P}$. For example, in the program $\mathcal{P}_3$ the atoms o and e occur only in the bodies of rules. Hence, $\mathcal{A}_{\mathcal{P}_3} = \{e \leftarrow \top, \ e \leftarrow \bot, \ o \leftarrow \top, \ o \leftarrow \bot\}$. To avoid that a consequent abduces itself, $A \leftarrow \top$ is deleted from $\mathcal{A}_{\mathcal{P}}$ if the atom A occurs in the consequent $\mathcal{C}$ and $A \leftarrow \bot$ is deleted from $\mathcal{A}_{\mathcal{P}}$ if the negated atom $\neg A$ occurs in $\mathcal{C}$. It may suffice that only a subset $\mathcal{O}$ of $\mathcal{C}$ needs to be explained by $\mathcal{X}$ as long as the least model $\mathcal{M}_{\mathcal{P} \cup \mathcal{X}}$ of the weak completion of the program $\mathcal{P}$ along with the explanation $\mathcal{X}$ maps $\mathcal{C}$ to true. In this case a new conditional can be derived, where the antecedent is extended by all atoms A such that $A \leftarrow \top$ occurs in the explanation $\mathcal{X}$ and all negated atoms $\neg A$ such that $A \leftarrow \bot$ occurs in $\mathcal{X}$. Of course, we need to check that the antecedent of the new conditional is strongly relevant to the consequent $\mathcal{C}$ with respect to the program $\mathcal{P} \cup \mathcal{X}$.

We have already discussed various applications of the extended MRFA procedure in this paper. The conditional *if she has an essay to write and the library stays open, then she will study late in the library* has been derived from the conditional *if she has an essay to write, then she will study late in the library* and the program $\mathcal{P}_4$. The given conditional being unknown, the explanation $\mathcal{X} = \{o \leftarrow \top\}$ explains that she will study late in the library (ℓ). In the last section, it was shown that the least model of the weak completion of $\mathcal{P}_{10} = \mathcal{P}_4 \cup \mathcal{X}$ maps ℓ to true and, moreover, that the atoms e and o are strongly relevant to ℓ.

The conditional *if Oswald did not shoot Kennedy in Dallas and no one else shot, then no one else would have* cannot be derived from the conditional *if Oswald did not shoot Kennedy in Dallas, then no one else would have* and the program $\mathcal{P}_6$. The given conditional being unknown, we may be tempted to apply abduction. The set of abducibles for $\mathcal{P}_6$ is $\mathcal{A}_{\mathcal{P}_6} = \{ses \leftarrow \top, \; ses \leftarrow \bot\}$. However, $ses \leftarrow \bot$ must be deleted from the set of abducibles because the consequent is $\neg ses$ and we do not want consequents to abduce themselves. After the deletion the consequent cannot be abduced anymore.

On the other hand, the conditional *if Oswald did not shoot Kennedy in Dallas and nobody else did, then Kennedy was not killed* can be derived from the conditional *if Oswald did not shoot Kennedy in Dallas, then Kennedy was not killed* and program $\mathcal{P}_6$. The given conditional being unknown, the explanation $\mathcal{X} = \{ses \leftarrow \bot\}$ explains $\neg k$ because the least model of the weak completion of $\mathcal{P}_6 \cup \mathcal{X}$ maps $\neg k$ to true. It still needs to be checked that $\{\neg os, \neg ses\}$ are strongly relevant to $\neg k$ with respect to the program $\mathcal{P}_6 \cup \mathcal{X}$, but this does hold.

Finally, the conditional *if she is studying late in the library then lightning will occur* will be evaluated as meaningless with respect to the program $\mathcal{P}_2 \cup \{lightning \leftarrow \top\}$. Both, antecedent and consequent, are mapped to true in the least model of the weak completion of $\mathcal{P}_2 \cup \{lightning \leftarrow \top\}$, but the antecedent ℓ is not strongly relevant to the consequent *lightning*.

8   Conclusion

In this paper we have pursued the idea to apply abduction in order to find an explanation for an unknown consequent of a conditional whose antecedent is true. If such an explanation can be abduced then new conditionals can be generated which are known to be true. We identified two problems with this idea which can be solved by disallowing consequents to abduce themselves and by requiring that an antecedent is strongly relevant to the consequent of a conditional. The definition of strongly relevant is with respect to the models of a program and, thus, deviates from the mostly proof theoretic definitions of relevance in relevance theory.

We are unaware of any experimental data supporting our claim that humans are unsatisfied if they cannot assign true or false to the consequent of a conditional whose antecedent is true. Likewise, we are unaware of any experimental data supporting our idea that in this case, humans construct novel and true conditionals by applying abduction to explain an unknown consequence. However, in the context of legal reasoning, Bob Kowalski has argued that legal experts understand conditionals like *if she has an essay to write, then she will study late in the library* and *if the library stays open, then she will study late in the library* often as the context dependent rule *if she has an essay to write and the library stays open, then she will study late in the library* [22]. In this paper we have shown that exactly this context dependent rule can be derived by the

Weak Completion Semantics using the extended *minimal revision followed by abduction* procedure.

We have not yet thoroughly investigated on how precisely the different theories of relevance mentioned in Sect. 3 correspond to the notion of strong relevance developed in Sect. 6. This is a topic for future research.

The presented approach is based on the three-valued logic of Łukasiewicz [24]. It is nonmonotonic. It can deal with inconsistencies when confronted with a counterfactual and, in this case, revision is applied to remove the inconsistency. Moreover, as shown in [9], the *Weak Completion Semantics* can be computed in a connectionist or articifical neural network setting. In particular, the semantic operator used to compute the least model of a weakly completed program can itself be computed by a feed-forward connectionist network. As shown in [12] such semantic operators can be learned by backpropagation given appropriate training data. Once the network has been trained, a novel logic program can be extracted using appropriate rule extraction techniques (see e.g. [11]). Hence, programs can be learned. We strongly believe that the *new, multi-valued, and nonmonotonic paradigm* should be extensively studied in the context of human reasoning.

Acknowledgements. I would like to thank Emmanuelle-Anna Dietz Saldanha and Luís Moniz Pereira for many discussions, comments and ideas on conditionals and the *Weak Completion Semantics*. This paper is a revised and extended version of our joint effort [6]. Many thanks also to Meghna Bhadra for many suggestions and corrections.

Appendix: The MRFA Procedure

In [6] the MRFA procedure was specified as follows:

If $\mathcal{M}_\mathcal{P}$ maps $\mathcal{A}$ to true
    then the value of the conditional *if $\mathcal{A}$ then $\mathcal{C}$* is $\mathcal{M}_\mathcal{P}(\mathcal{C})$.

If $\mathcal{M}_\mathcal{P}$ maps $\mathcal{A}$ to false
    then evaluate *if $\mathcal{A}$ then $\mathcal{C}$* with respect to $\mathcal{M}_{rev(\mathcal{P},\mathcal{S})}$, where
        $\mathcal{S} = \{L \in \mathcal{A} \mid \mathcal{M}_\mathcal{P}\, L = \bot\}$ and $rev(\mathcal{P},\mathcal{S}) = (\mathcal{P} \setminus def(\mathcal{P},\mathcal{S})) \cup \mathcal{S}^\uparrow$.

If $\mathcal{M}_\mathcal{P}$ maps $\mathcal{A}$ to unknown
    then evaluate *if $\mathcal{A}$ then $\mathcal{C}$* with respect to $\mathcal{M}_{\mathcal{P}'}$, where
        $\mathcal{P}' = rev(\mathcal{P},\mathcal{S}) \cup \mathcal{X}$
        and $\mathcal{S}$ is a smallest subset of $\mathcal{A}$
        and $\mathcal{X} \subseteq \mathcal{A}_{rev(\mathcal{P},\mathcal{S})}$ is an explanation for $\mathcal{A} \setminus \mathcal{S}$
        such that $\mathcal{M}_{\mathcal{P}'}$ maps $\mathcal{A}$ to true.

In this paper, the first step is extended as specified in Sect. 7.

References

1. Adams, E.W.: Subjunctive and indicative conditionals. Found. Lang. **6**(1), 89–94 (1970)

2. Bollen, A.W.: Conditional Logic Programming. Ph.D. thesis, Australian National University (1988)
3. Byrne, R.M.J.: Suppressing valid inferences with conditionals. Cognition **31**(1), 61–83 (1989)
4. Clark, K.L.: Negation as failure. In: Gallaire, H., Minker, J. (eds.) Logic and Databases, pp. 293–322. Plenum, New York (1978)
5. Dietz, E.-A., Hölldobler, S.: A new computational logic approach to reason with conditionals. In: Calimeri, F., Ianni, G., Truszczynski, M. (eds.) LPNMR 2015. LNCS (LNAI), vol. 9345, pp. 265–278. Springer, Cham (2015). https://doi.org/10.1007/978-3-319-23264-5_23
6. Dietz, E.A., Hölldobler, S., Pereira, L.M.: On conditionals. In: Gottlob, G., Sutcliffe, G., Voronkov, A. (eds.) Global Conference on Artificial Intelligence. Epic Series in Computing, vol. 36, pp. 79–92. EasyChair (2015)
7. Dietz, E.A., Hölldobler, S., Ragni, M.: A computational logic approach to the suppression task. In: Miyake, N., Peebles, D., Cooper, R.P. (eds.) Proceedings of the 34th Annual Conference of the Cognitive Science Society, pp. 1500–1505. Cognitive Science Society (2012)
8. Dietz, E.A., Hölldobler, S., Ragni, M.: A computational logic approach to the abstract and the social case of the selection task. In: Proceedings Eleventh International Symposium on Logical Formalizations of Commonsense Reasoning (2013). http://commonsensereasoning.org/2013/proceedings.html
9. Dietz Saldanha, E.A., Hölldobler, S., Kencana Ramli, C.D.P., Palacios Medinacelli, L.: A core method for the weak completion semantics with skeptical abduction. J. Artif. Intell. Res. **63**, 51–86 (2018)
10. Dunn, J.M., Restall, G.: Relevance logic. In: Gabbay, D., Guenthner, F. (eds.) Handbook of Phylosophical Logic, vol. 6, chap. 2, pp. 1–128. Kluwer, Doedrecht (2002)
11. d'Avila Garcez, A.S., Broda, K.B., Gabbay, D.M.: Neural-Symbolic Learning Systems: Foundations and Applications. Springer, Heidelberg (2002)
12. d'Avila Garcez, A.S., Zaverucha, G., de Carvalho, L.A.V.: Logic programming and inductive learning in artificial neural networks. In: Herrmann, C., Reine, F., Strohmaier, A. (eds.) Knowledge Representation in Neural Networks, pp. 33–46. Logos Verlag, Berlin (1997)
13. Goodman, N.: Fact, Fiction, and Forecast. Harvard University Press, Cambridge (1954)
14. Grice, H.P.: Logic and conversation. In: Cole, P., Morgan, J.L. (eds.) Syntax and Semantics, vol. 3, pp. 41–58. Academic Press, New York (1975)
15. Hölldobler, S.: Logik und Logikprogrammierung, vol. 1: Grundlagen. Synchron Publishers GmbH, Heidelberg (2009)
16. Hölldobler, S.: Weak completion semantics and its applications in human reasoning. In: Furbach, U., Schon, C. (eds.) Bridging 2015 - Bridging the Gap between Human and Automated Reasoning. CEUR Workshop Proceedings, vol. 1412, pp. 2–16. CEUR-WS.org (2015). http://ceur-ws.org/Vol-1412/
17. Hölldobler, S., Kencana Ramli, C.D.P.: Logic programs under three-valued Łukasiewicz's semantics. In: Hill, P.M., Warren, D.S. (eds.) Logic Programming. Lecture Notes in Computer Science, vol. 5649, pp. 464–478. Springer, Heidelberg (2009)
18. Johnson-Laird, P.N.: Mental Models: Towards a Cognitive Science of Language, Inference, and Consciousness. Cambridge University Press, Cambridge (1983)
19. Johnson-Laird, P.N., Byrne, R.M.J.: Deduction. Lawrence Erlbaum Associates, Hove and London (UK) (1991)

20. Kakas, A.C., Kowalski, R.A., Toni, F.: Abductive logic programming. J. Logic Computat. **2**(6), 719–770 (1993)
21. Khemlani, S., Johnson-Laird, P.N.: Theories of the syllogism: a meta-analysis. Psychol. Bull. **138**(3), 427–457 (2012)
22. Kowalski, R.A.: Computational Logic and Human Thinking: How to be Artificially Intelligent. Cambridge University Press, Cambridge (2011)
23. Lloyd, J.W.: Foundations of Logic Programming. Springer, Heidelberg (1993). https://doi.org/10.1007/978-3-642-96826-6
24. Łukasiewicz, J.: O logice trójwartościowej. Ruch Filozoficzny **5**, 169–171 (1920), English translation: On Three-Valued Logic. In: Borkowski, L. (ed.) Jan Łukasiewicz Selected Works, North Holland, 87–88, 1990
25. MacColl, H.: 'if' and 'imply'. Mind **17**(151–152), 453–455 (1908)
26. Mares, E.: Relevance logic. In: Zalta, E.N. (ed.) The Stanford Encyclopedia of Philosophy. Metaphysics Research Lab, Stanford University, Summer 2020 edn (2020)
27. Nickerson, R.S.: Conditional Reasoning. Oxford University Press, Oxford (2015)
28. Oaksford, M., Chater, N.: New paradigms in the psychology of reasoning. Ann. Rev. Psychol. **71**, 12.1–12.26 (2020)
29. Oliviera da Costa, A., Dietz Saldanha, E.A., Hölldobler, S., Ragni, M.: A computational logic approach to human syllogistic reasoning. In: Gunzelmann, G., Howes, A., Tenbrink, T., Davelaar, E.J. (eds.) Proceedings of the 39th Annual Conference of the Cognitive Science Society, pp. 883–888. Cognitive Science Society, Austin, TX (2017)
30. Pearl, J.: Causality: Models, Reasoning, and Inference. Cambridge University Press, New York (2000)
31. Polk, T.A., Newell, A.: Deduction as verbal reasoning. Psychol. Rev. **102**(2), 533–566 (1995)
32. Rips, L.J.: The Psychology of Proof: Deductive Reasoning in Human Thinking. MIT Press, Cambridge (1994)
33. Stenning, K., van Lambalgen, M.: Semantic interpretation as computation innonmonotonic logic: the real meaning of the suppression task. Cogn. Sci. **29**(919–960), 1996–2005 (2005)
34. Stenning, K., van Lambalgen, M.: Human Reasoning and Cognitive Science. MIT Press, Cambridge (2008)

HTN Plan Repair via Model Transformation

Daniel Höller[1,4(✉)], Pascal Bercher[2,4], Gregor Behnke[3,4], and Susanne Biundo[4]

[1] Saarland University, Saarland Informatics Campus, Saarbrücken, Germany
hoeller@cs.uni-saarland.de
[2] The Australian National University, Canberra, Australia
pascal.bercher@anu.edu.au
[3] University of Freiburg, Freiburg, Germany
behnkeg@cs.uni-freiburg.de
[4] Institute of Artificial Intelligence, Ulm University, Ulm, Germany
susanne.biundo@uni-ulm.de

Abstract. To make planning feasible, planning models abstract from many details of the modeled system. When executing plans in the actual system, the model might be inaccurate in a critical point, and plan execution may fail. There are two options to handle this case: the previous solution can be modified to address the failure (plan repair), or the planning process can be re-started from the new situation (re-planning). In HTN planning, discarding the plan and generating a new one from the novel situation is not easily possible, because the HTN solution criteria make it necessary to take already executed actions into account. Therefore all approaches to repair plans in the literature are based on specialized algorithms. In this paper, we discuss the problem in detail and introduce a novel approach that makes it possible to use unchanged, off-the-shelf HTN planning systems to repair broken HTN plans. That way, no specialized solvers are needed.

Keywords: HTN Planning · Plan repair · Re-planning

1 Introduction

When generating plans that are executed in a real-world system, the planning system needs to be able to deal with execution failures, i.e. with situations during plan execution that are not consistent with the predicted state. Since planning comes with several assumptions that may not hold the real system, such situations may arise for several reasons like non-determinism in the problem, exogenous events, or actions of other agents. When we speak of an execution failure, we mean that the outcome of an action is not like anticipated by the planning model (e.g. due to the given reasons).

Two mechanisms have been developed to deal with such situations: Systems that use *re-planning* discard the original plan and generate a new one from the novel situation. Systems using *plan repair* adapt the original plan so that it can

© Springer Nature Switzerland AG 2020
U. Schmid et al. (Eds.): KI 2020, LNAI 12325, pp. 88–101, 2020.
https://doi.org/10.1007/978-3-030-58285-2_7

deal with the unforeseen change. In classical planning, the sequence of already executed actions implies no changes other than state transition. The motivation for plan repair in this setting has e.g. been *efficiency* [20] or *plan stability* [18], i.e. finding a new plan that is as similar as possible to the original one.

In hierarchical task network (HTN) planning [8,17], the hierarchy has wide influence on the set of solutions and it makes the formalism also more expressive than classical planning [21,22]. The hierarchy can e.g. enforce that certain actions might only be executed in combination. By simply re-starting the planning process from the new state, those implications are discarded, thus simple re-planning is no option and plans have to be repaired, i.e., the implications have to be taken into account. Several approaches have been proposed in the literature, all of them use special repair algorithms to find the repaired plans.

In this paper we make the following contributions (some of the work has been presented before in a workshop version of the paper [25]):

– We discuss the issues that arise when using a re-planning approach that re-starts the planning process from the new state in HTN planning.
– We survey the literature on plan repair in HTN planning.
– Based on a transformation for plan and goal recognition [23], we introduce a transformation-based approach that makes it possible to use unchanged HTN planning systems to repair broken HTN plans.

Outline. We first introduce HTN planning and specify the plan repair problem (Sect. 2), discuss issues with repairing HTN plans (Sect. 3), summarize related work (Sect. 4), and give our transformation (Sect. 5) and its properties (Sect. 6).

2   Formal Framework

This section introduces HTN planning and specifies the repair problem.

2.1   HTN Planning

In HTN planning, there are two types of tasks: *primitive* tasks equal classical planning actions, which cause state transitions. *Abstract* tasks describe more abstract behavior. They can not be applied to states directly, but are iteratively split into sub-tasks until all tasks are primitive.

We use the formalism by Geier and Bercher [19,22]. A classical planning problem is defined as a tuple $P_c = (L, A, s_0, g, \delta)$, where L is a set of propositional state features, A a set of action names, and $s_0, g \in 2^L$ are the initial state and the goal definition. A state $s \in 2^L$ is a *goal state* if $s \supseteq g$. The tuple $\delta = (prec, add, del)$ defines the preconditions *prec* as well as the add and delete effects (add, del) of actions, all are functions $f : A \to 2^L$. An action a is applicable in a state s if and only if $\tau : A \times 2^L$ with $\tau(a, s) \Leftrightarrow prec(a) \subseteq s$ holds. When an (applicable) action a is applied to a state s, the resulting state is defined as $\gamma : A \times 2^L \to 2^L$ with $\gamma(a, s) = (s \setminus del(a)) \cup add(a)$. A sequence of actions

$(a_0 a_1 \ldots a_l)$ is applicable in a state s_0 if and only if for each a_i it holds that $\tau(a_i, s_i)$, where s_i is for $i > 0$ defined as $s_i = \gamma(a_{i-1}, s_{i-1})$. We call the state s_{l+1} the resulting state from the application. A sequence of actions $(a_0 a_1 \ldots a_l)$ is a solution if and only if it is applicable in s_0 and results in a goal state.

An HTN planning problem $P = (L, C, A, M, s_0, tn_I, g, \delta)$ extends a classical planning problem by a set of abstract (also called compound) task names C, a set of decomposition methods M, and the tasks that need to be accomplished which are given in the so-called initial task network tn_I. The other elements are equivalent to the classical case. The tasks that need to be done as well as their ordering relation are organized in *task networks*. A task network $tn = (T, \prec, \alpha)$ consists of a set of identifiers T. An identifier is just a unique element that is mapped to an actual task by a function $\alpha : T \to A \cup C$. This way, a single task can be in a network more than once. $\prec : T \times T$ is a set of ordering constraints between the task identifiers. Two task networks are called to be *isomorphic* if they differ solely in their task identifiers. An abstract task can by decomposed by using a (decomposition) method. A method is a pair (c, tn) of an abstract task $c \in C$ that specifies to which task the method is applicable and a task network tn, the method's subnetwork. When decomposing a task network $tn_1 = (T_1, \prec_1, \alpha_1)$ that includes a task $t \in T_1$ with $\alpha_1(t) = c$ using a method (c, tn), we need an isomorphic copy of the method's subnetwork $tn' = (T', \prec', \alpha')$ with $T_1 \cap T' = \emptyset$. The resulting task network tn_2 is then defined as

$$\begin{aligned}
tn_2 &= ((T_1 \setminus \{t\}) \cup T', \prec' \cup \prec_D, (\alpha_1 \setminus \{t \mapsto c\}) \cup \alpha') \\
\prec_D &= \{(t_1, t_2) \mid (t_1, t) \in \prec_1, t_2 \in T'\} \cup \\
&\quad \{(t_1, t_2) \mid (t, t_2) \in \prec_1, t_1 \in T'\} \cup \\
&\quad \{(t_1, t_2) \mid (t_1, t_2) \in \prec_1, t_1 \neq t \wedge t_2 \neq t\}
\end{aligned}$$

We will write $tn \to^* tn'$ to denote that a task network tn can be decomposed into a task network tn' by applying an arbitrary number of methods in sequence.

A task network $tn = (T, \prec, \alpha)$ is a solution to a planning problem P if and only if 1. all tasks are primitive, $\forall t \in T : \alpha(t) \in A$, 2. it was obtained via decomposition, $tn_I \to^* tn$, 3. there is a sequence of the task identifiers in T in line with the ordering whose application results in a goal state.

2.2 Plan Repair Problem in HTN Planning

Next we specify the plan repair problem, i.e., the problem occurring when plan execution fails (that could be solved by plan repair or re-planning), please be aware the ambiguity of the term *repair* naming the problem and a way to resolve it. A plan repair problem consists of three core elements: The original HTN planning problem P, its original solution plus its already executed prefix, and the execution error, i.e., the state deviation that occurred during executing the prefix of the original solution.

Most HTN approaches that can cope with execution failures do not just rely on the original solution, but also require the modifications that transformed the initial task network into the failed solution. How these modifications look like depends on the planning system, e.g., whether it is a progression-based system [24, 26, 28] or a plan-space planner [11, 16]. To have a general definition, we include the so-called decomposition tree (DT) of the solution. A DT is a tree representation of the decompositions leading to the solution [19]. Its nodes represent tasks; each abstract task is labeled with the method used for decomposition, the children in the tree correspond to the subtasks of that specific method. Ordering constraints are also represented, such that a DT dt yields the solution tn it represents by restricting the elements to dt's leaf nodes.

Definition 1 (Plan Repair Problem). *A plan repair problem can now be defined as a tuple $P_r = (P, tn_s, dt, exe, F^+, F^-)$ with the following elements. P is the original planning problem. $tn_s = (T, \prec, \alpha)$ is the failed solution for it, dt the DT as a witness that tn_s is actually a refinement of the original initial task network, and $exe = (t_0, t_1, \dots t_n)$ is the sequence of already executed task identifiers, $t_i \in T$. Finally, the execution failure is represented by the two sets $F^+ \subseteq L$ and $F^- \subseteq L$ indicating the state features that were (not) holding contrary to the expected state after execution the solution prefix exe.*

Notice that not every divergence of the state predicted by the model and the actual state during execution prevents further execution of the plan. A technique detecting whether repair is necessary is e.g. described by Bercher et al. [10].

Though they have been introduced before, we want to make the terms replanning and plan repair more precise.

Definition 2 (Re-Planning). *The old plan is discarded, a new plan is generated starting from the current state of the system that caused the execution failure.*

Definition 3 (Plan Repair). *The system modifies the non-executed part of the original solution such that it can cope with the unforeseen state change.*

3   About Re-planning in HTN Planning

In classical planning, a prefix of a plan that has already been executed does not imply any changes to the environment apart from the actions' effects. It is therefore fine to discard the current plan and generate a new one from scratch from the (updated) state of the system. HTN planning provides the domain designer a second means of modeling: the hierarchy. Like preconditions and effects, it can be used to model either physics *or* advice. Figure 1 illustrates the Toll Domain. A car moves in a road network. The red square indicates the city center (the toll area). Whenever the car takes a road segment starting inside the center, a toll has to be paid at a position marked with a credit card. Since the car may want to use a segment more than once (e.g. because the driver wants to visit certain shops in a specific ordering), it is not sufficient to mark *which* segments have been used, they need to be counted. For simplicity, we assume that the toll area

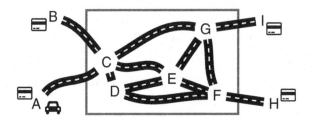

Fig. 1. The Toll domain. (Color figure online)

is left at the end (i.e. the final position is outside). An HTN domain is given in Figure 2.

It contains five methods. Actions are given in boxes, abstract tasks are non-boxed. The *driveTA* action is only applicable inside the toll area, *drive* only outside it and the *payToll* action only at positions marked with a credit card. Whenever *driveTA* is added to the plan, an instance of the *payToll* task is added and the toll for that single segment is paid when the toll area is left. The domain is a simple example for a context-free language-like structure. When described in STRIPS, one has to commit to a maximum number of visits or encode it using a richer classical model (e.g. supporting numeric variables).

Consider a car starting at position A and driving to H. A planning system could come up with the following plan:

$$drive(A, C), driveTA(C, G), driveTA(G, F),$$
$$driveTA(F, H), payToll(), payToll(), payToll()$$

Consider an execution failure after the first *driveTA* action: being at location G: the driver gets aware that the road to F is closed. Re-planning is triggered. The planning system comes up with the following new plan:

$$driveTA(G, E), driveTA(E, F), driveTA(F, H),$$
$$payToll(), payToll(), payToll()$$

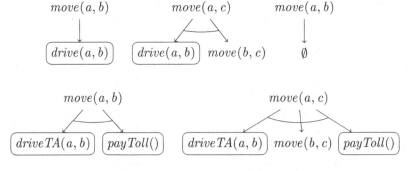

Fig. 2. Sketch of an HTN model for the Toll domain.

The driver executes the plan and reaches H, but while four segments are used, the toll gets only paid three times.

As we have seen, the hierarchy assures that certain properties hold in every plan and the domain designer might rely on these properties. There are different ways to ensure them during a repair process:

1. The responsibility can be shifted to the domain designer, i.e., the domain must be created in a way that the planning process can be started from any state of the real-world system. This leads to a higher effort for the domain expert and it might also be more error-prone, because the designer has to consider possible re-planning in every intermediate state of the system.
2. The reasoning system that triggers planning and provides the planning problem is responsible to incorporate additional tasks to make the system safe again. This shifts the problem to the creator of the execution system. This is even worse, since this might not even be a domain expert, and the execution system has to be domain-specific, i.e., the domain knowledge is split.
3. The repair system generates a solution that has the properties assured by the hierarchy. This solution leads to a single model containing the knowledge, the planning domain; and the domain designer does not need to consider every intermediate state of the real system.

Since it represents a fully domain-independent approach, we consider the last solution to be the best. This leads us to a core requirement of a system that solves the plan repair problem: regardless of whether it technically uses plan repair or re-planning, it needs to generate solutions that start with the same prefix of actions that have already been executed. Otherwise, the system potentially discards "physics" that have been modeled via the hierarchy. Therefore we define a solution to the plan repair problem as follows.

Definition 4 (Repaired Plan). *Given a plan repair problem* $P_r = (P, tn_s, dt, exe, F^+, F^-)$ *with* $P = (L, C, A, M, s_0, tn_I, g, \delta)$, $tn_s = (T, \prec, \alpha)$ *and* $exe = (t_0, t_1, \ldots t_n)$, *a repaired plan is a plan that*

1. *can be executed in* s_0
2. *is a refinement of* tn_I,
3. *has a linearization with a prefix* $(\alpha(t_0), \alpha(t_1), \ldots \alpha(t_n))$ *followed by tasks executable despite the unforeseen state change, resulting in a goal state.*

4   HTN Plan Repair: Related Work

Before we survey practical approaches on plan repair in HTN planning, we recap the theoretical properties of the task. Modifying existing HTN solutions (in a way so that the resulting solution lies still in the decomposition hierarchy) is undecidable even for quite simple modifications [5] and even deciding the question whether a given sequence of actions can be generated in a given HTN problem is NP-complete [6,7]. Unsurprisingly, the task given here – finding a solution that starts with a given sequence of actions – is undecidable [6].

We now summarize work concerned with plan repair or re-planning in hierarchical planning in chronological order.

One of the first approaches dealing with execution failures in hierarchical planning is given by Kambhampati and Hendler [27]. It can be seen as *plan repair*, since it repairs the already-found solution with the least number of changes. There are two properties we want to point out regarding our classification: (1) Though they assume a hierarchical model, (i.e., they also feature abstract tasks and decomposition methods for refining them), the planning goals are not defined in terms of an initial task network, but as a state-based goal. Abstract tasks use preconditions and effects so that they can be inserted as well. The plan that is repaired is a primitive plan, but it was generated by a hierarchical planner. (2) They do not base their work on an execution error, such as an unexpected change of a current situation, but instead assume that the problem description changes, i.e., the initial state and a goal description.

Drabble et al. [15] introduced algorithms to repair plans in case of action execution failure and unexpected world events by modifying the existing plan.

Boella and Damiano [14] propose a repair algorithm for a reactive agent architecture. Though they refer to it as re-planning, it can be seen as plan repair according to our classification. The original problem is given in terms of an initial plan that needs to be refined. Repair starts with a given primitive plan. They take back performed refinements until finding a more abstract plan that can be refined into a new primitive one with an optimal expected utility.

Warfield et al. [31] propose the RepairSHOP system, which extends the progression-based HTN planner SHOP [29] to cope with unexpected changes to the current state. Their *plan repair* approach shows some similarities with the previous one, as they backtrack decompositions up to a point where different options are available that allow a refinement in which the unexpected change does not violate executability. To do this, the authors propose the *goal graph*, which is a representation of the commitments that the planner has already made to find the executed solution.

Bidot et al. [12] propose a *plan repair* algorithm to cope with execution failures. The same basic idea has later been described in a more dense way relying on a simplified formalism [13]. Their approach also shows similarities to the previous two, as they also start with the failed plan and take planning decisions back, starting with those that introduced failure-associated plan elements, thereby re-using much of the planning effort already done. The already executed plan elements (steps and orderings) are marked with so-called *obligations*, a new flaw class in the underlying flaw-based planning system.

The previous plan repair approach has been further simplified by Bercher et al. [9,10]. Their approach uses obligations to state which plan elements must be part of any solution due to the already executed prefix. In contrast to the approaches given before, it starts with the initial plan and searches for refinements that achieve the obligations. Technically, it can be regarded *re-planning*, because it starts planning from scratch and from the *original* initial state while ensuring that new solutions start with the executed prefix. It was implemented in the plan-space-based planning system PANDA [11] and practically in use in the described assembly scenario, but never systematically evaluated empirically.

The most recent approach for HTN *plan repair* is the one by Barták and Vlk [4]. It focuses on *scheduling*, i.e., the task of allocating resources to actions and determine their execution time. In case of an execution error (a changed problem specification), another feasible schedule is found via backjumping (conflict-directed backtracking).

All these approaches address execution failures by a specialized algorithm. In the next section, we propose a novel approach that solves the problem *without* relying on specialized algorithms. Instead, it encodes the executed plan steps and the execution error into a standard HTN problem, which allows to use standard HTN solvers instead.

5   Plan Repair via Domain Transformation

Technically, the task is similar to *plan recognition as planning* (PGR) and we heavily build on the transformation-based PGR approach by Höller et al. [23]. The encoding of actions used by Höller et al. is similar to the one introduced by Ramírez and Geffner [30] in plan recognition in the context of classical planning.

Let $P_r = (P, tn_s, dt, exe, F^+, F^-)$ be the plan repair problem, $P = (L, C, A, M, s_0, tn_I, g, \delta)$ with $\delta = (prec, add, del)$ the original HTN planning problem, $exe = (a_1, a_2, \ldots, a_m)$ the sequence of already executed actions[1], and $F^+, F^- \in 2^L$ the sets of the unforeseen positive and negative facts, respectively. We define the following HTN planning problem $P' = (L', C', A', M', s'_0, tn'_I, g', \delta')$ with $\delta' = (prec', add', del')$ that solves the plan repair problem.

First, a set of new propositional symbols is introduced that indicate the position of some action in the enforced plan prefix. We denote these facts as l_i with $0 \leq i \leq m$ and $l_i \notin L$ and define $L' = L \cup \{l_i \mid 0 \leq i \leq m\}$.

For each task a_i with $1 \leq i < m - 1$ in the prefix of executed actions, a new task name a'_i is introduced with

$$prec'(a'_i) \mapsto prec(a_i) \cup \{l_{i-1}\},$$
$$add'(a'_i) \mapsto add(a_i) \cup \{l_i\} \text{ and}$$
$$del'(a'_i) \mapsto del(a_i) \cup \{l_{i-1}\}.$$

The last action in the executed prefix a_m needs to have additional effects, it performs the unforeseen state change.

$$prec'(a'_m) \mapsto prec(a_m) \cup \{l_{m-1}\},$$
$$add'(a'_m) \mapsto \big(add(a_m) \setminus F^-\big) \cup F^+ \cup \{l_m\} \text{ and}$$
$$del'(a'_m) \mapsto del(a_m) \cup F^- \cup \{l_{m-1}\}.$$

---

[1] To simplify the following definitions, the definition is slightly different from Definition 1, where it is a sequence of identifiers mapped to the tasks. The latter makes it possible to identify which decomposition resulted in an action, which is not needed here.

The original actions shall be ordered after the prefix, i.e., $\forall a \in A : prec'(a) \mapsto prec(a) \cup \{l_m\}$. The new set of actions is defined as $A' = A \cup \{a_i' \mid 1 \leq i \leq m\}$. To make the first action of the prefix applicable in the initial state, the symbol l_0 is added, i.e., $s_0' = s_0 \cup \{l_0\}$. We enforce that every solution starts with the entire prefix, i.e. $g' = g \cup \{l_m\}$.

Having adapted the non-hierarchical part of the problem, the newly introduced actions now need to be made reachable via the hierarchy. Since they simulate their duplicates from the prefix of the original plan, the planner should be allowed to place them at the same positions. This can be enabled by introducing a new abstract task for each action appearing in the prefix, replacing the original action at each position it appears, and adding methods such that this new task may be decomposed into the original or the new action. Formally, the transformation is defined in the following way.

$$C' = C \cup \{c_a' \mid a \in A\}, c_a' \notin C \cup A,$$
$$M^c = \{(c, (T, \prec, \alpha')) \mid (c, (T, \prec, \alpha)) \in M\}, \text{ where}$$
$$= \forall t \in T \text{ with } \alpha(t) = k \text{ we define } \alpha'(t) = \begin{cases} k, & \text{if } k \in C \\ c_k', & \text{else.} \end{cases}$$
$$M^a = \{(c_a', (\{t\}, \emptyset, \{t \mapsto a\})) \mid \forall a \in A\},$$

So far the new abstract tasks can only be decomposed into the original action. Now we allow the planner to place the new actions at the respective positions by introducing a new method for every action in $exe = (a_1, a_2, \ldots, a_m)$, decomposing a new abstract task c_{a_i}' into the executed action a_i:

$$M^{exe} = \{(c_{a_i}', (\{t\}, \emptyset, \{t \mapsto a_i'\})) \mid a_i \in exe\}$$

The set of methods is defined as $M' = M^c \cup M^a \cup M^{exe}$.

Figure 3 illustrates the method encoding. On the left, a method m is given that decomposes an abstract task c into another abstract task c' and an action a. When we assume that a is contained in the prefix once, the given approach will result in three new methods in the new model that are given on the right. In the original method m, the action a is replaced by a new abstract task c_a (the resulting method is named m_1). When a is contained in other methods, it is replaced in the same way as given here. The abstract task c_a can be decomposed using one of the two methods m_2 and m_3. They replace c_a either by the original action a or by the newly introduced copy a'. That way, a' can be added into the solution at exactly the positions where a has been possible before.

Figure 4 shows the schema of plans generated from our transformation: The structure of preconditions and effects results in a totally ordered sequence of actions in the beginning that is equal to these actions already executed. The last action (a_m') has additional effects that realize the unforeseen state change. Afterwards the planner is free to generate any partial ordering of tasks as allowed by the original domain. The newly introduced goal feature forces the prefix to be in the plan.

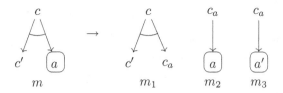

Fig. 3. Encoding of methods.

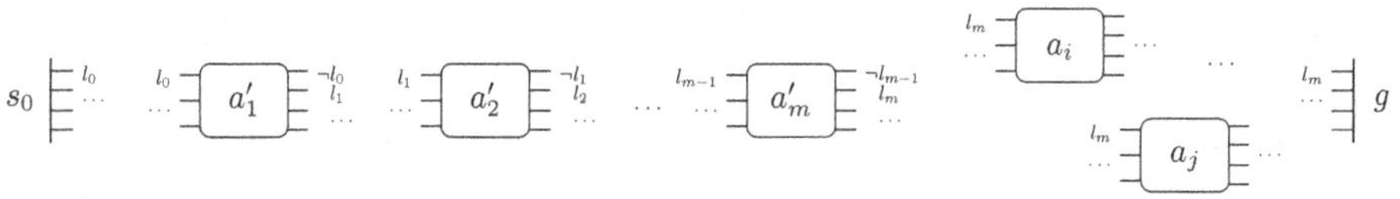

Fig. 4. Schema of the overall plan generated from our transformation.

Now we come back to our example. Starting the planner after the execution failure on the transformed model, it might now come up with the following plan that is executed starting with the third action. Now the toll is paid correctly.

$$drive(A, C)', drive\,TA(C, G)', drive\,TA(G, E),$$
$$drive\,TA(E, F), drive\,TA(F, H),$$
$$pay\,Toll(), pay\,Toll(), pay\,Toll(), pay\,Toll()$$

Like the approach given by Bercher et al. [9], our transformation is a mixture between re-planning and repair. The planning process is started from scratch, but the system generates a solution that starts with the executed prefix and incorporates constraints induced by the hierarchy. Since it enforces the properties by using a transformation, the system that generates the actual solution can be a standard HTN planning system. For future work, it might be interesting to adapt the applied planning heuristic to increase plan stability (though this would, again, lead to a specialized system).

A problem class related to HTN planning where our transformation may also be used is HTN planning with task insertion [2,8,19] (TIHTN planning). Here, the planning system is allowed to add actions apart from the decomposition process. This makes the issues described in Sect. 3 less obvious, since the sequence of already executed actions might simply be considered *inserted*. However, a TIHTN planner needs to include all actions that are enforced via the hierarchy into the plan. Consider an action that can only be executed once and that has already been executed. When the prefix is considered inserted and planning is done from scratch, the planner needs to insert it again and no executable plan is found. Using our techniques (with minor changes) will prevent such situations.

6   Theoretical Properties of the Transformation

We do not give an empirical evaluation of the encoding. Instead we analyze the theoretical properties of the transformation.

We first show that the common sub-classes of HTN planning are closed under the transformation, i.e., that the transformed problem is in the same class as the original problem. We consider the following sub-classes:

1. Full HTN planning – The full formalism without restrictions.
2. Totally ordered HTN planning [1,17] – The subtasks of all methods as well as the initial task network are totally ordered.
3. Tail-recursive HTN planning [1,3] – In this class, there exists a pre-order on all tasks in the domain (not to be confused with the partial order on tasks within task networks). For all methods, the following holds: All subtasks except the distinct last task (if there is one) have to be smaller than the decomposed task with respect to the pre-order. The last task may not be greater. Intuitively, there are layers of tasks and all but the last task are in lower layers. The last task may be in the same layer. It is always possible to put primitive tasks on a single lowest layer.
4. Acyclic HTN planning – There is no recursion, i.e. (one or more steps of) decomposition of a task can not end up with the same task.

Afterwards, we show that the size of the transformed problem is – in the worst case – quadratic when considering the executed prefix part of the input (as done in our definition, cf. Definition 1). Please be aware, however, that the transformed problem can become arbitrary large in comparison to the original planning problem when the prefix is not considered part of the input.

6.1   Closure Properties

We first show closure properties of the given HTN sub-classes.

Full HTN Models. Since the model resulting from the transformation is a common HTN model, it is obvious that this class is closed under the transformation.

Totally Ordered HTN Models. When we have a look at the transformation, we see that (1) the ordering of modified methods is exactly as it was before and that (2) new methods contain a single subtask (making them totally ordered, i.e. maximally restricted in the ordering). Surely we do not change properties related to method ordering and the transformation resulting from a totally ordered model as input will also be totally ordered.

Tail-recursive HTN Models. The newly introduced abstract tasks form a decomposition layer between the original abstract tasks and the original and newly introduced actions: when such a new abstract task is reached, it is not possible to reach any abstract task anymore, only actions are reachable from it.

Given there was an ordering of the tasks with the given properties before the transformation, we can define one on the transformed model by inserting a new "layer" between the original actions and the original abstract tasks and put the new abstract tasks on this layer. So if there was a pre-order with the given properties on all tasks in the first place (making the problem tail-recursive) the new model will still possess such a pre-order, i.e. it is still tail-recursive.

Acyclic Models. We do not introduce recursive decomposition structures. When a model is non-recursive before, it will also be non-recursive afterwards.

6.2 Model Size

Next we show that the transformation is in the worst case quadratic in the input. Let n be the size of the HTN model and m the size of the already executed prefix. We consider both model and prefix as part of the input. For each step in the prefix, the transformation adds to the model:

1. a single state feature,
2. a single new action,
3. up to two methods (with constant size), and
4. at most a single abstract task.

Due to the (rather artificial) case that the actions included in the prefix dominate the size of the HTN model (e.g. if they have every state feature as precondition/effect and the elements defining the hierarchy, i.e. abstract tasks and methods are small in comparison to the actions) the size of the transformation is bounded by $n \times m$ (caused by adding a new action m times). In practice, it should be much smaller, though.

Even in this artificial kind of domain, the size of the encoding will only be quadratic for a certain prefix length. When the prefix is very small, the size of the input model will dominate the size of the resulting model, if it becomes very large, the prefix dominates the size. Only when they are of similar size we end up with quadratic model size.

7 Conclusion

In this paper we introduced a novel approach to repair broken plans in HTN planning. We discussed that simply re-starting the planning process is no option since this discards constraints implied by the hierarchy. Instead, systems need to come up with a new plan that starts with the actions that have already been executed. All systems in the literature tackle the given problem by specialized algorithms. We provided a transformation-based approach that enables the use of unchanged HTN planning systems.

Acknowledgments. Gefördert durch die Deutsche Forschungsgemeinschaft (DFG) – Projektnummer 232722074 – SFB 1102 / Funded by the Deutsche Forschungsgemeinschaft (DFG, German Research Foundation) – Project-ID 232722074 – SFB 1102.

References

1. Alford, R., Bercher, P., Aha, D.W.: Tight bounds for HTN planning. In: Proceedings of the 25th International Conference on Automated Planning and Scheduling (ICAPS), pp. 7–15. AAAI Press (2015)
2. Alford, R., Bercher, P., Aha, D.W.: Tight bounds for HTN planning with task insertion. In: Proceedings of the 24th International Joint Conference on Artificial Intelligence (IJCAI). pp. 1502–1508. AAAI Press (2015)
3. Alford, R., Shivashankar, V., Kuter, U., Nau, D.S.: HTN problem spaces: structure, algorithms, termination. In: Proceedings of the 5th Annual Symposium on Combinatorial Search (SoCS), pp. 2–9. AAAI Press (2012)
4. Barták, R., Vlk, M.: Hierarchical task model for resource failure recovery in production Scheduling. In: Sidorov, G., Herrera-Alcántara, O. (eds.) MICAI 2016. LNCS (LNAI), vol. 10061, pp. 362–378. Springer, Cham (2017). https://doi.org/10.1007/978-3-319-62434-1_30
5. Behnke, G., Höller, D., Bercher, P., Biundo, S.: Change the plan - how hard can that be? In: Proceedings of the 26th International Conference on Automated Planning and Scheduling (ICAPS), pp. 38–46. AAAI Press (2016)
6. Behnke, G., Höller, D., Biundo, S.: On the complexity of HTN plan verification and its implications for plan recognition. In: Proceedings of the 25th International Conference on Automated Planning and Scheduling (ICAPS), pp. 25–33. AAAI Press (2015)
7. Behnke, G., Höller, D., Biundo, S.: This is a solution! (...but is it though?) - Verifying solutions of hierarchical planning problems. In: Proceedings of the 27th International Conference on Automated Planning and Scheduling (ICAPS), pp. 20–28. AAAI Press (2017)
8. Bercher, P., Alford, R., Höller, D.: A survey on hierarchical planning - one abstract idea, many concrete realizations. In: Proceedings of the 28th International Joint Conference on Artificial Intelligence (IJCAI), pp. 6267–6275. IJCAI Organization (2019)
9. Bercher, P., et al.: Plan, repair, execute, explain - how planning helps to assemble your home theater. In: Proceedings of the 24th International Conference on Automated Planning and Scheduling (ICAPS), pp. 386–394. AAAI Press (2014)
10. Bercher, P., Höller, D., Behnke, G., Biundo, S.: User-centered planning. In: Biundo, S., Wendemuth, A. (eds.) Companion Technology. CT, pp. 79–100. Springer, Cham (2017). https://doi.org/10.1007/978-3-319-43665-4_5
11. Bercher, P., Keen, S., Biundo, S.: Hybrid planning heuristics based on task decomposition graphs. In: Proceedings of the 7th Annual Symposium on Combinatorial Search (SoCS), pp. 35–43. AAAI Press (2014)
12. Bidot, J., Schattenberg, B., Biundo, S.: Plan repair in hybrid planning. In: Dengel, A.R., Berns, K., Breuel, T.M., Bomarius, F., Roth-Berghofer, T.R. (eds.) KI 2008. LNCS (LNAI), vol. 5243, pp. 169–176. Springer, Heidelberg (2008). https://doi.org/10.1007/978-3-540-85845-4_21
13. Biundo, S., Bercher, P., Geier, T., Müller, F., Schattenberg, B.: Advanced user assistance based on AI planning. Cogn. Syst. Res. **12**(3–4), 219–236 (2011)
14. Boella, G., Damiano, R.: A replanning algorithm for a reactive agent architecture. In: Scott, D. (ed.) AIMSA 2002. LNCS (LNAI), vol. 2443, pp. 183–192. Springer, Heidelberg (2002). https://doi.org/10.1007/3-540-46148-5_19
15. Drabble, B., Dalton, J., Tate, A.: Repairing plans on-the-fly. In: Proceedings of the NASA Workshop on Planning and Scheduling for Space, pp. 13.1–13.8 (1997)

16. Dvořák, F., Barták, R., Bit-Monnot, A., Ingrand, F., Ghallab, M.: Planning and acting with temporal and hierarchical decomposition models. In: Proceedings of the 26th International Conference on Tools with Artificial Intelligence (ICTAI), pp. 115–121. IEEE (2014)

17. Erol, K., Hendler, J.A., Nau, D.S.: Complexity results for HTN planning. Ann. Math. Artif. Intell. **18**(1), 69–93 (1996)

18. Fox, M., Gerevini, A., Long, D., Serina, I.: Plan stability: replanning versus plan repair. In: Proceedings of the 16th International Conference on Automated Planning and Scheduling (ICAPS), pp. 212–221. AAAI Press (2006)

19. Geier, T., Bercher, P.: On the decidability of HTN planning with task insertion. In: Proceedings of the 22nd International Joint Conference on Artificial Intelligence (IJCAI), pp. 1955–1961. IJCAI/AAAI (2011)

20. Gerevini, A., Serina, I.: Fast plan adaptation through planning graphs: local and systematic search techniques. In: Proceedings of the 5th International Conference on Artificial Intelligence Planning Systems (AIPS), pp. 112–121. AAAI Press (2000)

21. Höller, D., Behnke, G., Bercher, P., Biundo, S.: Language classification of hierarchical planning problems. In: Proceedings of the 21st European Conference on Artificial Intelligence (ECAI), pp. 447–452. IOS Press (2014)

22. Höller, D., Behnke, G., Bercher, P., Biundo, S.: Assessing the expressivity of planning formalisms through the comparison to formal languages. In: Proceedings of the 26th International Conference on Automated Planning and Scheduling (ICAPS), pp. 158–165. AAAI Press (2016)

23. Höller, D., Behnke, G., Bercher, P., Biundo, S.: Plan and goal recognition as HTN planning. In: Proceedings of the 30th IEEE International Conference on Tools with Artificial Intelligence (ICTAI), pp. 466–473. IEEE Computer Society (2018)

24. Höller, D., Bercher, P., Behnke, G., Biundo, S.: A generic method to guide HTN progression search with classical heuristics. In: Proceedings of the 28th International Conference on Automated Planning and Scheduling (ICAPS). AAAI Press (2018)

25. Höller, D., Bercher, P., Behnke, G., Biundo, S.: HTN plan repair using unmodified planning systems. In: Proceedings of the 1st ICAPS Workshop on Hierarchical Planning (HPlan), pp. 26–30 (2018)

26. Höller, D., Bercher, P., Behnke, G., Biundo, S.: HTN planning as heuristic progression search. J. Artif. Intell. Res. **67**, 835–880 (2020)

27. Kambhampati, S., Hendler, J.A.: A validation-structure-based theory of plan modification and reuse. Artif. Intell. **55**, 193–258 (1992)

28. Nau, D.S., et al.: SHOP2: an HTN planning system. J. Artif. Intell. Res. **20**, 379–404 (2003)

29. Nau, D.S., Cao, Y., Lotem, A., Muñoz-Avila, H.: The SHOP planning system. AI Mag. **22**(3), 91–94 (2001)

30. Ramírez, M., Geffner, H.: Plan recognition as planning. In: Proceedings of the 21st International Joint Conference on Artificial Intelligence (IJCAI), pp. 1778–1783. AAAI Press (2009)

31. Warfield, I., Hogg, C., Lee-Urban, S., Muñoz-Avila, H.: Adaptation of hierarchical task network plans. In: Proceedings of the 20th International Florida Artificial Intelligence Research Society Conference (FLAIRS), pp. 429–434. AAAI Press (2007)

Nonmonotonic Inferences with Qualitative Conditionals Based on Preferred Structures on Worlds

Christian Komo[(⊠)] and Christoph Beierle

Department of Computer Science, FernUniversität in Hagen, 58084 Hagen, Germany
Christian.Komo@web.de, christoph.beierle@fernuni-hagen.de

Abstract. A conditional knowledge base $\mathcal{R}$ is a set of conditionals of the form "If A then usually B". Using structural information derived from the conditionals in $\mathcal{R}$, we introduce the preferred structure relation on worlds. The preferred structure relation is the core ingredient of a new inference relation called system W inference that inductively completes the knowledge given explicitly in $\mathcal{R}$. We show that system W exhibits desirable inference properties like satisfying system P and avoiding, in contrast to, e.g., system Z, the drowning problem. It fully captures and strictly extends both system Z and skeptical c-inference. In contrast to skeptical c-inference, it does not require to solve a complex constraint satisfaction problem, but is as tractable as system Z.

1 Introduction

In the area of knowledge representation and reasoning, conditionals play a prominent role. Nonmonotonic reasoning investigates qualitative conditionals of the form *"If A then usually B"*. Various semantical approaches for inferences based on sets of such conditionals as well as criteria and postulates for evaluating the obtained inference relations have been proposed (cf. [1,4,7,8,10,12,14,19–22]). Among the different semantical models of conditional knowledge bases are Spohn's ordinal conditional functions (OCFs) [24,25], also called ranking functions. An OCF κ assigns a degree of surprise (or degree of implausibility) to each world ω, the higher the value $\kappa(\omega)$ assigned to ω, the more surprising ω. Each κ that accepts a set $\mathcal{R}$ of conditionals, called a knowledge base, induces a nonmonotonic inference relation that inductively completes the explicit knowledge given in $\mathcal{R}$.

Two inference relations which are defined based on specific OCFs obtained from a knowledge base $\mathcal{R}$ have received some attention: system Z [13,23] and c-representations [14,15], or the induced inference relations, respectively, both show excellent inference properties. System Z is based upon the ranking function κ^Z, which is the unique Pareto-minimal OCF that accepts $\mathcal{R}$. The definition of κ^Z crucially relies on the notions of *tolerance* and of *inclusion-maximal ordered partition* of $\mathcal{R}$ obtained via the tolerance relation [13,23]. Among the OCF models of $\mathcal{R}$, c-representations are special models obtained by assigning an individual impact to each conditional and generating the world ranks as the

© Springer Nature Switzerland AG 2020
U. Schmid et al. (Eds.): KI 2020, LNAI 12325, pp. 102–115, 2020.
https://doi.org/10.1007/978-3-030-58285-2_8

sum of impacts of falsified conditionals [14,15]. While for each consistent $\mathcal{R}$, the system Z ranking function κ^Z is uniquely determined, there may be many different c-representations of $\mathcal{R}$. Skeptical c-inference [2,5] is the inference relation obtained by taking all c-representations of $\mathcal{R}$ into account.

It is known that system Z and skeptical c-inference both satisfy system P [5,13,19] and other desirable properties. Furthermore, there are system Z inferences that are not obtained by skeptical c-inference, and on the other hand, there are skeptical c-inferences that are not system Z inferences [5]. Another notable difference between system Z and skeptical c-inference is that the single unique system Z model [23] can be computed much easier than skeptical c-inference which involves many models obtained from the solutions of a complex constraint satisfaction problem [5]. In recently published work [18], we showed that the exponential lower bound 2^{n-1} is needed as possible impact factor for c-representations to fully realize skeptical c-inference, supporting the observation that skeptical c-inference is less tractable than system Z inference (cf. [5,13]).

Inspired by our findings in [18], here we develop the *preferred structure* relation on worlds and propose the new nonmonotonic *system W inference* based on it. The main contributions of this paper are:

- We introduce the *preferred structure relation* $<^{\mathsf{w}}_{\mathcal{R}}$ on worlds based on the notions of tolerance and verification/falsification behavior of a knowledge base $\mathcal{R}$.
- By exploiting $<^{\mathsf{w}}_{\mathcal{R}}$, we develop a new inference relation, called *system W inference*, which is as tractable as system Z.
- We prove that system W inference captures and strictly extends both system Z inference and skeptical c-inference.
- We show that system W inference exhibits desirable inference properties like satisfying the axioms of system P and avoiding the drowning problem.

The rest of the paper is organized as follows. After briefly recalling the required background in Sect. 2, we introduce the preferred structure on worlds and prove several of its properties in Sect. 3. In Sect. 4, we give the formal definition of system W, illustrate it with various examples and show its main properties. In Sect. 5, we conclude and point out future work.

2   Conditional Logic, System Z, and C-Representations

Let $\Sigma = \{v_1, ..., v_m\}$ be a propositional alphabet. A *literal* is the positive (v_i) or negated ($\overline{v_i}$) form of a propositional variable, $\dot{v}_i$ stands for either v_i or $\overline{v_i}$. From these we obtain the propositional language $\mathcal{L}$ as the set of formulas of Σ closed under negation $\neg$, conjunction $\wedge$, and disjunction $\vee$. For shorter formulas, we abbreviate conjunction by juxtaposition (i.e., AB stands for $A \wedge B$), and negation by overlining (i.e., $\overline{A}$ is equivalent to $\neg A$). Let Ω_Σ denote the set of possible worlds over $\mathcal{L}$; Ω_Σ will be taken here simply as the set of all propositional interpretations over $\mathcal{L}$ and can be identified with the set of all complete conjunctions over Σ; we will often just write Ω instead of Ω_Σ. For $\omega \in \Omega$, $\omega \models A$

means that the propositional formula $A \in \mathcal{L}$ holds in the possible world ω. With $\Omega_A = \{\omega \in \Omega_\Sigma \mid \omega \models A\}$, we denote the set of all worlds in which A holds, and $\equiv$ denotes propositional equivalence.

A *conditional* $(B|A)$ with $A, B \in \mathcal{L}$ encodes the defeasible rule "if A then normally B" and is a trivalent logical entity with the evaluation [11,14]

$$[\![(B|A)]\!]_\omega = \begin{cases} \mathsf{v} & \text{iff} \quad \omega \models AB & \text{(verification)}, \\ \mathsf{f} & \text{iff} \quad \omega \models A\overline{B} & \text{(falsification)}, \\ - & \text{iff} \quad \omega \models \overline{A} & \text{(not applicable)}. \end{cases} \tag{1}$$

An *ordinal conditional function* (OCF, ranking function) [24,25] is a function $\kappa : \Omega \to \mathbb{N}_0 \cup \{\infty\}$ that assigns to each world $\omega \in \Omega$ an implausibility rank $\kappa(\omega)$: the higher $\kappa(\omega)$, the more surprising ω is. OCFs have to satisfy the normalization condition that there has to be a world that is maximally plausible, i.e., $\kappa^{-1}(0) \neq \emptyset$. The rank of a formula A is defined by $\kappa(A) = \min\{\kappa(\omega) \mid \omega \models A\}$ where $\min \emptyset = \infty$. An OCF κ *accepts* a conditional $(B|A)$, denoted by $\kappa \models (B|A)$, if the verification of the conditional is less surprising than its falsification, i.e., $\kappa \models (B|A)$ iff $\kappa(AB) < \kappa(A\overline{B})$. This can also be understood as a nonmonotonic inference relation between the premise A and the conclusion B: Basically, we say that A κ-*entails* B, written $A \mathrel{\mid\!\sim}^\kappa B$, if κ accepts $(B|A)$; formally, this is given by

$$A \mathrel{\mid\!\sim}^\kappa B \quad \text{iff} \quad A \equiv \bot \text{ or } \kappa(AB) < \kappa(A\overline{B}). \tag{2}$$

Note that the reason for including the disjunctive condition in (2) is to ensure that $\mathrel{\mid\!\sim}^\kappa$ satisfies supraclassicality, i.e., $A \models B$ implies $A \mathrel{\mid\!\sim}^\kappa B$, also for the case $A \equiv \bot$ as it is required, for instance, by the reflexivity axiom $A \mathrel{\mid\!\sim} A$ of system P [1,19]. Let us remark that κ-entailment is based on the total preorder on possible worlds induced by a ranking function and can be expressed equivalently by:

$$A \mathrel{\mid\!\sim}^\kappa B \quad \text{iff} \quad \forall \omega' \in \Omega_{A\overline{B}} \, \exists \omega \in \Omega_{AB} \, \kappa(\omega) < \kappa(\omega'). \tag{3}$$

The acceptance relation is extended as usual to a set $\mathcal{R}$ of conditionals, called a *knowledge base*, by defining $\kappa \models \mathcal{R}$ iff $\kappa \models (B|A)$ for all $(B|A) \in \mathcal{R}$. This is synonymous to saying that κ is *admissible* with respect to $\mathcal{R}$ [13], or that κ is a *ranking model* of $\mathcal{R}$. $\mathcal{R}$ is *consistent* iff it has a ranking model.

Two inference relations which are defined by specific OCFs obtained from a knowledge base $\mathcal{R}$ have received some attention: system Z [23] and c-representations [14,15], or the induced inference relations, respectively, both show excellent inference properties. We recall both approaches briefly.

System Z [23] is based upon the ranking function κ^Z, which is the unique Pareto-minimal OCF that accepts $\mathcal{R}$. The definition of κ^Z crucially relies on the notion of *tolerance*. A conditional $(B|A)$ is *tolerated* by a set of conditionals $\mathcal{R}$ if there is a world $\omega \in \Omega$ such that $\omega \models AB$ and $\omega \models \bigwedge_{i=1}^n (\overline{A_i} \vee B_i)$, i.e., iff ω verifies $(B|A)$ and does not falsify any conditional in $\mathcal{R}$. For every consistent knowledge base, the notion of tolerance yields an ordered partition $(\mathcal{R}_0, ..., \mathcal{R}_k)$ of $\mathcal{R}$, where each $\mathcal{R}_i$ is tolerated by $\bigcup_{j=i}^k \mathcal{R}_j$. The *inclusion-maximal partition* of $\mathcal{R}$, in the following denoted by $OP(\mathcal{R}) = (\mathcal{R}_0, \dots, \mathcal{R}_k)$, is the ordered partition of $\mathcal{R}$ where each $\mathcal{R}_i$ is the (with respect to set inclusion) maximal subset of $\bigcup_{j=i}^{k} \mathcal{R}_j$ that is tolerated by $\bigcup_{j=i}^{k} \mathcal{R}_j$. This partitioning is unique due to the maximality and can be computed using the consistency test algorithm given in [13]; for an inconsistent knowledge base $\mathcal{R}$, $OP(\mathcal{R})$ does not exist. Using $OP(\mathcal{R}) = (\mathcal{R}_0, \ldots, \mathcal{R}_k)$, the system Z ranking function κ^Z is defined by

$$
\kappa^Z(\omega) := \begin{cases} 0, & \text{if } \omega \text{ does not falsify any conditional } r \in \mathcal{R}, \\ 1 + \max_{\substack{1 \leqslant i \leqslant n \\ \omega \models A_i \overline{B_i}}} Z(r_i), & \text{otherwise,} \end{cases}
$$

(4)

where the function $Z : \mathcal{R} \to \mathbb{N}_0$ is given by $Z(r_i) = j$ if $r_i \in \mathcal{R}_j$.

Definition 1 (system Z inference, $\sim^Z_{\mathcal{R}}$ [13]). *Let $\mathcal{R}$ be a knowledge base and let A, B be formulas. We say that B can be inferred from A by system Z in the context of $\mathcal{R}$, denoted by $A \sim^Z_{\mathcal{R}} B$, iff $A \sim^{\kappa^Z} B$ holds.*

Among the OCF models of $\mathcal{R}$, c-representations are special models obtained by assigning an individual impact to each conditional and generating the world ranks as the sum of impacts of falsified conditionals. For an in-depth introduction to c-representations and their use of the principle of conditional preservation ensured by respecting conditional structures, we refer to [14,15]. The central definition is the following:

Definition 2 (c-representation [14]). *A c-representation of a knowledge base $\mathcal{R}$ is a ranking function $\kappa_{\vec{\eta}}$ constructed from $\vec{\eta} = (\eta_1, \ldots, \eta_n)$ with integer impacts $\eta_i \in \mathbb{N}_0, i \in \{1, \ldots, n\}$ assigned to each conditional $(B_i | A_i)$ such that κ accepts $\mathcal{R}$ and is given by:*

$$
\kappa_{\vec{\eta}}(\omega) = \sum_{\substack{1 \leqslant i \leqslant n \\ \omega \models A_i \overline{B_i}}} \eta_i
$$

(5)

We will denote the set of all c-representations of $\mathcal{R}$ by $\mathcal{O}(CR(\mathcal{R}))$.

As every ranking model of $\mathcal{R}$, each c-representation $\kappa_{\vec{\eta}}$ gives rise to an inference relation according to (2). While for each consistent $\mathcal{R}$, the system Z ranking function κ^Z is uniquely determined, there may be many different c-representations of $\mathcal{R}$. C-inference [2,5] is an inference relation taking all c-representations of $\mathcal{R}$ into account.

Definition 3 (c-inference, $\sim^c_{\mathcal{R}}$ [2]). *Let $\mathcal{R}$ be a knowledge base and let A, B be formulas. B is a (skeptical) c-inference from A in the context of $\mathcal{R}$, denoted by $A \sim^c_{\mathcal{R}} B$, iff $A \sim^{\kappa} B$ holds for all c-representations κ for $\mathcal{R}$.*

In [5] a modeling of c-representations as solutions of a constraint satisfaction problem $CR(\mathcal{R})$ is given and shown to be sound and complete with respect to the set of all c-representations of $\mathcal{R}$.

Definition 4 (CR(R) [2]). *Let* $\mathcal{R} = \{(B_1|A_1), \ldots, (B_n|A_n)\}$. *The constraint satisfaction problem for c-representations of* $\mathcal{R}$, *denoted by* $CR(\mathcal{R})$, *on the constraint variables* $\{\eta_1, \ldots, \eta_n\}$ *ranging over* $\mathbb{N}_0$ *is given by the conjunction of the constraints, for all* $i \in \{1, \ldots, n\}$:

$$\eta_i \geqslant 0 \tag{6}$$

$$\eta_i > \min_{\substack{\omega \models A_i B_i}} \sum_{\substack{j \neq i \\ \omega \models A_j \overline{B_j}}} \eta_j - \min_{\substack{\omega \models A_i \overline{B_i}}} \sum_{\substack{j \neq i \\ \omega \models A_j \overline{B_j}}} \eta_j \tag{7}$$

A solution of $CR(\mathcal{R})$ is an n-tuple $(\eta_1, \ldots, \eta_n) \in \mathbb{N}_0^n$. For a constraint satisfaction problem CSP, the set of solutions is denoted by $Sol(CSP)$. Thus, with $Sol(CR(\mathcal{R}))$ we denote the set of all solutions of $CR(\mathcal{R})$.

Proposition 1 (soundness and completeness of $CR(\mathcal{R})$ [5]). *Let* $\mathcal{R} = \{(B_1|A_1), \ldots, (B_n|A_n)\}$ *be a knowledge base. With* $\kappa_{\vec{\eta}}$ *as in (5), we then have:*

$$\mathcal{O}(CR(\mathcal{R})) = \{\kappa_{\vec{\eta}} \mid \vec{\eta} \in Sol(CR(\mathcal{R}))\} \tag{8}$$

Example 1 ($\mathcal{R}_{bird}$). To illustrate the definitions and concepts presented in this paper let us consider an instance of the well known penguin bird example. This example is our running example and it will be continued and extended throughout the paper. Consider the propositional alphabet $\Sigma = \{p, b, f\}$ representing whether something is a penguin (p), whether it is a bird (b), or whether it can fly (f). Thus, the set of worlds is $\Omega = \{pbf, pb\overline{f}, p\overline{b}f, p\overline{b}\overline{f}, \overline{p}bf, \overline{p}b\overline{f}, \overline{p}\overline{b}f, \overline{p}\overline{b}\overline{f}\}$. The knowledge base $\mathcal{R}_{bird} = \{r_1, r_2, r_3, r_4\}$ contains the conditionals

$$r_1 = (f|b) \quad \text{"Birds usually fly"},$$
$$r_2 = (\overline{f}|p) \quad \text{"Penguins usually do not fly"},$$
$$r_3 = (\overline{f}|bp) \quad \text{"Penguins which are also birds usually do not fly"},$$
$$r_4 = (b|p) \quad \text{"Penguins are usually birds"}.$$

For $\mathcal{R}_0 = \{(f|b)\}$ and $\mathcal{R}_1 = \mathcal{R}_{bird} \setminus \mathcal{R}_0$ we have the ordered partitioning $(\mathcal{R}_0, \mathcal{R}_1)$ such that every conditional in $\mathcal{R}_0$ is tolerated by $\mathcal{R}_0 \cup \mathcal{R}_1 = \mathcal{R}_{bird}$ and every conditional in $\mathcal{R}_1$ is tolerated by $\mathcal{R}_1$. For instance, $(f|b)$ is tolerated by $\mathcal{R}_{bird}$ since there is, for example, the world $\overline{p}bf$ with $\overline{p}bf \models bf$ as well as $\overline{p}bf \models (p \Rightarrow \overline{f}) \wedge (pb \Rightarrow \overline{f}) \wedge (p \Rightarrow b)$. Furthermore $(\mathcal{R}_0, \mathcal{R}_1)$ is indeed the inclusion-maximal partition of $\mathcal{R}$. Therefore, $\mathcal{R}$ is consistent. An OCF κ that accepts $\mathcal{R}_{bird}$ is:

ω	pbf	$pb\overline{f}$	$p\overline{b}f$	$p\overline{b}\overline{f}$	$\overline{p}bf$	$\overline{p}b\overline{f}$	$\overline{p}\overline{b}f$	$\overline{p}\overline{b}\overline{f}$
$\kappa(\omega)$	2	1	2	2	0	1	0	0

For instance, we have $\kappa \models (f|b)$ since $\kappa(bf) = \min\{\kappa(pbf), \kappa(\overline{p}bf)\} = \min\{2, 0\} = 0$ and $\kappa(b\overline{f}) = \min\{\kappa(pb\overline{f}), \kappa(\overline{p}b\overline{f})\} = \min\{1, 1\} = 1$ and therefore $\kappa(bf) < \kappa(b\overline{f})$.

3   Preferred Structure on Worlds

Aiming at developing a nonmonotonic inference relation combining advantages of system Z like tractability and of skeptical c-inference like, for instance, avoidance of the downing problem [9,23], we first introduce the new notion of preferred structure on worlds with respect to a knowledge base $\mathcal{R}$. The idea is to take into account both the tolerance information expressed by the ordered partition of $\mathcal{R}$ and the structural information which conditionals are falsified.

Definition 5 (ξ^j, ξ, preferred structure $<^{\text{w}}_{\mathcal{R}}$ on worlds). *Consider a consistent knowledge base* $\mathcal{R} = \{r_i = (B_i|A_i) \mid i \in \{1,\ldots,n\}\}$ *with* $OP(\mathcal{R}) = (\mathcal{R}_0,\ldots,\mathcal{R}_k)$. *For* $j \in \{0,\ldots,k\}$, ξ^j *and* ξ *are the* functions *mapping worlds to the set of falsified conditionals from the tolerance partition* $\mathcal{R}_j$ *and from* $\mathcal{R}$, *respectively, given by*

$$\xi^j(\omega) := \{r_i \in \mathcal{R}_j \mid \omega \models A_i\overline{B_i}\}, \tag{9}$$

$$\xi(\omega) := \{r_i \in \mathcal{R} \mid \omega \models A_i\overline{B_i}\}. \tag{10}$$

The preferred structure on worlds *is given by the binary relation* $<^{\text{w}}_{\mathcal{R}} \subseteq \Omega \times \Omega$ *defined by, for any* $\omega, \omega' \in \Omega$,

$$\omega <^{\text{w}}_{\mathcal{R}} \omega' \quad \textit{iff} \quad \textit{there exists } m \in \{0,\ldots,k\} \textit{ such that}$$
$$\xi^i(\omega) = \xi^i(\omega') \quad \forall i \in \{m+1,\ldots,k\}, \textit{ and} \tag{11}$$
$$\xi^m(\omega) \subsetneqq \xi^m(\omega').$$

Thus, $\omega <^{\text{w}}_{\mathcal{R}} \omega'$ if and only if ω falsifies strictly less conditionals than ω' in the partition with the biggest index m where the conditionals falsified by ω and ω' differ. The preferred structure on worlds will be the basis for defining a new inference relation induced by $\mathcal{R}$. Before formally defining this new inference relation and elaborating its properties, we proceed by illustrating the preferred structure on worlds for a knowledge base $\mathcal{R}$, relating it to c-representations of $\mathcal{R}$, and proving a set of its properties that will be useful for investigating the characteristics and properties of the resulting inference relation.

Example 2 ($<^{\text{w}}_{\mathcal{R}_{bird}}$). Let us determine the preferred structure on worlds $<^{\text{w}}_{\mathcal{R}_{bird}}$ for the knowledge base $\mathcal{R}_{bird}$ from Example 1 whose verification/falsification behavior is shown in Table 1. The inclusion-maximal partition $OP(\mathcal{R}_{bird}) = (\mathcal{R}_0, \mathcal{R}_1)$ is given by $\mathcal{R}_0 = \{r_1 = (f|b)\}$ and $\mathcal{R}_1 = \{r_2 = (\overline{f}|p), r_3 = (\overline{f}|bp), r_4 = (b|p)\}$. Figure 1 shows the preferred structure on worlds $<^{\text{w}}_{\mathcal{R}_{bird}}$ for the knowledge base $\mathcal{R}_{bird}$. An edge $\omega \to \omega'$ between two worlds indicates that $\omega <^{\text{w}}_{\mathcal{R}_{bird}} \omega'$. The full relation $<^{\text{w}}_{\mathcal{R}_{bird}}$ is obtained from the transitive closure of $\to$ in Fig. 1.

The following proposition can be seen as a generalization of a result from [6]. It extends [6, Proposition 15] to the relation $<^{\text{w}}_{\mathcal{R}}$ and to arbitrary knowledge bases, not just knowledge bases only consisting of conditional facts as in [6, Proposition 15]. It tells us that the set of c-representations is rich enough to guarantee the existence of a particular c-representation $\kappa_{\vec{\eta}} \in \mathcal{O}(CR(\mathcal{R}))$ fulfilling the ordering constraints given in the proposition.

Table 1. Verification/falsification behavior of the knowledge base $\mathcal{R}_{bird}$; (v) indicates verification, (f) falsification, and (−) non-applicability. The OCF κ^Z is the ranking function obtained from $\mathcal{R}_{bird}$ using system Z.

ω	pbf	$pb\overline{f}$	$p\overline{b}f$	$p\overline{b}\,\overline{f}$	$\overline{p}bf$	$\overline{p}b\overline{f}$	$\overline{p}\,\overline{b}f$	$\overline{p}\,\overline{b}\,\overline{f}$
$r_1 = (f\mid b)$	v	f	−	−	v	f	−	−
$r_2 = (\overline{f}\mid p)$	f	v	f	v	−	−	−	−
$r_3 = (\overline{f}\mid pb)$	f	v	−	−	−	−	−	−
$r_4 = (b\mid p)$	v	v	f	f	−	−	−	−
$\kappa^Z(\omega)$	2	1	2	2	0	1	0	0

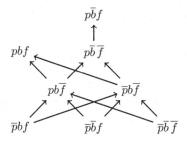

Fig. 1. The preferred structure relation $<^{w}_{\mathcal{R}_{bird}}$ on worlds for the knowledge base $\mathcal{R}_{bird}$.

Proposition 2. *Let* $\mathcal{R} = \{r_i = (B_i\mid A_i) \mid i = 1,\dots,n\}$ *be a consistent knowledge base, let* $\omega' \in \Omega$ *and let* $\Omega_V \subseteq \Omega$. *Assume that* $\omega \not<^{w}_{\mathcal{R}} \omega'$ *for all* $\omega \in \Omega_V$. *Then there exists a solution* $\vec{\eta} \in Sol(CR(\mathcal{R}))$ *and thus a c-representation,* $\kappa_{\vec{\eta}} \in \mathcal{O}(CR(\mathcal{R}))$ *such that, for all* $\omega \in \Omega_V$, *we have:*

$$\kappa_{\vec{\eta}}(\omega') \leqslant \kappa_{\vec{\eta}}(\omega) \tag{12}$$

Proof. (Sketch) Due to lack of space, we give a sketch of the proof. The claim follows by combining the following two statements:

(i) If $\eta_i \in \mathbb{N}, i \in \{1,\dots,n\}$, satisfy

$$\eta_i > \sum_{\substack{j\in\{1,\dots,n\} \\ r_j\in\bigcup_{l=0}^{m-1}\mathcal{R}_l}} \eta_j \tag{13}$$

for all $i \in \{1,\dots,n\}$ where $m = m(i) \in \{0,\dots,k\}$ with $r_i \in \mathcal{R}_m$ then $\vec{\eta} = (\eta_1,\dots,\eta_n)$ is a solution of $CR(\mathcal{R})$ and so $\kappa_{\vec{\eta}}$ defined as in (5) is a c-representation of $\mathcal{R}$.

(ii) Because of $\omega \not<^{w}_{\mathcal{R}} \omega'$ for all $\omega \in \Omega_V$ we can choose $\vec{\eta} = (\eta_1,\dots,\eta_n)$ satisfying (13) such that $\kappa_{\vec{\eta}}$ defined as in (5) satisfies (12) for all $\omega \in \Omega_V$.

A complete proof that (i) and (ii) hold is given in the full version of this paper [17].   □

The rest of this section is dedicated to the investigation of further properties of the relation $<^{\mathsf{w}}_{\mathcal{R}}$. Let us start with a lemma that tells us that worlds falsifying the same sets of conditionals are equivalent with respect to $<^{\mathsf{w}}_{\mathcal{R}}$.

Lemma 1. *Let* $\mathcal{R} = \{(B_i|A_i) \mid i = 1,\dots,n\}$ *be a knowledge base, and let* $\omega_1, \omega_2 \in \Omega$ *falsify the same sets of conditionals, i.e., for all* $i \in \{1,\dots,n\}$, *we have* $\omega_1 \models A_i\overline{B}_i$ *iff* $\omega_2 \models A_i\overline{B}_i$. *Then* ω_1, ω_2 *behave exactly the same way with respect to* $\mathcal{R}$, *i.e., for all* $\omega \in \Omega$, *the following equivalences hold:*

$$\omega <^{\mathsf{w}}_{\mathcal{R}} \omega_1 \quad \text{iff} \quad \omega <^{\mathsf{w}}_{\mathcal{R}} \omega_2,$$
$$\omega_1 <^{\mathsf{w}}_{\mathcal{R}} \omega \quad \text{iff} \quad \omega_2 <^{\mathsf{w}}_{\mathcal{R}} \omega.$$

Proof. The claim follows from $\xi^i(\omega_1) = \xi^i(\omega_2)$ for all $i \in \{0,\dots,k\}$.   □

In general, the relation $<^{\mathsf{w}}_{\mathcal{R}}$ cannot be obtained from a ranking function.

Lemma 2. *There exists a knowledge base* $\mathcal{R}$ *such that there is no ranking function* $\kappa : \Omega \to \mathbb{N}_0^\infty$ *with* $\omega_1 <^{\mathsf{w}}_{\mathcal{R}} \omega_2$ *iff* $\kappa(\omega_1) < \kappa(\omega_2)$.

Proof. The proof is by contradiction. Assume there is a ranking function $\kappa : \Omega \to \mathbb{N}_0^\infty$ with $\omega_1 <^{\mathsf{w}}_{\mathcal{R}} \omega_2$ iff $\kappa(\omega_1) < \kappa(\omega_2)$ for $\mathcal{R}_{bird}$. For $<^{\mathsf{w}}_{\mathcal{R}}$ (cf. Fig. 1) we have $p\,b\,f \not<^{\mathsf{w}}_{\mathcal{R}_{bird}} p\,\overline{b}\,f$ and $p\,\overline{b}\,f \not<^{\mathsf{w}}_{\mathcal{R}_{bird}} p\,b\,f$ and furthermore $p\,b\,f \not<^{\mathsf{w}}_{\mathcal{R}_{bird}} p\,\overline{b}\,\overline{f}$ and $p\,\overline{b}\,\overline{f} \not<^{\mathsf{w}}_{\mathcal{R}_{bird}} p\,b\,f$. Therefore, we obtain $\kappa(p\,b\,f) = \kappa(p\,\overline{b}\,f)$ and $\kappa(p\,b\,f) = \kappa(p\,\overline{b}\,\overline{f})$. Thus, $\kappa(p\,\overline{b}\,f) = \kappa(p\,\overline{b}\,\overline{f})$ which is a contradiction to $p\,\overline{b}\,\overline{f} <^{\mathsf{w}}_{\mathcal{R}_{bird}} p\,\overline{b}\,f$.   □

Let us end this subsection by proving that $<^{\mathsf{w}}_{\mathcal{R}}$ defines a strict partial order.

Lemma 3. *The relation* $<^{\mathsf{w}}_{\mathcal{R}}$ *is irreflexive, asymmetric, and transitive, meaning that* $<^{\mathsf{w}}_{\mathcal{R}}$ *is a strict partial order.*

Proof. Condition (11) immediately yields that $<^{\mathsf{w}}_{\mathcal{R}}$ is irreflexive and asymmetric. It remains to show that $<^{\mathsf{w}}_{\mathcal{R}}$ is transitive. Define $a := \max\{i \in \{0,\dots,k\} \mid \xi^i(\omega_1) \neq \xi^i(\omega_2)\}$ and $b := \max\{i \in \{0,\dots,k\} \mid \xi^i(\omega_2) \neq \xi^i(\omega_3)\}$. Then $\omega_1 <^{\mathsf{w}}_{\mathcal{R}} \omega_2$ and $\omega_2 <^{\mathsf{w}}_{\mathcal{R}} \omega_3$ is equivalent to $\xi^a(\omega_1) \subsetneq \xi^a(\omega_2)$ and $\xi^b(\omega_2) \subsetneq \xi^b(\omega_3)$.

If $a = b$ then $\xi^a(\omega_1) \subsetneq \xi^a(\omega_3)$ and $a = \max\{i \in \{0,\dots,k\} \mid \xi^i(\omega_1) \neq \xi^i(\omega_3)\}$ and so $\omega_1 <^{\mathsf{w}}_{\mathcal{R}} \omega_3$. If $a < b$ then $\xi^b(\omega_1) \subsetneq \xi^b(\omega_3)$ and $b = \max\{i \in \{0,\dots,k\} \mid \xi^i(\omega_1) \neq \xi^i(\omega_3)\}$ and so $\omega_1 <^{\mathsf{w}}_{\mathcal{R}} \omega_3$. If $a > b$ then $\xi^i(\omega_2) = \xi^i(\omega_3)$ for all $i \in \{b+1,\dots,k\}$ and $b+1 \leqslant a \leqslant k$; therefore $\xi^a(\omega_1) \subsetneq \xi^a(\omega_3)$ and $a = \max\{i \in \{0,\dots,k\} \mid \xi^i(\omega_1) \neq \xi^i(\omega_3)\}$ and so $\omega_1 <^{\mathsf{w}}_{\mathcal{R}} \omega_3$.   □

4   System W

The preferred structure $<^{\mathsf{w}}_{\mathcal{R}}$ on worlds for a knowledge base $\mathcal{R}$ is defined using both the tolerance information provided by the inclusion-maximal ordered partition $OP(\mathcal{R})$ and information on the set of falsified conditionals. Inference based on $<^{\mathsf{w}}_{\mathcal{R}}$ is called *system W* inference and is defined as follows.

Definition 6 (system W, $\vdash\!\!\!\sim^{\text{w}}_{\mathcal{R}}$). *Let $\mathcal{R}$ be a knowledge base and A, B be formulas. Then B is a* system W inference *from A (in the context of $\mathcal{R}$), denoted*

$$A \vdash\!\!\!\sim^{\text{w}}_{\mathcal{R}} B \quad iff \quad \forall \omega' \in \Omega_{A\overline{B}} \,\exists \omega \in \Omega_{AB} \; \omega <^{\text{w}}_{\mathcal{R}} \omega'. \tag{14}$$

A consequence of this definition is that system W inference is as tractable as system Z because the preferred structure on worlds is obtained directly from the ordered partition of $\mathcal{R}$ and the verification/falsification behavior of $\mathcal{R}$. We apply the definition of system W to our running example.

Example 3 ($\mathcal{R}_{bird}$, cont.). Consider again $\mathcal{R}_{bird}$ from Example 1. Let us show that for $A = b\,f$ and $B = \overline{p}$ we have $A \vdash\!\!\!\sim^{\text{w}}_{\mathcal{R}_{bird}} B$, i.e., that flying birds are usually not penguins. Due to $\xi(b\,f\,\overline{p}) = \varnothing$ and $\xi(b\,f\,p) = \{r_2, r_3\}$ (see Table 1) it follows that $b\,f\,\overline{p} <^{\text{w}}_{\mathcal{R}_{bird}} b\,f\,p$. Therefore, since $\Omega_{AB} = \{b\,f\,\overline{p}\}$ and $\Omega_{A\overline{B}} = \{b\,f\,p\}$, from (14) it follows that indeed $b\,f \vdash\!\!\!\sim^{\text{w}}_{\mathcal{R}_{bird}} \overline{p}$.

Note that $b\,f \vdash\!\!\!\sim^{\text{c}}_{\mathcal{R}_{bird}} \overline{p}$, i.e., this inference is also a skeptical c-inference (cf. [5, Example 5]). Therefore, Example 3 presents a c-inference that is also a system W inference. The following proposition tells us that $A \vdash\!\!\!\sim^{\text{c}}_{\mathcal{R}} B$ always implies $A \vdash\!\!\!\sim^{\text{w}}_{\mathcal{R}} B$.

Proposition 3 (system W captures c-inference). *Let $\mathcal{R}$ be a consistent knowledge base. Then we have for all formulas $A, B \in \mathcal{L}$:*

$$If \quad A \vdash\!\!\!\sim^{\text{c}}_{\mathcal{R}} B \quad then \quad A \vdash\!\!\!\sim^{\text{w}}_{\mathcal{R}} B. \tag{15}$$

Proof. The proof of (15) is by contraposition. Assume $A \not\vdash\!\!\!\sim^{\text{w}}_{\mathcal{R}} B$ and thus

$$\exists \omega' \in \Omega_{A\overline{B}} \,\forall \omega \in \Omega_{AB} \; \omega \not<^{\text{w}}_{\mathcal{R}} \omega'. \tag{16}$$

Our goal is to show $A \not\vdash\!\!\!\sim^{\text{c}}_{\mathcal{R}} B$. Let us fix $\omega' \in \Omega_{A\overline{B}}$ such that (16) holds. Let us define $\Omega_V := \Omega_{AB}$. Then $\omega \not<^{\text{w}}_{\mathcal{R}} \omega'$ for all $\omega \in \Omega_V$. Due to Lemma 2 there exists a c-representation $\kappa_{\vec{\eta}} \in \mathcal{O}(CR(\mathcal{R}))$ such that $\kappa_{\vec{\eta}}(\omega') \leqslant \kappa_{\vec{\eta}}(\omega)$ for all $\omega \in \Omega_{AB}$. This means that $A \not\vdash\!\!\!\sim^{\kappa_{\vec{\eta}}}_{\mathcal{R}} B$ and so indeed $A \not\vdash\!\!\!\sim^{\text{c}}_{\mathcal{R}} B$. $\qquad\square$

Furthermore, every system Z inference is also a system W inference.

Proposition 4 (system W captures system Z). *Let $\mathcal{R}$ be a consistent knowledge base. Then we have for all formulas $A, B \in \mathcal{L}$*

$$If \quad A \vdash\!\!\!\sim^{\text{Z}}_{\mathcal{R}} B \quad then \quad A \vdash\!\!\!\sim^{\text{w}}_{\mathcal{R}} B. \tag{17}$$

Proof. Inspecting (4) and (11) and given any worlds $\omega, \omega' \in \Omega$, we conclude that $\kappa^Z(\omega) < \kappa^Z(\omega')$ implies $\omega <^{\text{w}}_{\mathcal{R}} \omega'$. Therefore, comparing (3), applied to the ranking function κ^Z, with (14), shows that (17) is fulfilled. $\qquad\square$

In [16], a preference relation on worlds is defined that is based on structural information by preferring a world ω to a world ω' if ω falsifies fewer conditionals than ω' and ω' falsifies at least all conditionals falsified by ω. Using this preference relation, the following entailment relation along the scheme as given by (3) is obtained; we present the definition from [16] in a slightly modified form adapted to our notion $\xi(\omega)$ for the set of conditionals from $\mathcal{R}$ falsified by ω.

Definition 7 ($\sigma_{\mathcal{R}}$-structural inference [16]**).** *Let $\mathcal{R} = \{r_1, \ldots, r_n\}$ with $r_i = (B_i|A_i)$ for $i = 1, \ldots, n$ be a knowledge base, A, B formulas, and let $<_{\mathcal{R}}^{\sigma}$ be the relation on worlds given by $\omega <_{\mathcal{R}}^{\sigma} \omega'$ iff $\xi(\omega) \subsetneq \xi(\omega')$. Then B can be structurally inferred, or $\sigma_{\mathcal{R}}$-inferred, from A, written as*

$$A \mathrel{\vdash\!\!\!\sim}_{\mathcal{R}}^{\sigma} B \quad \textit{iff} \quad \forall \omega' \in \Omega_{A\overline{B}} \; \exists \omega \in \Omega_{AB} \; \omega <_{\mathcal{R}}^{\sigma} \omega'. \tag{18}$$

We can show that every $\sigma_{\mathcal{R}}$-structural inference is also a system W inference.

Proposition 5 (system W captures $\sigma_{\mathcal{R}}$-structural inference). *Let $\mathcal{R}$ be a consistent knowledge base. Then we have for all formulas $A, B \in \mathcal{L}$*

$$\textit{If} \quad A \mathrel{\vdash\!\!\!\sim}_{\mathcal{R}}^{\sigma} B \quad \textit{then} \quad A \mathrel{\vdash\!\!\!\sim}_{\mathcal{R}}^{\mathrm{w}} B. \tag{19}$$

Proof. Inspecting (11) and the definition of $<_{\mathcal{R}}^{\sigma}$, we conclude that $\omega <_{\mathcal{R}}^{\sigma} \omega'$ implies $\omega <_{\mathcal{R}}^{\mathrm{w}} \omega'$ for all $\omega, \omega' \in \Omega$. Combining (11) and (18) yields (19). □

The following proposition summarizes Propositions 3, 4, and 5 and shows aditionally that system W strictly extends skeptical c-inference, system Z, and structural inference by licensing more entailments than each of these three inference modes.

Proposition 6 (system W) *For every consistent knowledge base $\mathcal{R}$*

$$\mathrel{\vdash\!\!\!\sim}_{\mathcal{R}}^{c} \subseteq \mathrel{\vdash\!\!\!\sim}_{\mathcal{R}}^{\mathrm{w}}, \quad \mathrel{\vdash\!\!\!\sim}_{\mathcal{R}}^{Z} \subseteq \mathrel{\vdash\!\!\!\sim}_{\mathcal{R}}^{\mathrm{w}} \quad \textit{and} \quad \mathrel{\vdash\!\!\!\sim}_{\mathcal{R}}^{\sigma} \subseteq \mathrel{\vdash\!\!\!\sim}_{\mathcal{R}}^{\mathrm{w}}. \tag{20}$$

Furthermore, there are knowledge bases $\mathcal{R}_1, \mathcal{R}_2, \mathcal{R}_3$ such that the inclusions in (20) are strict, i.e.:

$$\mathrel{\vdash\!\!\!\sim}_{\mathcal{R}_1}^{c} \subsetneq \mathrel{\vdash\!\!\!\sim}_{\mathcal{R}_1}^{\mathrm{w}} \tag{21}$$

$$\mathrel{\vdash\!\!\!\sim}_{\mathcal{R}_2}^{Z} \subsetneq \mathrel{\vdash\!\!\!\sim}_{\mathcal{R}_2}^{\mathrm{w}} \tag{22}$$

$$\mathrel{\vdash\!\!\!\sim}_{\mathcal{R}_3}^{\sigma} \subsetneq \mathrel{\vdash\!\!\!\sim}_{\mathcal{R}_3}^{\mathrm{w}} \tag{23}$$

Proof. The inclusions in (20) are shown in Propositions 3, 4, and 5. Thus, we are left to show that the inclusions in (21)–(23) are strict.

1. For proving the strictness part of (21), consider the knowledge base $\mathcal{R}^* = \{(b|a), (b\,c|a)\}$ whose verification/falsification behavior is given by Table 2. First, due to $\xi(a\,b\,\overline{c}) = \{(b\,c|a)\} \subsetneq \{(b|a), (b\,c|a)\} = \xi(a\,\overline{b}\,\overline{c})$, we obtain $a\,\overline{c} \mathrel{\vdash\!\!\!\sim}_{\mathcal{R}^*}^{\mathrm{w}} b$. Making use of the verification/falsification behavior stated in Table 2, for $CR(\mathcal{R}^*)$ we obtain $\eta_1 > -\eta_2$ and $\eta_2 > 0$. Now consider the solution vector $\vec{\eta} = (\eta_1, \eta_2) = (0, 1)$. For the associated c-representation $\kappa_{\vec{\eta}}$ (see Table 2) we then obtain $\kappa_{\vec{\eta}}(a\,b\,\overline{c}) = \eta_2 = \eta_1 + \eta_2 = \kappa_{\vec{\eta}}(a\,\overline{b}\,\overline{c})$ and thus $a\,\overline{c} \mathrel{\not\vdash\!\!\!\sim}_{\mathcal{R}^*}^{c} b$.

Table 2. Verification/falsification behavior and (generic) c-representation of the knowledge base $\mathcal{R}^*$ in the proof of Proposition 6; (v) indicates verification, (f) falsification and $(-)$ non-applicability.

ω	abc	$ab\overline{c}$	$a\overline{b}c$	$a\overline{b}\,\overline{c}$	$\overline{a}bc$	$\overline{a}b\overline{c}$	$\overline{a}\,\overline{b}c$	$\overline{a}\,\overline{b}\,\overline{c}$
$r_1 = (b\|a)$	v	v	f	f	$-$	$-$	$-$	$-$
$r_2 = (bc\|a)$	v	f	f	f	$-$	$-$	$-$	$-$
$\kappa_{\vec{\tau}}(\omega)$	0	η_2	$\eta_1 + \eta_2$	$\eta_1 + \eta_2$	0	0	0	0

2. For proving the strictness part of (22), consider the knowledge base $\mathcal{R}_{bird}$ from Example 1. Let us show that for $A = p\overline{b}$ and $B = \overline{f}$ we have $A \mathrel{\mathop{\vdash}\limits^{w}_{\mathcal{R}_{bird}}} B$, i.e., that penguins which are no bird usually do not fly. According to Example 2, we have $p\overline{b}\,\overline{f} <^{w}_{\mathcal{R}_{bird}} p\overline{b}f$. Therefore, since $\Omega_{AB} = \{p\overline{b}\,\overline{f}\}$ and $\Omega_{A\overline{B}} = \{p\overline{b}f\}$ it follows from (14) that indeed $p\overline{b} \mathrel{\mathop{\vdash}\limits^{w}_{\mathcal{R}_{bird}}} \overline{f}$. Looking at Table 1, we observe $\kappa^Z(AB) = 2 = \kappa^Z(A\overline{B})$ and thus $p\overline{b} \mathrel{\mathop{\not\vdash}\limits^{Z}_{\mathcal{R}_{bird}}} \overline{f}$.

3. For proving the strictness part of (23), consider again $\mathcal{R}_{bird}$ with $OP(\mathcal{R}_{bird}) = (\mathcal{R}_0, \mathcal{R}_1)$ where $\mathcal{R}_0 = \{(f|b)\}$ and $\mathcal{R}_1 = \{(\overline{f}|p), (\overline{f}|bp), (b|p)\}$ (cf. Example 2). For $\omega = pbf$, we get (cf. Table 1) that $\xi(\omega) = \{(\overline{f}|p), (\overline{f}|pb)\}$, $\xi(p\overline{b}\,\overline{f}) = \{(f|b)\}$ and $\xi(p\overline{b}\,\overline{f}) = \{(b|p)\}$. Thus, there is no world $\omega' \in \Omega$ with $\omega' \models p\overline{f}$ and $\omega' <^{\sigma}_{\mathcal{R}_{bird}} \omega$ (which is equivalent to $\xi(\omega') \subsetneq \xi(\omega)$). Therefore, $p \mathrel{\mathop{\not\vdash}\limits^{\sigma}_{\mathcal{R}_{bird}}} \overline{f}$. To show $p \mathrel{\mathop{\vdash}\limits^{w}_{\mathcal{R}}} \overline{f}$ fix any $\omega \in \Omega$ with $\omega \models pf$. Then $(\overline{f}|p) \in \xi(\omega)$ where $(\overline{f}|p) \in \mathcal{R}_1$. For $\omega' = pb\overline{f}$ we have $\omega' <^{w}_{\mathcal{R}} \omega$ due to $\xi(\omega') = \{(f|b)\}$ where $(f|b) \in \mathcal{R}_0$. Thus, indeed $p \mathrel{\mathop{\vdash}\limits^{w}_{\mathcal{R}}} \overline{f}$. □

After comparing system W with other established inference methods let us deal with further of its properties.

Proposition 7. *In general, system W inference cannot be obtained from a ranking function, i.e., there exists a knowledge base $\mathcal{R}$ such that there is no ranking function $\kappa : \Omega \to \mathbb{N}_0^\infty$ with $\mathrel{\mathop{\vdash}\limits^{w}_{\mathcal{R}}} = \mathrel{\mathop{\vdash}\limits^{\kappa}}$.*

Proof. This follows immediately from Lemma 2. □

Nonmonotonic inference relations are usually evaluated by means of properties. In particular, the axiom system P [1,19] provides an important standard for plausible, nonmonotonic inferences.

Proposition 8. *System W inference satisfies System P.*

Proof. According to Lemma 3, $<^{w}_{\mathcal{R}}$ is a strict transitive relation. Furthermore, since Ω is finite, the triple $\mathcal{M}^w(\mathcal{R}) = [\Omega, \models, <^{w}_{\mathcal{R}}]$ is a stoppered classical preferential model [22]. Thus, the definition of system W given by (14) in Definition 6 ensures that system W inference is a preferential inference, hence satisfying system P (cf. [19,22]). □

An inference relation suffers from the *Drowning Problem* [9,23] if it does not allow to infer properties of a superclass for a subclass that is exceptional with respect to another property because the respective conditional is "drowned" by others. E.g., penguins are exceptional birds with respect to flying but not with respect to having wings. So we would reasonably expect that penguins have wings.

Example 4 ($\mathcal{R}^*_{bird}$[5]). We extend the alphabet $\Sigma = \{p, b, f\}$ of our running example knowledge base $\mathcal{R}_{bird}$ from Example 1 with the variable w for *having wings*, the variable a for *being airborne*, and the variable r for *being red*, obtaining the alphabet $\Sigma^* = \{p, b, f, w, a, r\}$. We use the knowledge base

$$\mathcal{R}^*_{bird} = \{(f|b), (\overline{f}|p), (b|p), (w|b), (a|f)\}$$

where the conditional $(w|b)$ encodes the rule that birds usually have wings, and the conditional $(a|f)$ encodes the rule that flying things are usually airborne; the other three conditionals $(f|b)$, $(\overline{f}|p)$, $(b|p)$ are the same as in $\mathcal{R}_{bird}$.

The Drowning Problem distinguishes between inference relations that allow for subclass inheritance only for non-exceptional subclasses (like system Z inference) and inference relations that allow for subclass inheritance for exceptional subclasses (like skeptical c-inference [5, Observation 1] and inference with minimal c-representations, cf. [16,26]). As an illustration for the drowning problem, consider $\mathcal{R}^*_{bird}$ from Example 4. Here, we have $\kappa^Z(p\,\overline{w}) = 1 = \kappa^Z(p\,w)$, and consequently $p \not\hspace{-2pt}\sim^Z_{\mathcal{R}^*_{bird}} w$ (cf. [5, Example 9]), illustrating that system Z suffers from the drowning problem. In contrast, the following observation shows that system W licenses the inference that penguins usually have wings and thus avoids this drowning phenomenon.

Observation 1 *System W inference does not suffer from the drowning problem in Example 4, i.e., we have $p \hspace{1pt}\sim^W_{\mathcal{R}^*_{bird}} w$.*

Proof. The inclusion-maximal partition $OP(\mathcal{R}^*_{bird}) = (\mathcal{R}_0, \mathcal{R}_1)$ of $\mathcal{R}^*_{bird}$ in Example 4 is given by $\mathcal{R}_0 = \{(f|b), (w|b), (a|f)\}$ and $\mathcal{R}_1 = \{(\overline{f}|p), (b|p)\}$.

Consider $\omega \in \Omega$ with $\omega \models p\overline{w}$. Choose an arbitrary $\omega' \in \Omega$ with $\omega' \models p\,b\,\overline{f}w$. We will show $\omega' <^W_{\mathcal{R}^*_{bird}} \omega$. Obviously, ω' falsifies only the conditional $(f|b)$ which is in $\mathcal{R}_0$, written as a formula $\xi(\omega) = \{(f|b)\}$. Since $\omega \models p\overline{w}$, we can distinguish the following two cases:

(i) If $\omega \models p\,\overline{w}\,f$ then the conditional $(\overline{f}|p)$ from $\mathcal{R}_1$ is falsified.
(ii) If $\omega \models p\,\overline{w}\,\overline{f}$ then we can again distinguish two cases:
   (a) If $\omega \models p\,\overline{w}\,\overline{f}\,\overline{b}$ then $(b|p)$ from $\mathcal{R}_1$ is falsified.
   (b) If $\omega \models p\,\overline{w}\,\overline{f}\,b$ then at least $(f|b), (w|b)$ (both from $\mathcal{R}_0$) are falsified.

Due to (11), we thus get $\omega' <^W_{\mathcal{R}^*_{bird}} \omega$ in every case, implying $p \hspace{1pt}\sim^W_{\mathcal{R}^*_{bird}} w$. $\qquad\square$

5   Conclusions and Future Work

In this paper, we introduced system W and its underlying preferred structure of worlds. System W inference captures both System Z inference and skeptical c-inference and exhibits desirable properties. For instance, in contrast to system Z, it avoids the drowning problem. In contrast to skeptical c-inference, it does not require to solve a complex constraint satisfaction problem, but is as tractable as system Z because the preferred structure on worlds is obtained directly from the ordered partition of $\mathcal{R}$ and the verification/falsification behavior of $\mathcal{R}$. In future work, we will empirically evalute system W with the reasoning platform InfOCF [3] and investigate further inference properties of it.

References

1. Adams, E.W.: The Logic of Conditionals: An Application of Probability to Deductive Logic. Synthese Library. Springer, Dordrecht (1975)
2. Beierle, C., Eichhorn, C., Kern-Isberner, G.: Skeptical inference based on C-representations and its characterization as a constraint satisfaction problem. In: Gyssens, M., Simari, G. (eds.) FoIKS 2016. LNCS, vol. 9616, pp. 65–82. Springer, Cham (2016). https://doi.org/10.1007/978-3-319-30024-5_4
3. Beierle, C., Eichhorn, C., Kutsch, S.: A practical comparison of qualitative inferences with preferred ranking models. KI - Künstliche Intelligenz **31**(1), 41–52 (2017)
4. Beierle, C., Kern-Isberner, G.: Semantical investigations into nonmonotonic and probabilistic logics. Ann. Math. Artif. Intell. **65**(2–3), 123–158 (2012)
5. Beierle, C., Eichhorn, C., Kern-Isberner, G., Kutsch, S.: Properties of skeptical c-inference for conditional knowledge bases and its realization as a constraint satisfaction problem. Ann. Math. Artif. Intell. 247–275 (2018). https://doi.org/10.1007/s10472-017-9571-9
6. Beierle, C., Kutsch, S.: Computation and comparison of nonmonotonic skeptical inference relations induced by sets of ranking models for the realization of intelligent agents. Appl. Intell. **49**(1), 28–43 (2018). https://doi.org/10.1007/s10489-018-1203-5
7. Benferhat, S., Dubois, D., Prade, H.: Representing default rules in possibilistic logic. In: Proceedings 3th International Conference on Principles of Knowledge Representation and Reasoning KR 1992, pp. 673–684 (1992)
8. Benferhat, S., Dubois, D., Prade, H.: Possibilistic and standard probabilistic semantics of conditional knowledge bases. J. Logic Comput. **9**(6), 873–895 (1999)
9. Benferhat, S., Cayrol, C., Dubois, D., Lang, J., Prade, H.: Inconsistency Management and Prioritized Syntax-Based Entailment. In: Proceedings of the Thirteenth International Joint Conference on Artificial Intelligence (IJCAI 1993), vol. 1, pp. 640–647. Morgan Kaufmann Publishers, San Francisco (1993)
10. Dubois, D., Prade, H.: Conditional objects as nonmonotonic consequence relationships. Special Issue Condit. Event Algebra IEEE Trans. Syst. Man Cybern. **24**(12), 1724–1740 (1994)
11. de Finetti, B.: La prévision, ses lois logiques et ses sources subjectives. Ann. Inst. H. Poincaré **7**(1), 1–68 (1937). English translation in Studies in Subjective Probability, ed. H. Kyburg and H.E. Smokler, 1974, 93–158. New York: Wiley & Sons

12. Goldszmidt, M., Pearl, J.: On the consistency of defeasible databases. Artif. Intell. **52**(2), 121–149 (1991)
13. Goldszmidt, M., Pearl, J.: Qualitative probabilities for default reasoning, belief revision, and causal modeling. Artif. Intell. **84**(1–2), 57–112 (1996)
14. Kern-Isberner, G.: Conditionals in Nonmonotonic Reasoning and Belief Revision. LNCS (LNAI), vol. 2087. Springer, Heidelberg (2001). https://doi.org/10.1007/3-540-44600-1
15. Kern-Isberner, G.: A thorough axiomatization of a principle of conditional preservation in belief revision. Ann. Math. Artif. Intell. **40**(1–2), 127–164 (2004)
16. Kern-Isberner, G., Eichhorn, C.: Structural inference from conditional knowledge bases. Studia Logica, Special Issue Logic Probabil. Reason. Uncertain Environ. **102**(4), 751–769 (2014). http://dx.doi.org/10.1007/s11225-013-9503-6
17. Komo, C., Beierle, C.: Realization of nonmonotonic reasoning from conditional knowledge bases by skeptical c-inference and by preferred structures on worlds. Manuscript, May 2020. 32 pp
18. Komo, C., Beierle, C.: Upper and lower bounds for finite domain constraints to realize skeptical c-inference over conditional knowledge bases. In: International Symposium on Artificial Intelligence and Mathematics (ISAIM 2020), Fort Lauderdale, FL, USA, January 6–8 (2020)
19. Kraus, S., Lehmann, D., Magidor, M.: Nonmonotonic reasoning, preferential models and cumulative logics. Artif. Intell. **44**, 167–207 (1990)
20. Lehmann, D., Magidor, M.: What does a conditional knowledge base entail? Artif. Intell. **55**, 1–60 (1992)
21. Lewis, D.: Counterfactuals. Harvard University Press, Cambridge (1973)
22. Makinson, D.: General patterns in nonmonotonic reasoning. In: Gabbay, D., Hogger, C., Robinson, J. (eds.) Handbook of Logic in Artificial Intelligence and Logic Programming, vol. 3, pp. 35–110. Oxford University Press (1994)
23. Pearl, J.: System Z: A natural ordering of defaults with tractable applications to nonmonotonic reasoning. In: Parikh, R. (ed.) Proceedings of the 3rd conference on Theoretical Aspects of Reasoning About Knowledge (TARK 1990), pp. 121–135. Morgan Kaufmann Publishers Inc., San Francisco (1990)
24. Spohn, W.: Ordinal conditional functions: a dynamic theory of epistemic states. In: Harper W.L., Skyrms B. (eds.) Causation in Decision, Belief Change and Statistics: Proceedings of the Irvine Conference on Probability and Causation. The Western Ontario Series in Philosophy of Science, vol. 42, pp. 105–134. Springer, Dordrecht (1988). https://doi.org/10.1007/978-94-009-2865-7_6
25. Spohn, W.: The Laws of Belief: Ranking Theory and Its Philosophical Applications. Oxford University Press, Oxford (2012)
26. Thorn, P.D., Eichhorn, C., Kern-Isberner, G., Schurz, G.: Qualitative probabilistic inference with default inheritance for exceptional subclasses. In: Beierle, C., Kern-Isberner, G., Ragni, M., Stolzenburg, F. (eds.) Proceedings of the 5th Workshop on Dynamics of Knowledge and Belief (DKB-2015) and the 4th Workshop KI & Kognition (KIK-2015) co-located with 38th German Conference on Artificial Intelligence (KI-2015). CEUR Workshop Proceedings, vol. 1444 (2015)

Positive Free Higher-Order Logic and Its Automation via a Semantical Embedding

Irina Makarenko$^{(\boxtimes)}$ and Christoph Benzmüller

Freie Universität Berlin, Berlin, Germany
rna.mkr@gmail.com, c.benzmueller@gmail.com

Abstract. Free logics are a family of logics that are free of any existential assumptions. Unlike traditional classical and non-classical logics, they support an elegant modeling of nonexistent objects and partial functions as relevant for a wide range of applications in computer science, philosophy, mathematics, and natural language semantics. While free first-order logic has been addressed in the literature, free higher-order logic has not been studied thoroughly so far. The contribution of this paper includes (i) the development of a notion and definition of free higher-order logic in terms of a positive semantics (partly inspired by Farmer's partial functions version of Church's simple type theory), (ii) the provision of a faithful shallow semantical embedding of positive free higher-order logic into classical higher-order logic, (iii) the implementation of this embedding in the Isabelle/HOL proof-assistant, and (iv) the exemplary application of our novel reasoning framework for an automated assessment of Prior's paradox in positive free quantified propositional logics, i.e., a fragment of positive free higher-order logic.

Keywords: Knowledge representation and reasoning · Interactive and automated theorem proving · Philosophical foundations of AI · Partiality and undefinedness · Prior's paradox.

1 Introduction

The proper handling of nonexistence and partiality constitutes a key challenge not only for applications of formal methods in philosophy and mathematics but also for computational approaches to artificial intelligence and natural language [15–17]. In a so-called *free logic*, terms do not necessarily have to denote existing objects allowing for theories involving both partial and total functions. For that reason, free higher-order logics provide elegant solutions to the handling of some well-known paradoxes in knowledge representation and reasoning, many of which are beyond first-order logic. Moreover, free logics are well suited to represent abstract objects and to support hypothetical reasoning with fictive (and concrete) entities, and can therefore also be applied in metaphysics, ethics, and law.

© Springer Nature Switzerland AG 2020
U. Schmid et al. (Eds.): KI 2020, LNAI 12325, pp. 116–131, 2020.
https://doi.org/10.1007/978-3-030-58285-2_9

Modern interactive and automated theorem provers, however, are typically developed for classical notions of logic, in which only total functions are supported natively. Instead of investing time and effort in the development of new theorem provers for free first-order and higher-order logics, a promising approach for the implementation of such logics in existing higher-order theorem provers are *shallow semantical embeddings* (SSEs) [5]. The contribution of this paper is four-fold: We (i) developed a notion and definition of free higher-order logic in terms of a positive semantics (partly inspired by Farmer's partial functions version of Church's simple type theory [14]), (ii) provided a faithful shallow semantical embedding of positive free higher-order logic into classical higher-order logic, (iii) implemented this embedding in the Isabelle/HOL proof-assistant, and (iv) applied our novel reasoning framework for an automated assessment of Prior's paradox [29] in positive free quantified propositional logics, i.e., a fragment of positive free higher-order logic. Furthermore, we are currently integrating the results reported in this paper in the LogiKEy framework [9] for expressive, pluralistic normative reasoning.

Prior, coinciding with Kaplan [19], showed that paradoxes can arise quickly in particular philosophical theories that include both sets and propositions. Bacon, Hawthorne, and Uzquiano [3] discovered that universal instantiation, or, better, the rejection of it, is key to blocking certain paradoxes inherent in such higher-order logics. Logics without existential assumptions, i.e., free logics, just naturally reject the principle of universal instantiation. The family of paradoxes considered by Bacon et al. is represented by what we will call Prior's paradox in this paper. Prior's paradox states:

$$Q\,\forall p.\ (Q\,p \to \neg p)\ \to\ \exists p.\ (Q\,p \wedge p) \wedge \exists p.\ (Q\,p \wedge \neg p)\,.$$

Reading $Q\,p$ as, e.g., 'Kaplan says at midnight that p', Prior's paradox implies that if Kaplan says at midnight that everything Kaplan says at midnight is false, then Kaplan has said a true and a false thing at midnight. We end up with a logical self-contradiction that, as we will discuss and demonstrate later in this paper, is indeed resolved in free higher-order logic.

The paper structure is as follows: Sect. 2 briefly recaps *classical higher-order logic* (HOL), before *positive free higher-order logic* (PFHOL) is introduced in Sect. 3. Section 4 presents a faithful embedding of PFHOL in HOL, and Sect. 5 discusses its encoding in Isabelle/HOL. Section 6 applies the encoded embedding to "solve" Prior's paradox, and the last section concludes the paper.

2   Classical Higher-Order Logic (HOL)

Church's *simple type theory* [13] is a classical higher-order logic defined on top of the simply typed λ-calculus. Church's original definitions, as generalized by Henkin [18] to *extensional type theory*, the logical basis of most automated theorem proving systems for higher-order logic, are summarized below.

2.1 Syntax

The main components of Church's type theory are types and terms; more precisely, typed terms. The set of *simple types* $\mathcal{T}$ is freely generated from a set of two base types, $\{o, i\}$, and the right-associative function type constructor $\rightarrow$. Intuitively, o is the type of standard truth values, and i is the type of individuals.[1] $\mathcal{T}$ is thus defined by $\alpha, \beta := o \mid i \mid (\alpha \rightarrow \beta)$. $\mathcal{T}_o \subsetneq \mathcal{T}$, the set of *simple types of (goal) type o*, is given by $\beta := o \mid (\alpha \rightarrow \beta)$ (with $\alpha \in \mathcal{T}$). $\mathcal{T}_i \subsetneq \mathcal{T}$, the set of *simple types of (goal) type i*, is analogously given by $\beta := i \mid (\alpha \rightarrow \beta)$ (with $\alpha \in \mathcal{T}$).

Starting with some nonempty countable sets of typed constant symbols C_α and some nonempty countable sets of typed variable symbols V_α, the *simply typed terms* of HOL are defined by the following formation rules (where $\alpha, \beta \in \mathcal{T}$, $P_\alpha \in C_\alpha$, and $x_\alpha \in V_\alpha$):

$$s, t := P_\alpha \mid x_\alpha \mid (s_{\alpha \rightarrow \beta} t_\alpha)_\beta \mid (\lambda x_\alpha . s_\beta)_{\alpha \rightarrow \beta} .$$

We assume the following constant symbols to be part of our "signature": $\neg_{o \rightarrow o} \in C_{o \rightarrow o}$, $\vee_{o \rightarrow o \rightarrow o} \in C_{o \rightarrow o \rightarrow o}$, $=_{\alpha \rightarrow \alpha \rightarrow o} \in C_{\alpha \rightarrow \alpha \rightarrow o}$, $\forall_{(\alpha \rightarrow o) \rightarrow o} \in C_{(\alpha \rightarrow o) \rightarrow o}$, and $\iota_{(\alpha \rightarrow o) \rightarrow \alpha} \in C_{(\alpha \rightarrow o) \rightarrow \alpha}$ with $\alpha \in \mathcal{T}$. These constant symbols, which we call logical constants, have a fixed interpretation according to their intuitive meaning.[2] For example, the definite description $(\iota_{(\alpha \rightarrow o) \rightarrow \alpha} (\lambda x_\alpha . s_o)_{\alpha \rightarrow o})_\alpha$ denotes the unique object x of type $\alpha \in \mathcal{T}$ satisfying s_o if such an object exists and some fixed but arbitrary object of type α otherwise. It offers the possibility to define an if-then-else operator as follows (with $\alpha \in \mathcal{T}$):

$$ite_{o \rightarrow \alpha \rightarrow \alpha \rightarrow \alpha} := \lambda s_o . \lambda x_\alpha . \lambda y_\alpha . \iota(\lambda z_\alpha . (s \rightarrow z = x) \wedge (\neg s \rightarrow z = y)) .$$

Further logical constants can be introduced as abbreviations, e.g., $\wedge_{o \rightarrow o \rightarrow o} := \lambda x_o . \lambda y_o . \neg(\neg x \vee \neg y)$ and $\exists_{(\alpha \rightarrow o) \rightarrow o} := \lambda p_{\alpha \rightarrow o} . \neg \forall (\lambda x_\alpha . \neg(p x))$ with $\alpha \in \mathcal{T}$. Terms of type o are *formulas*, nonformula terms of type $\alpha \in \mathcal{T}_o$ are called *predicates*. Formulas whose leftmost nonparenthesis symbol is either equality or some nonlogical constant or variable are called *atomic formulas*. A variable x is *bound* in a term s if it occurs in the scope of the binder λ in s. x is *free* in s when it is not bound in s.

Type information may be omitted if clear from the context. For each binary operator op with prefix notation $((op\, s)\, t)$ we may fall back to its infix notation $(s\, op\, t)$ to improve readability. Likewise, the binder notation $\{\forall, \iota\}(x.\, s)$ may be used as shorthand for $\{\forall, \iota\}(\lambda x.\, s)$. In the remainder of this paper, a matching pair of parentheses in a type or term may be dropped when they are not

---

[1] There is no serious restriction to a two-valued base set so that further base types could be added [8].

[2] The set of primitive logical constants could be a much smaller one, e.g., equality is known to be sufficient in order to define all remaining logical constants of classical higher-order logic apart from the description operator [6].

necessary, assuming that, in addition to the generally known rules, $s\,t$, function application, and $\lambda x.\,s$, function abstraction, are left- and right-associative[3], respectively, and that application has a smaller scope than abstraction.

2.2   Semantics

A *frame* $D = \{D_\alpha : \alpha \in \mathcal{T}\}$ is a set of nonempty sets (or *domains*) D_α, such that D_i is chosen freely, $D_o = \{T, F\}$ where $T \neq F$ and T represents truth and F represents falsehood, and $D_{\alpha \to \beta}$ is the set of all total functions from domain D_α to codomain D_β. A *standard model* is a tuple $M = \langle D, I \rangle$ where D is a frame and I is a family of typed interpretation functions, i.e., $I = \{I_\alpha : \alpha \in \mathcal{T}\}$. Each *interpretation function* I_α maps constants of type α to appropriate objects of D_α. The logical constants $=, \neg, \vee, \forall$, and ι are interpreted as follows:

$$I(=_{\alpha \to \alpha \to o}) \;:=\; id \quad \in D_{\alpha \to \alpha \to o} \quad \text{s.t. for all } d, d' \in D_\alpha:$$
$$id(d, d') = T \text{ iff } d \text{ is identical to } d',$$

$$I(\neg_{o \to o}) \qquad := \; not \; \in D_{o \to o} \qquad \text{s.t. } not(T) = F \text{ and } not(F) = T,$$

$$I(\vee_{o \to o \to o}) \;:=\; or \quad \in D_{o \to o \to o} \quad \text{s.t. } or(v_1, v_2) = T \text{ iff } v_1 = T \text{ or } v_2 = T,$$

$$I(\forall_{(\alpha \to o) \to o}) := all \; \in D_{(\alpha \to o) \to o} \; \text{s.t. for all } f \in D_{\alpha \to o}:$$
$$all(f) = T \text{ iff } f(d) = T \text{ for all } d \in D_\alpha,$$

$$I(\iota_{(\alpha \to o) \to \alpha}) := desc \in D_{(\alpha \to o) \to \alpha} \; \text{s.t. for all } f \in D_{\alpha \to o}:$$
$$desc(f) = d \in D_\alpha \text{ if } f(d) = T \text{ and for}$$
$$\text{all } d' \in D_\alpha: \text{ if } f(d') = T, \text{ then } d' = d,$$
$$\text{otherwise } desc(f) = e \text{ where } e \text{ is a}$$
$$\text{fixed but arbitrary object in } D_\alpha.$$

g_α is a *variable assignment* mapping variables of type α to corresponding objects in D_α. Thus, $g = \{g_\alpha : \alpha \in \mathcal{T}\}$ is a family of typed variable assignments. $g\,[x \to d]$ denotes the variable assignment that is identical to g, except for variable x_α, which is now mapped to d_α. The *value* $[\![\,s_\alpha\,]\!]^{M,g}$ of a HOL term s_α in a standard model M under variable assignment g is an object $d \in D_\alpha$ and defined as follows:

$$[\![\,P_\alpha\,]\!]^{M,g} \qquad\qquad := \quad I(P_\alpha),$$

$$[\![\,x_\alpha\,]\!]^{M,g} \qquad\qquad := \quad g(x_\alpha),$$

$$[\![\,(s_{\alpha \to \beta}\,t_\alpha)_\beta\,]\!]^{M,g} \quad := \quad [\![\,s_{\alpha \to \beta}\,]\!]^{M,g}([\![\,t_\alpha\,]\!]^{M,g}),$$

$$[\![\,(\lambda x_\alpha.\,s_\beta)_{\alpha \to \beta}\,]\!]^{M,g} \;:= \quad \text{the function } f \text{ from } D_\alpha \text{ into } D_\beta$$
$$\text{s.t. for all } d \in D_\alpha: f(d) = [\![\,s_\beta\,]\!]^{M,g[x \to d]}.$$

A formula s_o is *true* in a standard model M under variable assignment g, denoted by $M, g \models s$, if and only if $[\![\,s_o\,]\!]^{M,g} = T$. A formula s_o is *valid in* M, denoted by

---

[3] For an abstraction, being right-associative means that its body extends as far right as possible. For instance, $\lambda x.s\,t$ corresponds to $\lambda x.\,(s\,t)$ and not $(\lambda x.\,s)\,t$.

$M \vDash s$, if and only if $M, g \vDash s$ for all variable assignments g. Moreover, a formula s_o is *(generally) valid*, denoted by $\vDash s_o$, if and only if s_o is valid in all standard models M.

As a consequence of Gödel's incompleteness theorem, Church's type theory with respect to the ordinary semantics based on standard models is incomplete. However, Henkin [18] introduced a generalized notion of a model in which the function domains contain enough but not necessarily all functions: In a standard model, a domain $D_{\alpha \to \beta}$ is defined as the set of all total functions from D_α to D_β. In a *Henkin model* (or *general model*) the domains $D_{\alpha \to \beta}$ in the underlying frame are some nonempty sets of total functions, $D_{\alpha \to \beta} \subseteq \{ f \mid f : D_\alpha \to D_\beta \}$, containing at least sufficiently many of them such that the valuation function remains total.

For Henkin's generalized notion of semantics, sound and complete proof calculi exist [1,2,18]. Any standard model is obviously also a Henkin model. Hence, any formula that is valid in all Henkin models must be valid in all standard models as well. Therefore, the semantics employed in this paper are Henkin's general models. For truth, validity, and general validity in a Henkin model, the above definitions are adapted in the obvious way.

For further details on the semantics of HOL, we refer to the literature [6,7].

3   Positive Free Higher-Order Logic (PFHOL)

Free logic, a term coined by Lambert [21], refers to a family of logics that are free of existential presuppositions in general and with respect to the denotation of terms in particular. Terms of free logic may denote existent[4] objects, but are not necessarily required to do so. Quantification and definite descriptions are treated as in classical logic, meaning that quantifiers and description operators range over the existing objects only. In the following, we will pursue an *inner-outer dual-domain approach* for the representation of the relationship between existing and nonexisting objects. The inner-outer dual-domain approach postulates that some domain D contains both existing and nonexisting objects whereas the quantification domain E, a subdomain of D, contains solely the existing ones.

A free logic is known to be positive if it allows atomic formulas containing terms that refer to nonexisting objects to be either true or false [22,32]. For example, even though $isHuman(Pegasus)$ is, in general, denied, $hasLegs(Pegasus)$ may be regarded as a valid formula since the denotation of $Pegasus$ is a mythological creature that is usually depicted in the form of a winged horse (with legs).

3.1   Syntax

Except for terms, all definitions and terminology for PFHOL correspond to those presented in Sect. 2.1 for HOL. Simply typed terms of PFHOL have essentially

---

[4] In the paper at hand, the terms existent/existing and defined are used interchangeably even though a differentiation is advisable. The same applies to the terms nonexistent/nonexisting and undefined.

the same structure as terms of HOL, but we additionally include the nonlogical constant symbol $E!_{\alpha \to o} \in C_{\alpha \to o}$ in the "signature". Apart from that, the interpretation of the universal quantifier changes since free logical quantification is traditionally limited to existing objects only. Moreover, not only quantifiers have existential import: Definite descriptions of free logic denote a unique object satisfying some property if and only if such an object exists and is defined [4].

3.2   Semantics

The following proposal of a positive semantics for free higher-order logic combines two sophisticated concepts that go back to Benzmüller and Scott [10] and Farmer [14].

While a frame is defined exactly as in HOL, a *subframe* $E = \{E_\alpha : \alpha \in \mathcal{T}\}$ is a set of nonempty sets (or *domains*) E_α such that $E_\alpha \subsetneq D_\alpha$ for each $\alpha \in \mathcal{T}_i$ and $E_\alpha = D_\alpha$ for each $\alpha \in \mathcal{T}_o$.[5] We assume, inspired by Farmer, that $\bot_\alpha \in D_\alpha \setminus E_\alpha$ for all $\alpha \in \mathcal{T}_i$ with $\bot_{\alpha \to \beta}(d) := \bot_\beta$ for all $d \in D_\alpha$. Furthermore, each domain D_α with $\alpha \in \mathcal{T}_o$ contains the element F_α defined inductively by $F_o := F$ and $F_{\alpha \to \beta}(d) := F_\beta$ for all $d \in D_\alpha$. The purpose of these objects is to propagate the nondenotation or falsehood of a term up through all terms containing it with $\bot_i$ symbolizing 'the undefinedness' among individuals. Their intended use will be explained in the further course of this section. Exemplary schematics of some of the domains can be found in Fig. 1. A *standard model* is a triple $M = \langle D, E, I \rangle$ where D is a frame, E is a subframe, and I is a family of typed interpretation functions, i.e., $I = \{I_\alpha : \alpha \in \mathcal{T}\}$. Each *interpretation function* I_α maps constants of type α to appropriate elements of D_α. The nonlogical constant $E!$ and the logical constants $=, \neg, \vee, \forall$, and ι are interpreted as follows:

$I(E!_{\alpha \to o}) \quad := ex \quad \in E_{\alpha \to o} \qquad$ s.t. for all $d \in D_\alpha$: $ex(d) = \mathrm{T}$ iff $d \in E_\alpha$,

$I(=_{\alpha \to \alpha \to o}) \quad := id \quad \in E_{\alpha \to \alpha \to o} \qquad$ s.t. for all $d, d' \in D_\alpha$:
$$id(d, d') = \mathrm{T} \text{ iff } d \text{ is identical to } d',$$

$I(\neg_{o \to o}) \quad := not \ \in E_{o \to o} \qquad$ s.t. $not(\mathrm{T}) = \mathrm{F}$ and $not(\mathrm{F}) = \mathrm{T}$,

$I(\vee_{o \to o \to o}) \quad := or \ \in E_{o \to o \to o} \qquad$ s.t. $or(v_1, v_2) = \mathrm{T}$ iff $v_1 = \mathrm{T}$ or $v_2 = \mathrm{T}$,

$I(\forall_{(\alpha \to o) \to o}) := all \ \in E_{(\alpha \to o) \to o}$ s.t. for all $f \in D_{\alpha \to o}$:
$$all(f) = \mathrm{T} \text{ iff } f(d) = \mathrm{T} \text{ for all } d \in E_\alpha,$$

$I(\iota_{(\alpha \to o) \to \alpha}) := desc \in E_{(\alpha \to o) \to \alpha}$ s.t. for all $f \in D_{\alpha \to o}$:
$$desc(f) = d \in E_\alpha \text{ if } f(d) = \mathrm{T} \text{ and for}$$
$$\text{all } d' \in E_\alpha: \text{ if } f(d') = \mathrm{T}, \text{ then } d' = d,$$
$$\text{otherwise } desc(f) = \bot_\alpha \text{ if } \alpha \in \mathcal{T}_i \text{ and}$$
$$desc(f) = F_\alpha \text{ if } \alpha \in \mathcal{T}_o.$$

---

[5] Restricting nondenotation to the domain of individuals, i.e., to define $E_i \subsetneq D_i$ and for all $\alpha \neq i$, $E_\alpha = D_\alpha$, is reasonable but complicates the definition of strict functions.

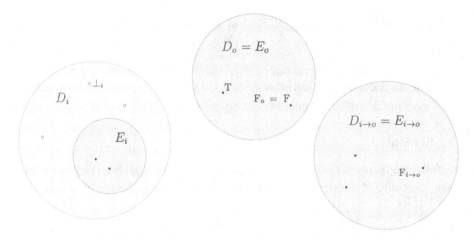

Fig. 1. Schematics of domains D_i, D_o and $D_{i\to o}$

As for HOL, g_α is a *variable assignment* mapping variables of type α to corresponding objects in D_α. The value $[\![s_\alpha]\!]^{M,g}$ of a PFHOL term s_α in a standard model M under the variable assignment g is an object $d \in D_\alpha$ and evaluated as follows:

$$[\![P_\alpha]\!]^{M,g} \quad := \quad I(P_\alpha),$$

$$[\![x_\alpha]\!]^{M,g} \quad := \quad g(x_\alpha),$$

$$[\![(s_{\alpha\to\beta}\, t_\alpha)_\beta]\!]^{M,g} \quad := \quad [\![s_{\alpha\to\beta}]\!]^{M,g}([\![t_\alpha]\!]^{M,g}),$$

$$[\![(\lambda x_\alpha.\, s_\beta)_{\alpha\to\beta}]\!]^{M,g} \quad := \quad \text{the function } f \text{ from } D_\alpha \text{ into } D_\beta$$
$$\text{s.t. for all } d \in D_\alpha\colon f(d) = [\![s_\beta]\!]^{M,g[x\to d]}.$$

The application is hereby defined in a nonstrict manner. A strict function application would be defined like this (with $\alpha \to \beta \in \mathcal{T}_i$):[6]

$$[\![(s_{\alpha\to\beta}\, t_\alpha)_\beta]\!]^{M,g} \quad := \quad \begin{cases} [\![s_{\alpha\to\beta}]\!]^{M,g}([\![t_\alpha]\!]^{M,g}) & \text{if } [\![t_\alpha]\!]^{M,g} \in E_\alpha \\ \bot_\beta & \text{else.} \end{cases}$$

A strictly applied function results in undefined if one of its arguments is undefined. In simple type theory, arguments are typically processed one after another. To be able to pass the undefined state of a once applied argument through any other possibly following arguments, the objects $\bot_\alpha$ were added to each relevant domain D_α. $\bot_{\alpha\to\beta}$ maps any argument of type α to $\bot_\beta$ until $\bot_i$ appears. This way, undefinedness is transmitted until the evaluation of the application has reached its end.[7] Predicates, on the other hand, do not generally require such

---

[6] Farmer also checked the function itself for existence. But since the distinction between existing and nonexisting functions – in contrast to existing/nonexisting individuals – is unusual and not well-defined, this was left out.

[7] Restraining applications like this could lead to malformed evaluations, i.e., evaluated terms might not receive the actually intended value. For instance, the *ite* operator must be handled separately when the then- or else-parts are meant to be undefined.

a special treatment. In positive free logic, atomic formulas may denote truth or falsehood even if one of the arguments is undefined. Otherwise, the objects F_α could be used for transmitting falsehood.

The definitions of truth, validity, and general validity in PFHOL are equivalent to the corresponding definitions in HOL. The partiality characteristic for free logic is implemented by a trick that exploits the objects $\perp_\alpha$, enabling the functions in each domain $D_{\alpha \to \beta}$ to remain total. Hence, the generalization of standard models to Henkin models is equally applicable to PFHOL.[8]

4 Embedding of PFHOL in HOL

To provide a shallow semantical embedding of PFHOL in HOL, the "signature" of HOL has to be enriched with an additional nonlogical constant $E_{\alpha \to o} \in C_{\alpha \to o}$ denoting a unary predicate that enables an explicit distinction of existing and nonexisting objects in the domain D_α. In addition, we include the object e_α in each domain D_α with $\alpha \in \mathcal{T}$, which is meant to be the error object that is returned by the definite description $(\iota_{(\alpha \to o) \to \alpha}(\lambda x_\alpha. s_o)_{\alpha \to o})_\alpha$ if no such object exists. We redefine the interpretation of ι thus as follows:

$$I(\iota_{(\alpha \to o) \to \alpha}) := desc \in D_{(\alpha \to o) \to \alpha} \text{ s.t. for all } f \in D_{\alpha \to o}:$$
$$desc(f) = d \in D_\alpha \text{ if } f(d) = \text{T and for}$$
$$\text{all } d' \in D_\alpha: \text{ if } f(d') = \text{T, then } d' = d,$$
$$\text{otherwise } desc(f) = e_\alpha.$$

Obviously, for all $\alpha \in \mathcal{T}_o$: $(\forall x_\alpha. (E_{\alpha \to o} x_\alpha)_o)_o = \text{T}$, and $(E_{\alpha \to o} e_\alpha)_o = \text{F}$ for each $\alpha \in \mathcal{T}_i$. Then, a HOL term $[s_\alpha]$ is assigned to each PFHOL term s_α according to the following translation function:[9]

$$[P_\alpha] \qquad\qquad = P_\alpha,$$

$$[x_\alpha] \qquad\qquad = x_\alpha,$$

$$[(E!_{\alpha \to o} s_\alpha)_o] \qquad\qquad = (E_{\alpha \to o}[s_\alpha])_o,$$

$$[((=^F_{\alpha \to \alpha \to o} s_\alpha)_{\alpha \to o} t_\alpha)_o] \qquad = ((=^H_{\alpha \to \alpha \to o}[s_\alpha])_{\alpha \to o}[t_\alpha])_o,$$

$$[(\neg^F_{o \to o} s_o)_o] \qquad\qquad = (\neg^H_{o \to o}[s_o])_o,$$

$$[((\wedge^F_{o \to o \to o} s_o)_{o \to o} t_o)_o] \qquad = ((\wedge^H_{o \to o \to o}[s_o])_{o \to o}[t_o])_o,$$

$$[(\forall^F_{(\alpha \to o) \to o}(\lambda x_\alpha. s_o)_{\alpha \to o})_o] = (\forall^H_{(\alpha \to o) \to o}(\lambda x_\alpha. ((E x)_o \to^H_{o \to o \to o}[s_o])_o)_{\alpha \to o})_o,$$

$$[(\iota^F_{(\alpha \to o) \to \alpha}(\lambda x_\alpha. s_o)_{\alpha \to o})_\alpha] = (\iota^H_{(\alpha \to o) \to \alpha}(\lambda x_\alpha. ((E x)_o \wedge^H_{o \to o \to o}[s_o])_o)_{\alpha \to o})_\alpha,$$

$$[(s_{\alpha \to \beta} t_\alpha)_\beta] \qquad\qquad = ([s_{\alpha \to \beta}][t_\alpha])_\beta,$$

---

[8] As shown by Farmer and Schütte [31], it is possible to give a Henkin-style completeness proof for free higher-order logic defined based on a partial valuation function.

[9] A similar translation, although for free first-order logic, was provided and proved to be sound and complete by Meyer and Lambert [26] and Benzmüller and Scott [10].

$$[(\lambda x_\alpha.\ s_\beta)_{\alpha\to\beta}] \qquad = (\lambda x_\alpha.\ [s_\beta])_{\alpha\to\beta}.$$

Note that operators of HOL and PFHOL are annotated with ^{H} and ^{F}, respectively.

The main trick of this translation is that the existential import of the universal quantifier and the description operator is secured by cleverly exploiting the additional predicate $E_{\alpha\to o}$ as a guard. When mapping definite descriptions, $[(\iota^F_{(\alpha\to o)\to\alpha}(\lambda x_\alpha.\ s_o)_{\alpha\to o})_\alpha]$ could also be translated into

$$\begin{aligned}
(ite^H_{o\to\alpha\to\alpha\to\alpha} \\
(\exists^H_{(\alpha\to o)\to o}(\lambda x_\alpha. \\
(((E_{\alpha\to o}\,x_\alpha)_o \wedge^H_{o\to o\to o} [s_o])_o \\
\wedge^H_{o\to o\to o}(\forall^H_{(\alpha\to o)\to o}(\lambda y_\alpha.(((E_{\alpha\to o}\,y_\alpha)_o \to^H_{o\to o\to o} [s_o])_o \\
\to^H_{o\to o\to o}(y_\alpha =^H_{\alpha\to\alpha\to o} x_\alpha)_o)_o)_{\alpha\to o})_o)_o)_{\alpha\to o})_o \\
(\iota^H_{(\alpha\to o)\to\alpha}(\lambda x_\alpha.\ ((E_{\alpha\to o}\,x_\alpha)_o \wedge^H_{o\to o\to o} [s_o])_o)_{\alpha\to o})_\alpha \\
e_\alpha)_\alpha
\end{aligned}$$

using the if-then-else operator ite to ensure that the classical definite description definitely returns the error object e_α in case of no such existing object. But due to our previously done redefinition of the classical description operator, this is not really necessary here. Furthermore, it is noteworthy that any term $\exists^F x.\ s$ is translated into $\neg^H\forall^H x.\ E\,x \to^H \neg^H s$, which is the same as $\exists^H x.\ E\,x \wedge^H s$.

Next, we establish the faithfulness of this embedding.

Theorem 1. $\vDash_{PFHOL} s_o$ *if and only if* $\vDash_{HOL} [s_o]$.

The proof of Theorem. 1 is sketched in the appendix. For full details, see Makarenko [25].

5   Implementation in Isabelle/HOL

In this section, the encoding of the embedding from Sect. 4 in Isabelle/HOL [27] is presented. The general syntax and semantics of Isabelle/HOL can be found in the specified literature and is therefore omitted here. The encoding starts with a declaration of the base type i for individuals while the type o of HOL is associated with the predefined type **bool** in Isabelle/HOL.

typedecl i

Next, we introduce an existence predicate, E, for each of the base and compound types. In the signature, the single quote in 'a indicates that this is a type variable, meaning that the definition given hereupon is polymorphic.

consts fExistence :: "'a ⇒ bool" ("E")

Then, for each type, we define another new constant, **e**, and, in accordance with the definitions in Sect. 4, we postulate **e** of type **i** to be nonexistent and **e** of type **bool** to be **False**. Furthermore, **True** and **False** are declared as existent.

```
consts fUndef :: "'a" ("e")
axiomatization where fUndefIAxiom: "¬E (e::i)"
axiomatization where fFalsehoodBAxiom: "(e::bool) = False"
axiomatization where fTrueAxiom: "E True"
axiomatization where fFalseAxiom: "E False"
```

The embedding of the logical constants $=$, $\neg$, and $\vee$ is straightforward. PFHOL operators are presented in bold-face fonts to distinguish them from HOL operators.

```
definition fIdentity :: "'a ⇒ 'a ⇒ bool" (infixr "=" 56)
    where "φ = ψ ≡ φ = ψ"
definition fNot :: "bool ⇒ bool" ("¬_" [52]53)
    where "¬φ ≡ ¬φ"
definition fOr :: "bool ⇒ bool ⇒ bool" (infixr "V" 51)
    where "φ V ψ ≡ φ ∨ ψ"
```

Now, for the embedding of the existential import of the universal quantifier, we utilize the existence predicate **E** of the respective type exactly as discussed in Sect. 4. Isabelle/HOL supports the introduction of syntactic sugar for binding notations, which we adopt in the following definition in order to support the more intuitive notation $\forall x.\, P\, x$ instead of writing $\forall(\lambda x.\, P\, x)$ or $\forall P$.

```
definition fForall :: "('a ⇒ bool) ⇒ bool" ("∀")
    where "∀Φ ≡ ∀x. E x ⟶ Φ x"
definition fForallBinder:: "('a ⇒ bool) ⇒ bool" (binder "∀" [8]9)
    where "∀x. φ x ≡ ∀φ"
```

For encoding the PFHOL operator ι, we rely on Isabelle/HOL's own definite description operator **THE**. Unlike the embedding from Sect. 4, we must here specify the object that will be returned if there is no unique object that has the desired properties. We use Isabelle/HOL's if-then-else operator for this.

```
definition fThat :: "('a ⇒ bool) ⇒ 'a" ("I")
    where "IΦ ≡ if ∃x. E x ∧ Φ x ∧ (∀y. (E y ∧ Φ y) ⟶ (y = x))
              then THE x. E x ∧ Φ x
              else e"
definition fThatBinder:: "('a ⇒ bool) ⇒ 'a" (binder "I" [8]9)
    where "Ix. φ x ≡ Iφ"
```

We also introduced binder notation for **I**. Further PFHOL operators are embedded as abbreviations.

```
definition fAnd :: "bool ⇒ bool ⇒ bool" (infixr "∧" 52)
  where "φ ∧ ψ ≡ ¬(¬φ ∨ ¬ψ)"
definition fImp :: "bool ⇒ bool ⇒ bool" (infixr "→" 49)
  where "φ → ψ ≡ ¬φ ∨ ψ"
definition fEquiv :: "bool ⇒ bool ⇒ bool" (infixr "↔" 50)
  where "φ ↔ ψ ≡ φ → ψ ∧ ψ → φ"
definition fExists :: "('a ⇒ bool) ⇒ bool" ("∃")
  where "∃Φ ≡ ¬(∀(λy. ¬(Φ y)))"
definition fExistsBinder :: "('a ⇒ bool) ⇒ bool" (binder "∃" [8]9)
  where "∃x. φ x ≡ ∃φ"
```

For experiments, tests, and for the Isabelle/HOL sources, see Makarenko [25].[10]

6   Automated Assessment of Prior's Paradox

In our practical studies, we benefit from the fact that Isabelle/HOL integrates powerful reasoning tools such as the model finder Nitpick [11] and the meta-prover Sledgehammer [28], which, in turn, invokes third-party resolution provers, SMT solvers, and higher-order provers as Satallax [12] and Leo-III [34]. Applying Sledgehammer together with our embedding of PFHOL in HOL to Prior's paradox, we end up with the following result.

```
axiomatization where fTrueAxiom: "E True"
axiomatization where fFalseAxiom: "E False"

lemma "(Q (∀p. (Q p → (¬p)))) → ((∃p. Q p ∧ p) ∧ (∃p. Q p ∧ (¬p)))"
  using Defs by (smt fFalseAxiom fTrueAxiom)
```

The theorem is valid. But as can be clearly seen, the theorem is proved by using the axioms fTrueAxiom and fFalseAxiom imposing that both truth values are defined. We try it again without these.

```
lemma "(Q (∀p. (Q p → (¬p)))) → ((∃p. Q p ∧ p) ∧ (∃p. Q p ∧ (¬p)))"
  nitpick [user_axioms=true, show_all, format=2]
  oops
```

```
Nitpick found a counterexample for card i = 3:

  Free variable:
    Q = (λx. _)(True := True, False := True)
  Constants:
    E = (λx. _)(True := True, False := False)
    E = (λx. _)(i₁ := False, i₂ := False, i₃ := True)
    e = i₂
    e = False
```

This time the model finder Nitpick actually found a countermodel. Observe that in this countermodel one of the two truth values is undefined, namely False. This

---

[10] The Isabelle/HOL sources are also available at https://github.com/stilleben/Free-Higher-Order-Logic.

coincides with the countermodel provided by Bacon, Hawthorne, and Uzquiano. However, on a metaphysical level, it is highly questionable to shift even one of the truth values into the undefined range. Bacon et al. themselves did not find this approach for overcoming the paradox very promising and have constructed other countermodels as a substitute, which we could not reproduce with our embedding of PFHOL in HOL. For these countermodels, at least three different truth values are needed, and hence trivalent or other many-valued free higher-order logics should be used for that. Research has already been conducted in this direction, which, so far, has concentrated mainly on using deep embeddings [35] as opposed to adapting shallow ones [33].

An alternative option, already explored and implemented by Makarenko [25], is to embed and automate the free semantics specially developed by Bacon et al. to overcome this particular paradox. The semantical theory they introduced is a positive free higher-order logic based on set theory where only (possible) worlds are taken as primitive, and the validity of propositions is then modeled as world dependent. The embedding of this 'modal' positive free logic has proved useful and adequate in dealing with the paradox, as was confirmed by verifying further, more reasonable countermodels to Prior's paradox. Moreover, it is worth mentioning that there is currently a growing interest to further adapt the definitions of Sect. 3 and the embedding of Sect. 4 to develop proper notions of modal and intensional positive free higher-order logic and to embed them faithfully in HOL. An interesting application, and related ongoing work, includes the exploitation of free logic machinery in Kirchner's embedding of hyperintensional second-order modal logic and abstract object theory in Isabelle/HOL [20, Footnote 7 and Sect. 5] utilized for the encoding, assessment, and further investigation of Zalta's *Principia Logico-Metaphysica* [36].

7   Conclusion

Positive free higher-order logic and its characteristics of nonexistent objects and partial functions have been faithfully represented in an adequately modified version of simple type theory. A key point of the inner-outer dual-domain approach is that partiality is only simulated instead of inherently accomodating it, such that a classical logic environment could be maintained. Subsequently, our embedding was implemented in Isabelle/HOL to support interactive and automated reasoning. We applied this embedding to Prior's paradox and reconstructed some of the results Bacon, Hawthorne, and Uzquiano provided in dealing with the theorem. This shows that certain paradoxes can fruitfully be addressed in free higher-order logic. However, we were also able to verify that two-valued free logic is not enough to resolve the issue. Our ongoing research has therefore also been concerned with other variants of free logic. Traditionally, the family of free logics involves not only positive free logic, but also negative [30], neutral [24], and supervaluational [4] free logic whose semantics differ in the way how atomic formulas with terms that refer to nonexistent objects are treated. Furthermore, free many-valued logic or a logic with more than one notion and/or degree of nonexistence could be imagined. Some of these variants have already been successfully embedded and tested in Isabelle/HOL, as for example negative free higher-order logic and partly also supervaluational free higher-order logic [25], others are still under development. Of special interest are in particular neutral free higher-order logic and, as indicated in the previous section, many-valued (positive) free higher-order logic. Obviously, a mixture between shallow and deep embedding appears conceivable in this context and worth investigating. Fact is, nondenoting terms have always been and will always be an intriguing subject in logic, and, considering the lack of theorem provers for free logic, the development of an appropriate definition of free logic suited for embedding in HOL as well as the automation of free logic via a semantical embedding seems more important than ever.

Acknowledgments. We thank the anonymous reviewers whose insightful comments and suggestions have helped to improve this manuscript.

Appendix

For the proof of Theorem 1, we first need to elaborate how to transform a PFHOL model M into a HOL model M^*, and a PFHOL variable assignment g into a HOL variable assignment g^*. We assume that $D_\alpha^* = D_\alpha$ and $C_\alpha^* \setminus \{E_{\alpha \to o}\} = C_\alpha \setminus \{E!_{\alpha \to o}\}$ for all $\alpha \in \mathcal{T}$, and set $e_\alpha = \bot_\alpha$ for each $\alpha \in \mathcal{T}_i$ and $e_\alpha = F_\alpha$ for each $\alpha \in \mathcal{T}_o$. Then, $M = \langle D, E, I \rangle$ corresponds to the model $M^* = \langle D^*, I^* \rangle$ where I^* is a family of interpretation functions that assigns the standard interpretation to the logical constants $=, \neg, \vee, \forall,$ and ι of HOL as described in Sect. 2. For all other constants $P_\alpha \neq E_{\alpha \to o}$, $P_\alpha \in C_\alpha^*$: $I^*(P_\alpha) = I(P_\alpha)$. The nonlogical constant $E_{\alpha \to o} \in C_\alpha^*$ is interpreted as follows:

$$I^*(E_{\alpha \to o}) \quad := ex \quad \in D_{\alpha \to o}^* \qquad \text{s.t. for all } d \in D_\alpha^* : ex(d) = \mathrm{T} \text{ iff } d \in E_\alpha.$$

We further assume $V_\alpha^* = V_\alpha$ for all $\alpha \in \mathcal{T}$, and hence, for all $x_\alpha \in V_\alpha^*$ and $\alpha \in \mathcal{T}$, $g_\alpha^*(x_\alpha) = g_\alpha(x_\alpha)$.

Next, we first need to establish the following lemma.

Lemma 1. *For all PFHOL models M and PFHOL variable assignments g,*

$$[\![s_\alpha]\!]^{M,g} = [\![[s_\alpha]]\!]^{M^*,g^*}.$$

The detailed proof of this lemma can be found in Makarenko [25].

Theorem 1. $\vDash_{PFHOL} s_o$ *if and only if* $\vDash_{HOL} [s_o]$.

Proof.

($\rightarrow$) The proof is by contraposition:

Assume $\nvDash_{PFHOL} s_o$. Then, there exists a PFHOL model M and a variable assignment g such that $[\![s_o]\!]^{M,g} = F$. By Lemma 1, $[\![s_o]\!]^{M,g} = [\![[s_o]]\!]^{M^*,g^*} = F$. Hence, $\nvDash_{HOL} [s_o]$.

($\leftarrow$) Analogous to above by contraposition and Lemma 1.

Therefore, the embedding of PFHOL in HOL is sound and complete.

References

1. Andrews, P.B.: General models and extensionality. J. Symbol. Logic **37**(2), 395–397 (1972)
2. Andrews, P.B.: General models, descriptions, and choice in type theory. J. Symbol. Logic **37**(2), 385–394 (1972)
3. Bacon, A., Hawthorne, J., Uzquiano, G.: Higher-order free logic and the Prior-Kaplan paradox. Canadian J. Philos. **46**(4–5), 493–541 (2016)
4. Bencivenga, E.: Free logics. In: Gabbay, D.M., Günthner, F. (eds.) Handbook of Philosophical Logic. Volume III: Alternatives in Classical Logic, pp. 373–426. Springer, Netherlands, Dordrecht (1986)
5. Benzmüller, C.: Universal (Meta-)logical reasoning: recent successes. Sci. Comput. Program. **172**, 48–62 (2019)
6. Benzmüller, C., Andrews, P.B.: Church's type theory. In: Zalta, E.N. (ed.), The Stanford Encyclopedia of Philosophy. Metaphysics Research Lab, Stanford University, summer 2019 edition (2019)
7. Benzmüller, C., Brown, C.E., Kohlhase, M.: Higher-order semantics and extensionality. J. Symbol. Logic **69**(4), 1027–1088 (2004)
8. Benzmüller, C., Miller, D.: Automation of higher-order logic. In: Gabbay, D.M., Siekmann, J.H., Woods, J. (eds.) Computational Logic. Handbook of the History of Logic, vol. 9, pp. 215–254. Elsevier, North Holland (2014)
9. Benzmüller, C., Parent, X., van der Torre, L.: Designing normative theories for ethical and legal reasoning: LogiKEy framework, methodology, and tool support. Artif. Intell. **287**, 103348 (2020)
10. Benzmüller, C., Scott, D.S.: Automating free logic in HOL, with an experimental application in category theory. J. Autom. Reason. **64**(1), 53–72 (2019). https://doi.org/10.1007/s10817-018-09507-7
11. Blanchette, J.C., Nipkow, T.: Nitpick: a counterexample generator for higher-order logic based on a relational model finder. In: Kaufmann, M., Paulson, L.C. (eds.) ITP 2010. LNCS, vol. 6172, pp. 131–146. Springer, Heidelberg (2010). https://doi.org/10.1007/978-3-642-14052-5_11
12. Brown, C.E.: Satallax: an automatic higher-order prover. In: Gramlich, B., Miller, D., Sattler, U. (eds.) IJCAR 2012. LNCS (LNAI), vol. 7364, pp. 111–117. Springer, Heidelberg (2012). https://doi.org/10.1007/978-3-642-31365-3_11
13. Church, A.: A formulation of the simple theory of types. J. Symbol. Logic **5**(2), 56–68 (1940)

14. Farmer, W.M.: A Partial Functions Version of Church's Simple Theory of Types. J. Symbol. Log. **55**, 1269–1291 (1990)
15. Feferman, S.: Logics for termination and correctness of functional programs. In: Moschovakis, Y.N. (ed.) Logic from Computer Science, pp. 95–127. Springer, New York (1992). https://doi.org/10.1007/978-1-4612-2822-6_5
16. Gumb, R.D.: Free logic in program specification and verification. In: Morscher, E., Hieke, A. (eds.) New Essays in Free Logic. In Honour of Karel Lambert, vol. 23, pp. 157–193. In Honour of Karel Lambert. Springer, Dordrecht (2001). https://doi.org/10.1007/978-94-015-9761-6_9
17. Gumb, R.D., Lambert, K.: Definitions in nonstrict positive free logic. Modern Logic **7**(1), 25–55 (1997)
18. Henkin, L.: Completeness in the theory of types. J. Symbol. Logic **15**(2), 81–91 (1950)
19. Kaplan, D.: A problem in possible worlds semantics. In: Sinnott-Armstrong, W., Raffman, D., Asher, N. (eds.) Modality, Morality and Belief: Essays in Honor of Ruth Barcan Marcus, pp. 41–52. Cambridge University Press, Cambridge (1995)
20. Kirchner, D., Benzmüller, C., Zalta, E.N.: Mechanizing principia Logico-Metaphysica in functional type theory. Rev. Symbol. Logic **13**(1), 206–218 (2020)
21. Lambert, K.: The Definition of E! in Free Logic. The International Congress for Logic, Methodology and Philosophy of Science, Abstracts (1960)
22. Lambert, K.: Free logic and the concept of existence. Notre Dame J. Formal Logic **1–2**(8), 133–144 (1967)
23. Lambert, K.: Philosophical Applications of Free Logic. Oxford University Press, Oxford (1991)
24. Lehmann, S.: 'No Input, No Output' Logic. In: Morscher, E., Hieke, A. (eds.) New Essays in Free Logic. In Honour of Karel Lambert, vol. 23, pp. 147–155. Springer, Netherlands, Dordrecht (2001). https://doi.org/10.1007/978-94-015-9761-6_8
25. Makarenko, I.: Free Higher-Order Logic - Notion, Definition and Embedding in HOL. Master's thesis, Freie Universität Berlin (2020)
26. Meyer, R.K., Lambert, K.: Universally free logic and standard quantification theory. J. Symbol. Logic **33**(1), 8–26 (1968)
27. Nipkow, T., Paulson, L.C., Wenzel, M.: Isabelle/HOL – A Proof Assistant for Higher-Order Logic (2019). http://isabelle.in.tum.de/doc/tutorial.pdf. Accessed 30 Dec 2019
28. Paulson, L.C., Blanchette, J.C.: Three years of experience with sledgehammer, a practical link between automatic and interactive theorem provers. In: Proceedings of the 8th International Workshop on the Implementation of Logics, pp. 131–146 (2015)
29. Prior, A.N.: On a Family of Paradoxes. Notre Dame J. Formal Logic **2**(1), 16–32 (1961)
30. Schock, R.: Logics Without Existence Assumptions. Almqvist & Wiksell, Stockholm (1968)
31. Schütte, K.: Syntactical and semantical properties of simple type theory. J. Symbol. Logic **25**(4), 305–326 (1960)
32. Dana Scott. Existence and Description in Formal Logic. In Ralph Schoenman, editor, Bertrand Russell: Philosopher of the Century, pages 181–200. Little, Brown & Company, Boston, 1967. Repr. in [23], pp. 28–48
33. Steen, A., Benzmüller, C.: Sweet SIXTEEN: automation via embedding into classical higher-Order Logic. Logic Logical Philos. **25**(4), 535–554 (2016)

34. Steen, A., Benzmüller, C.: The higher-order prover Leo-III. In: Galmiche, D., Schulz, S., Sebastiani, R. (eds.) IJCAR 2018. LNCS (LNAI), vol. 10900, pp. 108–116. Springer, Cham (2018). https://doi.org/10.1007/978-3-319-94205-6_8
35. Villadsen, J., Schlichtkrull, A.: Formalization of many-valued logics. In: Christiansen, H., Dolores Jiménez-López, M., Loukanova, R., Moss, L.S. (eds.), Partiality and Underspecification in Information, Languages, and Knowledge, pp. 219–256. Cambridge Scholars Press (2017)
36. Zalta, E.N.: Principia Logico-Metaphysica. http://mally.stanford.edu/principia.pdf. Draft/Excerpt; Accessed 31 May 2020

Low-Rank Subspace Override
for Unsupervised Domain Adaptation

Christoph Raab$^{(\boxtimes)}$ and Frank-Michael Schleif$^{(\boxtimes)}$

University for Applied Sciences Würzburg-Schweinfurt,
Sanderheinrichsleitenweg 20, Würzburg, Germany
{christoph.raab,frank-michael.schleif}@fhws.de

Abstract. Current supervised learning models cannot generalize well across domain boundaries, which is a known problem in many applications, such as robotics or visual classification. Domain adaptation methods are used to improve these generalization properties. However, these techniques suffer either from being restricted to a particular task, such as visual adaptation, require a lot of computational time and data, which is not always guaranteed, have complex parameterization, or expensive optimization procedures. In this work, we present an approach that requires only a well-chosen snapshot of data to find a single domain invariant subspace. The subspace is calculated in closed form and overrides domain structures, which makes it fast and stable in parameterization. By employing low-rank techniques, we emphasize on descriptive characteristics of data. The presented idea is evaluated on various domain adaptation tasks such as text and image classification against state of the art domain adaptation approaches and achieves remarkable performance across all tasks.

Keywords: Transfer learning · Domain-adaptation · Single value decomposition · Nyström approximation · Subspace Override

1 Introduction

Supervised learning and, in particular, classification is an essential task in machine learning with a broad range of applications. The obtained models are used to predict the labels of unseen test samples. A basic assumption in supervised learning is that the underlying domain or distribution is not changing between training and test samples. If the domain is changing from one task to a related but different task, one would like to reuse the available learning model. Domain differences are quite common in real-world scenarios and, eventually, lead to substantial performance drops [32].

In image classification, a domain adaptation problem exists when the source and target data come from different cameras, as shown in Fig. 1. The domain adaptation problem occurs due to different camera characteristics between training and evaluation since cameras have different rendering and focus properties.

© Springer Nature Switzerland AG 2020
U. Schmid et al. (Eds.): KI 2020, LNAI 12325, pp. 132–147, 2020.
https://doi.org/10.1007/978-3-030-58285-2_10

More formally, let $\mathbf{X}_s = \{\mathbf{x}_s^i\}_{i=1}^m \in \mathbb{R}^d$ be m source data samples in a d-dimensional feature space from the source domain distribution $p(x_s)$ with labels $Y_s = \{y_s^i\}_{i=1}^m \in \mathcal{Y} = \{1, 2, .., C\}$ and let $\mathbf{X}_t = \{\mathbf{x}_t^j\}_{j=1}^n \in \mathbb{R}^d$ be n target samples from the target domain distribution $p(x_t)$ with labels $Y_t = \{y_t^j\}_{j=1}^n \in \mathcal{Y}$. Traditional machine learning assumes similar distributions, i.e. $p(x_s) \sim p(x_t)$, but domain adaptation assumes different distributions, i.e. $p(x_s) \neq p(x_t)$.

Fig. 1. Objects from different domains [8]

Various domain adaptation techniques have already been proposed, following different strategies and improving the prediction performance of underlying classification algorithms in test scenarios [20,32]. State of the art domain adaptation approaches [7,16,18,31,34] require a large number of source or target samples, which is indeed a disadvantage of many domain adaptation approaches and is not guaranteed in restricted environments where labeling is expensive [32]. In this work, we show that only a well-chosen subset of samples is necessary to approximate domain structures.

Despite the popularity of kernelized subspace adaptations [15,31,34] or manifold embeddings [7,8,19,31] for domain alignment, it was shown in [2,6] that least-squares approaches are at least competitive to more complicated settings, where domain differences are explicitly solved using least-squares to find a common subspace. Solutions to least-square problems are intuitive and theoretically justified. However, if both domains do not lie in a common subspace, this technique fails to transfer knowledge effectively [24]. We address this problem and evaluate a domain invariant subspace, where both domains are explicitly part of the target subspace, which neglects the mentioned drawback.

The main contribution of this work is to derive a *subspace* closed-form solution of the least-squares domain adaptation problem by finding a suitable domain invariant projection operator called Subspace Override (SO). The approach constructs a target subspace representation for both domains, which transfers target basis information to source data. We show that a well-chosen snapshot of the data is sufficient to approximate the domain characteristics by approximating the optimal solution of the least-squares problem. For the first time in domain adaptation, a Nyström approximation is used on *subspace* domain adaptation. The resulting method has a better prediction performance with stable parameterization and is easy to apply. Further, it is the fastest subspace domain adaptation algorithm in terms of computational complexity compared to related approaches, while maintaining its very good performance.

The rest of the paper is organized as follows: We give an overview of related work in Sect. 2. The proposed approach is discussed in Sect. 3, followed by an experimental part in Sect. 4, addressing the classification performance, computational time and the stability of the approach. The underlying mathematical concepts can be looked up at Appendix B in [22]. A summary with a discussion of open issues is provided in the conclusion at the end of the paper. **Source code, including all experiments and plots, is available at** https://github.com/ChristophRaab/nso.

2   Related Work

In general, homogeneous transfer learning [32] or domain adaptation (DA) approaches, distinguish roughly between the following strategies:

The *feature adaptation* techniques [32] are trying to find a common latent subspace for source and target domain to reduce distribution differences, such that the underlying structure of the data is preserved in the subspace. A baseline approach for feature adaptation is Transfer Component Analysis (TCA) [19]. TCA finds a suitable subspace transformation called transfer components via minimizing the Maximum Mean Discrepancy (MMD) in the Reproducing Kernel Hilbert Space (RKHS). Joint Distribution Adaptation (JDA) [15] also considers MMD but incorporates class-dependent distributions. These works considered a subspace projection based on a combined eigendecomposition for both domains, which fails to include domain-specific attributes into the subspace. The Joint Geometrical Subspace Alignment (JGSA) [34] tackled this issue by searching MMD based subspaces for the domains individually. However, these methods rely on kernels and are not able to explore the full characteristics of the original feature space and are computationally intensive. Proposed work relies on original space and uses only a snapshot of data for computational efficiency.

Least-Squares (LS) adaptation is closely related to us, aligning both domains by finding a solution to the LS problem and use this solution as a feature transformation matrix. The transformation directly modifies the data or finds a subspace projection based on the eigenvectors of the domains. Subspace Alignment (SA) [6] computes a target subspace representation by direct modification of the correlation matrices of both domains. The Correlation Alignment (CORAL) [26] technique transfers second-order statistics of the target domain into whitened source data and project source and target data via principal component analysis (PCA) into the subspace. The Landmarks Selection-based Subspace Alignment (LSSA) [1] is a successor of SA and selects only a subset of both domains, which are near to domain borders to align these borders in the subspace explicitly. However, LSSA cannot capture the whole domain characteristic, and in supervised classification problems, the landmark sample is prone to omit class-information. Our work considers a uniform and class-wise sample strategy to capture the whole domain.

The work of Shao et al. [25] proposed that least-squares approaches, as above, are unable for effective adaptation, because the source and target data may lay not in a single subspace. In this work, we *override* the orthogonal basis of the source domain with the target one. With this, we model the source subspace domain as part of the target subspace, and subspace differences do not exist because both must lie in the same subspace by construction.

The considered domain adaptation methods have approximately a complexity of $\mathcal{O}(n^2)$, where n is the highest number of samples concerning target or source. All these algorithms require some *unlabeled test data* to be available at training time. These transfer-solutions cannot be directly used as predictors, but instead, are wrappers for classification algorithms.

3 Subspace Override

The task of domain adaptation is to align distribution differences with the goal that underlying statistics will be similar afterward. As in prior work [1,5,6,12, 16,21,25], we assume that similar matrices will lead to similar distributions. Hence, we strive for aligning the domain data matrices in a suitable subspace and model the source data to be part of the target data, and therefore it *must* be in the same (single) subspace.

To draw both domains closer together, represented by their respective samples $\mathbf{X}_s$ and $\mathbf{X}_t$, consider the following optimization function

$$\underset{\mathbf{M}}{\operatorname{argmin}} ||\mathbf{MX}_s - \mathbf{X}_t||_F^2, \tag{1}$$

$$s.t. \ \ \mathbf{MM}^T = \mathbf{I}. \tag{2}$$

The goal is to learn $\mathbf{M}$ to adapt $\mathbf{X}_s$ to the target domain. Further, we also make sure that the obtained projection operator is an orthogonal basis. This formulation has two flaws.

First, if sample sizes of source and target are not the same, i.e. $m \neq n$, the above formula is invalid. We address the problem by a simple data augmentation strategy. If $m < n$, $\mathbf{X}_s$ is enriched by sampling new source data from the estimated Gaussian distribution of $\mathbf{X}_s$ and assign random source labels until $m = n$. If $n < m$, source samples are randomly removed until sample sizes are equal. Hence, from know we assume $m = n$.

Further, (1) prevents effective domain adaptation, because the transformation $\mathbf{M}$ may project the data in different spaces [25]. However, if we model $\mathbf{M}$ to be directly related to the target domain, the projection operator will be domain invariant. To get this kind of solution for problem (1), it must be rewritten that source data is part of the target subspace.

Let us consider the relationship between singular- and eigendecomposition and rewrite the PCA in terms of SVD. Given a rectangular matrix $\mathbf{X} \in \mathbb{R}^{n \times d}$ we can rewrite the eigendecomposition to

$$\mathbf{X}^T\mathbf{X} = (\mathbf{V}\boldsymbol{\Sigma}^T\mathbf{U}^T)(\mathbf{U}\boldsymbol{\Sigma}\mathbf{V}^T) = \mathbf{V}\boldsymbol{\Sigma}^2\mathbf{V}^T, \tag{3}$$

with $\boldsymbol{\Sigma} \in \mathbb{R}^{n \times d}$ as singular values and $\mathbf{U} \in \mathbb{R}^{n \times n}$ are singular vectors of $\mathbf{X}$. Further, $\boldsymbol{\Sigma}^2 = \boldsymbol{\Sigma}^T\boldsymbol{\Sigma} \in \mathbb{R}^{d \times d}$ as eigenvalues and $\mathbf{V} \in \mathbb{R}^{d \times d}$ as eigenvectors of

$\mathbf{X}^T\mathbf{X}$. A low rank solution and a reduction of dimensionality is integrated into the new data matrix by sorting $\boldsymbol{\Sigma}$ and $\mathbf{V}$ in descending order with respect to $\boldsymbol{\Sigma}$ and choose only the biggest l eigenvalues and corresponding eigenvectors

$$\mathbf{X}^l = \mathbf{X}\mathbf{V}^l = \mathbf{U}^l\boldsymbol{\Sigma}^l\mathbf{V}^{l^T}\mathbf{V}^l = \mathbf{U}^l\boldsymbol{\Sigma}^l \in \mathbb{R}^{n\times l}, \tag{4}$$

with $\mathbf{U}^l \in \mathbb{R}^{n\times l}$ and $\boldsymbol{\Sigma}^l \in \mathbb{R}^{l\times l}$ and $\mathbf{V}^l \in \mathbb{R}^{d\times l}$. $\mathbf{X}^l$ is the reduced target matrix and only the most relevant data w.r.t. to variance is kept. In (3) a linear covariance or kernel is used, but non-linear kernels like the RBF kernel could be integrated as well.

With the insights of (3) and (4), we rewrite the optimization problem in (1) to a low-rank subspace version and state the **main optimization problem**:

$$\underset{\mathbf{M}}{\operatorname{argmin}} \|\mathbf{M}\mathbf{U}_s^l\boldsymbol{\Sigma}_s^l - \mathbf{U}_t^l\boldsymbol{\Sigma}_t^l\|_F^2, \tag{5}$$

$$s.t. \quad \mathbf{M}\mathbf{M}^T = \mathbf{I}. \tag{6}$$

Based on domain relatedness and standardization techniques, we assume that singular values are similar, i.e. $\boldsymbol{\Sigma}_s^l \simeq \boldsymbol{\Sigma}_t^l$ and fix them. Naturally, this assumption does not always hold. See Sect. 3.2 for a discussion. *If they are fixed, then* the optimal solution to (5) is easily obtained by solving the linear equation and obtain the solution $\mathbf{M} = \mathbf{U}_t^l\mathbf{U}_s^{l^T}$. By applying $\mathbf{M}$ to (5) the source data becomes

$$\mathbf{X}_s^l = \mathbf{M}\mathbf{U}_s^l\boldsymbol{\Sigma}_s^l = \mathbf{U}_t^l\mathbf{U}_s^{l^T}\mathbf{U}_s^l\boldsymbol{\Sigma}_s^l = \mathbf{U}_t^l\boldsymbol{\Sigma}_s^l \in \mathbb{R}^{n\times l} \tag{7}$$

and is used for training an invariant classifier. The resulting model can be evaluated on $\mathbf{X}_t^l = \mathbf{U}_t^l\boldsymbol{\Sigma}_t^l \in \mathbb{R}^{n\times l}$. This overrides the source basis and prevents the source subspace to be arbitrarily different from the target due to the affiliation to the target space. The solution also fulfills the constrains because $\mathbf{M}$ is an orthogonal matrix due to the orthogonal matrices $\mathbf{U}_t^l$ and $\mathbf{U}_s^{l^T}$. In particular, (7) projects the source data onto the principal components of the subspace basis of $\mathbf{X}_t$. If data matrices $\mathbf{X}_t$ and $\mathbf{X}_s$ are standardized, the geometric interpretation is a rotation of source data w.r.t to angles of the target basis. We call this procedure Subspace Override (SO).

This procedure requires a complete eigenspectrum and scales to $\mathcal{O}(n^3)$ in worst case [33]. Further, all available data is required for this approach. Using Nyström techniques, we show that only a subset of the data is required, which simultaneously reduces computational complexity and eliminates the need to examine all singular values.

3.1   Nyström Extension

For clarity, the following notation will overlap with the previous section but keeps things simple. We assume the reader is familiar with Nyström SVD techniques. Otherwise, the reader may consider Appendix B in [22] for an introduction to the Nyström approximation.

In short, the Nyström SVD technique is a low-rank approximation which decomposes a given matrix $\mathbf{K} \in \mathbb{R}^{n \times d}$ into the constitution

$$\mathbf{K} = \begin{bmatrix} \mathbf{A} & \mathbf{B} \\ \mathbf{C} & \mathbf{F} \end{bmatrix}, \tag{8}$$

with $\mathbf{A} \in \mathbb{R}^{l \times l}$, $\mathbf{B} \in \mathbb{R}^{l \times (d-l)}$, $\mathbf{C} \in \mathbb{R}^{(n-l) \times l}$ and $\mathbf{F} \in \mathbb{R}^{(n-l) \times (d-l)}$. The matrix $\mathbf{A}$ contains the random samples called the landmark matrix. Given $\mathbf{K}$, the singular value decomposition $\mathbf{A} = \mathbf{U}\boldsymbol{\Sigma}\mathbf{V}^T$, and $\mathbf{C}$, the full SVD of $\mathbf{K}$ is reconstructable, which is similar to the following approach.

Consider $\mathbf{X}_s$ and $\mathbf{X}_t$ with the decomposition as in (8). For a Nyström SVD, we sample from both matrices l rows/columns obtaining landmarks matrices $\mathbf{A}_s = \mathbf{U}_s\boldsymbol{\Sigma}_s\mathbf{V}_s^T \in \mathbb{R}^{l \times l}$ and $\mathbf{A}_t = \mathbf{U}_t\boldsymbol{\Sigma}_t\mathbf{V}_t^T \in \mathbb{R}^{l \times l}$. The target data is projected into the subspace as in (4) via the Nyström technique (Appendix B in [22]) and keeps only the most relevant data structures via

$$\tilde{\mathbf{X}}_t^l = \tilde{\mathbf{U}}_t\boldsymbol{\Sigma}_t = \begin{bmatrix} \mathbf{U}_t \\ \hat{\mathbf{U}}_t \end{bmatrix} \boldsymbol{\Sigma}_t = \begin{bmatrix} \mathbf{U}_t \\ \mathbf{C}_t\mathbf{V}_t\boldsymbol{\Sigma}_t^{-1} \end{bmatrix} \boldsymbol{\Sigma}_t \in \mathbb{R}^{n \times l}. \tag{9}$$

Analogously, the source data could be approximated by $\mathbf{X}_s^l = \tilde{\mathbf{U}}_s\boldsymbol{\Sigma}_s \in \mathbb{R}^{n \times l}$. The Nyström technique is also used to approximate the solution to the optimization problem with $\mathbf{M} = \tilde{\mathbf{U}}_t\tilde{\mathbf{U}}_s^{-1}$ and project the source data into the target subspace via

$$\tilde{\mathbf{X}}_s^l = \mathbf{M}\tilde{\mathbf{U}}_s\boldsymbol{\Sigma}_s = \tilde{\mathbf{U}}_t\tilde{\mathbf{U}}_s^{-1}\tilde{\mathbf{U}}_s\boldsymbol{\Sigma}_s = \tilde{\mathbf{U}}_t\boldsymbol{\Sigma}_s \in \mathbb{R}^{n \times l}. \tag{10}$$

Hence, it is sufficient to only compute a Singular Value Decomposition (SVD) of $\mathbf{A}_t$ and $\mathbf{A}_s$ instead of $\mathbf{X}_t$ and $\mathbf{X}_s$ with $l \ll m, d, n$ and therefore is considerably lower in computational complexity.

By definition of the Nyström approximation, it is $\tilde{\mathbf{U}}_s\tilde{\mathbf{U}}_s^T = \tilde{\mathbf{U}}_t\tilde{\mathbf{U}}_t^{-1} = \mathbf{I}$ and $\tilde{\mathbf{U}}_t$ is an orthogonal basis. Therefore, the subspace projections are orthogonal transformations and fulfill the constrains of (5).

Besides small sample requirements, the major advantage of using the approximated low-rank solution in favor of the optimal solution is that singular values that are closer to zero are set to zero, reducing the noise of the data in the subspace. Therefore the approach focuses on intrinsic data characteristics, which should lead to better classification performance.

Subsequently, this approach is denoted as Nyström Subspace Override (NSO). The matrix $\mathbf{X}_s^l$ is used for training, and $\mathbf{X}_t^l$ is used for testing. But uniform sampling may not be optimal for Nyström, given a classification task [23]. Therefore, we subsequently integrate class-wise sampling in the following. Pseudo code shown in Algorithm 1.

3.2 Sampling Strategy

The standard technique to create Nyström landmark matrices is to sample uniformly or find clusters in the data [28]. In supervised classification with more than two classes, class-wise sampling should be utilized to properly include class-depending attributes of a matrix into the approximation [23]. However, a decomposition as in (8), required for Nyström SVD, is intractable with class-wise sampling, because respective matrices are non-square. Let $\mathbf{X}_s \in \mathbb{R}^{m \times d}$ with $m \neq d$ and landmark indices $I = \{i_1, \ldots, i_s\}$ with at least one $i_j > d$ and if $m > d$, then it is undefined. Therefore, we sample rows class-wise and obtain $\mathbf{A}_s^d \in \mathbb{R}^{l \times d}$ instead of $\mathbf{A}_s \in \mathbb{R}^{l \times l}$, making it possible to sample from the whole range of source data. The sampling from test data $\mathbf{X}_t$ is done uniformly row-wise, because of missing class information. The resulting singular value decompositions, i.e. $\mathbf{A}_t^d = \mathbf{U}_t^d \boldsymbol{\Sigma}_t^d \mathbf{V}_t^{dT}$ and $\mathbf{A}_s^d = \mathbf{U}_s^d \boldsymbol{\Sigma}_s^d \mathbf{V}_s^{dT}$, are utilized for successive Nyström approximations.

However, the possible numerical range of $\boldsymbol{\Sigma}_{(\cdot)}^d$ and $\boldsymbol{\Sigma}_{(\cdot)}$ is naturally not the same, which is easily shown by the Gerschgorin Bound [10] (See Appendix B in [22] for an introduction). It scales approximated matrices $\mathbf{X}_{(\cdot)}^l$ different by $\boldsymbol{\Sigma}_{(\cdot)}^d$ and accurate scaling of the singular vectors cannot be guaranteed. Therefore, we apply a post-processing correction and standardize the approximated matrices to transform the data back to mean zero and variance one. The singular vectors also have an approximation error. However, both subspace projections are based on the same transformation matrix, hence making an identical error, and as a result, the error should not affect the classification.

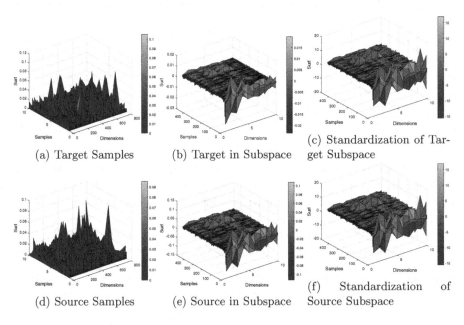

(a) Target Samples   (b) Target in Subspace   (c) Standardization of Target Subspace

(d) Source Samples   (e) Source in Subspace   (f) Standardization of Source Subspace

Fig. 2. Process of *Nyström Subspace Override* with ten landmark samples applied to *Caltech vs Amazon* image dataset encoded with surf features as a surface plot. Best viewed in color.

The process of Nyström Subspace Override (NSO) is given in Fig. 2. The first column visualizes the samples of Nyström to create the approximated set of subspace projection operators. The second column shows the data after the subspace projection. The similarity in structure but dissimilarity in scaling, as discussed above, is visible. The last column shows the data after applying post-correction and leading to a high similarity afterward. The pseudo code of NSO is shown in Algorithm 1.

Algorithm 1. Nyström Subspace Override

Require: $\mathbf{X}_s$ as m sized training; $\mathbf{X}_t$ as n sized test set; $\mathbf{Y}$ as m sized training label vector; l as number of landmarks parameter.
Ensure: New Source $\tilde{\mathbf{X}}_s^l$; new Target $\tilde{\mathbf{X}}_t^l$;
1: $\mathbf{X}_s, \mathbf{Y}_s = $ augmentation$(\mathbf{X}_s, \mathbf{Y}_s, n)$
2:              ▷ Gaussian sampling or random removal to make $\mathbf{X}_s$ equally sized to $\mathbf{X}_t$.
3: $\mathbf{A}_t^d, \mathbf{A}_s^d, \mathbf{C}_t = $ decomposition$(\mathbf{X}_t, \mathbf{X}_s, \mathbf{Y}, l)$ ▷ Eq.(8)
4: $\mathbf{\Sigma}_s^d = SVD(\mathbf{A}_s^d)$;
5: $\mathbf{U}_t^d, \mathbf{\Sigma}_t^d, \mathbf{V}_t^d = SVD(\mathbf{A}_t^d)$;
6: $\tilde{\mathbf{U}}_t = \left[\mathbf{U}_t^d \, \mathbf{C}_t \mathbf{V}_t^d \mathbf{\Sigma}_t^{d-1}\right]^T$ ▷ Eq. (9)
7: $\tilde{\mathbf{X}}_t^l = \tilde{\mathbf{U}}_t \mathbf{\Sigma}_t^d$ ▷ Eq. (9)
8: $\tilde{\mathbf{X}}_s^l = \tilde{\mathbf{U}}_t \mathbf{\Sigma}_s^d$ ▷ Eq. (10)
9: $\tilde{\mathbf{X}}_s^l, \tilde{\mathbf{X}}_t^l = $ standardization$(\tilde{\mathbf{X}}_s^l, \tilde{\mathbf{X}}_t^l)$ ▷ Effect as in Fig. 2

3.3 Properties of Nyström Subspace Override

The computational complexity of Nysröm Subspace Override (NSO) is composed of economy-size SVD of landmark matrices $\mathbf{A}_s^d$ and $\mathbf{A}_t^d$ with complexity $\mathcal{O}(2l^2)$. The matrix inversion of diagonal matrix $\mathbf{\Sigma}_t^{d-1}$ in (9) can be neglected. The remaining k matrix multiplications are of complexity $\mathcal{O}(kl^2)$ and are therefore contributing to the overall complexity of NSO, which is $O(l^2)$ with $l \ll n, m, d$. This makes NSO the fastest subspace domain adaptation solution in terms of computational complexity in comparison to *compared methods in Sect. 4*.

The **out-of-sample extension** for unseen target/source samples, e. g. $\mathbf{x} \in \mathbb{R}^d$, is analog to (9). Based on (4), a subspace projection via (approximated) right singular vectors is also valid. Hence, a sample can be projected into the subspace via

$$\mathbf{x}^l = \mathbf{x}\tilde{\mathbf{V}}_t^T = x\left[\mathbf{V}_t \, \mathbf{\Sigma}_t^{-1}\mathbf{U}^T\mathbf{B}_t\right] \tag{11}$$

and be evaluated by an arbitrary classifier learned in the subspace.

The difference between source and target domain after SO, i. e. approximation error of source by target domain is bounded by

$$E_{SO} = \left\|\mathbf{X}_s^l - \mathbf{X}_t^l\right\|_F^2 < \sum_{i=1}^{l+1}(\sigma_i(\mathbf{X}_s) - \sigma_i(\mathbf{X}_t))^2 < \left\|\mathbf{X}_s - \mathbf{X}_t\right\|_F^2. \tag{12}$$

where $\sigma_i(\cdot)$ is the i-th singular value in descending order of $\mathbf{X}_s$ and $\mathbf{X}_t$ respectively and $1 < l < min(n, d)$. The proof can be found in Appendix A. As in prior LS approaches [1,6,26], we want NSO to minimize the difference between the source and target data. In Eq. (12) is shown that NSO has a lower norm to the original data and proves that the matrices are aligned during NSO, making them numerically more similar. Note that similar matrices not necessarily indicate a good classification performance in terms of accuracy by an arbitrary classifier in a domain adaptation setting. The classification performance is evaluated in the following.

4   Experiments

We follow the experimental design typical for domain adaptation algorithms [1,3,6,8,14–16,18–20,26,34]. The tests are conducted on the common datasets Reuters, Newsgroup and Office-Caltech. A crucial characteristic of datasets for domain adaptation is that domains for training and testing are different but related, e. g. sharing the same categories. The NSO approach is evaluated against the common and state of the art domain adaptation methods TCA [19], GFK [8], JDA [15], SA [6], CORAL [26], EasyTL [30], SCA [7], MEDA [31] and JGSA [34]. We extend the object detection study by also evaluating against deep DA networks. We follow [31] and use the Alexnet [11] as the baseline for Deep-Coral [27], JAN [17], DAN [13] and DDC [29]. The networks are always trained on original images. The parameters for the respective method are determined for the best performance in terms of accuracy via grid search. In the experiments, the Support Vector Machine (SVM) independent of being a baseline or underlying classifier for domain adaptation methods uses the RBF-Kernel. All experiments are done via the standard sampling protocol [17] and use all available source and target data. We did 20 test runs and summarized the result as mean accuracy.

4.1   Dataset Description

A summary of all datasets is shown in Table 1. Regardless of the dataset, it has been standardized to standard mean and variance.

Reuters-21578 [3]: A collection of Reuters news-wire articles collected in 1987 as TFIDF features. The three top categories *organization (orgs)*, *places* and *people* are used in our experiment.

To create a transfer problem, a classifier is not tested with the same categories as it is trained on, e. g. it is trained on some subcategories of organization and people and tested on others. Six datasets are generated: *orgs vs. places, orgs vs. people, people vs. places, places vs. orgs, people vs. places* and *places vs. people*. They are two-class problems with the top categories as the positive and negative class and with subcategories as training and testing examples.

20-Newsgroup [14]: The original collection has approximately 20.000 text documents from 20 Newsgroups and is nearly equally distributed in 20 subcategories.

The top four categories are *comp, rec, talk* and *sci*, each containing four subcategories. We follow a data sampling scheme introduced by [16] and generate 216 cross domain datasets based on subcategories, which are summarized as mean over all test runs as *comp vs rec, comp vs talk, comp vs sci, rec vs sci, rec vs talk* and *sci vs talk*.

Caltech-Office (OC) [8]: The first, Caltech (*C*), is an extensive dataset of images and contains 30.607 images within 257 categories. The Office dataset is a collection of images drawn from three sources, which are from *amazon (A)*, digital SLR camera *(DSLR)* and *webcam (W)*. They vary regarding camera, light situation and size, but ten similar object classes, e. g. computer or printer, are extracted for a classification task. We use SURF [8] and DeCaf [4] features.

Table 1. Overview of the dataset characteristics containing numbers of samples, features and labels.

Dataset	Subsets	#Samples	#Features	#Classes
Caltech	C	1123	800 (4096)	10
Office	A, W, D	1123	800 (4096)	10
Newsgroup	Comp, Rec, Sci, Talk	4857, 3967, 3946, 3250	25804	2
Reuters	Orgs, People, Places	1237, 1208, 1016	25804	2

4.2   Performance Results

The results are shown per dataset separately. The results on Newsgroup in Table 2, Reuters in Table 3, OC with Surf features in Table 4, OC with decaf and deep DA methods in Table 5. Summarizing, our NSO algorithm is basically the best on Reuters and Newsgroup data. The only competitive algorithm is SA on Reuters data with similar results to ours. SA is also an LS subspace approach. However, SA is outperformed by NSO at Newsgroup. NSO demonstrates its usefulness for large sparse matrices that are given at these datasets. At the OC-Surf dataset, the NSO outperforms on many datasets and has the best mean accuracy. Only at OC-Decaf features, NSO is midfield in performance, but it is still competitive. We assume that the Decaf features are very dense feature matrices in terms of descriptive information even if the singular values are small. Therefore, the low-rank approximation is contra-productive.

The intriguing part of this evaluation comes with the cross-task evaluation. While SA is very good at Reuters and Newsgroup, it has bad performance on OC datasets. While MEDA and JGSA have poor performance at Reuters and Newsgroup, they are good at OC datasets. Our NSO approach is in three out of four tasks the recommendable choice showing convincing task-independent performance. In Fig. 3, the parameter sensitivity is shown and demonstrates that the parameterization (number of landmarks) of NSO is stable, simple to optimize and supports the Nyström error expectation.

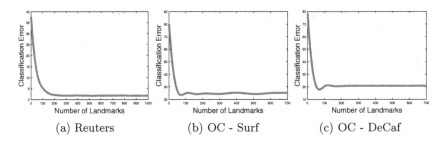

(a) Reuters   (b) OC - Surf   (c) OC - DeCaf

Fig. 3. Relationship between the number of landmarks and mean error on Reuters and Office-Caltech datasets.

Table 2. Mean accuracy of traditional DA methods on Newsgroup text dataset.

Dataset	SVM	TCA	JDA	GFK	SA	CORAL	CGCA	SCA	EasyTL	JGSA	MEDA	NSO (ours)
Comp vs Rec	77.6	78.9	83.1	75.1	78.5	79.4	84.0	56.1	42.2	88.3	49.1	**90.2**
Comp vs Sci	71.1	62.0	75.5	64.1	80.2	71.8	73.2	72.4	25.2	78.4	49.2	**98.4**
Comp vs Talk	84.4	75.0	87.7	83.8	91.1	90.5	87.0	89.5	41.1	91.2	54.4	**96.7**
Rec vs Sci	69.3	79.6	79.0	64.4	81.1	75.0	74.0	71.4	33.8	80.5	50.0	**99.0**
Rec vs Talk	74.5	86.6	82.0	72.9	79.7	81.6	77.3	78.3	41.6	80.8	55.0	**96.4**
Sci vs Talk	70.9	77.6	70.5	64.2	76.0	74.2	69.0	72.2	41.1	77.7	53.7	**96.4**
Mean	74.6	76.6	79.6	70.7	81.1	78.7	77.4	73.3	37.5	82.8	51.9	**96.2**

Table 3. Mean accuracy of traditional DA methods on Reuters text dataset.

Dataset	SVM	TCA	JDA	GFK	SA	CORAL	CGCA	SCA	EasyTL	JGSA	MEDA	NSO (ours)
Orgs vs People	78.1	79.5	76.6	75.3	**99.9**	77.5	78.0	77.8	39.2	76.5	48.0	99.6
People vs Orgs	79.2	82.7	80.0	71.6	**99.9**	78.2	78.6	79.8	37.9	74.2	47.3	98.5
Orgs vs Place	69.2	72.9	70.0	60.5	97.3	70.3	70.1	69.8	28.9	72.2	43.2	**98.6**
Place vs Orgs	66.3	71.1	65.6	61.5	**97.2**	66.5	67.7	65.3	27.0	64.4	41.4	**97.2**
People vs Place	55.7	57.4	57.0	57.5	**97.4**	57.8	57.0	57.3	22.4	52.6	40.9	**97.4**
Place vs People	57.4	48.9	60.7	56.2	**97.4**	56.3	54.4	58.2	18.3	55.5	38.5	**97.4**
Mean	67.7	68.7	68.3	63.8	**98.1**	67.7	67.6	68.0	28.9	65.9	43.2	**98.1**

Table 4. Mean accuracy of traditional DA on Caltech-Office with surf features.

Dataset	SVM	TCA	JDA	GFK	SA	CORAL	CGCA	SCA	EasyTL	JGSA	MEDA	NSO (ours)
C vs A	53.1	53.9	55.2	41.8	52.2	52.1	54.1	33.1	50.1	51.8	56.5	**88.5**
C vs W	41.7	42.4	46.8	40.7	18.3	38.6	43.1	24.9	49.5	46.1	53.9	**81.0**
C vs D	47.8	46.5	49.7	39.5	15.9	36.3	37.6	33.1	48.4	44.6	50.3	**79.0**
A vs C	41.7	45.4	43.5	39.0	60.0	45.1	44.9	26.3	43.0	39.7	43.9	**61.5**
A vs W	31.9	37.6	44.4	36.9	29.2	44.4	43.9	27.6	40.7	46.1	53.2	**81.0**
A vs D	44.6	40.1	31.2	33.1	28.0	39.5	36.3	25.5	38.9	47.8	45.9	**79.0**
W vs C	21.2	31.2	31.5	27.4	23.2	33.7	33.8	15.6	29.7	30.2	34.2	**63.5**
W vs A	27.6	34.7	31.7	31.2	29.5	35.9	37.6	21.1	35.2	40.0	42.7	**95.8**
W vs D	78.3	83.4	92.4	82.8	78.3	86.6	88.5	41.4	77.1	**91.1**	88.5	79.0
D vs C	26.5	36.2	32.6	27.2	21.9	33.9	35.4	17.2	31.3	30.3	34.8	**66.6**
D vs A	26.2	37.1	36.7	30.9	26.5	37.7	38.9	17.2	31.9	38.2	40.6	**93.1**
D vs W	52.5	83.1	88.5	71.9	**89.8**	84.7	87.1	32.5	69.5	91.5	87.5	83.1
Mean	41.1	47.6	48.7	41.9	39.4	47.4	48.4	26.3	45.4	49.8	52.7	**79.3**

Table 5. Mean accuracy of traditional and deep DA on Caltech-Office with Decaf and original images (Deep Learning approaches), respectively.

	Traditional Methods												Deep Domain Adaptation				
Dataset	SVM	TCA	JDA	GFK	SA	CORAL	CGCA	SCA	EasyTL	JGSA	MEDA	NSO (ours)	Alexnet	DDC-MMD	JAN	DAN	Deep-CORAL
C vs A	90.6	90.2	92.4	85.6	92.0	91.5	90.1	48.0	90.2	92.1	**93.5**	88.9	92.5	92.5	93.4	92.9	92.8
C vs W	79.0	78.3	81.7	76.6	73.2	78.6	75.9	35.3	76.9	86.4	**93.6**	81.3	74.8	74.9	85.0	86.6	84.3
C vs D	83.4	89.8	87.3	82.8	79.0	84.7	85.4	46.1	81.5	92.4	**93.0**	79.0	74.9	74.8	83.0	82.6	78.1
A vs C	81.9	81.2	82.7	76.6	83.8	83.2	81.6	43.0	81.7	85.1	**87.5**	61.6	85.3	84.9	84.1	84.1	80.0
A vs W	74.2	78.0	72.9	67.8	77.3	75.9	71.2	36.5	74.2	79.0	**88.1**	81.2	65.1	65.2	85.5	84.5	84.3
A vs D	80.9	80.9	79.6	73.9	81.5	81.5	74.8	43.6	84.7	79.6	**91.1**	79.0	78.0	75.8	83.3	85.4	65.6
W vs C	63.0	69.5	74.0	61.1	76.0	67.9	73.7	27.9	66.3	84.9	**88.3**	63.6	70.9	69.8	78.4	78.6	60.8
W vs A	73.8	74.6	79.7	71.2	86.1	76.0	80.5	29.8	73.6	90.3	93.1	**96.2**	80.0	77.6	84.5	83.4	73.6
W vs D	100.0	100.0	100.0	100.0	98.7	100.0	100.0	51.1	98.1	100.0	100.0	79.0	98.8	98.8	99.7	99.5	99.4
D vs C	52.7	68.8	80.2	61.2	75.9	68.0	75.5	24.2	69.1	85.0	**87.1**	66.7	77.3	77.8	79.6	78.1	66.5
D vs A	62.5	79.7	88.9	69.5	87.3	77.2	86.9	26.2	76.3	91.9	**93.2**	92.8	82.8	82.3	84.4	85.1	77.4
D vs W	89.8	97.6	99.3	98.6	95.6	98.3	99.0	33.7	93.9	99.7	**99.0**	83.1	99.0	98.8	98.7	98.6	99.0
Mean	77.7	82.4	84.9	77.1	83.9	81.9	82.9	37.1	80.5	88.9	**92.3**	79.4	81.6	81.1	86.6	86.6	80.1

Table 6. Mean computational time in seconds of subspace DA methods.

Dataset	TCA	JDA	GFK	SA	CORAL	CGCA	SCA	JGSA	MEDA	NSO (ours)
Newsgroup	21.4	4.8	214.4	59.7	705.8	11977.0	59.0	3637.0	3447.0	**2.64**
Reuters	6.5	1.5	2.6	3.0	15.4	225.6	14.8	122.1	53.2	**0.6**
CO - Surf	3.2	0.9	0.6	0.7	0.4	6.4	12.2	10.8	6.3	**0.2**
CO - Decaf	1.8	0.4	1.1	1.3	10.6	99.8	10.3	79.8	45.0	**0.2**
Overall	8.2	1.9	54.7	16.2	183.1	3077.2	24.1	962.4	887.9	0.9

4.3 Time Results

The mean time results of the subspace DA methods in seconds are shown in the Table 6. The deep DA methods are not presented as they are unrivaled to the traditional methods. The experiments shows that our NSO approach is task-independent, the fastest algorithm. Compared to recent MEDA, JGSA and CGCA, the NSO approach needs substantially less time. The related SA approach is also fast, but as theoretically derived, the override of a subspace basis approximated by Nyström leads to a boost in computational performance. In summary, the NSO approach is efficient and should be favored with regard to Green AI.

5 Conclusion

We proposed a low-rank domain approximation algorithm called Nyström Subspace Override. It overrides the source basis with the target basis, which is designed as a domain invariant subspace projection operator. Due to the affiliation of the operator to the target space, we make sure that both domains lie in the same subspace. It requires only a subset of domain data from both domains and provides a subspace variant of the domain adaptation-related least-squares problem. The Nyström based projection, paired with smart class-wise sampling, showed its reliability and robustness in this study. Validated on common domain adaptation tasks and data, it showed a convincing performance. Additionally, NSO has the lowest computational complexity and time consumption compared to discussed solutions, which makes the approach favorable in the light of Green

AI. The next steps are a theoretically evaluation of the Nyström approximation error with the proposed decomposition.

Acknowledgment. We are thankful for support in the FuE program Informations- und Kommunikationstechnik of the StMWi, project OBerA, grant number IUK-1709- 0011// IUK530/010.

A   Appendix A Proof of Subspace Override Bound

Theorem 1. *Given two rectangular matrices* $\mathbf{X}_t, \mathbf{X}_s \in \mathbb{R}^{n \times d}$ *with* $n, d > 1$ *and rank of* $\mathbf{X}_t$ *and* $\mathbf{X}_s > 1$. *The norm* $\left\| \mathbf{X}_s^l - \mathbf{X}_t^l \right\|_F^2$ *in the subspace* $\mathbb{R}^l$ *induced by normalized subspace projector* $\mathbf{M} \in \mathbb{R}^{n \times l}$ *with* $\mathbf{M}^T \mathbf{M} = \mathbf{I}$ *is bounded by*

$$E_{SO} = \left\| \mathbf{X}_s^l - \mathbf{X}_t^l \right\|_F^2 < \sum_{i=1}^{l+1} (\sigma_i(\mathbf{X}_s) - \sigma_i(\mathbf{X}_t))^2 \le \left\| \mathbf{X}_s - \mathbf{X}_t \right\|_F^2. \quad (13)$$

Following [9] the squared Frobenius norm of a matrix difference between two matrices can be bounded by

$$\sum_{i=1}^{q} (\sigma_i(\mathbf{X}_s) - \sigma_i(\mathbf{X}_t))^2 \le \left\| \mathbf{X}_s - \mathbf{X}_t \right\|_F^2, \quad (14)$$

where $q = min(n, d)$ and $\sigma_i(\cdot)$ is the i-th singular value of the respective matrix in descending order. However, the subspace matrices $\mathbf{X}_s^l$ and $\mathbf{X}_t^l$ are a special case due to the subspace override of the projector $\mathbf{M} = \mathbf{U}_t^l \mathbf{U}_s^{l-1}$, because

$$\left\| \mathbf{X}_s^l - \mathbf{X}_t^l \right\|_F^2 = \left\| \mathbf{M} \mathbf{U}_s^l \boldsymbol{\Sigma}_s^l - \mathbf{U}_t^l \boldsymbol{\Sigma}_t^l \right\|_F^2 = \left\| \mathbf{U}_t^l \boldsymbol{\Sigma}_s^l - \mathbf{U}_t^l \boldsymbol{\Sigma}_t^l \right\|_F^2 \quad (15)$$

$$= \left\| \mathbf{U}_t^l \boldsymbol{\Sigma}_s^l \right\|_F^2 + \left\| \mathbf{U}_t^l \boldsymbol{\Sigma}_t^l \right\|_F^2 - 2Tr(\boldsymbol{\Sigma}_s^{l^T} \mathbf{U}_t^{l^T} \mathbf{U}_t^l \boldsymbol{\Sigma}_t^l) \quad (16)$$

$$= \left\| \boldsymbol{\Sigma}_s^l \right\|_F^2 + \left\| \boldsymbol{\Sigma}_t^l \right\|_F^2 - 2Tr(\boldsymbol{\Sigma}_s^{l^T} \boldsymbol{\Sigma}_t^l) \quad (17)$$

$$= \sum_{i=1}^{l} \sigma_i^2(\mathbf{X}_s^l) + \sum_{i=1}^{l} \sigma_i^2(X_t^l) - 2 \sum_{i=1}^{l} (\sigma_i(X_s^l) \cdot \sigma_i(X_t^l)) \quad (18)$$

$$= \sum_{i=1}^{l} (\sigma_i(\mathbf{X}_s^l) - \sigma_i(\mathbf{X}_t^l))^2. \quad (19)$$

The important fact in the right part of Eq. (16) and (17) is that we do not rely on the bound of the Frobenius inner product as in the proof for Eq. (14) [9, p. 459], because $\mathbf{U}_t^{l^T} \mathbf{U}_t^l = \mathbf{I}$. Therefore, we can directly compute the Frobenius inner product of the the diagonal matrices $\boldsymbol{\Sigma}_s^l$ and $\boldsymbol{\Sigma}_t^l$, which is simply the sum of the product of the singular values. Consequently follows for $l + 1$ and $(\sigma_{l+1}(\mathbf{X}_s) - \sigma_{l+1}(\mathbf{X}_t))^2 \neq 0$,

$$\left\| \mathbf{X}_s^l - \mathbf{X}_t^l \right\|_F^2 < \sum_{i=1}^{l+1} (\sigma_i(\mathbf{X}_s) - \sigma_i(\mathbf{X}_t))^2 < \sum_{i=1}^{q} (\sigma_i(\mathbf{X}_s) - \sigma_i(\mathbf{X}_t))^2 \leq \left\| \mathbf{X}_s - \mathbf{X}_t \right\|_F^2,$$
(20)

where again $q = min(n, d)$ and $1 < l < q$.

B   Appendix B Component Analysis

We inspect the performance contribution of the different parts of the NSO approach. First, the exact solution to the optimization problem is called Subspace Override (SO). The approximation with uniform sampling is evaluated to study the impact of class-wise sampling on the performance. To show the efficiency of the subspace projection in original space, we include a kernelized version where we approximate the RBF-kernels of $\mathbf{X}_s$ and $\mathbf{X}_t$, respectively. The results are given in Table 7 and show that the Nyström approximation independent of the sampling strategy yields the best performance. This comes from the approximation of the subspace projection, where small values are likely to be zero, hence reducing noise further. The kernelized version is not recommended due to bad performance. Overall, as proposed, the class-wise NSO is recommended, because it is slightly better.

Table 7. Component evaluation of NSO in mean accuracy.

Dataset	SO	$NSO_{uniform}$	$NSO_{classwise}$	NSO_{ker}
Reuters	94.8	**97.6**	**97.6**	80.8
Newsgroup	93.0	96.1	**97.4**	94.3
CO - Surf	**79.3**	79.1	**79.3**	56.5
CO - Decaf	79.2	**79.4**	**79.4**	76.4
Overall	86.2	**88.1**	**88.4**	77.0

References

1. Aljundi, R., Emonet, R., Muselet, D., Sebban, M.: Landmarks-based kernelized subspace alignment for unsupervised domain adaptation. In: 2015 IEEE Conference on Computer Vision and Pattern Recognition (CVPR), 07–12 June, pp. 56–63. IEEE, June 2015
2. Blitzer, J., Foster, D., Kakade, S.: Domain adaptation with coupled subspaces. J. Mach. Learn. Res. **15**, 173–181 (2011)

3. Dai, W., Yang, Q., Xue, G.R., Yu, Y.: Boosting for transfer learning. In: Proceedings of the 24th International Conference on Machine Learning - ICML 2007, pp. 193–200. ACM Press, New York (2007)
4. Donahue, J., et al.: DeCAF: a deep convolutional activation feature for generic visual recognition. In: 31st International Conference on Machine Learning, ICML 2014, vol. 2, pp. 988–996 (2014)
5. Elhadji-Ille-Gado, N., Grall-Maes, E., Kharouf, M.: Transfer learning for large scale data using subspace alignment. In: 2017 16th IEEE International Conference on Machine Learning and Applications (ICMLA), vol. 2018-January, pp. 1006–1010. IEEE, December 2017
6. Fernando, B., Habrard, A., Sebban, M., Tuytelaars, T.: Unsupervised visual domain adaptation using subspace alignment. In: Proceedings of the IEEE International Conference on Computer Vision, pp. 2960–2967 (2013)
7. Ghifary, M., Balduzzi, D., Kleijn, W.B., Zhang, M.: Scatter component analysis: a unified framework for domain adaptation and domain generalization. IEEE Trans. Pattern Anal. Mach. Intell. **39**(7), 1414–1430 (2017)
8. Gong, B., Shi, Y., Sha, F., Grauman, K.: Geodesic flow kernel for unsupervised domain adaptation. In: Proceedings of the IEEE Computer Society Conference on Computer Vision and Pattern Recognition, pp. 2066–2073 (2012)
9. Horn, R.A., Johnson, C.R.: Matrix Analysis. Cambridge University Press, Cambridge (2012)
10. Kierzkowski, J., Smoktunowicz, A.: Block normal matrices and Gershgorin-type discs. Electron. J. Linear Algebra **22**(October), 1059–1069 (2011)
11. Krizhevsky, A., Sutskever, I., Hinton, G.E.: ImageNet classification with deep convolutional neural networks. In: Pereira, F., Burges, C.J.C., Bottou, L., Weinberger, K.Q. (eds.) Advances in Neural Information Processing Systems 25, pp. 1097–1105. Curran Associates, Inc. (2012)
12. Liu, P., Yang, P., Huang, K., Tan, T.: Uniform low-rank representation for unsupervised visual domain adaptation. In: 2015 3rd IAPR Asian Conference on Pattern Recognition (ACPR), pp. 216–220, November 2015
13. Long, M., Cao, Y., Cao, Z., Wang, J., Jordan, M.I.: Transferable representation learning with deep adaptation networks. IEEE Trans. Pattern Anal. Mach. Intell. **PP**(c), 1 (2018)
14. Long, M., Wang, J., Ding, G., Pan, S.J., Yu, P.S.: Adaptation regularization: a general framework for transfer learning. IEEE Trans. Knowl. Data Eng. **26**(5), 1076–1089 (2014)
15. Long, M., Wang, J., Ding, G., Sun, J., Yu, P.S.: Transfer feature learning with joint distribution adaptation. In: Proceedings of the IEEE International Conference on Computer Vision, pp. 2200–2207 (2013)
16. Long, M., Wang, J., Sun, J., Yu, P.S.: Domain invariant transfer kernel learning. IEEE Trans. Knowl. Data Eng. **27**(6), 1519–1532 (2015)
17. Long, M., Zhu, H., Wang, J., Jordan, M.I.: Deep transfer learning with joint adaptation networks. In: Proceedings of the 34th International Conference on Machine Learning - Volume 70, ICML 2017, pp. 2208–2217. JMLR.org (2017)
18. Mahadevan, S., Mishra, B., Ghosh, S.: A unified framework for domain adaptation using metric learning on manifolds. In: Berlingerio, M., Bonchi, F., Gärtner, T., Hurley, N., Ifrim, G. (eds.) ECML PKDD 2018. LNCS (LNAI), vol. 11052, pp. 843–860. Springer, Cham (2019). https://doi.org/10.1007/978-3-030-10928-8_50
19. Pan, S.J., Tsang, I.W., Kwok, J.T., Yang, Q.: Domain adaptation via transfer component analysis. IEEE Trans. Neural Netw. **22**(2), 199–210 (2011)

20. Pan, S.J., Yang, Q.: A survey on transfer learning. IEEE Trans. Knowl. Data Eng. **22**(10), 1345–1359 (2010)
21. Raab, C., Schleif, F.-M.: Sparse transfer classification for text documents. In: Trollmann, F., Turhan, A.-Y. (eds.) KI 2018. LNCS (LNAI), vol. 11117, pp. 169–181. Springer, Cham (2018). https://doi.org/10.1007/978-3-030-00111-7_15
22. Raab, C., Schleif, F.M.: Low-Rank Subspace Override for Unsupervised Domain Adaptation. arXiv:1907.01343 (2019)
23. Schleif, F., Gisbrecht, A., Tiño, P.: Supervised low rank indefinite kernel approximation using minimum enclosing balls. Neurocomputing **318**, 213–226 (2018)
24. Shao, J., Huang, F., Yang, Q., Luo, G.: Robust prototype-based learning on data streams. IEEE Trans. Knowl. Data Eng. **30**(5), 978–991 (2018)
25. Shao, M., Kit, D., Fu, Y.: Generalized transfer subspace learning through low-rank constraint. Int. J. Comput. Vis. **109**(1–2), 74–93 (2014). https://doi.org/10.1007/s11263-014-0696-6
26. Sun, B., Feng, J., Saenko, K.: Return of frustratingly easy domain adaptation. In: Proceedings of the Thirtieth AAAI Conference on Artificial Intelligence, Phoenix, Arizona, USA, 12–17 February 2016, pp. 2058–2065 (2016)
27. Sun, B., Saenko, K.: Deep CORAL: correlation alignment for deep domain adaptation. In: Hua, G., Jégou, H. (eds.) ECCV 2016. LNCS, vol. 9915, pp. 443–450. Springer, Cham (2016). https://doi.org/10.1007/978-3-319-49409-8_35
28. Talwalkar, A., Kumar, S., Mohri, M.: Sampling methods for the Nyström method. J. Mach. Learn. Res. **13**, 981–1006 (2012)
29. Tzeng, E., Hoffman, J., Zhang, N., Saenko, K., Darrell, T.: Deep Domain Confusion: Maximizing for Domain Invariance. CoRR abs/1412.3 (2014)
30. Wang, J., Chen, Y., Yu, H., Huang, M., Yang, Q.: Easy transfer learning by exploiting intra-domain structures. In: 2019 IEEE International Conference on Multimedia and Expo (ICME), pp. 1210–1215. IEEE, July 2019
31. Wang, J., Feng, W., Chen, Y., Yu, H., Huang, M., Yu, P.S.: Visual domain adaptation with manifold embedded distribution alignment. In: 2018 ACM Multimedia Conference on Multimedia Conference - MM 2018, pp. 402–410. ACM Press, New York (2018)
32. Weiss, K., Khoshgoftaar, T.M., Wang, D.D.: A survey of transfer learning. J. Big Data **3**(1), 1–40 (2016). https://doi.org/10.1186/s40537-016-0043-6
33. Williams, C., Seeger, M.W.: Using the Nystrom method to speed up Kernel machines. In: Leen, T.K., Dietterich, T.G., Tresp, V. (eds.) NIPS Proceedings, vol. 13, pp. 682–688. MIT Press, Cambridge (2001)
34. Zhang, J., Li, W., Ogunbona, P.: Joint geometrical and statistical alignment for visual domain adaptation. In: 2017 IEEE Conference on Computer Vision and Pattern Recognition (CVPR), pp. 5150–5158. IEEE, July 2017

Expressive Explanations of DNNs by Combining Concept Analysis with ILP

Johannes Rabold[1]([✉]) [iD], Gesina Schwalbe[1,2] [iD], and Ute Schmid[1] [iD]

[1] Cognitive Systems, University of Bamberg, Bamberg, Germany
{johannes.rabold,gesina.schwalbe,ute.schmid}@uni-bamberg.de
[2] Holistic Engineering and Technologies, Artificial Intelligence,
Continental AG, Regensburg, Germany
gesina.schwalbe@continental-corporation.com

Abstract. Explainable AI has emerged to be a key component for black-box machine learning approaches in domains with a high demand for reliability or transparency. Examples are medical assistant systems, and applications concerned with the General Data Protection Regulation of the European Union, which features transparency as a cornerstone. Such demands require the ability to audit the rationale behind a classifier's decision. While visualizations are the de facto standard of explanations, they come short in terms of expressiveness in many ways: They cannot distinguish between different attribute manifestations of visual features (e.g. eye open vs. closed), and they cannot accurately describe the influence of *absence* of, and *relations* between features. An alternative would be more expressive symbolic surrogate models. However, these require symbolic inputs, which are not readily available in most computer vision tasks. In this paper we investigate how to overcome this: We use inherent features learned by the network to build a global, expressive, verbal explanation of the rationale of a feed-forward convolutional deep neural network (DNN). The semantics of the features are mined by a concept analysis approach trained on a set of human understandable visual concepts. The explanation is found by an Inductive Logic Programming (ILP) method and presented as first-order rules. We show that our explanation is faithful to the original black-box model (The code for our experiments is available at https://github.com/mc-lovin-mlem/concept-embeddings-and-ilp/tree/ki2020).

Keywords: Explainable AI · Concept analysis · Concept embeddings · Inductive Logic Programming

1 Introduction

Machine learning went through several changes of research perspective since its beginnings more than fifty years ago. Initially, machine learning algorithms were inspired by human learning [14]. Inductive Logic Programming (ILP) [17] and

© Springer Nature Switzerland AG 2020
U. Schmid et al. (Eds.): KI 2020, LNAI 12325, pp. 148–162, 2020.
https://doi.org/10.1007/978-3-030-58285-2_11

explanation-based generalization [16] were introduced as integrated approaches which combine reasoning in first-order logic and inductive learning.

With the rise of statistical approaches to machine learning, focus shifted from human-like learning to optimizing learning for high predictive accuracy. Deep learning architectures [7] resulted in data-intensive, black-box approaches with impressive performances in domains such as object recognition, machine translation, and game playing. However, since machine learning more and more is moving from the lab to the real world, researchers and practitioners alike realize that interpretable, human-like approaches to machine learning are necessary to allow developers as well as end-users to evaluate and understand classifier decisions or possibly also the learned models themselves.

Consequently there is a growing number of approaches to support explainability of black-box machine learning [1]. Explainable AI (XAI) approaches are proposed to support developers to recognize oversampling and problems with data quality such as number of available data, class imbalance, expensive labeling, and sampling biases [2,13]. For many application domains, it is a legal as well as an ethical obligation to make classifier decisions transparent and comprehensible to end-users who need to make sense of complex information, for instance in medical diagnosis, automotive safety, or quality control.

A main focus of research on explanations for image classifications is on visual explanations, that is, highlighting of relevant pixels such as LRP [23] or showing relevant areas in the image such as LIME [21]. However, visual explanations can only show which conjunction of information in an image is relevant. In many domains, more sophisticated information needs to be taken into account [24]:

- **Feature values:** highlighting the area of the eye in an image is not helpful to understand that it is important for the class decision that the lids are tightened (indicating pain) in contrast to eyes which are wide open (indicating startle, [29]);
- **Quantification:** highlighting all blowholes on the supporting parts of a rim does not make clear that the rim is not a reject because *all* blowholes are smaller than 0,5 mm;
- **Negation:** highlighting the flower in the hand of a person does not transport the information that this person is *not* a terrorist because he or she does *not* hold a weapon;
- **Relations:** highlighting all windows in a building cannot help to discriminate between a tower, where windows are *above* each other and a bungalow, where windows are *beside* each other [19];
- **Recursion:** highlighting all stones within a circle of stones cannot transport the information that there must be a sequence of an arbitrary number of stones with increasing size [20].

Such information can only be expressed in an expressive language, for instance some subset of first-order logic [18]. In previous work, it has been shown how ILP can be applied to replace the simple linear model agnostic explanations of LIME [3,19,20,25]. Alternatively, it is investigated how knowledge can be incorporated into deep networks. For example, capsule networks [22] are proposed to model hierarchical relationships and embeddings of knowledge graphs allow to grasp relationships between entities [8].

In this paper, we investigate how symbolic knowledge can be extracted from the inner layers of a deep convolutional neural network to uncover and extract relational information to build an expressive global explanation for the network. In the following, we first introduce concept embedding analysis (to extract visual concepts) and ILP (to build the explanation). In Sect. 3, the proposed approach to model-inherent generation of symbolic relational explanations is presented. We present a variety of experiments on a new "Picasso" data set of faces with permuted positions of sub-parts such as eyes, mouth, and nose. We conclude with an outlook to extend this first, preliminary investigation in the future.

2   Theoretical Background

2.1   Concept Embedding Analysis

To understand the process flow of an algorithm, it is of great value to have access to interpretable intermediate outputs. The goal of concept embedding analysis is to answer *whether, how well, how,* and with what *contribution to the reasoning* information about semantic concepts is embedded into the latent spaces (intermediate outputs) of DNNs, and to provide the result in an explainable way. Focus currently lies on finding embeddings in either the complete output of a layer (image-level concepts), or single pixels of an activation map of a convolutional DNN (concept segmentation). To answer the *whether*, one can try to find a decoder for the information about the concept of interest, the *concept embedding*. This means, one is looking for a classifier on the latent space that can predict the presence of the concept. The performance of the classifier provides a measure of *how well* the concept is embedded. For an explainable answer of *how* a concept is embedded, the decoder should be easily interpretable. One constraint to this is introduced by the rich vector space structure of the space of semantic concepts respectively word vector spaces [15]: The decoder map from latent to semantic space should preserve at least a similarity measure. For example, the encodings of "cat" and "dog" should be quite similar, whereas that of a "car" should be relatively distant from the two. The methods in literature can essentially be grouped by their choice of distance measure $\langle -, - \rangle$ used on the latent vector space. A concept embedding classifier E_c predicting the presence of concept c in the latent space L then is of the form $E_c(v) = \langle v_c, v \rangle > t_c$ for $v \in L$, where $v_c \in L$ is the concept vector of the embedding, and $t_c \in \mathbb{R}$.

Automated concept explanations [6] uses L_2 distance as similarity measure. They discover concepts in an unsupervised fashion by k-means clustering of the latent space representations of input samples. The concept vectors of the discovered concepts are the cluster centers. In TCAV [11] it is claimed that the mapping from semantic to latent space should be linear for best interpretability. To achieve this, they suggest to use linear classifiers as concept embeddings. This means they try to find a separation hyperplane between the latent space representations of positive and negative samples of the concept. A normal vector of the hyperplane then is their concept vector, and the distance to the hyperplane is used as distance measure. As method to obtain the embedding they use support vector machines (SVMs). TCAV further investigated the contribution of concepts to given output classes by sensitivity analysis. A very similar approach to TCAV, only instead relying on logistic regression, is followed by Net2Vec [5]. As a regularization, they add a filter-specific cut-off before the concept embedding analysis to remove noisy small activations. The advantage of Net2Vec over the SVMs in TCAV is that they can more easily be used in a convolutional setting: They used a 1×1-convolution to do a prediction of the concept for each activation map pixel, providing a segmentation of the concept. This was extended by [26], who suggested to allow larger convolution windows to ensure that the receptive field of the window can cover the complete concept. This avoids a focus on local patterns. A measure that can be applied to concept vectors of the same layer regardless of the analysis method, is that of *completeness* suggested in [31]. They try to measure, how much of the information relevant to the final output of the DNN is covered by a chosen set of concepts vectors. They also suggested a metric to compare the attribution of each concept to the completeness score of a set of concepts.

2.2 Inductive Logic Programming

Inductive Logic Programming (ILP) [17] is a machine learning technique that builds a logic theory over positive and negative examples (E^+, E^-). The examples consist of symbolic background knowledge (BK) in the form of first-order logic predicates, e.g. contains(Example, Part), isa(Part, nose). Here the upper case symbols are variables and the lower case symbol is a constant. The given BK describes that example Example contains a part Part which is a nose. Based on the examples, a logic theory can be learned. The hypothesis language of this theory consists of logic Horn clauses that contain predicates from the BK. We write the Horn clauses as implication rules, e.g.

```
face(Example):- contains(Example, Part), isa(Part, nose).
```

For this work we obey the syntactic rules of the Prolog programming language. The :- denotes the logic implication ($\leftarrow$). We call the part before the implication the *head* of a rule and the part after it the *body* or *preconditions* of a rule.

We use the framework Aleph [28] for this work since it is a flexible and adaptive general purpose ILP toolbox. Aleph's built in algorithm attempts to induce a logic theory from the given BK to cover as many positive examples E^+ as possible while avoiding covering the negative examples E^-. The general algorithm of Aleph can be summarized as follows [28]:

1. As long as positive examples exist, select one. Otherwise halt.
2. Construct the most-specific clause that entails the selected example and is within the language constraints.
3. Find a more general clause which is a subset of the current literals in the clause.

4. Remove examples covered by the current clause.
5. Repeat from step 1.

3   Explaining a DNN with Concept Localization and ILP

When building explanations for a DNN via approximate rule sets, the underlying logic and predicates of the rules should reflect the capabilities of the model. For example, spatial relations like top_of or right_of should be covered, as e.g. dense layers of a DNN are capable of encoding these. Spatial relations cannot be represented by current visualization methods for explainable AI, which only feature predicates of the form contains(Example, Part) and at_position(Part, xy). Rule-based methods like ILP are able to incorporate richer predicates into the output. However, their input must be symbolic background knowledge about the training and inference samples which is formulated using these predicates *explicitly*. For computer vision tasks with pixel-level input, this encoding of the background knowledge about samples is not available. To remedy this, we propose to use existing concept mining techniques for extraction of the required background knowledge:

1. Associate pre-defined visual semantic concepts with intermediate output of the DNN. Concepts can be local, like parts and textures, or image-level.
2. Automatically infer the background knowledge about a sample Ex given the additional concept output, which defines predicates isa(C, concept), and isa(Ex, C) (image-level) or contains(Ex, C) with at_position(C, xy). From this, spatial relations and negations can be extracted.
3. Given background knowledge for a set of training samples, apply an inductive logic programming approach to learn an expressive set of rules for the DNN.

The approach presented in this paper differs from the previous work outlined in [19] by the following main aspects:

- We will find a global verbal explanation for a black-box decision in contrast to a local explanation.
- We directly make use of information stored in the building blocks of the DNN instead of relying on the linear surrogate model generated by LIME.

3.1   Enrich DNN Output via Concept Embedding Analysis

We directly built upon the concept detection approach from [5,26], suggesting some further improvements. Net2Vec bilinearly upscaled the predicted masks before applying the sigmoid for logistic regression. This overrates the contribution to the loss by pixels at the edges from positive to negative predicted pixels. We instead apply upscaling after applying the sigmoid. Instead of the suggested IoU penalty from [26], we propose a more stable Dice loss to fit the overlap objective, supported by a small summand of the balanced binary cross-entropy (bBCE) suggested in Net2Vec to ensure pixel-wise accuracy.

One major disadvantage of the linear model approaches over the clustering ones is their instability, i.e. several runs for the same concept yield different concept vectors. Reasons may be dependence on the outliers of the concept cluster (SVM); non-unique solutions due to a margin between the clusters; and inherent variance of the used optimization methods. To decrease dependence on the training set selection and ordering, and the initialization values, we for now simply use ensembling. For this we define a hyperplane H as the zero set of the distance function $d_H(v) = (v - b_H \cdot v_H) \circ v_H$ for the normal vector v_H and the support vector $b_H v_H$, $b_H \in \mathbb{R}$. Then, the zero set of the mean $\frac{1}{N} \sum_{i=1}^{N} d_{H_i}$ of the distance functions of hyperplanes H_i again defines a hyperplane with

$$v_H = \frac{1}{N} \sum_{i=1}^{N} v_{H_i} \qquad \text{and} \qquad b_H = \frac{1}{\|v_H\|^2} \frac{1}{N} \sum_{i=1}^{N} (b_{H_i} \|v_{H_i}\|^2) \,.$$

Note, that hyperplanes with longer normal vectors (i.e. higher confidence values) are overrated in this calculation. To remedy this, concept vectors are normalized before ensembling, using the property $(w - b \cdot v) \circ v = \|v\| \cdot (w - (b\|v\|)) \frac{v}{\|v\|}) \cdot \frac{v}{\|v\|}$ of the distance function for scalar b and vectors v, w.

3.2 Automatic Generation of Symbolic Background Knowledge

The output of the concept analysis step (binary masks indicating the spatial location of semantic concepts) can be used to build a symbolic global explanation for the behavior of the original black-box model. We obtain the explanation by finding a first-order logic theory with the ILP approach Aleph (see Sect. 2.2). Since Aleph needs a set of positive and negative examples (E^+, E^-), the first step is to obtain these examples along with their corresponding symbolic background knowledge (BK). In order to obtain a good approximation of the behavior of the model, we sample N^+ binary masks from positively predicted images and N^- binary masks from negatively predicted images that lie close to the decision boundary of the original black-box model using the concept analysis model described above. Let M^+, M^- be the set of positive and negative binary masks. Let $m^+ \in M^+$, $m^- \in M^-$ be single masks. Each mask (e.g. m^+) consists of multiple mask layers (e.g. $l_c \in m^+$, $c \in C$) for the different human understandable concepts from the pool of concepts C. These mask layers are sparse matrices upsampled to the same size as the original images they are masking. The matrices have the value 1 at all the positions where the concept analysis model detected the respective concept and 0 at all other positions.

The symbolic explanation of the original model should consist of logic rules that establish the prototypical constellation of visual parts of an image that resembles the positive class as seen by the DNN. We therefore need not only the information about occurrence of certain visual parts in the sampled examples but also the different relations that hold between the parts. In the next sections we adhere to the following general workflow:

1. Find positions of visual parts in the examples and name them.
2. Find relations between parts.
3. Build BK with the information from step 1 and 2.
4. Induce a logic theory with Aleph.

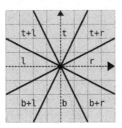

Fig. 1. Potential positions of an object to be only top of, right of, bottom of, or left of a reference object located in the origin. Also the four overlapping regions are indicated.

Find Visual Parts. One mask layer l_c contains possibly multiple contiguous clusters of concept propositions. Therefore, as a denoising step, we only take the cluster with the largest area into account. As a proposition for the position of the concept c in the picture, in this cluster we take the mean point of the area A_{max} of 1's in l_c. We therefore find the position $p_c = (x, y)$ with $x = (\min_x(A_{max}) + \max_x(A_{max}))/2$ and $y = (\min_y(A_{max}) + \max_y(A_{max}))/2$. This procedure can be followed for all masks l_c that are contained in all $m^+ \in M^+$ and $m^- \in M^-$.

Find Relations Between Parts. By taking relationships between the parts into account, we strive for more expressive explanations. For this work we limit ourselves to spatial relationships that hold between the parts that were found in the previous steps. We assume that pairs of two parts can be in the following four relationships to each other: `left_of`, `right_of`, `top_of`, `bottom_of`. We declare part A to be `top_of` part B if the vertical component y_A of the position p_A is above y_B and the value for the horizontal offset $\Delta x = x_A - x_B$ does not diverge from the value for the vertical offset $\Delta y = y_A - y_B$ by more than double. The other spatial relations can be formalized in an analogous manner. Thus, the relations that can hold between two parts A and B can be visualized as in Fig. 1.

Inferring Global Symbolic Explanations. After the inference of visual parts and the relationships that hold between them, we can build the BK needed for Aleph. Part affiliation to an example can be declared by the `contains` predicate. We give all parts a unique name over all examples. Suppose part A is part of a particular example E and describes the human understandable concept $c \in C$. Then the example affiliation can be stated by the predicates `contains(E, A)`, `isa(A, c)`. Likewise for the relations we can use 2-ary predicates that state the constellation that holds between the parts. When part A is left of part B we incorporate the predicate `left_of(A, B)` in the BK and likewise for the other relations. When the BK for the positive and negative examples E^+ and E^- is found, we can use Aleph's induction mechanism to find the set of rules that best fit the examples. The complete algorithm for the process is stated in Algorithm 1.

Algorithm 1. Verbal Explanation Generation for DNNs

1: **Require:** Positive and negative binary masks M^+, M^-
2: **Require:** Pool of human understandable concepts C
3: $E^+ \leftarrow \{\}$
4: $E^- \leftarrow \{\}$
5: **for each** $\odot \in \{+, -\}$ **do**
6:     **for each** $m^\odot \in M^\odot$ **do**
7:         $P \leftarrow \{\}$
8:         **for each** $l_c \in m^\odot$ where $c \in C$ **do**
9:             $p_c \leftarrow calculatePartPosition(l_c)$
10:            $P \leftarrow P \cup \{\langle c, p_c \rangle\}$
11:        $R \leftarrow calculateRelations(P)$
12:        $E^\odot \leftarrow E^\odot \cup \langle P, R \rangle$
13: $T \leftarrow \text{Aleph}(E^+, E^-)$
14: **return** T

---

4 Experiments and Results

We conducted a variety of experiments to audit our previously described approach. As a running example we used a DNN which we trained on images from a generated dataset we dubbed *Picasso Dataset*. The foundation are images of human faces we took from the FASSEG dataset [9,10]. The Picasso Dataset contains collage images of faces with the facial features (eyes, mouth, nose) either in the correct constellation (positive class) or in a mixed-up constellation (negative class). See Fig. 2 for examples. No distinction is made between originally left and right eyes.

Fig. 2. Examples from the Picasso Dataset (*left:* positive class, *right:* negative).

In order to not establish a divergence in the image space of the two classes, the positive and negative classes contain facial features that were cut out of a set of images from the original FASSEG dataset. As a canvas to include the features, we took a set of original faces and got rid of the facial features by giving the complete facial area a similar skin-like texture. Then we included the cut out facial features onto the original positions of the original features in the faces.

The face images in Fig. 2 show that the resulting dataset is rather constructed. This however will suffice for a proof of concept to show that our approach in fact exploits object parts and their relations. In the future we plan on moving towards more natural datasets.

4.1   Analyzed DNNs

We evaluated our method on three different architectures from the pytorch model-zoo[1]: AlexNet [12], VGG16 [27], and ResNeXt-50 [30]. The convolutional parts of the networks were initialized with weights pre-trained on the ImageNet dataset. For fine-tuning the DNNs for the Picasso Dataset task, the output dimension was reduced to one and the in- and output dimension of the second to last hidden dense layer was reduced to 512 for AlexNet and VGG16. Then the dense layers and the last two convolutional layers (AlexNet, VGG16) respectively bottleneck blocks (ResNeXt) were fine-tuned. The fine-tuning was conducted in one epoch on a training set of 18,002 generated, 224 × 224-sized picasso samples with equal distribution of positive and negative class. All models achieved accuracy greater than 99% on a test set of 999 positive and 999 negative samples.

4.2   Training the Concept Models

In our example we determined the best ensembled detection concept vectors for the concepts EYES, MOUTH and NOSE amongst the considered layers. We excluded layers with low receptive field, as they are assumed to hold only very local features (for the layers used see Fig. 3). Convolutional output was only considered after the activation. For each concept, 452 training/validation, and 48 test picasso samples with segmentation masks were used. The training objective was: Predict at each activation map pixel whether the kernel window centered there lies "over" an instance of the concept. Over meant that the fuzzy intersection of the concept segmentation and the kernel window area exceeds a threshold (*intersection encoding*). This fuzzy definition of a box center tackles the problem of sub-optimal intersections in later layers due to low resolution. Too high values may lead to elimination of an instance, and thresholds were chosen to avoid such issues with values 0.5/0.8/0.7 for nose/mouth/eye. We implemented the encoding via a convolution. As evaluation metric we use set IoU (sIoU) between the detection masks and the intersection encoded masks as in Net2Vec. On each dataset and each layer, 15 concept models were trained in three 5-fold-cross-validation runs with the following settings: Adam optimization with mean best learning rate of 0.001, a weighting of 5:1 of Dice to bBCE loss, batch size of 8, and two epochs (all layers showed quick convergence).

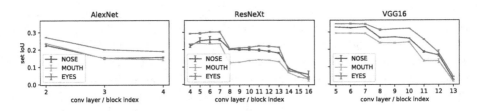

Fig. 3. The layer-wise mean set IoU results of the concept analysis runs.

[1] https://pytorch.org/docs/stable/torchvision/models.html.

Results. Our normalized ensembling approach proved valuable as it yielded mean or slightly better performance compared to the single runs. For the considered models, meaningful embeddings of all concepts could be found (see Table 1): The layers all reached sIoU values greater than 0.22 despite of the still seemingly high influence of sub-optimal resolutions of the activation maps. Figure 4 shows some exemplary outputs. The concepts were best embedded in earlier layers, while different concepts did not necessarily share the same layer.

Table 1. Results for ensemble embeddings with set IoU (sIoU), mean cosine distance to the runs (Cos.d.), and index of conv layer or block (L) (cf. Fig. 3).

AlexNet	L	sIoU	Cos.d.	VGG16	L	sIoU	Cos.d.	ResNeXt	L	sIoU	Cos.d.
NOSE	2	0.228	0.040	NOSE	7	0.332	0.104	NOSE	6	0.264	0.017
MOUTH	2	0.239	0.040	MOUTH	6	0.296	0.154	MOUTH	5	0.237	0.020
EYES	2	0.272	0.058	EYES	6	0.350	0.197	EYES	7	0.302	0.020

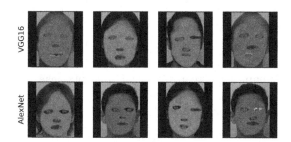

Fig. 4. Ensemble embedding outputs of NOSE (green), MOUTH (blue), EYES (red). (Color figure online)

4.3 Example Selection for ILP Training

The goal of the ILP model is to approximate the behavior of the main DNN, i.e. its decision boundary. For this, few but meaningful training samples and their DNN output are needed: class-prototypes as well as ones that tightly frame the DNN decision boundary. From the 1,998 samples in the picasso test set, in total 100 samples were chosen from the DNN test set to train the ILP model. The DNN confidence score here was used to estimate the proximity of a data point to the decision boundary. For each class, we selected the 50 samples predicted to be in this class and with confidence closest to the class boundary of 0.5. In our setup this provided a wide range of confidence values (including 0 and 1).

4.4 Finding the Symbolic Explanation

In order to find the background knowledge needed for Aleph to generate the explanation, we need to extract the information about the facial features and their constellations from the masks of the samples drawn in the previous step. Abiding the procedure described in Sect. 3.2, we first find contiguous clusters in the mask layers to then infer the positional information for them. This is straight-forward for the nose and the mouth but imposes a problem for the eyes, since we do not want to have a single position proposal for them in the eye that produces the biggest cluster in the mask layer. Thus, we allow for the top two biggest clusters to infer a position. Although we give them unique constants in the BK, we both give them the type eye $\in C$.

The next step consists of the extraction of the spatial features between the found parts. Since the relation pair left_of/right_of as well as top_of/bottom_of can be seen as the inverses of the respective other relation, we omit the relations right_of and bottom_of in the BK. This is possible, because the *Closed World Assumption* holds (Everything that is not stated explicitly is false).

Once the BK is found for all examples, we can let Aleph induce a theory of logic rules. Consider the induced theory for the trained VGG16 network:

```
face(F):- contains(F, A), isa(A, nose), contains(F, B), isa(B, mouth),
        top_of(A, B), contains(F, C), top_of(C, A).
```

The rule explicitly names the required facial concepts nose and mouth and the fact that the nose has to be above the mouth in order for an image to be a face. Further there is another unnamed component C required which has to be placed above the nose. By construction this has to be one of the eyes. The rule makes sense intuitively as it describes a subset of correct constellations of the features of a human face.

To further test the fidelity of the generated explanations to the original black-box network, we calculated several performance metrics for a test set of 1998 test images (999 positive and 999 negative examples). We handled the learned explanation rules as binary classification model for the test images in BK representation. If an image representation is covered by the explanation rules, it is predicted to be positive, otherwise negative. We now can handle the binary output of the black-box model as ground truth to our explanation predictions. The performance metrics together with the induced explanation rules for several DNN architectures are listed in Table 2. It can be seen that the explanations stay true to the original black-box model.

Table 2. Learned rules for different architectures and their fidelity scores (accuracy and F1 score wrt. to the original model predictions). Learned rules are of common form
`face(F):- contains(F, A), isa(A, nose), contains(F, B), isa(B, mouth), distinctPart`

Arch.	Accuracy	F1	Distinct rule part
VGG16	99.60%	99.60%	`top_of(A, B), contains(F, C), top_of(C, A)`
AlexNet	99.05%	99.04%	`contains(F, C), left_of(C, A), top_of(C, B), top_of(C, A)`
ResNext	99.75%	99.75%	`top_of(A, B), contains(F, C), top_of(C, A)`

5   Conclusion and Future Work

Within the described simple experiment we showed that expressive, verbal surrogate models with high fidelity can be found for DNNs using the developed methodology. We suggest that the approach is promising and worth future research and optimization.

The proposed concept detection approach requires a concept to have little variance in its size. It should easily extend to a concept with several size categories (e.g. close by and far away faces) by merging the result for each category. A next step for the background knowledge extraction would be to extend it to an arbitrary number of concept occurrences per image, where currently the algorithm assumes a fixed amount (exactly one mouth, one nose, two eyes). This could e.g. be achieved by allowing a maximum number per sliding window rather than an exact amount per image. In cases, where the predicates cannot be pre-defined, one can learn the relations as functions on the DNN output from examples as demonstrated in [4].

We further did not consider completeness (cf. Sect. 2.1) of the chosen concepts: They may not be well aligned with the decision relevant features used by the DNN, infringing fidelity of the surrogate model. We suggest two ways to remedy this: One could rely on (possibly less interpretable) concepts found via concept mining [6]. Or, since ILP is good at rejecting irrelevant information, one can start with a much larger set of pre-defined, domain related concepts. We further assume that best fidelity can only be achieved with the *minimal* complete sub-set of most decision-relevant concepts, which fosters uniqueness of the solution. For a decision relevance measure see e.g. [6].

It may be noted that the presented concept analysis approach is not tied to image classification: As long as the ground truth for concepts in the form of masks or classification values is available, the method can be applied to any DNN latent space (imagine e.g. audio, text, or video classification). However, spatial or temporal positions and relations are currently inferred using the receptive field information of convolutional DNNs. This restriction may again be resolved by learning of relations.

Lastly, in order to examine the understandability of the induced explanation in a real world scenario, we need to let explanations be evaluated in a human user study. For this matter, subjective evaluation measures have to be specifically designed for verbal explanations.

References

1. Adadi, A., Berrada, M.: Peeking inside the black-box: a survey on explainable artificial intelligence (XAI). IEEE Access **6**, 52138–52160 (2018)
2. Arya, V., et al.: One explanation does not fit all: a toolkit and taxonomy of AI explainability techniques. CoRR (2019). http://arxiv.org/abs/1909.03012
3. Dai, W.Z., Xu, Q., Yu, Y., Zhou, Z.H.: Bridging machine learning and logical reasoning by abductive learning. In: Advances in Neural Information Processing Systems, pp. 2811–2822 (2019)
4. Donadello, I., Serafini, L., d'Avila Garcez, A.S.: Logic tensor networks for semantic image interpretation. In: Proceedings of the 26th International Joint Conference on Artificial Intelligence, pp. 1596–1602. ijcai.org (2017). https://doi.org/10.24963/ijcai.2017/221
5. Fong, R., Vedaldi, A.: Net2Vec: quantifying and explaining how concepts are encoded by filters in deep neural networks. In: Proceedings of the 2018 IEEE Conference on Computer Vision and Pattern Recognition, pp. 8730–8738. IEEE (2018). https://doi.org/10.1109/CVPR.2018.00910
6. Ghorbani, A., Wexler, J., Zou, J.Y., Kim, B.: Towards automatic concept-based explanations. In: Advances in Neural Information Processing Systems 32, pp. 9273–9282 (2019). http://papers.nips.cc/paper/9126-towards-automatic-concept-based-explanations
7. Goodfellow, I., Bengio, Y., Courville, A.: Deep Learning. MIT Press, Cambridge (2016)
8. Ji, G., He, S., Xu, L., Liu, K., Zhao, J.: Knowledge graph embedding via dynamic mapping matrix. In: Proceedings of the 53rd Annual Meeting of the Association for Computational Linguistics and the 7th International Joint Conference on Natural Language Processing (Vol. 1: Long Papers), pp. 687–696 (2015)
9. Khan, K., Mauro, M., Leonardi, R.: Multi-class semantic segmentation of faces. In: Proceedings of the 2015 IEEE International Conference on Image Processing (ICIP), pp. 827–831. IEEE (2015)
10. Khan, K., Mauro, M., Migliorati, P., Leonardi, R.: Head pose estimation through multi-class face segmentation. In: Proceedings of the 2017 IEEE International Conference on Multimedia and Expo (ICME). pp. 175–180. IEEE (2017)
11. Kim, B., et al.: Interpretability beyond feature attribution: Quantitative testing with concept activation vectors (TCAV). In: Proceedings of the 35th International Conference on Machine Learning. Proceedings of Machine Learning Research, vol. 80, pp. 2668–2677. PMLR (2018). http://proceedings.mlr.press/v80/kim18d.html
12. Krizhevsky, A.: One weird trick for parallelizing convolutional neural networks. CoRR (2014). http://arxiv.org/abs/1404.5997
13. Lapuschkin, S., Wäldchen, S., Binder, A., Montavon, G., Samek, W., Müller, K.R.: Unmasking clever hans predictors and assessing what machines really learn. Nat. Commun. **10**(1), 1–8 (2019)

14. Michalski, R.S., Carbonell, J.G., Mitchell, T.M. (eds.): Machine Learning - An Artificial Intelligence Approach. Tioga, Palo Alto (1983)

15. Mikolov, T., Yih, W.T., Zweig, G.: Linguistic regularities in continuous space word representations. In: Proceedings of the 2013 Conference on North American Chapter Association for Computational Linguistics: Human Language Technologies, pp. 746–751. Association for Computational Linguistics (2013). https://www.aclweb.org/anthology/N13-1090

16. Mitchell, T.M., Keller, R.M., Kedar-Cabelli, S.T.: Explanation-based generalization: a unifying view. Mach. Learn. **1**(1), 47–80 (1986). https://doi.org/10.1023/A:1022691120807

17. Muggleton, S.: Inductive logic programming. New Gener. Comput. **8**(4), 295–318 (1991)

18. Muggleton, S., Schmid, U., Zeller, C., Tamaddoni-Nezhad, A., Besold, T.: Ultrastrong machine learning: comprehensibility of programs learned with ILP. Mach. Learn. **107**(7), 1119–1140 (2018). https://doi.org/10.1007/s10994-018-5707-3

19. Rabold, J., Deininger, H., Siebers, M., Schmid, U.: Enriching visual with verbal explanations for relational concepts-combining lime with Aleph. arXiv preprint arXiv:1910.01837 (2019)

20. Rabold, J., Siebers, M., Schmid, U.: Explaining black-box classifiers with ILP – empowering LIME with Aleph to approximate non-linear decisions with relational rules. In: Riguzzi, F., Bellodi, E., Zese, R. (eds.) ILP 2018. LNCS (LNAI), vol. 11105, pp. 105–117. Springer, Cham (2018). https://doi.org/10.1007/978-3-319-99960-9_7

21. Ribeiro, M.T., Singh, S., Guestrin, C.: Why should i trust you?: Explaining the predictions of any classifier. In: Proceedings of the 22nd ACM SIGKDD International Conference on Knowledge Discovery and Data Mining, pp. 1135–1144. ACM (2016)

22. Sabour, S., Frosst, N., Hinton, G.E.: Dynamic routing between capsules. In: Advances in Neural Information Processing Systems, pp. 3856–3866 (2017)

23. Samek, W., Wiegand, T., Müller, K.R.: Explainable artificial intelligence: understanding, visualizing and interpreting deep learning models. CoRR (2017). http://arxiv.org/abs/1708.08296

24. Schmid, U.: Inductive programming as approach to comprehensible machine learning. In: Proceedings of the 6th Workshop KI & Kognition, KIK-2018. Co-located with KI 2018 (2018). http://ceur-ws.org/Vol-2194/schmid.pdf

25. Schmid, U., Finzel, B.: Mutual explanations for cooperative decision making in medicine. KI - Künstliche Intelligenz, Special Issue Challenges in Interactive Machine Learning 34 (2020)

26. Schwalbe, G., Schels, M.: Concept enforcement and modularization as methods for the ISO 26262 safety argumentation of neural networks. In: Proceedings of the 10th European Congress Embedded Real Time Software and Systems (2020). https://hal.archives-ouvertes.fr/hal-02442796

27. Simonyan, K., Zisserman, A.: Very deep convolutional networks for large-scale image recognition. In: Proceedings of the 3rd International Conference on Learning Representations (2015). http://arxiv.org/abs/1409.1556

28. Srinivasan, A.: The Aleph Manual (2004). https://www.cs.ox.ac.uk/activities/programinduction/Aleph

29. Weitz, K., Hassan, T., Schmid, U., Garbas, J.U.: Deep-learned faces of pain and emotions: elucidating the differences of facial expressions with the help of explainable AI methods. tm-Technisches Messen **86**(7–8), 404–412 (2019)

30. Xie, S., Girshick, R.B., Dollár, P., Tu, Z., He, K.: Aggregated residual transformations for deep neural networks. In: Proceedings of the 2017 IEEE Conference on Computer Vision and Pattern Recognition, pp. 5987–5995. IEEE (2017). https://doi.org/10.1109/CVPR.2017.634

31. Yeh, C.K., Kim, B., Arik, S.O., Li, C.L., Pfister, T., Ravikumar, P.: On completeness-aware concept-based explanations in deep neural networks. CoRR (2020). http://arxiv.org/abs/1910.07969

Stable Resolving - A Randomized Local Search Heuristic for MaxSAT

Julian Reisch[1,2]([⊠]), Peter Großmann[1], and Natalia Kliewer[2]

[1] Synoptics GmbH, Chemnitzer Str. 48b, 01187 Dresden, Germany
{julian.reisch,peter.grossmann}@synoptics.de
[2] Freie Universität Berlin, Garystraße 21, 14195 Berlin, Germany
natalia.kliewer@fu-berlin.de
http://www.synoptics.de/

Abstract. Many problems from industrial applications and AI can be encoded as Maximum Satisfiability (MaxSAT). Often, it is more desirable to produce practicable results in very short time compared to optimal solutions after an arbitrary long computation time. In this paper, we propose Stable Resolving (SR), a novel randomized local search heuristic for MaxSAT with that aim. SR works for both weighted and unweighted instances. Starting from a feasible initial solution, the algorithm repeatedly performs the three steps of perturbation, improvements and solution checking. In the perturbation, the search space is explored at the cost of possibly worsening the current solution. The local improvements work by repeatedly flipping signs of variables in over-satisfied clauses. Finally, the algorithm performs a solution checking in a simulated annealing fashion. We compare our approach to state-of-the-art MaxSAT solvers and show by numerical experiments on benchmark instances from the annual MaxSAT competition that SR performs comparable on average and is even the best solver for particular problem instances.

Keywords: Maximum Satisfiability · MaxSAT · Incomplete solving · Randomized algorithm · Local search algorithm · Simulated annealing

1 Introduction

We consider the Constraint Satisfaction Problem of Maximum Satisfiability (MaxSAT). Many NP-hard optimization problems from applications in industry and AI can be encoded as MaxSAT and existing solution algorithms have proved to yield results that are competitive to domain specific solvers. The applications vary from periodic scheduling [15], to causal discovery [18], Bayesian network structure learning [9], correlation clustering [8], reasoning over bionetworks [16], probabilistic inference [20] and many more. A MaxSAT encoding consists a Boolean formula that we assume to be in conjunctive normal form (CNF) which means that the literals are grouped in clauses where they are connected disjunctively (*or*) and the clauses are connected conjunctively (*and*).

© Springer Nature Switzerland AG 2020
U. Schmid et al. (Eds.): KI 2020, LNAI 12325, pp. 163–175, 2020.
https://doi.org/10.1007/978-3-030-58285-2_12

Example. A Boolean formula in CNF: $F = (\neg x \vee \neg y) \wedge (\neg y \vee \neg z)$.

A literal is a variable together with a positive or negative sign. A clause is satisfied if at least one of its literals has the same sign as the variable in the solution. We also say the literal is *true* and denote the number of true literals in a clause its *stability*. An unsatisfied clause has a stability of zero. When a clause has a stability greater than 1, we say that the clause is over-satisfied. A solution is an assignment of the variables to *true* or *false* and is called *feasible* if all hard clauses are satisfied. We assume the formula to consist of both hard clauses and (possibly weighted) soft clauses. The sum of (the weights of) satisfied soft clauses is the objective function value. Then, the task is to find a feasible solution maximizing the objective function value.

Example. Let $F = H_1 \wedge H_2 \wedge S_1 \wedge S_2 \wedge S_3$ where

$$
\begin{aligned}
H_1 &: \ \neg x \vee \neg y \\
H_2 &: \ \neg y \vee \neg z \\
S_1 &: \ x && weight(S_1) = 2 \\
S_2 &: \ y && weight(S_2) = 3 \\
S_3 &: \ z && weight(S_3) = 2
\end{aligned}
$$

are hard and soft clauses with according weights respectively. Then, the optimal solution of value 4 is $x = z = true$ and $y = false$.

Due to its generic form, almost any problem from combinatorial optimization and many optimization problems in AI can be encoded as MaxSAT and practice shows that this conversion often works well. In this paper, we propose a novel heuristic solution approach to the MaxSAT problem called Stable Resolving (SR). The aim is to solve even large problem instances with millions of clauses and variables within short time, that is, up to 60 s, to a practicable solution. To do so, SR repeatedly performs the three steps of perturbation, improvements and solution checking, starting from an initial feasible solution. In the perturbation, the search space is explored by satisfaction of randomly picked unsatisfied (soft) clauses at the cost of other clauses becoming unsatisfied. More precisely, we consider the randomly picked clauses as hard clauses and call a SAT solver on them, together with the original hard clauses. If other, formerly satisfied soft clauses become unsatisfied by this perturbation, we write them in a list of unsatisfied candidate clauses. Then, in the improvement part, a local search technique is employed that builds on the clauses' stabilities. Starting with the first member of the list of unsatisfied candidate clauses, clauses with stability zero are being satisfied by flipping the sign of a randomly chosen variable. Flipping the sign of one of its variables increases the clause's stability by 1 but might cause other clauses to become unsatisfied. These unsatisfied clauses are added to the (local) search space and will be tried to be satisfied later. On the other hand, if flipping a variable's sign increases other clauses' stabilities to a number larger 1, that is, they become over-satisfied, they can have at least one literal falsified without becoming unsatisfied. This falsification can hence satisfy yet other clauses that contain the same variable with opposite sign and improve the objective function again. In this way, the local search space grows until all unsatisfied clauses have been tried to satisfy. Then, the improvement step ends and if the objective function value has decreased, the previous solution is restored. Else, newly unsatisfied clauses are added to the list of unsatisfied candidate clauses. As candidate clauses are only added when the objective function value increases, and one candidate is erased when it decreases, this list will eventually be empty. Then, the solution checking part begins. Here, a worsening of the objective value is allowed with a probability that decreases during the run of the algorithm.

The outline of the paper will be as follows. After a literature overview over existing approaches in Sect. 2, we explain the algorithm in detail in Sect. 3. In Sect. 4, we present and discuss our results on common benchmark instances and finally give a conclusion and outlook in Sect. 5.

2   Related Work

There are numerous solution approaches for the MaxSAT problem both exact and heuristic ones. Let us point out the differences between SR and other state-of-the-art MaxSAT solvers. In the 2019's MaxSAT competition [1], the solver Loandra performed best in the incomplete unweighted track. It combines a core-guided approach for finding a lower bound [7] and a linear algorithm for an upper bound. As the linear algorithm, the authors use LinSBPS [13] that performs a neighborhood search in a complete algorithmic setting by repeatedly calling the SAT Solver glucose [4]. In contrast to LinSPBS, we only call glucose once at the beginning for an initial solution and for the perturbation of a solution but not in order to achieve an improvement. Moreover, we do not calculate lower bounds at all. The local search algorithms MaxRoster (a description can be found in [5]) which is based on Ramp [14] and SATLike [19] which iteratively flips the sign of variables that bring the best improvement work differently than our solver in the respect that they adapt weights of clauses in order to leave local optima. We, however, perturb a current solution for that purpose and instead of changing weights. (Max-)WalkSAT and GSAT [23] are local search approaches similar to SR in the sense that unsatisfied clauses are picked at random and one of their variables' sign is flipped. The difference to our approach is that SR searches a larger neighborhood with a more complex improvement heuristics based on stabilities. In fact, one can consider SR a large neighborhood search, as pursued in the OR world (cf. e.g. [21]), with the difference that SR finds improvements in the neighborhood heuristically and without calling an exact solver whereas the repair procedure in large neighborhood searches often involve an exact solver. At the end of each iteration, SR checks the solution in a simulated annealing fashion. Simulated annealing with reset has been used also for MaxSAT [10,17]. Finally, let us point out that the splitting of our algorithm into perturbation, improvement and solution checking was introduced for a state-of-the-art Maximum Independent Set (MIS) heuristic [3] that in a previous work, we have been able to extend by a different improvement technique and simulated annealing solution checking in order to solve MaxSAT instances that have been transformed to MIS [22]. In contrast, in this paper we propose an algorithm that works directly on the Boolean formula.

3 Algorithm

The overall procedure of SR is shown in Algorithm 1. We first apply a SAT-based preprocessing on the formula. That is, we label the soft clauses meaning that each soft clause gets an additional variable l and will be considered a hard clause. In addition, for each label, we introduce a unit soft clause $\neg l$ with the weight the original soft clause had [6]. For the obtained equivalent formula, we apply unit clause propagation and bounded variable elimination (cf. e.g. [12]) on the hard clauses, as long as it is possible. Note that the label variables are excluded from the propagations since these operations are only sound for hard clauses. Then, for an initial feasible solution the SAT solver glucose [4] is called.

The algorithm then repeatedly executes the three steps of perturbation, improvement and solution checking.

Algorithm 1. StableResolving()

Preprocess()
CalculateInitialSolution()
while *timeout has not been reached* **do**
   | Perturb()
   | StableImprove()
   | CheckSolution()
end

Let us explain the single parts in greater detail. In the perturbation part shown in Algorithm 2, we explore the search space. More precisely, we first sample a random number k from the geometric distribution with parameter p and select k unsatisfied clauses uniformly at random. Then, we call the SAT solver glucose on all hard clauses and the selected clauses. Additionally, we give the previous solution as an initial solution to the solver in order to speed up the computation. If this formula is feasible, we have altered the solution, but maybe at the cost of a lower objective function value because formerly satisfied clauses are now unsatisfied. These unsatisfied clauses are added to the back of a list of *candidates* that potentially can be satisfied by improvements. We keep and update this list throughout the algorithm.

Algorithm 2. Perturb()

---

k = random number where $\mathbb{P}[k = i] = p(1 - p)^{i-1}$
$\mathcal{C}$ = set of k unsatisfied clauses picked uniformly at random
Call SAT solver on $\mathcal{C}$ and all hard clauses and overwrite the solution
Add newly unsatisfied clauses to the back of *candidates*

Example. Consider the example formula F from above. An initial feasible solution is given by all variables set to $false$. The perturbation might set $k = 1$, choose the unsatisfied clause $C = S_2$ and the SAT solver returns the feasible solution of $y = true$ and $x = z = false$. No clause gets unsatisfied by this step.

Remark. In some large instances from industrial applications, sampling a random unsatisfied clause is computationally expensive when all clauses are iterated through in order to detect the unsatisfied ones and sample among them. This is why we keep a superset of the unsatisfied clauses where every time a clause gets unsatisfied, it is added to. Moreover, we apply a heuristic in this superset and sample 1000 clause indices at random and only return if the corresponding clause indeed is unsatisfied. Only if all 1000 sampled clauses are satisfied, we iterate through the superset to find the unsatisfied clauses and sample among them.

Algorithm 3. StableImprove()

---

while $candidates \neq \emptyset$ **do**
   C = pop first clause from $candidates$
   Init $A = \emptyset$ and $\mathcal{C} = \{C\}$
   while $\exists v = variable\ picked\ uniformly\ at\ random\ in\ vars(\mathcal{C}) \setminus A$ **do**
      Flip sign of v and add v to A
      Add newly unsatisfied clauses to $\mathcal{C}$
      $Stab_{1\to2}$ = set of clauses whose stability has grown to 2
      foreach $S \in Stab_{1\to2}$ **do**
         w = variable of second true literal in S
         if w is in no clause of stability 1 nor in A **then**
            | Flip sign of w and add w to A
         end
      end
   end
   if objective function value has decreased **then**
      | Revert flips of variables in A
   end
   else
      | Add $\mathcal{C}$ at the back of $candidates$
   end
end

In the improvement part shown in Algorithm 3, we iteratively pick a variable uniformly at random of an unsatisfied clause (at first from the candidates and later from the clauses that have been unsatisfied during this improvement step) and flip its sign. A flip might lead to other clauses becoming unsatisfied now and we store them in the set $\mathcal{C}$. Note that also hard clauses can become temporarily unsatisfied. On the other hand, there might be a set $Stab_{1\to2}$ of clauses whose stability grows from 1 to 2 which means that there exists now a second true literal whose variable's sign can now be flipped without unsatisfying this clause.

This optimization technique of considering variables in over-satisfied constraints is well-known in mathematical optimization (cf. e.g. Simplex Method [11]) and we apply it here as a local improvement heuristics. In our algorithm, the clauses in $Stab_{1\to 2}$ are iterated through and checked for such an improvement. When no more variables are found that can be flipped, either because C is empty or all variables from C, denoted $vars(C)$, are flipped already, the improvement step ends. Either the objective function value has increased, then the now unsatisfied clauses are added to the candidates, or it has not and the flips, stored in A, are reverted. Note that the feasible solution remains feasible as the objective function value cannot increase when hard clauses have become unsatisfied. The improvement part ends when there are no more candidate clauses.

Remark. In some test instances, the set C monotonously grows and never shrinks because there are more new unsatisfied clauses than clauses that can either be satisfied or whose variables have all been considered for an improvement. In order to avoid that we spend too much time in a single local improvement step, we set an iterations limit of 25 for the inner while-loop.

Note that both while-loops terminate. For the outer one, candidate clauses are only added if the objective function value has increased which cannot be infinitely often as MaxSAT instances are always bounded. The inner one ends - besides the iterations limit - when A contains all variables.

Example. Consider the example formula F with solution

$$(x, y, z) = (false, true, false)$$

from above. The stabilities of the following steps are illustrated in Fig. 1. S_1 is unsatisfied and might be the first candidate clause (a). Flipping the sign of its

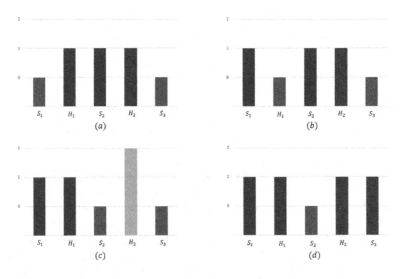

Fig. 1. Stabilities of clauses during an improvement step.

only variable x unsatisfies H_1 because y has been set to *true* in the perturbation already (b). Hence, H_1 gets added to $\mathcal{C}$ and x to A. Flipping the sign of one of the variables of H_1 (the only clause in $\mathcal{C}$) that has not already been flipped (i.e. that is not in A) means flipping y to *false*. Note that H_2 has now stability 2 and gets added to $Stab_{1 \to 2}$ as both variables y and z are *false* (c). The variable z is the second *true* literal that has been *true* before, so its sign gets flipped because no further clause is being unsatisfied by that flip. The improvement step ends with a objective function value that has increased from 3 to 4 (d).

Let us mention that during an improvement step (and after the perturbation), it is possible that formerly satisfied hard clauses become unsatisfied. Hard clauses have a weight greater than the sum of the weights of the soft clauses. Therefore, breaking hard clauses (without satisfying other formerly unsatisfied hard clauses) worsens the solution. In order to leave local optima, however, a worsening is possible in our algorithm - with decreasing probability according to the simulated annealing step, as will be explained in the remainder of this section.

Algorithm 4. CheckSolution()

---

if *objective function value has increased to the best one ever seen* **then**
  | Save new best solution
end
else if *objective function value has decreased* **then**
  | **if** *number of iterations without improvement has exceeded m* **then**
  | | Restore best solution
  | **end**
  | **else**
  | | Restore previous solution with probability $exp(-prob)$
  | **end**
end

After the improvements we have arrived in a local optimum. The current solution might be of smaller objective function value than the previous solution from before this iteration of Algorithm 1 if the improvements could not compensate the perturbation. Still, we sometimes allow such a worsening in the simulated annealing approach shown in Algorithm 4 in order to be able to leave local optima. More precisely, we restore the previous solution if it had a better objective function value with a probability growing exponentially with a factor *prob* that decreases linearly during the course of the algorithm from 1 to 0 and represents the temperature of the simulated annealing. If, however, the number of iterations without an improvement exceeds a parameter m, we reset to the best solution ever seen. When SR terminates, this best solution is returned.

4   Experimental Results

We have applied SR to problem instances and compared it to results that are taken from the 2019's MaxSAT competition[1] [1]. The instances encode various industrial applications' and theoretical problems, such as scheduling, fault diagnosis, tree-width computation, max clique problems, causal discovery, Ramsey number approximation and many more. An overview of the competing solvers can be found in [5]. For all calculations, we set the parameters for the geometric distribution and maximum steps in SR to $p = 0.75$ and $m = 1000$, respectively, because they yield the best results on average. We performed all computations on an Intel Core i7-8700K and with a time limit of 60 s. Note that if a solver from [1] yields worse results on our machine than in the results of the 2019's MaxSAT competition where computations were performed on the StarExec Cluster [2], we include the better results for the analysis here. We mark such solvers with an asterisk*.

Table 1. Sum of scores by solver on unweighted instances

Loandra	LinSBPS 2018	SR	SATLike*	Open WBO g	sls mcs*	sls mcs lsu*	Open WBO ms
251.7327	238.3298	231.1436	227.4589	204.1828	202.7803	202.7158	190.9274

Table 1 and Table 2 show the sum of scores of the competing solvers on the unweighted and weighted benchmark instances, respectively, from the incomplete track of the MaxSAT competition against the scores of SR. The score of a solver on an instance is calculated in the following way. Maximizing the sum

Table 2. Sum of scores by solver on weighted instances

Loandra	236.2272
TT Open WBO Inc*	233.4784
LinSBPS2018	231.6581
Open WBO Inc (inc bmo satlike)*	220.3607
Open WBO Inc (inc bmo complete)*	218.6454
SR	213.3262
Open WBO g*	212.1081
SATLike*	210.6802
sls mcs2*	203.1498
Open WBO ms*	194.5451
sls mcs*	191.4503
uwrmaxsat inc*	190.7841

---

[1] We have submitted SR to the 2020's MaxSAT competition.

(of weights) of satisfied soft clauses is equivalent to minimizing the sum (of weights) of unsatisfied soft clauses, which is denoted by the *gap*. The score of a solver on an instance is the fraction of the best gap known divided by the gap of the particular solver. If a solver's solution violates a hard clause, its score is zero and its gap infinity.

Example. Consider the example above. In the optimal solution, only S_2 is unsatisfied which yields the optimal gap of 3. If solver A has achieved this optimum, solvers B and C satisfy only S_2 and not S_1 and S_3, then their scores are $3/4$ while solver A has the maximal score of 1 on this instance.

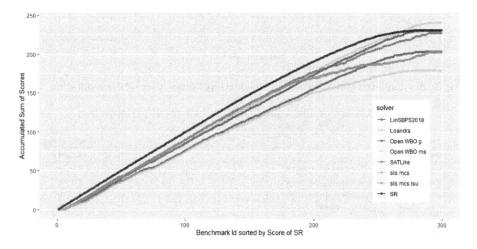

Fig. 2. Accumulated sum of scores of unweighted instances after 60 s computation time

The score hence reflects the ratio of the achieved result to the optimal (or best known) one. In Fig. 2 and Fig. 3, we see the accumulated sum of scores of the single instances, ordered by SR's scores and grouped by the competing solvers for the unweighted and weighted instances, respectively. The figures illustrate that SR (black) has the highest sum of scores on a large subset of instances. Counting all instances, including those where SR has low scores, we conclude that SR still has a competitive performance. More precisely, in 210 and 179 of the 299 unweighted and 297 weighted instances, SR has a score at least the mean of the other solvers. Furthermore, SR performs especially well on the unweighted instances, in comparison to the other solvers.

What is more, SR often has the best result among all solvers for particular instances. We observe that in the unweighted case, SR performs especially well on instances from *atcos*, *extension enforcement* and *set covering*. In the weighted case, SR is best on many instances encoding the *Minimum Weight Dominating Set Problem*. See Tables 3 and 4 for complete lists of such instances in the unweighted and weighted case, respectively. For a better comparison, we include a column showing the gaps of the winning solver Loandra, as well.

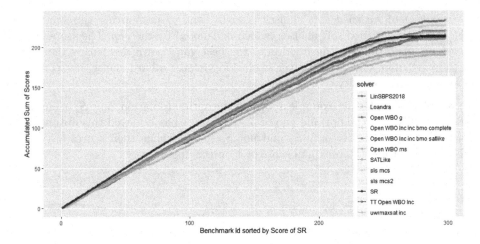

Fig. 3. Accumulated sum of scores of weighted instances after 60 s computation time

Table 3. Gaps of unweighted instances where SR performs best

	Benchmark	SR	Loandra
1	aes/sbox-8.wcnf.gz	443	690
2	atcoss/mesat/atcoss-mesat-04.wcnf.gz	97	Inf
3	atcoss/mesat/atcoss-mesat-05.wcnf.gz	74	Inf
4	atcoss/mesat/atcoss-mesat-10.wcnf.gz	32	40
5	atcoss/mesat/atcoss-mesat-18.wcnf.gz	80	Inf
6	atcoss/sugar/atcoss-sugar-15.wcnf.gz	133	Inf
7	extension-enforcement/extension-enforcement-non-strict-stb-200-0.05-1-10-0.wcnf.gz	7	18
8	extension-enforcement/extension-enforcement-non-strict-stb-200-0.05-2-10-2.wcnf.gz	12	20
9	extension-enforcement/extension-enforcement-non-strict-stb-200-0.05-3-10-1.wcnf.gz	8	9
10	extension-enforcement/extension-enforcement-non-strict-stb-200-0.05-3-10-4.wcnf.gz	10	16
11	extension-enforcement/extension-enforcement-non-strict-stb-200-0.05-4-10-1.wcnf.gz	7	17
12	extension-enforcement/extension-enforcement-non-strict-stb-200-0.05-4-10-2.wcnf.gz	6	13
13	extension-enforcement/extension-enforcement-non-strict-stb-200-0.05-4-10-4.wcnf.gz	8	18
14	min-fill/MinFill-R3-miles1000.wcnf.gz	3634	3755
15	optic/gen-cvc-add7to3-9999.wcnf.gz	197	204
16	pseudoBoolean/garden/normalized-g100x100.opb.msat.wcnf.gz	2163	2526
17	railway-transport/d4.wcnf.gz	8296	8524
18	SeanSafarpour/wb-4m8s1.dimacs.filtered.wcnf.gz	58	282
19	SeanSafarpour/wb-4m8s4.dimacs.filtered.wcnf.gz	220	230
20	set-covering/crafted/scpclr/scpclr13-maxsat.wcnf.gz	27	28
21	set-covering/crafted/scpcyc/scpcyc07-maxsat.wcnf.gz	145	149
22	set-covering/crafted/scpcyc/scpcyc08-maxsat.wcnf.gz	363	390
23	set-covering/crafted/scpcyc/scpcyc09-maxsat.wcnf.gz	835	972
24	set-covering/crafted/scpcyc/scpcyc10-maxsat.wcnf.gz	1967	2242
25	set-covering/crafted/scpcyc/scpcyc11-maxsat.wcnf.gz	4771	5623
26	uaq/uaq-ppr-nr200-nc66-n5-k2-rpp4-ppr12-plb100.wcnf.gz	75	78
27	xai-mindset2/liver-disorder.wcnf.gz	316	318

Table 4. Gaps of weighted instances where SR performs best

	Benchmark	SR	Loandra
1	causal-discovery/causal-Water-10-1000.wcnf.gz	11339025	16041455
2	causal-discovery/causal-Wdbc-8-569.wcnf.gz	1446339	2541316
3	correlation-clustering/Rounded-CorrelationClustering-Vowel-BINARY-N740-D0.200.wcnf.gz	120199215	130874895
4	correlation-clustering/Rounded-CorrelationClustering-Vowel-BINARY-N760-D0.200.wcnf.gz	120800405	132256968
5	drmx-cryptogen/geffe128-7.wcnf.gz	812	846
6	min-width/MinWidthCB-mitdbsample-100-43-1k-5s-2t-5.wcnf.gz	32010	32200
7	min-width/MinWidthCB-mitdbsample-200-64-1k-2s-1t-4.wcnf.gz	76975	78325
8	min-width/MinWidthCB-mitdbsample-300-43-1k-6s-1t-8.wcnf.gz	45780	45825
9	MinimumWeightDominatingSetProblem/delaunay-n24.wcnf.gz	304532225	350820532
10	MinimumWeightDominatingSetProblem/hugebubbles-00020.wcnf.gz	694937186	753286458
11	MinimumWeightDominatingSetProblem/inf-road-usa.wcnf.gz	840126999	903206743
12	MinimumWeightDominatingSetProblem/sc-rel9.wcnf.gz	15590036	16746750
13	MinimumWeightDominatingSetProblem/web-wikipedia2009.wcnf.gz	28120892	37674803
14	pseudoBoolean/miplib/normalized-mps-v2-20-10-p0548.opb.msat.wcnf.gz	12451	25494
15	spot5/log/1401.wcsp.log.wcnf.gz	463106	469110
16	spot5/log/1407.wcsp.log.wcnf.gz	459591	465638

5 Conclusion and Outlook

In this paper, we have proposed a novel local search algorithm for solving large MaxSAT problems in short time. We could prove by numeric experiments on benchmark instances encoding problems from combinatorial optimization and AI that our algorithm yields results that are comparable to and for some problem families even better than state-of-the-art solvers.

As a possible prospect, we aim at developing more sophisticated improvement methods that take into account not single over-satisfied clauses but sets of such. Also, we can think of caching unsuccessful local improvements so that they will never be performed a second time. Finally, we want to analyse the different components of our algorithm by replacing each of the perturbation, stable improvements and simulated annealing by a naive technique. This will give an insight into the contribution of each component to the solvers performance.

References

1. MaxSAT Evaluation 2019. https://maxsat-evaluations.github.io/2019/index.html
2. Starexec Cluster. https://www.starexec.org/starexec/public/about.jsp. Accessed 2019
3. Andrade, D.V., Resende, M.G.C., Werneck, R.F.F.: Fast local search for the maximum independent set problem. J. Heuristics **18**(4), 525–547 (2012). https://doi.org/10.1007/s10732-012-9196-4
4. Audemard, G., Simon, L.: Predicting learnt clauses quality in modern SAT solvers. In: Proceedings of the 21st International Joint Conference on Artificial Intelligence, IJCAI 2009, San Francisco, CA, USA, pp. 399–404 (2009)

5. Bacchus, F., Järvisalo, M., Martins, R.: MaxSAT evaluation 2018: new developments and detailed results. J. Satisf. Boolean Model. Comput. **11**, 99–131 (2019). https://doi.org/10.3233/SAT190119

6. Belov, A., Morgado, A., Marques-Silva, J.: SAT-based preprocessing for MaxSAT. In: McMillan, K., Middeldorp, A., Voronkov, A. (eds.) LPAR 2013. LNCS, vol. 8312, pp. 96–111. Springer, Heidelberg (2013). https://doi.org/10.1007/978-3-642-45221-5_7

7. Berg, J., Demirović, E., Stuckey, P.J.: Core-boosted linear search for incomplete MaxSAT. In: Rousseau, L.-M., Stergiou, K. (eds.) CPAIOR 2019. LNCS, vol. 11494, pp. 39–56. Springer, Cham (2019). https://doi.org/10.1007/978-3-030-19212-9_3

8. Berg, J., Järvisalo, M.: Cost-optimal constrained correlation clustering via weighted partial maximum satisfiability. Artif. Intell. **244**, 110–142 (2017). https://doi.org/10.1016/j.artint.2015.07.001. Combining Constraint Solving with Mining and Learning

9. Berg, J., Järvisalo, M., Malone, B.: Learning optimal bounded treewidth Bayesian networks via maximum satisfiability. In: Kaski, S., Corander, J. (eds.) Proceedings of the Seventeenth International Conference on Artificial Intelligence and Statistics. Proceedings of Machine Learning Research, vol. 33, pp. 86–95. PMLR, Reykjavik, 22–25 April 2014

10. Bouhmala, N.: Combining simulated annealing with local search heuristic for MaxSAT. J. Heuristics **25**(1), 47–69 (2019). https://doi.org/10.1007/s10732-018-9386-9

11. Dantzig, G.B.: Linear Programming and Extensions. Princeton University Press, Princeton (1963)

12. Davis, M., Putnam, H.: A computing procedure for quantification theory. J. ACM **7**(3), 201–215 (1960). https://doi.org/10.1145/321033.321034

13. Demirović, E., Stuckey, P.J.: Techniques inspired by local search for incomplete MaxSAT and the linear algorithm: varying resolution and solution-guided search. In: Schiex, T., de Givry, S. (eds.) CP 2019. LNCS, vol. 11802, pp. 177–194. Springer, Cham (2019). https://doi.org/10.1007/978-3-030-30048-7_11

14. Fan, Y., Ma, Z., Su, K., Sattar, A., Li, C.: Ramp: a local search solver based on make-positive variables. In: MaxSAT Evaluation (2016)

15. Großmann, P., Hölldobler, S., Manthey, N., Nachtigall, K., Opitz, J., Steinke, P.: Solving periodic event scheduling problems with SAT. In: Jiang, H., Ding, W., Ali, M., Wu, X. (eds.) IEA/AIE 2012. LNCS (LNAI), vol. 7345, pp. 166–175. Springer, Heidelberg (2012). https://doi.org/10.1007/978-3-642-31087-4_18

16. Guerra, J., Lynce, I.: Reasoning over biological networks using maximum satisfiability. In: Milano, M. (ed.) CP 2012. LNCS, pp. 941–956. Springer, Heidelberg (2012). https://doi.org/10.1007/978-3-642-33558-7_67

17. Hoos, H.H.: Solving hard combinatorial problems with GSAT—A case study. In: Görz, G., Hölldobler, S. (eds.) KI 1996. LNCS, vol. 1137, pp. 107–119. Springer, Heidelberg (1996). https://doi.org/10.1007/3-540-61708-6_53

18. Hyttinen, A., Eberhardt, F., Järvisalo, M.: Constraint-based causal discovery: conflict resolution with answer set programming. In: Proceedings of the 30th Conference on Uncertainty in Artificial Intelligence, pp. 340–349 (2014)

19. Lei, Z., Cai, S.: Solving (weighted) partial MaxSAT by dynamic local search for sat. In: Proceedings of the Twenty-Seventh International Joint Conference on Artificial Intelligence, IJCAI 2018, pp. 1346–1352. International Joint Conferences on Artificial Intelligence Organization, July 2018. https://doi.org/10.24963/ijcai.2018/187

20. Park, J.D.: Using weighted Max-SAT engines to solve MPE. In: Proceedings of the 18th National Conference on Artificial Intelligence, pp. 682–687 (2002)
21. Pisinger, D., Ropke, S.: Large neighborhood search. In: Gendreau, M., Potvin, J.Y. (eds.) Handbook of Metaheuristics. International Series in Operations Research & Management Science, vol. 146, pp. 399–419. Springer, Boston (2010). https://doi.org/10.1007/978-1-4419-1665-5_13
22. Reisch, J., Großmann, P., Kliewer, N.: Conflict resolving - a maximum independent set heuristics for solving MaxSAT. In: Proceedings of the 22nd International Multiconference Information Society, vol. 1, pp. 67–71 (2019)
23. Selman, B., Kautz, H., Cohen, B.: Local search strategies for satisfiability testing. In: DIMACS Series in Discrete Mathematics and Theoretical Computer Science, pp. 521–532 (1995)

A Virtual Caregiver for Assisted Daily Living of Pre-frail Users

Jennifer Renoux[1]($\boxtimes$), Matteo Luperto[2], Nicola Basilico[2], Marta Romeo[3],
Marios Milis[4], Francesca Lunardini[5], Simona Ferrante[5], Amy Loutfi[1],
and N. Alberto Borghese[2]

[1] Center for Applied Autonomous Sensor Systems,
Örebro University, Örebro, Sweden
{jennifer.renoux,amy.loutfi}@oru.se
[2] Applied Intelligent Systems Lab, University of Milan, Milan, Italy
{matteo.luperto,nicola.basilico,alberto.borghese}@unimi.it
[3] University of Manchester, Manchester, UK
marta.romeo@manchester.ac.uk
[4] SignalGeneriX Ltd, Lemesos, Cyprus
marios.milis@signalgenerix.com
[5] NearLab, Department of Electronics, Information and Bioengineering,
Politecnico di Milano, Milan, Italy
{francesca.lunardini,simona.ferrante}@polimi.it

Abstract. As Europe sees its population aging dramatically, Assisted Daily Living for the elderly becomes a more and more important and relevant research topic. The Movecare Project focuses on this topic by integrating a robotic platform, an IoT system, and an activity center to provide assistance, suggestions of activities and transparent monitoring to users at home. In this paper, we describe the Virtual Caregiver, a software component of the Movecare platform, that is responsible for analyzing the data from the various modules and generating suggestions tailored to the user's state and needs. A preliminary study has been carried on over 2 months with 15 users. This study suggests that the presence of the Virtual Caregiver encourages people to use the Movecare platform more consistently, which in turn could result in better monitoring and prevention of cognitive and physical decline.

Keywords: Virtual Caregiver · Assisted Daily Living · Ambient intelligence

1 Introduction

As the overall population in Europe is aging remarkably [5], developing solutions allowing users to stay cognitively and physically healthier becomes critical. A

Supported by the MoveCare Project (ID 732158), funded by the European Commission under the H2020 Framework. Programme H2020-ICT-26b-2016.

lack of cognitive and physical stimuli has been shown to encourage the appearance of Mild Cognitive Impairment (MCI), a condition that may later develop in dementia [12]. The development of the Internet of Things, robotic platforms, and communication technologies in general offers new possibilities for innovative solutions to provide such stimuli while monitoring the user's cognitive and physical state and evolution. This is the goal pursued by the MoveCare project. However, such systems need to be proactive and encourage the users to interact with the different tools provided so that they can be monitored efficiently while being prevented with relevant stimulus.

In this paper, we describe the Virtual Caregiver, a software component of the MoveCare platform, whose role is to analyze data collected by a monitoring system and generate interventions to assist and encourage the user to use the digital tools part of the MoveCare ecosystem. The remainder of this paper is organized as follows. Section 2 presents the overall MoveCare project and platform, explaining the interaction between the Virtual Caregiver and the rest of the platform. Section 3 presents the architecture of the Virtual Caregiver and Sect. 4 presents a pilot study performed in the context of MoveCare, which allowed us to test the feasibility and efficiency of the Virtual Caregiver. Finally, Sect. 5 present studies and systems related to ours, and Sect. 6 concludes this paper with a discussion of the limitations and opportunities created by our system.

2   The MoveCare project

The MoveCare project is an H2020 European project aiming at creating a complete solution to provide transparent monitoring, assistance and tailored recommendations to elders at home. The MoveCare platform, presented on Fig. 1, integrates an activity center, along with a virtual community, an assistive robot (the Giraff platform[1]), and environmental sensors and smart objects

In MoveCare, data is collected from three different types of sources: environmental sensors, smart objects and a Community Based Activity Center (CBAC).

The set of environmental sensors include motion sensors in each room of the user's house, accelerometers under couches and beds, door sensors, and a smart scale. Two objects have been "smartified": a pen, which allows to measure handwriting-related parameters, and a ball, which is associated to an exergame on the CBAC to measure the user's grip force.

The CBAC is an interactive application that can be used from a Tablet or a TV and allows the user to play to a certain number of games, both cognitive (cards games, pictionary) and physical (exergames) and record their score. Games can be single or multi-player. In case of multi-player games, a video chat system allows the players to interact with each other while playing. This video chat system is also available as an application of its own.

The Virtual Caregiver (VC) gathers data from all the monitoring components, analyzes it and provides feedback, assistance, and recommendations.

---

[1] http://www.giraff.org/.

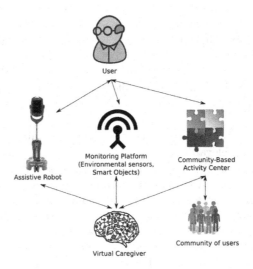

Fig. 1. The Movecare platform

The assistive robot is the main face of the system. It will deliver interventions generated by the VC to the user and interact with them through voice interaction.

In the remainder of this paper, we will describe the architecture of the Virtual Caregiver as well as the different algorithms that it encompasses.

3 The Virtual Caregiver

3.1 Overview

The goal of the Virtual Caregiver is to gather all information provided from the different components in the system and create *interventions* for the user. An *intervention* is defined as a proactive action of the system which aims at helping the user in their everyday life. Each intervention triggers an action from the robot and/or a display on the CBAC for the user to read. Interventions are tailored to the user's needs and past behaviors and engineered to maintain their physical, cognitive and social health. Interventions are characterized by the following elements: (a) an intervention code, describing the type of intervention. (b) a priority, manually defined for each intervention type. Priorities range from 0 (lowest priority) to 7 (highest priority). (c) other data specific to this intervention. The structure of the Virtual Caregiver, presented in Fig. 2, has been designed around scenarios characterized by their clinical value and interest for the user.

The movecare modules are separated in two categories: (a) the *scenarios* modules, which implement functionalities specific to each scenario, and (b) the *utility* modules which implement functionalities used across the different scenarios.

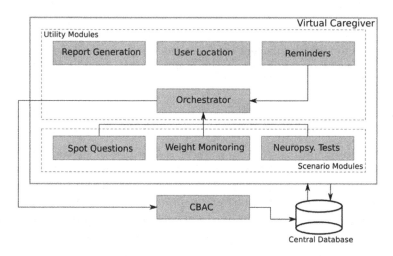

Fig. 2. The overall architecture of the Virtual Caregiver

The modules in the VC follow two types of workflows, which differ only by the way data is received. Workflows are not mutually exclusive and one module can implement both for different functions. In one case, which we call the *Reactive Workflow*, the module receives data from other components (monitoring system, robot, CBAC) in real-time, analyzes it, and generates an intervention. This is for instance the case for the analysis of weight in the Weight Monitoring or the User Location module. In the second case, which is the *Periodic Workflow*, the module "wakes up" after a pre-determined amount of time (usually daily or weekly), collects data from the database, analyzes it, and generates an intervention. This is for instance the case for the function that reminds the user to measure their weight in the Weight Monitoring module, or for the whole Reminder module. All modules send the intervention they generate immediately to the Orchestrator, who is in charge of timing the actual delivery to the user according context and pre-defined constraints.

To communicate within the VC and with the other components of the system, a set of MQTT[2] channels have been implemented. These channels are of a publish/subscribe type, and allow the VC to receive data from sensors and send interventions to the rest of the system. Within the VC, one channel has been implemented to send interventions from the different module to the orchestrator.

In the remainder of this section, we will describe in more details all the VC modules. We will first focus on the scenarios modules (Sect. 3.2) and then describe the set of Utility Modules (Sect. 3.3).

---

[2] http://mqtt.org/.

3.2 The Scenarios Modules

The scenarios modules implement the functionalities needed by the different scenarios. Scenarios have been designed focusing on their interest for the clinical aspect of the MoveCare project, their interest for the end-user, and their technical feasibility. Three separate scenarios have been implemented, described in the following.

Spot Questions. In this scenario, the user is expected to answer several questions related to their previous activities, the current context (current day, current month) or an event in the past. This scenario has a high clinical value as it allows to monitor the user's cognitive state and to detect changes in the long-term. The types of spot questions, their purpose, and examples of such questions are presented in Table 1. The role of the Virtual Caregiver in this scenario is to select a question to ask according to a predefined frequency decided by the clinical partners of the projects and presented on Table 2. The delivery of the selected spot questions is made by the robot, through voice interaction. The robot also records the user's answer, transcript to text thanks to a speech-to-text module and send it to the global database.

Table 1. Type of spot questions

Type of question	Aim	Examples of questions
Episodic memory	Recovery related to different activities previously performed by the user	"To be able to offer you more varied exercises, can you tell me if you played cards in the last 3 days?"
		"Do you remember how much you weighed yesterday?"
Apathy	User's self-evaluation of their physical and cognitive states	"Are you more tired than usual today?"
		"Are you more irritable than usual?"
Temporal orientation	Recovery related to current time	"What weekday is it today?"
		"Which month is the current one?"
Confabulation	Trigger recovery of long-term memory	"Do you remember how you spent the day of your 25th birthday?"
		Do you remember what you were doing a month ago at the same time?"

Table 2. Frequency at which spot questions must be asked

Week 1	1 question per day for 4 consecutive days
Week 2	2 questions days 1 and 3, 1 question day 5
Week 3	4 questions during one randomly selected day
Week 4	1 question per day for 5 consecutive days

The Spot Question module follows the periodic workflow. Algorithm 1 presents the general algorithm used by the VC. For space reasons, we did not detail all of the functions used but only summarized them.

Data: fqcy: representation of Table 2
listAvailableQuestions: the list of available questions allSpotQuestions: the list of all possible questions
Result: dailySpotQuestions: a list of interventions SQ, corresponding to the spot questions for the day with the corresponding correct answer (if any) and the time they should be asked
1 **if** *listAvailableQuestions.length ¡= 3* **then**
2 | listAvailableQuestions = allSpotQuestions ;
3 **end**
4 nbQuestions = getNumberOfQuestionForCurrentDay();
5 delta = calculateDeltaBetweenQuestions() ;
6 **for** *0 ≤ i < nbQuestions* **do**
7 | question = selectQuestion(listAvailableQuestions) ;
8 | answer = retrieveAnswerFromQuestion(question) ;
9 | listAvailableQuestions.remove(question) ;
10 | dailySpotQuestions.add(question, answer, currentTime + i*delta) ;
11 **end**
12 **return** *dailySpotQuestions*

Algorithm 1: Spot Questions main algorithm. The function getNumberOfQuestionForCurrentDay calculates how many spot questions are supposed to be asked on the current day according to the frequency given in Table 2. The function calculateDeltaBetweenQuestions distributes the questions evenly during the day and returns the minimum amount of time between two questions. The function retrieveAnswerFromQuestion retrieves the expected answer for each spot question and its implementation is tightly linked to the type of question selected by selectQuestion.

Weight Monitoring. Sudden change of weight is an important indicator of frailty. For this reason, monitoring the user's weight variations has a high clinical value. The role of the VC in this scenario is twofold: it reminds the user to measure their weight and analyzes the measurement. In case an important change is detected (i.e., a gain or loss of at least 2% of the previous weight), then an alert is sent to the clinicians through the Report Generation module (see Sect. 3.3).

The Weight Monitoring module implements both the reactive and the periodic workflows. The reactive workflow is used when a new measure is received from the smart scale to analyze it. The periodic workflow is used to remind the user to measure their weight if they haven't done so in a week.

Neuropsychological Tests. The user is expected to perform regularly two neuropsychological tests commonly used to detect early signs of cognitive impairment [9]. The role of the VC in this scenario is to detect when the tests need to be performed and present them for the user to perform. The Neuropsychological Tests module implements exclusively the periodic workflow. Algorithm 2 describes the main loop of the module.

Data: deltaTests: the number of days between two sets of tests
Result: Intervention CT to perform neuropsychological tests
1 Module wakes up every day at 01:00am ;
2 latestTests = getDateLatestTestsFromBD() ;
3 **if** *no latestTests or latestTests are more than deltaTests days ago* **then**
4   sendIntervention(CT) ;
5 **end**
6 sleepUntilNextDay() ;

Algorithm 2: The main loop for the neuropsychological tests.

3.3   The Utility Modules

The utility modules of the Virtual Caregiver implement functionalities that are not tied to any specific scenario but are of use for various situations and components. Five separate utility modules were developed, described in the following sub-sections.

Reminders. The monitoring of the users is done through three components: environmental sensors, smart objects and activities played in the CBAC. If the monitoring through environmental sensors is completely transparent for the user, they still need to remember to use the Smart Objects and the CBAC. The VC can detect if they are doing so and remind them if needed through the Reminders module. The Reminders module uses exclusively the periodic workflow and creates interventions according to a set of rules and priorities summarized in Table 3. To avoid overwhelming the users, it has been decided that only one reminder should be sent per day (if needed). If several reminders were necessary for the current day, then the reminder with highest priority is sent.

In addition to reminding the user of several elements, this module also provides "positive feedback": every three days, a message is sent through the CBAC with an encouraging message of what the user has been using a lot during this period of time (e.g., "You have been using your smart pen a lot lately. It's important for me to be able to monitor your handwriting. Keep doing it!").

Report Generation. The report generation component generates reports to send weekly to the clinician responsible for the study. These reports contain the user's answers to the confabulation questions as well as alerts that might have been detected during the week. In the pilot study described in Sect. 4, we only generated upon abnormal weight measurement.

Table 3. Rules and priority for each type of reminders. Priority ranges from 1 (lowest) to 5 (highest)

Reminder name	Context	Rule	Priority
Grip Force game	The Grip Force game is an activity developed during the MoveCare project that aims at monitoring the user's grip force, a loss of grip force being a common sign of frailty	There is not grip force data in the DB for the past 7 days	5
Smart Pen	The Smart Pen allows to monitor changes in handwriting, which can be signs of frailty	There is no smart pen data in the DB for the past 7 days	1
Cognitive Games	Cognitive games in the CBAC allow to monitor changes in the user's cognitive state	There is no report of cognitive games played in the DB for the past 7 days	2
Physical activity	Maintaining a good level of physical activity is important for pre-frail users. Physical activity includes exergames from the CBAC and going outdoor	There is no report of exergames in the DB and the user has not been outdoor for the past 3 days	3
Social games	Multi-player games in the CBAC allow the users to socialize with peers while playing	There is no report of multi-player games in the DB for more than 3 days	4

User Location. Being able to locate the user inside the home is a central functionality for a system such as the MoveCare platform. This information is used by the robot to navigate to the user and by the Virtual Caregiver itself to infer some user's activity and context. In the MoveCare platform, the Virtual Caregiver infers the topological position of the user (i.e. the room in which they currently are) based on motion sensors only. The User Location module implements the reactive workflow and Algorithm 3 is called each time an event is received from one of the motion sensors. An event corresponds to the sensor turning on or the sensor turning off. The sensors map, i.e., the map between sensor IDs and the room they are located in, is supposed to be known. We also assume that one sensor monitors entrances of the user's apartment. In the case of the MoveCare platform, this sensor is a contact sensor installed on the main entrance door. Algorithm 3 can be summarized as follows: each new activation of a motion sensor in a room where the robot is not moving is added to a list of past locations and the user is located to the most recent location. When a sensor turns off, then all the occurrences of locations corresponding to this sensor are removed from the list. If the user cannot be located in the home (all the sensors are off), they are either considered outside (if the entrance sensor has been activated recently) or their position is unknown. This last case can happen when the user is in a room which is not monitored (for instance the bathroom) or too still for the sensors to be activated (for instance sitting on a chair).

Data: sensorEvent: event from one sensor, containing the sensor ID and the
        value (OFF or ON)
robotPosition: the room in which the robot currently is
robotState: the state of the robot (IDLE, NAVIGATING)
pastLocations: the list of past known locations
latestDoorActivation: timestamp of the latest time the entrance sensor was
activated
Result: userLocation: the room in which the user is present

```
 1  eventLocation = getLocationFromSensorMap(sensorEvent.id) ;
 2  if event.value is OFF then
 3  |    pastLocations.removeAll(eventLocation) ;
 4  else
 5  |    if robotState is IDLE or robotPosition is not eventLocation then
 6  |    |    pastLocations.headInsert(eventLocation) ;
 7  |    end
 8  end
 9  if pastLocations is not empty then
10  |    return pastLocations.firstElement() ;
11  else
12  |    if latestDoorActivation ¡ currentTime - 5min then
13  |    |    return OUTDOOR ;
14  |    else
15  |    |    return UNKNOWN ;
16  |    end
17  end
```

Algorithm 3: The main user location algorithm.

The Orchestrator. At the center of the Virtual Caregiver, the Orchestrator receives all intervention requests from the different modules and send them to the other components of the MoveCare system when appropriate. To do so, the Orchestrator uses a policy, based on rules and temporal constraints, presented in Table 4, to detect the appropriate time to send interventions. Rules are either context-based or ad-hoc.

Table 4. Rules and constraints implemented in the Orchestrator

Number	Name	Type	Description
1	Resting	Context-based	No intervention is sent if the user is detected in the bedroom
2	Night time	Ad-Hoc	No intervention between 21:00 and 08:00. This rule has been implemented to ensure that the user won't be disturbed by the robot while sleeping, should the context from rule 1 not be detected properly
3	User at home	Context-based	No intervention is sent if the user is OUTDOOR
4	In bathroom	Context-based	No intervention is sent if the user is in the bathroom
5	Max. number of interventions	Ad-hoc	There should be a maximum of 5 interventions per day
6	Min. time between interventions	Ad-hoc	There should be at least 1 hour between 2 interventions

The orchestrator implements both a reactive and a periodic workflow: Algorithm 4 is called in three cases: (1) when the orchestrator receives an intervention request from another VC module, (2) when the user's location is updated from OUTDOOR to another location in the home, (3) every hour between 08:00 and 21:00.

When the orchestrator receives a new intervention, it queues it in a list of pending interventions. It then selects the intervention with highest priority, and checks that all the rules from Table 4 apply before actually sending the intervention through MQTT. At the end of the day, the list of pending interventions is cleared. Since all periodic modules wake up at regular intervals, interventions that have not been sent will be regenerated the next day.

Data: requestedIntervention: the intervention requested by one of the VC
        modules (when real time),
pendingInterventionList: the list of all pending interventions,
Result: Publishes an intervention on the corresponding MQTT topic if
        constraints are met.

```
 1 if intervention not null then
 2 │   pendingInterventionList.add(intervention) ;
 3 │   pendingInterventionList.sortBy(priority) ;
 4 end
 5 if Rules 1 to 6 are OK then
 6 │   intervention = getFirst() ;
 7 │   publish(intervention) ;
 8 │   pendingInterventionList.remove(intervention) ;
 9 end
10 if currentTime > 21:00 then
11 │   pendingInterventionList.clear() ;
12 end
```

Algorithm 4: The Orchestrator's main loop.

4   Pilot Study

The developed system has been tested during a pilot study involving 15 users for 2 months. Users were situated in Italy (7 users) and Spain (8 users) and were recruited following interviews from clinicians, which allowed to categorize them in the pre-frail state. Among these users, 8 of them (4 in Italy and 4 in Spain) have been provided with the full MoveCare platform (environmental sensors, smart objects, CBAC, and robot) and 7 (3 in Italy and 4 in Spain) have been equipped with the platform without the robot. This separation allowed us to test whether the presence of the robot (the "face" of the Virtual Caregiver) had a positive impact on the use of the monitoring platform (smart objects and CBAC). Figure 3a shows the number of measurement corresponding to the use of the CBAC (code ARU), the use of the smart scale (code BWT), the use of the smart ball (code EXG) and the use of the smart pen (code PEN).

We can see that the presence of a robot systematically increases the use of the Smart Objects and the CBAC. However, when analyzing the number of interventions delivered to users with robots compared to number of actual measurements from the same users (Fig. 3b) we can see that the users are interacting with the monitoring system much more than they are reminded to. This suggest that either the physical presence of the robot, or the few times the robot actually reminded them to use the object were sufficient to encourage users to use the monitoring system. This could also result from the fact that users that have been equipped with a robot are more engaged with the study, and therefore more likely to use the system.

5   Related Work

The development of Virtual Caregivers to assist elders at home has been a hot topic of research for several years now. Early work focused on the development of robotic platforms capable of assisting the user [11,13] and providing social interaction [10,14]. Other studies focused on creating platforms for rehabilitation, in which robots can help the patient train specific tasks [6,8]. These systems are focused on user's assistance and do not consider user monitoring.

With the recent booming of the Internet of Things and Ambient Sensing, many systems have been developed to monitor elders in Smart Homes and assess their cognitive and physical states, promoting independent living. Work as early as the one presented in [15] acknowledge the added value of monitoring users to provide better care and allow them to stay at home. Since, many studies relied on IoT and ambient intelligent systems to recognize user's patterns [1], activities [4] and habits [2].

When combining the monitoring and assistive aspects of elderly care at home, some systems preferred the use of "ambient actions" (actions to devices connected to the system) [16] or favored the use of Smart TVs [3,7].

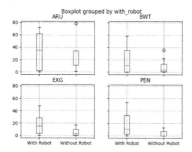 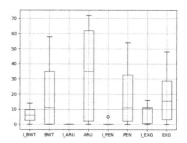

(a) Number of measurements recorded during the study for groups of users with and without a robot. ARU corresponds to the activities in the CBAC (all types of activities), BWT is the weight measurement, EXG is the use of the smart ball and PEN is the use of the smart pen.

(b) Number of interventions reminding the users to use a certain component and number of actual use of this component. ARU corresponds to the activities in the CBAC (all types of activities), BWT is the weight measurement, EXG is the use of the smart ball and PEN is the use of the smart pen. I_X correspond to the intervention reminding the user to use X.

Fig. 3. Results of the pilot study

6 Conclusion

In this paper, we presented the Virtual Caregiver, a software component that analyzes data gathered from a monitoring system and generates interventions, with the goal of monitoring and assisting the user of the system. The VC uses context elements and constraints to decide when to send an intervention, thus providing assistance in an non-intrusive way. The system has been implemented and tested during a pilot study involving 15 users over 2 months, and results suggest that such a proactive component is beneficial for the system as a whole. Indeed, users equipped with the robot (which acted as the face of the Virtual Caregiver and delivered interventions) were more engaged with the platform as a whole. The main limitation of this study is in its size. The number of users and the duration of the study does not allow us to strongly conclude whether the presence of the system was beneficial overall to the users. Longer and bigger studies would be required. However, the results are encouraging and open a lot of possibilities for future improvement. The main line of future work concerns long-term analysis of the user's cognitive and physical state. In the current implementation of the Virtual Caregiver, only short term analysis was used to detect interventions. Some trend and pattern detection have been performed during the project after the end of the pilot, but were not considered during the pilot. Identifying trends and patterns in the user's state as the system runs would allow for more tailored recommendations.

References

1. Adami, A., Hayes, T., Pavel, M.: Unobtrusive monitoring of sleep patterns. In: Proceedings of the 25th Annual International Conference of the IEEE Engineering in Medicine and Biology Society (IEEE Cat. No. 03CH37439), vol. 2, pp. 1360–1363. IEEE (2003)
2. Chimamiwa, G., Alirezaie, M., Banaee, H., Köckemann, U., Loutfi, A.: Towards habit recognition in smart homes for people with dementia. In: Chatzigiannakis, I., De Ruyter, B., Mavrommati, I. (eds.) AmI 2019. LNCS, vol. 11912, pp. 363–369. Springer, Cham (2019). https://doi.org/10.1007/978-3-030-34255-5_29
3. Costa, C.R., Anido-Rifón, L.E., Fernández-Iglesias, M.J.: An open architecture to support social and health services in a smart TV environment. IEEE J. Biomed. Health Inform. **21**(2), 549–560 (2017)
4. Debes, C., Merentitis, A., Sukhanov, S., Niessen, M., Frangiadakis, N., Bauer, A.: Monitoring activities of daily living in smart homes: understanding human behavior. IEEE Sig. Process. Mag. **33**(2), 81–94 (2016)
5. European Commission: Population aging in Europe: facts, implications, and policies (2014)
6. Guidali, M., Duschau-Wicke, A., Broggi, S., Klamroth-Marganska, V., Nef, T., Riener, R.: A robotic system to train activities of daily living in a virtual environment. Med. Biol. Eng. Comput. **49**(10), 1213–1223 (2011). https://doi.org/10.1007/s11517-011-0809-0
7. Hossain, M.A., Ahmed, D.T.: Virtual Caregiver: an ambient-aware elderly monitoring system. IEEE Trans. Inf. Technol. Biomed. **16**(6), 1024–1031 (2012)

8. Johnson, M.J., Wisneski, K.J., Anderson, J., Nathan, D., Smith, R.O.: Development of Adler: the activities of daily living exercise robot. In: The First IEEE/RAS-EMBS International Conference on Biomedical Robotics and Biomechatronics, BioRob 2006, pp. 881–886 (2006)

9. Lunardini, F., et al.: Validity of digital trail making test and bells test in elderlies. In: 2019 IEEE EMBS International Conference on Biomedical & Health Informatics (BHI), pp. 1–4. IEEE (2019)

10. Matsuyama, Y., Taniyama, H., Fujie, S., Kobayashi, T.: System design of group communication activator: an entertainment task for elderly care. In: 2009 4th ACM/IEEE International Conference on Human-Robot Interaction (HRI), pp. 243–244. IEEE (2009)

11. Montemerlo, M., Pineau, J., Roy, N., Thrun, S., Verma, V.: Experiences with a mobile robotic guide for the elderly. In: AAAI/IAAI 2002, pp. 587–592 (2002)

12. Petersen, R.C., Caracciolo, B., Brayne, C., Gauthier, S., Jelic, V., Fratiglioni, L.: Mild cognitive impairment: a concept in evolution. J. Intern. Med. **275**(3), 214–228 (2014)

13. Pineau, J., Montemerlo, M., Pollack, M., Roy, N., Thrun, S.: Towards robotic assistants in nursing homes: challenges and results. Robot. Auton. Syst. **42**(3–4), 271–281 (2003)

14. Tamura, T., et al.: Is an entertainment robot useful in the care of elderly people with severe dementia? J. Gerontol. Ser. A: Biol. Sci. Med. Sci. **59**(1), M83–M85 (2004)

15. Tang, P., Venables, T.: 'Smart' homes and telecare for independent living. J. Telemed. Telecare **6**(1), 8–14 (2000)

16. Zhou, F., Jiao, J.R., Chen, S., Zhang, D.: A case-driven ambient intelligence system for elderly in-home assistance applications. IEEE Trans. Syst. Man Cybern. Part C (Apl. Rev.) **41**(2), 179–189 (2010)

Exploring the Effects of Role Design on Agent Learning

Lukas Reuter[1]([envelope]), Jan Ole Berndt[1], and Ingo J. Timm[1,2]

[1] Business Informatics I, Trier University, Trier, Germany
{reuter,berndt,itimm}@uni-trier.de
[2] German Research Center for Artificial Intelligence,
SDS Branch Trier (Cognitive Social Simulation),
Behringstraße 21, 54296 Trier, Germany

Abstract. In multiagent organizations, the coordination of problem-solving capabilities builds the foundation for processing complex tasks. Roles provide a structured approach to consolidate task-processing responsibilities. However, designing roles remains a challenge since role configurations affect individual and team performance. On the one hand, roles can be specialized on certain tasks to allow for efficient problem solving. On the other hand, this reduces task processing flexibility in case of disturbances. As agents gain experience knowledge by enacting certain roles, switching roles becomes difficult and requires training. Hence, this paper explores the effects of different role designs on learning agents at runtime. We utilize an adaptive Belief-Desire-Intention agent architecture combined with a reinforcement learning approach to model experience knowledge, task-processing improvement, and decision-making in a stochastic environment. The model is evaluated using an emergency response simulation in which agents manage fire departments for which they configure and control emergency operations. The results show that specialized agents learn to process their assigned tasks more efficient than generalized agents.

Keywords: Adaptive agents · Role design · Reinforcement learning · Multiagent systems

1 Introduction

In modern organizations, the automation of processes and distribution of knowledge is rising. For instance in the context of an "Industry 4.0" setting where autonomous Cyber-Physical-Systems (CPS) control processes by a decentralized decision-making. From an artificial intelligence perspective, these CPS are modeled by virtual representatives in form of intelligent agents. In order to enact according to organizational goals, these agents have to be part of the organizational structure as well. That is, agents adopt predefined roles and act according to their definition. Roles define, on the one hand, the responsibility of a role

© Springer Nature Switzerland AG 2020
U. Schmid et al. (Eds.): KI 2020, LNAI 12325, pp. 190–203, 2020.
https://doi.org/10.1007/978-3-030-58285-2_14

owner for various tasks and, on the other hand, the expected behavior towards other members of the organization to perform these tasks [5,12]. In addition, the execution of a role requires certain capabilities for processing the tasks in the area of responsibility. The application of these capabilities can be improved upon multiple execution, i.e., learning by collecting information about the environment and its change [24]. Reinforcement learning approaches allow agents to learn from their experience to decide which action should be selected in a specific situation. As learning applications arise, the organizational structure in general and the role design in particular must take into account the behavior and effects of learning systems. Especially since roles specifically define an agents responsibilities and therefore its abilities of gaining experience to learn from.

Hence, this paper analyses the effects of role design on agent learning. In theory, specialization allows for a more efficient gain of experience because the agent responsibilities are focused on a narrow task set [12]. Contrastingly, cross-training agents to process various tasks increases robustness and scalability [7,12]. In this paper we extend a Belief-Desire-Intention (BDI) agent architecture by a reinforcement learning approach to improve action execution in a given situation. The agent learns a policy to process different kind of task types. Since BDI plans consists of a finite set of actions, the policy provides an action selection function for a given state. In order to evaluate different role designs, an emergency response environment is utilize in which agents control fire departments and allocate resources to emergencies. As an example for dynamic environments, emergency response requires adaptation to changing environmental situations and therefore suits for a demanding learning application.

The remainder of this paper is structured as follows. Section 2 introduces organizational structures and different approaches for designing roles as well as presents current research on assigning roles in multiagent systems. Section 3 is divided into Sect. 3.1 and Sect. 3.2. In Sect. 3.1 the overall adaptive agent framework is presented to give a broader outlook role adaptation. Section 3.2 introduces the BDI learning model. Section 4.1 describes the emergency response framework and environment as well as Sect. 4.2 shows and analyses the simulation results for different role designs. Section 5 concludes this article.

2   Foundations and Challenges of Role Design

From an artificial intelligence perspective, distributed task processing is a key functionality of multiagent systems (MAS) due to their intelligent and autonomous behavior. MAS organizations support successful coordination of problem solving capabilities [4,6] and provide a rigid structure to reduce complexity in coordination [21]. MAS organizations are defined as "complex entities where a multitude of agents interact, within a structured environment aiming at some global purpose" [4, p. 4]. Designing collaborative structures for efficient and effective teamwork is a core challenge in designing MAS [7]. A common approach is to encapsulate task processing responsibilities in roles. Hence, roles define expected behavior for processing certain tasks [3,7,11,12]. Organizational research distinguishes between roles and role enactment [5]. As a consequence, agents need to be aware of organizational structures and their roles which they are enacting. When agents decide which action to perform next, their behavior need to be aligned with organizational structures and goals. In multiagent organizations, the main purpose of an agent is enacting its role(s).

In organizational research, role configurations can be categorized by two dimensions, namely generalist or specialist configurations. Completely specialized roles are defined by their limited set of responsibilities for task-processing [12]. Generalist role configurations (cross-training) allows for a more robust configuration in which members of the organization share responsibilities and capabilities [2]. According to Ferber, the performance of an agent organization is dependent on the degree of specialization and redundancy [7]. Hence, he distinguishes four different types of organizational role design [7]: (1) not redundant hyper specialized organizations in which each agent is specialized on one task and each task can be performed by one agent only, (2) redundant specialized organizations in which each agent is specialized on one task but each task can be solved by several agents, (3) redundant generalized organization in which every agent can solve all types of tasks and each task can be solved by every agent, and (4) not redundant generalized organization in which an agent is able to perform all kind of tasks but each task can be processed by exactly one agent. However, type (4) is special configuration in which only one totipotent agent operates [7].

On the one hand, sharing problem-solving capabilities increases the robustness of the work process against disturbances. For instance, if an agent becomes unavailable, tasks can be reassigned to other team members (organizational types (2) and (3)). Furthermore, cross-training allows for better task processing scalability and workload balancing which is necessary if some types of tasks occur more frequently (type (3)). On the other hand, sharing of the entire knowledge among all team members results in an increased amount of information that needs to be processed by each agent individually. By specialization on specific tasks team members can focus on their specific expertise which reduces the load of information being processed (type (1) & (2)). However, this potentially makes the team as a system more fragile as it lacks the required redundancy of knowledge to avoid conflicts and failures.

Besides the role design itself, role allocation also addresses the issue of specialization and generalization indirectly. In role allocation, there is a finite set of roles R and a finite set of agents Ag to which resources have to be assigned to. Therefore an allocation function $a : R \times Ag \rightarrow (R, Ag)$ defines the assignment of a role to an agent. Campbell and Wu provide an overview of role allocation problem formalizations and solutions in their overview article [1]. They present three different formalizations in form of the iterative Optimal Assigning Problem (OAP) [9,10], the Extended Generalized Assigning Problem (E-GAP) [20] as well as Role-based Markov Team Decision Problem (RMTDP) [15]. In the OAP approach, a finite set of roles is allocated to agents but each agent can only enact one role. In order to allow for multi role allocation, the E-GAP approach allocates severals roles to an agent. In their papers, Nair et al. utilize MDP to search for a role allocation policy in a multiagent team [14,15]. They utilize role taking and role execution actions to optimize team work for BDI agents and learn a policy for role taking and execution.

However, role allocation problems and formalizations rely on previously defined roles. That is, true specialization is only possible if individual roles are specialized on tasks beforehand. Otherwise this would be a specialization of agents to certain roles but not on tasks itself. Moreover, role allocation is mostly determined based on fixed capability and fixed cost functions for enacting roles.

3 Adaptive Organizational Agent Model

In dynamic environments agents need to adapt their decision-making to situational changes. Hence, Sect. 3.1 introduces an adaptive agent framework for adapting organizational structures in multiagent systems to increase performance. The framework builds the foundation and the overall objective for analyzing role designs for learning agents. Section 3.2 describes the learning BDI agent architecture in detail.

3.1 Adaptive MAS Framework

The vision of adaptive agent organizations is to allow multiagent teams to dynamically adapt their structure based on current workload at runtime. Hence, an adaptation framework is introduced and Fig. 1 provides an overview of its components. The framework consists of three different components: (1) organizational structure, (2) performance measurement, and (3) adaptation mechanisms. The basis builds an organizational structure which provides definitions for roles, tasks, and communication. According to this structure, agents adopt roles to process tasks. In this framework, agents are modeled by a Belief-Desire-Intention architecture (cf. Sect. 3.2). The selection of utilizing BDI is driven by two main advantages: (1) handling multiple goals and (2) its intentionality. Participating in an organization requires the consideration of various point of views and aims of different actors. Furthermore, the special feature of directed adaptation lies in intentional situation evaluation of individual agents.

The performance model provides key figures to evaluate the agents' current effectivity and efficiency. These measures can either be referring to individual performance or team performance as a whole. Potential performance indicators could be the mean task processing durations or as in a reinforcement learning the reward obtained from the environment. Based on their performance and workload, the adaptation of the organizational structure can be initiated. This framework manipulates organizational structures mainly by their role definitions. That is, role designs directly influence task responsibilities and therefore task processing as well. For instance, if the certain tasks may occur unforeseen, single agents can be overloaded by their workload. In this case other agents can support by adopting their current role(s). The adaptation of the organizational structures

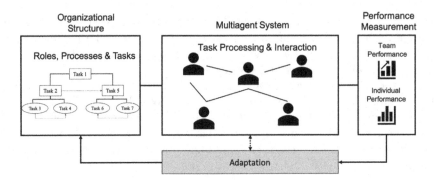

Fig. 1. Adaptive agent framework

should increase the team and individual performance. Therefore, it requires a detailed evaluation of the current workforce to anticipate future behavior.

In previous research we could show that the role design itself has a significant influence on the team performance [18,26,27]. In the experiments, specialized teams and the adaptation to specialized teams are processing tasks more effective and efficient. However, enacting roles facilitates the generation of experience knowledge and agents improve their skills by processing tasks more often. Especially in dynamic environments untrained agents suffer from the lack of experience because task processing requirements may change rapidly over time. Hence, the next Sect. 3.2 extends previous research by introducing a learning component to a BDI agent model to accommodate for experience and improving skills in a stochastic environment. Hence, analyzing the interdependency of role design and learning behavior is a the next step towards the goal of adaptive multiagent organizations.

3.2 Learning BDI Model

Belief-Desire-Intention agents are well-known for their rational decision-making [29]. Each agent is driven by three different mental states, i.e., its beliefs B, its desires D, and intentions I. Beliefs store knowledge about the current situation, desires store goals it can attempt to achieve and the intentions connect goals its has committed to achieve with actual plans. Due to their architecture, BDI agents are suitable for handling multiple or conflicting goals [16,25]. Figure 2 shows the learning BDI model at the center and its dynamic environment at the top. For describing the basic BDI architecture we utilize the formalization for the discourse agent by Timm [25] and extend previous defined knowledge distribution approaches [19] by a learning approach. The core of the agent model is its localstate L which includes the set of its beliefs B, desires D, and intentions I as well as the set of plans $Plan$. Plans are based on the total set of actions Act of the agent. Hence, each plan definition uses a (sub-)set of Act. The localstate is initialized with l_0. In order to reason about its environment, the agent has a *see*-function which converts the environment to a perception ($see: Env \rightarrow Perc$).

Based on the perception, the localstate is then being revised by $reflect\colon L \times Perc \to L^*$. $decide$ is a deliberation function which transforms the localstate to an action plan ($decide\colon L \to L$) and $execute$ executes a single action from an action plan ($execute\colon L \to Act$).

Due to the organizational context, the environment of an agent consists of multiple tasks. Which task an agent can perceive is defined by its role definition. The task processing is model as a stochastic process in form of a Markov Decision Process (MDP). A Markov Decision Process is a tuple of $\langle S, A, T, R \rangle$ where S is a finite set of states, A is a finite set of actions, T is a transition model $T\colon S \times A \to S$, and R is a reward function $r\colon S \times A \to \mathbb{R}$ [23]. MDP represent probabilistic state transitions based on predefined actions. For executing an action, a reward is being obtained from the following state. Hence, each state of the MDP represents an individual state of a task. The actions allowed within the MDP are represented by the actions available for a particular plan. The transition model represents the dynamic environment. Individual tasks are represented by individual MDPs.

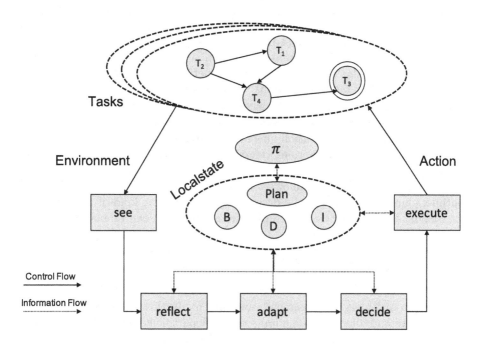

Fig. 2. BDI decision-making process

In this context, we utilize BDI agents for a task driven decision-making. That is, each agent chooses their actions based on its current task. Hence, the agent has a plan for each type of task it is responsible for. In this model, plans are represented by a set of *actions*, functions for its *status* and *action selection*. Furthermore, each plan has φ_{pre} and φ_{post} to represent pre- and post-condition of a plan corresponding to the STRIPS[1] notation [8]. In order to solve a task the agent can perform actions in the environment.

To chose an action in a given state, a policy $\pi : S \to A$ maps a single state to an action. In literature, different learning approaches are applied to BDI agents dealing with stochastic environments [13,17,23,28]. Hence, π implements the action selection function in a plan. φ_{pre} and φ_{post} are modeled by start and goal states of the MDP and are determined by the beliefs of the agent. The set of actions which the agent can perform are determined by each plan. To learn a policy for action selection the Q-learning algorithm is used. Q-learning is a model free approach and is common in reinforcement learning applications [24]. Q-learning models the quality of state-action-pairs (S and A) by a real valued function $Q \colon S \times A \to \mathbb{R}$. Q-values are updated according to Eq. 1 in which α represents the learning rate, γ defines the discount factor, and r represents the reward the agent achieves [22].

$$Q_{k+1}(s_t, a_t) = Q(s_t, a_t) + \alpha(r_t + \gamma maxQ_k(s_{t+1}, a_{t+1}) - Q_k(s_t, a_t)) \quad (1)$$

For adapting organizational structures (cf. adaptation mechanism Sect. 3.1), i.e, to specialize or to cross-train agents, an adaptation function *adapt* for task-related knowledge is introduced. The function modifies an agent's set of actions by adding or removing actions. Given sets of actions to add (Act^i_{add}) or remove (Act^i_{remove}) for agent i, the agent's adaptation operations for task-related knowledge are defined as: *add*: $Act^{i'} = Act^i \cup Act^i_{add}$ and *remove*: $Act^{i'} = Act^i \setminus Act^i_{remove}$. This adaptation affects the available actions for the plans and to specialize an agent, all actions referring to a particular task types can be removed. On the other hand, adding actions extends an agent's capabilities. This representation of adaptation allows for enacting according to role designs and runtime adaptation. That is, the desire for processing the kind of task remains but without the necessary action repertoire no intention can be instantiated.

4 Emergency Response Simulation

In order to test the adaptive agent model, a dynamic resource allocation problem is utilized in an emergency response environment. In this scenario, agents have to coordinate and allocate rescue units of fire departments. Hence, agents learn to assign a set of resources R (vehicles and fire station operators) to a set of emergencies E. The next Sections provide an overview of the simulation model (Sect. 4.1) as well as simulation experiments and results (Sect. 4.2).

4.1 Emergency Response Scenario

This scenario model distinguishes between emergencies E, stations S, vehicles V, and operators O. Each station has a finite set of vehicles and a finite set of

---

[1] Stanford Research Institute Problem Solver.

operators. Each operator has individual qualifications and each vehicle has a list
of required qualifications for an emergency. In this specific simulation setup each
agent is controlling a station and needs to assign vehicles to operations. Each
individual operation corresponds to an emergency. Figure 3 gives an overview
of the mentioned concepts on the left side and shows a part of the environment
on the right side. The scenario environment is represented by realistic map data
which is provided by OpenStreetMap[2] to allow for a more detailed and complex
model of emergency operations.

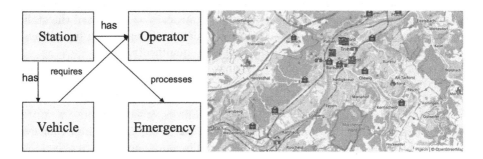

Fig. 3. Simulation entity model (left) and environmental setting (right)

As described in Sect. 3, each emergency is modeled as a stochastic process and
is categorized as *small*, *medium*, or *big*. If an emergency is not handled correctly,
its state, i.e., category changes which is defined by the transition probabilities.
For instance a small emergency would evolve into a medium one. If an emergency occurs, the agent selects suitable vehicles based on the policy and defines
an operation. The action an agent can take in this environment is defined by
configuring and starting operations. Each operation is defined by its vehicles in a
vector representation, e.g., the vector <2, 3, 2> describes sending two vehicles of
type A, three type B, and two type C vehicles. Hence, the learning task is to find
a suitable operation configuration for a given emergency. The optimal configuration consists of the minimal set of vehicles to finish the emergency. Sending too
many vehicles will also finish the task but is rewarded less due to the over use
of resources. In contrast, sending not enough units results in negative rewards
since the emergency task escalates.

4.2 Simulation Configuration and Results

For evaluation purposes, the simulation environment is configured as follows.
Each agent controls a fire station containing three different types of vehicles,
namely: heavy rescue vehicles, water tenders, and fire trucks with turntable
ladder. The station has a total of 15 vehicles (five vehicles of each type).

---

[2] https://www.openstreetmap.de/.

A fire station is responsible for three different types of emergencies: (1) fire, (2) transporting dangerous goods, and (3) technical support. Each type of emergency requires a different operation configuration, for instance a small fire can be extinguished by two water tenders, a fire truck with turntable ladder, and a heavy rescue vehicle which corresponds to an action vector of <2, 1, 1>. The other small types of emergencies require operations such <1, 2, 1> and <1, 1, 2> respectively. Medium tasks require operations such as: <4, 2, 2>, <2, 4, 2>, and <2, 2, 4>. Large emergency operations consists of: <5, 4, 4>, <4, 5, 4>, and <4, 4, 5>. The types of emergencies, the type of vehicles, and the configuration of operations are inspired by the requirements and classifications for german fire departments and operations. For simplicity purposes we neglected the staff allocation problem in this scenario. Hence, a vehicle in an operation has always the right amount of operators with the necessary qualifications.

In order to test the effects of specializing agents, roles are defined based on the three emergency types. Specialized agents are responsible for exactly one type and a generalized agent is able to process all kind of emergencies. Hence, the learning task is scaled based on the responsibilities of each agent.

The reward for the learning task is specified based on the required vehicles and the vehicles provided within the operation. The maximum reward is 500 for sending the minimal required amount. Sending not enough vehicles or the wrong type results in a linear negative reward from zero and for each vehicle missing or wrong type of -20. Sending too many vehicles reduces the maximum reward by 20 for each unnecessary or wrong vehicle. Equation 2 models the rewards for an action A and the amount of arrived vehicles in a State S ($N_{arrived} \in \mathbb{N}$) as well as the amount of required vehicles in S ($N_{req} \in \mathbb{N}$).

$$Reward(A, S) = \begin{cases} 500 & N_{req} = N_{arrived} \\ 500 - 20 * (N_{arrived} - N_{req}) & N_{req} < N_{arrived} \\ 0 - 20 * (N_{req} - N_{arrived}) & N_{req} > N_{arrived} \end{cases} \quad (2)$$

At the beginning of each simulation, the Q values are initialized with random values. To explore the environment an ϵ-greedy strategy is utilized. ϵ defines the probability at which the highest Q-Value from the table is used or a random action is applied to explore the environment.

For evaluating the effects of specialization on agent learning, a sensitivity analysis is conducted. The sensitivity analysis considers the ϵ parameter (interval [0.5; 0.9]), the learning rate (interval [0.5; 1.0]), the discount factor (interval [0.5; 1.0]) as well as the role design in the spectrum of specialization and full generalization. Each simulation consists of 1000 individual learning episodes and each configuration has been run 10 times. In this evaluation, we investigate two scenarios: (1) learning specialist vs. learning generalist role designs and (2) adaptation performance of learning agents in a modified environment.

Specialist Versus Generalists. In Fig. 4 the mean rewards for the specialist and generalist role designs are shown. The runs were executed using a linear

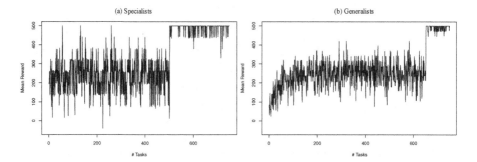

Fig. 4. Rewards: (a) mean rewards specialists and (b) mean rewards generalists

increasing ϵ value starting at 0.5 and a learning rate of 0.9 to allow for an exploration of the environment at the beginning. The discount factor is set to 1. In these specific runs, emergencies of all categories are equally distributed. Specialist role configurations are achieving the maximum reward faster than generalist structures because the training of generalists is delayed by the change between different task types.

In Fig. 5 shows the difference between specialist and generalist mean rewards from Fig. 4. The dotted blue line shows the mean value of the difference (49, 24). This shows an advantage in reward for specialist roles. The dotted red line describes a linear regression model of the difference data which also indicates specialist efficiency. It confirms the hypothesis that specialist are reaching the maximum reward faster since they gain more experience. Running a t-test shows that specialist and generalist mean rewards are significantly distinct (p-value = 0.006827). Then the average reward normalizes as both generalists and specialists reach the maximum reward amount.

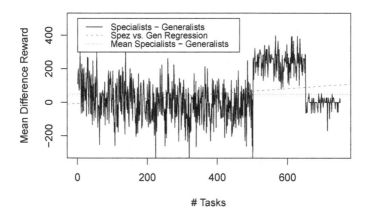

Fig. 5. Specialist vs. generalist rewards

Adaptation of Task Requirements. In this context, the dynamics of a system is defined not only by the stochastic change of states but also by the change of task requirements. Hence, in order to demonstrate and analyze learning in dynamic environments, the requirements for accomplishing a small emergency task are modified. By this modification an agent need to send resources as it would for a medium operation. For instance, one could argue that strong wind would spread a fire much faster so one would need more units to fight the fire.

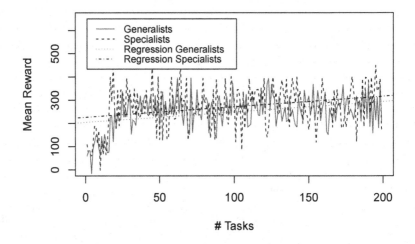

Fig. 6. Adaptation performance

In this experiment a total of 700 emergencies have to be operated. After a learning period of 500 emergencies, the requirements for a successful operation are changed. Figure 6 shows the mean rewards of generalist and specialist role designs. For comparing the recovery performance for the two role designs a linear regression is conducted. The resulting linear models shows a stronger recovery for specialist roles (linear models: $Reg_{spec} = 0.46 * x + 226.40$ and $Reg_{gen} = 0.44 * x + 203.99$). The linear regression shows almost equivalent gradients but the intercept for generalist role designs is lower. This indicates a higher impact of dynamic environment on generalist roles in comparison to specialized ones. A T-test reveals a significant distinction of the test series with a p-value of 0.0057. Overall, specialized role designs allow for a more efficient learning than generalist role designs in this experimental setting.

5   Conclusions

Task processing in dynamic environments is a major challenge for designing multiagent systems. This paper addresses the challenge by analyzing learning agents in organizational structures and the impact of specializing agents on learning performance. Hence, we extend a Belief-Desire-Intention agent architecture with a Q-learning approach to learn action selection for agent plans to incorporate experience and environmental feedback into task-related knowledge. Different role designs are tested using an emergency response simulation environment in which agents control fire departments and assign rescue units to emergency operations.

The two main conclusions from the simulation experiments are that (1) specialist roles gain maximum reward values faster than generalist ones and consequently (2) specialized agents recover more efficient from environmental changes. These observation refer to the average reward gained trough various learning episodes. However, these first tests are limited to the simulation scenario and its structure but allow for first quantifications of learning costs which build the basis for adapting agent roles at runtime. In future research, a continuation of the adaptive agent framework is planned in which these findings can be complemented with an optimization approach. The adaptation aims at balancing specialist role designs for allowing more efficient adaptation to changing environments with a cross-training approach to accommodate for robustness.

Acknowledgements. The project *AdaptPRO: Adaptive Process and Role Design in Organizations* (TI 548/-1) is funded by the German Research Foundation (DFG) within the Priority Program "Intentional Forgetting in Organizations" (SPP 1921).

References

1. Campbell, A., Wu, A.S.: Multi-agent role allocation: issues, approaches, and multiple perspectives. Auton. Agents Multi Agent Syst. **22**(2), 317–355 (2011)
2. Chung, J., White, K.P.: Cross-trained versus specialized agents in an inbound call centre: a simulation-based methodology for trade-off analysis. J. Simul. **2**(3), 162–169 (2008). https://doi.org/10.1057/jos.2008.6
3. Coutinho, L.R., Sichman, J.S., Boissier, O.: Modelling dimensions for agent organizations. In: Handbook of Research on Multi-Agent Systems: Semantics and Dynamics of Organizational Models, pp. 18–50. IGI Global (2009)
4. Dignum, V.: The role of organization in agent systems. In: Handbook of Research on Multi-Agent Systems: Semantics and Dynamics of Organizational Models, pp. 1–16. IGI Global (2009)
5. Dignum, V., Dignum, F.: A logic of agent organizations. Log. J. IGPL **20**(1), 283–316 (2012)
6. Dunin-Keplicz, B., Verbrugge, R.: Teamwork in Multi-Agent Systems: A Formal Approach, vol. 21. Wiley, Hoboken (2011)
7. Ferber, J.: Multi-Agent Systems: An Introduction to Distributed Artificial Intelligence. Addison-Wesley, Harlow (1999)
8. Fikes, R., Nilsson, N.J.: STRIPS: a new approach to the application of theorem proving to problem solving. In: Cooper, D.C. (ed.) Proceedings of the 2nd International Joint Conference on Artificial Intelligence, London, UK, September 1–3, 1971, pp. 608–620. William Kaufmann (1971)
9. Gale, D.: The Theory of Linear Economic Models. University of Chicago Press, Chicago (1989)

10. Gerkey, B.P., Matarić, M.J.: On role allocation in RoboCup. In: Polani, D., Browning, B., Bonarini, A., Yoshida, K. (eds.) RoboCup 2003. LNCS (LNAI), vol. 3020, pp. 43–53. Springer, Heidelberg (2004). https://doi.org/10.1007/978-3-540-25940-4_4

11. Hannoun, M., Sichman, J.S., Boissier, O., Sayettat, C.: Dependence relations between roles in a multi-agent system. In: Sichman, J.S., Conte, R., Gilbert, N. (eds.) MABS 1998. LNCS (LNAI), vol. 1534, pp. 169–182. Springer, Heidelberg (1998). https://doi.org/10.1007/10692956_12

12. Kieser, A., Walgenbach, P.: Organisation. Schäffer-Poeschel (October 2010)

13. Kuo, J.Y., Tsai, M.L., Hsueh, N.L.: Goal evolution based on adaptive Q-learning for intelligent agent. In: 2006 IEEE International Conference on Systems, Man and Cybernetics, vol. 1, pp. 434–439 (October 2006). https://doi.org/10.1109/ICSMC.2006.384421

14. Nair, R., Tambe, M.: Hybrid BDI-POMDP framework for multiagent teaming. J. Artif. Intell. Res. 23(1), 367–420 (2005)

15. Nair, R., Tambe, M., Marsella, S.: Role allocation and reallocation in multiagent teams: towards a practical analysis. In: Proceedings of the Second International Joint Conference on Autonomous Agents and Multiagent Systems, AAMAS 2003, pp. 552–559. Association for Computing Machinery, Melbourne (July 2003)

16. Rana, O.F., Winikoff, M., Padgham, L., Harland, J.: Applying conflict management strategies in BDI agents for resource management in computational grids. In: Proceedings of the Twenty-Fifth Australasian Conference on Computer Science, ACSC 2002, vol. 4, pp. 205–214. Australian Computer Society Inc., Melbourne (January 2002)

17. Rens, G., Moodley, D.: A hybrid POMDP-BDI agent architecture with online stochastic planning and plan caching. Cogn. Syst. Res. 43, 1–20 (2017)

18. Reuter, L., Berndt, J.O., Timm, I.J.: Towards simulation-based role optimization in organizations. In: Kern-Isberner, G., Fürnkranz, J., Thimm, M. (eds.) KI 2017. LNCS (LNAI), vol. 10505, pp. 359–365. Springer, Cham (2017). https://doi.org/10.1007/978-3-319-67190-1_32

19. Reuter, L., Berndt, J.O., Ulfert, A.-S., Antoni, C.H., Ellwart, T., Timm, I.J.: Intentional forgetting in distributed artificial intelligence. KI - Künstliche Intell. 33(1), 69–77 (2018). https://doi.org/10.1007/s13218-018-0566-4

20. Scerri, P., Farinelli, A., Okamoto, S., Tambe, M.: Allocating roles in extreme teams. In: Proceedings of the Third International Joint Conference on Autonomous Agents and Multiagent Systems, vol. 3, pp. 1502–1503 (2004)

21. Schillo, M., Fley, B., Florian, M., Hillebrandt, F., Hinck, D.: Self-organization in multiagent systems: from agent interaction to agent organization. In: Third International Workshop on Modelling Artificial Societies and Hybrid Organisations (MASHO), pp. 37–46 (2002)

22. Schwartz, H.M.: Multi-Agent Machine Learning: A Reinforcement Approach. Wiley, Hoboken (2014)

23. Simari, G.I., Parsons, S.D.: Markov Decision Processes and the Belief-Desire-Intention Model: Bridging the Gap for Autonomous Agents. Springer, Heidelberg (2011). https://doi.org/10.1007/978-1-4614-1472-8

24. Sutton, R.S., Barto, A.G.: Reinforcement learning: an introduction (2011)

25. Timm, I.J.: Dynamisches Konfliktmanagement Als Verhaltenssteuerung Intelligenter Agenten. Ph.D. thesis, University of Bremen (2004)

26. Timm, I.J., Berndt, J.O., Reuter, L., Ellwart, T., Antoni, C.H., Ulfert, A.S.: Towards multiagent-based simulation of knowledge management in teams. In: Tagungsband Der 9. Konferenz Professionelles Wissensmanagement (Professional Knowledge Management), Karlsruhe, Germany, April 5–7, 2017, pp. 25–40 (2017)

27. Timm, I.J., Reuter, L., Berndt, J.O.: Role assignment adaptation: an intentional forgetting approach. In: 53rd Hawaii International Conference on System Sciences, HICSS 2020, Maui, Hawaii, USA, January 7–10, 2020, pp. 1–10. ScholarSpace (2020)

28. Wan, Q., Liu, W., Xu, L., Guo, J.: Extending the BDI model with Q-learning in uncertain environment. In: Proceedings of the 2018 International Conference on Algorithms, Computing and Artificial Intelligence, ACAI 2018, pp. 1–6. Association for Computing Machinery, Sanya (December 2018). https://doi.org/10.1145/3302425.3302432

29. Wooldridge, M.: Reasoning about Rational Agents. MIT Press, Cambridge (2000)

Descriptor Revision for Conditionals: Literal Descriptors and Conditional Preservation

Kai Sauerwald$^{(\boxtimes)}$ ⓘ, Jonas Haldimann ⓘ, Martin von Berg,
and Christoph Beierle

FernUniversität in Hagen, 58084 Hagen, Germany
{kai.sauerwald,jonas.haldimann,christoph.beierle}@fernuni-hagen.de

Abstract. Descriptor revision by Hansson is a framework for addressing the problem of belief change. In descriptor revision, different kinds of change processes are dealt with in a joint framework. Individual change requirements are qualified by specific success conditions expressed by a belief descriptor, and belief descriptors can be combined by logical connectives. This is in contrast to the currently dominating AGM paradigm shaped by Alchourrón, Gärdenfors, and Makinson, where different kinds of changes, like a revision or a contraction, are dealt with separately. In this article, we investigate the realisation of descriptor revision for a conditional logic while restricting descriptors to the conjunction of literal descriptors. We apply the principle of conditional preservation developed by Kern-Isberner to descriptor revision for conditionals, show how descriptor revision for conditionals under these restrictions can be characterised by a constraint satisfaction problem, and implement it using constraint logic programming. Since our conditional logic subsumes propositional logic, our approach also realises descriptor revision for propositional logic.

1 Introduction

The work by Alchourrón, Gärdenfors, and Makinson [1] (AGM) and its successors have shaped the currently dominating paradigm for belief change. By AGM, mainly three main kinds of belief changes are subject of interest: *revision* (incorporating new beliefs into an agent's belief state while maintaining consistency), *contraction* (removing beliefs from the agent's belief state), and *expansion* (incorporating new beliefs into an agent's belief state without maintaining consistency). The most prominent difference between these kinds of changes is their success condition. The approach to the problem of belief change by AGM is top-down, starting from the axiomatisation of each of the three kinds of changes and then investigating the representational issues through representation theorems.

In the last 20 years, the AGM theory has been extended into several directions and has been deeply investigated. This gives new insights on the requirements

© Springer Nature Switzerland AG 2020
U. Schmid et al. (Eds.): KI 2020, LNAI 12325, pp. 204–218, 2020.
https://doi.org/10.1007/978-3-030-58285-2_15

of representation and conceptual problems of (AGM) belief change. In particular, for Hansson [16], the requirement of epistemic states for iterative belief change [8], the central role of conditionals in belief change and non-monotonic logic [23,24] and problems like the non-finite representability of the result of a contraction [14] or concerns about the "select-and-intersect" approach of AGM [16] were a motivation to design a new framework for belief change. Descriptor revision by Hansson [10] follows the top-down approach to belief change, but, in contrast to the AGM paradigm, in descriptor revision, different kinds of changes are expressible in one joint framework. For this, Hansson introduced a language for success conditions, called belief descriptors. Through belief descriptors, success conditions become an explicit part of the change process, instead of hiding them in distinct kinds of operations having different success conditions. This allows to express and analyse change processes that go beyond the classical AGM operations, e.g., a change process where a contraction of a belief α and a revision by β appear at the same time. Descriptor revision has been broadly investigated by Hansson [11–16], but did not gain as much attention as AGM [26]. In particular, to the best of our knowledge, until now, no approach to the realisation of descriptor revision is available.

In this article, we investigate descriptor revision for a conditional logic while using ordinal conditional functions [25], also called ranking functions, as representation for epistemic states. We outline how to instantiate the framework of descriptor revision for this logic and design an approach for its realisation. Furthermore, for descriptor revision we use and adapt the sophisticated principle of conditional preservation by Kern-Isberner [18,19] for ranking functions. In summary, the main contributions of this article are:

- Introduction of conditional descriptor revision, which introduces the principle of conditional preservation to the framework of descriptor revision.
- A sound and complete characterisation of conditional descriptor revision for elementary descriptors by a constraint satisfaction problem.
- Implementation of elementary descriptor revision using constraint logic programming and by employing the developed characterisation.

The article is organised as follows. In Sect. 2, we present logical preliminaries. We recall descriptors and descriptor revision in Sect. 3. Section 4 introduces our framework of conditional descriptor revision. Section 5 develops a characterisation of conditional descriptor revision for elementary descriptors by a constraint satisfaction problem. The implementation of this approach is sketched in Sect. 6. We conclude and point out future work in Sect. 7.

2   Logical Preliminaries

Let Σ be a propositional signature (non-empty finite set of propositional variables) and $\mathcal{L}^{\mathrm{prop}}$ the propositional language over Σ. With upper case letters $A, B, C, \ldots$, we denote formulas in $\mathcal{L}^{\mathrm{prop}}$ and with lower case letters $a, b, c, \ldots$ propositional variables from Σ. We allow the typical abbreviation $A \to B$ for

$\neg A \vee B$, abbreviate $A \wedge B$ by AB and write $\overline{A}$ for $\neg A$. With $\top$, we denote a propositional tautology and with $\perp$ a propositional falsum. The set of propositional interpretations $\Omega = \mathcal{P}(\Sigma)$, also called set of worlds, is identified with the set of corresponding complete conjunctions over Σ, where $\mathcal{P}(\cdot)$ is the powerset operator. Propositional entailment is denoted by $\models$, the set of models of A with $Mod(A)$, and $Cn(A) = \{B \mid A \models B\}$ is the deductive closure of A. For a set X, we define $Cn(X) = \{B \mid X \models B\}$ and say X is deductively closed if $X = Cn(X)$. In the context of belief change, a deductively closed set is also called a *belief set*.

A function $\kappa : \Omega \rightarrow \mathbb{N}$ such that $\kappa^{-1}(0) \neq \emptyset$ is a called a *ordinal conditional function (OCF)*, also called a *ranking function* [25]. It expresses degrees of implausibility of interpretations. This is lifted to propositional formulas A by defining $\kappa(A) := \min\{\kappa(\omega) \mid \omega \models A\}$, where $\min \emptyset = \infty$, yielding a function $\kappa : \mathcal{L} \rightarrow \mathbb{N} \cup \{\infty\}$ which specifies a degree of implausibility for each formula. With $Mod(\kappa) = \{\omega \mid \kappa(\omega) = 0\}$ we denote the minimal interpretations with respect to κ, and $Bel(\kappa)$ denotes the theory of propositional formulas that hold in all $\omega \in Mod(\kappa)$.

Over Σ and $\mathcal{L}^{\mathrm{prop}}$, we define the set of conditionals $\mathcal{L}^{\mathrm{cond}} = \{(B|A) \mid A, B \in \mathcal{L}\}$. A conditional $(B|A)$ formalizes *"if A then usually B"* and establishes a plausible connection between the *antecedent* A and the *consequent* B. Conditionals with tautological antecedents are taken as plausible statements about the world. Because conditionals go well beyond classical logic, they require a richer setting for their semantics than classical logic. Following De Finetti [9], a conditional $(B|A)$ can be *verified (falsified)* by a possible world ω iff $\omega \models AB$ ($\omega \models A\overline{B}$). If $\omega \not\models A$, then we say the conditional is *not applicable* to ω.

Ranking functions serve here as interpretations in a model theory for a conditional logic. We say a conditional $(B|A)$ is accepted in a ranking function κ, written as $\kappa \models (B|A)$, iff $\kappa(AB) < \kappa(A\overline{B})$, i.e., iff the verification AB of the conditional is more plausible than its falsification $A\overline{B}$. For a propositional formula A, we define $\kappa \models A$ if $\kappa \models (A|\top)$, i.e., iff $\kappa(A) < \kappa(\overline{A})$ or equivalently iff $\kappa(\overline{A}) > 0$, since at least one of $\kappa(A), \kappa(\overline{A})$ must be 0 due to $\kappa^{-1}(0) \neq \emptyset$. The models of a conditional $(B|A)$ are the set of all ranking functions accepting $(B|A)$, i.e. $Mod((B_1|A_1)) = \{\kappa \mid \kappa \models (B|A)\}$. A conditional $(B_1|A_1)$ entails $(B_2|A_2)$, written $(B_1|A_1) \models (B_2|A_2)$, if $Mod((B_1|A_1)) \subseteq Mod((B_2|A_2))$ holds. Furthermore, we define the set of consequences for $X \subseteq \mathcal{L}^{\mathrm{cond}}$ by $Cn(X) = \{(B|A) \mid X \models (B|A)\}$. As usual, $X \subseteq \mathcal{L}^{\mathrm{cond}}$ is called deductively closed if $X = Cn(X)$. This ranking function based semantics can be mapped to, and can also be obtained from, other semantics of conditionals [4].

Example 1 (adapted [5]). Let $\Sigma = \{p, b, f\}$ with p meaning "penguin", b "bird" and f "able to fly". "Birds normally fly" is modelled with the conditional $r_1 = (f|b)$, "penguins normally do not fly" with $r_2 = (\overline{f}|p)$, and "penguins are normally birds" with $r_3 = (b|p)$. Consider the ranking function κ_p from Table 1, which will act as our running example for the following sections (where we will also elaborate the other ranking function and conditionals shown in Table 1). Table 1 also contains the verifying and falsifying interpretations of the conditional $(\overline{f}|p)$.

The ranking function κ_p accepts all conditionals in $\mathcal{R}_{pen} = \{r_1, r_2, r_3\}$, i.e. $\kappa_p \models r_i$ for all $1 \leqslant i \leqslant 3$. For example, $\kappa \models r_1$ because $\kappa(bf) = 0 < 1 = \kappa(b\overline{f})$ holds. For the rest of the article, we will assume that the ranking function κ_p is the initial belief state representing the beliefs about penguins, flying, and birds of our agent.

Table 1. Verifying (v) and falsifying (f) interpretations for the conditionals $(p|b)$, $(f|p)$, and $(\overline{f}|p)$, and the ranking functions for the running penguin example.

ω	Conditionals			Belief states	
	$(p\|b)$	$(f\|p)$	$(\overline{f}\|p)$	$\kappa_p(\omega)$	$\kappa_p^\circ(\omega)$
$b\,f\,p$	v	v	f	2	1
$b\,f\,\overline{p}$	f			0	2
$b\,\overline{f}\,p$	v	f	v	1	1
$b\,\overline{f}\,\overline{p}$	f			1	3
$\overline{b}f\,p$		v	f	4	3
$\overline{b}f\,\overline{p}$				0	0
$\overline{b}\,\overline{f}\,p$		f	v	2	2
$\overline{b}\,\overline{f}\,\overline{p}$				0	0

3   Descriptors and Descriptor Revision

The main building blocks of descriptor revision are belief descriptors, which provide a language for expressing membership constraints for a belief set.

Definition 1 (Descriptor [15]). *Let $\mathcal{L}$ be a logical language. For any sentence $\varphi \in \mathcal{L}$ the expression $\mathfrak{B}\varphi$ is an atomic descriptor (over $\mathcal{L}$). Any connection of atomic descriptors with disjunction, conjunction and negation is called a molecular descriptor (over $\mathcal{L}$). A composite descriptor (over $\mathcal{L}$) is a set of molecular descriptors (over $\mathcal{L}$).*

As stated by Hansson [15], composite descriptors are just denoted as *descriptors*. A molecular descriptor of the form $\mathfrak{B}\varphi$ or $\neg\mathfrak{B}\varphi$ is called a *literal descriptor*. An *elementary descriptor* is a set of literal descriptors (and therefore a descriptor).

Definition 2 (Descriptor Semantics [15]). *An atomic descriptor $\mathfrak{B}\varphi$ holds in a belief set X, written $X \Vdash \mathfrak{B}\varphi$, if $\varphi \in X$. This is lifted to molecular descriptors truth-functionally. A descriptor Ψ holds in X, likewise written $X \Vdash \Psi$, if $X \Vdash \alpha$ holds for every molecular descriptor $\alpha \in \Psi$.*

For an example of descriptors, consider the following example.

Example 2. Assume that $\mathcal{L}_{ab}$ is the propositional language over $\Sigma = \{a, b\}$ and $X = Cn(a \vee b)$. Then, $\neg\mathfrak{B}a$ expresses that a is not part of the belief set, whereas $\mathfrak{B}\neg a$ states that the formula $\neg a$ is part of the belief set, e.g. $X \Vdash \neg\mathfrak{B}a$ and $X \nVdash \mathfrak{B}\neg a$. Likewise, $\mathfrak{B}a \vee \mathfrak{B}b$ expresses that a or b is believed, whereas $\mathfrak{B}(a \vee b)$ states that the formula $a \vee b$ is believed, e.g. $X \Vdash \mathfrak{B}(a \vee b)$ and $X \nVdash \mathfrak{B}a \vee \mathfrak{B}b$.

For the setting of belief change, we assume that every agent is equipped with a belief state, also called epistemic state, which contains all information necessary for performing belief change operations. We denote belief states by $K, K_1, K_2, \ldots$ following the notion of Hansson [15]. General descriptor revision does not specify what a belief state is, but assumes that a belief set $Bel(K)$ is immanent for every epistemic state K. To make descriptors compatible with belief states, we naturally lift the semantics to belief states, i.e. $K \Vdash \Psi$ if $Bel(K) \Vdash \Psi$.

Example 3 (Continued). Assume ranking functions as a representation of belief states. Let κ_p be the belief state from Table 1 and let $\Psi = \{\mathfrak{B}\overline{p}, \mathfrak{B}(b \to f), \neg\mathfrak{B}b\overline{f}\}$ be an elementary descriptor. The descriptor Ψ expresses belief in $\overline{p}$ (it is not a penguin) and $b \to f$ (a bird flies) and not believing $b\overline{f}$ (it is a non-flying bird). The immanent belief set of κ_p is $Bel(\kappa_p) = Cn(\overline{p} \wedge (b \to f))$. The descriptor Ψ holds in κ_p, i.e. $\kappa_p \Vdash \Psi$, since $\overline{p} \in Bel(\kappa_p)$, $b \to f \in Bel(\kappa_p)$ and $b\overline{f} \notin Bel(\kappa_p)$.

AGM theory [1] focuses on properties of revision (or contraction) operations by examining the interconnection between prior belief state, new information and posterior belief state of a change. Descriptor revision examines the interconnection between prior belief state and posterior belief states that satisfy a particular descriptor. Let $\mathbb{K}_K$ denote the set of all reasonable conceivable successor belief states for a belief state K. A descriptor revision by a descriptor Ψ is the process of choosing a state K' from $\mathbb{K}_K$ such that $K' \Vdash \Psi$. We abstract from the internal process of how $\mathbb{K}_K$ is obtained and define descriptor revision[1] as follows.

Definition 3. (Descriptor Revision, Adapted [15]). *Let K be a belief state, $\mathbb{K}_K$ a set of belief states and $C : \mathcal{P}(\mathbb{K}_K) \to \mathbb{K}_K$ be a choice function. Then the change from K to $K^\circ = K \circ \Psi$ is called a descriptor revision by Ψ realised by C over $\mathbb{K}_K$ if the following holds:*

$$K \circ \Psi = C(\{K' \in \mathbb{K}_K \mid K' \Vdash \Psi\}) \tag{1}$$

We say that the change from K to K° is a descriptor revision (by Ψ), if C and $\mathbb{K}_K$ (and Ψ) exist such that the change from K to K° is realised by C over $\mathbb{K}_K$. We also say K° is the result of the descriptor revision of K (by Ψ under $\mathbb{K}_K$).

---

[1] In the original framework by Hansson this is much more elaborated. By the terminology of Hansson, here we present a form of local deterministic monoselective descriptor revision [15]. Moreover, we primarily focus on one change, while Hansson designs the framework for change operators.

Descriptors allow to express a variety of different success conditions, e.g.

$\{\mathfrak{B}\varphi\}$ Revision by φ
$\{\neg\mathfrak{B}\varphi\}$ Contraction by φ (also called revocation [16])
$\{\neg\mathfrak{B}\varphi, \neg\mathfrak{B}\neg\varphi\}$ Giving up the judgement on φ (also called ignoration [5]).

Additionally, Hansson provides the following examples [16]:

$\{\mathfrak{B}\varphi_1, \ldots, \mathfrak{B}\varphi_n\}$ Package revision by $\{\varphi_1, \ldots, \varphi_n\}$
$\{\neg\mathfrak{B}\varphi, \mathfrak{B}\psi\}$ Replacement of φ by ψ
$\{\mathfrak{B}\varphi_1 \vee \ldots \vee \mathfrak{B}\varphi_n\}$ Choice revision by $\{\varphi_1, \ldots, \varphi_n\}$
$\{\mathfrak{B}\varphi \vee \mathfrak{B}\neg\varphi\}$ Making up one's mind about φ.

Note that all given examples, except for choice revision and "making up one's mind", are elementary descriptors. In particular, elementary descriptor revision subsumes operations of AGM, and, furthermore, also allows to express changes which lead to a revision and a contraction at the same time. For a concrete example, we continue our running example.

Example 4 (Continued). Let κ_p and κ_p° be as in Table 1, let $\mathbb{K}_{\kappa_p}$ be the set of all ranking functions, let C be a choice function such that $C(X) = \kappa_p^\circ$ if $\kappa_p^\circ \in X$, and let $\Psi = \{\mathfrak{B}\bar{b} \vee \mathfrak{B}p, \neg\mathfrak{B}bf\}$ be a descriptor. The descriptor Ψ expresses posterior belief in $\bar{b}$ or belief in p and disbelief in bf. In particular, $\neg\mathfrak{B}bf$ expresses a contraction with bf (it is a flying bird), but for $\mathfrak{B}\bar{b} \vee \mathfrak{B}p$ (it is not a bird or it is a penguin), there is no straight counterpart in the AGM framework. Note that we have $Bel(\kappa_p^\circ) = Cn(\bar{b} \wedge \bar{p})$, and thus, it holds that $\bar{b} \in Bel(\kappa_p^\circ)$ and $bf \notin Bel(\kappa_p^\circ)$, and therefore, the descriptor Ψ holds in κ_p°. Thus, the change from κ_p to κ_p° is a descriptor revision by Ψ realised by C over $\mathbb{K}_{\kappa_p}$.

4   Conditional Descriptor Revision

We instantiate descriptor revision for the case in which the underlying logic is the conditional logic $\mathcal{L}^{\mathrm{cond}}$ and ranking functions serve as a representation for epistemic states. Furthermore, we adapt the principle of conditional preservation by Kern-Isberner [18] to the requirements of descriptor revision.

4.1   Adaptions for Conditionals in $\mathcal{L}^{\mathrm{cond}}$

In the formal framework of descriptor revision by Hansson, as recalled in Sect. 3, semantics of a descriptor refer to a belief set, containing formulas of the underlying logic. Thus, when using the logic $\mathcal{L}^{\mathrm{cond}}$, we need to refer to the set of conditionals accepted by a ranking function κ when choosing ranking functions as representations for epistemic states. However, the belief set $Bel(\kappa)$ of a ranking function κ is a set of propositional beliefs, i.e. $Bel(\kappa) \subseteq \mathcal{L}^{\mathrm{prop}}$. We define the set of conditional beliefs for a ranking function κ as follows:

$$Bel^{cond}(\kappa) = \{(B|A) \mid \kappa \models (B|A)\}$$

Clearly, the set $Bel^{cond}(\kappa)$ is a deductively closed set for every ranking function κ and therefore a belief set. Descriptors and descriptor revision for $\mathcal{L}^{cond}$ then refer to the set of conditional beliefs $Bel^{cond}(\kappa)$, and their formal definition can be easily obtained by correspondingly modifying Definitions 1, 2 and 3.

Note that the conditional logic $\mathcal{L}^{cond}$ embeds the propositional logic $\mathcal{L}^{prop}$, hence every proposition $A \in \mathcal{L}^{prop}$ can be represented by $(A|\top)$. Moreover, the definition of $Bel^{cond}(\kappa)$ ensures compatibility of propositional beliefs with the conditional beliefs, i.e. $\{(A|\top) \mid A \in Bel(K)\} \subseteq Bel^{cond}(K)$. Thus, our approach to descriptor revision by conditionals, presented in the following, subsumes descriptor revision for propositions.

4.2   Conditional Preservation

When an agent performs a belief change, the change might not only affect explicit beliefs, but also implicit beliefs. Boutilier proposed that belief change should also minimize the effect on conditional beliefs [6]. Kern-Isberner introduced the principle of conditional preservation (PCP) and gave a thorough axiomatisation of PCP [17,18] in a very general manner.

Note that the principle of conditional preservation is usually defined as a property of a change by a set of conditionals $\mathcal{R}$. However, when having a descriptor revision, the underlying change framework and its parameters and capabilities might be hidden. Thus, we abstract from the assumption that the change is done by a set of conditionals $\mathcal{R}$, and just state that a change satisfies PCP with respect to a set of conditionals $\mathcal{R}$. This allows us to say that a change satisfies the principle of conditional preservation without assuming the involvement of specific parameters in the underlying change framework. In the following, we present our relaxed variant of the principle of conditional preservation for the special case of ranking functions.

Definition 4. (PCP for OCF Changes, Adapted [20]). *A change of a ranking function κ to a ranking function κ° fulfils the principle of conditional preservation with respect to the conditionals $\mathcal{R} = \{(B_1|A_1), \ldots, (B_n|A_n)\}$, if for every two multisets of propositional interpretations $\Omega_1 = \{\omega_1, \ldots, \omega_m\}$ and $\Omega_2 = \{\omega_1', \ldots, \omega_m'\}$ with the same cardinality m such that the multisets Ω_1 and Ω_2 contain the same number of interpretations which verify, respectively falsify, each conditional $(B_i|A_i)$ in $\mathcal{R}$, the ranking functions κ and κ° are balanced in the following way:*

$$\sum_{i=1}^{m} \kappa(\omega_i) - \sum_{i=1}^{m} \kappa(\omega_i') = \sum_{i=1}^{m} \kappa^{\circ}(\omega_i) - \sum_{i=1}^{m} \kappa^{\circ}(\omega_i') \qquad (2)$$

Example 5 (Continued). Assume our agent lives in Antarctica and she starts to question her beliefs about penguins and birds. The only birds she sees in Antarctica are penguins, and moreover, she observes, through her window, a lot of penguins jumping off a cliff, and thus, flying for a moment. Her belief state is changing from κ_p to κ_p° from Table 1. Consider now the conditional

$(p|b)$ expressing that *birds are usually penguins*, the conditional $(f|p)$ expressing that *penguins usually fly*, and the conditional $(\overline{f}|p)$ expressing that *penguins usually don't fly*. The change from κ_p to κ_p° satisfies the principle of conditional preservation with respect to the conditionals in $\mathcal{R} = \{(p|b), (f|p), (\overline{f}|p)\}$. For instance, the two multisets $\Omega_1 = \{bfp, \overline{b}\,\overline{f}p\}$ and $\Omega_2 = \{b\overline{f}p, \overline{b}fp\}$, containing for every conditional in $\mathcal{R}$ the same number of verifying and falsifying worlds, and their values under κ_p and κ_p° are balanced according to Eq. (2), i.e.

$$\kappa_p(bfp) + \kappa_p(\overline{b}\,\overline{f}p) - \kappa_p(b\overline{f}p) - \kappa_p(\overline{b}fp) = 2 + 2 - 1 - 4 = -1$$
$$= 1 + 2 - 1 - 3 = \kappa_p^\circ(bfp) + \kappa_p^\circ(\overline{b}\,\overline{f}p) - \kappa_p^\circ(b\overline{f}p) - \kappa_p^\circ(\overline{b}fp).$$

The definition of the principle of conditional preservation, as given in Definition 4, does not require information about the success condition of a change. Thus, the notion of the principle of conditional preservation is directly available for descriptor revision of conditionals when we provide a set of conditionals. A natural choice are the conditionals appearing in a descriptor Ψ. For a descriptor Ψ over $\mathcal{L}^{\mathrm{cond}}$, we define the set of conditionals in Ψ, denoted by $cond(\Psi)$, as follows:

- for $\Psi = \emptyset$ let $cond(\Psi) = \emptyset$,
- for $\Psi = \{\mathfrak{B}(B|A)\}$ let $cond(\Psi) = \{(B|A)\}$,
- for $\Psi = \{\alpha, \beta, \ldots\}$ let $cond(\Psi) = cond(\{\alpha\}) \cup cond(\{\beta, \ldots\})$,
- for $\Psi = \{\alpha \vee \beta\}$ let $cond(\Psi) = cond(\{\alpha\}) \cup cond(\{\beta\})$,
- for $\Psi = \{\alpha \wedge \beta\}$ let $cond(\Psi) = cond(\{\alpha\}) \cup cond(\{\beta\})$, and
- for $\Psi = \{\neg\alpha\}$ let $cond(\Psi) = cond(\{\alpha\})$.

In the following, we use a central characterisation [19,20] of the principle of conditional preservation to obtain a characterisation of the principle of conditional preservation for descriptor revisions.

Proposition 1. (PCP for Descriptor Revision, Adapted [20]). *Let Ψ be a descriptor over $\mathcal{L}^{\mathrm{cond}}$ and $cond(\Psi) = \{(B_1|A_1), \ldots, (B_n|A_n)\}$ be the set of conditionals in Ψ, and let κ° be the result of the descriptor revision of κ by Ψ. Then this change satisfies the* principle of conditional preservation *with respect to the conditionals in $cond(\Psi)$ if and only if there are integers[2] $\kappa_0, \gamma_i^+, \gamma_i^- \in \mathbb{Z}$, $1 \leqslant i \leqslant n$, such that:*

$$\kappa^\circ(\omega) = \kappa_0 + \kappa(\omega) + \sum_{\substack{1 \leqslant i \leqslant n \\ \omega \models A_i B_i}} \gamma_i^+ + \sum_{\substack{1 \leqslant i \leqslant n \\ \omega \models A_i \wedge \neg B_i}} \gamma_i^- \qquad (3)$$

The proof of Proposition 1 is directly obtainable from a proof given by Kern-Isberner [19, Theorem 4.6.1], since no specific information on the success condition for the conditionals in the descriptor was used in Proposition 1. The idea underlying Proposition 1 is that interpretations that are verifying and falsifying

---

[2] As noted by Kern-Isberner [20], all $\kappa_0, \gamma_i^+, \gamma_i^-$ can be rational, but κ° has to satisfy the requirements for OCF, in particular, all $\kappa^\circ(\omega)$ must be non-negative integers.

the same conditionals are treated in the same way. Thus, for every conditional $(B_i|A_i) \in cond(\Psi)$, the two constants γ_i^+ and γ_i^- handle how interpretations are shifted over the change process. The constant κ_0 acts as a normalizer, ensuring that κ° is indeed a ranking function, i.e. there is at least one world ω such that $\kappa^\circ(\omega) = 0$.

Example 6 (Continued). Consider the change from κ_p to κ_p°, both given in Table 1. As shown in Example 5, this change satisfies the principle of conditional preservation with respect to the conditionals in $\mathcal{R} = \{(p|b), (f|p), (\overline{f}|p)\}$. Indeed, as stated in Proposition 1, we can obtain κ_p° from κ_p via Eq. (3) by choosing $\kappa_0 = 0$, $\gamma_1^+ = 0$, $\gamma_1^- = -1$, $\gamma_2^+ = 0$, $\gamma_2^- = 2$, $\gamma_3^+ = 0$, and $\gamma_3^- = 0$.

4.3 Descriptor Revision with Conditional Preservation

The principle of conditional preservation is a powerful basic principle of belief change and it is natural to demand satisfaction of this principle. The principle demands a specific relation between the conditionals in the prior belief state K, the conditionals in the posterior state K° and the conditionals in the descriptor Ψ. Remember that by Definition 3, a descriptor revision from K to K° is determined by a choice function C, the descriptor Ψ and the set $\mathbb{K}_K$ such that Eq. (1) holds, but none of these components allow to express a direct relation between K, K° and Ψ. Thus, there is no possibility to express conditional preservation by the means of descriptor revision. The principle of conditional preservation is somewhat orthogonal to descriptor revision, which gives rationale to the following definition of conditional descriptor revision.

Definition 5 (Conditional Descriptor Revision). *Let κ be a ranking function. A descriptor revision of κ to κ° by a descriptor Ψ over $\mathcal{L}^{cond}$ (realised by C over $\mathbb{K}_\kappa$) is called a* conditional descriptor revision *of κ to κ° by Ψ (realised by C over $\mathbb{K}_\kappa$) if the change from κ to κ° satisfies the principle of conditional preservation with respect to $cond(\Psi)$.*

In Definition 5, we choose ranking functions as representations for belief states, but note that the principle of conditional preservation also applies to other representations [19]. Thus, for other kinds of representations of belief states one might give a definition of conditional descriptor revision similar to the one given here. However, for the rest of the article, we focus on ranking functions. Moreover, we assume $\mathbb{K}_\kappa$ to be the set of all ranking functions, i.e. when revising by a descriptor over Ψ, we choose over the set of all ranking functions.

Example 7 (Continued). Consider κ_p to κ_Ψ° given in Table 1. The change from κ_p to κ_Ψ° is a conditional descriptor revision by $\Psi = \{\mathfrak{B}(p|b), \neg\mathfrak{B}(f|p), \neg\mathfrak{B}(\overline{f}|p)\}$. Note that $cond(\Psi) = \{(p|b), (f|p), (\overline{f}|p)\}$, and therefore, as stated in Example 5, the change from κ_p to κ_Ψ° satisfies the principle of conditional preservation with respect to $cond(\Psi)$. Note that Ψ holds in κ_p°, i.e. $\kappa_p^\circ \Vdash \Psi$. In particular, it is the case that $\kappa_p^\circ \Vdash \neg\mathfrak{B}(\overline{f}|p)$, which is equivalent to $\kappa_p^\circ \not\models (\overline{f}|p)$, i.e. $\kappa_p^\circ(\overline{f}p) \not< \kappa_p^\circ(fp)$.

5   Characterisation of Conditional Descriptor Revision with Elementary Descriptors by CSPs

The arithmetic nature of ranking functions and the characterisation of the principle of conditional preservation by Proposition 1 allow us to give a constraint, expressing the success condition of a literal descriptor.

Definition 6. (Constraint for Literal Descriptors, $CR_D(\kappa, \alpha, \Psi)$). *Let κ be a ranking function, let $\Psi = \{\alpha_1, \ldots, \alpha_m\}$ be an elementary descriptor over $\mathcal{L}^{\text{cond}}$ with $\text{cond}(\Psi) = \{(B_1|A_1), \ldots, (B_n|A_n)\}$, and let α be a literal descriptor in Ψ. The constraint for α in κ under Ψ, denoted by $CR_D(\kappa, \alpha, \Psi)$, on the constraint variables $\gamma_1^+, \gamma_1^-, \ldots, \gamma_n^+, \gamma_n^-$ ranging over $\mathbb{Z}$, is given for a positive literal $\alpha = \mathcal{B}(B_i|A_i)$ descriptor by*

$$
\gamma_i^- - \gamma_i^+ > \Big(\min_{\omega \models A_i B_i} \kappa(\omega) + \sum_{\substack{j \neq i \\ \omega \models A_j B_j}} \gamma_j^+ + \sum_{\substack{j \neq i \\ \omega \models A_j \bar{B}_j}} \gamma_j^- \Big)
$$
$$
- \Big(\min_{\omega \models A_i \bar{B}_i} \kappa(\omega) + \sum_{\substack{j \neq i \\ \omega \models A_j B_j}} \gamma_j^+ + \sum_{\substack{j \neq i \\ \omega \models A_j \bar{B}_j}} \gamma_j^- \Big) \quad \text{for } i = 1, \ldots, n
$$

(4)

and for a negative literal descriptor $\alpha = \neg \mathcal{B}(B_i|A_i)$ by

$$
\gamma_i^- - \gamma_i^+ \leqslant \Big(\min_{\omega \models A_i B_i} \kappa(\omega) + \sum_{\substack{j \neq i \\ \omega \models A_j B_j}} \gamma_j^+ + \sum_{\substack{j \neq i \\ \omega \models A_j \bar{B}_j}} \gamma_j^- \Big)
$$
$$
- \Big(\min_{\omega \models A_i \bar{B}_i} \kappa(\omega) + \sum_{\substack{j \neq i \\ \omega \models A_j B_j}} \gamma_j^+ + \sum_{\substack{j \neq i \\ \omega \models A_j \bar{B}_j}} \gamma_j^- \Big) \quad \text{for } i = 1, \ldots, n.
$$

(5)

The rationale for Definition 6 is that a positive literal descriptor $\{\mathcal{B}(B|A)\}$ holds in the posterior state κ° if $(B|A)$ is accepted by κ°, more formally $\kappa^\circ \models (B|A)$, i.e. $\kappa^\circ(AB) < \kappa^\circ(A\bar{B})$. Likewise, a negative literal descriptor $\{\neg\mathcal{B}(B|A)\}$ corresponds to $\kappa^\circ \not\models (B|A)$, i.e. $\kappa^\circ(AB) \geqslant \kappa^\circ(A\bar{B})$. Combining all the constraints obtained for each literal descriptor in Ψ yields a constraint satisfaction problem.

Definition 7. (CSP for Elementary Descriptors, $CR_D(\kappa, \Psi)$). *Let κ be a ranking function and Ψ be an elementary belief descriptor with $\text{cond}(\Psi) = \{(A_1|B_1), \ldots, (A_n|B_n)\}$. The constraint satisfaction problem for κ and Ψ, on the constraint variables $\gamma_1^+, \gamma_1^-, \ldots, \gamma_n^+, \gamma_n^-$ ranging over $\mathbb{Z}$, denoted by $CR_D(\kappa, \Psi)$, is given by the conjunction of the constraints $CR_D(\kappa, \alpha, \Psi)$ for each $\alpha \in \Psi$.*

With $Sol(CR_D(\kappa, \Psi))$, we denote the solutions of the constraint satisfaction problem $CR_D(\kappa, \Psi)$. Each solution $\vec{\gamma} = \langle \gamma_1^+, \gamma_1^-, \ldots, \gamma_n^+, \gamma_n^- \rangle \in Sol(CR_D(\kappa, \Psi))$ induces a unique ranking function $\kappa_{\vec{\gamma}}$ obtained from Eq. (3) in Theorem 1 by choosing κ_0 as the smallest integer such that the equation yields a ranking function, i.e., there is a propositional interpretation $\omega \in \Omega$ such that $\kappa_{\vec{\gamma}}(\omega) = 0$ and for all $\omega \in \Omega$ the value $\kappa_{\vec{\gamma}}(\omega)$ is a non-negative integer.

Example 8 (Continued). Consider κ_p from Table 1 and the elementary descriptor $\Psi = \{\mathfrak{B}(p|b), \neg\mathfrak{B}(f|p), \neg\mathfrak{B}(\overline{f}|p)\}$. The CSP $CR_D(\kappa, \Psi)$ is given by:

$$CR_D(\kappa_p, \mathfrak{B}(p|b), \Psi): \quad \gamma_1^- - \gamma_1^+ > \min\{\kappa_p(bfp) + \gamma_2^+ + \gamma_3^-, \ \kappa_p(b\overline{f}p) + \gamma_3^+ + \gamma_2^-\}$$
$$- \min\{\kappa_p(bf\overline{p}), \kappa_p(b\overline{f}\overline{p}))\}$$
$$CR_D(\kappa_p, \neg\mathfrak{B}(f|p), \Psi): \quad \gamma_2^- - \gamma_2^+ \leqslant \min\{\kappa_p(bfp) + \gamma_1^+ + \gamma_3^-, \ \kappa_p(\overline{b}fp) + \gamma_3^-\}$$
$$- \min\{\kappa_p(b\overline{f}p) + \gamma_1^+ + \gamma_3^+, \kappa_p(\overline{b}\,\overline{f}p)) + \gamma_3^+\}$$
$$CR_D(\kappa_p, \neg\mathfrak{B}(\overline{f}|p), \Psi): \quad \gamma_3^- - \gamma_3^+ \leqslant \min\{\kappa_p(b\overline{f}p) + \gamma_1^+ + \gamma_2^-, \ \kappa_p(\overline{b}\,\overline{f}p) + \gamma_2^-\}$$
$$- \min\{\kappa_p(bfp) + \gamma_1^+ + \gamma_2^+, \kappa_p(\overline{b}fp)) + \gamma_2^+\}$$

The vector $\vec{\gamma} = \langle \gamma_1^+, \gamma_1^-, \gamma_2^+, \gamma_2^-, \gamma_3^+, \gamma_3^- \rangle$ with $\gamma_1^+ = 0$, $\gamma_1^- = -1$, $\gamma_2^+ = 0$, $\gamma_2^- = 2$, $\gamma_3^+ = 0$, and $\gamma_3^- = 0$ is a solution of $Sol(CR_D(\kappa_p, \Psi))$, i.e. $\vec{\gamma} \in Sol(CR_D(\kappa_p, \Psi))$. We obtain the ranking function $\kappa_p^\circ = \kappa_{\vec{\gamma}}$ given in Table 1.

We examine whether our approach is sound and complete with respect to conditional descriptor revision.

Theorem 1. (Soundness of $CR_D(\kappa, \Psi)$). *Let κ be an ordinal conditional ranking function, Ψ be an elementary belief descriptor, and let $\vec{\gamma} \in Sol(CR_D(\kappa, \Psi))$. Then, the change from κ to $\kappa_{\vec{\gamma}}$ is a conditional descriptor revision by Ψ (over all ranking functions).*

Note that a ranking function κ° is a c-representation [19] for a set of conditionals $\mathcal{R}$ if and only if κ° is the result of a conditional descriptor revision starting form a ranking function κ such that $\kappa(\omega) = 0$ for every $\omega \in \Omega$ with a descriptor $\Psi = \{\mathfrak{B}(B|A) \mid (B|A) \in \mathcal{R}\}$. The construction of a c-representation can be characterised by a constraint-satisfaction problem similar to the one given in Definition 7 [3,19]. The soundness proof transfers to a proof of Theorem 1.

Theorem 2. (Completeness of $CR_D(\kappa, \Psi)$). *Let Ψ be an elementary belief descriptor and κ, κ° be ordinal conditional functions. If the change from κ to κ° is a conditional descriptor revision by Ψ (over all ranking functions), then there exists a vector $\vec{\gamma} \in Sol(CR_D(\kappa, \Psi))$ such that $\kappa^\circ = \kappa_{\vec{\gamma}}$.*

Proof (Sketch). Because of Proposition 1, there exists κ_0 and $\vec{\gamma} = \langle \gamma_1^+, \gamma_1^-, \ldots \rangle$ such that the ranking function κ° is representable as stated in Eq. (3). Therefore, we have $\kappa^\circ = \kappa_{\vec{\gamma}}$. It remains to show that $\vec{\gamma} \in Sol(CR_D(\kappa, \Psi))$. Note that by our assumptions $\kappa^\circ \Vdash \alpha$ holds for each $\alpha \in \Psi$. Suppose that α is a positive literal descriptor, i.e. $\alpha = \mathfrak{B}(B|A)$, and thus, $\kappa^\circ(AB) < \kappa^\circ(A\overline{B})$. By employing Eq. (3), we obtain Eq. (4) from $\kappa^\circ(AB) < \kappa^\circ(A\overline{B})$ by algebraic transformations [19]. In an analogue way, one can obtain Eq. (5) from a negative literal descriptor. Note that these are exactly the inequalities in $CR_D(\kappa, \Psi)$. Therefore, the vector $\vec{\gamma}$ is a solution for $Sol(CR_D(\kappa, \Psi))$.

6   Implementation by ChangeOCF

We implemented descriptor revision for conditionals and elementary descriptors under the principle of conditional preservation. Given a ranking function κ and an elementary descriptor Ψ, our system, called ChangeOCF, calculates a list of possible outcomes of a revision of κ with Ψ. To calculate the possible outcomes of the revision, ChangeOCF uses a constraint system based on $CR_D(\kappa, \Psi)$ introduced in Sect. 5. Following the Propositions 1 and 2, the solutions of this constraint system correspond to the outcomes of a conditional descriptor revision. A straightforward approach would be to solve $CR_D(\kappa, \Psi)$ for the given κ and Ψ. Then, for each $\vec{\gamma} \in Sol(CR_D(\Psi))$ the corresponding ranking function $\kappa_{\vec{\gamma}}$ is calculated.

In general, $Sol(CR_D(\Psi))$ may contain infinite elements, but there is only a finite number of equivalence classes with respect to the acceptance of conditionals. Therefore, it is possible to restrict the set of solutions to finitely many without losing interesting results. To do this, we used an approach inspired by *maximal impacts* for c-representations [3] that addresses a similar problem for the enumeration of c-representations. The idea of maximal impacts is to add explicit bounds for the value of each γ_i^+, γ_i^-. This reduces the set of possible solutions to a finite set, without losing equivalent solutions when choosing the bounds appropriately. ChangeOCF limits the value of $\gamma_1^+, \gamma_1^-, \ldots, \gamma_n^+, \gamma_n^-$ to an individual finite domain by extending the constraint system $CR_D(\kappa, \Psi)$ with constraints $u_i^{\min -} \leqslant \gamma_i^- \leqslant u_i^{\max -}$ and $u_i^{\min +} \leqslant \gamma_i^+ \leqslant u_i^{\max +}$ for $1 \leqslant i \leqslant n$. We denote this extended constraint system by $CR_D^{\vec{u}}(\kappa, \Psi)$ with $\vec{u} = \langle u_1^{\min -}, u_1^{\max -}, u_1^{\min +}, u_1^{\max +}, \ldots, u_n^{\max +} \rangle$. Like for c-representations [21], it is an open problem which values for $\vec{u}$ guarantee that a representative for each equivalence class of solutions with respect to the acceptance of conditionals is found for a given κ and Ψ.

The implementation of ChangeOCF is build upon by InfOCF-Lib [22], a Java library for reasoning with conditionals and ranking functions. InfOCF-Lib calculates the c-representations of a conditional knowledge base by solving a constraint system similar to $CR_D^{\vec{u}}(\kappa, \Psi)$. The interface of ChangeOCF is implemented in Java. To solve $CR_D^{\vec{u}}(\kappa, \Psi)$, we use SICStus Prolog and its constraint logic programming library for finite domains [7]. The Prolog implementation is an adaption of the implementation of InfOCF [2] to the more general case of belief change.

Example 9 (Continued).   Consider again the descriptor revision of κ_p from Table 1 with the elementary descriptor $\Psi = \{\mathfrak{B}(p|b), \neg\mathfrak{B}(f|p), \neg\mathfrak{B}(\overline{f}|p)\}$. The corresponding constraint satisfaction problem $CR_D^{\vec{u}}(\kappa, \Psi)$ is given by the conjunction of $CR_D(\kappa, \Psi)$ from Example 8 with the following constraints:

$$u_1^{\min -} \leqslant \gamma_1^- \leqslant u_1^{\max -} \qquad u_2^{\min -} \leqslant \gamma_2^- \leqslant u_1^{\max -} \qquad u_3^{\min -} \leqslant \gamma_3^- \leqslant u_3^{\max -}$$
$$u_1^{\min +} \leqslant \gamma_1^+ \leqslant u_1^{\max +} \qquad u_2^{\min +} \leqslant \gamma_2^+ \leqslant u_1^{\max +} \qquad u_3^{\min +} \leqslant \gamma_3^+ \leqslant u_3^{\max +}$$

If we choose for example $\vec{u} = \langle -2, 0, 0, 2, -1, 1, -1, 1, 0, 0, 0, 0 \rangle$, there are nine solutions to $CR_D^{\vec{u}}(\kappa, \Psi)$. One of the solutions is $\vec{\gamma} = \langle 0, 2, -1, 0, 0, 0 \rangle$, which corresponds to $\kappa_{\vec{\gamma}} = \kappa_p^\circ$ from Table 1.

7   Summary and Future Work

In this article, we investigated descriptor revision for a conditional logic and its realisation. We defined elementary descriptors, a large fragment of the full descriptor language, allowing to express a multitude of different kinds of change processes. In particular, elementary descriptors cover the success conditions of AGM revision and AGM contraction. We introduced conditional descriptor revision, which is an extension of descriptor revision for conditionals obeying the principle of conditional preservation by Kern-Isberner. We gave a characterisation by a constraint satisfaction problem and an implementation of conditional descriptor revision with elementary descriptors was presented.

For future work, we plan to give a characterisation of conditional descriptor revision with descriptors with disjunction. This requires a more fine-grained handling of the interaction of the constraints, and might require transformations of a descriptor into a normal form. Another open problem is the determination of maximal impacts for the constraint problem such that all solutions up to equivalence with respect to acceptance of conditionals are captured.

Acknowledgements. This work was supported by DFG Grant BE 1700/9-1 awarded to Christoph Beierle as part of the priority program "Intentional Forgetting in Organizations" (SPP 1921). Kai Sauerwald is supported by this Grant. We thank the anonymous reviewers for their valuable hints and comments that helped us to improve the paper.

References

1. Alchourrón, C.E., Gärdenfors, P., Makinson, D.: On the logic of theory change: partial meet contraction and revision functions. J. Symb. Log. **50**(2), 510–530 (1985)
2. Beierle, C., Eichhorn, C., Kutsch, S.: A practical comparison of qualitative inferences with preferred ranking models. KI - Künstliche Intell. **31**(1), 41–52 (2017)
3. Beierle, C., Eichhorn, C., Kern-Isberner, G., Kutsch, S.: Properties of skeptical c-inference for conditional knowledge bases and its realization as a constraint satisfaction problem. Ann. Math. Artif. Intell. **83**, 247–275 (2018). https://doi.org/10.1007/s10472-017-9571-9
4. Beierle, C., Kern-Isberner, G.: Semantical investigations into nonmonotonic and probabilistic logics. Ann. Math. Artif. Intell. **65**(2–3), 123–158 (2012). https://doi.org/10.1007/s10472-012-9310-1
5. Beierle, C., Kern-Isberner, G., Sauerwald, K., Bock, T., Ragni, M.: Towards a general framework for kinds of forgetting in common-sense belief management. KI - Künstliche Intell. **33**(1), 57–68 (2018). https://doi.org/10.1007/s13218-018-0567-3
6. Boutilier, C.: Iterated revision and minimal change of conditional beliefs. J. Philos. Log. **25**(3), 263–305 (1996)

7. Carlsson, M., Ottosson, G., Carlson, B.: An open-ended finite domain constraint solver. In: Glaser, H., Hartel, P., Kuchen, H. (eds.) PLILP 1997. LNCS, vol. 1292, pp. 191–206. Springer, Heidelberg (1997). https://doi.org/10.1007/BFb0033845
8. Darwiche, A., Pearl, J.: On the logic of iterated belief revision. Artif. Intell. **89**, 1–29 (1997)
9. de Finetti, B.: La prévision, ses lois logiques et ses sources subjectives. In: Kyburg, H., Smokler, H.E. (eds.) Annales de l'institut Henri Poincaré, vol. 7, pp. 93–158. Wiley, New York (1937). English translation in Studies in Subjective Probability (1964)
10. Hansson, S.O.: Descriptor revision. Stud. Logica **102**(5), 955–980 (2014)
11. Hansson, S.O.: A monoselective presentation of AGM revision. Stud. Logica **103**(5), 1019–1033 (2015). https://doi.org/10.1007/s11225-015-9604-5
12. Hansson, S.O.: Blockage revision. J. Log. Lang. Inf. **25**(1), 37–50 (2015). https://doi.org/10.1007/s10849-015-9223-6
13. Hansson, S.O.: Iterated descriptor revision and the logic of ramsey test conditionals. J. Philos. Log. **45**(4), 429–450 (2015). https://doi.org/10.1007/s10992-015-9381-7
14. Hansson, S.O.: AGM contraction is not reconstructible as a descriptor operation. J. Log. Comput. **27**(4), 1133–1141 (2017). https://doi.org/10.1093/logcom/exv076
15. Hansson, S.O.: Descriptor Revision. Springer, Heidelberg (2017). https://doi.org/10.1007/978-3-319-53061-1
16. Hansson, S.O.: Back to basics: belief revision through direct selection. Stud. Logica **107**(5), 887–915 (2018). https://doi.org/10.1007/s11225-018-9807-7
17. Kern-Isberner, G.: The principle of conditional preservation in belief revision. In: Eiter, T., Schewe, K.-D. (eds.) FoIKS 2002. LNCS, vol. 2284, pp. 105–129. Springer, Heidelberg (2002). https://doi.org/10.1007/3-540-45758-5_8
18. Kern-Isberner, G.: A thorough axiomatization of a principle of conditional preservation in belief revision. Ann. Math. Artif. Intell. **40**(1–2), 127–164 (2004)
19. Kern-Isberner, G. (ed.): Conditionals in Nonmonotonic Reasoning and Belief Revision. LNCS (LNAI), vol. 2087. Springer, Heidelberg (2001). https://doi.org/10.1007/3-540-44600-1
20. Kern-Isberner, G., Bock, T., Sauerwald, K., Beierle, C.: Iterated contraction of propositions and conditionals under the principle of conditional preservation. In: Benzmüller, C., Lisetti, C., Theobald, M. (eds.) 3nd Global Conference on Artificial Intelligence, GCAI 2017, Miami, USA, October 20–22, 2017. EPiC Series in Computing, vol. 50. EasyChair (October 2017). https://easychair.org/publications/volume/GCAI_2017
21. Komo, C., Beierle, C.: Upper and lower bounds for finite domain constraints to realize skeptical c-inference over conditional knowledge bases. In: International Symposium on Artificial Intelligence and Mathematics (ISAIM 2020), Fort Lauderdale, FL, USA, January 6–8 (2020)
22. Kutsch, S.: InfOCF-Lib: a Java library for OCF-based conditional inference. In: Beierle, C., Ragni, M., Stolzenburg, F., Thimm, M. (eds.) Proceedings of the 8th Workshop on Dynamics of Knowledge and Belief (DKB-2019) and the 7th Workshop KI & Kognition (KIK-2019) Co-Located with 44nd German Conference on Artificial Intelligence (KI 2019), Kassel, Germany, September 23, 2019. CEUR Workshop Proceedings, vol. 2445, pp. 47–58. CEUR-WS.org (2019)
23. Makinson, D., Gärdenfors, P.: Relations between the logic of theory change and nonmonotonic logic. In: Fuhrmann, A., Morreau, M. (eds.) The Logic of Theory Change. LNCS, vol. 465, pp. 183–205. Springer, Heidelberg (1991). https://doi.org/10.1007/BFb0018421

24. Sauerwald, K., Kern-Isberner, G., Beierle, C.: A conditional perspective for iterated belief contraction. In: Giacomo, G.D. (ed.) ECAI 2020–24nd European Conference on Artificial Intelligence, August 29th–September 8th, 2020, Santiago de Compostela, Spain. IOS Press (2020)

25. Spohn, W.: Ordinal conditional functions: a dynamic theory of epistemic states. In: Harper, W.L., Skyrms, B. (eds.) Causation in Decision, Belief Change, and Statistics. The University of Western Ontario Series in Philosophy of Science (A Series of Books in Philosophy of Science, Methodology, Epistemology, Logic, History of Science, and Related Fields), vol. 42. Springer, Dordrecht. https://doi.org/10.1007/978-94-009-2865-7_6

26. Zhang, L.: Believability relations for select-direct sentential revision. Stud. Logica **105**(1), 37–63 (2017)

Multi-agent Path Finding Modulo Theory with Continuous Movements and the Sum of Costs Objective

Pavel Surynek[(⊠)]

Faculty of Information Technology, Czech Technical University in Prague,
Thákurova 9, 160 00 Praha 6, Czechia
pavel.surynek@fit.cvut.cz

Abstract. Multi-agent path finding with continuous movements and time (denoted MAPF$^\mathcal{R}$) is addressed. The task is to navigate agents that move smoothly between predefined positions to their individual goals so that they do not collide. Recently a novel solving approach for obtaining makespan optimal solutions called SMT-CBS$^\mathcal{R}$ based on *satisfiability modulo theories* (SMT) has been introduced. We extend the approach further towards the sum-of-costs objective which is a more challenging case in the yes/no SMT environment due to more complex calculation of the objective. The new algorithm combines collision resolution known from conflict-based search (CBS) with previous generation of incomplete SAT encodings on top of a novel scheme for selecting decision variables in a potentially uncountable search space. We experimentally compare SMT-CBS$^\mathcal{R}$ and previous CCBS (continuous conflict-based search) algorithm for MAPF$^\mathcal{R}$.

Keywords: Path finding · Multiple agents · Robotic agents · Logic reasoning · Satisfiability modulo theory · Sum-of-costs optimality

1 Introduction

In *multi-agent path finding* (MAPF) [6, 15, 24–27, 30, 37] the task is to navigate agents from given starting positions to given individual goals. The problem takes place in an undirected graph $G = (V, E)$ where agents from set $A = \{a_1, a_2, ..., a_k\}$ are placed in vertices with at most one agent per vertex. The navigation task can be then expressed formally as transforming an initial configuration of agents $\alpha_0: A \to V$ to a goal configuration $\alpha_+: A \to V$ using instantaneous movements across edges assuming no collision occurs.

To reflect various aspects of real-life applications, variants of MAPF have been introduced such as those considering *kinematic constraints* [9], *large agents* [17], *generalized costs* of actions [36], or *deadlines* [19] - see [18,28] for more variants. Particularly in this work we are dealing with an extension of MAPF introduced only recently [1,33] that considers continuous movements and time (MAPF$^\mathcal{R}$). Agents move smoothly along predefined curves interconnecting predefined positions placed arbitrarily in some continuous space. It is natural in MAPF$^\mathcal{R}$ to assume geometric agents of

© Springer Nature Switzerland AG 2020
U. Schmid et al. (Eds.): KI 2020, LNAI 12325, pp. 219–232, 2020.
https://doi.org/10.1007/978-3-030-58285-2_16

various shapes that occupy certain volume in the space - circles in the 2D space, polygons, spheres in the 3D space etc. In contrast to MAPF, where the collision is defined as the simultaneous occupation of a vertex or an edge by two agents, collisions are defined as any spatial overlap of agents' bodies in MAPF$^{\mathcal{R}}$.

The motivation behind introducing MAPF$^{\mathcal{R}}$ is the need to construct more realistic paths in many applications such as controlling fleets of robots or aerial drones [7, 10] where continuous reasoning is closer to the reality than the standard MAPF.

The contribution of this paper consists in generalizing the previous makespan optimal approach for MAPF$^{\mathcal{R}}$ [31,33] that uses satisfiability modulo theory (SMT) reasoning [5,20] for the sum-of-costs objective. The SMT paradigm constructs decision procedures for various complex logic theories by decomposing the decision problem into the propositional part having arbitrary Boolean structure and the complex theory part that is restricted on the conjunctive fragment. Our SMT-based algorithm called SMT-CBS$^{\mathcal{R}}$ combines the Conflict-based Search (CBS) algorithm [8,25] with previous algorithms for solving the standard MAPF using incomplete encodings [32] and continuous reasoning.

1.1 Previous Work

Using reductions of planning problems to propositional satisfiability has been coined in the SATPlan algorithm and its variants [11–14]. Here we are trying to apply a similar idea in the context of MAPF$^{\mathcal{R}}$. So far MAPF$^{\mathcal{R}}$ has been solved by a modified version of CBS that tries to solve MAPF lazily by adding collision avoidance constraints on demand. The adaptation of CBS for MAPF$^{\mathcal{R}}$ consists in implementing continuous collision detection while the high-level framework of the algorithm remains the same as demonstrated in the CCBS algorithm [1] (*continuous conflict-based search*).

We follow the idea of CBS too but instead of searching the tree of possible collision eliminations at the high-level we encode the requirement of having collision free paths as a propositional formula [4] and leave it to the SAT solver as done in [34]. We construct the formula *lazily* by adding collision elimination refinements following [32] where the lazy construction of incomplete encodings has been suggested for the standard MAPF within the algorithm called SMT-CBS. SMT-CBS works with propositional variables indexed by *agent a*, *vertex v*, and *time step t* with the meaning that if the variable is *TRUE a* in *v* at time step *t*. In MAPF$^{\mathcal{R}}$ we however face major technical difficulty that we do not know necessary decision (propositional) variables in advance and due to continuous time we cannot enumerate them all. Hence we need to select from a potentially uncountable space those variables that are sufficient for finding the solution.

The previous application of SMT in MAPF$^{\mathcal{R}}$ [33] focused on the makespan optimal solutions where the shortest duration of the plan is required. The **sum-of-costs** is another important objective used in the context of MAPF [26,36]. Calculated as the summation over all agents of times they spend moving before arriving to the goal. Due to its more complex calculation, the sum-of-costs objective is more challenging to be integrated in the SMT-based solving framework.

1.2   MAPF with Continuous Movements and Time

We use the definition of MAPF with continuous movements and time denoted MAPF$^\mathcal{R}$ from [1]. MAPF$^\mathcal{R}$ shares components with the standard MAPF: undirected graph $G = (V, E)$, set of agents $A = \{a_1, a_2, ..., a_k\}$, and the initial and goal configuration of agents: $\alpha_0 : A \rightarrow V$ and $\alpha_+ : A \rightarrow V$. A simple 2D variant of MAPF$^\mathcal{R}$ is as follows:

Definition 1. *(MAPF$^\mathcal{R}$) Multi-agent path finding with continuous time and space is a 5-tuple $\Sigma^\mathcal{R} = (G = (V, E), A, \alpha_0, \alpha_+, \rho)$ where G, A, α_0, α_+ are from the standard MAPF and ρ determines continuous extensions:*

- $\rho.x(v), \rho.y(v)$ *for $v \in V$ represent the position of vertex v in the 2D plane*
- $\rho.speed(a)$ *for $a \in A$ determines constant speed of agent a*
- $\rho.radius(a)$ *for $a \in A$ determines the radius of agent a; we assume that agents are circular discs with omni-directional ability of movements.*

For simplicity we assume circular agents with constant speed and instant acceleration. The major difference from the standard MAPF where agents move instantly between vertices (disappears in the source and appears in the target instantly) is that smooth continuous movement between a pair of vertices (positions) along the straight line interconnecting them takes place in MAPF$^\mathcal{R}$. Hence we need to be aware of the presence of agents at some point in the 2D plane at any time.

Collisions may occur between agents in MAPF$^\mathcal{R}$ due to their volume; that is, they collide whenever their bodies **overlap**. In contrast to MAPF, collisions in MAPF$^\mathcal{R}$ may occur not only in a single vertex or edge being shared by colliding agents but also on pairs of edges (lines interconnecting vertices) that are too close to each other and simultaneously traversed by large agents.

A solution to given MAPF$^\mathcal{R}$ $\Sigma^\mathcal{R}$ is a collection of temporal plans for individual agents $\pi = [\pi(a_1), \pi(a_2), ..., \pi(a_k)]$ that are **mutually collision-free**. A temporal plan for agent $a \in A$ is a sequence $\pi(a) = [((\alpha_0(a), \alpha_1(a)), [t_0(a), t_1(a))); ((\alpha_1(a), \alpha_2(a)), [t_1(a), t_2(a))); ...; ((\alpha_{m(a)-1}(a), \alpha_{m(a)}(a)), [t_{m(a)-1}(a), t_{m(a)}(a)))]$ where $m(a)$ is the length of individual temporal plan and each pair $(\alpha_i(a), \alpha_{i+1}(a)), [t_i(a), t_{i+1}(a)))$ corresponds to traversal event between a pair of vertices $\alpha_i(a)$ and $\alpha_{i+1}(a)$ starting at time $t_i(a)$ and finished at $t_{i+1}(a)$.

It holds that $t_i(a) < t_{i+1}(a)$ for $i = 0, 1, ..., m(a) - 1$. Moreover consecutive events in the individual temporal plan must correspond to edge traversals or waiting actions, that is: $\{\alpha_i(a), \alpha_{i+1}(a)\} \in E$ or $\alpha_i(a) = \alpha_{i+1}(a)$; and times must reflect the speed of agents for non-wait actions.

The duration of individual temporal plan $\pi(a)$ is called an *individual makespan*; denoted $\mu(\pi(a)) = t_{m(a)}$. The overall *makespan* of π is defined as $\max_{i=1}^k \{\mu(\pi(a_i))\}$. The individual makespan is sometimes called an *individual cost*. A *sum-of-cost* for given temporal plan $\pi(a)$ is defined as $\sum_{i=1}^k \mu(\pi(a_i))$ An example of MAPF$^\mathcal{R}$ and makespan/sum-of-costs optimal solution is shown in Fig. 1.

Through straightforward reduction of MAPF to MAPF$^\mathcal{R}$ it can be observed that finding a makespan or sum-of-costs optimal solution with continuous time is an NP-hard problem [22, 38].

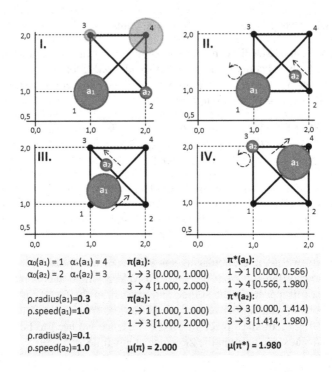

Fig. 1. An example of MAPF$^{\mathcal{R}}$ instance with two agents. A feasible makespan sub-optimal solution π (makespan $\mu(\pi) = 2.0$) and makespan optimal solution $\pi*$ (makespan $\mu(\pi*) = 1.980$) are shown.

2 Solving MAPF with Continuous Time

Let us recall CCBS [1], a variant of CBS [25] modified for MAPF$^{\mathcal{R}}$. The idea of CBS algorithms is to resolve conflicts lazily.

2.1 Conflict-Based Search

The high-level of CCBS searches a *constraint tree* (CT) using a priority queue ordered according to the sum-of-costs in the breadth first manner. CT is a binary tree where each node N contains a set of collision avoidance constraints $N.cons$ - a set of triples $(a_i, (u, v), [t_0, t_+))$ forbidding agent a_i to start smooth traversal of edge $\{u, v\}$ (line) at any time between $[t_0, t_+)$, a solution $N.\pi$ - a set of k individual temporal plans, and the sum-of-costs $N.\xi$ of $N.\pi$.

The low-level in CCBS associated with node N searches for individual temporal plan with respect to set of constraints $N.cons$. For given agent a_i, this is the standard single source shortest path search from $\alpha_0(a_i)$ to $\alpha_+(a_i)$ that at time t cannot start to traverse any $\{(u, v) \in E \mid (a_i, (u, v), [t_0, t_+)) \in N.cons \land t \in [t_0, t_+)\}$. Various intelligent single source shortest path algorithms such as SIPP [21] can be used here.

Algorithm 1: CCBS algorithm for solving $\text{MAPF}^{\mathcal{R}}$ for the sum-of-costs objective.

---

1 $\text{CBS}^{\mathcal{R}}$ ($\Sigma^{\mathcal{R}} = (G = (V,E), A, \alpha_0, \alpha_+, \rho))$

2 $\quad R.cons \leftarrow \emptyset$

3 $\quad R.\pi \leftarrow \{\text{shortest temporal plan from } \alpha_0(a_i) \text{ to } \alpha_+(a_i) \mid i = 1, 2, ..., k\}$

4 $\quad R.\xi \leftarrow \sum_{i=1}^{k} \mu(N.\pi(a_i))$

5 $\quad \text{OPEN} \leftarrow \emptyset$

6 $\quad \text{insert } R \text{ into OPEN}$

7 $\quad \textbf{while } \text{OPEN} \neq \emptyset \textbf{ do}$

8 $\quad\quad N \leftarrow \min_{\xi}(\text{OPEN})$

9 $\quad\quad \text{remove-Min}_{\xi}(\text{OPEN})$

10 $\quad\quad collisions \leftarrow \text{validate-Plans}(N.\pi)$

11 $\quad\quad \textbf{if } collisions = \emptyset \textbf{ then}$

12 $\quad\quad\quad \textbf{return } N.\pi$

13 $\quad\quad \textbf{let } (m_i \times m_j) \in collisions \text{ where } m_i = (a_i, (u_i, v_i), [t_i^0, t_i^+)) \text{ and }$
$\quad\quad\quad m_j = (a_j, (u_j, v_j), [t_j^0, t_j^+))$

14 $\quad\quad ([\tau_i^0, \tau_i^+); [\tau_j^0, \tau_j^+)) \leftarrow \text{resolve-Collision}(m_i, m_j)$

15 $\quad\quad \textbf{for } each\ m \in \{(m_i, [\tau_i^0, \tau_i^+)), (m_j, [\tau_j^0, \tau_j^+))\} \textbf{ do}$

16 $\quad\quad\quad \textbf{let } ((a, (u, v), [t_0, t_+)), [\tau_0, \tau_+)) = m$

17 $\quad\quad\quad N'.cons \leftarrow N.cons \cup \{(a, (u, v), [\tau_0, \tau_+))\}$

18 $\quad\quad\quad N'.\pi \leftarrow N.\pi$

19 $\quad\quad\quad \text{update}(a, N'.\pi, N'.cons)$

20 $\quad\quad\quad N'.\xi \leftarrow \sum_{i=1}^{k} \mu(N'.\pi(a_i))$

21 $\quad\quad\quad \text{insert } N' \text{ into OPEN}$

CCBS stores nodes of CT into priority queue OPEN sorted according to the ascending makespan. At each step CBS takes node N with the lowest makespan from OPEN and checks if $N.\pi$ represents non-colliding temporal plans. If there is no collision, the algorithms returns valid solution $N.\pi$. Otherwise the search branches by creating a new pair of nodes in CT - successors of N. Assume that a collision occurred between a_i traversing (u_i, v_i) during $[t_i^0, t_i^+)$ and a_j traversing (u_j, v_j) during $[t_j^0, t_j^+)$. This collision can be avoided if either agent a_i or agent a_j waits after the other agent passes. We can calculate for a_i so called maximum *unsafe interval* $[\tau_i^0, \tau_i^+)$ such that whenever a_i starts to traverse (u_i, v_i) at some time $t \in [\tau_i^0, \tau_i^+)$ it ends up colliding with a_j assuming a_j did not try to avoid the collision. Hence a_i should wait until τ_i^+ to tightly avoid the collision with a_j. Similarly we can calculate maximum unsafe interval for a_j: $[\tau_j^0, \tau_j^+)$. These two options correspond to new successor nodes of N: N_1 and N_2 that inherit set of constraints from N as follows: $N_1.cons = N.cons \cup \{(a_i, (u_i, v_i), [\tau_i^0, \tau_i^+))\}$ and $N_2.cons = N.cons \cup \{(a_j, (u_j, v_j), [\tau_j^0, \tau_j^+))\}$. $N_1.\pi$ and $N_1.\pi$ inherits plans from $N.\pi$ except those for agents a_i and a_j respectively that are recalculated with respect to the constraints. After this N_1 and N_2 are inserted into OPEN.

2.2 A Satisfiability Modulo Theory Approach

A recent algorithm called SMT-CBS$^{\mathcal{R}}$ [33] rephrases CCBS as problem solving in *satisfiability modulo theories* (SMT) [5,35]. The basic use of SMT divides the satisfiability problem in some complex theory T into a propositional part that keeps the Boolean structure of the problem and a simplified procedure $DECIDE_T$ that decides fragment of T restricted on *conjunctive formulae*. A general T-formula Γ being decided for satisfiability is transformed to a *propositional skeleton* by replacing its atoms with propositional variables. The standard SAT solver then decides what variables should be assigned $TRUE$ in order to satisfy the skeleton - these variables tells what atoms hold in Γ. $DECIDE_T$ then checks if the conjunction of atoms assigned $TRUE$ is valid with respect to axioms of T. If so then satisfying assignment is returned. Otherwise a conflict from $DECIDE_T$ (often called a *lemma*) is reported back to the SAT solver and the skeleton is extended with new constraints resolving the conflict. More generally not only new constraints are added to resolve the conflict but also new atoms can be added to Γ.

T will be represented by a theory with axioms describing movement rules of MAPF$^{\mathcal{R}}$; a theory we will denote $T_{MAPF^{\mathcal{R}}}$. $DECIDE_{MAPF^{\mathcal{R}}}$ can be naturally represented by the plan validation procedure from CCBS (validate-Plans).

2.3 RDD: Real Decision Diagram

The key question in the propositional logic-based approach is what will be the decision variables. In the standard MAPF, time expansion of G for every time step can be done resulting in a multi-value decision diagram (MDD) [34] representing possible positions of agents at any time step. Since MAPF$^{\mathcal{R}}$ is no longer discrete we cannot afford to use a decision variable for every time moment. We show how to restrict the decision variables on finitely many important moments only without compromising soundness nor optimality of the approach.

Analogously to MDD, we introduce *real decision diagram* (RDD). RDD$_i$ defines for agent a_i its space-time positions and possible movements. Formally, RDD_i is a directed graph (X^i, E^i) where X_i consists of pairs (u, t) with $u \in V$ and $t \in \mathbb{R}_0^+$ is time and E_i consists of directed edges of the form $((u, t_u); (v, t_v))$. Edge $((u, t_u); (v, t_v))$ correspond to agent's movement from u to v started at t_u and finished at t_v. Waiting in u is possible by introducing edge $((u, t_u); (v, t'_u))$. Pair $(\alpha_0(a_i), 0) \in X_i$ indicates start and $(\alpha_+(a_i), t)$ for some t corresponds to reaching the goal position.

RDDs for individual agents are constructed with respect to collision avoidance constraints. If there is no collision avoidance constraint then RDD$_i$ simply corresponds to a shortest temporal plan for agent a_j. But if a collision avoidance constraint is present, say $(a_i, (u, v), [\tau_0, \tau_+))$, and we are considering movement starting in u at t that interferes with the constraint, then we need to generate a node into RDD$_i$ that allows agent to wait until the unsafe interval passes by, that is node (u, τ^+) and edge $((u, \tau^+); (u, \tau^+))$ are added.

Similarly for wait constraints $(a_i, (u, u), [\tau_0, \tau_+))$ that forbid waiting in u during $[\tau_0, \tau_+)$. In such a case, we need to anticipate the constraint before entering u, that is we can wait until $\tau_+ - t_x$ in the source vertex before entering u where t_x is the time needed to traverse the edge towards u.

The process of building RDDs is formalized is described in details in [33]. An example of RDDs is shown in Fig. 2.

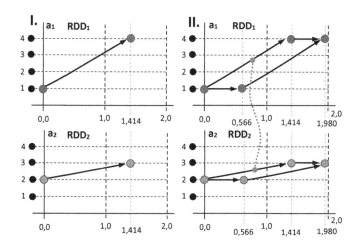

Fig. 2. Real decision diagrams (RDDs) for agents a_1 and a_2 from MAPF$^{\mathcal{R}}$ from Fig. 1. Decisions corresponding to shortest paths for agents a_1 and a_2 moving diagonally towards their goals are shown: $a_1 : 1 \to 4$, $a_2 : 2 \to 3$ (left). This however results in a collision whose resolution is either waiting for agent a_1 in vertex 1 from 0.000 until 0.566 or waiting for agent a_2 in vertex 2 from 0.000 until 0.566; reflected in the next RDDs (right). Mutex is depicted using dotted line connecting arcs form RDD$_1$ and RDD$_2$.

2.4   SAT Encoding from RDD

We introduce a decision variable for each node and edge $[RDD_1, ..., RDD_k]$; RDD$_i$ = (X^i, E^i): we have variable $\mathcal{X}_u^t(a_i)$ for each $(u, t) \in X^i$ and $\mathcal{E}_{u,v}^{t_u;t_v}(a_i)$ for each directed edge $((u, t_u); (v, t_v)) \in E^i$. The meaning of variables is that $\mathcal{X}_u^t(a_i)$ is *TRUE* if and only if agent a_i appears in u at time t and similarly for edges: $\mathcal{E}_{u,v}^{t_u;t_v}(a_i)$ is *TRUE* if and only if a_i moves from u to v starting at time t_u and finishing at t_v.

MAPF$^{\mathcal{R}}$ rules are encoded on top of these variables so that eventually we want to obtain formula $\mathcal{F}(\mu)$ that encodes existence of a solution of makespan μ to given MAPF$^{\mathcal{R}}$. We need to encode that agents do not skip but move along edges, do not disappear or appear from nowhere etc. We show below constraints stating that if agent a_i appears in vertex u at time step t_u then it has to leave through exactly one edge connected to u (constraint (2) although Pseudo-Boolean can be encoded using purely propositional means):

$$\mathcal{X}_u^{t_u}(a_i) \Rightarrow \bigvee_{(v,t_v) \mid ((u,t_u),(v,t_v)) \in E^i} \mathcal{E}_{u,v}^{t_u,t_v}(a_i), \tag{1}$$

$$\sum_{(v,t_v) \,|\, ((u,t_u),(v,t_v)) \in E^i} \mathcal{E}_{u,v}^{t_u,t_v}(a_i) \leq 1 \tag{2}$$

$$\mathcal{E}_{u,v}^{t_u,t_v}(a_i) \Rightarrow \mathcal{X}_v^{t_v}(a_i) \tag{3}$$

Analogously to (2) we have constraint allowing a vertex to accept at most one agent through incoming edges; plus we need to enforce agents starting in α_0 and finishing in α_+. Let us summarize soundness of the encoding in the following proposition (proof omitted).

Proposition 1. *Any satisfying assignment of $\mathcal{F}(\mu)$ correspond to valid individual temporal plans for $\Sigma^{\mathcal{R}}$ whose makespans are at most μ.*

We a-priori do not add constraints for eliminating collisions; these are added lazily after assignment/solution validation. Hence, $\mathcal{F}(\mu)$ constitutes an *incomplete model* for $\Sigma^{\mathcal{R}}$: $\Sigma^{\mathcal{R}}$ is solvable within makespan μ then $\mathcal{F}(\mu)$ is satisfiable. The opposite implication does not hold since satisfying assignment of $\mathcal{F}(\mu)$ may lead to a collision.

From the perspective of SMT, the propositional level does not understand geometric properties of agents so cannot know what simultaneous variable assignments are invalid. This information is only available at the level of theory $T = \text{MAPF}^{\mathcal{R}}$ through $DECIDE_{MAPF^{\mathcal{R}}}$. We also leave the bounding of the sum-of-costs at the level of $DECIDE_{MAPF^{\mathcal{R}}}$.

2.5   Lazy Encoding of Mutex Refinements and Sum-of-Costs Bounds

The SMT-based algorithm itself is divided into two procedures: SMT-CBS$^{\mathcal{R}}$ representing the main loop (Algorithm 2) and SMT-CBS-Fixed$^{\mathcal{R}}$ solving the input MAPF$^{\mathcal{R}}$ for a fixed maximum makespan μ and sum-of-costs ξ (Algorithm 3).

Procedures *encode-Basic* and *augment-Basic* in Algorithm 3 build formula $\mathcal{F}(\mu)$ according to given RDDs and the set of collected collision avoidance constraints. New collisions are resolved **lazily** by adding *mutexes* (disjunctive constraints). A collision is avoided in the same way as in CCBS; that is, one of the colliding agent waits. Collision eliminations are tried until a valid solution is obtained or until a failure for current μ and ξ which means to try bigger makespan and sum-of-costs.

For resolving a collision we need to: **(1)** eliminate simultaneous execution of colliding movements and **(2)** augment the formula to enable avoidance (waiting). Assume a collision between agents a_i traversing (u_i, v_i) during $[t_i^0, t_i^+)$ and a_j traversing (u_j, v_j) during $[t_j^0, t_j^+)$ which corresponds to variables $\mathcal{E}_{u_i,v_i}^{t_i^0,t_i^+}(a_i)$ and $\mathcal{E}_{u_j,v_j}^{t_j^0,t_j^+}(a_j)$. The collision can be eliminated by adding the following **mutex** (disjunction) to the formula: $\neg\mathcal{E}_{u_i,v_i}^{t_i^0,t_i^+}(a_i) \vee \neg\mathcal{E}_{u_j,v_j}^{t_j^0,t_j^+}(a_j)$. Satisfying assignments of the next $\mathcal{F}(\mu)$ can no longer lead to this collision. Next, the formula is augmented according to new RDDs that reflect the collision - decision variables and respective constraints are added.

After resolving all collisions we check whether the sum-of-costs bound is satisfied by plan π. This can be done easily by checking if $\mathcal{X}_u^{t_u}(a_i)$ variables across all agents together yield higher cost than ξ or not. If cost bound ξ is exceeded then corresponding nogood is recorded and added to $\mathcal{F}(\mu)$ and the algorithm continues by searching for a new satisfying assignment to $\mathcal{F}(\mu)$. The nogood says that $X_u^{t_u}(a_i)$ variables that jointly exceed ξ cannot be simultaneously set to *TRUE*.

Algorithm 2: High-level of SMT-CBS$^\mathcal{R}$ for the sum-of-costs objective.

1 **SMT-CBS$^\mathcal{R}$** $(\Sigma^\mathcal{R} = (G = (V,E), A, \alpha_0, \alpha_+, \rho))$
2        $constraints \leftarrow \emptyset$
3        $\pi \leftarrow \{\pi^*(a_i)$ a shortest temporal plan from $\alpha_0(a_i)$ to $\alpha_+(a_i) \mid i = 1,2,...,k\}$
4        $\mu \leftarrow \max_{i=1}^k \mu(\pi(a_i)); \xi \leftarrow \sum_{i=1}^k \mu(\pi(a_i))$
5   **while** *TRUE* **do**
6            $(\pi, constraints, \mu_{next}, \xi_{next}) \leftarrow$ SMT-CBS-Fixed$^\mathcal{R}(\Sigma^\mathcal{R}, constraints, \mu, \xi)$
7   **if** $\pi \neq$ *UNSAT* **then**
8   **return** π
9            $\mu \leftarrow \mu_{next}; \xi \leftarrow \xi_{next}$

The set of pairs of collision avoidance constraints is propagated across entire execution of the algorithm. Constraints originating from a single collision are grouped in pairs so that it is possible to introduce mutexes for colliding movements discovered in previous steps.

Algorithm 2 shows the main loop of SMT-CBS$^\mathcal{R}$. The algorithm checks if there is a solution for $\Sigma^\mathcal{R}$ of makespan μ and sum-of-costs ξ. It starts at the lower bound for μ and ξ obtained as the duration of the longest from shortest individual temporal plans ignoring other agents and the sum of these lengths respectively.

Then μ and ξ are iteratively increased in the main loop following the style of SAT-Plan [14]. The algorithm relies on the fact that the solvability of MAPF$^\mathcal{R}$ w.r.t. cumulative objective like the sum-of-costs or makespan behaves as a non decreasing function. Hence trying increasing makespan and sum-of-costs eventually leads to finding the optimum provided we do not skip any relevant value.

We need to ensure important property in the makespan/sum-of-costs increasing scheme: any solution of sum-of-costs ξ has the makespan of at most μ. The next sum-of-costs to try is be obtained by taking the current sum-of-costs plus the smallest duration of the continuing movement (lines 17–27 of Algorithm 3).

The following proposition is a direct consequence of soundness of CCBS and soundness of the encoding (Proposition 1) and soundness of the makespan/sum-of-costs increasing scheme (proof omitted).

Proposition 2. *The SMT-CBS$^\mathcal{R}$ algorithm returns sum-of-costs optimal solution for any solvable MAPF$^\mathcal{R}$ instance $\Sigma^\mathcal{R}$.*

Algorithm 3: Low-level of SMT-CBS$^\mathcal{R}$

---

1 **SMT-CBS-Fixed**$^\mathcal{R}(\Sigma^\mathcal{R}, cons, \mu, \xi)$
2   RDD ← build-RDDs($\Sigma^\mathcal{R}, cons, \mu$); $\mathcal{F}(\mu)$ ← encode-Basic(RDD, $\Sigma^\mathcal{R}, cons, \mu$)
3   **while** *TRUE* **do**
4   *assignment* ← consult-SAT-Solver($\mathcal{F}(\mu)$)
5   **if** *assignment* $\neq UNSAT$ **then**
6   π ← extract-Solution(*assignment*)
7   *collisions* ← validate-Plans(π)
8   **if** *collisions* $= \emptyset$ **then**
9   **while** *TRUE* **do**
10   *nogoods* ← validate-Cost(π, ξ)
11   **if** *nogoods* $= \emptyset$ **then**
12   **return** $(\pi, \emptyset, UNDEF, UNDEF)$
13                     $\mathcal{F}(\mu)$ ← $\mathcal{F}(\mu) \cup nogoods$
14   *assignment* ← consult-SAT-Solver($\mathcal{F}(\mu)$)
15   **if** *assignment* $= UNSAT$ **then**
16   (μ_{next}, ξ_{next}) ← calc-Next-Bounds($\mu, \xi, cons, $RDD)
17   **return** $(UNSAT, cons, \mu_{next}, \xi_{next})$
18   π ← extract-Solution(*assignment*)
19   **else**
20   **for** *each* $(m_i \times m_j) \in collisions$ *where* $m_i = (a_i, (u_i, v_i), [t_i^0, t_i^+))$ *and*
                     $m_j = (a_j, (u_j, v_j), [t_j^0, t_j^+))$ **do**
21                     $\mathcal{F}(\mu) \leftarrow \mathcal{F}(\mu) \wedge (\neg \mathcal{E}_{u_i, v_i}^{t_i^0, t_i^+}(a_i) \vee \neg \mathcal{E}_{u_j, v_j}^{t_j^0, t_j^+}(a_j))$
22                     $([\tau_i^0, \tau_i^+); [\tau_j^0, \tau_j^+))$ ← resolve-Collision(m_i, m_j)
23                     $cons \leftarrow cons \cup \{[(a_i, (u_i, v_i), [\tau_i^0, \tau_i^+)); (a_j, (u_j, v_j), [\tau_j^0, \tau_j^+))]\}$
24   RDD ←build-RDDs($\Sigma^\mathcal{R}, cons, \mu$); $\mathcal{F}(\mu)$ ← augment-Basic(RDD, $\Sigma^\mathcal{R}, cons$)
25   **else**
26   (μ_{next}, ξ_{next}) ← calc-Next-Bounds($\mu, \xi, cons, $RDD)
27   **return** $(UNSAT, cons, \mu_{next}, \xi_{next})$

---

3 Experimental Evaluation

We implemented SMT-CBS$^\mathcal{R}$ in C++ to evaluate its performance and compared it with CCBS[1]. SMT-CBS$^\mathcal{R}$ was implemented on top of Glucose 4 SAT solver [2] which ranks among the best SAT solvers according to recent SAT solver competitions [3]. The solver is consulted in the incremental mode if the formula is extended with new clauses. In case of CCBS, we used the existing C++ implementation [1].

---

[1] To enable reproducibility of presented results we will provide complete source code of our solvers on the author's website.

3.1   Benchmarks and Setup

SMT-CBS$^{\mathcal{R}}$ and CCBS were tested on benchmarks from the movinai.com collection [29]. We tested algorithms on three categories of benchmarks:

(i) **small** empty grids (presented representative benchmark empty-16-16),
(ii) **medium** sized grids with regular obstacles (presented maze-32-32-4),
(iii) **large** game maps (presented ost003d).

In each benchmark, we interconnected cells using the 2^K-neighborhood [23] for $K = 3, 4, 5$ - the same style of generating benchmarks as used in [1] ($K = 2$ corresponds to MAPF hence omitted). Instances consisting of k agents were generated by taking first k agents from random scenario files accompanying each benchmark on movinai.com. Having 25 scenarios for each benchmarks this yields to 25 instances per number of agents.

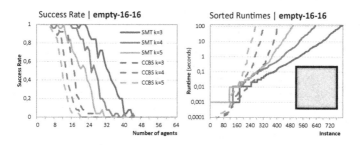

Fig. 3. Comparison of SMT-CBS$^{\mathcal{R}}$ and CCBS on empty-16-16.

Part of the results obtained in our experimentation is presented in this section[2]. For each presented benchmark we show *success rate* as a function of the number of agents. That is, we calculate the ratio out of 25 instances per number of agents where the tested algorithm finished under the timeout of 120 s. In addition to this, we also show concrete runtimes sorted in the ascending order. Results for one selected representative benchmark from each category are shown in Figs. 3, 4, and 5.

The observable trend is that the difficulty of the problem increases with increasing size of the $K-$neighborhood with notable exception of maze-32-32-4 for $K = 4$ and $K = 5$ which turned out to be easier than $K = 3$ for SMT-CBS$^{\mathcal{R}}$.

Throughout all benchmarks SMT-CBS$^{\mathcal{R}}$ tends to outperform CCBS. The dominance of SMT-CBS$^{\mathcal{R}}$ is most visible in medium sized benchmarks. CCBS is, on the other hand, faster in instances containing few agents. The gap between SMT-CBS$^{\mathcal{R}}$ and CCBS is smallest in large maps where SMT-CBS$^{\mathcal{R}}$ struggles with relatively big overhead caused by the big size of the map (the encoding is proportionally big). Here SMT-CBS$^{\mathcal{R}}$ wins only in hard cases.

---

[2] All experiments were run on a system with Ryzen 7 3.0 GHz, 16 GB RAM, under Ubuntu Linux 18.

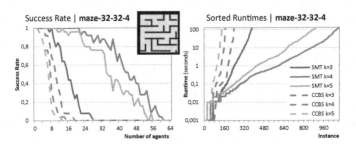

Fig. 4. Comparison of SMT-CBS$^{\mathcal{R}}$ and CCBS on `maze-32-32-4`.

4   Discussion and Conclusion

We extended the approach based on *satisfiability modulo theories* (SMT) for solving MAPF$^{\mathcal{R}}$ from the makespan objective towards the sum-of-costs objective. Our approach builds on the idea of treating constraints lazily as suggested in the CBS algorithm but instead of branching the search after encountering a conflict we refine the propositional model with the conflict elimination disjunctive constraint as it has been done in previous application of SMT in the standard MAPF. Bounding the sum-of-costs is done in similar lazy way through introducing nogoods incrementally. If it is detected that a conflict free solution exceeds given cost bound then decisions that jointly induce cost greater than given bound are forbidden via a nogood (that is, at least one of these decisions must not be taken).

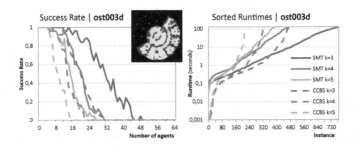

Fig. 5. Comparison of SMT-CBS$^{\mathcal{R}}$ and CCBS on `ost003d`.

We compared SMT-CBS$^{\mathcal{R}}$ with CCBS [1], currently the only alternative algorithm for MAPF$^{\mathcal{R}}$ that modifies the standard CBS algorithm, on a number of benchmarks. The outcome of our comparison is that SMT-CBS$^{\mathcal{R}}$ performs well against CCBS. The best results SMT-CBS$^{\mathcal{R}}$ are observable on medium sized benchmarks with regular obstacles. We attribute the better runtime results of SMT-CBS$^{\mathcal{R}}$ to more efficient handling of disjunctive conflicts in the underlying SAT solver through *propagation*, *clause learning*, and other mechanisms. On the other hand SMT-CBS$^{\mathcal{R}}$ is less efficient on large instances with few agents.

We plan to extend the RDD generation scheme to directional agents where we need to add the third dimension in addition to space (vertices) and time: *direction* (angle). The work on MAPF$^{\mathcal{R}}$ could be further developed into multi-robot motion planning in continuous configuration spaces [16].

Acknowledgement. This research has been supported by GAČR - the Czech Science Foundation, grant registration number 19-17966S. We would like to thank anonymous reviewers for their valuable comments.

References

1. Andreychuk, A., Yakovlev, K.S., Atzmon, D., Stern, R.: Multi-agent pathfinding with continuous time. In: Proceedings of IJCAI, vol. 2019, pp. 39–45 (2019)
2. Audemard, G., Simon, L.: Predicting learnt clauses quality in modern SAT solvers. In: IJCAI, pp. 399–404 (2009)
3. Balyo, T., Heule, M.J.H., Järvisalo, M.: SAT competition 2016: recent developments. In: AAAI, vol. 2017, pp. 5061–5063 (2017)
4. Biere, A., Heule, M., van Maaren, H., Walsh, T.: Handbook of Satisfiability. IOS Press, Amsterdam (2009)
5. Bofill, M., Palahí, M., Suy, J., Villaret, M.: Solving constraint satisfaction problems with SAT modulo theories. Constraints **17**(3), 273–303 (2012)
6. Botea, A., Surynek, P.: Multi-agent path finding on strongly biconnected digraphs. In: Proceedings of AAAI, vol. 2016, pp. 2024–2030 (2015)
7. Cáp, M., Novák, P., Vokrínek, J., Pechoucek, M.: Multi-agent RRT: sampling-based cooperative pathfinding. In: Proceedings of AAMAS, vol. 2013, pp. 1263–1264 (2013)
8. Felner, A., et al.: Adding heuristics to conflict-based search for multi-agent path finding. In: Proceedings of ICAPS 2018, pp. 83–87 (2018)
9. Hönig, W., et al.: Summary: Multi-agent path finding with kinematic constraints. In: Proceedings of IJCAI, vol. 2017, pp. 4869–4873 (2017)
10. Janovsky, P., Cáp, M., Vokrínek, J.: Finding coordinated paths for multiple holonomic agents in 2-D polygonal environment. In: Proceedings of AAMAS, vol. 2014, pp. 1117–1124 (2014)
11. Kautz, H.A.: Deconstructing planning as satisfiability. In: Proceedings, The Twenty-First National Conference on Artificial Intelligence and the Eighteenth Innovative Applications of Artificial Intelligence Conference, 2006, pp. 1524–1526. AAAI Press (2006)
12. Kautz, H.A., Selman, B.: Planning as satisfiability. In: Proceedings ECAI, vol. 1992, pp. 359–363 (1992)
13. Kautz, H.A., Selman, B.: Pushing the envelope: planning, propositional logic and stochastic search. In: Proceedings of AAAI, vol. 1996, pp. 1194–1201 (1996)
14. Kautz, H.A., Selman, B.: Unifying sat-based and graph-based planning. In: Proceedings of IJCAI, vol. 1999, pp. 318–325 (1999)
15. Kornhauser, D., Miller, G.L., Spirakis, P.G.: Coordinating pebble motion on graphs, the diameter of permutation groups, and applications. In: FOCS, vol. 1984, pp. 241–250 (1984)
16. LaValle, S.M.: Planning Algorithms. Cambridge University Press, Cambridge (2006)
17. Li, J., Surynek, P., Felner, A., Ma, H., Koenig, S.: Multi-agent path finding for large agents. In: Proceedings of AAAI 2019. AAAI Press (2019)
18. Ma, H., et al.: Overview: generalizations of multi-agent path finding to real-world scenarios. CoRR arxiv:1702.05515 (2017)
19. Ma, H., Wagner, G., Felner, A., Li, J., Kumar, T.K.S., Koenig, S.: Multi-agent path finding with deadlines. In: Proceedings of IJCAI, vol. 2018, pp. 417–423 (2018)

20. Nieuwenhuis, R.: SAT modulo theories: getting the best of SAT and global constraint filtering. In: Proceedings of CP, vol. 2010, pp. 1–2 (2010)
21. Phillips, M., Likhachev, M.: SIPP: safe interval path planning for dynamic environments. In: Proceedings of ICRA, vol. 2011, pp. 5628–5635 (2011)
22. Ratner, D., Warmuth, M.K.: Nxn puzzle and related relocation problem. J. Symb. Comput. **10**(2), 111–138 (1990)
23. Rivera, N., Hernández, C., Baier, J.A.: Grid pathfinding on the 2k neighborhoods. In: Proceedings of AAAI, vol. 2017, pp. 891–897 (2017)
24. Ryan, M.R.K.: Exploiting subgraph structure in multi-robot path planning. J. Artif. Intell. Res. (JAIR) **31**, 497–542 (2008)
25. Sharon, G., Stern, R., Felner, A., Sturtevant, N.: Conflict-based search for optimal multi-agent pathfinding. Artif. Intell. **219**, 40–66 (2015)
26. Sharon, G., Stern, R., Goldenberg, M., Felner, A.: The increasing cost tree search for optimal multi-agent pathfinding. Artif. Intell. **195**, 470–495 (2013)
27. Silver, D.: Cooperative pathfinding. In: AIIDE, pp. 117–122 (2005)
28. Stern, R.: Multi-agent path finding – an overview. In: Osipov, G.S., Panov, A.I., Yakovlev, K.S. (eds.) Artificial Intelligence. LNCS (LNAI), vol. 11866, pp. 96–115. Springer, Cham (2019). https://doi.org/10.1007/978-3-030-33274-7_6
29. Sturtevant, N.R.: Benchmarks for grid-based pathfinding. Comput. Intell. AI Games **4**(2), 144–148 (2012)
30. Surynek, P.: A novel approach to path planning for multiple robots in bi-connected graphs. In: ICRA, vol. 2009, pp. 3613–3619 (2009)
31. Surynek, P.: Multi-agent path finding with continuous time and geometric agents viewed through satisfiability modulo theories (SMT). In: Surynek, P., Yeoh, W. (eds.) Proceedings of the Twelfth International Symposium on Combinatorial Search, SOCS 2019, pp. 200–201. AAAI Press (2019)
32. Surynek, P.: Unifying search-based and compilation-based approaches to multi-agent path finding through satisfiability modulo theories. In: Proceedings of IJCAI, vol. 2019, pp. 1177–1183 (2019)
33. Surynek, P.: On satisfisfiability modulo theories in continuous multi-agent path finding: Compilation-based and search-based approaches compared. In: Rocha, A.P., Steels, L., van den Herik, H.J. (eds.) Proceedings of the 12th International Conference on Agents and Artificial Intelligence, ICAART 2020, vol. 2, pp. 182–193. SCITEPRESS (2020)
34. Surynek, P., Felner, A., Stern, R., Boyarski, E.: Efficient SAT approach to multi-agent path finding under the sum of costs objective. In: ECAI, pp. 810–818 (2016)
35. Tinelli, C.: Foundations of satisfiability modulo theories. In: Dawar, A., de Queiroz, R. (eds.) WoLLIC 2010. LNCS (LNAI), vol. 6188, pp. 58–58. Springer, Heidelberg (2010). https://doi.org/10.1007/978-3-642-13824-9_6
36. Walker, T.T., Sturtevant, N.R., Felner, A.: Extended increasing cost tree search for non-unit cost domains. In: Proceedings of IJCAI, vol. 2018, pp. 534–540 (2018)
37. Wang, K., Botea, A.: MAPP: a scalable multi-agent path planning algorithm with tractability and completeness guarantees. JAIR **42**, 55–90 (2011)
38. Yu, J., LaValle, S.M.: Optimal multi-robot path planning on graphs: structure and computational complexity. CoRR arxiv:1507.03289 (2015)

Abstracts of Pre-published Papers

Cones, Negation, and All That

Özgür Lütfü Özçep[1](✉) [ID], Mena Leemhuis[1] [ID], and Diedrich Wolter[2] [ID]

[1] University of Lübeck, Lübeck, Germany
oezcep@ifis.uni-luebeck.de,
mena.leemhuis@student.uni-luebeck.de
[2] University of Bamberg, Bamberg, Germany
diedrich.wolter@uni-bamberg.de

Abstract. This paper summarizes results on embedding ontologies expressed in the $\mathcal{ALC}$ description logic into a real-valued vector space, comprising restricted existential and universal quantifiers, as well as concept negation and concept disjunction. The main result states that an $\mathcal{ALC}$ ontology is satisfiable in the classical sense iff it is satisfiable by a partial faithful geometric model based on cones. The line of work to which we contribute aims to integrate knowledge representation techniques and machine learning. The new cone-model of $\mathcal{ALC}$ proposed in this work gives rise to conic optimization techniques for machine learning, extending previous approaches by its ability to model full $\mathcal{ALC}$.

This is an extended abstract of the paper "Cone Semantics for Logics with Negation" to be published in the proceedings of the 29th International Joint Conference on Artificial Intelligence (IJCAI 2020).

1 Introduction

This extended abstract reports on results related to the general framework of cone-based semantics as developed in [15]. The framework relies on the idea of embedding ontologies into low-dimensional continuous vector spaces. This idea goes back to the idea of embedding words into low-dimensional continuous vector spaces which has been implemented successfully in various algorithms with various applications in the realm of information retrieval [6,12,16]. However, these approaches are insensitive to the relational structure of documents. The embedding idea was pushed further (see, e.g., [3,14] and, for an overview, [17]) in order to design embeddings of knowledge graphs or embeddings of ontologies consisting of axioms in some (expressive) logic [8,10,13].

The main aim of our framework is to find embeddings of ontologies that give a better compromise between the geometrical models that can be constructed by means of learning and the (expressivity and consistency) demands of ontologies. *Convex cones* are an ideal data structure for such embeddings, as they combine two desirable properties: On the one hand, computational feasibility is ensured by convexity (see work on convex or conic optimization, e.g., [4] as well as work on conceptual spaces [5]). And on the other hand, sufficient expressivity is ensured by conicity; cones have a well-defined polarity operation that behaves

U. Schmid et al. (Eds.): KI 2020, LNAI 12325, pp. 235–239, 2020.
https://doi.org/10.1007/978-3-030-58285-2_17

as a negation operator, in fact as an orthonegation operator [7,9]. Arbitrary convex sets do not provide a well-defined negation operation (convex sets are closed under intersection but not under set-complement or set-union.) The main result of [15] states that an ontology defined over the description logic $\mathcal{ALC}$ [1], which provides full concept negation, is satisfiable in a classical sense iff it is satisfiable by a geometric model that interprets all concept descriptions as axis-aligned cones, for short *al-cones*. And one can even ensure that the embedding is faithful: The cone-based geometric models used in [15] are partial and thus allow some uncertainty to be retained, i.e., if x is only known to be a member of the union of two atomic concepts, then our partial model will not commit to saying to which atomic concept x belongs. A *faithful* partial model will represent exactly those axioms derivable from the ontology.

2   Embedding $\mathcal{ALC}$ Ontologies with Al-Cones

The core of our cone-based semantics evolves around the notion of the polarity operator, which is defined for arbitrary convex cones X, i.e. sets fulfilling: If $v, w \in X$, then also $\lambda v + \mu w \in X$ for all $\lambda, \mu \geq 0$. The *polar cone* X° for X is defined for Euclidean spaces with a scalar (dot) product $\langle \cdot, \cdot \rangle$ as follows:

$$X^\circ = \{v \in \mathbb{R}^n \mid \forall w \in X : \langle v, w \rangle \leq 0\}$$

The use of the polarity operation for concept negation $\neg$ is motivated by the idea of providing an operator that always maps a concept to a disjoint concept such that the disjoint concept is maximally so w.r.t. the underlying similarity structure $\langle \cdot, \cdot \rangle$ (see also Farkas' classical lemma on polarity).

Interpreting set intersection as concept-conjunction $\sqcap$ and using de Morgan's rule to define concept-disjunction $\sqcup$ one already has the main ingredients to interpret arbitrary Boolean $\mathcal{ALC}$ concepts. But, as arbitrary cones do not fulfil the distributivity property of $\mathcal{ALC}$ concepts w.r.t. $\sqcap$ and $\sqcup$ (Fig. 1, lhs), our embeddings are constrained to axis-aligned cones, for short *al-cones*:

$$X \text{ is al-cone} :\Leftrightarrow X = X_1 \times \cdots \times X_n, X_i \in \{\mathbb{R}, \mathbb{R}_+, \mathbb{R}_-, \{0\}\}$$

As a simple example for embedding (Boolean) $\mathcal{ALC}$ ontologies we consider the case of all concept descriptions over two atomic symbols A, B (Fig. 1, rhs). In the al-cone embedding of Fig. 1 the A is interpreted by the left upper quadrant and B by the right upper quadrant. This induces uniquely the positions of all other hyperoctants corresponding to the other boolean concepts.

One can check that the concepts are associated with appropriate al-cones. For example, the negation $\neg A$ of A is indeed the polar cone of the quadrant of A. Similarly, consider $B \sqcap \neg A$, which is interpreted as the positive x-axis $\mathbb{R}_+ \times \{0\}$.

The example demonstrates also the partiality of al-cone models. Consider, e.g., the difference between a_2 and a_3 in the geometric model on the rhs of Fig. 1.

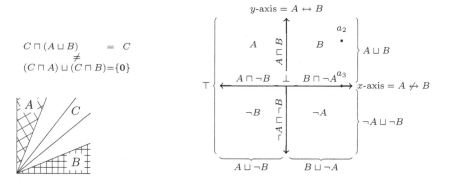

Fig. 1. Counterexample distributivity (lhs) and example al-cone model (rhs)

The individual a_3 is completely identified w.r.t. the given concepts A, B: it lies in the extension of B and in the extension of $\neg A$. For a_2 we "only" know that it must be an B, but we do not know whether it is also an A.

Using the construction idea of the example one can prove that a Boolean $\mathcal{ALC}$ ontology is classically satisfiable iff it satisfiable by an al-cone based model. And one can guarentee faithfulness: The geometric model encodes all and only the information of the ontology. Using some more thoughts on how to deal with relations (roles) one can generalize the result to hold for arbitrary $\mathcal{ALC}$ ontologies.

Proposition 1. *$\mathcal{ALC}$ ontologies are classically satisfiable iff they are satisfiable by a faithful geometric model on some $\mathbb{R}^n$ using sets of the form $b_1 \times \cdots \times b_n$ with $b_i \in \{\{0\}, \mathbb{R}_+, \mathbb{R}_-, \mathbb{R}\}$.*

This result has important consequences for possible supervised learning algorithms relying on al-cone based geometric models (such as the prototypical multi-labelling algorithm described in [11]): If the algorithm is not able to find a model fitting the training data, this is due to a small feature dimension n chosen in the beginning or due to inconsistencies of the ontology. The inconsistency cannot be due to the fact that concepts are represented as al-cones.

3   Conclusion and Outlook

By interpreting negation as a polarity operator it is possible to find embeddings of $\mathcal{ALC}$ ontologies that interpret all concepts as axis-aligned cones. This result adds an interesting alternative to embeddings considered so far.

In [15] we only consider the case where the logic ($\mathcal{ALC}$) has been specified beforehand, not the case of investigating logics induced by the intersection and polarity operators for arbitrary cones. In ongoing work we are investigating non-distributive logics suitable for arbitrary cones. These logics are extensions of so-called orthologics [7]—which describe lattices equipped with an orthonegation. We are able to identify non-trivial rules (weakenings of orthomodularity, a property used for minimal quantum logic [2]) that are fulfilled by cones.

References

1. Baader, F.: Description logic terminology. In: Baader, F., Calvanese, D., McGuinness, D., Nardi, D., Patel-Schneider, P. (eds.) The Description Logic Handbook, pp. 485–495. Cambridge University Press (2003)
2. Birkhoff, G., von Neumann, J.: The logic of quantum mechanics. Ann. Math. **37**(4), 823–843 (1936)
3. Bordes, A., Usunier, N., García-Durán, A., Weston, J., Yakhnenko, O.: Translating embeddings for modeling multi-relational data. In: Burges, C.J.C., Bottou, L., Ghahramani, Z., Weinberger, K.Q. (eds.) Advances in Neural Information Processing Systems 26: 27th Annual Conference on Neural Information Processing Systems 2013. Proceedings of a meeting held December 5–8, 2013, Lake Tahoe, Nevada, United States, pp. 2787–2795 (2013). http://papers.nips.cc/paper/5071-translating-embeddings-for-modeling-multi-relational-data
4. Boyd, S., Vandenberghe, L.: Convex Optimization. Cambridge University Press, Cambridge (2004)
5. Gärdenfors, P.: Conceptual Spaces: The Geometry of Thought. The MIT Press, Cambridge (2000)
6. Goldberg, Y., Levy, O.: word2vec explained: deriving Mikolov et al.'s negative-sampling word-embedding method. ArXiv e-prints (February 2014)
7. Goldblatt, R.I.: Semantic analysis of orthologic. J. Philos. Logic **3**(1), 19–35 (1974). https://doi.org/10.1007/BF00652069
8. Gutiérrez-Basulto, V., Schockaert, S.: From knowledge graph embedding to ontology embedding? An analysis of the compatibility between vector space representations and rules. In: Thielscher, M., Toni, F., Wolter, F. (eds.) Principles of Knowledge Representation and Reasoning: Proceedings of the Sixteenth International Conference, KR 2018, Tempe, Arizona, 30 October - 2 November 2018, pp. 379–388. AAAI Press (2018). https://aaai.org/ocs/index.php/KR/KR18/paper/view/18013
9. Hartonas, C.: Reasoning with incomplete information in generalized galois logics without distribution: the case of negation and modal operators. In: Bimbó, K. (ed.) J. Michael Dunn on Information Based Logics. OCL, vol. 8, pp. 279–312. Springer, Cham (2016). https://doi.org/10.1007/978-3-319-29300-4_14
10. Kulmanov, M., Liu-Wei, W., Yan, Y., Hoehndorf, R.: El embeddings: geometric construction of models for the description logic EL++. In: Proceedings of the Twenty-Eighth International Joint Conference on Artificial Intelligence (IJCAI-2019) (2019)
11. Leemhuis, M., Özçep, O.L., Wolter, D.: Multi-label learning with a cone-based geometric model. In: Proceedings of the 25th International Conference on Conceptual Structures (ICCS 2020) (2020)
12. Levy, O., Goldberg, Y.: Neural word embedding as implicit matrix factorization. In: Ghahramani, Z., Welling, M., Cortes, C., Lawrence, N.D., Weinberger, K.Q. (eds.) Advances in Neural Information Processing Systems 27: Annual Conference on Neural Information Processing Systems 2014, December 8–13 2014, Montreal, Quebec, Canada, pp. 2177–2185 (2014). http://papers.nips.cc/paper/5477-neural-word-embedding-as-implicit-matrix-factorization
13. Kazemi, S.M., Poole, D.: SimpLE embedding for link prediction in knowledge graphs. arXiv e-prints arXiv:1802.04868 (February 2018)

14. Nickel, M., Tresp, V., Kriegel, H.P.: A three-way model for collective learning on multi-relational data. In: Proceedings of the 28th International Conference on International Conference on Machine Learning, ICML 2011, pp. 809–816. Omnipress, USA (2011). http://dl.acm.org/citation.cfm?id=3104482.3104584

15. Özçep, Ö.L., Leemhuis, M., Wolter, D.: Cone semantics for logics with negation. In: Proceedings of the Twenty-Ninth International Joint Conference on Artificial Intelligence, IJCAI-2020 (2020)

16. Pennington, J., Socher, R., Manning, C.D.: Glove: global vectors for word representation. In: EMNLP, vol. 14, pp. 1532–1543 (2014). https://nlp.stanford.edu/pubs/glove.pdf

17. Wang, Q., Mao, Z., Wang, B., Guo, L.: Knowledge graph embedding: a survey of approaches and applications. IEEE Trans. Knowl. Data Eng. **29**(12), 2724–2743 (2017). https://doi.org/10.1109/TKDE.2017.2754499

Swarm-Based Cluster Analysis for Knowledge Discovery

Michael C. Thrun[1,2]($\boxtimes$) (iD) and Alfred Ultsch[1]($\boxtimes$)

[1] Databionics Research Group, Philipps-University of Marburg, Marburg, Germany
`{mthrun,ultsch}@informatik.uni-marburg.de`
[2] Department of Hematology, Oncology and Immunology, Philipps-University Marburg, Marburg, Germany

Abstract. The Databionic swarm (DBS) is a flexible and robust clustering framework that consists of three independent modules: swarm-based projection, high-dimensional data visualization, and representation guided clustering. The first module is the parameter-free projection method Pswarm, which exploits concepts of self-organization and emergence, game theory, and swarm intelligence. The second module is a parameter-free high-dimensional data visualization technique called topographic map. It uses the generalized U-matrix, which enables to estimate first, if any cluster tendency exists and second, the estimation of the number of clusters. The third module offers a clustering method that can be verified by the visualization and vice versa. Benchmarking w.r.t. conventional algorithms demonstrated that DBS can outperform them. Several applications showed that cluster structures provided by DBS are meaningful. This article is an abstract of Swarm Intelligence for Self-Organized Clustering [1].

Keywords: Cluster analysis · Swarm intelligence · Self-organization · Emergence · Dimensionality reduction

1 Introduction

The term knowledge discovery refers to the general process of finding valid, novel, potentially useful, and understandable patterns in data [2]. Here, the focus lies on data-driven methods that find specific patterns in data. These patterns identify homogeneous groups of objects if the objects are heterogonous between the groups or so-called clusters [3]. In this sense, cluster analysis can be seen as one step in the knowledge discovery process, and the clusters are often specified as "natural" clusters [4, 5]. The question that arises is how to recognize structures that define clusters in high-dimensional data without prior assumptions because clustering algorithms most-often use a global objective function that implicitly assumes specific cluster structures in data [4–8]. Moreover, cluster analysis has two additional challenges. For the clustering process, a wide variety of indices have been proposed to find the optimal number of clusters [9] and one of many statistical approaches has to be selected to test for the clustering tendency or so-called

© Springer Nature Switzerland AG 2020
U. Schmid et al. (Eds.): KI 2020, LNAI 12325, pp. 240–244, 2020.
https://doi.org/10.1007/978-3-030-58285-2_18

clusterability [10, 11]. After an extensive review of algorithms of behavior-based systems in unsupervised machine learning performed in [1], two interesting concepts are addressed, which are called self-organization and swarm intelligence. Additionally, two missing links are identified: emergence [12, 13] and game theory [14].

The irreducible structures of high-dimensional data can emerge through self-organization in a phenomenon called emergence. Exploiting the Nash equilibrium concept from game theory [15] through the use of a swarm of intelligent agents, the data-driven approach presented in this work can outperform the optimization of a global objective function in the tasks of clustering and discover new knowledge. This is demonstrated using a collection of datasets offering a variety of real-world challenges, such as outliers or density vs. distance-defined clusters [16].

2   Databionic Swarm (DBS)

The algorithms of DBS consists of three modules: focusing projection with Pswarm, visualization via a topographic map of projected points and clustering. Focusing projection methods first adapt to global structures, and as time progresses, structure preservation shifts from global optimization to the preservation of local neighbor-hoods. Projections of this type (e.g., NerV, CCA, ESOM, t-SNE) usually require parameters to be set because this phase, which is also called the learning phase, requires an annealing scheme. This task is challenging if no prior knowledge about the data exists.

In contrast to all other conventional projection methods, Pswarm neither does have any global objective function nor requires any input parameters other than the data set of interest. In this case, Euclidean distances are used in the input space. Alternatively, a user may also provide Pswarm with a matrix defined in terms of a particular dissimilarity measure, which is typically a distance but may also be a non-metric measure.

The intelligent agents of Pswarm, called DataBots [17], operate on a toroid grid, where positions are coded into polar coordinates to allow for the precise definition of their movement, neighborhood function, and annealing scheme. The size of the grid and, in contrast to other focusing projection methods, the annealing scheme is data-driven. During learning, each agent moves across the grid or stays in its current position in the search for the most potent scent emitted by other DataBots. Hence, agents search for other agents carrying data with the most similar features to themselves with a data-driven decreasing search radius. The movement of every agent is modeled using a game-theory approach, and the radius decreases only if a Nash equilibrium is found [15]. After the self-organization of agents is finished, the output of the Pswarm algorithm is a scatter plot of projected points.

The goal of this scatter plot is a visualization of distance and density-based structures, which is often used in cluster analysis [6, 18–20]. However, it is stated by the Johnson–Lindenstrauss lemma [21] that the two-dimensional similarities in the scatter plot cannot coercively represent high-dimensional structures. For example, similar data points can be mapped onto far-separated points, or a pair of closely neighboring positions represents a pair of distant data points.

Therefore, the generalized U-matrix [22, 23] is exploited on this projection in the second step using emergence through an unsupervised artificial neural network called a simplified (because parameter-free) emergent self-organizing map. The generalized U-matrix generates the visualization of a topographic map with hypsometric tints, which can be vividly described as a virtual 3D landscape with a specific color scale chosen with an algorithm defining the contour lines [24]. The topographic map addresses the central problem in clustering, i.e., the correct estimation of the number of clusters. It allows the assessment of the number of clusters [24] by inspecting the 3D landscape. The color scale and contour lines imitate valleys, ridges, and basins: blue colors indicate small distances (sea level), green and brown colors indicate middle distances (low hills), and shades of gray and white indicate vast distances (high mountains covered with snow and ice). Valleys and basins represent clusters, and the watersheds of hills and mountains represent the borders between clusters. In this 3D landscape, the borders of the visualization are cyclically connected with a periodicity defined by two parameters (L, C). One example of a topographic map can be found on GitHub (https://github.com/Mthrun/DatabionicSwarm).

The semi-automated clustering is performed by calculating the shortest paths [25] of the Delaunay graph between all projected points weighted with high-dimensional distances. This is possible because it was shown that the U-matrix is an approximation of the abstract U-matrix [26], which is based on Voronoi cells. Voronoi cells define a Delaunay graph where the edges between every projected point are weighted by the high-dimensional distances of the corresponding data points.

The clustering approach itself involves one of two choices. For each choice, a dendrogram can be visualized, which shows the ultrametric portion of the distance used is visualized (c.f. [27]). Large changes in fusion levels of the ultrametric portion of the distance indicate the best cut, but the resulting clustering should always be evaluated by the topographic map.

2.1 Open Source Access

There is a general need for open-source implementations in swarm intelligence algorithms [28]. Thus, DBS is available as the R package "DatabionicSwarm" on CRAN (https://CRAN.R-project.org/package=DatabionicSwarm). Datasets are available in [16]. The top 50 clustering algorithms are summarized in the R package "FCPS" on CRAN (https://CRAN.R-project.org/package=FCPS). A small subset of algorithms was selected for benchmarking in [1] because the implicit assumptions were known for this subset in literature.

3 Conclusion

By exploiting the missing links between swarm-based algorithms and emergence as well as game theory, the main advantage of DBS is its robustness regarding very different types of distance and density-based structures of clusters. As a technique that uses swarm intelligence, DBS clustering is more robust with respect to outliers than conventional algorithms. DBS enables even a non-professional in the field of data mining to integrate its algorithms for visualization and/or clustering in their knowledge discovery process because no prior knowledge about the data is required, and no implicit assumptions about the data are made.

References

1. Thrun, M.C., Ultsch, A.: Swarm intelligence for self-organized clustering. Artif. Intell. (2020). https://doi.org/10.1016/j.artint.2020.103237
2. Fayyad, U.M., et al.: Advances in Knowledge Discovery and Data Mining, vol. 21. American Association for Artificial Intelligence Press, Menlo Park, p. 611 (1996)
3. Bonner, R.E.: On some clustering technique. IBM J. Res. Dev. 8(1), 22–32 (1964)
4. Duda, R.O., Hart, P.E., Stork, D.G.: Pattern Classification, 2nd edn. Wiley, Ney York (2001)
5. Theodoridis, S., Koutroumbas, K.: Pattern Recognition, 4th edn., vol. 961. Elsevier, Canada (2009)
6. Everitt, B.S., Landau, S., Leese, M.: Cluster Analysis, 4th edn. Arnold, London (2001)
7. Handl, J., Knowles, J., Kell, D.B.: Computational cluster validation in post-genomic data analysis. Bioinformatics 21(15), 3201–3212 (2005)
8. Ultsch, A., Lötsch, J.: Machine-learned cluster identification in high-dimensional data. J. Biomed. Inform. 66(C), 95–104 (2017)
9. Charrad, M., et al.: NbClust package: finding the relevant number of clusters in a dataset. J. Stat. Softw. 61(6), 1–36 (2012)
10. Adolfsson, A., Ackerman, M., Brownstein, N.C.: To cluster, or not to cluster: an analysis of clusterability methods. Pattern Recogn. 88, 13–26 (2019)
11. Thrun, M.C.: Improving the sensitivity of statistical testing for clusterability with mirrored-density plot. In: Archambault, D., Nabney, I., Peltonen, J. (eds.) Machine Learning Methods in Visualisation for Big Data. The Eurographics Association, Norrköping (2020). https://doi.org/10.2312/mlvis.20201102
12. Goldstein, J.: Emergence as a construct: history and issues. Emergence 1(1), 49–72 (1999)
13. Ultsch, A.: Data mining and knowledge discovery with emergent self-organizing feature maps for multivariate time series. In: Oja, E., Kaski, S. (eds.) Kohonen Maps, pp. 33–46. Elsevier (1999)
14. Nash, J.F.: Non-cooperative games. Ann. Math. 54, 286–295 (1951)
15. Nash, J.F.: Equilibrium points in n-person games. Proc. Nat. Acad. Sci. USA 36(1), 48–49 (1950)
16. Thrun, M.C., Ultsch, A.: Clustering benchmark datasets exploiting the fundamental clustering problems. Data Brief 30(C), 105501 (2020)
17. Ultsch, A.: Clustering with DataBots. In: International Conference on Advances in Intelligent Systems Theory and Applications (AISTA), pp. 99–104. IEEE ACT Section, Canberra (2000)
18. Hennig, C., et al.: Handbook of cluster analysis. In: Hennig, C., et al. (eds.) Handbook of Modern Statistical Methods, vol. 730. Chapman & Hall/CRC Press, New York (2015)
19. Mirkin, B.G.: Clustering: a data recovery approach. In: Lafferty, J., et al. (eds.) Computer Science and Data Analysis Series. Chapman & Hall/CRC, Boca Raton (2005)
20. Ritter, G.: Robust cluster analysis and variable selection. In: Monographs on Statistics and Applied Probability. Chapman & Hall/CRC Press, Passau (2014)
21. Dasgupta, S., Gupta, A.: An elementary proof of a theorem of Johnson and Lindenstrauss. Random Struct. Algorithms 22(1), 60–65 (2003)
22. Thrun, M.C.: Projection Based Clustering through Self-Organization and Swarm Intelligence. Springer, Heidelberg (2018). https://doi.org/10.1007/978-3-658-20540-9
23. Ultsch, A., Thrun, M.C.: Credible visualizations for planar projections. In: Cottrell, M. (ed.) 12th International Workshop on Self-Organizing Maps and Learning Vector Quantization, Clustering and Data Visualization (WSOM), pp. 1–5. IEEE, Nany (2017)
24. Thrun, M.C., et al.: Visualization and 3D printing of multivariate data of biomarkers. In: Skala, V. (ed.) International Conference in Central Europe on Computer Graphics, Visualization and Computer Vision (WSCG), Plzen, pp. 7–16 (2016)

25. Dijkstra, E.W.: A note on two problems in connexion with graphs. Numer. Math. **1**(1), 269–271 (1959)
26. Lötsch, J., Ultsch, A.: Exploiting the structures of the U-matrix. In: Villmann, T., Schleif, F.-M., Kaden, M., Lange, M. (eds.) Advances in Self-Organizing Maps and Learning Vector Quantization. AISC, vol. 295, pp. 249–257. Springer, Cham (2014). https://doi.org/10.1007/978-3-319-07695-9_24
27. Murtagh, F.: On ultrametricity, data coding, and computation. J. Classif. **21**(2), 167–184 (2004)
28. Martens, D., Baesens, B., Fawcett, T.: Editorial survey: swarm intelligence for data mining. Mach. Learn. **82**(1), 1–42 (2011)

Draw with Me: Human-in-the-Loop for Image Restoration

Thomas Weber[1], Zhiwei Han[2]([⊠]), Stefan Matthes[2], Heinrich Hußmann[1], and Yuanting Liu[2]

[1] Ludwig-Maximilians-University Munich, Munich, Germany
{thomas.weber,heinrich.hussmann}@ifi.lmu.de
[2] fortiss GmbH, Munich, Germany
{han,matthes,liu}@fortiss.org

Abstract. The purpose of image restoration is to recover the original state of damaged images. To mitigate the disadvantages of the manual image restoration process such as the high time consumption, we present **interactive Deep Image Prior** by extending **Deep Image Prior** with a user interface to an interactive process with the human in the loop. In this process, a human can iteratively embed knowledge to provide guidance and control for the automated inpainting process.

Our evaluation shows that, even with very little human guidance, our interactive approach has a restoration performance on par or superior to other methods. Meanwhile, very positive results of our user study suggest that learning systems with the human-in-the-loop positively contribute to user satisfaction.

Keywords: Interactive machine learning · Image inpainting · Computer Vision

1 Problem and Challenges

Image inpainting is a process that fills missing sections in images, such that the restored images are visually plausible. In order to distinguish from the general image inpainting tasks, we consider image restoration of damaged or corrupted art works in this paper.

A typical scenario for image restoration is heritage protection. The Dunhuang grottoes dataset [7] of damaged murals from the Mogao Grottoes which we use in our work is a popular example for both heritage protection and image restoration [5]. Traditionally, the restoration requires a professional to paint manually, which requires much experience and effort.

In order to quickly and reliably restore digital copies of historical artifacts, numerous automated frameworks have been proposed for this digital image

---

We submit this paper as an abstract paper. The original paper was published as a conference paper in IUI'20 [1]

T. Weber and Z. Han—The first two authors contributed equally to this research.

© Springer Nature Switzerland AG 2020
U. Schmid et al. (Eds.): KI 2020, LNAI 12325, pp. 245–248, 2020.
https://doi.org/10.1007/978-3-030-58285-2_19

restoration in the recent years. The inpainting frameworks proposed by prior works can be categorized into two main classes: exemplar-based [2] and learning-based methods [4]. Those frameworks offer a digital restoration process which showed decent results for many image inpainting tasks while being significantly less time-intensive. However, exemplar-based methods have trouble in recovering complex images, since they only copy existing patches from the same image. And while Deep Learning (DL) works well when trained on a large dataset, DL-based approaches severely suffer from over-fitting when only a small training set is available. The fact that such datasets are rarely available prevents learning-based methods from being adopted into many domains.

2   Approach

When missing image features are obvious from semantic but not structural context, humans can easily deduce these missing features than many algorithms. To incorporate human knowledge in image restoration and improve the restoration quality, we present interactive Deep Image Prior (iDIP), a collaborative, interactive image restoration system which enables humans to iteractively guide and correct an automated restoration process.

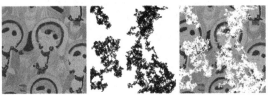

Fig. 1. Left to right: the damaged image from the Mogao Grotto dataset [7], a mask specifying damaged regions, and a restoration by iDIP.

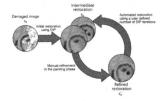

Fig. 2. iDIP performs an initial restoration using DIP and then cycles through interactive inpainting phases.

iDIP restores images by alternately and iteratively exploiting the image prior and human knowledge. The underlying algorithm updates the image iteratively, incrementally, and focused onto specific masked regions (see Fig. 1). Refinement by the user can come in two forms: First, the user can edit the mask and therefore direct the DIP to include or exclude specific regions in the restoration process. Second, the user can paint onto the current increment to provide information that may not be restorable by structural information alone. This may for example be features that can be deduced from image semantics. Blending hand painted image features into the structure of the original image can be hard though. With the collaborative approach, this can be left to the DIP algorithm.

The results of the human involvement are fed back into the DIP system which continues training – and therefore refinement of the image prior – until the next increment is reached. The human is in control of how many training iterations should be performed for the next increment, giving more control and making degradation due to overfitting less likely.

Figure 2 visualizes the stages of iDIP:

1. To provide some base information, the first increment x_0 is given without the user refining it.
2. From then on the user always receives the current increment x_n restored by iDIP.
3. In the following painting phase, the user paints onto the image x_n to refine it, yielding the refined image x'_n.
4. The refined image x'_n is fed back to the DIP algorithm for another training phase where a set number of training iterations are applied.
5. After training, the system generates the next increment x_{n+1} from the further trained generator. At this point the process starts anew.

With the iterative nature we intend for DIP and human knowledge to jointly boost each other. Besides, this approach should also give users greater control on the output: by trial-and-error they can determine what impact their actions have to better gauge their actions for the next increment.

3   Results and Conclusion

To compare the reconstructed image to the baselines we used established measures for the comparison of images: We compute the Dissimilarity Structural Similarity Index Measure (DSSIM) [6] and the Local Mean Squared Error (LMSE) [3] between the restored and ground truth images (Table 1).

Table 1. Results for the restoration metrics. Lower values are better. Significance levels for comparison to iDIP using Mann-Whitney-U test.

Metrics/Methods	EdgeConnect	PartialConv	PatchMatch	PatchOffset	DIP	iDIP
LMSE	629.65***	2550.02***	185.68	558.05***	214.23	**207.37**
DSSIM	0.2803***	0.2816***	0.2423	0.2247*	0.2228	**0.2227**

While significant improvement would have been more desirable, we see these results as an indicator that our approach achieves at least performance on par with these baselines regarding the objective measures. These results look promising, indicating that added interactivity is a positive influence on image restoration. Consequently we decided to conduct a user study with two goals: to evaluate the subjective quality of our image reconstruction as described below and to receive feedback on the overall usability of the tool and method. For the details of user study, we refer to our original papers [1].

In this paper we have described iDIP, our Human-in-the-Loop framework for interactive image restoration. This framework allows users to interactively contribute their knowledge to a DIP-based image restoration process such that both image prior and human knowledge are used as a collaborative iML system. We have outlined our implementation of this system as well as how we evaluated whether the interactive approach improves output quality and how it is perceived by users. Our experiments show that the interactivity positively affects the output quality as iDIP is on par with or better than the five state of the art baselines.

References

1. IUI 2020: Proceedings of the 25th International Conference on Intelligent User Interfaces. Association for Computing Machinery, New York, NY, USA (2020)
2. Criminisi, A., Perez, P., Toyama, K.: Object removal by exemplar-based inpainting. In: 2003 Proceedings of the IEEE Computer Society Conference on Computer Vision and Pattern Recognition, 2003, vol. 2, pp. II-II. IEEE (2003)
3. Grosse, R., Johnson, M.K., Adelson, E.H., Freeman, W.T.: Ground truth dataset and baseline evaluations for intrinsic image algorithms. In: 2009 IEEE 12th International Conference on Computer Vision, pp. 2335–2342. IEEE (2009)
4. Liu, G., Reda, F.A., Shih, K.J., Wang, T.C., Tao, A., Catanzaro, B.: Image inpainting for irregular holes using partial convolutions. In: Proceedings of the European Conference on Computer Vision (ECCV), pp. 85–100 (2018)
5. Wang, H., Li, Q., Zou, Q.: Inpainting of dunhuang murals by sparsely modeling the texture similarity and structure continuity. J. Comput. Cultural Heritage (JOCCH) **12**(3), 17 (2019)
6. Wang, Z., Bovik, A.C., Sheikh, H.R., Simoncelli, E.P., et al.: Image quality assessment: from error visibility to structural similarity. IEEE Trans. Image Process. **13**(4), 600–612 (2004)
7. Yu, T., Zhang, S., Lin, C., You, S.: Dunhuang grotto painting dataset and benchmark. arXiv preprint arXiv:1907.04589 (2019)

Technical Contributions

Reasonable Machines: A Research Manifesto

Christoph Benzmüller[1](✉)[iD] and Bertram Lomfeld[2][iD]

[1] Institute of Computer Science, Freie Universität Berlin, Berlin, Germany
c.benzmueller@fu-berlin.de
[2] Department of Law, Freie Universität Berlin, Berlin, Germany
bertram.lomfeld@fu-berlin.de

Abstract. Future intelligent autonomous systems (IAS) are inevitably deciding on moral and legal questions, e.g. in self-driving cars, health care or human-machine collaboration. As decision processes in most modern sub-symbolic IAS are hidden, the simple political plea for transparency, accountability and governance falls short. A sound ecosystem of trust requires ways for IAS to autonomously justify their actions, that is, to learn giving and taking reasons for their decisions. Building on social reasoning models in moral psychology and legal philosophy such an idea of »REASONABLE MACHINES« requires novel, hybrid reasoning tools, ethico-legal ontologies and associated argumentation technology. Enabling machines to normative communication creates trust and opens new dimensions of AI application and human-machine interaction.

Keywords: Trustworthy and explainable AI · Ethico-legal governors · Social reasoning model · Pluralistic and expressive normative reasoning

1 Introduction

Intelligent autonomous systems (IASs) are rapidly entering applications in industry, military, finance, governance, administration, healthcare, etc., leading to a historical transition period with unprecedented dynamics of innovation and change, and with unpredictable outcomes. Politics, regulatory bodies, indeed society as a whole, are challenged not only with keeping pace with these potentially disruptive developments, but also with staying ahead and wisely guiding the transition. Fostering positive impacts, while preventing negative side effects, is a balanced vision shared within most of the numerous ethical guidelines of the last years on trustworthy AI, including the European Commission's most recent White Paper on AI [6], proposing the creation of an *"ecosystem of excellence"* in combination with an *"ecosystem of trust"*.

We think that real *"Trustworthy AI by Design"* demands IASs, which are able to give and take reasons for their decisions to act. Such »REASONABLE MACHINES« require novel, hybrid reasoning tools, upper ethico-legal ontologies

© Springer Nature Switzerland AG 2020
U. Schmid et al. (Eds.): KI 2020, LNAI 12325, pp. 251–258, 2020.
https://doi.org/10.1007/978-3-030-58285-2_20

and associated argumentation technology to be utilised in practice for assessing, justifying and controlling (externally and internally) the behaviour of IASs with respect to explicitly encoded legal and ethical regulation. We envision this technology to be integrated with an on-demand, cloud-based workbench for pluralistic, expressive regulatory reasoning. This would foster knowledge transfer with industry, research, and educational institutions, it would enable access to critical AI infrastructure at scale with little risk and minimal costs, and, in the long run, it could support dynamic adjustments of regulating code for IASs in the cloud via politically and socially legitimated processes.

Paper structure: Sect. 2 formulates objectives for REASONABLE MACHINES, and Sect. 3 provides models for them building on moral psychology and legal philosophy. Section 4 outlines modular steps for research and implementation of REASONABLE MACHINES; this leverages own prior work such as the LOGIKEY methodology and framework for designing normative theories for ethical and legal reasoning [4], which needs to be combined and extended with an upper-level value ontology [17] and further domain-level regulatory theories for the assessment and explanation of ethical and legal conflicts and decisions in IASs.

2   REASONABLE MACHINES: Objectives

The need for some form of "moral machines" [22] is no science fiction scenario at all. With the rise of autonomous systems in all fields of life including highly complex and ethically critical applications like self-driving cars, weapon systems, healthcare assistance in triage and pandemic plans, predictive policing, legal judgement supports or credit scoring tools, involved AI systems are inevitably confronted with, and deciding on, moral and legal questions. One core problem with ethical and legal accountability or even governance of autonomous systems is the hidden decision process (black box) in modern (sub-symbolic) AI technologies, which hinders transparency as well as direct intervention. The simple plea for transparency disregards technological realities or even restrains much needed further developments.[1]

Inspired by moral psychology and cognitive science, we envision the solution in the development of independent, symbolic logic based safety-harnesses in future AI systems [9]. Such "ethico-legal governors" encapsulate and interact with black box AI systems, and they will use symbolic AI techniques in order to

---

[1] While interpreting, modeling and explaining the inner functioning of black box AI systems is relevant also with respect to our REASONABLE MACHINES vision, such research alone cannot completely solve the trust and control challenge. Sub-symbolic AI black box systems (e.g. neural architectures) are suffering from various issues (including adversarial attacks and influence of bias in data) which cannot be easily eliminated by interpreting, modeling and explaining them. Offline, forensic processes are then required such that the whole enterprise of turning black box AI systems into fully trustworthy AI systems becomes a challenging multi-step engineering process, and such an approach is significantly further complicated when online learning capabilities are additionally foreseen.

search for possible justifications, i.e. reasons, for their decisions and (intended) actions with regard to some formally encoded ethico-legal theories defined by regulating bodies. The symbolic justifications computed at this abstract level thus provide a basis for generating explanations about why a decision/action (proposed by an AI black box system) is ethico-legally legitimate and compliant with respect to the encoded ethico-legal regulation.

Such an approach is complementary to, and as an additional measure more promising than, explaining the inner (mis-)functioning of the black box AI system itself. Symbolic justifications in turn enable the development of further means towards a meaningful and robust control and towards human-understandable explanation and human-machine interaction. The REASONABLE MACHINES idea outlines a genuine approach of trustworthiness by design proposing, in psychological terminology [14], a slow, rational (i.e. symbolic) "System 2" layer in responsible IASs to justify and control their fast, *"intuitive"*, but opaque (subsymbolic), "System 1" layer computations.

REASONABLE MACHINES research aims at analyzing and constructing ways how intelligent machines could socially justify their actions at abstract level, i.e. give and take moral and legal reasons for their decisions to act. Reason is based on reasons. This is true as much for artificial as for human intelligent agents. The "practical reasonableness" of intelligent agents depends on their moral abilities to communicate socially acceptable reasons for their behavior [11]. Thus, the exploration of methods and tools enabling machines to generate normative reasons (which may be independent of underlying black box architectures and opaque algorithms) smoothes the way for more comprehensive artificial moral agency and new dimensions of human-machine communication.

The core objectives of REASONABLE MACHINES technology are:

- enabling argument-based explanations & justifications of IAS decisions,
- enabling ethico-legal reasoning about, and public critique of, IAS decisions,
- facilitating political and legal governance of IAS decision making,
- evolving ethico-legal agency and communicative capacity of IASs,
- enabling trustworthy human-interaction by normative communication,
- fostering development of novel neuro-symbolic AI architectures.

3   Artificial Social Reasoning Model (aSRM)

The black box governance problem has an interesting parallel in human decision making. Most actual models in moral psychology consider emotional intuition to be *the* (or at least one) initial driving force of human action which is only afterwards (or with a second significantly slower system) rationalized with reasons [12,14]. Within a social framework of giving and taking reasons (e.g. moral convention or a legal system) the initial motivation of a single human agent could be ignored if his actions and his post-hoc reasoning comply with given social (moral or legal) standards [16]. Communicating reasons within such a post-hoc *"Social Reasoning Model"* (SRM) is not superfluous, but essential, as only they guarantee the coherence of a moral or legal order in an increasingly pluralistic world. The remaining difference is the relative independence of rational reasoning from the motivational impulse to act. Even so, in the long run the inner-subjective or social feedback loop with rational reasons might also change the agents' motivational (emotional) disposition.

This post-hoc SRM is transferable to AI decision processes as *"artificial Social Reasoning Model" (aSRM)*. The black box of an opaque AI system functions like an AI intuition. Following the SRM model, transparency is not needed as long as the system generates post-hoc reasons for its action. Moral and legal accountability and governance could instead be enabled through symbolic or sub-symbolic aSRMs.

A symbolic solution would try to reconstruct (or justify with an alternative argument) the intuitive decision of the black box with deontic logical reasoning applying moral or legal standards. A pluralistic, expressive "normative reasoning infrastructure", such as LogiKEy [4], should e.g. be able to support this process.

A sub-symbolic solution could create an independent (second) neural network to produce reasons for the output of the (first) decision network (e.g. autonomous driving control). Of course, the structure of this "reasoning net" process is again hidden. Yet, if the outcoming reasons coherently comply with prescribed social and ethico-legal standards the lack of transparency in the second black box constitutes less of a problem.

Robust solutions for aSRMs could even seek to integrate and align these two options. Moreover, in both scenarios the introduced feedback loop of giving and taking reasons could be integrated as learning environment (self-supervised learning) for the initial, intuitive layer of autonomous decision making, with the eventual effect that differences at both layers may gradually dissolve.

Allowing various kinds of reasons, SRMs & aSRMs advance normative pluralism and may integrate different (machine-)ethical traditions: deontological, consequentialist and virtue ethics. "Reasonable pluralism" in recent moral and political philosophy defines reasonableness by meta-level procedures like "reflective equilibrium" and "overlapping consensus" [20] or "rational discourse" [11]. Contemporary legal philosophy and theory has enfolded how law could act as democratic real-world implementation of these meta-procedures, structuring public deliberation and argumentation over conflicting reasons [1,15]. Constructing a pluralist aSRM substantially widens the mostly consequentialist contemporary approaches [5,9] to machine ethics and moral IAS.

4   REASONABLE MACHINES: Implementation

The implementation of REASONABLE MACHINES requires expertise from different areas: pluralistic normative reasoning, formal ethics and legal theory, expressive ontologies and semantic web taxonomies, human-computer interaction, rule-based systems, automated theorem proving, argumentation technology, neural architectures and machine learning. Acknowledging the complexity of each field, REASONABLE MACHINES research should complement top-down construction of responsible machine architecture with bottom-up developments starting from existing works in different domains. More concretely, we propose a modular and stepwise implementation of our research scheme based on the following modules:

M1: Responsible Machine Architecture. The vision of an aSRM and its parallel to human SRM needs to be further explored to guide and refine the overall architectural design of REASONABLE MACHINES based on respective system components responsible for generating justifications, for conducting compliance checks and for governing the action executions of an IAS.

M2: Ethico-Legal Ontologies. Ethico-legal ontologies constitute a core ingredient to enable the computation, assessment and communication of aSRM-based rational justifications in the envisioned ethico-legal governance components for IASs, and they are also key for black box independent user-explanations in form of rational arguments. We propose the development of expressive ethico-legal upper-level ontologies to guide and connect the encoding of concrete ethico-legal domain-level theories (regulatory codes) [8,13]. Moreover, we propose the concrete regulatory codes to be complemented with an abstract ethico-legal value ontology, for example, as "discoursive grammar" of justification [17].

M3: Symbolic Reasoning Tools. For the implementation of pluralistic, expressive and paradox-free normative reasoning at the upper-level, the LogiKEy framework [4] can e.g. be adapted and further advanced. LogiKEy works with shallow semantical embeddings (SSEs) of (combinations of) non-classical logics in classical higher-order logic (HOL). HOL thereby serves as a meta-logic, rich enough to support the encoding of a plurality of "object logics" (e.g. conditional, deontic or epistemic logics and combinations thereof). The embedded "object logics" are used for the iterative, experimental encoding of normative theories. This generic approach shall ideally be integrated with specialized solutions based e.g. on semantic web reasoning, logic programming, answer set programming, and with formalized argumentation for ethical [21] or legal [3] systems design.

M4: Interpretable AI Systems. Sub-symbolic solutions to SRM-based accountability and governance challenge could develop a hidden reasoning net, which might be trained with legal and ethical use-cases. Moreover, techniques in "explainable AI" [10] have to be assessed and, if possible, integrated with the symbolic aSRM tools to be developed in M3 in order to provide guidance to their computations and search processes. The more information can be obtained about the particular information bits that trigger the decisions of the black box systems we want to govern, the easier the corresponding reasoning tasks, i.e. the search for justifications, should become in the associated, symbolic aSRM tool.

M5: Human-Machine Communication and Interaction. The intended aSRM-based justifications generated by the tools developed in M3 and M4 require arguments and rational explanation which are understandable for different AI ecosystems [19], including human users, collect decision scenarios between machines and independent verification tools. Here, the development of respective techniques could build on argumentation theory in combination with recent advances towards a computational hermeneutics [7]. An overarching objective of REASONABLE MACHINES is to contribute to trustful and fruitful interaction between human and IASs.

M6: Cloud-based Reasoning Workbench. To facilitate access to the proposed knowledge representation and reasoning solutions, and also to host the ethico-legal theories, a cloud-based reasoning workbench should be implemented. This workbench would (i) integrate the bottom-up construed components and tools from M2-M5 and (ii) implement instances of the top-down governance architecture(s) developed in M1 based on (i). This cloud-based solution could be developed in combination with, or as an alternative to, more independent solutions based e.g. on agent-based development frameworks [23].

M7: Use Cases and Empirical Studies. The overall system framework needs to be adequately prepared to support changing use cases and empirical studies. Concrete use cases with high ethical and legal potential must be defined and employed to guide the research and development work, as for example the representative issue on self-driving cars [5]. Empirical studies should support and inform the constructive development process. For testing the ethico-legal value ontology in M2, for example, we could try to demonstrate that it can make sense out of the rich MIT Moral Machine experiment data [2]. When its architecture evolves, it would be highly valuable to design a genuine aSRM experiment.

5   Conclusion

The REASONABLE MACHINES vision and research requires the integration of heterogeneous and interdisciplinary expertise to be fruitfully implemented. The cloud-based framework we envision would ideally be widely available and reusable, and it could become part of related, bigger initiatives towards the sharing of critical AI infrastructure (such as the claire-ai.org vision towards a CERN for AI). The implementation of the depicted program requires substantial resources and investment in foundational AI research and in practical system development, but it reflects the urgent and timely need for the development of trustworthy AI technology.

The possible outreach of the REASONABLE MACHINES idea is even far beyond an ecosystem of trust. To enable machines to give normative reasons for their decisions and actions means to capacitate them of communicative action [11], or at least to engage in constitutive communication of social systems [18]. The capacity to give and take reasons is a crucial step towards fully autonomous normative (moral and legal) agency. Moreover, our research, in the long run, paves way for interesting further studies and experiments on integrated neuro-symbolic AI architectures and on the emergence of patterns of self-reflection in intelligent autonomous machines.

Acknowledgement. We thank David Fuenmayor and the anonymous reviewers for their helpful comments to this work.

References

1. Alexy, R.: Theorie der juristischen Argumentation. Suhrkamp, Frankfurt/M (1978)
2. Awad, E.: The moral machine experiment. Nature **563**(7729), 59–64 (2018)
3. Benzmüller, C., Fuenmayor, D., Lomfeld, B.: Encoding legal balancing: automating an abstract ethico-legal value ontology in preference logic. In: MLR 2020. Preprint: https://arxiv.org/abs/2006.12789 (2020)
4. Benzmüller, C., Parent, X., van der Torre, L.: Designing normative theories for ethical and legal reasoning: LogiKEy framework, methodology, and tool support. Artif. Intell. **287**, 103348 (2020). https://doi.org/10.1016/j.artint.2020.103348
5. Bonnefon, J.-F., Shariff, A., Rahwan, I.: The social dilemma of autonomous vehicles. Science **352**(6293), 1573–1576 (2016)
6. European Commission, On Artificial Intelligence - A European approach to excellence and trust. European Commission White Paper, COM (2020) 65 final (2020)
7. Fuenmayor, D., Benzmüller, C.: A computational-hermeneutic approach for conceptual explicitation. In: Nepomuceno-Fernández, Á., Magnani, L., Salguero-Lamillar, F.J., Barés-Gómez, C., Fontaine, M. (eds.) MBR 2018. SAPERE, vol. 49, pp. 441–469. Springer, Cham (2019). https://doi.org/10.1007/978-3-030-32722-4_25
8. Fuenmayor, D., Benzmüller, C.: Harnessing higher-order (meta-)logic to represent and reason with complex ethical theories. In: Nayak, A.C., Sharma, A. (eds.) PRICAI 2019. LNCS (LNAI), vol. 11670, pp. 418–432. Springer, Cham (2019). https://doi.org/10.1007/978-3-030-29908-8_34
9. Greene, J., Rossi, F., Tasioulas, J., Venable, K.B., Williams, B.C.: Embedding ethical principles in collective decision support systems. In: Schuurmans, D., Wellman, M.P. (eds.) Proceedings of the Thirtieth AAAI Conference on Artificial Intelligence, pp. 4147–4151. AAAI Press (2016)
10. Guidotti, R.: A survey of methods for explaining black box models. ACM Comput. Surv. **51**(5), 1–42 (2018)
11. Habermas, J.: Theorie des kommunikativen Handelns. Suhrkamp, Frankf./M (1981)
12. Haidt, J.: The emotional dog and its rational tail: a social intuitionist approach to moral judgment. Psychol. Rev. **108**(4), 814–34 (2001)
13. Hoekstra, R., Breuker, J., Bello, M.D., Boer, A.: LKIF core: principled ontology development for the legal domain. In: Breuker, J., et al. (eds.) Law, Ontologies and the Semantic Web - Channelling the Legal Information Flood, Frontiers in Artificial Intelligence and Applications, pp. 21–52. IOS Press (2009)
14. Kahnemann, D.: Thinking, Fast and Slow. Farrar, Straus and Giroux, New York City (2013)
15. Lomfeld, B.: Die Gründe des Vertrages: Eine Diskurstheorie der Vertragsrechte. Mohr Siebeck, Tübingen (2015)
16. Lomfeld, B.: Emotio Iuris. Skizzen zu einer psychologisch aufgeklärten Methodenlehre des Rechts. In: Köhler, Müller-Mall, Schmidt, Schnädelbach, (eds.) Recht Fühlen, pp. 19–32. Fink, München (2017)
17. Lomfeld, B.: Grammatik der Rechtfertigung: Eine kritische Rekonstruktion der Rechts(fort)bildung. Kritische Justiz **52**(4) (2019)
18. Luhmann, N.: Soziale Systeme: Grundlage einer allgemeinen Theorie. Suhrkamp, Frankfurt/M (1984)
19. Rahwan, I.: Machine behaviour. Nature **568**(7753), 477–486 (2019)

20. Rawls, J.: Justice as Fairness: A Restatement. Harvard University Press, Cambridge
21. Verheij, B.: Formalizing value-guided argumentation for ethical systems design. Artif. Intell. Law **24**(4), 387–407 (2016). https://doi.org/10.1007/s10506-016-9189-y
22. Wallach, W., Allen, C.: Moral Machines: Teaching Robots Right from Wrong. Oxford University Press, Oxford (2008)
23. Wisniewski, M., Steen, A., Benzmüller, C.: LEOPARD—A generic platform for the implementation of higher-order reasoners. In: Kerber, M., Carette, J., Kaliszyk, C., Rabe, F., Sorge, V. (eds.) CICM 2015. LNCS (LNAI), vol. 9150, pp. 325–330. Springer, Cham (2015). https://doi.org/10.1007/978-3-319-20615-8_22

A Heuristic Agent in Multi-Agent Path Finding Under Destination Uncertainty

Lukas Berger$^{(\boxtimes)}$, Bernhard Nebel, and Marco Ragni

Foundations of AI and Cognitive Computation Lab, Faculty of Engineering,
Albert-Ludwigs-University, Freiburg im Breisgau, Germany
lukas.berger@uranus.uni-freiburg.de
{nebel,ragni}@cs.uni-freiburg.de

Abstract. Humans are capable of recognizing intentions by solely observing another agent's actions. Hence, in a cooperative planning task, i.e., where all agents aim for all other agents to reach their respective goals, to some extend communication or a central planning instance are not necessary. In epistemic planning a recent research line investigates multi-agent planning problems (MAPF) with goal uncertainty. In this paper, we propose and analyze a round-based variation of this problem, where each agent moves or waits in each round. We show that simple heuristics from cognition can outperform in some cases an adapted formal approach on computation time and solve some new instances in some cases. Implications are discussed.

1 Introduction

Autonomous aircraft towing [6], airport ground traffic [5], and robots in warehouses [12] require the interaction of multiple agents acting in the same environment. But how good can agents reach their goal, if they have no direct communication about their goals and actions? Analyzing this problem allows to learn about how much intention can be recognized by an agent's action and when some form of coordination by communication is required. Let us consider a warehouse as an example. The warehouse is represented by a grid graph $G = (V, E)$ (see, Fig. 1). The vertices are the corridors and the edges describe how they are connected with each other. Located in the warehouse are robots, which we call *agents* $A = \{a_0, a_1, ..., a_m\}$. They all have a distinct position and there can never be more than one agent on the same vertex. In each round $R = \{0, 1, ..., n\}$ each agent can stay at its vertex or move at most to the next one. They move in a specific move order $MO = (a_o, a_1, ..., a_m), a_i \in A$ which describes the order in which the agents can make actions after each other in each round. Since the shelves are so narrow, no agent can move into a corridor in which another agent is located, therefore the agents are able to block each others paths. Every agent has a set of corridors it is responsible for. Let $\beta : A \rightarrow 2^V$ be the function which maps the agents to their possible goals. In our example the red robot has the set of items $\beta(\text{Red Robot}) = \{\text{cables}, \text{toys}\}$. It might be going to either one of those corridors,

© Springer Nature Switzerland AG 2020
U. Schmid et al. (Eds.): KI 2020, LNAI 12325, pp. 259–266, 2020.
https://doi.org/10.1007/978-3-030-58285-2_21

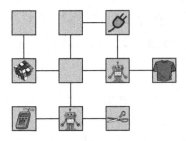

Fig. 1. A sample representation of the warehouse as a graph. The vertices are the corridors of the warehouse. The two agents are represented as red and blue robots (Color figure online).

but in reality there is always only one goal an agent wants to reach, which we will call $\alpha^*(i) \in \beta(i)$, the *"true goal"*. On the other hand, we will call goals that will not be pursued by i : *"false goals"*. Furthermore, let $B \subseteq V$ be the set of all goals of all agents. How solutions to this problem can be found when no direct communication between the agents is allowed has been already investigated. A generalization of the well known multi-agent path finding problem, where multiple agents are located on the same problem instance trying to reach their destinations, has been investigated [9]. Instead of having a stream of tasks in a life-long environment [7], this analysis focuses on a one-shot framework, i.e., where goals do not change over time. The analysis is based on the general problem of *Distributed MAPF*, where each agent plans to solve the instance itself, planning also actions of the other agents, instead of having a central entity to solve the instance. *Optimally eager agents* [2], i.e., agents that always plan to act first whenever this results in a shortest execution path, can solve any solvable *MAPF* instance, perhaps replanning when other agents do something unanticipated. *Conservative eager agents*, i.e., agents that always plan to act first and only replan their actions from the already executed execution forward, can solve any *MAPF* instance given the instance is solvable. In the first case, the agents have to solve NP-complete problems, in the second case, they may have to remember exponentially many moves. A further generailzation of this framework is *MAPF with Destination Uncertainty* (MAPF/DU), where one drops the assumption that the goal configuration is common knowledge between the agents. Instead of having only one goal, each agent is assigned a set of goals it might reach, but only one of those goals is the agent's true destination. By having this kind of uncertainty, the execution plans are no longer linear sequences, but they have to be branching plans. Agents branch on their real goals and make perspective shifts in order to generate plans for the other agents. A crucial concpet for understanding the structure of these branching plans are *stepping stones*, which are states where an agent can move towards its goal without other agents having to move, not blocking the further success of the plan. Utilizing these stepping stones, pne can show that when agents are *conservative and optimally eager*, then they will solve every instance, given it is solvable, with an execution length polynomially bounded. The computational complexity of generating such plans is PSPACE-complete problem, however. The problem we consider differs from the previous scenario. It is round based, i.e., in each round any agent can perform one or none action at all. This variant allows the agents to interpret each others actions and to adapt to it respectively, something which is has not been utilized in the MAPF/DU approach (but cf. [8]).

2   Outline of a Heuristic Agent

Let us stick to the warehouse example. How can an agent in the warehouse know where the other agents goal is? Let us take a look at how a human would approach this situation: Since the only clues we are given is the position and the movement of the other agents, we can use a form of *Theory of Mind* reasoning to interpret the other agents actions. Theory of Mind has been introduced by a heuristic agent's ability to represent and reason about another agent's state of mind [10], being now in the research focus of AI and Cognitive Science [1,11]. We will now outline, based on the introduced problem instance, rational and plausible mechanisms that a typical cognitive reasoning agent, i.e., an agent that has a form of symbolic representation and reasons about it, may employ.

2.1   Movement and Waiting

In each round the agent moves either towards its goal, or towards an escape (see Subsect. 2.2) by using Dijkstras-Algorithm [3] to calculate the path. An agent can either move one vertex per round or it does not move at all. Introducing the possibility of waiting is a crucial action of this agent. One can surely imagine a lot of scenarios where waiting for a robot in the warehouse to pass, before using the corridor it came from, can be beneficial for the success of the plan. But what can we interpret about the direction they came from? Since the agents are moving (or not moving) across G, we can use this information and make estimates about the agents true goal. For example: If the red robot is moving away from the toys

(a) An instance at some time t (b) The instance with a $t' > t$

Fig. 2. A possible instance from the perspective of the **red agent** (the red circle). Notice that the possible goal (the white rhombus at the top left vertex) of the **blue agent** (blue rhombus) in 2a disappears in 2b, because the **red agent** ignored the goal as a possible destination (Color figure online).

section in the warehouse, we can assume that toys might not be the item the robot is going to retrieve for the order. We can therefore *"ignore"* toys from its list of possible items until it begins to move back to them. An agent a_i ignores the goal k of another agent a_j, if a_j moved away from this specific goal (see Fig. 2) or a_i is interpreting a_j as waiting. What might be a suitable place for the agent to wait (a so called *"Escape"*), will be discussed in the next section.

2.2   Escaping

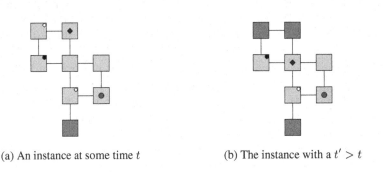

(a) An instance at some time t (b) The instance with a $t' > t$

Fig. 3. A possible instance from the perspective of the **red agent** (the red circle). The vertices suitable for an escape are marked in green. Notice that this set does change over time, depending on the movement of an agent and its perspective. (Color figure online)

Just waiting alone might not be enough, since standing in the way of another robot and doing nothing seems not to be very productive. In order for the waiting to be useful, a suitable place needs to be found. An agent a_i knows the possible goals of all agents and it can therefore calculate $\pi_{a_j,k}(t) = (v_0, v_1, ..., k)$, where $k \in \beta(a_j)$ is the k-th goal of agent a_j. $\pi_{a_j,k}(t)$ is called a *"goal path"*. An escape is a vertex which is not a part of any *goal path* of any agent that is not waiting. In our example a suitable escape (the green vertices in Fig. 3) might be a corridor which is not assigned to any robot at the moment. Since agents know the goals of each other, it is somewhat possible for them to predict their movement across the graph. In order to avoid agents blocking each other, an early escape mechanism is needed. By looking at an agent's movement, some goals can be ignored. If two paths of different agents collide, which means that there is least one vertex on both paths, one of them will try to escape the colliding path beforehand. An agent a_i is checking whether or not there are conflicting paths between it and another agent a_j that is not being ignored by a_i. If no conflict between the paths of the agents is found, they will pursue their *true goal path* without having to move out of the way. If there is at least one conflicting path between two agents, however, they will check if one of them is closer to an escape. The one who is closest will then proceed to move to said escape. If both agents have the same distance to the nearest escape, the agent earlier in the move order will move to its escape. Note that vertices suitable for an escape will change over time depending on the waiting or movements of the agents. This can lead to agents blocking a real goal path. In reality, two agents might be next to each other, blocking each others paths, waiting for something to happen. When this occurs, the first agent to notice the other agent waiting will move to a neighboring vertex. We will call this an *immediate escape*. If an agent manages to reach its *true goal* it will immediately stop and present a success statement. This is the only form of direct communication that is allowed between the agents, otherwise it would be impossible to determine whether an agent is waiting on a *false goal* or if it has already reached its goal.

2.3   A Runtime Estimation

The agent will either pursue its goal path, escape immediately, or it will do a planned escape. Since the latter one is the most complex in terms of time, we will estimate its time complexity. The agent checks for every agent $a_i \in A$ if there is a conflict. Because $B \subseteq V$ there can be at most $|V|$ goals and therefore at most $|V|$ paths to the goals. Since the paths are calculated using the *Dijkstra-Algorithm* [3], they will not contain any cycles and are therefore at most $|V - 1|$ long. All vertices are then compared to the own goal path which, as mentioned before, is also at most $|V|$ long. Hence checking for a conflict has a time complexity of $\mathcal{O}(|V|^3)$. The agent then searches the graph for a suitable escape. It iterates over all vertices and all paths and compares them to each other, resulting in it being in $\mathcal{O}(|V|^3)$. It then iterates through the previously calculated escapes and determines which one is the closest (has the shortest path) to an escape for the agents. This is again in $\mathcal{O}(|V|^3)$. So every round and every agent has to solve a problem in $\mathcal{O}(|A| * |V|^3)$.

3   Evaluation

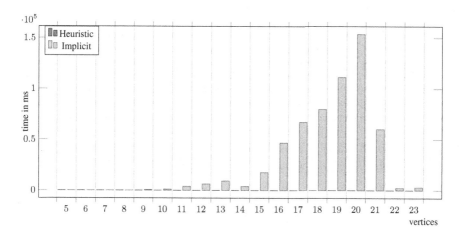

Fig. 4. Average solution time required by the heuristic agent and implicit planner (Color figure online).

Table 1. Comparison between the heuristic agent and the implicitly coordinated planner.

	2 Agents		3 Agents		4 Agents		5 Agents	
	Heu.	Impl.	Heu.	Impl.	Heu.	Impl.	Heu.	Impl.
Average solution rate of the resp. models	95.6%	99.2%	91.6%	99.5%	89.7%	N/A	81.3%	N/A
Proportion of solved to total no. of models	$\frac{19242}{20125}$	$\frac{19958}{20125}$	$\frac{13837}{15103}$	$\frac{14348}{15103}$	$\frac{7179}{8000}$	N/A	$\frac{6505}{8000}$	N/A
Average time	2.0 ms	48.4 ms	6.8 ms	49841.3 ms	19.7 ms	N/A	37.3 ms	N/A
Median time	1 ms	25 ms	5 ms	860 ms	15 ms	N/A	29 ms	N/A

In this section, we present a comparison of the heuristic agent with the implicitly coordinated planner [9]. We generated[1] test instances by creating an $n \times n$, $n \in \{3, 4, 5\}$ grid-graph and randomly assigning $m \in \{2, 3\}$ agents with $k \in \{2, 3\}$ and goals on the grid. Afterwards some vertices were deleted from the grid. For every combination of those values, instances were created (including duplicates), resulting in $N = 35,228$ instances including unsolvable instances. Both approaches were tested on the same problem instances, measuring the time the agents needed to reach their respective goals and their total solution rate (see Table 1). Since the runtime of the implicitly coordinated planner was by an order of magnitude slower, only the heuristic agent was able to solve additional 16000 instances with $m \in \{4, 5\}$ agents, $n \in \{4, 5\}$ grid size, and $k \in \{2, 3\}$ goals. Figure 4 shows the average amount of time needed for solvable instances only. Noticeable is the large average solution time at about 13 and 20 vertices. With a higher number of agents, both approaches require a higher and higher time for solving the instances. Table 1 demonstrates that there is an inverse correlation between the solution rate and the number of agents.

4   Conclusion

Given the right instances, the heuristic agent we developed is able to solve instances by an order of magnitude faster than the implicitly coordinated approach. But as any heuristic based approach, there are some instances that cannot be solved by our approach. Our approach uses just a few heuristics and is in line with other efficient heuristic approaches (e.g., [4]) that were able, for decision-making, to outperform complex algorithms. The implicitly coordinated planner, in contrast to our presented approach, was not designed to work in a round-based framework, it did not take into account past observations (but cf. [8]), and its main intention was to provide a method that is provably complete and correct.

---

[1] The implementation and a more in-depth explanation of the benchmark set and generated data can be found at: https://github.com/Grintel/Cognitive-MAPFDU.

Nevertheless, it is an interesting comparison since it is the only MAPF planner around that deals with goal uncertatinty. We are looking forward to apply similar heuristics in an asynchronous setting as this planner does. Refining the success conditions of the agents and a more sophisticated searching of escapes may increase the performance more. Additionally, by extending the implicitly coordinating planner with the new heuristic approach a hybrid system could be built, leading to a significant speed-up.

Acknowledgements. This paper was supported by DFG grants RA 1934/9-1, RA 1934/4-1, and RA 1934/3-1.

References

1. Baker, C., Tenenbaum, J.: Modeling human plan recognition using Bayesian theory of mind. In: Sukthankar, G., Geib, C., Bui, H.H., Pynadath, D.V., Goldman, R.P. (eds.) Plan, Activity, and Intent Recognition: Theory and Practice, vol. 7, pp. 177–204. Elsevier (2014). https://doi.org/10.1016/B978-0-12-398532-3.00007-5
2. Bolander, T., Engesser, T., Mattmüller, R., Nebel, B.: Better eager than lazy? How agent types impact the successfulness of implicit coordination. In: Principles of Knowledge Representation and Reasoning: Proceedings of the Sixteenth International Conference (KR-2018), pp. 445–453 (2018). https://aaai.org/ocs/index.php/KR/KR18/paper/view/18070
3. Dijkstra, E.W.: A note on two problems in connexion with graphs. Numerische Mathematik **1**(1), 269–271 (1959). https://doi.org/10.1007/BF01386390
4. Gigerenzer, G., Todd, P.M.: Simple Heuristics that Make us Smart. Oxford University Press, Oxford (1999)
5. Hatzack, W., Nebel, B.: Solving the operational traffic control problem. In: Cesta, A. (ed.) Proceedings of the 6th European Conference on Planning (ECP-01), pp. 37–48. AAAI Press (2013). https://www.aaai.org/ocs/index.php/ECP/ECP01/paper/view/7284
6. Hönig, W., et al.: Multi-agent path finding with kinematic constraints. In: Proceedings of the Twenty-Sixth International Conference on Automated Planning and Scheduling (ICAPS-2016), pp. 477–485 (2016). http://www.aaai.org/ocs/index.php/ICAPS/ICAPS16/paper/view/13183
7. Ma, H., Li, J., Kumar, T.S., Koenig, S.: Lifelong multi-agent path finding for online pickup and delivery tasks. In: Proceedings of the 16th Conference on Autonomous Agents and MultiAgent Systems (AAMAS-2017), pp. 837–845 (2017). http://dl.acm.org/citation.cfm?id=3091243
8. Nebel, B.: Some thoughts on forward induction in multi-agent-path finding under destination uncertainty. In: Description Logic, Theory Combination, and All That - Essays Dedicated to Franz Baader on the Occasion of His 60th Birthday, pp. 431–440. Springer, Heidelberg (2019). https://doi.org/10.1007/978-3-030-22102-7_20
9. Nebel, B., Bolander, T., Engesser, T., Mattmüller, R.: Implicitly coordinated multi-agent path finding under destination uncertainty: success guarantees and computational complexity. J. Artif. Intell. Res. **64**, 497–527 (2019). https://doi.org/10.1613/jair.1.11376
10. Premack, D., Woodruff, G.: Does the chimpanzee have a theory of mind? Behav. Brain Sci. **1**(4), 515–526 (1978). https://doi.org/10.1017/S0140525X00076512

11. Rabinowitz, N.C., Perbet, F., Song, H.F., Zhang, C., Eslami, S.M.A., Botvinick, M.: Machine theory of mind. In: Proceedings of the 35th International Conference on Machine Learning (ICML-2018). pp. 4215–4224 (2018). http://proceedings.mlr.press/v80/rabinowitz18a.html
12. Wurman, P.R., D'Andrea, R., Mountz, M.: Coordinating hundreds of cooperative, autonomous vehicles in warehouses. AI Magazine **29**(1), 9–20 (2008). http://www.aaai.org/ojs/index.php/aimagazine/article/view/2082

Earnings Prediction with Deep Leaning

Lars Elend[1]([☒])[ID], Sebastian A. Tideman[2][ID], Kerstin Lopatta[2][ID], and Oliver Kramer[1][ID]

[1] Computational Intelligence Group, Department of Computer Science, Carl von Ossietzky University of Oldenburg, 26111 Oldenburg, Germany
{lars.elend,oliver.kramer}@uni-oldenburg.de
[2] Chair of Accounting, Auditing and Sustainability, University of Hamburg, 20146 Hamburg, Germany
{sebastian.tideman,kerstin.lopatta}@uni-hamburg.de

Abstract. In the financial sector, a reliable forecast the future financial performance of a company is of great importance for investors' investment decisions. In this paper we compare long-term short-term memory (LSTM) networks to temporal convolution network (TCNs) in the prediction of future earnings per share (EPS). The experimental analysis is based on quarterly financial reporting data and daily stock market returns. For a broad sample of US firms, we find that both LSTMs outperform the naive persistent model with up to 30.0% more accurate predictions, while TCNs achieve and an improvement of 30.8%. Both types of networks are at least as accurate as analysts and exceed them by up to 12.2% (LSTM) and 13.2% (TCN).

Keywords: Finance · Earnings prediction · EPS forecasts · Long short term memory · Temporal convolutional network.

1 Introduction

Investors rely first and foremost on earnings predictions when making investment decisions, e.g., buy, hold, or sell a firm's shares. Besides using own projections, they heavily rely on earnings forecasts provided by financial analysts. Consequently, forecasting earnings is one of the main tasks of financial analysts working at major financial institutions, e.g., broker firms. Analysts invest significant resources to provide accurate forecasts. However, forecasting is a difficult undertaking as numerous factors have an influence on the prediction performance. In this paper, we predict publicly listed US firms' quarterly earnings per share with state-of-the-art techniques from the field of deep neural networks based on companies' time series data.

We structure the remainder of this paper as follows. In Sect. 2, we present related work on prediction of financial data. The base time series model and quality measures are introduced in Sect. 3. We describe the data preprocessing process in Sect. 4. Objective of our work is to compare LSTM networks with TCNs, which will be introduced in Sect. 5. Section 6 presents the experimental analysis, and Sect. 7 draws conclusions.

© Springer Nature Switzerland AG 2020
U. Schmid et al. (Eds.): KI 2020, LNAI 12325, pp. 267–274, 2020.
https://doi.org/10.1007/978-3-030-58285-2_22

2   Related Work

Analyst forecasts are often used to benchmark the accuracy of earnings predictions obtained from models. However, due to recent regulation on financial analysts working conditions, e.g., limiting the private access to management, a drop in analyst coverage has been observed [1]. Automated earnings prediction models supported by artificial intelligence may fill this gap. While there is already significant work on predictions of stock market price and returns (which is an aggregate of several factors such as firm-, industry-, country-level variables) using neural networks [7], empirical evidence is missing whether artificial intelligence can provide meaningful earnings forecasts as a direct measure of firm success.

Some evidence exists that fraud, e.g., illegal manipulation of earnings, can be predicted using machine learning [4]. In their study, Bao *et al.* (2020) find that ensemble learning with raw accounting numbers has predictive power for future fraud cases. Their approach outperforms logistic regression models based on financial ratios commonly used by prior research [6] as well as a support-vector-machine model [5], where a financial kernel maps raw accounting numbers into a set of financial ratios. Yet, the prediction of restatements is relatively less challenging as it is a binary decision tree (future restatement vs. no future restatement). To the contrary, predicting future earnings is more challenging as all discrete values are theoretically possible and information from multiple sources, e.g., financial statements, stock market data, have to be considered.

To our knowledge, no study has yet predicted future earnings using artificial intelligence. Closest to this study is the work of Ball and Ghysels (2018) [3]. They use a mixed data sampling regression method (but no neural networks) to predict future earnings and find that their predictions beat analysts' predictions in certain cases, e.g., when the firm size is smaller and analysts' forecast dispersion is high.

3   Time Series Model

The goal in data-driven prediction based on time series is to find a function ϕ that yields a future value y based on the data of the past β time steps $x = (q_{t-\beta+1}, \ldots, q_t)$ (Fig. 1). In this paper, the time-span between two time steps is 3 months. A non-perfect predictor $\hat{\phi}(x) = \hat{y}$ can be evaluated using the mean squared error (MSE) to the real value y.

To evaluate our model we compare it with the persistent model and the analysts forecast. The persistence model is a simple baseline that uses the current value as a prediction for the next time step. For each model the MSE is calculated. Therefore, larger deviations are more punished than smaller ones.

Since the difficulty of forecasting the given data varies greatly over time and between different companies, the error value in itself is not meaningful. Therefore

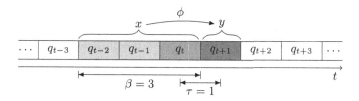

Fig. 1. Illustration of time series model for prediction of earnings of a company with quarterly reports q_t at time step t. We seek a mapping ϕ from pattern x of earning data of the past to label y of the predicted earning for the future $t = t + \tau$. The window size β describes the time span of considered past earnings.

we use a relative comparison between the different models, namely the skill score (SS) [12]:

$$\text{SS}_{\text{MSE}} = 1 - \frac{\text{MSE}(m)}{\text{MSE}(\text{base})}, \qquad (1)$$

where $\text{MSE}(m)$ is MSE of the own model m (LSTM, TCN) and MSE(base) is the MSE of the comparison model: persistent model[1] pa or analyst forecast a. The model under consideration is better (worse) than the reference model if the skill score is greater (less) than 0 [12].

4   Data Preprocessing

As input data, we use accounting data (e.g., total assets and cost of goods sold) from COMPUTSTAT QUARTERLY as well as daily stock market price and return data from CRSP (DAILY SHARES) as these are the most commonly used databases in accounting and finance research. At first both datasets COMPUTSTAT QUARTERLY and DAILY SHARES are reduced to the most important parameters[2] per time-step and firm. Different value ranges of individual parameters x are "normalized" and scaled using the total assets `atq`:

$$x' = \frac{x}{\max\{1, \texttt{atq}\}} \qquad (2)$$

and studentized:

$$z'_i = \frac{z_i - \bar{z}}{\sqrt{\frac{1}{n}\sum_i (z_i - \bar{z})^2}}, \qquad (3)$$

where $\bar{z}$ is the mean of z_i. Outliers of `eps` which are partially erroneous are removed by using the first (last) percentile as minimum (maximum). We create

---

[1] For the comparisons only data points are used for which analyst forecasts exist.

[2] The following parameters of the data records are used. The parameters in brackets are only used for the assignment and selection of the samples. COMPUTSTAT QUARTERLY: (`cusip`, `fpedats`, `ffi5`, `ffi10`, `ffi12`, `ffi48`, `financialfirm`, `EPS_Mean_Analyst`), `rdq`, `epsfiq`, `atq`, `revtq`, `nopiq`, `xoprq`, `apq`, `gdwlq`, `rectq`, `xrdq`, `cogsq`, `rcpq`, `ceqq`, `niq`, `oiadpq`, `oibdpq`, `dpq`, `ppentq`, `piq`, `txtq`, `gdwlq`, `xrdq`, `rcpq`
DAILY SHARES: (`cusip`, `date`), `ret`, `prc`, `vol`, `shrout`, `vwretd`.

company samples of a given window size (number of quarters). Smaller data gaps a filled using linear interpolation, while samples with larger gaps are rejected. The quarterly data are merged with the corresponding daily stock data DAILY SHARES, which are also being studentized.

5   Deep Neural Networks

An LSTM network [9] belongs to the family of recurrent neural networks. It employs backward connections, which allow saving information in time. LSTM cells internally consists of three gates: forget, input, and output gates, see Fig. 2. An LSTM cell employs internal states h and s propagated through time. Yellow boxes represent ANN layers, orange circles represent element wise operations. Input x_t is concatenated with h_{t-1} and fed to the forget, input, and output gates. The forget gate determines which information should be forgotten, the input gate specifies to which amount the new input data is taken into account, and the output gate state specifies the information to output based on the internal state. With these functional components, an LSTM is well suited for time series data. LSTM networks have successfully been applied to numerous domains, e.g., for wind power prediction [13] and for speech recognition [8].

A TCN [2] is a special kind of convolutional neural network [10]. While convolutional neural networks are primarily used for classification tasks in image, text or speech, TCNs can be applied to time series data. TCNs extend their counterparts by causal convolutions and dilated convolutions. The TCN has a one-dimensional time series input. Causal convolutions only use the current and past information for each filter. The dilation defines the distance between the used input data elements of each filter. An example for both concepts is visualized in Fig. 3 with a dilated causal convolution with kernel size $k = 2$ and dilations 1, 2, 4. In our experiments we increase d exponentially, i.e. $d_i = 2^i$ and select an appropriate number of layers to cover the given time span. TCNs also find numerous applications, e.g., in satellite image time series classification [11].

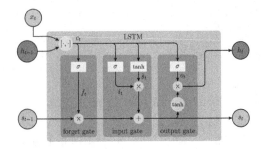

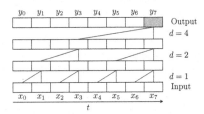

Fig. 2. Illustration of LSTM cell   **Fig. 3.** Dilated causal convolution

6 Experimental Analysis

For our experiments we employed two datasets: **A** for the choice of a proper architecture and parameters and **B** for the final experiment with the selected best architecture. The training set of A includes all samples whose predicted EPS values lie in the period 2012 to end of 2016. The last 10% of the training set is used for validation only. The test set is in the following half year after the training, so it is independent and has no unfair knowledge. For data set B, the period is extended by half a year, so that its test data have not been seen before.

Each model is trained with a batch size 1024 for 1000 epochs and a dropout rate of 0.3 for each intermediate layer and the recurrent edges of an LSTM layer. Dense layers apply tanh as activation function, except for the last layer using a linear one. The window size of Computstat Quarterly and Daily Shares is set to 20, i.e., the last 20 quarters of earning reports and the last 20 daily stock market returns form a pattern. The model is optimized using Adam and MSE as loss. Each epoch's best model w.r.t. validation error is used for testing. Each experiment is repeated five times. Statistics include mean and standard deviation.

Furthermore, we have experimentally selected the best architectures as representatives for LSTM and TCN (Fig. 4). Computstat Quarterly and Daily Shares are used as input (green). The dimensions are given in parentheses. Since the shares data is put into a dense layer (D), the time input 20 × 22 is flattened to 220. After a few layers the two inputs are joined by a merge layer. For the TCN 32 filters and a kernel size of 3 were used. The last dense layer with only one neuron outputs the predicted EPS value.

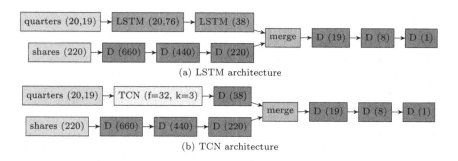

(a) LSTM architecture

(b) TCN architecture

Fig. 4. Visualization of selected LSTM and TCN architectures (Color figure online).

As financial and non-financial companies show a significantly different behavior in many regards, we analyze the prediction in independent experiments. Table 1 compares the prediction performance with three different sets of companies: all companies (all), no financial companies (nofin), only financial companies (onlyfin). The data sets without financial firms usually give the best results. The worst results are achieved when only financial companies are taken into account.

Table 1. Selected architectures and parameters for three groups of companies: financial (onlyfin), non-financial (nofin), and all.

		SS_{MSE}	
type	comp	(m, pa)	(m, a)
LSTM	all	0.466±0.030	0.119±0.050
	nofin	**0.543**±0.013	**0.146**±0.024
	onlyfin	0.378±0.025	0.100±0.036
TCN	all	0.355±0.058	-0.065±0.096
	nofin	**0.547**±0.015	**0.154**±0.028
	onlyfin	-0.001±0.155	-0.450±0.225

We test the best model an independent dataset B. Table 2 shows the results of the bests configurations of Table 1. The results for the non-financial companies are similar to the results observed before with an MSE that is 12–13% better than the analysts' predictions. The predictions for all companies are slightly better, but worse than on dataset A.

Table 2. Results on dataset B of optimal architectures and parameters grouped by financial sector affiliation.

		SS_{MSE}	
type	comp	(m, pa)	(m, a)
LSTM	nofin	**0.300**±0.012	**0.122**±0.015
TCN	nofin	**0.308**±0.014	**0.132**±0.018

These results suggest that LSTM networks and TCNs are indeed able to provide meaningful earnings predictions. Even after acknowledging for the variation across the repetitions (e.g., standard errors based on three repetitions), the range of significance (e.g., mean estimate plus/minus standard error) is well above zero in all cases. This is remarkable, as we only used widely available public data on companies such as balance sheet information and stock market price and return data. Hence, we can conclude that our networks outperform both the persistent model and the mean forecast of financial analysts based on a subsample of non-financial firms (e.g., manufacturing firms).

7   Conclusion

Our experimental analysis has shown that LSTM networks and TCNs are powerful models in the application of earnings prediction. We base our prediction models on quarterly accounting data such as cost of goods sold and total assets as well as stock market price and return data. Using these widely available time series data, the persistent model was significantly outperformed. The LSTMs performed slightly better in our analysis using the same set of variables. In the future, we will extend the experimental analysis to further data sets and integrate further domain knowledge to improve the financial predictions. Our findings are relevant to both broker firms and investors. Broker firms may want to consider developing LSTM networks and TCN to supplement their analysts' forecast. Investors could build up their own forecast models using artificial intelligence, particularly when there are no forecasts available from financial analysts, which became a more urgent issue recently due to the drop in analyst coverage induced by regulation.

References

1. Anantharaman, D., Zhang, Y.: Cover me: managers' responses to changes in analyst coverage in the post-regulation FD period. Account. Rev. **86**(6), 1851–1885 (2011). https://doi.org/10.2308/accr-10126
2. Bai, S., Kolter, J.Z., Koltun, V.: An Empirical Evaluation of Generic Convolutional and Recurrent Networks for Sequence Modeling. CoRR abs/1803.01271 (2018)
3. Ball, R.T., Ghysels, E.: Automated earnings forecasts: beat analysts or combine and conquer? Manage. Sci. **64**(10), 4936–4952 (2017). https://doi.org/10.1287/mnsc.2017.2864
4. Bao, Y., Ke, B., Li, B., Yu, Y.J., Zhang, J.: Detecting accounting fraud in publicly traded U.S. firms using a machine learning approach. J. Account. Res. **58**(1), 199–235 (2020). https://doi.org/10.1111/1475-679X.12292
5. Cecchini, M., Aytug, H., Koehler, G.J., Pathak, P.: Detecting management fraud in public companies. Manage. Sci. **56**(7), 1146–1160 (2010). https://doi.org/10.1287/mnsc.1100.1174
6. Dechow, P.M., Ge, W., Larson, C.R., Sloan, R.G.: Predicting material accounting misstatements. Contemporary Account. Res. **28**(1), 17–82 (2011). https://doi.org/10.1111/j.1911-3846.2010.01041.x
7. dos Santos Pinheiro, L., Dras, M.: Stock market prediction with deep learning: a character-based neural language model for event-based trading. Proc. Australasian Lang. Technol. Assoc. Workshop **2017**, 6–15 (2017)
8. Graves, A., Jaitly, N.: Towards end-to-end speech recognition with recurrent neural networks. In: Proceedings of the 31st International Conference on International Conference on Machine Learning, vol. 32. pp. II-1764-II-1772. ICML 2014, JMLR.org, Beijing, China (2014)
9. Hochreiter, S., Schmidhuber, J.: Long short-term memory. Neural Comput. **9**(8), 1735–1780 (1997). https://doi.org/10.1162/neco.1997.9.8.1735
10. LeCun, Y., et al.: Backpropagation applied to handwritten zip code recognition. Neural Comput. **1**(4), 541–551 (1989). https://doi.org/10.1162/neco.1989.1.4.541
11. Pelletier, C., Webb, G.I., Petitjean, F.: Temporal convolutional neural network for the classification of satellite image time series. Remote Sens. **11**(5), 523 (2019). https://doi.org/10.3390/rs11050523

12. Roebber, P.J.: The regime dependence of degree day forecast technique, skill, and value. Weather Forecast. **13**(3), 783–794 (1998). https://doi.org/10.1175/1520-0434(1998)013⟨0783:TRDODD⟩2.0.CO;2
13. Woon, W.L., Oehmcke, S., Kramer, O.: Spatio-temporal wind power prediction using recurrent neural networks. In: Liu, D., Xie, S., Li, Y., Zhao, D., El-Alfy, E.S.M. (eds.) Neural Information Processing, pp. 556–563. Lecture Notes in Computer Science, Springer, Cham (2017). https://doi.org/10.1007/978-3-319-70139-4_56

Integrating Keywords into BERT4Rec for Sequential Recommendation

Elisabeth Fischer$^{(\boxtimes)}$, Daniel Zoller, Alexander Dallmann, and Andreas Hotho

Data Science Chair, Julius-Maximilians University Würzburg, Würzburg, Germany
{elisabeth.fischer,zoller,dallmann,hotho}@informatik.uni-wuerzburg.de

Abstract. A crucial part of recommender systems is to model the user's preference based on her previous interactions. Different neural networks (e.g., Recurrent Neural Networks), that predict the next item solely based on the sequence of interactions have been successfully applied to sequential recommendation. Recently, BERT4Rec has been proposed, which adapts the BERT architecture based on the Transformer model and training methods used in the Neural Language Modeling community to this task. However, BERT4Rec still only relies on item identifiers to model the user preference, ignoring other sources of information. Therefore, as a first step to include additional information, we propose KeBERT4Rec, a modification of BERT4Rec, which utilizes keyword descriptions of items. We compare two variants for adding keywords to the model on two datasets, a Movielens dataset and a dataset of an online fashion store. First results show that both versions of our model improves the sequential recommending task compared to BERT4Rec.

Keywords: Sequential recommendation · Bidirectional Transformer · Item recommendation

1 Introduction

The knowledge of a user's preferences is of great interest for a recommender system. With explicit information about the user's interest often missing, the only clue is the history of previous interactions. To model the preference based on a sequence of historic interactions a number of neural network architectures have been developed, for example, Recurrent Neural Networks (RNNs) [5] or Convolutional Neural Networks (CNNs) [8]. Most of the methods so far model the sequence unidirectional, only taking the previous interactions into account at each step. The recently introduced BERT4Rec method [7] overcomes this limitation by using a bidirectional Transformer [2], allowing it to take context from both sides into account. To build a sequential representation the model relies only on the item identifiers. Other information, like keywords describing items, although available, is not used, but could improve the recommendation of next items in the sequence. For example, if a user has viewed the movie "The Lion King", the information that the item is an "animation", a "musical" and

© Springer Nature Switzerland AG 2020
U. Schmid et al. (Eds.): KI 2020, LNAI 12325, pp. 275–282, 2020.
https://doi.org/10.1007/978-3-030-58285-2_23

(not only) for "children", would be helpful to recommend the next item, because it is more likely that she might be interested in "The Jungle Book" than in "IT". Similar, the information that someone clicked on a page showing some "running shoe", is quite useful for recommending other items of interest.

Previous work has shown that including additional information of items in models like RNNs or CNNs can improve the performance of the recommendation model (e.g., [4,10]). Therefore, as a first step to include additional information into the new state-of-the-art model BERT4Rec, we introduce KeBERT4Rec, a modification, that allows to add keywords describing items (e.g., genres of a movie). To that end, we modify the representation of the sequence items encoded by the Transformer. We evaluate our approach on a Movielens dataset, and a new dataset created from real-world clickstreams of a big online fashion store. The two main contributions of this paper are: 1) We propose two different approaches to include keyword descriptions into the sequential recommendation model BERT4Rec. 2) We compare the two options on two real-world datasets. First results on both datasets show, that our approach of integrating keywords improves the sequential recommendation task.

The remainder of this paper is structured as follows: In Sect. 2 we define the task, followed by a description of our approach in Sect. 3. After reviewing related work in Sect. 4, we describe our datasets, and evaluation setup, and report our results in Sect. 5. Finally, we conclude the paper in Sect. 6.

2   Problem Setting

In this paper we tackle the problem of recommending an item for a user based on her previous sequence of interactions (i.e., previous rated movies or previous clicks in an online shop). Following [2], we denote the set of users with $\mathcal{U} = \{u_1, u_2, \ldots, u_{|\mathcal{U}|}\}$, the set of items with $\mathcal{V} = \{v_1, v_2, \ldots, v_{|\mathcal{V}|}\}$ and the list of interactions of user $u \in \mathcal{U}$ with $S_u = \{v_1^u, v_2^u \ldots, v_{n_u}^u\}$, where user u has interacted with item $v_t^u \in \mathcal{V}$ at the relative time step t. Additionally, we have for every item $v \in \mathcal{V}$ a set of keywords $K_v = \{k_1, k_2, \ldots, k_{|K_v|}\}$ describing each item v. We denote with $\mathcal{K}$ the set of all possible keywords. The recommendation task is now to predict, given the history $\mathcal{S}_u$ with the additional meta information $K_{v_t^u}$ for every $v_t^u \in \mathcal{S}_u$, the next item $v_{n_u+1}^u$ in the sequence of the user's interaction.

3   KeBERT4Rec

Our model builds upon the sequential recommendation model BERT4Rec [7], that transfers the idea of the deep bidirectional self-attention model BERT [2], which is used for language modeling, to the sequential recommendation task. The modified model is shown in Fig. 1, which consists of three different layers, like BERT4Rec: (i) an *embedding layer*, that learns a representation of the inputs (i.e., identifier and keywords), and is fed to (ii) a *Transformer layer*, that consists of L Transformer blocks (see [11] for more details) and (iii) a *projection layer*, that projects the learned hidden representation by the previous layer to the item

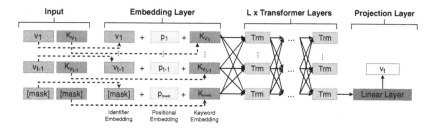

Fig. 1. Model architecture of KeBERT4Rec. In contrast to BERT4Rec, we add an embedding for the keywords of the items and replace the projection layer with a linear layer.

space for prediction using a softmax layer. The Cloze task [9] is used for training, where the model has to predict randomly masked items in the interaction sequence. For evaluation the item to be predicted will be masked. To include keyword descriptions of items as an additional input, we make the following two modifications to the BERT4Rec model:

Embedding Layer: The embedding layer of BERT4Rec, which has a size of d, consists of two different embeddings: (i) an embedding $E_\mathcal{V} \in \mathbb{R}^{|\mathcal{V}| \times d}$ of the item identifier and (ii) an auxiliary embedding $E_P \in \mathbb{R}^{N \times d}$ for the position of the items in the sequence, to encode the position for the Transformer blocks, where N is the configurable maximum input sequence length. For every sequence step t, the item embedding $e_t = v_t E_\mathcal{V}$ of item v_t and the positional embedding $p_t = t E_P$, the sum $h_t^0 = e_t + p_t$ is used as input for the Transformer layer. Following this idea, we add an additional embedding k_t of the keywords K_{v_t} of item v_t as summand: $h_t^0 = e_t + p_t + k_t$. We propose two different methods to embed multiple keywords into k_t: (i) KE_m merges all keywords of item v_t into a super keyword $K_{v_t}^{u *}$ and than embeds this using $E_{\mathcal{K}^*} \in \mathbb{R}^{|\mathcal{K}^*| \times d}$, where $\mathcal{K}^*$ is the set of all possible keyword combinations. (ii) KE_l encodes the categories as a multi-hot vector, which is scaled to the embedding size d using a linear layer. The keyword descriptions are masked accordingly while training and evaluation.

Projection Layer: Given the last hidden state of the L-th Transformer layer h_t^L of the masked item v_t at time step t, BERT4Rec uses a linear layer and the item embedding $E_\mathcal{V}$ for projection: $o = \sigma(h_t^L W) E_\mathcal{V}^\top$ (bias omitted for readability), where $W \in \mathbb{R}^{|\mathcal{V}| \times d}$ is the weight matrix of the linear layer and σ the GELU activation function [3]. To remove the coupling of the item embedding with the projection layer, we only use a linear layer with parameter matrix $\bar{W} \in \mathbb{R}^{d \times |\mathcal{V}|}$ for projection, $o = h_t^L \bar{W}$, which is also in line with the original BERT model [2].

4 Related Work

Different neural network architectures have been introduced to model the user's interactions for sequential recommendation. These architectures include

Table 1. Statistics of the two preprocessed datasets ML-20m and Fashion.

Dataset	$|\mathcal{U}|$	$|\mathcal{V}|$	$|\mathcal{K}|$	#Interactions	Avg.length	Density
ML-20m	138,493	26,744	20	20 m	144,4	0,54%
Fashion	47,158	63,706	301	1.2 m	24.4	0.02%

CNNs [8], RNNs [5], recurrent CNNs [12] and self-attention networks [6]. Recently, [7] introduced BERT4Rec, that adapts the BERT [2] model based on bidirectional Transformers [11], that are currently one of the state-of-the-art architectures for modeling sequences in Natural Language Processing, to the sequential recommendation task. Their method outperforms previous work on four datasets.

Also, modifications to these different neural networks have been proposed to include additional information. For example, [10] adapts CNNs to add textual descriptions of the items using 3D convolutions, or [4] extended the work of [5] by parallel encoding different features (e.g., title, identifier) using different RNNs to improve the recommendation task. A uni-directional Transformer model, that integrates sparse item features, has been presented in [1] to improve the Clickthrough-Rate of an e-commerce online shop.

Instead of using unidirectional models like RNNs, we extend the current state-of-the-art bidirectional model BERT4Rec for sequence recommendation by adding keyword descriptions available for each item into the model. In contrast to [1], we use a bidirectional instead of a unidirectional Transformer and evaluate two different approaches of incorporating item keyword information.

5 Experiments

In this section we introduce the datasets and the setup used in our experiments. At last, we present the results of our evaluation.

5.1 Experimental Setup

Datasets: We evaluate our model on two datasets. As an established dataset for sequential recommendation we use the ML-20m[1] dataset. ML-20m contains movie ratings from an online platform for movie recommendation. We utilize the list of genres of each movie as keyword descriptions. To create interaction sequences, we apply the same preprocess steps as [7]. Our second dataset is from a big online fashion store (Fashion), which consists of user interactions with store pages over the duration of two days. For this dataset we have keywords assigned to each page (e.g., "training pants"). We removed all technical pages (e.g., account pages) and keep only interactions with pages showing one or multiple items. Furthermore, we drop sequences with less than 5 and more than

---

[1] https://grouplens.org/datasets/movielens/20m/.

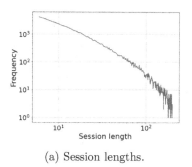

(a) Session lengths.

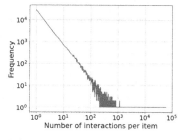

(b) Number of item interactions.

Fig. 2. Different frequency distributions for the Fashion dataset.

200 interactions. The resulting frequency distribution of the session length is displayed in Fig. 2a. We observe very few long sessions and an average session length of 24.4 clicks. In Fig. 2b we show the frequency distribution of clicks per items. With most items being rarely visited and only a few frequent items, we only observe a density (avg. number of unique items rated/clicked per user) of 0.02%. In contrast, ML-20m has more ratings per user, but fewer items, so the overall density is a bit higher. Also, a movie can only appear once in a sequence while a page can be visited repeatedly in the Fashion dataset. This happens often, as we treat all paginations of a page as one single page.

Statistics about the two preprocessed datasets are reported in Table 1.

Evaluation Setup: To show that KeBERT4Rec improves the recommendations with the inclusion of keyword descriptions, we compare it with BERT4Rec. For both datasets we used the hyper-parameters reported in [7], and for comparison of the approaches we used the same hyper-parameters for every model.[2] We apply the same evaluation protocol as [7] (i.e., *leave-one-out* evaluation; for more details see [7]) and we use the evaluation metrics *Hit Ratio (HR)* and *Normalized Discounted Cumulative Gain (NDCG)* at various cut-off values k. We apply the Student's t-test to test the statistical significance difference between the results.

Baselines: We also report two baselines in our evaluation: (i) Most-Popular (POP), which recommends items just based on their popularity in the interactions, and (ii) Last-Item (LI), which recommends the previous last item in the sequence. This baseline is only applicable for the Fashion dataset.

5.2 Results

Table 2 shows the recommendation results on our two evaluation datasets.[3] As expected, the performance of POP is far below all other methods on both

---

[2] We only adapted the batch size to our hardware restrictions and increased the number of epochs for training, because first experiments indicated that our models need more training time. Our code is available at https://dmir.org/KeBERT4Rec.

[3] We train all models on the ML-20m for 200 epochs. Our numbers for BERT4Rec are better than the ones reported in [7], as they train shorter.

Table 2. Results of the two baselines, BERT4Rec and our two versions of KeBERT4Rec on the two evaluation datasets. Both variants of KeBERT4Rec are significantly better than BERT4Rec ($\alpha \leq 0.01$). KE_l marked with * is significant better than KE_m with $\alpha \leq 0.01$ and $^+$ with $\alpha \leq 0.05$.

Dataset	Metric	POP	Bert4Rec	KE_m	KE_l
ML-20m	HR@1	0.022	0.528	0.536	**0.542***
	HR@5	0.081	0.871	0.876	**0.877**$^+$
	HR@10	0.138	0.943	**0.946**	0.945
	NDCG@5	0.051	0.715	0.722	**0.725***
	NDCG@10	0.070	0.739	0.745	**0.747***
Fashion (LI: 0.294)	HR@1	0.029	0.476	0.642	**0.648**$^+$
	HR@5	0.066	0.700	**0.824**	0.823
	HR@10	0.089	0.795	0.871	0.871
	NDCG@5	0.048	0.048	0.741	**0.743***
	NDCG@10	0.056	0.625	0.757	**0.759**$^+$

datasets. The other baseline LI recommends on average about 29% correct on the Fashion dataset. The high HR can be explained by pagination inside the shop. BERT4Rec outperforms the two baselines on Fashion and POP on ML-20m. Both versions of our model KeBERT4Rec achieve better results than BERT4Rec on both datasets, for example, increasing the HR@1 from 0.528 to 0.542 on ML-20m and from 0.476 to 0.648 on Fashion. This proves that including keyword descriptions of items with KeBERT4Rec can improve the sequential recommendation. Moreover, we observe a larger gain on all metrics on the Fashion dataset compared to the ML-20m dataset (on average about 22% vs. 1%). The keywords in the Fashion dataset might be more distinctive, as there are about six times more keywords relative to the number of items. When comparing the variants KE_m and KE_l, we observe, that KE_l outperforms KE_m significantly (only at a level of 0.05 for HR@5) on the ML-20m dataset, except for HR@10, where the difference is not significant. On the Fashion dataset, KE_l is only significantly better than KE_m regarding NDCG@5 (α-level 0.01) and NDCG@5 and HR@1 (α-level 0.05), but regarding the other metrics there is no significant difference.

6 Conclusion

In this paper we introduced KeBERT4Rec, an extension based on BERT4Rec, that includes additional keyword descriptions of items as a first step to integrate additional information about items into BERT4Rec. We evaluated two different approaches to include keywords into the model and compared these with the BERT4Rec model on two datasets. Our evaluation shows that both versions lead to significant improved results in next item recommendation, demonstrating that the inclusion of additional information about the items is a promising way of improvement. To better understand and improve the model further analysis of the results is needed, especially analyzing the keyword distributions. There are also more options we would like to explore for embedding keywords (e.g., a pre-trained BERT). Data about the items (e.g., title) could also be embedded, requiring an adaption of the proposed model.

References

1. Chen, Q., Zhao, H., Li, W., Huang, P., Ou, W.: Behavior sequence transformer for e-commerce recommendation in Alibaba. In: Proceedings of the 1st International Workshop on Deep Learning Practice for High-Dimensional Sparse Data. ACM, August 2019. https://doi.org/10.1145/3326937.3341261
2. Devlin, J., Chang, M.W., Lee, K., Toutanova, K.: BERT: Pre-training of deep bidirectional transformers for language understanding. In: Proceedings of the 2019 Conference of the North American Chapter of the Association for Computational Linguistics: Human Language Technologies, Volume 1 (Long and Short Papers), pp. 4171–4186. Association for Computational Linguistics, Minneapolis, Minnesota, June 2019. https://doi.org/10.18653/v1/N19-1423
3. Hendrycks, D., Gimpel, K.: Gaussian error linear units (GELUs) (2016). http://arxiv.org/abs/1606.08415, cite arxiv:1606.08415. Comment: Trimmed version of 2016 draft
4. Hidasi, B., Quadrana, M., Karatzoglou, A., Tikk, D.: Parallel recurrent neural network architectures for feature-rich session-based recommendations. In: Proceedings of the 10th ACM Conference on Recommender Systems. RecSys 2016, pp. 241–248. ACM, New York (2016). https://doi.org/10.1145/2959100.2959167
5. Hidasi, B., Karatzoglou, A., Baltrunas, L., Tikk, D.: Session-based recommendations with recurrent neural networks. In: Bengio, Y., LeCun, Y. (eds.) ICLR (Poster) (2016)
6. Kang, W.C., McAuley, J.: Self-attentive sequential recommendation. In: 2018 IEEE International Conference on Data Mining (ICDM), pp. 197–206. IEEE (2018)
7. Sun, F., Liu, J., Wu, J., Pei, C., Lin, X., Ou, W., Jiang, P.: BERT4Rec: sequential recommendation with bidirectional encoder representations from transformer. In: Proceedings of the 28th ACM International Conference on Information and Knowledge Management - CIKM 2019. ACM Press (2019). https://doi.org/10.1145/3357384.3357895
8. Tang, J., Wang, K.: Personalized top-n sequential recommendation via convolutional sequence embedding. In: Proceedings of the Eleventh ACM International Conference on Web Search and Data Mining - WSDM 2018. ACM Press (2018). https://doi.org/10.1145/3159652.3159656
9. Taylor, W.L.: "cloze procedure": a new tool for measuring readability. J. Mass Commun. Quart. **30**, 415–433 (1953)
10. Tuan, T.X., Phuong, T.M.: 3D convolutional networks for session-based recommendation with content features. In: Proceedings of the Eleventh ACM Conference on Recommender Systems, RecSys 2017, pp. 138–146. ACM, New York (2017). https://doi.org/10.1145/3109859.3109900

11. Vaswani, A., et al.: Attention is all you need. In: Advances in neural information processing systems, pp. 5998–6008 (2017)
12. Xu, C., Zhao, P., Liu, Y., Xu, J., S.Sheng, V.S., Cui, Z., Zhou, X., Xiong, H.: Recurrent convolutional neural network for sequential recommendation. In: The World Wide Web Conference - WWW 2019. ACM Press (2019). https://doi.org/10.1145/3308558.3313408

Modelling and Reasoning in Biomedical Applications with Qualitative Conditional Logic

Jonas Philipp Haldimann$^{(\boxtimes)}$ (ID), Anna Osiak, and Christoph Beierle

FernUniversität in Hagen, 58084 Hagen, Germany
{jonas.haldimann,christoph.beierle}@fernuni-hagen.de, anna.osiak@yahoo.de

Abstract. Different approaches have been investigated for the modelling of real-world situations, especially in the medical field, many of which are based on probabilities or other numerical parameters. In this paper, we show how real world situations from the biomedical domain can be conveniently modelled with qualitative conditionals by presenting three case studies: modelling the classification of certain mammals, modelling infections with the malaria pathogen, and predicting the outcome of chronic myeloid leukaemia. We demonstrate that the knowledge to be modelled can be expressed directly and declaratively using qualitative conditional logic. For instance, it is straightforward to handle exceptions to a general rule as conditionals support nonmonotonic reasoning. Each of the knowledge bases is evaluated with example queries and with respect to different inference mechanisms that have been proposed for conditional knowledge, including p-entailment, system Z, and various inference relations based on c-representations. Comparing the obtained inference results with the answers expected from human experts demonstrates the feasibility of the modelling approach and also provides an empirical evaluation of the employed nonmonotonic inference relations in realistic application scenarios.

Keywords: Conditional · Nonmonotonic reasoning · Biomedical domain

1 Introduction

While there are different systems that use symbolic reasoning in the medical domain (e.g. MYCIN [4] or ADA [15]), many approaches in the biomedical field deal with statistical and probabilistic methods [17,21]. In this paper, we present and evaluate three conditional knowledge bases from the biomedical domain that demonstrate the applicability of qualitative conditional logic to real-world situations. The main contributions of this short paper are:

- Demonstration of the applicability of conditionals to real-world examples.
- Three case studies modelling biomedical knowledge with conditional logic (classification of mammals, malaria infections, and chronic myeloid leukaemia).

U. Schmid et al. (Eds.): KI 2020, LNAI 12325, pp. 283–289, 2020.
https://doi.org/10.1007/978-3-030-58285-2_24

– Empirical evaluation and comparison of established inference methods in biomedical applications (p-entailment; system Z; skeptical, weakly skeptical, and credulous c-inference over all and over minimal c-representations).

2 Background: Reasoning with Conditionals

Let $\mathcal{L}$ be a propositional language over a finite signature Σ. We write AB for $A \wedge B$ for formulas $A, B \in \mathcal{L}$. We denote the set of all interpretations over $\mathcal{L}$ as Ω. For $\omega \in \Omega$, $\omega \models A$ means that $A \in \mathcal{L}$ holds in ω. We define the set $(\mathcal{L} \mid \mathcal{L}) = \{(B|A) \mid A, B \in \mathcal{L}\}$ of *conditionals* over $\mathcal{L}$. The intuition of a conditional $(B|A)$ is that if A holds then usually B holds, too. As semantics for conditionals, we use functions $\kappa : \Omega \to \mathbb{N}$ such that $\kappa(\omega) = 0$ for at least one $\omega \in \Omega$, called *ordinal conditional functions (OCF)* [19]. They express degrees of plausibility of possible worlds where a lower degree denotes "less surprising". Each κ uniquely extends to a function mapping sentences to $\mathbb{N} \cup \{\infty\}$ given by $\kappa(A) = \min\{\kappa(\omega) \mid \omega \models A\}$ where $\min \emptyset = \infty$. An OCF κ *accepts* a conditional $(B|A)$, written $\kappa \models (B|A)$, if $\kappa(AB) < \kappa(A\overline{B})$. A finite set $\mathcal{R} \subseteq (\mathcal{L}|\mathcal{L})$ of conditionals is called a *knowledge base*. An OCF κ accepts $\mathcal{R}$ if κ accepts all conditionals in $\mathcal{R}$, and $\mathcal{R}$ is *consistent* if an OCF accepting $\mathcal{R}$ exists [7].

There are different answers to the question of what a conditional knowledge base entails. We consider three common approaches to inference with conditionals here: p-entailment [7], system Z [18], and c-inference [2]. For a knowledge base $\mathcal{R}$, $(B|A)$ is a *system Z inference* if the (uniquely determined) Pareto-minimal OCF accepting $\mathcal{R}$ accepts $(B|A)$. For a knowledge base $\mathcal{R}$, $(B|A)$ is a *skeptical* (resp. *credulous*) *c-inference* [2] if every (resp. at least one) c-representation [12] of $\mathcal{R}$ accepts $(B|A)$, and it is a *weakly skeptical c-inference* if at least one c-representation of $\mathcal{R}$ accepts $(B|A)$ and no c-representation of $\mathcal{R}$ accepts $(\overline{B}|A)$ [1]. Variations of c-inference do not take all but only minimal ranking functions with respect to different notions of minimality (cw min, sum min, ind min) into account [1].

3 Modelled Scenarios

Mammals can be divided into three major groups depending on their mode of reproduction. Most mammals are placentals. Approximately 95% of all mammalian species belong to this group. Their embryos are nourished by complex placentas and are born after a relatively long gestation period. Therefore, their offspring is well-developed at birth [11]. Another group of mammals are marsupials. The marsupials' offspring is born in a very early, embryo-like state. Afterwards it is carried in a marsupium where it matures. Most marsupials do not develop a complex placenta [16]. The third group of mammals are monotremes. In contrast to the two other groups, monotremes are not viviparous but lay eggs. Hence, they do not have a placenta. Platypuses belong to this group of mammals [9]. For modelling the mammal's modes of reproduction, we use the signature $\Sigma = \{m, v, c, e, k\}$. The variable m is true if the animal is a mammal, e if it is a marsupial, and k if it is a monotreme. The variable v expresses that the animal is viviparous, and c that the animal has a placenta. The knowledge base $\mathcal{KB}_{\mathrm{mammal}}$ contains the conditionals:

$(v\|m)$	Mammals are usually viviparous.
$(c\|m)$	Mammals usually have a placenta.
$(m\|e)$	Marsupials are mammals.
$(\neg c\|e)$	Marsupials usually do not have placentas.
$(m\|k)$	Monotremes are mammals.
$(\neg v\neg c\|k)$	Monotremes are neither viviparous nor have a placenta.

To test this knowledge base, we apply different inference modes to queries and compare the resulting answers to the answers a human expert would give. The first query is "Are marsupials viviparous?", i.e. does $\mathcal{KB}_{\mathrm{mammal}}$ entail $(v\|e)$. The second query is "Do marsupials have a placenta?", i.e. does $\mathcal{KB}_{\mathrm{mammal}}$ entail $(c\|e)$. The answers to these queries with respect to different inference methods are displayed in the upper part of Table 1.

While every mode of c-inference answers the query $(v\|e)$ as expected, p-entailment and system Z yield non-plausible results. This is due to the effect that is described as *drowning problem* in literature [3]. The three different notions of minimality for c-representations all yield a single ranking function for $\mathcal{KB}_{\mathrm{mammal}}$; therefore, the results for skeptical, weakly skeptical, and credulous c-inference over the minimal c-representations coincide. Both queries were answered in less than a second for each of the inference types by InfOCF-Lib [14] on a usual home computer[1]. Note that the knowledge base $\mathcal{KB}_{\mathrm{mammal}}$ can be easily extended. We have different versions of this knowledge base that contain more information about different groups of animals and their properties. The largest knowledge base contains 24 conditionals and 21 propositional variables. However, reasoning with larger knowledge bases takes more computational effort. Skeptical c-inference over all c-representations for an extended knowledge base with eleven variables and twelve conditionals takes more than 30 min with the current version of InfOCF-Lib while system Z takes only two seconds.

Malaria tropica is a widespread and life-threatening disease in Sub-Saharan Africa. It is caused by an infection with the single-celled parasite *Plasmodium falciparum*. This malaria pathogen is transmitted by *Anopheles* mosquitoes [20]. But not everyone infected with *P. falciparum* gets seriously sick with malaria: Some humans carry a hereditary form of the haemoglobin gene called sickle cell allele. Two copies of this defect gene cause a malformation of the red blood cells and sickle cell anaemia in humans, whereas one copy does not affect the function of red blood cells. However, humans carrying one copy of the sickle cell gene usually do not get seriously sick with malaria despite being infected with the malaria pathogen, thus having a survival advantage against malaria fatality over humans with normal haemoglobin [5]. Different approaches have been developed to protect humans from malaria. The two most important strategies to prevent

---

[1] The queries were answered on a computer with an Intel Core i5 Processor at 2.3 GHz and 8 GB RAM.

malaria are the avoidance of mosquito bites and therefore infections (exposure prophylaxis) and the use of medication to control the spread of the malaria pathogen inside the body after an infection (chemoprophylaxis). Humans who are treated with chemoprophylaxis usually do not get seriously sick with malaria even if infected. An exception to this rule are infections with a malaria pathogen that is resistant against the used chemoprophylaxis [13].

For modelling the situation for a patient infected with the malaria pathogen, we use the signature $\Sigma = \{m, s, p, r\}$ with the following semantic. The variable m is true if the patient gets sick with malaria. The variable s expresses that the patient has the sickle cell allele. A chemoprophylaxis is modelled by p and an infection with a resistant malaria pathogen is modelled by r. As we assume that the patient is already infected with the malaria pathogen, we do not have to introduce a variable for this. The knowledge base $\mathcal{KB}_{malaria}$ contains:

$(\neg s | \top)$ Patients usually do not have the sickle cell allele.
$(m | \neg s)$ Infected patients without the sickle cell allele usually get sick.
$(\neg m | s)$ Infected patients with the sickle cell allele usually do not get sick.
$(\neg m | p)$ Infected patients with a chemoprophylaxis usually do not get sick.
$(m | pr)$ Patients with a chemoprophylaxis that are infected with a resistant malaria pathogen usually get sick.

We evaluated the knowledge base with the following queries among others.

$(m | \top)$ Does a patient (infected with malaria) usually get sick?
$(m | rp)$ Does a patient who got a chemoprophylaxis but is infected with a resistant malaria pathogen usually get sick?
$(m | rsp)$ Does a patient who got a chemoprophylaxis, is infected with a resistant malaria pathogen, and has the sickle cell allele usually get sick?

The first query should be answered with *yes* as patients usually do not have the sickle cell allele and therefore get sick with malaria. The second query should be answered with *yes* as well, as this conditional is in the knowledge base. The last query is most interesting, as it includes two reasons not to get malaria (i.e., the sickle cell allele and the chemoprophylaxis) of which the chemoprophylaxis is not applicable in this situation as the malaria pathogen is resistant. The plausible answer is *yes* because the patient has the sickle cell allele while the chemoprophylaxis does not help against the resistant malaria pathogen. Comparing the second and the third query also shows that non-monotonic reasoning is covered by conditionals: As we add s to our query, we cannot infer m any more.

The answers of different inference methods to these queries are displayed in the middle part of Table 1. For $(m | \top)$ and $(m | rp)$, all inference modes yield the expected answer. For $(m | rsp)$, both system Z and credulous c-inference over all c-representations yield implausible answers. All minimal c-representions coincide and yield the expected answer.

Table 1. Results of queries to knowledge bases with different inference types

	Query	Inf. Mode	c-inference				p-entailment	System Z	Expert opinion
			all	cw min	sum min	ind min			
$\mathcal{KB}_{\mathrm{mammal}}$	$(v\|e)$	sk.	yes	yes	yes	yes	no	no	yes
		ws.	yes	yes	yes	yes			
		cr.	yes	yes	yes	yes			
	$(c\|e)$	sk.	no	no	no	no	no	no	no
		ws.	no	no	no	no			
		cr.	no	no	no	no			
$\mathcal{KB}_{\mathrm{malaria}}$	$(m\|\top)$	sk.	yes	yes	yes	yes	yes	yes	yes
		ws.	yes	yes	yes	yes			
		cr.	yes	yes	yes	yes			
	$(m\|rp)$	sk.	yes	yes	yes	yes	yes	yes	yes
		ws.	yes	yes	yes	yes			
		cr.	yes	yes	yes	yes			
	$(m\|rsp)$	sk.	no	no	no	no	no	yes	no
		ws	no	no	no	no			
		cr	yes	no	no	no			
$\mathcal{KB}_{\mathrm{CML}}$	$(g\|c)$	sk.	yes	yes	yes	yes	no	yes	yes
		ws.	yes	yes	yes	yes			
		cr.	yes	yes	yes	yes			
	$(g\|a)$	sk.	no	no	no	no	no	no	no
		ws.	no	no	no	no			
		cr.	no	no	no	no			
	$(g\|am)$	sk.	yes	yes	yes	yes	no	no	yes
		ws.	yes	yes	yes	yes			
		cr.	yes	yes	yes	yes			
	$(g\|amr)$	sk.	no	no	no	no	no	no	no
		ws.	no	no	no	no			
		cr.	no	no	no	no			

Chronic Myeloid Leukemia (CML) is one of the four common forms of leukaemia and is caused by a specific genetic defect in a single cell. In most cases of CML, it is a translocation between chromosomes 9 and 22. Part of the BCR gene from chromosome 22 is fused with the ABL gene on chromosome 9. The resulting fusion gene BCR-ABL leads to an uncontrolled proliferation of the affected cell. The use of targeted medication allows treatment of CML caused by a BCR-ABL translocation and results in improved long-term survival rates [10]. Approximately 5% of the CML cases are atypical CML (aCML), which is not caused by a BCR-ABL translocation. The recommended treatment for aCML is a hematopoetic stem cell transplantation (HSCT) which is associated with severe side effects [8], e.g. the Graft-versus-Host-Disease (GvHD), a reaction where the transplanted immune cells recognise the tissues of the recipient as foreign. While the patient can benefit from a mild form of GvHD, a severe form of GvHD is likely to cause heavy organ damage or the patient's death. A severe form of GvHD occurs only in about 10% of all HSCTs [6].

For modelling this knowledge about CML, we use $\Sigma = \{c, a, b, g, m, r\}$. The variable c indicates that the patient has CML, and a indicates that the patient has aCML. The variable b is true if the patient has the BCR-ABL translocation.

The variable g models that the patient has a good chance to survive the CML. The variable m means that the patient gets a HSCT, r that the patient suffers from severe GvHD. The knowledge base $\mathcal{KB}_{\text{CML}}$ contains:

$(b\|c)$	CML is usually caused by a BCR-ABL translocation.
$(g\|b)$	Patients with a BCR-ABL translocation usually have good survival chances.
$(c\|a)$	aCML is a form of CML.
$(\neg b\|a)$	aCML usually coincides with no BCR-ABL translocation.
$(g\|m)$	Patients getting a HSCT usually have good survival chances.
$(\neg g\|mr)$	Patients getting a HSCT and suffering from severe GvHD usually have poor survival chances.

This knowledge base was evaluated with the following queries:

$(g|c)$ Has a patient with CML good chances to survive?
$(g|a)$ Has a patient with aCML good chances to survive?
$(g|am)$ Has a patient with aCML who gets a HSCT good chances to survive?
$(g|amr)$ Has a patient with aCML who gets a HSCT and suffers from severe GvHD good chances to survive?

The first query checks if conditionals are combined to answer a query. We expect this conditional to be answered with *yes*. The other queries verify that exceptions and exceptions of exceptions are handled as expected. An expert's answer to $(g|a)$ would be *no*, to $(g|am)$ *yes*, and to $(g|amr)$ *no* again. The answers of different inference methods to these queries are displayed in the lower part of Table 1. While the different types of c-inference yield plausible results, p-entailment and system Z do not always provide the expected answer. P-entailment cannot derive the first queried conditional as it does not handle combinations of plausible conditionals well.

4   Conclusions and Further Work

We demonstrated how knowledge from different biomedical scenarios can be expressed directly and declaratively using qualitative conditional logic. We developed knowledge bases for the classification of mammals, for malaria infections, and for the outcome of CML, and evaluated them by answering queries with respect to different reasoning methods. While p-entailment, system Z, and credulous c-inference over all c-representations yield implausible results in some cases, the results of skeptical and weakly skeptical c-inference (over all and over minimal c-representations) coincided with the answers human experts would give. In all three case studies, using only minimal c-representations was a proper substitute for skeptical and weakly skeptical c-inference over all c-representations.

In future work, we will extend our case studies and address the reasoning and the computational aspects when using larger signatures and knowledge bases containing more conditionals. We will also broaden our case studies by modelling further applications scenarios, in particular from the medical domain.

References

1. Beierle, C., Eichhorn, C., Kern-Isberner, G., Kutsch, S.: Skeptical, weakly skeptical, and credulous inference based on preferred ranking functions. In ECAI-2016, vol. 285, pp. 1149–1157. IOS Press (2016)
2. Beierle, C., Eichhorn, C., Kern-Isberner, G., Kutsch, S.: Properties of skeptical c-inference for conditional knowledge bases and its realization as a constraint satisfaction problem. Ann. Math. Artif. Intell. **83**(3–4), 247–275 (2018)
3. Benferhat, S., Cayrol, C., Dubois, D., Lang, J., Prade, H.: Inconsistency management and prioritized syntax-based entailment. In: Proceedings of the IJCAI 1993, vol. 1, pp. 640–647. Morgan Kaufmann Publishers, San Francisco (1993)
4. Buchanan, B., Shortliffe, E.: Rule-Based Expert Systems. The MYCIN Experiments of the Stanford Heuristic Programming Project. Addison-Wesley, Reading (1984)
5. Ferreira, A., et al.: Sickle hemoglobin confers tolerance to plasmodium infection. Cell **145**(3), 398–409 (2011)
6. Ghimire, S., Weber, D., Mavin, E., Wang, X.-N., Dickinson, A., Holler, E.: Pathophysiology of GVHD and other HSCT-related major complications. Front. Immunol. **8**, 03 (2017)
7. Goldszmidt, M., Pearl, J.: Qualitative probabilities for default reasoning, belief revision, and causal modeling. Artif. Intell. **84**, 57–112 (1996)
8. Gotlib, J.: How I treat atypical chronic myeloid leukemia. Blood **129**(7), 838–845 (2017)
9. Griffiths, M.: The Biology of the Monotremes. Elsevier, New York (2012)
10. Jabbour, E., Kantarjian, H.: Chronic myeloid leukemia: 2018 update on diagnosis, therapy and monitoring. Am. J. Hematol. **93**(3), 442–459 (2018)
11. Kemp, T.S.: The Origin and Evolution of Mammals. Oxford University Press, Oxford (2005)
12. Kern-Isberner, G.: A thorough axiomatization of a principle of conditional preservation in belief revision. Ann. Math. and Artif. Intell. **40**(1–2), 127–164 (2004)
13. Kollaritsch, H.: Malaria-prophylaxe. Österreich. Ärztezeitung **2018**(9), 28–36 (2018)
14. Kutsch, S.: InfOCF-Lib: a Java library for OCF-based conditional inference. In: Proceedings of the DKB/KIK-2019, CEUR Workshop Proceedings, vol. 2445, pp. 47–58. CEUR-WS.org (2019)
15. Kühnel, S., Jovanović, M., Hoffmann, H., Schneider, L., Golde, S., Hirsch, M.: Introduction of a pathophysiology-based diagnostic decision support system and its potential impact on the use of AI in healthcare. Stud. Health Technol. inform. **264**, 1696–1697 (2019)
16. McKenna, M.C., Bell, S.: Classification of Mammals - Above the Species Level. Columbia University Press, New York (2000)
17. Merkl, R., Waack, S.: Bioinformatik Interaktiv. Wiley, Weinheim (2009)
18. J. Pearl. System Z: A natural ordering of defaults with tractable applications to nonmonotonic reasoning. In: Proceedings of the TARK 1990, pp. 121–135. Morgan Kaufmann Publ. Inc. (1990)
19. Spohn, W.: The Laws of Belief: Ranking Theory and Its Philosophical Applications. Oxford University Press, Oxford (2012)
20. WHO: World Malaria Report 2019. WHO (2019)
21. Yu, K.-H., Beam, A., Kohane, I.: Artificial intelligence in healthcare. Nat. Biomed. Eng. **2**, 10 (2018)

Conformal Rule-Based Multi-label Classification

Eyke Hüllermeier[1]([✉]), Johannes Fürnkranz[2], and Eneldo Loza Mencia[3]

[1] Paderborn University, Paderborn, Germany
eyke@upb.de
[2] Johannes Kepler University, Linz, Austria
[3] Technical University Darmstadt, Darmstadt, Germany

Abstract. We advocate the use of conformal prediction (CP) to enhance rule-based multi-label classification (MLC). In particular, we highlight the mutual benefit of CP and rule learning: Rules have the ability to provide natural (non-)conformity scores, which are required by CP, while CP suggests a way to calibrate the assessment of candidate rules, thereby supporting better predictions and more elaborate decision making. We illustrate the potential usefulness of calibrated conformity scores in a case study on lazy multi-label rule learning.

1 Introduction

The setting of multi-label classification (MLC), which generalizes standard multi-class classification by relaxing the assumption of mutual exclusiveness of classes, has received a lot of attention in machine learning, and various methods for tackling this problem have been proposed in the literature [15]. A *rule-based approach* to MLC is appealing and comes with a number of interesting properties. For example, rules are potentially interpretable and can provide explanations of a prediction [7]. Moreover, due to their local nature, rule-based predictors are very expressive and can adapt to local properties of the data in a flexible way.

In the context of MLC, the local nature of rules may also cause difficulties, however. In particular, due to the imbalance between positive and negative labels, which is typical for MLC, "good" rules with positive predictions that can stand up to negative rules are difficult to find. Here, we advocate the combination of multi-label rule learning with conformal prediction (CP) to mitigate this problem.

2 Multilabel Classification

Let $\mathcal{X}$ denote an instance space, and let $\mathcal{L} = \{\lambda_k\}_{k=1}^{K}$ be a finite set of class labels. We assume that an instance $x \in \mathcal{X}$ is (probabilistically) associated with a subset of labels $\Lambda = \Lambda(x) \in 2^{\mathcal{L}}$; this subset is often called the set of relevant (positive) labels, while the complement $\mathcal{L} \setminus \Lambda$ is considered as irrelevant (negative) for x.

© Springer Nature Switzerland AG 2020
U. Schmid et al. (Eds.): KI 2020, LNAI 12325, pp. 290–296, 2020.
https://doi.org/10.1007/978-3-030-58285-2_25

We identify a set Λ of relevant labels with a binary vector $\boldsymbol{y} = (y_1, \ldots, y_K)$, where $y_k = [\![\lambda_k \in \Lambda]\!]$.[1] By $\mathcal{Y} = \{0,1\}^K$ we denote the set of possible labelings.

Given training data $\mathcal{D} = \{(\boldsymbol{x}_n, \boldsymbol{y}_n)\}_{n=1}^N \subset \mathcal{X} \times \mathcal{Y}$, the goal in MLC is to learn a predictive model in the form of a multilabel classifier $\boldsymbol{h}$, which is a mapping $\mathcal{X} \longrightarrow \mathcal{Y}$ that assigns a (predicted) label subset to each instance $\boldsymbol{x} \in \mathcal{X}$. Thus, the output of a classifier $\boldsymbol{h}$ is a vector of predictions $\boldsymbol{h}(\boldsymbol{x}) = (h_1(\boldsymbol{x}), \ldots, h_K(\boldsymbol{x})) \in \{0,1\}^K$, also denoted as $\hat{\boldsymbol{y}} = (\hat{y}_1, \ldots, \hat{y}_K)$. For measuring the (generalization) performance of such a model, a large spectrum of loss functions or performance metrics have been proposed in the literature, including the Hamming loss $\ell_H(\boldsymbol{y}, \hat{\boldsymbol{y}}) := \frac{1}{K} \sum_{k=1}^K [\![y_k \neq \hat{y}_k]\!]$ and the F1-measure [4].

3   Conformal Prediction

Conformal prediction [3,6,12,13] is a framework for reliable prediction that is rooted in classical frequentist statistics and hypothesis testing. Given a sequence of training observations $(\boldsymbol{x}_1, y_1), (\boldsymbol{x}_2, y_2), \ldots, (\boldsymbol{x}_N, y_N), (\boldsymbol{x}_{N+1}, \bullet)$ and a new query $\boldsymbol{x}_{N+1}$ with unknown outcome y_{N+1}, the basic idea is to hypothetically replace $\bullet$ by each candidate, i.e., to test the hypothesis $y_{N+1} = y$ for all $y \in \mathcal{Y}$. Only those outcomes y for which this hypothesis can be rejected at a predefined level of confidence are excluded, while those for which the hypothesis cannot be rejected are collected to form the prediction set or *prediction region* $Y \subseteq \mathcal{Y}$. By construction, the set-valued prediction $Y = Y(\boldsymbol{x}_{n+1})$ is guaranteed to cover the true outcome y_{N+1} with a pre-specified probability of $1 - \epsilon$ (for example 95%).

Hypothesis testing is done in a nonparametric way: Consider any "nonconformity" function $f : \mathcal{X} \times \mathcal{Y} \longrightarrow \mathbb{R}$ that assigns scores $\alpha = f(\boldsymbol{x}, y)$ to input/output tuples; the latter can be interpreted as a measure of "strangeness" of the pattern $(\boldsymbol{x}, y)$, i.e., the higher the score, the less the data point $(\boldsymbol{x}, y)$ conforms to what one would expect to observe. Applying this function to the sequence of observations, with a specific (though hypothetical) choice of $y = y_{N+1}$, yields a sequence of scores $\alpha_1, \alpha_2, \ldots, \alpha_N, \alpha_{N+1}$, where $\alpha_i = f(\boldsymbol{x}_i, y_i)$. Denote by σ the permutation of $\{1, \ldots, N+1\}$ that sorts the scores in increasing order, i.e., such that $\alpha_{\sigma(1)} \leq \ldots \leq \alpha_{\sigma(N+1)}$. Under the assumption that the hypothetical choice of y_{N+1} is in agreement with the true data-generating process, and that this process has the property of exchangeability (which is weaker than the assumption of independence and essentially means that the order of observations is irrelevant), every permutation σ has the same probability of occurrence. Consequently, the probability that α_{N+1} is among the $\epsilon\%$ highest nonconformity scores should be low. This notion can be captured by the p-values associated with the candidate y, defined as

$$p(y) := \frac{\#\{i \,|\, \alpha_i \geq \alpha_{N+1}\}}{N+1} \tag{1}$$

According to what we said, the probability that $p(y) < \epsilon$ (i.e., α_{N+1} is among the $\epsilon\%$ highest α-values) is upper-bounded by ϵ. Thus, the hypothesis $y_{N+1} = y$ can be rejected for those candidates y for which $p(y) < \epsilon$.

---

[1] $[\![\cdot]\!]$ is the indicator function, i.e., $[\![A]\!] = 1$ if the predicate A is true and $= 0$ otherwise.

Conformal prediction as outlined above realizes transductive inference, although inductive variants also exist [9], where the nonconformity scores in (1) are produced on a training resp. validation data set. The error bounds are valid and well calibrated by construction, regardless of the nonconformity function f. However, the choice of this function has an important influence on the *efficiency* of conformal prediction, that is, the size of prediction regions: The more suitably the nonconformity function is chosen, the smaller these sets will be.

4   Conformal Rule-Based MLC

A rule-based classifier in the context of MLC is understood as a collection $\mathcal{R} = \{r_1, \ldots, r_M\}$ of individual rules r_m, where each rule $r_m : H_m \leftarrow B_m$ is characterized by a *head* H_m and a *body* B_m. Roughly speaking, the rule head makes an assertion about the relevance of the labels λ_k, while the rule body specifies conditions under which this assertion is valid. It typically appears in the form of a logical predicate that specifies conditions on a query instance x, for example a logical conjunction of restrictions on some of the features (e.g., a numerical value must lie in a certain interval).

4.1   Lazy Rule Learning

Here, we consider a *lazy* approach to multi-label rule learning, in which, instead of (eagerly) inducing a complete model $\mathcal{R}$ from the training data $\mathcal{D}$, a single rule $r_q : H_q \leftarrow B_q$ is induced at prediction time [1,5]. This rule is specifically tailored to a query instance x_q, for which a prediction is sought. More concretely, considering a binary relevance approach, a separate rule $r_{q,k} : H_{q,k} \leftarrow B_{q,k}$ is constructed for each label $\lambda_k \in \mathcal{L}$. The rule head is of the form $\hat{y}_k = 0$ or $\hat{y}_k = 1$. In the first case, the rule is a negative rule that predicts λ_k to be irrelevant, in the second case a positive rule that predicts λ_k to be relevant.

The local nature of rules has advantages but may also cause difficulties, especially in the context of MLC, where the data is highly imbalanced. In many cases, only a tiny fraction of the labels is relevant (positive), while the majority is irrelevant (negative). In general, this makes it difficult to find a "good" rule with positive predictions in its head, where the quality of a rule is typically measured in terms of two criteria, namely support (the body should be general enough so as to cover many instances) and confidence (the covered instances should belong to the same class). On the contrary, the learner has a strong incentive to make negative predictions, especially for loss functions such as Hamming. For example, the default rule with empty body, which predicts all labels to be always negative, will often have a very low Hamming loss, because most labels will be negative in the test examples. At the same time, this rule has a large support. When learning a single rule, as opposed to a complete model with many rules, that single rule must at least be better than the default rule—which is difficult for positive rules, as these normally have a small support.

4.2 Conformity of Positive and Negative Predictions

In general, the evaluation of negative rules is systematically better than the evaluation of positive rules. This is a motivation for the use of conformal prediction, which, if applied in a per-class manner, could "calibrate" the evaluations. More specifically, for a query instance x_q and a label $\lambda_k \in \mathcal{L}$, we propose the conformity (instead of non-conformity) score

$$c(x_q, y_k) := \max_{r \in C(x_q, y_k)} eval(r), \tag{2}$$

where $y_k \in \{0, 1\}$, $C(x_q, y_k)$ is a set of candidate rules that cover x_q and predict y_k for the label λ_k, and $eval$ is an evaluation measure informing about the quality of the rule r. As already said, such measures typically depend on the confidence and the support of the rule. In our illustration below, we shall use the lower confidence bound $\hat{p} - \sqrt{1/n}$, where n is the number of examples covered by the rule and $\hat{p}$ the fraction of examples with the predicted label [2], though any other measure could be used as well. Practically, it might be difficult to determine the maximum in (2) exactly, as an exhaustive search of the candidate set $C(x_q, y_k)$ might be infeasible. Instead, greedy search techniques are often used to find an approximately optimal rule.

The measure (2) appears to be a very natural measure of conformity: The conformity of y_k for x_q is high if a high-quality rule can be found that predicts y_k. A measure of *plausibility* of this label is then given by

$$q(x_q, y_k) = 1 - p(x_q, y_k) = \frac{\#\{(x, y) \in \mathcal{D} \mid y = y_k, c(x_q, y_k) > c(x, y)\}}{\#\{(x, y) \in \mathcal{D} \mid y = y_k\}}, \tag{3}$$

where $\mathcal{D}$ is the training data and $c(x, y)$ the conformity of the training example (x, y) determined in a leave-one-out manner (i.e., the quality of the best rule for (x, y) found in $\mathcal{D} \setminus \{(x, y)\}$). In other words, if $q(x_q, 1) = \alpha$, it means that the quality of the best positive rule for x_q is better than the quality of $100\,\alpha\%$ of the rules found for the truly positive examples in the training data, and the same interpretation applies to $q(x_q, 0)$. Consequently, only low values close to 0 provide real evidence *against* a certain prediction. For example, if $q(x_q, 1) = 0.2$, it means that the positive rule found for x_q is still better than 20% of the rules for the truly positive examples in the training data. In the spirit of hypothesis testing, one would "reject" the positive class only if $q(x_q, 1) < t$ for some critical threshold t such as $t = 0.1$ or $t = 0.05$, and similarly for the negative class.

As an illustration, Fig. 1 shows the distribution of positive and negative conformity scores (2) and calibrated plausibilities (3) for the first label in the emotions data (on a randomly chosen training set of size 400), a common benchmark data set with 596 examples, 72 attributes, and 6 labels [14]. Here, simple rules in the form of Parzen windows [11] have been learned, searching the space of such rules in a greedy, bottom-up manner (starting with a small window around x_q and successively increasing its size). As expected, the positive examples tend to have a higher positive than negative plausibility, and vice versa for the negative

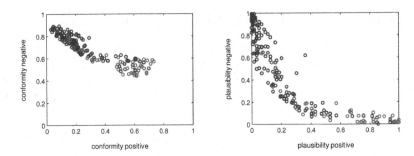

Fig. 1. Positive and negative conformity scores (2) and calibrated plausibilities (3) for the first label in the emotions data. Positive examples are plotted as red, negative examples as blue points. (Color figure online)

examples. Moreover, the sum of the two scores tends to be upper-bounded by 1 and sometimes takes values closer to 0, suggesting higher certainty in the true label in some cases and less in others, again confirming the appropriateness of the conformity measure (2).

4.3 Prediction and Decision Making

Given a query $\boldsymbol{x}_q$, the degrees $q(\boldsymbol{x}_q, 1)$ and $q(\boldsymbol{x}_q, 0)$ provide useful information about the plausibility of the positive and negative class, respectively, and hence a suitable basis for prediction and decision making. The arguably most obvious idea is to compare the two degrees and predict the label with higher plausibility, i.e., positive if $q(\boldsymbol{x}_q, 1) \geq q(\boldsymbol{x}_q, 0)$ and negative otherwise. Yet, since MLC losses are not necessarily symmetric, and the class distribution is imbalanced, one may also think of a more general decision rule of the form

$$\hat{y}_k = \llbracket q(\boldsymbol{x}_q, 1) \geq \theta \cdot q(\boldsymbol{x}_q, 0) \rrbracket , \tag{4}$$

where $\theta > 0$ is a parameter. Figure 2 (top) shows the average test performance[2] on the emotions data in terms of the Hamming loss and (micro) F1-measure. As can be seen, by tuning the threshold θ, the performance can indeed be optimized, although $\theta = 1$ is already close to optimal, confirming that the scores (3) are already well calibrated.

Recalling that conformal prediction is actually conceived for *set-valued* prediction, one may also think of using the two plausibilities to support more sophisticated decision making. One example is multi-label classification with (partial) abstention, where the learner is allowed to abstain on those labels on which it is not certain enough [8]. A natural reason to abstain, for example, is a low support for both options: $\max\{q(\boldsymbol{x}_q, 0), q(\boldsymbol{x}_q, 1)\} \leq \theta$, where θ is again a threshold. The effectiveness of such an approach is shown by the accuracy-rejection curves in Fig. 2 (bottom), which depict the average Hamming loss and F1-measure on

---

[2] 50 random splits into 400 training examples and 196 test examples.

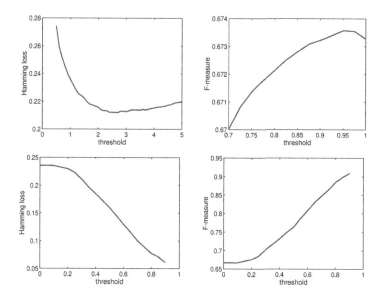

Fig. 2. Top: Hamming loss and F-measure on the emotions data, depending on the threshold θ in the decision rule (4). Bottom: Accuracy-rejection curves for Hamming loss and F1-measure on the same data.

those parts of the test data on which the learner does not abstain. The curves show a drastic increase in performance with an increasing amount of abstention (i.e., increasing θ), suggesting that the learner is indeed abstaining on the right labels, namely those that are most uncertain[3].

5   Conclusion and Outlook

The purpose of this paper is to highlight the potential usefulness of combining multi-label (rule) learning with conformal prediction. On the one side, rules provide a natural means for producing conformity scores of candidate labelings, very much like nearest neighbor methods, which are commonly used for CP [10]. On the other side, CP allows for producing meaningful and better calibrated measures of support in favor or label relevance, thus providing the basis for improved prediction, especially in advanced settings like MLC with abstention.

Exploiting the potential of this approach requires answers to a multitude of questions. One important building block, for example, is the class of candidate rules $C(\boldsymbol{x}_q, y)$ and the search in this class. Lazy rule learning as well as ensemble methods appear to be appealing in this regard. Moreover, to capture correlations and dependencies between different labels, the approach should be generalized toward the learning of rules with multi-label heads, predicting complete label combinations instead of individual labels.

---

[3] Note that the accuracy-rejection curve for random abstention is flat.

Acknowledgements. This work was supported by the German Research Foundation (DFG) under grant number 400845550.

References

1. Aha, D. (ed.): Lazy Learning. Kluwer Academic Publ., Dordrecht (1997)
2. Auer, P., Cesa-Bianchi, N., Fischer, P.: Finite-time analysis of the multiarmed bandit problem. Mach. Learn. **47**(2–3), 235–256 (2002)
3. Balasubramanian, V., Ho, S., Vovk, V. (eds.): Conformal Prediction for Reliable Machine Learning: Theory, Adaptations and Applications. Morgan Kaufmann, Waltham (2014)
4. Dembczynski, K., Waegeman, W., Cheng, W., Hüllermeier, E.: On label dependence and loss minimization in multi-label classification. Mach. Learn. **88**(1–2), 5–45 (2012)
5. Friedman, J., Kohavi, R., Yun, Y.: Lazy decision trees. In: Proceedings AAAI 1996. pp. 717–724. Morgan Kaufmann, Menlo Park, California (1996)
6. Gammerman, A., Vovk, V., Boström, H., Carlsson, L.: Conformal and probabilistic prediction with applications: editorial. Mach. Learn. **108**(3), 379–380 (2019)
7. Mencía, E.L., Fürnkranz, J., Hüllermeier, E., Rapp, M.: Learning interpretable rules for multi-label classification. In: Escalante, H.J., et al. (eds.) Explainable and Interpretable Models in Computer Vision and Machine Learning. TSSCML, pp. 81–113. Springer, Cham (2018). https://doi.org/10.1007/978-3-319-98131-4_4
8. Nguyen, V.L., Hüllermeier, E.: Reliable multi-label classification: Prediction with partial abstention. In: Proceedings of the AAAI 2020, Thirty-Fourth AAAI Conference on Artificial Intelligence, New York, USA(2020)
9. Papadopoulos, H.: Inductive conformal prediction: theory and application to neural networks. Tools Artif. Intel. **18**(2), 315–330 (2008)
10. Papadopoulos, H., Vovk, V., Gammerman, A.: Regression conformal prediction with nearest neighbours. J. Artif. Intell. Res. **40**, 815–840 (2011)
11. Parzen, E.: On estimation of a probability density function and mode. Ann. Math. Stat. **33**, 1065–1076 (1962)
12. Shafer, G., Vovk, V.: A tutorial on conformal prediction. J. Mach. Learn. Res. **9**, 371–421 (2008)
13. Vovk, V., Gammerman, A., Shafer, G.: Algorithmic Learning in a Random World. Springer, Boston (2003)
14. Wieczorkowska, A., Synak, P., Ras, Z.: Multi-label classification of emotions in music. In: Klopotek, M., Wierzchon, S., Trojanowski, K. (eds.) Intelligent Information Processing and Web Mining. Springer, Heidelberg (2006). https://doi.org/10.1007/3-540-33521-8_30
15. Zhang, M.L., Zhou, Z.H.: A review on multi-label learning algorithms. IEEE Trans. Knowl. Data Eng. **26**(8), 1819–1837 (2014)

Optimizing Constraint Satisfaction Problems by Regularization for the Sample Case of the Warehouse Location Problem

Sven Löffler[✉], Ke Liu, and Petra Hofstedt

Brandenburg University of Technology Cottbus-Senftenberg, Cottbus, Germany
Sven.Loeffler@b-tu.de

Abstract. The performance of a constraint problem can often be improved by converting a subproblem into a single regular constraint. We describe a new approach to optimize constraint satisfaction (optimization) problems using constraint transformations from different kinds of global constraints to regular constraints, and their combination. Our transformation approach has two aims: 1. to remove redundancy originating from semantically overlapping constraints over shared variables and 2. to remove origins of backtracks in the search during the solution process. Based on the case study of the Warehouse Location Problem we show that our new approach yields a significant speed-up.

Keywords: Constraint programming · CSP · Refinement · Optimizations · Regular membership constraint · Warehouse Location Problem

1 Introduction

Since the search space of constraint satisfaction problems CSPs, and consequently also the solution time, is very big, we are always interested in a speed-up of the solution process. There are various ways to describe a CSP in practice and consequently, the problem can be modeled by different combinations of constraints, which results in differences in resolution speed and behavior.

Hence, the diversity of models and constraints for a given CSP offers us an opportunity to improve the problem solving process by using another model in which a subset of constraints is replaced with a constraint which combines the original ones but offers a faster solution process [1,6–8]. In contrast to [1], which exploit the tabular constraint, our approach is based on the transformation of constraints into semantically equivalent regular constraints [7].

The solution speed and behavior of a CSP depends amongst other things on the number of backtracks in the depth-first search of the solution process and redundancy in the propagation of constraints. We developed a new approach for the optimization of CSPs, where singleton constraints or sets of constraints are

© Springer Nature Switzerland AG 2020
U. Schmid et al. (Eds.): KI 2020, LNAI 12325, pp. 297–304, 2020.
https://doi.org/10.1007/978-3-030-58285-2_26

substituted by regular constraints which are combined and minimized. The aim of this CSP reformulation is on the one hand to reduce slowing-down redundancy in constraints over shared variables and on the other hand to remove origins of backtracks in the search.

2   Preliminaries

In the following, we presuppose the notions of a deterministic finite automaton (DFA), directed acyclic graphs (DAGs), their minimization and intersection, see e.g.[5]. Furthermore, we consider *CSPs*, *CSOPs*, and *regular* constraints defined below. For the propagation algorithm of the regular constraint see [9].

CSP [3]. A constraint satisfaction problem (CSP) is defined as a 3-tuple $P = (X, D, C)$ with $X = \{x_1, \ldots, x_n\}$ is a set of variables, $D = \{D_1, \ldots, D_n\}$ a set of finite domains, where D_i is the domain of x_i, and $C = \{c_1, \ldots, c_m\}$ a set of primitive or global constraints covering between one and all variables of X.

CSOP [11]. A constraint satisfaction optimization problem (CSOP) $P_{opt} = (X, D, C, f)$ is defined as a CSP with an optimization function f that maps each solution to a numerical value to be minimized or maximized, respectively.

Regular Constraint [11, Chapter 6]. Let $M = (Q, \Sigma, \delta, q_0, F)$ be a DFA, let $X = \{x_1, \ldots, x_n\}$ be a set of variables with domains $D = \{D_1, D_2, \ldots, D_n\}$, $\forall i \in \{1, \ldots, n\} : D_i \subseteq \Sigma$. The regular constraint is defined as: $regular(X, M) = \{(w_1, \ldots, w_n) \mid \forall i \in \{1, \ldots, n\} : w_i \in D_i, (w_1 w_2 \ldots w_n) \in L(M)\}$.

3   Transformations of Global Constraints to Regular Constraints

Special transformations from several global constraints like *globalCardinality*, *count*, *stretch* and *table* constraints into regular constraints were already shown in previous work [7]. We introduce new transformations for *sum*, *scalar*, and *ifThen* constraints. First, we briefly explain our regularization procedure, before we show how such regularizations can improve the solution process of CSPs.

3.1   The Transformation Process

For the transformation of a constraint c into a regular constraint c_{reg}, we create a deterministic finite automaton (DFA) M which accepts a language L which is equivalent to the set of solutions of the original constraint c.

The Scalar and the Sum Constraint. The scalar constraint $scalar(X, C, \oplus, r)$ takes an array of variables $X = [x_1, ..., x_n]$, an array of corresponding integer coefficients $C = [c_1, ..., c_n]$, a relation $\oplus \in \{\leq, <, =, >, \geq, \neq\}$ and a result variable r as input. Its successful propagation ensures that the scalar product of X

and C is in relation $\oplus$ to the result r. For the reformulation of the *scalar* constraint we follow the idea of [12], where the DAG substitution of the knapsack problem is shown.

The sum constraint $sum(X, \oplus, r)$, where $X = [x_1, ..., x_n]$ is an array of variables, $\oplus \in \{\leq, <, =, >, \geq, \neq\}$ is a relation symbol and r is a result variable, can be interpreted as a special version of the scalar constraint, such that all coefficients c_i are equal to 1. Thus, we can use the same transformation as before.

The IfThen Constraint. The constraint $ifThen(c_{if}, c_{then})$ takes two constraints c_{if} and c_{then} as input and guarantees that, if the first constraint c_{if} is satisfied, also the second constraint c_{then} is fulfilled. At the moment, we only consider ifThen constraints, where the variables of both involved constraints are disjoint $(scope(c_{if}) \cap scope(c_{then}) = \emptyset)$. Furthermore, we expect that for both constraints $(c_{if}$ and $c_{then})$ transformations into regular constraints $(c_{r_{if}}$ and $c_{r_{then}})$ exist. Let be M_{if} the DAG used in $c_{r_{if}}$ and M_{then} the DAG used in $c_{r_{then}}$.

$$M_{ifThen} = (M_{if} \circ M_{then}) \vee (M_{\neg if} \circ M_{all}) \tag{1}$$

Equation 1 shows how an $ifThen$ automaton can be created by the use of the (DAG) automaton functions complement, concatenation and union. The resulting DAG M_{ifThen} accepts input words $w = w_1 w_2$ such that either w_1 is accepted by M_{if} and the remaining w_2 by M_{then} or w_1 is not in the language of M_{if} and w_2 is any word of length l, where l is the length of the accepted words of the *then* automaton M_{then}. The constraint $regular((scope(c_{if}) \cup scope(c_{then})), M_{ifThen})$ can be used as a replacement for the constraint $ifThen(c_{if}, c_{then})$.

3.2 The Benefit of Regularization

The transformation of constraints into regular constraints allows us to apply automaton methods like intersection and minimization, and this, furthermore, allows us to combine constraints which cover similar sets of variables. The algorithms from [1,8] can be used for the detection of parts in the CSP, which can be combined to a regular constraint. The combination of constraints is explained in [8], see the following two examples for clarification how they can reduce unwanted redundancy (Example 1) and origins of backtracks (Example 2).

Example 1. Figure 1 shows an example, where two automatons are intersected, such that the number of transitions is reduced. This yields an increase of the propagation speed of the CSP. Let M_1 and M_2 be two DAGs used in two regular constraints c_{r_1} and c_{r_2} which represent the two constraints $c_1 = (a \neq b) \wedge (a, b, c \in \{1, 2\})$ and $c_2 = (b \neq c) \wedge (a, b, c \in \{1, 2\})$. The necessary time to propagate the regular constraint depends primarily on the number of transitions in the used automaton [9], where transitions with k values count k times.

M_1 and M_2 have together 12 transitions, where six of them must be removed to find a solution. The intersected DAG M_3 has only 6 transitions and only three of them must be removed to find a solution (a singleton path from the start state to the final state). One reason for the reduction is, that we could reduce the unwanted redundancy, that both automatons M_1 and M_2 contain the path $(0,1,0)$ and $(1,0,1)$. In the combined automaton M_3 these paths must be considered only once.

Consequently, a CSP P with two regular constraints c_{r_1} and c_{r_2} based on M_1 and M_2 can be remodeled by substituting c_{r_1} and c_{r_2} with a regular constraint $regular(\{a,b,c\}, M_3)$, where we receive a semantically equivalent CSP P' which can propagate and solve faster.

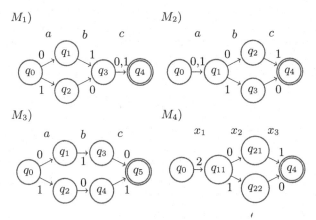

Fig. 1. The DAGs of Examples 1 and 2.

Example 2. Consider a CSP $P = (X, D, C)$, where $X = \{x_1, x_2, x_3\}, D = \{D_1, D_2, D_3 | D_1 = \{0,1,2\}, D_2 = D_3 = \{0,1\}\}$ and $C = \{c_1, c_2, c_3\}$, with $c_1 = (x_1 \neq x_2)$, $c_2 = (x_1 \neq x_3)$ and $c_3 = (x_2 \neq x_3)$. Some search strategies set x_1 to value 0 or 1, which cannot satisfy the CSP, so backtracking is necessary. If the well-known *alldifferent* constraint is used, then no backtracking is necessary. But what happens if we change c_1 to $x_1 > x_2$? It is no longer obvious that we can substitute c_1, c_2 and c_3 with an *alldifferent* constraint. But we still have the situation that common search strategies assign 1 to x_1, so that backtracking is necessary again. But, the constraints c_1, c_2 and c_3 can be substituted by one regular constraint $c_r = \{\{x_1, x_2, x_3\}, M_4\}$ which removes backtracking from the search. The DAG M_4 is created by the intersection of the three automatons of the regular representations of c_1, c_2 and c_3.

4   The Warehouse Location Problem

Now, we present an example to underline the benefits of our approach. We consider the Warehouse Location Problem (WLP) from the CSPlib [4]. We show an intuitive model of the problem and present experimental results.

4.1 Modeling the Warehouse Location Problem

The aim of the Warehouse Location Problem is to find a cheapest assignment of stores to warehouses with restricted capacities. Each store must be supplied by exactly one open warehouse. Each open warehouse has the same maintenance cost, and the supply cost to a store depends on the warehouse (e.g. distance, usually given as matrix M).

We consider n warehouses, s stores, fixed costs f_c per used warehouse, a supply cost matrix $M = Int^{n \times s}$ and the capacity vector $c = [c_1, ..., c_n]$ as explained in [4]. We use the following CSOP P to describe the problem: $P = (X, D, C, f)$, where $X = X^{ws} \cup X^{wc} \cup X^{sc} \cup \{x_{tc}\}$, $D = D^{ws} \cup D^{wc} \cup D^{sc} \cup \{D_{tc}\}$, $C = C^{scalar} \cup C^{count_s} \cup C^{count_w} \cup C^{ifThen} \cup \{c_{sum}\}$ and $f = minimize(x_{tc})$.

The variables $X^{ws} = \{x_{i,j}^{ws} | i \in \{1, ..., n\}, j \in \{1, ..., s\}\}$ are binary variables with $D^{ws} = \{D_{i,j}^{ws} = \{0, 1\} | i \in \{1, ..., n\}, j \in \{1, ..., s\}\}$, and represent, whether a warehouse i supplies a store j ($x_{i,j}^{ws} = 1$) or not ($x_{i,j}^{ws} = 0$).

Each binary variable $x_i^{wc} \in X^{wc}, \forall i \in \{1, ..., w\}$ with domain $D_i^{wc} = \{0, f_c\} \in D^{wc}$ describes the costs for warehouse i, whether it is used ($x_i^{wc} = f_c$) or not ($x_i^{wc} = 0$). Each variable $x_i^{sc} \in X^{sc}, \forall i \in \{1, ..., s\}$ with domain $D_i^{sc} = \{M_{i,*}\} \in D^{sc}$ describes the cost of a store based on the information by which warehouse it is supplied. For example, if store i is supplied by warehouse j then x_i^{sc} is instantiated by $M_{i,j}$. The variable x_{tc} with domain $D_{tc} = \{0, ..., \infty\}$ describes the total costs for supplying all stores. The goal is it to minimize these costs ($f = minimize(x_{tc})$). The constraints C of P are defined as follow:

$$C^{scalar} = \{c_j^{scalar} = scalar(x_{*,j}^{ws}, M_{*,j}, =, x_j^{sc}) \qquad | \forall j \in \{1, ..., s\}\}$$
$$C^{count_s} = \{c_j^{count_s} = count(1, \{x_{*,j}^{ws}\}, =, 1) \qquad | \forall j \in \{1, ..., s\}\}$$
$$C^{count_w} = \{c_i^{count_w} = count(0, \{x_{i,*}^{ws}\}, \geq, (s - c_i)) \qquad | \forall i \in \{1, ..., n\}\}$$
$$C^{ifThen} = \{c_i^{ifThen} = ifThen(sum(x_{i,*}^{ws}, \neq, 0), (x_i^{wc} = f_c)) \ | \forall i \in \{1, ..., n\}\}$$
$$c_{sum} = sum((X^{sc} \cup X^{wc}), =, x_{tc})$$

The constraints in C^{scalar} guarantee that each x_j^{sc} represents the cost of store j from warehouse supply. The constraints in C^{count_s} guarantee that each store is supplied by exactly one warehouse. The constraints in C^{count_w} guarantee that each warehouse i supplies at maximum as many stores as its capacity c_i allows. The constraints in C^{ifThen} set the costs x_i^{wc} of a warehouse i either to the fixed cost value f_c or to zero. The c_{sum} constraint models the total cost variable x_{tc} to be the sum of the costs of all warehouses (X^{wc}) and all stores (X^{sc}).

There are two notable overlaps in the constraints of the CSP: First, every c_j^{scalar} constraint has n overlapping variables with the corresponding $c_j^{count_s}$ constraint; second, every $c_i^{count_w}$ constraint has s overlapping variables with the corresponding c_i^{ifThen} constraint. These overlapping constraints are both: candidates for unwanted redundancy and candidates for being origins of backtracks. Using our approach, we substituted each pair of overlapping constraints with regular constraints by intersecting the concerning DAGs. The detection of overlapping constraints can be done using the algorithms presented in [1,8].

4.2 Experimental Results

For the benchmark suite from [4] we computed the different instances of the WLP
with different capacity vectors ($c_i = (i * 10, i * 10, ..., i * 10)$ $\forall i \in \{1, ..., 5\}$).
The algorithms are implemented in Java under JDK version 1.8.0_191 and Choco
Solver version 4.0.4 [10]. We used the *DowOverWDeg* search strategy which is
explained in [2] and used as default search strategy in the Choco Solver.

We run all instances in different versions: *Original*: The CSOP is solved as
modeled in Sect. 4.1. *IfCountInt*: Each c_i^{ifThen} constraint and each $c_i^{count_w}$ constraint were transformed and pairwise intersected. *ScalarCountInt*: Each c_j^{scalar}

Table 1. Speed-ups of the WLP using our new regularization approach.

Problem		Original	Scalar Count Inter.		Full Intersection	
Name	Cap.	t in s	t in s	Imp in %	t in s	Imp in %
cap101	10	1,800.292	7.669	99.574	2.601	99.856
cap131	10	1,800.288	249.089	86.164	20.649	98.853
cap44	10	1,800.275	2.594	99.856	1.493	99.917
cap63	10	1,800.280	6.980	99.612	5.890	99.673
cap71	10	1,800.276	4.193	99.767	854.154	52.554
cap101	20	1,800.278	17.115	99.049	4.124	99.771
cap131	20	1,800.292	313.592	82.581	24.235	98.654
cap44	20	1,800.280	3.300	99.817	5.186	99.712
cap63	20	1,800.279	3.221	99.821	18.230	98.987
cap71	20	1,232.520	0.001	99.999	0.001	99.999
cap101	30	1,800.288	23.806	98.678	4.815	99.733
cap131	30	1,800.291	298.942	83.395	18.827	98.954
cap44	30	1,764.474	0.001	99.999	0.001	99.999
cap63	30	1,800.275	3.271	99.818	5.138	99.715
cap71	30	635.064	0.001	99.999	0.001	99.999
cap101	40	1,800.283	25.243	98.598	3.771	99.791
cap131	40	1,800.291	310.353	82.761	19.582	98.912
cap44	40	1,800.275	2.625	99.854	3.018	99.832
cap63	40	1,800.275	2.766	99.846	3.790	99.789
cap71	40	561.218	0.001	99.999	0.001	99.999
cap101	50	1,800.273	24.575	98.635	3.704	99.794
cap131	50	1,800.294	346.415	80.758	16.629	99.076
cap44	50	1,800.276	1.975	99.890	3.295	99.817
cap63	50	1,800.280	2.773	99.846	2.681	99.851
cap71	50	552.281	0.001	99.999	0.001	99.999
A. i. in %				96.333		97.730

constraint and each $c_j^{count_s}$ constraint were transformed and pairwise intersected. *FullInt*: Both transformations from *IfCountInt* and *ScalarCountInt* are considered together.

Our test series figured out a small worsening of in average -0.146% for the IfCountInt approach. The versions ScalarCountInt and FullInt illustrate the advantages of our approach. It leads in average to a decrease of the optimization variable by 9.304% respectively 15.619%, by no worsening of one of the problem instances. Table 1 shows the real power of our approach. It shows for the versions ScalarCountInt and FullInt, resp. how much time is needed (in seconds) and saved (in percentage) to get a result which is at least as good as the result of the original model. We see significant time savings. Both approaches need approximately 97% less time than the original model to get the same results. Also note, all problems could find an adequate solution in at least half the time as the original approach.

5   Conclusion and Future Work

We presented a new way to optimize CSPs/CSOP by transformations from different kinds of constraints into regular constraints. By the use of intersection and minimization methods on the DAGs of regular constraints, new, more effective regular constraints can be created, which, in most cases, improve the solution speed of CSPs significantly. The existing list of transformations [7] was expanded and the use of the new transformations explained. We evaluated our approach by a benchmark suite based on the common Warehouse Location Problem [4]. The results show that our approach is appropriate for the optimization of a constraint network in short time.

In contrast to the tabulation approach presented in [1], our method does not have a strict threshold of 10,000 solutions per regularization process, as [1] have it for the tabulation process. For example, the C^{count_w} constraint for 50 stores with different capacities (10, 20, 30, 40, 50) can be created in less than one second and contains in all scenarios more than 10^{10} solutions. Future work includes a comparison and potentially an integration with work, e.g. the tabulation transformation of CSPs from [1].

References

1. Akgün, Ö., Gent, I.P., Jefferson, C., Miguel, I., Nightingale, P., Salamon, A.Z.: Automatic discovery and exploitation of promising subproblems for tabulation. In: Hooker, J. (ed.) CP 2018. LNCS, vol. 11008, pp. 3–12. Springer, Cham (2018). https://doi.org/10.1007/978-3-319-98334-9_1
2. Boussemart, F., Hemery, F., Lecoutre, C., Sais, L.: Boosting systematic search by weighting constraints. In: de Mántaras, R.L., Saitta, L. (eds.) 16th European Conference on Artificial Intelligence, ECAI 2004, PAIS 2004. IOS Press (2004)
3. Dechter, R.: Constraint Processing. Elsevier Morgan Kaufmann, Burlington (2003)
4. Hnich, B.: CSPLib problem 034: warehouse location problem. http://www.csplib.org/Problems/prob034. Accessed 28 Mar 2019

5. Hopcroft, J.E., Ullman, J.D.: Introduction to Automata Theory, Languages and Computation. Addison-Wesley, Boston (1979)

6. Löffler, S., Liu, K., Hofstedt, P.: The power of regular constraints in CSPs. In: 47 Jahrestagung der Gesellschaft für Informatik, Informatik 2017, Chemnitz, Germany, September 25–29, 2017, pp. 603–614 (2017)

7. Löffler, S., Liu, K., Hofstedt, P.: The regularization of CSPs for rostering, planning and resource management problems. In: Iliadis, L., Maglogiannis, I., Plagianakos, V. (eds.) AIAI 2018. IAICT, vol. 519, pp. 209–218. Springer, Cham (2018). https://doi.org/10.1007/978-3-319-92007-8_18

8. van den Herik, J., Rocha, A.P. (eds.): ICAART 2018. LNCS (LNAI), vol. 11352. Springer, Cham (2019). https://doi.org/10.1007/978-3-030-05453-3

9. Pesant, G.: A regular language membership constraint for finite sequences of variables. In: Wallace, M. (ed.) CP 2004. LNCS, vol. 3258, pp. 482–495. Springer, Heidelberg (2004). https://doi.org/10.1007/978-3-540-30201-8_36

10. Prud'homme, C., Fages, J.G., Lorca, X.: Choco documentation. TASC, INRIA Rennes, LINA CNRS UMR 6241, COSLING S.A.S. (2019). http://www.choco-solver.org/. Accessed 07 Nov 2019

11. Rossi, F., Beek, P.V., Walsh, T.: Handbook of Constraint Programming, 1st edn. Elsevier, Amsterdam (2006)

12. Trick, M.A.: A dynamic programming approach for consistency and propagation for knapsack constraints. Ann. OR **118**(1–4), 73–84 (2003)

Fast Pathfinding in Knowledge Graphs Using Word Embeddings

Leon Martin[✉][iD], Jan H. Boockmann[iD], and Andreas Henrich[iD]

University of Bamberg, An der Weberei 5, 96047 Bamberg, Germany
{leon.martin,jan.boockmann,andreas.henrich}@uni-bamberg.de

Abstract. Knowledge graphs, which model relationships between entities, provide a rich and structured source of information. Currently, search engines aim to enrich their search results by structured summaries, e.g., obtained from knowledge graphs, that provide further information on the entity of interest. While single entity summaries are available already, summaries on the relations between multiple entities have not been studied in detail so far. Such queries can be understood as a pathfinding problem. However, the large size of public knowledge graphs, such as Wikidata, as well as the large indegree of its major entities, and the problem of concept drift impose major challenges for standard search algorithms in this context.

In this paper, we propose a bidirectional pathfinding approach for directed knowledge graphs that uses the semantic distance between entity labels, which is approximated using word vectors, as a search heuristics in a parameterized A*-like evaluation function in order to find *meaningful* paths between two entities *fast*. We evaluate our approach using different parameters against a set of selected within- and cross-domain queries. The results indicate that our approach generally needs to explore fewer entities compared to its uninformed counterpart and qualitatively yields more meaningful paths.

Keywords: Knowledge graphs · Word embeddings · Pathfinding

1 Introduction

Modern web search engines aim to extend their core functionality by providing key information relevant to a queried entity in a structured way alongside with the ranked web pages. To do so, search engine providers leverage additional data sources that characterize the information of entities and the relationships among them. Google introduced the concept of a Knowledge Graph (KG) in their blog [11] as a tool for enhancing their search engine via three main features: the disambiguation of entities, the generation of summaries for entities, and the provision of links to related entities. The latter two are displayed as a knowledge panel [12] next to the vertical list of ranked web pages. Indeed, KGs provide the necessary information to construct knowledge panels, however, these panels are

© Springer Nature Switzerland AG 2020
U. Schmid et al. (Eds.): KI 2020, LNAI 12325, pp. 305–312, 2020.
https://doi.org/10.1007/978-3-030-58285-2_27

only constructed for queries that focus on a *single entity*. While such panels can meet the information need related to directly adjacent entities, e.g., 'inhabitants of Elva', a city in Estonia, they do not cover relationships between non-adjacent entities, e.g., 'Elva' and 'Europe'. However, the latter, so far unaddressed use case of *multiple entities* is a typical information need expressed by users.

Answering such dual-entity queries can be understood as pathfinding in KGs, e.g., the relationship between Elva and Europe is represented as the path(s) that exist between the KG entities 'Elva' and 'Europe'. Although pathfinding in general graphs is well studied [3], finding paths in KGs remains a non-trivial problem, given that paths should be found *fast* and yield a *meaningful* explanation of the entities' relationship, i.e., shorter paths are not necessarily more meaningful. The semantic focus of the query is left – a problem known as concept drift [4] – when a search algorithm decides to explore non-meaningful paths. In addition, general KGs, such as DBpedia [1] or Wikidata [13], comprise many entities and relationships yielding a large search space, i.e., the work in [9] observed that popular KGs comprise up to 18 million entities and that the approximate in-/outdegree of an entity ranges from 10/40 to 10/100.

The key challenge is the design of an appropriate search heuristics and the choice of an accompanying search algorithm suited for this particular use case where *meaningful* paths must be found *fast* in a large graph. In this paper, we thus investigate the following research question: "Does a bidirectional search algorithm using the semantic distance as a search heuristics lead to meaningful paths in KGs fast?"

2   Foundations

The central problem tackled in this paper is finding a path between the two entities v_{source} and v_{target} in a KG $= (V, E)$, as usual. As there does not exist a formal definition of a KG [5], we utilize the characterization of [8], according to which a KG encodes entities of the real world (*nodes*) and their relations (*edges*) taken from various domains in a graph representation. A schema, which links entities to classes and properties, may provide further type information.

A best-first search guided by an appropriate search heuristics is key to perform pathfinding in large KGs in a reasonable amount of time. We propose to use the semantic distance between the labels of entities as a search heuristics. Word embedding toolkits like word2vec [7] and fastText (FT) [2] produce vector representations of words in a metric space by training a model using a large textual corpus. In the remainder of this paper, we approximate the semantic distance of two KG entities v_1 and v_2 using the cosine distance $d(v_1, v_2) = 1 - cos(\theta)$, where θ is the angle between the word vectors of the corresponding entity labels. The cosine distance is derived from the cosine similarity $cos(\theta) = \frac{v_1 \cdot v_2}{||v_1|| \cdot ||v_2||}$, a standard measure used in information retrieval and natural language processing [6].

Algorithm 1. Our bidirectional pathfinding algorithm.

Require: $v_{source}, v_{target} \in Knowledge\ Graph$
 procedure FINDPATH(v_{source}, v_{target})
  $priorityqueue \leftarrow \langle v_{source}, v_{target} \rangle$
  $reachable_{source} \leftarrow \{v_{source}\}$
  $reachable_{target} \leftarrow \{v_{target}\}$
  while $priorityqueue \neq \varnothing$ **do**
   $entity \leftarrow dequeue(priorityqueue)$
   if $entity \in (reachable_{source} \cap reachable_{target})$ **then**
    return $reconstructPath(v_{source}, entity, v_{target})$
   end if
   $nextEntities \leftarrow getAdjacentEntities(entity)$
   $priorityqueue \leftarrow enqueueAll(priorityqueue, nextEntities)$
   if $entity \in reachable_{source}$ **then**
    $reachable_{source} \leftarrow reachable_{source} \cup nextEntities$
   else if $entity \in reachable_{target}$ **then**
    $reachable_{target} \leftarrow reachable_{target} \cup nextEntities$
   end if
  end while
 end procedure

---

3 Concept

Our bidirectional A*-like search algorithm (see Algorithm 1) is capable of finding direct paths, i.e., from v_{source} to v_{target} and vice versa, and paths where one entity is reachable from both v_{source} and v_{target}. A shared priority queue ensures that the least costly path is explored next.

Word embeddings, used as our search heuristics, allow to estimate the semantic distance using the cosine distance of vector representations of words, i.e., entity labels. Named entities like people and geographic points of interest account for a significant part of all encoded entities and pose a problem for traditional word embedding models that can only produce word vectors for words present in their training data. The ability to reliably compute the semantic distance between all entities is essential for our use case, because missing semantic distances lead to a biased path selection. Modern word embedding models provide additional functionalities, such as producing word vectors for unknown words, e.g., the herein employed FT model achieves this by computing word vectors based on vectors of substrings. In particular, we utilize the pre-trained English word vectors `cc.en.300.bin` as provided by FT.

Our approach is based on the assumptions that the semantic distance varies between adjacent entities and that entities in proximity show a lower semantic distance on average. Figure 1 shows the distribution of the semantic distance for a selection of sample entities. Note that the semantic distance is broadly distributed indicating that some neighboring entities are indeed more worthwhile to pursue than others. For example, the adjacent entities of 'river' include 'watercourse' with a semantic distance of 0.45, 'Template:Infobox river' with a

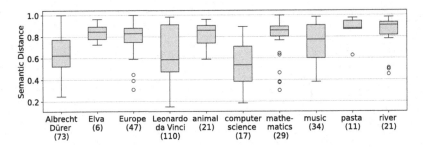

Fig. 1. Distribution of the semantic distance among the Wikidata entities reachable via a single non-reflexive outgoing edge; outdegree of an entity provided in parenthesis.

semantic distance of 0.91, and 'Explanatory Dictionary of the Living Great Russian Language' with a semantic distance of 0.98. Note that FT yields a higher semantic distance for less related entities, supporting our assumption for adjacent entities.

In the following, we consider paths meaningful that minimize the average semantic distance to the target, i.e., preventing concept drift. Hence, inspired by a general A* evaluation function, the function $f(p) = g(p) + h(p)$ denotes the costs of a path p with length n as follows:

$$g(p) := \alpha \cdot \overline{d}(p_{[1..n-1]}, v_{target}) + \beta \cdot n$$
$$h(p) := \gamma \cdot d(v_n, v_{target})$$
$$\text{where } p = \langle v_1, v_2, \ldots, v_n \rangle$$
$$\text{and } p_{[i..j]} \text{ is the sub-path } \langle v_i, \ldots, v_j \rangle$$

Formula $\overline{d}(p_{[1..n-1]}, v_{target})$ calculates the average of the semantic distances between each entity on the path – excluding the last one – and the target entity. Formula $d(v_n, v_{target})$ estimates the semantic distance between the last entity and the target entity. Note that this approach is a heuristic adaptation of the A* idea. The algorithm does not minimize the sum of the distances but focuses on the distance of all nodes on the path to the target node. The evaluation function is parameterized over variables α, β, and γ to enable component-based weight adjustments. Due to missing benchmarks for pathfinding in KGs, no parameter fitting could be performed. In the following, we explore the four sample evaluation function configurations:

1. *Uninformed* ($\alpha = \gamma = 0$, $\beta = 1$) neglects the semantic distances and only considers the prior path length, thus representing a baseline.
2. *Semantics-Only* ($\alpha = \gamma = 1$, $\beta = 0$) ignores the path length and only considers the semantic distances.
3. *Greedy* ($\alpha = \beta = 0$, $\gamma = 1$) does not consider prior path length and average semantic path costs, and estimates the remaining path costs using the semantic distance of the last entity to v_{target}.

4. *Balanced* ($\alpha = \gamma = 1$, $\beta = 0.5$) takes semantic distances and path length into account; $\beta < 1$ reduces the impact of path length on the overall costs.

4   Evaluation

Since there does not exist a standard benchmark for evaluating the performance of pathfinding in the Wikidata KG, we conduct a preliminary evaluation of the configurations above using a small handmade selection of diverse queries. This benchmark contains within- and cross-domain queries to observe how our approach performs in different search scenarios. Since the employed Wikidata SPARQL interface yields a timeout for many entities in our test set when requesting their incoming edges, this evaluation considers only outgoing edges.

Table 1 summarizes our results. First note that every query can be answered by at least one configuration that considers the semantic distance. With only a single unanswered query, the configurations *Uninformed* and *Balanced* yield the best coverage of the query set. However, the *Balanced* configuration needs to explore less entities to find a path and is also faster on average when excluding the outlier query from 'France' to 'air pollution', for which 270 entities had to be explored to find a path. Note that we forcefully stop a search that exceeds the limit of 500 explored entities. Despite the additional time necessary to properly enqueue elements into the priority queue, the runtime performance of any informed configuration is better than the uninformed configuration on average when ignoring forcefully stopped searches. In general, note that every configuration requires more time and has to visit more nodes in order to find a path for a cross-domain query compared to within-domain queries on average. Interestingly, despite having the most unanswered queries, only the configuration *Semantics-Only* found a path for the cross-domain query 'Bamberg, computer science'. Observe that this path spans 19 entities in total and could performance-wise not have been found by an uninformed search approach. Hence, the semantic distance appears to be a viable search heuristics to find paths in a large KG *fast*.

We conduct a qualitative analysis to assess the *meaningfulness* of the paths found by our configurations. The benchmark results show that our informed configurations can find useful paths, e.g., 'Elva' $\rightarrow$ 'Estonia' $\rightarrow$ 'Europe' and 'pasta' $\leftarrow$ 'flour' $\leftarrow$ 'pizza'. However, especially configurations that consider the path length find paths where the shared entity is an encyclopedia; the *meaningfulness* of such entities is debatable. Nevertheless, *meaningfulness* of paths strongly depends on an underlying definition, which is a subjective quality and may vary between different use cases. Hence, a ground truth, e.g., obtained from a user study, is necessary to properly assess the quality of found paths. From our point of view, the meaningfulness of the paths found using an informed configuration is mixed but promising considering that no parameter fitting has been done yet.

Note that the number of samples is way too small to draw a meaningful conclusion but suffices to motivate further investigation.

Table 1. Benchmark results for within- and cross-domain queries from v_{source} to v_{target} (entity label and Wikidata entity identifier) using the four evaluation function configurations. We provide information on the length of the found path (l) measured in the number of entities including source and target, and use symbols '♦', '♣', and '♠' in superscript to denote difference/equivalence among paths in the same row; we report on the number of explored entities (c) and the total runtime in seconds (t).

Queries		Uninformed			Semantics-Only			Greedy			Balanced		
	v_{source}, v_{target}	l	c	t	l	c	t	l	c	t	l	c	t
Within-Domain	Elva (Q213071), Europe (Q46)	3♦	131	123	3♦	3	8	3♦	3	8	3♦	3	8
	Albrecht Dürer (Q5580), Leonardo da Vinci (Q762)	3♦	74	71		c ≥ 500			c ≥ 500		3♦	19	30
	computer science (Q21198), mathematics (Q395)	3♦	21	19	4♣	4	7		c ≥ 500		3♦	19	19
	pasta (Q178), pizza (Q177)	3♦	31	34	3♦	7	9	3♦	9	10	3♦	8	10
	river (Q4022), ocean (Q9430)	3♦	27	24	5♣	9	13	5♦	10	12	3♦	21	31
	Ludwig v. Beethoven (Q255), Wolfgang A. Mozart (Q254)	2♠	34	33	2♦	2	7	2♦	2	3	2♠	2	6
Cross-Domain	Leonardo da Vinci (Q762), Italy (Q38)	3♦	117	110	3♦	3	15	3♦	3	6	3♦	3	13
	Bamberg (Q3936), computer science (Q21198)		c ≥ 500		19♦	29	43		c ≥ 500			c ≥ 500	
	air pollution (Q131123), France (Q142)	4♦	260	838		c ≥ 500		4♦	4	5	4♦	270	2312
	Loki (Q133147), Bible (Q1845)	3♦	108	70		c ≥ 500			c ≥ 500		3♦	8	10
	animal (Q729), building (Q41176)	4♦	212	161		c ≥ 500		16♦	54	134	3♦	6	5
	wood (Q287), music (Q638)	3♦	36	26		c ≥ 500		11♦	29	33	3♦	32	30

5   Conclusions

In this paper, we proposed the use of the semantic distance approximated using word embeddings as a heuristics to guide search in a KG. The introduced bidirectional A*-like search algorithm employs a parameterized evaluation function that considers path length *and* semantic distances.

For further optimization, we plan to explore which evaluation function configuration yields the best results with respect to a larger benchmark. Here, we assume that the semantic distance between v_{source} and v_{target} entity can be used as a decision criterion to allow for a query dependent parameter selection. Dropping unpromising paths from the path queue in a beam search fashion may enable to handle entities with many incoming/outgoing edges. A performance increase may also be achieved by using a manually trained FT model tailored to a particular domain, in contrast to the currently used pre-trained model. Furthermore, we want to extend our approach to also consider edge labels in the evaluation function and lift the support from dual-entity queries to multi-entity queries. Enriching our purely semantic heuristics with information on the graph's local structure, e.g., using RDF2Vec [10], is also worth to explore.

References

1. Auer, S., et al.: DBpedia: a nucleus for a web of open data. In: Aberer, K., et al. (eds.) ASWC/ISWC -2007. LNCS, vol. 4825, pp. 722–735. Springer, Heidelberg (2007). https://doi.org/10.1007/978-3-540-76298-0_52
2. Bojanowski, P., Grave, E., Joulin, A., Mikolov, T.: Enriching word vectors with subword information. Trans. Assoc. Comput. Linguistics **5**, 135–146 (2017). https://transacl.org/ojs/index.php/tacl/article/view/999
3. Bondy, J.A., Murty, U.S.R.: Graph Theory with Applications. Macmillan Education, UK (1976). https://doi.org/10.1007/978-1-349-03521-2
4. Dietz, L., Kotov, A., Meij, E.: Utilizing knowledge graphs for text-centric information retrieval. In: Collins-Thompson, K., Mei, Q., Davison, B.D., Liu, Y., Yilmaz, E. (eds.) 41st International ACM SIGIR Conference on Research & Development in Information Retrieval (SIGIR 2018), pp. 1387–1390. ACM (2018). https://doi.org/10.1145/3209978.3210187
5. Ehrlinger, L., Wöß, W.: Towards a definition of knowledge graphs. In: Martin, M., Cuquet, M., Folmer, E. (eds.) 12th International Conference on Semantic Systems (SEMANTiCS 2016). CEUR Workshop Proceedings, vol. 1695. CEUR-WS.org (2016). http://ceur-ws.org/Vol-1695/paper4.pdf
6. Gomaa, W.H., Fahmy, A.A., et al.: A survey of text similarity approaches. Int. J. Comput. Appl. **68**(13), 13–18 (2013)
7. Mikolov, T., Chen, K., Corrado, G., Dean, J.: Efficient estimation of word representations in vector space. In: Bengio, Y., LeCun, Y. (eds.) 1st International Conference on Learning Representations (ICLR 2013) (2013). http://arxiv.org/abs/1301.3781
8. Paulheim, H.: Knowledge graph refinement: a survey of approaches and evaluation methods. Semantic Web **8**(3), 489–508 (2017). https://doi.org/10.3233/SW-160218

9. Ringler, D., Paulheim, H.: One knowledge graph to rule them all? analyzing the differences between dbpedia, yago, wikidata & co. In: Kern-Isberner, G., Fürnkranz, J., Thimm, M. (eds.) 40th Annual German Conference on AI (KI 2017). LNCS, vol. 10505, pp. 366–372. Springer, Cham (2017). https://doi.org/10.1007/978-3-319-67190-1_33

10. Ristoski, P., Paulheim, H.: Rdf2vec: RDF graph embeddings for data mining. In: Groth, P.T., et al. (eds.) The Semantic Web - ISWC 2016–15th International Semantic Web Conference, Kobe, Japan, October 17–21, 2016, Proceedings, Part I. Lecture Notes in Computer Science, vol. 9981, pp. 498–514 (2016). https://doi.org/10.1007/978-3-319-46523-4_30

11. Singhal, A.: Introducing the Knowledge Graph: Things, not Strings (2012). https://googleblog.blogspot.com/2012/05/introducing-knowledge-graph-things-not.html

12. Stekkelpak, Z., Simonyi, G.: Providing customized content in knowledge panels, uS Patent App. 13/750, 354, 18 June 2015

13. Vrandecic, D., Krötzsch, M.: Wikidata: a free collaborative knowledgebase. Commun. ACM **57**(10), 78–85 (2014). https://doi.org/10.1145/2629489

A Visually Explainable Learning System for Skin Lesion Detection Using Multiscale Input with Attention U-Net

Duy Minh Ho Nguyen, Abraham Ezema, Fabrizio Nunnari$^{(\boxtimes)}$,
and Daniel Sonntag

German Research Center for Artificial Intelligence, Saarbrücken, Germany
{Ho_Minh_Duy.Nguyen,Abraham_Obinwanne.Ezema,
Fabrizio.Nunnari,Daniel.Sonntag}@dfki.de

Abstract. In this work, we propose a new approach to automatically predict the locations of visual dermoscopic attributes for Task 2 of the ISIC 2018 Challenge. Our method is based on the Attention U-Net with multi-scale images as input. We apply a new strategy based on transfer learning, i.e., training the deep network for feature extraction by adapting the weights of the network trained for segmentation. Our tests show that, first, the proposed algorithm is on par or outperforms the best ISIC 2018 architectures (LeHealth and NMN) in the extraction of two visual features. Secondly, it uses only 1/30 of the training parameters; we observed less computation and memory requirements, which are particularly useful for future implementations on mobile devices. Finally, our approach generates visually explainable behaviour with uncertainty estimations to help doctors in diagnosis and treatment decisions.

Keywords: Skin lesion · Diagnose features · Attention U-Net

1 Introduction

Skin cancer is one of the most frequently occurring diseases with more than one million positive diagnoses in the United States each year. The most dangerous type of skin cancer is the melanoma, causing over 9,000 deaths, and 76,380 new cases according to the American Cancer Society per year [12]. While melanoma at an early stage can be treated successfully, it still demands rigorous manual evaluations by the dermatologist for several skin lesion patterns. Hence, partly automatizing skin cancer detection plays an important role in the early diagnosis of skin cancer.

In recent years, the International Skin Imaging Collaboration (ISIC) [4] organizes competitions to seek the best algorithm that can diagnose melanoma automatically. Our work utilized the ISIC challenge data in 2018, which was composed of 3 subtasks. The first task was to segment the lesion and skin boundaries, next was the lesion attribute detection to predict the positions of five skin lesion

© Springer Nature Switzerland AG 2020
U. Schmid et al. (Eds.): KI 2020, LNAI 12325, pp. 313–319, 2020.
https://doi.org/10.1007/978-3-030-58285-2_28

attributes as a negative network, pigment network, milia-like cysts, streaks, and globules [4] (Fig. 2). The last task was the classification of images as melanoma, basal cell carcinoma, melanocytic nevus, actinic keratosis, benign keratosis, vascular lesion, and dermatofibroma. While image classification (Task 3) can be seen as a black box, the segmentation (Task 1) and lesion detection (Task 2) steps give visual feedback of known features that doctors can visually inspect and evaluate. In particular, the lesion attribute detection supports doctors to identify whether a lesion is benign or malignant. These visual features are described as a global distribution spanning over a massive area, or a local distribution in a small area, or multiple spots in the lesion. Therefore, the automatic detection and visualization of skin lesion attributes are critical and can be of tremendous support to doctors when diagnosing melanoma in an early phase while explaining the machine learning decisions.

In this paper, we propose a visually explainable learning system with uncertainty estimations for Task 2 of the ISIC Challenge 2018. Our approach adheres to the mental model of the doctor by leveraging the predictive power of deep learning approaches to reduce the bias of a doctor for lesion classification.

2   Related Works and Our Contribution

Several methods have been proposed for the extraction of features of skin lesions, all based on variants of the convolutional neural networks (CNN) such as XceptionNet [3], ResNet [6], U-Net [11]. However, unlike Task 1 and Task 3, the best performance in feature extraction (Task 2) was very low. The highest score (Jaccard index) was just above 30% compared to over 80% mean accuracy and 88% J-index in Task 1 and Task 3, respectively. The reasons behind are the lack of annotated data, imbalanced datasets, and complex structures with varying appearances per patient. To deal with these issues, most of the approaches utilized the transfer learning strategy and fine-tuned large pre-trained deep learning models; afterwards, stacking the networks into an ensemble to make final predictions. For instance, the second-ranked team (LeHealth) [14] adapted the ResNet architecture for PSPNet [13] to simultaneously predict the positions of five lesion attributes. The best method (NMN) [8] constructed an ensemble network based on five baseline architectures: Densenet169 [7], two versions of ResNet [6], Xception [3], and DeepLab-v3 [2], each predicting the position of a separate attribute. Unlike those works, we propose a new strategy for predicting the five skin lesion attributes based on a single variant of the U-Net called Attention U-Net [9], which has consistently shown to improve the performance of the U-Net architecture across different datasets.

In particular, our new approach differs from previous work in two aspects. First, instead of using existing models such as ResNet or XceptionNet, which were trained on a huge dataset like ImageNet [5] to initialize network parameters, we present a novel approach for training the Attention U-Net based on a transfer learning that first trains on the Task 1 (image boundary segmentation) and then uses the trained weights as initialization for Task 2 (lesion attributes prediction).

This idea is motivated by the key point that most of the lesion structures are located inside the lesion boundary, so initializing weights in this manner can be considered as a step to reduce the impact of the surrounding foreground–thus, the model can converge faster. Besides, by employing only the Attention U-Net architecture, we can downgrade the amount of memory for storing models on each device, which allows us to train the network without the difficulty of finding compatible devices.

Secondly, we utilize multi-scale images as a sequence of inputs rather than a single image, as conventional approaches do. This exploits the intermediate feature representations better. Experimental results on the ISIC 2018 challenge dataset show that our proposed method outperforms the second-ranked team (LeHealth) [14] and attains a close margin with the best team (NMN), thereby producing a much better performance-explainability trade-off that can be evaluated by doctors in future experiments.

3   Method

There are two principal ways to detect lesion attributes. The first one tries to train a network that can predict all five attributes together, while the second type focuses on training separate networks for each type of lesion attribute. In this work, we apply the second strategy for two main reasons. The first reason is to avoid the negative impact of the class imbalance in the dataset, while the second reason is that this approach leads to an uncertainty property whereby a pixel can be assigned to several classes with different probabilities depending on the input images. In those cases, the doctor can examine them carefully and make a final decision by visualizing the corresponding regions.

Datasets: We used two datasets downloaded from the ISIC 2018 challenge website (https://challenge2018.isic-archive.com/). The first dataset (for Task 1) includes 2594 images with corresponding ground-truth mask images for segmentation. A mask image is a 2-color image, black/white, whose resolution matches with the corresponding sample image, where pixels associated to a positive case are marked white. The second dataset (for Task 2) comprises of 2594 images with 12,970 ground-truth masks (one separate mask for each attribute). However, since most of the attributes do not appear together in an image, the corresponding masks are empty (all black) for the absent attributes. Table 1 represents in detail a distribution for each attribute, where the highest-occurring attribute are the pigment network and milia-like cysts with 58.7% and 26.3%, respectively. Streaks is the lowest-occurring attribute, with 2.9%. This imbalance makes the prediction task more complicated, that is a trained network will be severely biased towards the attributes with a lot of training data points as compared to attributes with fewer samples. This challenge motivated our choice to employ a separate model for each attribute prediction.

Network Architecture: The proposed method to predict masks for segmentation and for the five lesion attributes is illustrated in Fig. 1, where the main component is the Attention U-Net [9] with multi-scale images as input.

Table 1. Distribution of mask images

Lesion attributes	Pigment network	Globules	Milia-like cysts	Negative network	Streaks	Total images
Mask count	1522	602	681	189	100	2594
Rate	58.7%	23.2%	26.3%	7.3%	2.9%	100%

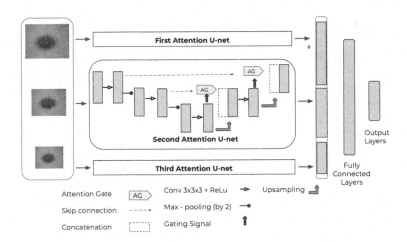

Fig. 1. Our proposed architecture with three blocks of Attention U-net.

The Attention U-Net is a modified version of U-Net [11], which has been proven to be very effective on small datasets. In particular, Attention U-net is equipped with Attention Gates (AG), which are used to recognize relevant spatial information from low-level features and passed to the decoding path. For each input feature map x^L at layer L, AG provides an attention coefficients α to transform the input feature map x^L to an output of semantical features $\hat{x}^L$, defined as: $\hat{x}^L = x^L \odot \alpha$, where $\odot$ denotes the element-wise product operator; α is the attention coefficient to identify salient image regions and prune feature responses to preserve only the activations relevant to the specific task. By leveraging AG, Attention U-Net focuses on target structures without additional supervision, thus enabling us to avoid an external object localization model.

We utilize a sequence of three images with different resolutions 180×180, 256×256, and 450×450 as the input of the three distinct Attention U-Nets. Such inputs are also referred to as the "Pyramid" feature [1], whereby the strength lies in the ability to search objects faster using a coarse-to-fine strategy, thus enabling the network to exploit more information of objects via the multiple resolution levels. Finally, we concatenate the feature vectors from the multi-scale images and pass them to a fully-connected layer before the final prediction layer. Pixel-level output is thresholded at 0.5 for black/white discrimination. The loss function is defined as the complement of the Jaccard index:

$$L = 1 - \frac{\sum y_{truth}\, y_{predict}}{\sum y_{truth}^2 + \sum y_{predict}^2 - \sum y_{truth}\, y_{predict} + \alpha} \tag{1}$$

where $y_{predict}$ and y_{truth} are the predicted pixel vector and its corresponding ground truth, and $\alpha = 1e - 05$ is a smoothing value to avoid divisions by zero.

Transfer Learning from Segmentation Task: While most recent works commonly initialized the parameters of their networks by transfer learning from ImageNet [5], we approach in a novel way through learning directly from the segmentation task. Specifically, we randomly sampled 70% of the total 2594 images of Task 1 as the training set, with the remaining 30% as the held-out set. For each image in the training set, we applied a pre-processing step to center the data by subtracting the mean per channel and constructing multi-scale versions with three corresponding sizes: 180×180, 256×256, and 450×450. At the next step, these images were fed into our architecture, as described in Sect. 3. We trained the proposed framework for 40 epochs with earlystopping. A Jaccard index score of about 76% was obtained on the test set of 780 images–closely matching the baseline results on the leaderboards from ISIC 2018 Task 1[1].

Lesion Attributes Detection: Given the trained segmentation network, we clone it into five new instances, one for each lesion attribute, thus each initialized with the segmentation task parameters. In other words, we model the prediction problem as five independent binary segmentation problems. Besides the advantages of avoiding the data imbalance problem (Table 1) and producing an uncertainty score; by further examination of the data, we discovered that most of the lesion attributes were located near the lesion boundary. Therefore, initializing weights from the segmentation network can be considered as a consequential preprocessing step to lessen the effect of the surrounding foreground. Consequently, the supporting model can predict more precisely the positions of lesion attributes.

4   Experiments and Results

During experiments, we build models with the Keras framework and using the AMSGrad optimisation algorithm [10] with a learning rate and weight decay of approximately 10^{-4}. A five-fold cross-validation scheme was applied for each lesion structure, with 60 epochs for each fold, then we computed the expected performance based on out-of-sample tests on the networks. To be consistent with the standard requirements of the ISIC challenge, we use the Jaccard index as the main score.

Figure 2 shows sample results in the detection of the globules lesion attribute.

We compare our cross-validation results with the two top methods: NMN's method [8] and LeHealth's method (see Table 2). Our average Jaccard index result is 0.278, which is 0.002 more compared to LeHealth's method and 0.029 less than the best approach. Nevertheless, our method surpasses both competitors in

---

[1] https://challenge2018.isic-archive.com/leaderboards/.

Fig. 2. Results for Globules where the blue regions indicate the ground-truth labels and the red regions indicate our visual predictions/explanations, respectively. (Color figure online)

Table 2. Comparing our results that uses network initialization from the segmentation network against the NMN and LeHealth team based on the Jaccard Index. The best-performing scores are in bold.

Method	Pigment network	Globules	Milia-like cysts	Negative network	Streaks	Average
Our method	0.535	**0.312**	0.162	0.187	**0.197**	0.278
Our method (without transfer)	0.493	0.221	0.145	0.156	0.118	0.227
NMN's method	**0.544**	0.252	**0.165**	**0.285**	0.123	**0.307**
LeHealth's method	0.482	0.239	0.132	0.225	0.145	0.276

two categories out of the five: globules and streaks. Furthermore, the experiment results prove the effectiveness of our transfer learning strategy as it improves the performance of all attributes; especially for the classes with the least data: Streaks (7.9%) and Negative Network (3.1%). Also, this approach improves our performance score from 0.227 to 0.278.

We quantify the computation and memory requirements. As a rough estimation, in our method each attention U-Net requires about $2320k$ parameters for each class. Hence, in total we trained approximately $2320k \times 5 = 11600k$, which is below 12 million parameters. On the other hand, ResNet [6] (the network architecture used by the winning team NWN) typically requires about $60344k$ parameters for a single class; hence $60344k \times 5 = 301721k$, which is more than 300 million parameters for five classes.

5   Conclusion

In this work, we proposed a novel approach for skin attributes detection based on Attention U-net with multi-scale image inputs. While our network only requires a small number of parameters compared to other state-of-the-art methods, it achieves performance on par or better compared to the best approaches for some classes. This advantage benefits from our effective transfer learning tactic that leverages the segmentation network as initialization. In term of the social impact, our system can contribute as a visually explainable system to doctors for the early diagnosis and treatment of skin cancer.

References

1. Bovik, A.C.: The Essential Guide to Image Processing. Academic Press, Cambridge (2009)
2. Chen, L.C., Papandreou, G., Schroff, F., Adam, H.: Rethinking atrous convolution for semantic image segmentation. arXiv preprint arXiv:1706.05587 (2017)
3. Chollet, F.: Xception: deep learning with depthwise separable convolutions. In: Proceedings of the IEEE Conference on Computer Vision and Pattern Recognition, pp. 1251–1258 (2017)
4. Codella, N., et al.: Skin lesion analysis toward melanoma detection 2018: a challenge hosted by the International Skin Imaging Collaboration (ISIC). arXiv preprint arXiv:1902.03368 (2019)
5. Deng, J., Dong, W., Socher, R., Li, L.J., Li, K., Fei-Fei, L.: ImageNet: a large-scale hierarchical image database. In: 2009 IEEE Conference on Computer Vision and Pattern Recognition, pp. 248–255. IEEE (2009)
6. He, K., Zhang, X., Ren, S., Sun, J.: Deep residual learning for image recognition. In: Proceedings of the IEEE Conference on Computer Vision and Pattern Recognition, pp. 770–778 (2016)
7. Huang, G., Liu, Z., Van Der Maaten, L., Weinberger, K.Q.: Densely connected convolutional networks. In: Proceedings of the IEEE Conference on Computer Vision and Pattern Recognition, pp. 4700–4708 (2017)
8. Koohbanani, N.A., Jahanifar, M., Tajeddin, N.Z., Gooya, A., Rajpoot, N.: Leveraging transfer learning for segmenting lesions and their attributes in dermoscopy images. arXiv preprint arXiv:1809.10243 (2018)
9. Oktay, O., et al.: Attention U-Net: learning where to look for the pancreas. arXiv preprint arXiv:1804.03999 (2018)
10. Reddi, S.J., Kale, S., Kumar, S.: On the convergence of Adam and beyond. arXiv preprint arXiv:1904.09237 (2019)
11. Ronneberger, O., Fischer, P., Brox, T.: U-Net: convolutional networks for biomedical image segmentation. In: Navab, N., Hornegger, J., Wells, W.M., Frangi, A.F. (eds.) MICCAI 2015. LNCS, vol. 9351, pp. 234–241. Springer, Cham (2015). https://doi.org/10.1007/978-3-319-24574-4_28
12. Siegel, R.L., Miller, K.D., Jemal, A.: Cancer statistics, 2016. CA: Cancer J. Clin. **66**(1), 7–30 (2016)
13. Zhao, H., Shi, J., Qi, X., Wang, X., Jia, J.: Pyramid scene parsing network. In: Proceedings of the IEEE Conference on Computer Vision and Pattern Recognition, pp. 2881–2890 (2017)
14. Zou, J., Ma, X., Zhong, C., Zhang, Y.: Dermoscopic image analysis for ISIC challenge 2018. arXiv preprint arXiv:1807.08948 (2018)

Evaluation of Deep Learning Accelerators for Object Detection at the Edge

Pascal Puchtler and René Peinl[(✉)]

iisys, Hof University, Alfons-Goppel-Platz1, 95028 Hof, Germany
`{pascal.puchtler,rene.peinl}@iisys.de`

Abstract. Deep learning is moving more and more from the cloud towards the edge. Therefore, embedded devices are needed that are reasonably cheap, energy-efficient and fast enough. In this paper we evaluate the performance and energy consumption of popular, off-the-shelf commercial devices for deep learning inferencing. We compare the Intel Neural Compute Stick 2, the Google Coral Edge TPU and the Nvidia Jetson Nano with the Raspberry Pi 4 for their suitability as a central controller in an autonomous vehicle for the formula student driverless.

Keywords: Object detection · Deep learning accelerator · Benchmark · Edge computing

1 Introduction

Deep learning has advanced the state of the art in many disciplines like object detection [1], or natural language understanding [2]. While most of the well-known deep learning solutions are running in the cloud on large server farms, the wish for doing the inferencing directly on edge devices grows stronger [3]. One reason for that is data protection of sensible data. Another one can be latency. Our goal is similar to [4]. We want to build a platform based on open source software and low cost hardware (<1.000 € as a target price) that is able to perform the tasks of the formula student driverless, but under adapted settings, since our prototyping hardware is only about $40 \times 30 \times 25$ cm (length, width, height) in size. Therefore, we are testing with lower distances between pylons and smaller track sizes. In this paper, we are reporting about the evaluation of suitable hardware for accelerating the inferencing of the deep neural network for object detection of the pylons that delimit the track in an edge computing scenario. The rest of the paper is organized as follows. We first report about related work in the formula student, deep learning accelerator and benchmarking area. Then we introduce our test setup, before reporting about the result. We end with a discussion and conclusion.

2 Related Work

One major task for competing in the formula student driverless is the recognition of the pylons that delimit the track [5]. The TU Vienna uses a ZED stereo camera together with

© Springer Nature Switzerland AG 2020
U. Schmid et al. (Eds.): KI 2020, LNAI 12325, pp. 320–326, 2020.
https://doi.org/10.1007/978-3-030-58285-2_29

a LIDAR for that [5], a Chinese team uses a similar combination, but does not report on the camera model [6]. The ETH Zurich, who won the first German competition in 2017 are using three cameras and a LIDAR [7]. All have a similar design, but we are trying to achieve the goals with low cost hardware such as a Raspberry Pi 4 (RPi 4) instead of high-end industrial PCs and an Arduino Mega as motion controller instead of an expensive embedded board.

Looking at commercial, low-cost off-the-shelf hardware for deep learning the RPi4 is certainly interesting due to its low price point and good CPU performance. Despite its improved CPU speed in v4 with its ARM Cortex A72 cores instead of the previous A53 cores, it is still only achieving 2.5 to 7.7 fps for deep learning inferencing [8]. Bahl et al. achieve not even 2 fps with the RPi4, whereas their implementation on an Altera Cyclone V 5CSXC6 FPGA achieves 7 fps at 100 MHz. In general, this could be sped up by offloading to the GPU [9, 10], but its VideoCore GPU is not supported by popular deep learning frameworks yet. The Nvidia Jetson Nano is an alternative with a CUDA compatible GPU that is supported and has a reasonable price [11], but it consumes significantly more power than a RPi4 and cannot be powered by a USB power bank. [4] are using it nevertheless in their car and power it by a 5000 mAh 7.2 V Ni-MH battery with banana 4.0 connector that needs to be transformed both regarding current and plug. The Jetson TX2 is slightly more efficient and has a 77% better performance [11], but is also nearly five times more expensive. Recently, the successor of the Jetson TX2 called Jetson Xavier NX was released, which is claimed to be 10 times faster than the TX2, but is still too expensive for us with it's 400 USD price point [12].

To speed up inferencing for deep learning compared to CPUs and GPUs, custom application-specific integrated circuits (ASICs), such as Google's tensor processing unit (TPU) are suggested [3] as well as field-programmable gate arrays (FPGAs) [13] due to their performance and energy-efficiency [14]. The Google Coral Edge TPU and Intels Neural Compute Stick (NCS) both come with a USB interface to plug them to any compatible computer [15]. The NCS was found to perform on par with the Nvidia TX1 (8 fps) and increased the performance of an Odroid XU4 by more than 400% [16]. However, accuracy also dropped around 2% points from around 60% mean average precision (mAP) when running the KITTI and LPS2017 validation datasets on the NCS instead of a PC [17].

Field-programmable gate array (FPGA)-based DNN accelerators are interesting since they can provide fast computation while maintaining re-configurability [3]. However, [18] found that the Xilinx ZC706 FPGA they tested performed poor in both performance and energy efficiency compared to an Nvidia Jetson TX1. In special settings and high optimization effort, they can however outperform ASICs like the NCS [19]. Hegde and Kapre also mention an important additional aspect. The GPU-based solution was "effortless to use" whereas the other alternatives suffered from a "high barrier to setup" or were "hard to program" [18]. This is also a relevant issue for the aforementioned USB accelerators. "Executing a model in the Edge TPU requires a prior translation (recompilation) of the TFLite model by means of the Edge TPU Compiler, that maps each TFLite operator to an available operator in the device; if the original operator is not compatible with the TPU, it is mapped to the CPU" [15]. For the NCS, the procedure is similar, but the Intel Model Optimizer is used instead, which is part of the OpenVINO

SDK [20]. Both devices are not able to run arbitrary models, but require certain prerequisites like quantization of parameters, so that only two out of six models of the MLperf benchmark could be run [15]. Libutti et al. found that the Coral was between three and seven times faster than the NCS 2 and at the same time 4–7 times more energy-efficient [15]. The NCS 2 does also require a larger idle power with 1.5 W compared to 1.0 W for the Coral. That led in our setup to the fact, that the NCS2 did not start properly with the battery attached and even had problems with our standard 5 V 3A power supply. We had to order a 5.1 V power supply to get it running with the RPi 4, whereas the Coral had no problems with both the USB powerbank and the standard power supply. Libutti et al. also observed a difference in accuracy of the inferences. The NCS 2 achieved 73.7% versus 70.6% attained by the Edge TPU on MobileNet v1. For InceptionV1, the accuracy decreased from 69% to 65.9% in average [15].

ShiDianNao [21] is another custom ASIC with a focus on efficient memory access in order to reduce latency and energy consumption for embedded devices [22]. Although it exhibits superior performance compared to CPUs and GPUs for CNN inferencing and is at the same time very energy-efficient, it is not further considered here due to its lacking commercial availability. With neuromorphic hardware, an even better efficiency is possible [23], but at the cost of accuracy.

3   Test Setup

For our tests, we used the RPi4 as a single board computer (SBC) and connected the cameras and USB-based accelerators to its USB 3.1 ports. For comparison, we also ran the tests on the GPU of the **Nvidia Jetson Nano**. As a camera, we started with the **Orbbec Astra**, an RGB-D camera with a resolution of 640 × 480 pixels at 30 fps (frames per second). Our first tests suggested that the accelerators would be able to evaluate more than 30 fps. Therefore, we included a **Logitech Brio** camera to find the upper limit. It can deliver up to 90 fps for resolutions up to 1280 × 720 and 30 fps up to 4 k resolution. However, we've used it with 640 × 480 pixels resolution as the Orbbec Astra. The inferencing was run on the CPU of the RPi4 or on either the **Intel Neural Compute Stick 2** (NCS2) or the **Google Coral Edge TPU** (Coral). For energy measurements, we've used a **UM34 USB meter** as power meter. It can be simply plugged between the camera and RPi4 or between the accelerator and RPi4 or between the RPi 4 and the power supply to measure the energy of a single device or the whole system.

On the software side, we've used Raspian Buster with kernel 4.19, CMake 3.14.4 and python 3.7.3. For accessing the camera, OpenCV version 4.1.2-openvino was installed.

For running the inferencing on the models on the CPU or Coral, Tensorflow Lite (TFlite) 2.1.0 was used. For the NCS2, we used OpenVINO version 2020.1.

We've used SSD MobileNet v2 as a basis for object detection. However, we could not simply use the same version in each scenario. For the test on the CPU, we used the pre-trained model from the Tensorflow model zoo in version "quantized coco", which is also one of the fastest models according to the table with 29 ms inferencing time[1]. We've converted it to be used with Tensorflow lite, which is known to be better suited

---

[1] https://github.com/tensorflow/models/blob/master/research/object_detection/g3doc/detection_model_zoo.md.

for SBCs like the RPi 4. For usage on the Google Coral stick, we had to convert it again. The same applies to the NCS2. We've used a version of SSD MobileNet v2 prepared by Intel[2], but still had to run it through Intel's model optimizer tool before it was running on the NCS2 and this was everything, but a straight forward process. Interestingly, we also had problems with running the original model on the Nvidia Jetson Nano. Therefore, we chose the ssdtf_fp16 model from the Nvidia website[3] for this case.

The power meter measures voltage and current with three valid digits each. These are multiplied and accumulated in a 2 Hz cycle. The resulting power average for a 60 s interval therefore delivers a power measurement with two valid digits.

The Python time function is used to measure the execution times. Each measurement happened under the same conditions. Wi-Fi was activated and connected and a VNC connection to our PC is active. The camera always pointed at the same unchanged background[4]. The FPS were determined without simultaneous current measurement. Each measurement took one minute, after which the average output power was calculated. The accuracy was calculated as mean average precision (mAP) against our own dataset.

4 Results

Performance measurements show, that the RPi 4 achieves not even four frames per second (fps) without an accelerator (see Fig. 1), which is only suitable to reliably steer the formula student car at low speeds. The car should see the situation at least once every meter which means it can drive with maximum speed of 13 km/h. The NCS 2 is more than five times faster than the RPi 4 and achieves 20 fps, whereas the Coral is obviously limited by the frame rate of the camera at slightly more than 29 fps when using the Orbbec Astra. Using the Logitech Brio instead, all systems perform better. The NCS2 achieves 23 fps, a the Coral 45 fps in normal mode and even 54.74 fps in high power mode. The performance of the Nivdia Jetson Nano was surprisingly bad, reaching only 15.90 fps with the Brio, which is equal to 57 km/h.

Regarding energy, the differences seem rather small, but could still make a difference for a certain combination of battery, board, camera and accelerator (see Fig. 2). The most energy saving version is the RPi 4 with the Brio camera that consumes a total of 6.5 W. The NCS2 needs 7.3 W altogether, whereas the combination of RPi 4, Brio and Coral accelerator uses 7.0 and 7.1 in normal and high power mode respectively. The Jetson Nano needs the most energy with a total of 9.0 W. Interestingly, the Orbbec camera increases the total power consumption only by 0.1 W compared to the Brio when used with the RPi 4 alone, although the measurement of the camera alone showed a difference of 0.4 W between the Brio and the Orbbec. Together with the NCS2 or Coral, the difference between the Brio and the Orbbec is 0.8 W.

---

[2] https://docs.openvinotoolkit.org/latest/_docs_MO_DG_prepare_model_convert_model_Conv ert_Model_From_TensorFlow.html.

[3] https://ngc.nvidia.com/catalog/models/nvidia:ssdtf_fp16.

[4] Previous measurements have shown that the type of background and the number of detected objects has no measurable influence on the operating time and energy consumption. We've published our dataset on https://github.com/iisys-hof/formula-student-dataset.

Table 1. Accuracy of object detection with the different deep learning accelerators

	RPi only INT8	RPi only FP32	RPi + NCS2 FP32	RPi + Coral INT8	Jetson Nano FP16
mAP	0.1891	0.2530	0.2459	0.2248	0.1988

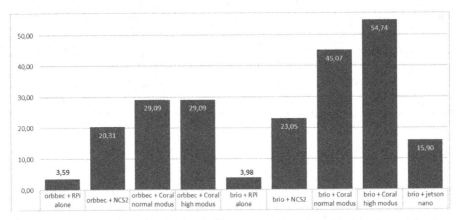

Fig. 1. Performance measurements for Raspberry Pi 4 with various deep learning accelerators

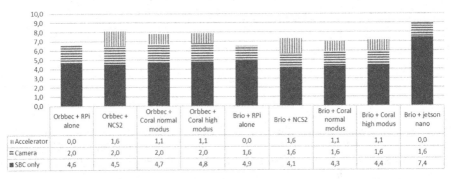

Fig. 2. Energy measurements for Raspberry Pi 4 with various deep learning accelerators

The energy consumption however reveals large differences, when looking at the energy in relation to the frame rate. The Jetson Nano seems even less attractive in this scenario compared to the Coral and the NCS2.

Finally, we need to look at the accuracy of the different candidates. One could naively expect that the accuracy is only depending on the network architecture, but the different transformation steps necessary to get the networks running on the accelerators lead to significant differences (see Table 1). The highest accuracy can be achieved on the RPi 4 with FP32. The NCS2 is very close to that. The Coral uses INT8 only and therefore falls behind in this category with 0.02 mAP less than the NCS2. The Jetson Nano performed worst with another drop of 0.025 mAP compared to the Coral, although it is using FP16. For our use case, however, we found that to be sufficient, since the pylons that are not recognized on one frame are usually recognized on the next.

5 Discussion and Conclusion

We've evaluated the inferencing speed and energy consumption of SSD MobileNet v2 pretrained with the COCO dataset on various hardware for an autonomous car. We found that the Raspberry Pi 4 is too slow for our use case with not even 4 fps, whereas the Google Coral Edge TPU performed best with nearly 55 fps. The Intel Neural Compute Stick 2 reached 23 fps, which could be sufficient for many use cases. The Nvidia Jetson Nano fell behind in our tests with only 16 fps. We expected it however to be the easiest device to use, since in theory it should be enough to switch a parameter in the Tensorflow runtime to let the network run on the GPU instead of the CPU. However, it turned out to be equally hard to get the model running on the Jetson Nano as it was on the Coral and the NCS2. It looks differently if we take the price into account. In this relation, the Jetson Nano is the cheapest solution if you consider the RPi 4 with 4 GB RAM as a fair comparison to the Jetson Nano that also comes with 4 GB RAM. However, the difference is not huge (120 € to 155 € for RPi 4 + Coral).

Summed up, the largest disappointment was the effort necessary to get the models running on the accelerators and the limitation regarding which models were suitable which we already encountered with the Jetson Nano for speech recognition [25].

References

1. Liu, L., Ouyang, W., Wang, X., Fieguth, P., Chen, J., Liu, X., Pietikäinen, M.: Deep learning for generic object detection: a survey. Int. J. Comput. Vis. **128**, 261–318 (2020)
2. Storks, S., Gao, Q., Chai, J.Y.: Recent Advances in Natural Language Inference: A Survey of Benchmarks, Resources, and Approaches. ArXiv Prepr. ArXiv190401172 (2019)
3. Chen, J., Ran, X.: Deep learning with edge computing: A review. Proc. IEEE **107**, 1655–1674 (2019)
4. Srinivasa, S.S., et al.: MuSHR: A Low-Cost, Open-Source Robotic Racecar for Education and Research. ArXiv Prepr. ArXiv190808031 (2019)
5. Zeilinger, M., Hauk, R., Bader, M., Hofmann, A.: Design of an autonomous race car for the formula student driverless (fsd). In: Oagm & Arw Joint Workshop (2017)
6. Jun, N.I., Jibin, H.U.: Autonomous driving system design for formula student driverless racecar. In: 2018 IEEE Intelligent Vehicles Symposium (IV). pp. 1–6. IEEE (2018)
7. Kabzan, J., et al.: Amz driverless: The full autonomous racing system. ArXiv Prepr. ArXiv190505150 (2019)
8. Bahl, G., Daniel, L., Moretti, M., Lafarge, F.: Low-power neural networks for semantic segmentation of satellite images. In: Proceedings of the IEEE International Conference on Computer Vision Workshops (2019)
9. Kristiani, E., Yang, C.-T., Huang, C.-Y.: iSEC: an optimized deep learning model for image classification on edge computing. IEEE Access. **8**, 27267–27276 (2020)
10. He, Q., Weaver, V., Segee, B.: Comparing power and energy usage for scientific calculation with and without GPU acceleration on a raspberry Pi model B + and 3B. In: International Conference on Internet Computing (ICOMP), pp. 3–9 (2018)

11. Peng, T., Zhang, D., Hettiarachchi, D.L.N., Loomis, J.: An evaluation of embedded GPU systems for visual SLAM algorithms. In: IS&T International Symposium on Electronic Imaging 2020: Intelligent Robotics and Industrial Applications using Computer Vision (2020)

12. Pinto, D.: NVIDIA Releases Jetson Xavier NX Developer Kit with Cloud-Native Support. http://nvidianews.nvidia.com/news/nvidia-releases-jetson-xavier-nx-developer-kit-with-cloud-native-support. Accessed 23 May 2020

13. Lee, M., Hwang, K., Park, J., Choi, S., Shin, S., Sung, W.: FPGA-based low-power speech recognition with recurrent neural networks. In: 2016 IEEE International Workshop on Signal Processing Systems (SiPS), pp. 230–235. IEEE (2016)

14. Reagen, B., et al.: Minerva: enabling low-power, highly-accurate deep neural network accelerators. In: 2016 ACM/IEEE 43rd Annual Intl. Symposium on Computer Architecture (ISCA), pp. 267–278. IEEE (2016)

15. Libutti, L.A., Igual, F.D., Pinuel, L., De Giusti, L., Naiouf, M.: Benchmarking performance and power of USB accelerators for inference with MLPerf⋆. In: 2nd Workshop on Accelerated Machine Learning (AccML), Valencia, Spain (2020)

16. Hossain, S., Lee, D.: Deep learning-based real-time multiple-object detection and tracking from aerial imagery via a flying robot with gpu-based embedded devices. Sensors. **19**, 3371 (2019)

17. Chen, C.-W., Ruan, S.-J., Lin, C.-H., Hung, C.-C.: Performance evaluation of edge computing-based deep learning object detection. In: 7th International Conference on Network, Communication and Computing, pp. 40–43 (2018)

18. Hegde, G., Kapre, N.: CaffePresso: accelerating convolutional networks on embedded SoCs. ACM Trans. Embed. Comput. Syst. TECS. **17**, 1–26 (2017)

19. Gao, C., Rios-Navarro, A., Chen, X., Delbruck, T., Liu, S.-C.: EdgeDRNN: Enabling Low-latency Recurrent Neural Network Edge Inference. ArXiv Prepr. ArXiv191212193 (2019)

20. Gorbachev, Y., Fedorov, M., Slavutin, I., Tugarev, A., Fatekhov, M., Tarkan, Y.: OpenVINO Deep Learning Workbench: Comprehensive Analysis and Tuning of Neural Networks Inference. In: IEEE Intl. Conf. on Computer Vision Workshops. (2019)

21. Du, Z., et al.: ShiDianNao: Shifting vision processing closer to the sensor. In: 42nd Annual International Symposium on Computer Architecture, pp. 92–104 (2015)

22. Chen, Y., Chen, T., Xu, Z., Sun, N., Temam, O.: DianNao family: energy-efficient hardware accelerators for machine learning. Commun. ACM **59**, 105–112 (2016)

23. Diehl, P.U., Zarrella, G., Cassidy, A., Pedroni, B.U., Neftci, E.: Conversion of artificial recurrent neural networks to spiking neural networks for low-power neuromorphic hardware. In: 2016 IEEE International Conference on Rebooting Computing (ICRC), pp. 1–8. IEEE (2016)

24. Lane, N.D., et al..: Deepx: a software accelerator for low-power deep learning inference on mobile devices. In: 15th ACM/IEEE International Conference on Info Proceeding in Sensor Nets (IPSN). pp. 1–12. IEEE (2016)

25. Peinl, R., Rizk, B., Szabad, R.: Open source speech recognition on edge devices. In: 10th International Conference on Advanced Computer Information Technologies, Deggendorf, Germany (2020)

Learning Choice Functions via Pareto-Embeddings

Karlson Pfannschmidt$^{(\boxtimes)}$ and Eyke Hüllermeier

Paderborn University, Paderborn, Germany
`kiudee@mail.upb.de`

Abstract. We consider the problem of learning to choose from a given set of objects, where each object is represented by a feature vector. Traditional approaches in choice modelling are mainly based on learning a latent, real-valued utility function, thereby inducing a linear order on choice alternatives. While this approach is suitable for discrete (top-1) choices, it is not straightforward how to use it for subset choices. Instead of mapping choice alternatives to the real number line, we propose to embed them into a higher-dimensional utility space, in which we identify choice sets with Pareto-optimal points. To this end, we propose a learning algorithm that minimizes a differentiable loss function suitable for this task. We demonstrate the feasibility of learning a Pareto-embedding on a suite of benchmark datasets.

Keywords: Choice function · Pareto-embedding · Generalized utility

1 Introduction

The quest for understanding and modeling human decision making has a long history in various scientific disciplines, including economics and psychology [4]. Starting with the seminal work by Arrow [1], *choice functions* have been analyzed as a key concept of a formal theory of choice. In simple terms, a decision maker is confronted with a (possibly varying) set of alternatives and the choices made are observed. The ultimate goal is to explain and predict the choice behavior.

In machine learning, the task of "learning to choose" is part of the broader field of *preference learning*, which attracted increased attention in recent years [5]. The task for a learner is to observe choices from multiple sets of objects, and to produce a function which maps from candidate sets to choice sets. An important special case is the setting in which the decision maker only chooses one object from each given set, which is known as *discrete choice*. A popular strategy to tackle the learning problem is to posit that the choice probabilities depend on an underlying real-valued utility function of the decision maker. Under this assumption, learning can be accomplished by identifying the parameters of such a function. The more general problem of predicting choices in the form of *subsets* of objects has been considered only very recently [2,11]. Extending the approach based on utility functions toward this setting turns out to be non-trivial. Either one faces combinatorial problems calculating the probabilities for many subsets [2], or has to resort to thresholding techniques [11].

© Springer Nature Switzerland AG 2020
U. Schmid et al. (Eds.): KI 2020, LNAI 12325, pp. 327–333, 2020.
https://doi.org/10.1007/978-3-030-58285-2_30

We propose to solve this problem by embedding the objects in a higher-dimensional utility space, in which subset choices are naturally identified by Pareto-optimal points (Sect. 3). To learn a suitable embedding function, we devise a differentiable loss function tailored to this task. We then utilize the loss function as part of a deep learning pipeline to investigate the feasibility of learning such a Pareto-embedding (Sect. 4).

2   Modeling Choice

We proceed from a reference set of objects (choice alternatives) $\mathcal{X} \subset \mathbb{R}^d$, which, for ease of exposition, is assumed to be finite. Each $\boldsymbol{x} \in \mathcal{X}$ is represented as a vector of real-valued features $(x_1, \ldots, x_d)$. We call a finite subset of objects $Q \subseteq \mathcal{X}$ a *choice task* and allow the size $|Q| \in \mathbb{N}$ to vary across tasks. For each choice task $Q = \{\boldsymbol{x}_1, \ldots, \boldsymbol{x}_m\}$, we assume that a preference is expressed in terms of a *choice set* $C \subseteq Q$. A useful representation of a choice set is in terms of a binary vector $\boldsymbol{c} \in \{0, 1\}^m$, where $c_i = 1$ if $\boldsymbol{x}_i \in C$ and $c_i = 0$ if $\boldsymbol{x}_i \notin C$.

One of the first approaches to explaining choices was to assume that a decision maker can assign a (latent) utility to each of the choice alternatives. Formally, we represent such a utility function as a function $\mathcal{X} \to \mathbb{R}$ from the space of objects to the real numbers. Based on these utilities, a rational decision maker will always pick the alternative with the highest utility, i. e., the top-1 object. To explain variability in choices, noise can be added to the utilities, which results in what is called a *random utility model* [7,8,12].

At first glance, it may appear that this approach can easily be generalized to modeling subset choices: Instead of only selecting the top-1 object, one could consider to select the top-k objects, where $1 \leq k \leq |Q|$. One major drawback of this approach is that the subset size is predetermined to be k, so it is not possible to produce subsets of varying size. Another possibility is to specify a threshold for the utilities, and to include all objects with a utility higher than the threshold in the choice set [11]. While this allows for the prediction of subsets of arbitrary size, the decision of whether to include an object in the choice set is now completely independent of all the other objects.

As we shall see in the next section, there is a natural way to define subset choices, if we embed the objects in a higher-dimensional utility space.

3   Pareto-Embeddings

The basic idea of a Pareto-embedding is illustrated in Fig. 1. On the left side, we depict the original set of objects in the object space $\mathcal{X}$. The function $\varphi \colon \mathcal{X} \to \mathcal{Z}$ maps each point into a new embedding space $\mathcal{Z} \subseteq \mathbb{R}^{d'}$. This space can be thought of as a higher-dimensional utility space, i. e., each dimension corresponds to the utility on a certain aspect or criterion. As we can see, the choice set C forms what is called a Pareto-set in this new space, i. e., the set of points that are not dominated by any other point.

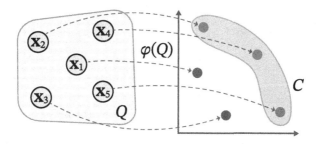

Fig. 1. A Pareto-embedding $\varphi(\cdot)$ maps a given set of objects Q into a higher-dimensional space $\mathcal{Z}$. The Pareto-optimal points in this space we define to be the choice set C.

More formally, let $Q = \{x_1, \ldots, x_m\} \subseteq \mathcal{X}$ be the original set of objects and $Z = \varphi(Q) = \{z_1, \ldots, z_m\} = \{\varphi(x_1), \ldots, \varphi(x_m)\}$ the corresponding points in the embedding space. A point z_i in the embedding space is *dominated* by another point z_j if $z_{i,k} \leq z_{j,k}$ for all $k \in [d']$ and $z_{i,k} < z_{j,k}$ for at least one such k. Then, a point z_i is called *Pareto-optimal* (with respect to Z), if it is not dominated by any other point $z_j \in Z$, $1 \leq j \neq i \leq m$. We denote by $P_\varphi(Q) \subseteq Q$ the subset of points that are Pareto-optimal in Q under the mapping φ, i.e., the points $x_i \in Q$ such that $\varphi(x_i)$ not dominated by any point in $\{\varphi(x_1), \ldots, \varphi(x_m)\}$.

It is interesting to note that the traditional one-dimensional utility always imposes a total order relation on the available objects, whereas the Pareto-embedding generalizes this to a partial order. Therefore, richer preference structures with multiple layers of incomparability can be modeled.

Given a set of observed choices $\mathcal{D} = \{(Q_n, C_n)\}_{n=1}^N$ as training data, where $Q_n \subseteq \mathcal{X}$ is a choice task and $C_n \subseteq Q_n$ the subset of objects selected, we are interested in learning a Pareto-embedding φ coherent with this data in the sense that $C_n \approx P_\varphi(Q_n)$ for all $n \in [N]$. Obviously, a function of that kind can then also be used for predictive purposes, i.e., to predict the choice for a new choice task. To induce φ from $\mathcal{D}$, we devise a general-purpose loss function, which can be used with any end-to-end trainable model, and hence should be differentiable almost everywhere.

The loss function we propose consists of several components, which we introduce step by step. Consider a choice C in a choice task Q, and denote by $c \in \{0,1\}^{|Q|}$ the vector encoding of C, i.e., $c_i = 1$ if $x_i \in C$ and $c_i = 0$ otherwise. In order to accomplish $C = P_\varphi(Q)$, the first constraint to be fulfilled by φ is to ensure that each point $x_j \in C$ will have an image in the embedding space which is Pareto-optimal in Z. Consider Fig. 2a, where the point in blue depicts the image $z_j = (z_{j,1}, \ldots, z_{j,d'})$ of x_j. The loss needs to penalize all points dominating z_j (shown in red). Formally, the first part of the loss function is defined as follows:

$$L_{\text{PO}}(Z, c) = \sum_{1 \leq i \neq j \leq |Z|} \max\left(0, c_j \cdot \min_{1 \leq k \leq d'} (1 + z_{i,k} - z_{j,k})\right) \tag{1}$$

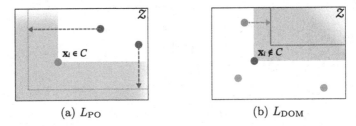

(a) L_{PO} (b) L_{DOM}

Fig. 2. Visualization of the effect of the loss terms L_{PO} and L_{DOM} in $\mathcal{Z}$ space. (Color figure online)

We project the points towards the blue region using the minimum term and penalize them in proportion from their distance to the boundary. Note that, to enforce a margin effect, we already penalize non-dominating points close to the boundary. This corresponds to using a hinge loss upper bound on the 0/1-binary loss, which is 1 if z_i dominates z_j and 0 otherwise.

Similarly, we define a loss that penalizes the embedding of a point $x_i \in Q \setminus C$ so that x_i is not dominated:

$$L_{\text{DOM}}(Z, c) = \sum_{i=1}^{|Z|} (1 - c_i) \min_{j \neq i} \left(\sum_{k=1}^{d'} \max\left(0, 1 + z_{i,k} - z_{j,k}\right) \right) \qquad (2)$$

The minimum selects the point which is closest to dominating z_i, while the inner sum penalizes all dimensions in which this point is not yet better than z_i.

With these two terms, we can ensure that if the loss is 0, we have a valid Pareto-embedding of the points. Furthermore, we add two more terms that are useful. To preserve as much of the original structure present in the object space $\mathcal{X}$, we use multidimensional scaling (MDS) [9]. It ensures that objects close to each other in the object space $\mathcal{X}$ will also be close in the embedding space $\mathcal{Z}$. In addition, all the losses so far are shift-invariant in the embedding space. To make the solution identifiable, we regularize the mapped points towards 0 using an L_2 loss. We define the complete Pareto-embedding loss as a convex combination

$$L(Q, Z, c) = \alpha_1 L_{\text{PO}}(Z, c) + \alpha_2 L_{\text{DOM}}(Z, c) + \alpha_3 L_{\text{MDS}}(Q, Z) + \alpha_4 \sum_{i=1}^{|Z|} \|z_i\|_2$$

with weights $\alpha_1, \alpha_2, \alpha_3, \alpha_4 \geq 0$ such that $\alpha_1 + \alpha_2 + \alpha_3 + \alpha_4 = 1$. These weights can be treated as hyperparameters of the learning algorithm. Given a space Φ of embedding functions, this algorithm seeks to find a minimizer

$$\varphi^* \in \operatorname*{argmin}_{\varphi \in \Phi} \sum_{n=1}^{N} L\big(Q_n, P_\varphi(Q_n), c_n\big)$$

of the overall loss on the training data $\mathcal{D}$.

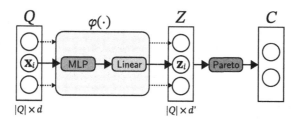

Fig. 3. Architecture of our approach. Each object is passed through a (deep) multi-layer perceptron followed by a linear output layer to produce the embedding. The Pareto-optimal points are selected to obtain a prediction C.

4 Empirical Evaluation

As for the space of embedding functions, any model class amenable to training by gradient descent can in principle be used. Here, as a proof of concept, we use a simple fully connected multi-layer perceptron as a learner. The architecture is depicted in Fig. 3. We take each object x_i for $1 \leq i \leq |Q|$ of the task Q and pass it through the (deep) multi-layer perceptron. Rectified linear units are used here as the nonlinearities. Batch normalization [6] is applied after each layer to speed up and stabilize training. In the final layer, we pass the output of the multi-layer perceptron through a linear layer with d' outputs. After the same network (using weight sharing) was applied to all objects in Q, we end up with the transformed set Z. To obtain the final prediction, we take the set Z and compute the corresponding Pareto-set. The network can be trained using standard backpropagation of the loss.

To ascertain the feasibility of learning a Pareto-embedding from data, we evaluate our approach on a suite of benchmark problems from the field of multi-criteria optimization. We use the well-known DTLZ test suite by Deb et al. [3] and the ZDT test suite by Zitzler et al. [13], containing datasets of varying difficulty. Adding a simple two-dimensional two parabola (TP) dataset, we end up with 14 benchmark problems in total. We generate 40 960 object sets of size 10 with 6 features each for every problem. Exceptions are the TP dataset with only 2 features and the ZDT5 dataset, which has 35 binary features by definition. For the DTLZ problems, we set the dimensionality of the underlying objective space to 5.

We evaluate our approach on every problem by 5 repetitions of a Monte Carlo cross validation with a 90/10% split into training and test data. The remaining instances are split into 1/9 validation instances and 8/9 training instances. We use the validation set to jointly optimize the hyperparameters of the learner, which are (a) the loss weights $\alpha_1, \alpha_2, \alpha_3, \alpha_4$, (b) the maximum learning rate of the cyclical learning rate scheduler, and (c) the number of hidden units and layers, using 60 iterations of Bayesian optimization. The neural network was trained for 500 epochs. The number of embedding dimensions d' we set to 2, since this allows us to move from a total order (only one utility dimension) to a partial order.

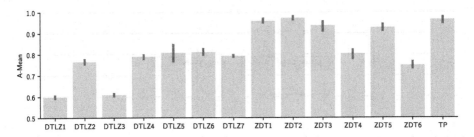

Fig. 4. Results of the empirical evaluation. The bars show the average performance in terms of A-mean across the 5 outer splits. The sticks show the estimated standard deviation.

Finally, we need a suitable metric to compare the ground truth subsets to the predicted ones. Since the shape of the Pareto-sets has an impact on how many points end up in the chosen subset, we have varying levels of positives across the datasets. Therefore, we choose a metric that is unbiased with respect to the prevalence of positives and well-suited for problems with class imbalance, called the *A-mean* [10], the arithmetic mean of the true positive and true negative rate.

The results are shown in Fig. 4. For five of the problems, the embedding approach is able to achieve an average A-mean of over 90%, indicating that for these problems we often identify the choice set correctly. This is important, as it shows that the loss function is able to steer the model parameters towards a valid Pareto-embedding. For comparison, a random selection in which each object is included in the choice set with a fixed probability (independently of the others) achieves an average A-mean of 50%. Thus, it is apparent that our learner is performing better than random guessing on all datasets. We also did an ablation experiment, where we removed the MDS term from the loss function and repeated the complete training procedure (including optimization of all the other hyperparameters). This resulted in a significant decrease in performance, showing that the MDS term is not only useful to preserve distances, but adds a helpful inductive bias.

5   Conclusion and Outlook

We proposed a novel way to tackle the problem of learning choice functions. Viewing it as an embedding problem and transforming the given objects into a utility space of more than one dimension, subset choice are naturally identified by the criterion of Pareto-optimality. To learn an embedding from a given set of observed choices as training data, we developed a suitable loss function that penalizes violations of the Pareto condition. Encouraged by the promising first results on benchmark problems, we are now looking forward to a more extensive empirical evaluation and applications to real-world choice problems.

References

1. Arrow, K.J.: Social Choice and Individual Values. Wiley, Hoboken (1951)
2. Benson, A.R., Kumar, R., Tomkins, A.: A discrete choice model for subset selection. In: Proceedings of the Eleventh ACM International Conference on Web Search and Data Mining, WSDM 2018, pp. 37–45. ACM (2018)
3. Deb, K., Thiele, L., Laumanns, M., Zitzler, E.: Scalable test problems for evolutionary multiobjective optimization. In: Abraham, A., Jain, L., Goldberg, R. (eds.) Evolutionary Multiobjective Optimization. Advanced Information and Knowledge Processing, pp. 105–145. Springer, London (2005). https://doi.org/10.1007/1-84628-137-7_6
4. Domshlak, C., Hüllermeier, E., Kaci, S., Prade, H.: Preferences in AI: an overview. Artif. Intell. **175**(7–8), 1037–1052 (2011)
5. Fürnkranz, J., Hüllermeier, E. (eds.): Preference Learning. Springer, Heidelberg (2010). https://doi.org/10.1007/978-3-642-14125-6
6. Ioffe, S., Szegedy, C.: Batch normalization: accelerating deep network training by reducing internal covariate shift. In: Proceedings of the 32nd International Conference on Machine Learning, ICML 2015, Lille, France, 6–11 July 2015. JMLR Workshop and Conference Proceedings, vol. 37, pp. 448–456. JMLR.org (2015)
7. Luce, R.D.: Individual Choice Behavior. Wiley, Hoboken (1959)
8. Marschak, J.: Binary choice constraints on random utility indicators. Technical report 74, Cowles Foundation for Research in Economics, Yale University (1959)
9. Mead, A.: Review of the development of multidimensional scaling methods. J. Roy. Stat. Soc. Ser. D (Stat.) **41**(1), 27–39 (1992)
10. Menon, A., Narasimhan, H., Agarwal, S., Chawla, S.: On the statistical consistency of algorithms for binary classification under class imbalance. In: Proceedings of the 30th International Conference on Machine Learning. Proceedings of Machine Learning Research, vol. 28, pp. 603–611. PMLR, Atlanta, 17–19 June 2013
11. Pfannschmidt, K., Gupta, P., Hüllermeier, E.: Learning Choice Functions: Concepts and Architectures. CoRR abs/1901.10860 (2019)
12. Thurstone, L.L.: A law of comparative judgment. Psychol. Rev. **34**(4), 273–286 (1927)
13. Zitzler, E., Deb, K., Thiele, L.: Comparison of multiobjective evolutionary algorithms: empirical results. Evol. Comput. **8**(2), 173–195 (2000)

Simulation-Based Validation of Robot Commands for Force-Based Robot Motions

Kim Wölfel$^{(\boxtimes)}$ and Dominik Henrich

Lehrstuhl Angewandte Informatik 3 (Robotik und Eingebettete Systeme),
Universität Bayreuth, Bayreuth, Germany
{kim.woelfel,dominik.henrich}@uni-bayreuth.de

Abstract. Speech-based robot instruction is a promising field in private households and in small and medium-sized enterprises. It facilitates the use of robot systems for experts as well as non-experts, especially while the user executes other tasks. Besides possible verbal ambiguities and uncertainties it has to be considered that the user may have no knowledge about the robot's capabilities. This can lead to faulty performances or even damage beyond repair which leads to a loss of trust in the robot. We present a framework, which validates verbally instructed, force-based robot motions using a physics simulation. This prevents faulty performances and allows a generation of motions even with exceptional outcomes. As a proof of concept the framework is applied to a household use-case and the results are discussed.

Keywords: Robotics · Natural language instruction · Validation

1 Introduction

One long term goal in current robotic research is the development of robot systems which have approximately the same cognitive, communicational, and handling abilities as humans. As part of this ongoing development, application domains for robot systems shall be expanded from industrial settings with separated working cells, fixed object positions, and preprogrammed motions towards a flexible usage in small or medium-sized enterprises or private households.

Speech-based instruction has been part of the research community for a few decades [8], which resulted in approaches reaching from pre-defined commands [3] to natural language based instructions [16] and spoken instructions [9]. Simulating robot motions as part of a reasoning process has also been investigated extensively, which led to comprehensive frameworks like *openEASE* [1].

Normally, motion parameters that lead to a successful manipulation regarding common sense, are derived from the simulation results. If no valid motion parameters are found, the motion is cancelled to omit faulty robot performances. As discussed in [7] preventing failures and showing the incapabilities of the used

© Springer Nature Switzerland AG 2020
U. Schmid et al. (Eds.): KI 2020, LNAI 12325, pp. 334–340, 2020.
https://doi.org/10.1007/978-3-030-58285-2_31

system is necessary to keep the users' trust in the system. In some cases, motions that seem unsuccessful regarding common sense may be still adequate in a specific situation.

Thus, the scientific contribution of this paper is an approach to verbally instructing force-based robot motions even with exceptional outcomes. Here, exceptional means that the result of the motion differs from its common result, i.e. an object falls over during shoving. Instructed force-based motions are simulated considering the accuracy of sensors and evaluated based on motion- and situation-specific knowledge. In the case of an exceptional outcome, the user is informed on occurring faults and asked if the motion should still be performed. Thus, an instruction of motions with such outcomes is also possible.

The remainder of this paper is structured as follows: Related work regarding reasoning about robot motions is presented (Sect. 2). The main part of this paper will cover the components of the presented approach (Sect. 3). Finally, the framework is applied to a household use-case as a proof of concept (Sect. 4), the scientific contribution is summarized and directions for future work are highlighted (Sect. 5).

2   Related Work

While performing and reasoning about the result of robot motions is the focus of this paper, a brief overview is given and the works closest to ours are discussed in more detail.

Approaches for reasoning about the outcome of robot motions can be divided into the three categories: Non-simulating [2,15], partly-simulating [5,12] and fully-simulating reasoning [6,13]. While the computational effort increases from non-simulating to fully-simulating, the accuracy normally decreases, because dynamic information about the workspace is estimated or not available. The first category contains approaches that do not use a physics simulation at all. Examples are symbolic reasoning [2] or approaches where a risk assessment based on sensor values is performed before a motion is executed [15].

Partly simulating a motion - a so called *projection* or *imagination* - during motion planning is a trade-off between the extremes regarding computational effort and accuracy. Here, a physics simulation is often used for computing collisions or check the stability of a build construct [12]. Nevertheless, as stated by [4], a limitation of this approach is that a successful plan depends highly on a correct belief state, which becomes more accurate in a complete simulation.

Besides approaches using simulations apart from the actual application in form of a test framework [5] or gaining user information [10], others use simulations on-line. The approaches of [13] and [6] are closest to ours. In [13] object parameters are monitored during the simulation and evaluated afterwards. Besides simulating the complete motion and logging parameters, [6] augments the simulation by defining environment objects as graph-like structures to even simulate the deformation or breaking of objects. Uncertainties regarding object transformations are also considered. The main difference to our approach is, that we focus on force-based motions and add a feedback component for the user.

3   Framework

In this section, we discuss the components of our framework in detail (see Fig. 1). Definitions necessary for a better understanding of each component are given, the simulation component and the interpreter are discussed, and the Parameter-of-Interest-Map is described.

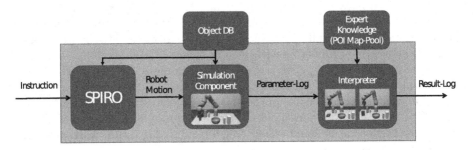

Fig. 1. System overview. An instruction is transformed into a robot motion by the *Spiro* framework [17], which is then simulated. Workspace parameters are logged and transformed into a result log by the interpreter.

3.1   Definitions

Each object state s is defined by dynamic properties $s = \{x, q, v, \omega, f, \tau\}$, where $x \in \mathbb{R}^3$ is the objects position, $q \in \mathbb{H}$ its orientation, $v \in \mathbb{R}^3$ its linear velocity, $\omega \in \mathbb{R}^3$ its angular velocity, $f \in \mathbb{R}^3$ forces applied to it and $\tau \in \mathbb{R}^3$ momentums applied to it. In the case of fixed objects, only f and τ change over time. The world state $w(t)$ at any time $t \in \mathbb{R}_0^+$ is then defined by $w(t) = \{s_0, \ldots, s_{n-1}, t\}$, where $n \in \mathbb{N}^+$ is the number of objects in the workspace.

Besides gravity, we assume that the robot arm movement is the main source of forces and momentums in the workspace. This movement is generated by transforming spoken instructions via the concept of *Combined Verbalized Effects* [17]. Verbs are connected to so called *Manipulation* or *Skill Primitives* ($\mathcal{MP}$) [11] that connect the concept of *Hybrid Motions* with tool commands and stop criteria. The concept of hybrid motions allows a definition of robot motions via position and sensor target values for each degree of freedom. We consider sensor values to be forces and torques. Thus, force-guided motions (scratching, wiping) and force-guarded motions (touching) can be realized.

Solving perception errors emerging from the accuracy of hardware used or environment conditions is still part of the current research [14]. In our case we model possible inaccuracies via defining a tolerance for an objects position and rotation instead of using a crisp transformation, which is then sampled in later steps. This simulates object detection errors as well as robot inaccuracies.

3.2 Parameters of Interest Map

A *Parameters of Interest Map* (POI-Map) holds the desired object parameters for the robot, the workpiece and the remaining objects in a scene for a robot motion. For each object state s_i, its parameters can either be limited via thresholds, e.g. $f_{min} < f \leq f_{max}$, or set as *insignificant* if they are of no interest in the current setting. The POI-Map then serves as a look-up-table for the interpreter component (Sect. 3.4) in a later step.

3.3 Simulation

To gain information about the dynamics while a motion is simulated, we implemented a simulation based on the *Bullet Physics Engine*[1]. Inputs are a workspace configuration, i.e. the set of objects, a data base storing the static object information, e.g. inertia tensors, and a set of motion commands. Controlling the robot is implemented via a torque control. The necessary joint torques are computed at each simulation step via extracting the position and force information for the robots *Tool Center Point* (TCP) from the current $\mathcal{MP}$ and transforming them to appropriate joint torques. The complete simulation is then run several times with varying initial object transformations to simulate the inaccuracy of the system. After every simulation step the world state $w(t)$ is logged in a parameter log $\mathcal{L}_P$. An alternative would be to log state parameters only if a deviation in accompanying POI values take place. In most cases, this would result in a smaller amount of data, but it can also lead to data loss if the threshold for identifying a deviation is set too high. A maximum duration for the motion is also passed to the simulation in order to prevent infinite loops.

3.4 Interpreter

The interpreter evaluates $\mathcal{L}_P$ regarding the POI-Map to find critical parameter values, i.e. values which extend the thresholds. For each entry in $\mathcal{L}_P$, its validity is checked regarding the POI-Map thresholds. If thresholds are exceeded, the simulation run is tagged as unsuccessful and critical values are stored in a result log $\mathcal{L}_R$ along with their timestamps and object IDs. The overall probability of success $p_s \in [0, 1]$ is then computed as the rate of successful to unsuccessful simulation runs. If $p_s = 1$ the instruction is accepted and the motion parameters are sent to the real world robot. If $p_{min} < p_s < 1$, $p_{min} \in [0, 1]$, the user is informed that the logged deviation may occur. If $p_s < p_{min}$ the user is informed that there is a high risk that the logged deviation occurs. In both cases the user is asked whether the motion should still be performed. Thus, even motions with exceptional goals can be instructed as well.

---

[1] https://github.com/bulletphysics/bullet3.

4   Experiment

As a proof of concept, the framework is evaluated by the household use-case *shoving* with two objects. The framework is used with varying sensor accuracies to gain information about their impact on the resulting motion, and the results are compared to their real-word motions to investigate the simulation's validity.

4.1   Experiment Set-Up

A user plans to make a cake and is currently mixing ingredients in front of the robot. While stirring, the user instructs the robot: 'Can you shove the obj_i towards me?'. Where $obj_i = \{cocoabox, milkbox\}$. A shoving motion is automatically initialized, consisting of approaching the object beneath the z-coordinate of its centroid, which usually results in a robust shoving motion. The motion is simulated $n = 9$ times and the minimum success rate is set to $p_{min} = 80\%$.

The robot arm used in this example is a *Franka Emika Panda*[2]. The POI-Map is set up indirectly through the shoving motion, i.e. translation into the y-direction, limited by a force that prevents damage of the box. The work-piece orientation is restricted by a threshold that ensures that it does not fall over during the manipulation. The remaining object states are tagged as insignificant. The sensor inaccuracy is modelled by varying the initial box centroid z- and y-coordinates by adding combinations of the accuracy $\epsilon \in [.1\ mm, \ldots, 1\ mm]$ in the y- and z-direction to it. The experiment was performed on a PC with the following specification: Intel Core i7-6700HQ processor and an NVIDIA GeForce GTX 960M graphics card (Fig. 2).

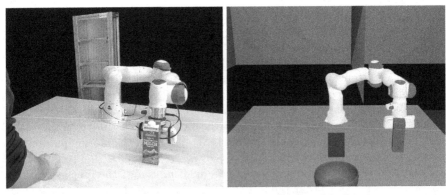

(a) Real world use-case   (b) Simulated use-case.

Fig. 2. Investigated household use-case with a milkbox (shoving an object).

---

[2] https://www.franka.de/de/.

4.2   Experimental Results

Insights on the computational effort are gained by measuring the time for each simulation step for a step size d_{step} and the overall duration of each simulation run. Overall a single simulation step with 1 ms without sub steps took 0.086 ms and a whole simulation run (simulation + torque computation + logging + interpreting) took about 909 ms for a motion that takes 13.39 s in real life. Thus, an acceleration by a factor of about 14 is possible in this use-case, which is an adequate time to inform the user about the outcome of the motion.

The success rates for the two use-cases can be seen in Table 1. In the milk box case an accuracy of 1 mm leads to a successful execution in all runs. The success rate decreases to by 12% for 2–8 mm and drops to 77% for 9 and 10 mm. In this case the user would be informed that something may go wrong if the given accuracy is below 1 mm. In the cocoa box case a success rate of 55% is reached for all accuracies.

We also executed the two motions on a real life robot arm[3]. The results are similar to our simulations, which leads us to the conclusion that our system is able to estimate the outcome of a robot motion.

Table 1. Success rates R_{milk} and R_{cocoa} for the sensor accuracies ϵ.

ϵ [mm]	1	2	3	4	5	6	7	8	9	10
R_{milk} [%]	100	88	88	88	88	88	88	88	77	77
R_{cocoa} [%]	55	55	55	55	55	55	55	55	55	55

5   Conclusion

In this paper an approach is presented which deals with the scientific question if and to what extent is it possible to validate force-based robot motions using a physics-based simulation. Software components for simulating, logging and interpreting logged object states are discussed and the system is evaluated by pushing manipulations in a household use case. Thus, the scientific contribution is an approach that allows an risk assessment of force-based motions as well as the execution of motions with exceptional outcomes.

Future directions could be to extend the approach to more object types, such as soft bodies or fluids as well as filling the POI-Maps more automatically.

Acknowledgements. This work has partly been supported by Deutsche Forschungs-gemeinschaft (DFG) under grant agreement He2696-18.

---

[3] https://www.ai3.uni-bayreuth.de/de/team/kim-woelfel/.

References

1. Beetz, M., Tenorth, M., Winkler, J.: Open-ease. In: 2015 IEEE International Conference on Robotics and Automation (ICRA), pp. 1983–1990. IEEE (2015)
2. Briggs, G.M., Scheutz, M.: "Sorry, I Can't Do That": developing mechanisms to appropriately reject directives in human-robot interactions. In: 2015 AAAI Fall Symposium Series (2015)
3. Bugmann, G., Pires, J.N.: Robot-by-voice: experiments on commanding an industrial robot using the human voice. Ind. Robot **32**, 505–511 (2005)
4. Kazhoyan, G., Beetz, M.: Specializing underdetermined action descriptions through plan projection. arXiv preprint arXiv:1812.08224 (2018)
5. Kresse, I.: A semantic constraint-based robot motion control for generalizing everyday manipulation actions (2017)
6. Kunze, L., Beetz, M.: Envisioning the qualitative effects of robot manipulation actions using simulation-based projections. Artif. Intell. **247**, 352–380 (2017)
7. Kwon, M., Huang, S.H., Dragan, A.D.: Expressing robot incapability. In: Proceedings of the 2018 ACM/IEEE International Conference on Human-Robot Interaction, pp. 87–95 (2018)
8. Liu, R., Zhang, X.: Methodologies realizing natural-language-facilitated human-robot cooperation: a review. CoRR arXiv:1701.08756 (2017)
9. Marge, M.: Miscommunication detection and recovery for spoken dialogue systems in physically situated contexts. Ph.D. thesis, Ph.D. Dissertation. Carnegie Mellon University, Pittsburgh, PA (2015)
10. Misra, D.K., Sung, J., Lee, K., Saxena, A.: Tell me dave: context-sensitive grounding of natural language to manipulation instructions. Int. J. Robot. Res. **35**(1–3), 281–300 (2016)
11. Mosemann, H., Wahl, F.M.: Automatic decomposition of planned assembly sequences into skill primitives. IEEE Trans. Robot. Autom. **17**(5), 709–718 (2001)
12. Mösenlechner, L., Beetz, M.: Fast temporal projection using accurate physics-based geometric reasoning. In: 2013 IEEE International Conference on Robotics and Automation, pp. 1821–1827. IEEE (2013)
13. Rockel, S., Konečný, Š., Stock, S., Hertzberg, J., Pecora, F., Zhang, J.: Integrating physics-based prediction with semantic plan execution monitoring. In: 2015 IEEE/RSJ International Conference on Intelligent Robots and Systems (IROS), pp. 2883–2888. IEEE (2015)
14. Sallami, Y., Lemaignan, S., Clodic, A., Alami, R.: Simulation-based physics reasoning for consistent scene estimation in an HRI context. In: IEEE/RSJ International Conference on Intelligent Robots and Systems (IROS 2019) (2019)
15. Sattar, J., Little, J.J.: Ensuring safety in human-robot dialog–a cost-directed approach. In: 2014 IEEE International Conference on Robotics and Automation (ICRA), pp. 6660–6666. IEEE (2014)
16. Tellex, S., et al.: Understanding natural language commands for robotic navigation and mobile manipulation. In: Twenty-fifth AAAI Conference on Artificial Intelligence (2011)
17. Wölfel, K., Henrich, D.: Grounding verbs for tool-dependent, sensor-based robot tasks. In: 2018 27th IEEE International Symposium on Robot and Human Interactive Communication (RO-MAN), pp. 378–383. IEEE (2018)

Demonstration Abstracts

Firefighter Virtual Reality Simulation for Personalized Stress Detection

Soeren Klingner[1(✉)], Zhiwei Han[1], Yuanting Liu[1], Fan Fan[1],
Bashar Altakrouri[2], Bruno Michel[3], Jonas Weiss[3], Arvind Sridhar[3],
and Sophie Mai Chau[3]

[1] fortiss GmbH, Munich, Germany
{klingner,han,liu,fan}@fortiss.org
[2] IBM Deutschland GmbH, Munich, Germany
altakrouri@de.ibm.com
[3] IBM Zurich Research Lab, Rüschlikon, Switzerland
{bmi,jwe,rvi,mai}@zurich.ibm.com

Abstract. Classifying stress in firefighters poses challenges, such as accurate personalized labeling, unobtrusive recording, and training of adequate models. Acquisition of labeled data and verification in cage mazes or during hot trainings is time consuming. Virtual Reality (VR) and Internet of Things (IoT) wearables provide new opportunities to create better stressors for firefighter missions through an immersive simulation. In this demo, we present a VR-based setup that enables to simulate firefighter missions to trigger and more easily record specific stress levels. The goal is to create labeled datasets for personalized multilevel stress detection models that include multiple biosignals, such as heart rate variability from electrocardiographic RR intervals. The multilevel stress setups can be configured, consisting of different levels of mental stressors. The demo shows how we established the recording of a baseline and virtual missions with varying challenge levels to create a personalized stress calibration.

Keywords: Virtual Reality · Machine learning · Dataset · Stress · Interactive experience · Biosignal processing · Internet of Things · Wearables

1 Introduction

Stress is the difficulty of organisms to maintain homeostasis under stimuli that causes an imbalance in the autonomic nervous system. This fight-or-flight response involves many biosignals including changes in heart rate variability

This research was co-funded by the Bavarian Ministry of Economic Affairs, Regional Development and Energy, project Dependable AI, IBM Deutschland GmbH, and IBM Research, and was carried out within the Center for AI jointly founded by IBM and fortiss.

(HRV) [6]. Reduced HRV shows an impaired regulatory capacity, stress, anxiety, or other health problems. Stress reduces the ability to make rational decisions if it exceeds a particular individual threshold, thus stressed workers are more likely to have accidents [5]. Early and reliable detection of stress helps to better manage team performance and health. Smoke divers in a firefighter mission, in particular, are susceptible to acute stress, and monitoring mental stress can prevent injuries and even death.

Building good models for stress classification based on real-world data captured in cage-maze sessions or "hot" training missions, where firefighters have to extinguish real fires are challenging. In these scenarios, firefighters are only stressed during a short time and only inaccurate labels can be acquired [6]. For these reasons, we suggest an approach based on VR and IoT to allow the acquisition of firefighter stress data with optimal labeling while providing a good level of immersion and realistic experience.

2   Related Work

With the advantages of eliciting a sense of presence [9] and grading the intensity of the stimulus by needs, VR has the potential to induce real physiological and emotional reactions. Social evaluative stress (TSST [3]) can be effectively induced in a virtual environment leading to stress reactions on several physiological measures [14]. Virtual reality exposure therapy has a large effect on affective domains [7]. Thus it is a relevant approach for anxiety-related treatments like anxiety disorder and post-traumatic stress disorder (PTSD) [1][10]. Models to distinguish and classify physical and mental stress using HRV analysis with low-cost wearables [8] were tested on 100 "Smoke divers" during their certification in a cage maze. Using unsupervised classification Oskooei [6] confirmed that 90% of the firefighters were mentally stressed. Our incentive is to bring this scenario into a controlled laboratory environment through VR technology, for accurate and robust labeling and sensor data recordings.

Furthermore, two public datasets SWELL [4] and WESAD [11] had been used for validation of stress monitoring methods. The SWELL dataset includes biosignals (e.g. ECG and EDA) from 25 subjects during office work, while the WESAD dataset was conducted with 15 subjects exposed to TSST [3]. Different from this previous work and datasets, we aim to study model generalizability on one specific subject under different physiological or physical conditions.

3   Concept and Implementation

We suggest a system to simulate firefighter missions to trigger and record specific stress levels. It can create labeled datasets for personalized multilevel stress detection models based on (a) biosignals such as HRV; (b) multi-level stress configurations (different levels of mental and physical stressors); (c) fully immersive VR experience; (d) automatic capturing and recording of labeled data. Different from existing datasets, our novel system aims at recording a baseline and virtual missions with varying challenge levels to create a personalized stress calibration and detection by combining biosignals and VR-tracking data.

3.1   Data Acquisition System

In our demo we base our implementation on an extensible RESTful web services architecture (Fig. 1), which consists of 6 software modules: (a) The firefighter sever is a nodeJS application that acts as a communication and orchestration hub; (b) VR Data Acquisition platform gathers real-time biosignal data using a Biosignalsplux sensor set[1], consisting of ECG, EDA, EMG, EEG, RESP, ACC and TMP sensors and VR-tracking data directly from Unity3D[2]. After synchronization, the collected data is sent to a firefighter server with a POST request; (c) Monitoring

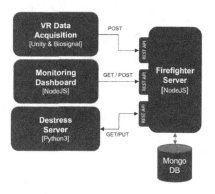

Fig. 1. System block diagram

Dashboard is a web application that displays the acquired biosignals from the subjects or participants in the VR experience. (d) Destress Server is a Python3 module that uses a stress classifier using the trained models from [8]; (e) a MongoDB database permanently stores data from all sensors.

To train and build better stress classification ML models, test subjects will also be exposed to mental exercises/games while on a bicycle home trainer. Initial results using a linear support vector machine (SVM) model, detected stress 87.3% of the time (sensitivity) and the relax state 80.5% of the time (specificity), resulting in an F-score of 82% [12].

3.2   Mission Simulation in VR

A firefighter mission simulation in VR developed with Unity3D puts the participant into different states of mental stress. Unlike common methods we do not equalize cognitive load with mental stress, such as using math questions, memorizing tasks, and the Stroop Color Word Test [2].

We realized the zero-stress state through a VR relaxation room with the 4-7-8 breathing technique [13]. To enable low to high-stress states, we implemented an apartment with 5 different rooms with configurable stressors that range from navigating inside an unknown environment with configurable visibility through thick dark smoke, disturbing sound effects and noises from victims, fire, breathing and communication system, time pressure by a limited amount of air for the life-saving respirator, to tasks such as rescuing a number of victims, extinguishing a fire, finding and turning off a gas tank, opening a water valve and

---

[1] https://biosignalsplux.com.
[2] https://unity.com.

windows. Throughout the VR experience, we simulate a communication system with a firefighter commander to give guidance during the simulation through audio instructions.

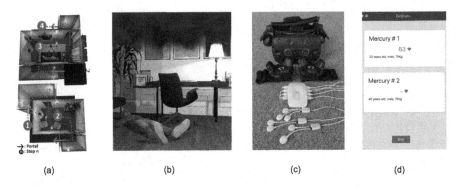

Fig. 2. VR simulation: (a) navigation concept; (b) one of the rescue tasks; (c) hardware (HTC Vive Pro Eye VR Headset and biosignalsplux); (d) stress monitoring dashboard

The navigation through the apartment is realized by physically walking from one room to the other inside a tracking space. We have developed an approach to map the limited VR tracking space (5×5 m) to a larger virtual space. A system of unnoticeable portals hidden inside doors had been implemented to redirect the participant from the edge of the tracking space back into the center as shown in Fig. 2(a).

4   Conclusion and Outlook

In this paper, we have presented a scaleable system for capturing reliable data about stress based on IoT and VR. We created a simulation to directly trigger different mental stress levels in VR with the capability to walk physically through the virtual environment. Moreover, it provides the opportunity to capture a baseline and a stress resilience parameter to allow a full personalization of stress classification. We are aiming to use the system to generate multiple datasets that will be made publicly available for researchers interested in building machine learning models for stress detection and management.

We analyze the strength and weaknesses of VR stress triggers and will compare them with physical stress triggering systems like cage maze or "hot pots" training locations where firefighters are exposed to fire with all senses (i.e smoke, extensive heat, sound, haptics for a backdraft). With the acquired data we can start to discuss the tradeoff between good labels and large volumes of data and gentle stress amplitudes vs. bad labels, little data but very strong stress triggers. Eventually, we will have to test the quality of the models in actual missions and build systems that continue to learn while on active duty to provide the best possible results.

References

1. Anderson, P.L., et al.: Virtual reality exposure therapy for social anxiety disorder: a randomized controlled trial. J. Consult. Clin. Psychol. **81**(5), 751 (2013)
2. Jensen, A.R., Rohwer Jr., W.D.: The stroop color-word test: a review. Acta Psychol. **25**, 36–93 (1966)
3. Kirschbaum, C., Pirke, K.M., Hellhammer, D.H.: The 'trier social stress test'-a tool for investigating psychobiological stress responses in a laboratory setting. Neuropsychobiology **28**(1–2), 76–81 (1993)
4. Koldijk, S., Sappelli, M., Verberne, S., Neerincx, M.A., Kraaij, W.: The swell knowledge work dataset for stress and user modeling research. In: Proceedings of the 16th International Conference on Multimodal Interaction, pp. 291–298 (2014)
5. McCraty, R., Shaffer, F.: Heart rate variability: new perspectives on physiological mechanisms, assessment of self-regulatory capacity, and health risk. Global Adv. Health Med. **4**(1), 46–61 (2015)
6. Oskooei, A., Chau, S.M., Weiss, J., Sridhar, A., Martínez, M.R., Michel, B.: Destress: deep learning for unsupervised identification of mental stress in firefighters from heart-rate variability (hrv) data. arXiv preprint arXiv:1911.13213 (2019)
7. Parsons, T.D., Rizzo, A.A.: Affective outcomes of virtual reality exposure therapy for anxiety and specific phobias: a meta-analysis. J. Behav. Ther. Exp. Psychiatry **39**(3), 250–261 (2008)
8. Pluntke, U., Gerke, S., Sridhar, A., Weiss, J., Michel, B.: Evaluation and classification of physical and psychological stress in firefighters using heart rate variability. In: 2019 41st Annual International Conference of the IEEE Engineering in Medicine and Biology Society (EMBC), pp. 2207–2212. IEEE (2019)
9. Riva, G., Waterworth, J.A., Waterworth, E.L., Mantovani, F.: From intention to action: the role of presence. New Ideas Psychol. **29**(1), 24–37 (2011)
10. Rothbaum, B.O., et al.: Virtual reality exposure therapy for PTSD Vietnam veterans: case study. J. Traumatic Stress Off. Publ. Int. Soc. Traumatic Stress Stud. **12**(2), 263–271 (1999)
11. Schmidt, P., Reiss, A., Duerichen, R., Marberger, C., Van Laerhoven, K.: Introducing WESAD, a multimodal dataset for wearable stress and affect detection. In: Proceedings of the 20th ACM International Conference on Multimodal Interaction, pp. 400–408 (2018)
12. Sierro, N.: Firefighter vital sign monitoring for predicting operational readiness. EPFL Master thesisa (2020)
13. Weil, A.: Three breathing exercises. Retrieved 15 May 2017 (2016)
14. Zimmer, P., Buttlar, B., Halbeisen, G., Walther, E., Domes, G.: Virtually stressed? a refined virtual reality adaptation of the trier social stress test (TSST) induces robust endocrine responses. Psychoneuroendocrinology **101**, 186–192 (2019)

The AI Domain Definition Language (AIDDL) for Integrated Systems

Uwe Köckemann[(✉)] [iD]

Center for Applied Autonomous Sensor Systems, Örebro University, Örebro, Sweden
uwe.koeckemann@oru.se

Abstract. As individual sub-fields of AI become more developed, it becomes increasingly important to study their integration into complex systems. In this paper, we provide a first look at the *AI Domain Definition Language (AIDDL)* as an attempt to provide a common ground for modeling problems, data, solutions, and their integration across all branches of AI in a common language. We look at three examples of how automated planning can be integrated with learning and reasoning.

1   Introduction

Many possibilities arise when combining the strengths of different AI methods. Automated planning, for instance, has been combined with machine learning or reasoning in various ways for mutual benefit [3,7,13]. However in most existing studies, the way the different models are combined highly depends on the problem at hand and cannot be generalized to other domains. In this work, we present the *AI Domain Definition Language (AIDDL)* and framework (available under www.aiddl.org), which aim at allowing AI system developers to easily integrate different AI models. AIDDL is domain-agnostic, flexible, and extendable, making it usable for a any type of problem. Using AIDDL, the integration of the different AI models is moved from implementation to model level. This means that integrated AI systems can be described independent of any programming language. This allows to easily exchange algorithms and solutions for individual sub-problem, which makes studying alternative combinations of solution easy. Thus, creating and maintaining AI systems will become easier as the developer can model interactions between the system's component without having to worry about implementation details.

In this paper, we give an overview of the AIDDL framework which is composed of the *AI Domain Definition Language (AIDDL)*, a core library (AIDDL Core), definitions and implementations of common AI algorithms (AIDDL Common), and a library of examples of integrated AI (AIDDL Examples).

2   The Language

The language is used to specify types (e.g., Planning Problem, Plan, Decision Tree, Supervised Learning Problem), data (instance of planning problem,

ⓒ Springer Nature Switzerland AG 2020
U. Schmid et al. (Eds.): KI 2020, LNAI 12325, pp. 348–352, 2020.
https://doi.org/10.1007/978-3-030-58285-2_33

instance of decision tree), functionalities (e.g., planner, decision tree learner), and requests (functionality calls and control flow).

Each AIDDL file starts with a module entry which states the self-reference (i.e., the term a module uses to refer to itself) and the module's URI. An *entry* generically specifies data as a tuple composed of type, name, and value. The following grammar defines the language:

```
<AiddlFile>   :: <Module> (<Entry>)*
<Module>      :: "(#mod" <Symbolic> <Symbolic> ")"
<Entry>       :: "("<Term> <Term> <Term>")"
<Term>        :: <Numerical> | <Collection> | <Tuple> | <Symbolic> | <String>
               | <Variable>  | <Reference> | <KeyValue>
<Numerical>   :: <Integer> | <Rational> | <Real> | <Infinity>
<Collection>  :: <List> | <Set>
<List>        :: "[" <Term>* "]"
<Set>         :: "{" <Term>* "}"
<Tuple>       :: "(" <Term>* ")"
<Reference>   :: <Term>"@"<Term> | "$"<Term>
<KeyValue>    :: <Term>":"<Term>
<Symbolic>    :: (("a"-"z"|"A"-"Z"|"#")("a"-"z"|"A"-"Z"|"0"-"9"|"_"|"."|"-"|"'")*)
               |"+"|"-"|"/"|"*"|"&"|"|"|"!"|"="|"<"|">"|"=>"|"<=>"|"^"|"!="|"<="|">="
<String>      :: "\"" [~\"]* "\""
<Variable>    :: <NamedVariable> | "_"
<NamedVariable> :: ?(("a"-"z"|"A"-"Z")("a"-"z"|"A"-"Z"|"0"-"9"|"_"|"."|"-"|"'")*)
<Integer>  :: ["-"]("0"|"1"-"9")("0"-"9")*
<Rational> :: ["-"]("0"|"1"-"9")("0"-"9")* "/" ("1"-"9"("0"-"9")*)
<Real> :: ["-"] ("0"|"1"-"9")("0"-"9")* "." ("0"-"9")+
<Infinity> :: ["+"|"-"]"INF"
```

3   AIDDL Core

The *AIDDL Core* is a library that makes AIDDL available for use with any of the supported programming languages[1]. It provides a parser to load AIDDL files as modules into an AIDDL container. It also includes an implementation of the evaluator (also used as type checker) and request handler.

Evaluator. The evaluator is a component of the AIDDL Core that recursively evaluates terms that can be interpreted as functions. All such terms are tuples and the first term of the tuple is a symbolic URI of the function. As an example, *(org.aiddl.eval.numerical.add 2 3)* is evaluated to 5. Namespaces are used to shorten overly long names. One of the default namespaces allows writing the above example as *(+2 3)*. The evaluator can be used to test if the value of an entry satisfies the stated type. It is also used to perform basic operations on data, e.g., to evaluate branching or loop conditions in requests or filtering lists or sets without having to implement a functionality.

Request Handler. Requests are AIDDL terms that allow to compose functionality in an imperative fashion. Unlike the strictly functional interpretation of the evaluator, requests require to specify where the result of function calls is stored (i.e., the name of entries to direct the output to). Any evaluator term that

---

[1] Currently Java. A Python Core is a work in progress.

appears in a request will be evaluated (as explained above) before the request is handled. This is often convenient for evaluating conditions. All examples presented in this paper were implemented using requests.

4 AIDDL Common

AIDDL Common consists of two elements: a library of type and functionality definitions, and a library of implementations. Type definitions are written in AIDDL and cover common AI problems and data types (e.g., planning/learning problems, learning data, graphs). Functionalities are defined for solvers of these common problems. Second, *AIDDL Common*. The library of implementations provides implementations of common AI functionalities and some commonly used data structures (such as graphs and matrices). These can be used as building blocks for setting up and testing integrated AI systems. Currently, the common library contains support for heuristic state-space planning [9] with fast forward [12] and causal graph [11] heuristics, decision tree learning and classification [14], basic Prolog reasoning [1], as well as basic graph algorithms and domain independent implementations of graph-based and tree-based search.

5 AIDDL Examples

AIDDL Examples refers to a growing collection of implementations of integrated AI systems. All three examples described below directly use components offered by the Common library. The resulting projects are compact and mainly consists of an AIDDL file that describes how components are combined via requests, initial data, and a few additional functionalities specific to the example. All examples are available open source at www.aiddl.org where a visualization of the integration can be found as well. The main point of these examples is not in the novelty of the integration they present, but that they are all realized in a common language and re-use common components.

Planning for Learning. Data is often difficult to acquire and data acquisition may require going through a complex process such as sending a robot to collect samples. In this example an automated planner is used to gather data from various locations for a machine learning system. Until the machine learning model performs well enough on a cross-validation, we generate data goals, plan to collect data, execute the plan, extract data, and then perform n-fold cross-validation. Similar integrations can be found in the literature [10,15,19]. For a more recent review see [13].

Learning for Planning. In this example we use learning for planning. Specifically, we start with an incomplete planning domain, generate data from executed actions and observed state transitions, and then learn new operators. If the problem cannot be solved a random action is chosen as an experiment. Otherwise we execute the next action of the plan. In either case, we execute the action, observe the outcome and generate data. Next, we try to learn a model that predicts the effects of actions on states. The resulting model is used to create operators for an updated planning domain. Once the domain is updated, we attempt to plan again and continue. This example can be seen as an extension of active learning [17]. Active learning uses queries to ask for specific instances of data to improve the performance of learning. Other ways of integrating planning and learning include learning heuristics for the search space of a planner [16], learning control knowledge to guide planning search [3], or configuring portfolio-based planning approaches [7].

Planning and Goal Reasoning. Our third example integrates automated planning with a form of goal reasoning. Here, we consider a planner that may be presented with a goal that it does not support directly. In case this happens, we call a reasoner to derive a goal that the planner can handle. As an example, consider that a planner may have a set of locations $\{l_1, \ldots, l_n\}$ and is presented with a goal to go to the location *kitchen*. We have a knowledge base of sub-class relations and instance relations and want to determine if any of the l_i locations known to the planner is a *kitchen*. This example can be seen as a form of goal reasoning [18] in form of goal transformation [4].

6 Related Work

Research on automated planning has lead to many changes and variations of the Planning Domain Definition Language (PDDL) [2,5,6,8] to consider, e.g., time, resources, or continuous change. The basic language, however, is designed to express planning problems. In this work we take a step back and suggest a domain definition language that can be extended to include any existing AI problem and also define how these problems are solved. Unlike languages such as Prolog, we do not assume anything about how problems are solved.

7 Conclusion

We proposed AIDDL as a language and framework to allow model-based integration of AI approaches across various domains. We discussed three examples that integrate planning with learning and reasoning by using our framework. This way of performing AI integration allows the resulting systems to benefit from a large body of existing implementations across all branches of AI. We also argue that a common domain definition language for AI allows to perform integration as done in this paper with minimal overhead. The first version of the AIDDL framework is available now and we plan to release new features as they become stable. If you are reading this paper and made it this far, we hope we spiked your curiosity. Feel free to contact us if you have any further questions, a use case, or would like to hook up your AI tools to the *AIDDL Framework* available under www.aiddl.org.

Acknowledgement. This work was funded by the project *AI4EU* (https://www. ai4eu.eu/) under the European Union's Horizon 2020 research and innovation programme (grant agreement 825619). Many thanks to Alessandro Saffiotti, Federico Pecora, and Jennifer Renoux for many interesting discussions, suggestions, and support.

References

1. Bratko, I.: Prolog Programming for Artificial Intelligence. Addison Wesley (2000)
2. Coles, A.J., Coles., A.I.: PDDL+ planning with events and linear processes. In: Proceedings of the 24th International Conference on Automated Planning and Scheduling (ICAPS) (2014)
3. Coles, A., Coles, A.J.: Marvin: a heuristic search planner with online macro-action learning. J. Artif. Intell. Res. **28**, 119–156 (2007)
4. Cox, M.T., Dannenhauer, D.: Goal transformation and goal reasoning. In: Proceedings of the 4th Workshop on Goal Reasoning at IJCAI-2016 (2016)
5. Fox, M., Long, D.: PDDL2.1: an extension to pddl for expressing temporal planning domains. J. Artif. Intell. Res. **20**, 61–124 (2003)
6. Gerevini, A., Long, D.: Plan Constraints and Preferences in PDDL3. Department of Electronics for Automation, University of Brescia, Ital, Technical report (2005)
7. Gerevini, A.E., Saetti, A., Vallati, M.: An automatically configurable portfolio-based planner with macro-actions: Pbp. In: Proceedings of the 19th International Conference on International Conference on Automated Planning and Scheduling (ICAPS), pp. 350–353. ICAPS 2009, AAAI Press (2009)
8. Ghallab, M., et al.: PDDL - the planning domain definition language. Technical report, CVC TR-98-003/DCS TR-1165, Yale Center for Computational Vision and Control (1998)
9. Ghallab, M., Nau, D., Traverso, P.: Automated Planning: Theory and Practice. Morgan Kaufmann (2004)
10. Gil, Y.: Acquiring domain knowledge for planning by experimentation. Ph.D. thesis, CMU, Pittsburgh, PA, USA (1992)
11. Helmert, M.: The fast downward planning system. J. Artif. Intell. Res. **26**(1), 191–246 (2006)
12. Hoffmann, J.: FF: the fast-forward planning system. AI Magazine **22**, 57–62 (2001)
13. Jiménez, S., De La Rosa, T., Fernández, S., Fernández, F., Borrajo, D.: A review of machine learning for automated planning. Knowl. Eng. Rev. **27**(4), 433–467 (2012)
14. Mitchell, T.M.: Machine Learning. McGraw-Hill, Inc., New York, NY, USA, 1 edn. (1997)
15. Shen, W.M., Simon, H.A.: Rule creation and rule learning through environmental exploration. In: Proceedings of the International Joint Conference on Artificial Intelligence, pp. 675–680 (1989)
16. Thayer, J.T., Dionne, A.J., Ruml, W.: Learning inadmissible heuristics during search. In: Bacchus, F., Domshlak, C., Edelkamp, S., Helmert, M. (eds.) Proceedings of the 21st International Conference on Automated Planning and Scheduling (ICAPS). AAAI (2011)
17. Tong, S.: Active learning: theory and applications. Ph.D. thesis, Stanford University (2001)
18. Vattam, S., Klenk, M., Molineaux, M., Aha, D.W.: Breadth of approaches to goal reasoning : a research survey. Goal Reasoning: Papers from the ACS Workshop, p. 111 (2013)
19. Wang, X.: Learning planning operators by observation and practice. In: International Conference on Artificial Intelligence Planning Systems (1994)

Abstract of a Pre-published Paper

Meta-Induction, Probability Aggregation, and Optimal Scoring

Christian J. Feldbacher-Escamilla$^{(\boxtimes)}$ ⓘ and Gerhard Schurz ⓘ

Duesseldorf Center for Logic and Philosophy of Science (DCLPS),
University of Duesseldorf, Universitaetsstr. 1, 40225 Duesseldorf, Germany
christian.feldbacher-escamilla@hhu.de, gerhard.schurz@phil.hhu.de

Abstract. In this paper, we combine the theory of probability aggregation with the theory of meta-induction and show that this allows for optimal predictions under expert advice. The full paper to this contribution is published as [3].

Keywords: Meta-induction · Probability aggregation · Brier score

1 Introduction

Probability aggregation is an expansion of the theory of judgment aggregation and addresses the question of how to aggregate probability distributions. In past, research in this field centred around the disciplines of economics and political science, law, and philosophy [4]. Recently, however, increasing work stems also from computer science and artificial intelligence [5].

We suggest to interpret the weights in characterisation results of linear probability aggregation (cf. Section 2) in a success-based way. By cashing out results on no-regret methods for prediction under expert advice of the field of online machine learning (cf. Section 3) we show that fixing the parameters in a success-based way allows for optimal probability aggregation (cf. Section 4).

2 Linear Probability Aggregation

The theory of probability aggregation deals with the problem of how to aggregate a set of probability distributions. Abstractly speaking, the question is how to characterise a probability aggregation rule f which takes as input a set of n probability distributions $P_1, \ldots, P_n$ and generates as output a/*the* aggregated probability distribution $P_{aggr} = f(P_1, \ldots, P_n)$. So-called "linear probability aggregation rules" have the following form of a weighted arithmetic mean:

$$P_{aggr} = \sum_{i=1}^{n} w_i \cdot P_i \text{ where } \mathrm{w_i} \geq 0 \text{ and } \mathrm{w_1} + \cdots + \mathrm{w_n} = 1 \quad \text{(AM)}$$

Different interpretations of the weights allow for different specifications. Here we want to argue for interpreting the weights in a regret-based way, because such an interpretation allows for optimal probability aggregation.

© Springer Nature Switzerland AG 2020
U. Schmid et al. (Eds.): KI 2020, LNAI 12325, pp. 355–357, 2020.
https://doi.org/10.1007/978-3-030-58285-2

3   Optimality in an Expert Advice Setting

In online machine learning, regret bounds of methods for predictions under expert advice are studied [2]. The idea is to consider a series of events (E) whose outcomes $(val_t(E))$ have to be predicted by so-called *experts* or *candidate* methods $(P_{1,t}, \ldots, P_{n,t}$ of n candidate methods). Given these predictions, the task is to construct a meta-inductive prediction method $P_{mi,t}$ that uses the candidate method's forecast as input and aims at optimality by approaching the predictive success of the best expert [6, 7].

We assume that all the mentioned values are within the unit interval. Then we define $P_{mi,t}$ by keeping track of the success rate s of a candidate method i via summing up its score (which is 1 minus the loss l of i's prediction—l is within $[0, 1]$ and convex) up to round t and then take the average. Afterwards, we define weights w via cutting off and normalisation [6, Sect. 1 and Sect. 7]:

$$s_{i,t} = \frac{\sum_{u=1}^{t} 1 - l(P_{i,u}, val_u(E))}{t} \qquad w_{i,t} = \frac{max(0, s_{i,t} - s_{mi,t})}{\sum_{j=1}^{n} max(0, s_{j,t} - s_{mi,t})}$$

If P_{mi} outperforms all other methods, averaging applies, so the weights are always positive and sum up to 1. Based on this, we can define a weighted-average meta-inductive method (MI) as a linear combination [2, 6, Sect. 2.1 resp. Sect. 7]:

$$P_{mi,t+1} = \sum_{i=1}^{n} w_{i,t} \cdot P_{i,t+1} \quad \text{(MI)}$$

Regarding the success rate of (MI) one can prove the following bound with respect to the success rates of the candidate methods [2, 6, Sect. 2. 1f resp. 7]:

Theorem 1. *Given the loss function l is convex it holds:*

$$s_{i,t} - s_{mi,t} \leq \sqrt{n/t} \ \ \forall i \in \{1, \ldots, n\}, \ so \ \lim_{t \to \infty} max(s_{1,t}, \ldots, s_{n,t}) - s_{mi,t} \leq 0$$

This theorem shows that (MI) is a no-regret method, and that its success rate converges to or outperforms that of the best performing candidate method.

4   Optimal Probability Aggregation

In *probabilistic* prediction games, each candidate method identifies the predicted real value with its credence of the predicted event. We expand the framework from above: Now it contains a series of events represented by random variables $\mathbf{E}_1, \mathbf{E}_2, \ldots$ within a space of discrete, mutually disjoint, and exhaustive values $v_1, \ldots, v_k$. In order to indicate which value a random variable took on at a specific round, we assume a valuation function val to be given by $val_t(v_m) = 1$ if the value of $\mathbf{E}_t$ is v_m and $val_t(v_m) = 0$ otherwise. Predictions are the credences of n

candidate methods for each event variable $\mathbf{E}_t$ in the series, represented by probability distributions $\mathbf{P}_1, \ldots, \mathbf{P}_n$ such that $\sum_{m=1}^{k} \mathbf{P}_{i,t}(v_m) = 1$ and $\mathbf{P}_{i,t}(v_m) \geq 0$. The probabilistic meta-inductive method $\mathbf{P}_{mi}$ is also represented by a probability distribution. In order to define it, we average the success-rates for the individual values of the value space. Let us first define such an average loss measure l_{av}:

$$l_{i,t}^{av} = \frac{\sum\limits_{m=1}^{k} l(\mathbf{P}_{i,t}(v_m), val_t(v_m))}{k}$$

Note that if l is the quadratic loss function, then l^{av} is the Brier score for a particular round [1]. The general Brier score can be calculated then by summing up all the scores up to round t and dividing them by t (that is the per round loss averaged over all values of the value space). Now we can define a measure for average success $s_{i,t}^{av}$ in analogy to s (simply replace l by l^{av} in the definition of $s_{i,t}$ above). Likewise, we define weights $w_{i,t}^{av}$ for the probabilistic predictions (simply replace s by s^{av} in the definition of $w_{i,t}$ above). Finally, we define the meta-inductive method for weighted average probability aggregation based on these weights in accordance with (AM): $\mathbf{P}_{mi,t+1} = \sum_{i=1}^{n} w_{i,t}^{av} \cdot \mathbf{P}_{i,t+1}$. Since we assumed that l is convex, also l^{av} is convex. To recognize this, we just have to hint to the mathematical fact that if the loss function l is convex with respect to all values of the value space, then also averaging among the losses with respect to all values of the value space is convex. Since the definition of $\mathbf{P}_{mi}$ is an instance of (MI), and since l^{av} used to determine the weights w^{av} is convex, we can transfer the no-regregt optimality result of P_{mi} to $\mathbf{P}_{mi}$ straightforwardly:

Theorem 2. *Given the loss function l is convex it holds:*

$$s_{i,t}^{av} - s_{mi,t}^{av} \leq \sqrt{n/t} \ \ \forall i \in \{1, \ldots, n\}, \ so \ \lim_{t \to \infty} max(s_{1,t}^{av}, \ldots, s_{n,t}^{av}) - s_{mi,t}^{av} \leq 0$$

To conclude: Success-based weighting allows for optimal probability aggregation.

References

1. Brier, G.W.: Verification of forecasts expressed in terms of probability. Mon. Weather Rev. **78**(1), 1–3 (1950)
2. Cesa-Bianchi, N., Lugosi, G.: Prediction, Learning, and Games. Cambridge University Press, Cambridge (2006)
3. Feldbacher-Escamilla, C.J., Schurz, G.: Optimal probability aggregation based on generalized brier scoring. Ann. Math. Artif. Intell. **88**(7), 717–734 (2019). https://doi.org/10.1007/s10472-019-09648-4
4. List, C., Pettit, P.: Aggregating sets of judgments: an impossibility result. Econ. Philos. **18**(01), 89–110 (2002)
5. Rossi, F., Venable, K.B., Walsh, T.: A short introduction to preferences. Between artificial intelligence and social choice. In: Synthesis Lectures on Artificial Intelligence and Machine Learning. Morgan & Claypool, Williston (2011)
6. Schurz, G.: The meta-inductivist's winning strategy in the prediction game: a new approach to hume's problem. Philos. Sci. **75**(3), 278–305 (2008)
7. Schurz, G.: Hume's Problem Solved. The Optimality of Meta-Induction. MIT Press, Cambridge (2019)

Author Index

Printed in the United States
By Bookmasters